Heavyweight Boxing
in the 1970s

Heavyweight Boxing in the 1970s
The Great Fighters and Rivalries

JOE RYAN

McFarland & Company, Inc., Publishers
Jefferson, North Carolina, and London

To my father James and my brother Michael,
two real fighters who set the bar very high
for those of us who must follow

LIBRARY OF CONGRESS CATALOGUING-IN-PUBLICATION DATA

Ryan, Joe, 1963–
Heavyweight boxing in the 1970s : the great
fighters and rivalries / Joe Ryan.
    p.   cm.
Includes bibliographical references and index.

ISBN 978-0-7864-7074-7
softcover : acid free paper ∞

1. Boxing — History — 20th century.   I. Title.
GV1121.R93 2013   796.8309 — dc23   2012050319

BRITISH LIBRARY CATALOGUING DATA ARE AVAILABLE

© 2013 Joe Ryan. All rights reserved

*No part of this book may be reproduced or transmitted in any form
or by any means, electronic or mechanical, including photocopying
or recording, or by any information storage and retrieval system,
without permission in writing from the publisher.*

On the cover: Boxer Muhammad Ali (right), against Ken Norton
in 1973 (Photofest); background image © 2013 Shutterstock

Manufactured in the United States of America

*McFarland & Company, Inc., Publishers
Box 611, Jefferson, North Carolina 28640
www.mcfarlandpub.com*

Contents

Acknowledgments vi
Preface 1

ONE. Comparing the Eras 3
TWO. The 1960s 23
THREE. 1970 42
FOUR. 1971 64
FIVE. 1972 91
SIX. 1973 110
SEVEN. 1974 142
EIGHT. 1975 176
NINE. 1976 198
TEN. 1977 229
ELEVEN. 1978 249
TWELVE. 1979 and Beyond 275

Chapter Notes 295
Bibliography 301
Index 307

Acknowledgments

There are so many people I would like to thank in making the completion of this book possible. First of all my wife Tracey, who has been supportive from the start, and my wonderful children, Meaghan, Joshua and Zachary, for putting up with the day-to-day lunacy it took to complete a project of this size. A special thanks to my youngest, Zachary, who, only twelve, has been my on-hand technical support man, and kept me from going crazy.

Thanks to my loving mother Mary, who has always made me feel that I could accomplish anything. To my big sister Cathy, my greatest example, constant supporter and lifelong friend.

A special thank you goes out to my good friend Charles R. Saunders, who has been my editor, advisor and source of material and encouragement throughout this endeavor. To Dave Somerton, who provided me through the years with the video needed to revisit these great fights. To my sister-in-law Tina Taylor, for all of her help. And to my new friend Clay Moyle, a fantastic author who has gone above and beyond in his assistance to me.

Preface

When I set out to write this book, my motivation was to revisit a period that gripped me throughout my youth. Muhammad Ali was the man who initially piqued my interest in boxing, as he did for many kids who grew up in the sixties and seventies. My interest eventually expanded to all of the eras and divisions in the sport. I would devour every book and magazine I could get my hands on. Combing old bookstores and tracking down movies of the old legends, I became an accomplished boxing historian. Seniors would regale me with tales of the old-timers, and I would listen intently. In time I could hold my own in conversations with fans fifty and sixty years my senior.

My university studies led me to a career in history, and a love of historical research. Summer employment at the National Museum of Man in Ottawa, Ontario, Canada, and provincial archives enhanced my knowledge of and desire for research. New avenues of research were opened to me and I began to utilize those skills to delve into my first love, boxing.

At this stage, I decided to write an in-depth study on the sport that intrigued me so much. With the age-old questions in mind as to who was the greatest heavyweight king, and which era was the best, I decided to formulate a set of criteria that would conclusively determine the true "golden age" of the heavyweights.

Approaching this task with an entirely unbiased focus, I tackled this old and controversial question. Using a fair and standard formula, I scrutinized, in great depth, every era from Jack Johnson up to and including the modern reign of the Klitschko brothers. Ironically, the conclusion brought me right back to the period and characters that captivated me in the first place, the heavyweights of the seventies.

I hope you will follow me on this sentimental journey back to the time of great fighters, great rivalries and an unprecedented interest in the sport of sports.

One

Comparing the Eras

In the world of sports, no event can capture the world's attention more readily than a major heavyweight title fight. The mystique that surrounds such a fight often transcends the boundaries of athletics. And few news items can command the level of media hype involved in a "Superfight."

The heavyweight championship of the world has been called the greatest prize sports can offer. A dominant champion is considered the supreme male, macho personified, the "baddest man on the planet."

The glitter and flash of modern, big-time boxing often disguises the true nature of the sport: organized violence. Although the fight game is more refined and better controlled than it was during the bare-knuckle days of the last century, the ultimate goal of its participants is the same as it has always been: to beat an opponent senseless.

Like it or not, this inherent barbarism is still one of boxing's main attractions. The majority of fans would rather see a brutal knockout than a scientific encounter that goes the distance. That's why a defensive stylist like Jimmy Young could never accumulate as many fans as crude sluggers like Earnie Shavers and George Foreman. The man who can put his opponents on the canvas is king at the box office.

In a way, the sport is an embodiment of Darwin's theory of survival of the strongest or the cleverest. Two men meet in a roped square of canvas, locked in deadly combat. Only one will emerge victorious.

By its very nature, boxing is a contest for territorial domination. Like two bucks fighting for control of the herd, boxers fight for supremacy in the ring. Boxing is an individual struggle of man against man, a fighter alone in the ring against a violent adversary. He must crush or be crushed.

Unlike team sports in which a weaker member can be helped by his teammates, a fighter must rely solely on his own abilities. A boxer who lacks the necessary strength, skill, and determination will be defeated and possibly injured. That's the risk a boxer takes every time he steps into the ring. For any fighter, regardless of his level of talent, that climb through the ropes represents an act of extreme courage.

The individual nature of the boxer's struggle leads to a more intimate relationship with the public. Though most of us are part of a larger group, be it a family, team, or work group, there are times when, like a boxer, we must overcome obstacles on our own. For that reason, it is natural for the average person to identify with a successful boxer. Also, boxers tend to come from humble beginnings, and most champions typify the "rags to riches" story.

Over the years, thousands of young men throughout the world have laced on the gloves with varying degrees of success. All fighters at some point in their careers entertain the idea of one day attaining the fame, glory, and economic rewards a world title can bring. Most are eventually forced to come to grips with the reality that they'll never come close to that pinnacle. They then readjust their professional objectives, set more realistic goals, and continue or end their careers.

Most fighters, however limited their abilities, manage to maintain a following even at a local level. On a higher plane, the champions represent the cream of the crop. Boxing champions, especially the heavyweights, have become legends in Western society, with fans numbering in the millions. They are perceived as real-life Supermen. Their lives have been immortalized and the tales of their accomplishments are told and retold long after their careers and lives have ended.

Comparisons of the styles and skills of these legendary heroes are inevitable. Throughout the years, boxing fans have carried on heated and ultimately futile debates comparing fighters from different eras who never met in the ring.

Pointless and inconclusive though such arguments may be, they are also inescapable. We all have our opinions, and I must admit to having engaged in more than one impassioned "Who was the greatest?" discussion.

In these verbal free-for-alls, I've found that older fans tend to favor the Dempseys and Louises, while younger ones support the Alis and the Tysons. It is, of course, impossible to accurately determine which heavyweight champion was the best in the absence of actual ring combat. Computer tournaments are a poor substitute that prove nothing.

On the other hand, it is possible to compare the quality of the eras in which the champions fought. I believe the decade of the 1970s is beyond a doubt the greatest era in heavyweight history. This conclusion is based not on sentiment. It can be established through the application of a standard set of criteria.

The first step one must take in assessing the past is to remove the rose-colored glasses. If we step away from biases and take an open and objective look at the facts, only one conclusion is possible: the seventies, that decade of Vietnam, Watergate, disco and mood rings, was the heavyweights' Golden Age.

In this introduction, we will examine the reigns of every heavyweight champion from Jack Johnson to the Klitschko brothers. The objective is to separate fact from fiction, not to detract from the accomplishments of non-seventies champions.

What, then, are the criteria by which boxing eras should be judged? First, a great era must possess more than one great fighter. Second, those great fighters must meet each other in the ring, preferably more than once. Third, the fights they produce must be memorable. Finally, the division must be steeped in talent, for truly great fighters prove themselves against a strong cast of contenders.

Now we'll examine how the eras before and after the 1970s measure up, beginning with the days of Jack Johnson, who was champion from 1908 to 1915. The exclusion of the champions who reigned before Johnson is not a denigration of their abilities. John L. Sullivan, James J. Corbett, Bob Fitzsimmons, Jim Jeffries, Marvin Hart, and Tommy Burns were remarkable fighters. But those men fought in a transitional period between the bare-knuckle days and the full application of the Marquess of Queensberry rules. Mouthpieces and protective cups hadn't been invented yet, and fights could last anywhere from four to twenty to the 61 three-minute rounds Corbett fought against Peter Jackson in 1891. Styles and techniques were still being established. And injuries that would cause bouts to be stopped today were then overlooked.

Until the light heavyweight division was established in 1903, anyone who weighed more than 158 pounds was a heavyweight. Champions would go for years without defending their titles, content to make easy money fighting exhibitions and appearing in badly written stage plays.

Also, boxing was illegal in many states until the early 1900s. To discourage betting, some states did not allow decisions to be rendered in fights that lasted the distance, a state of affairs that lasted well into the 1920s. To compare their time with today's is like comparing the modern National Football League to the days when players crashed into each other without helmets and the forward pass had not yet been invented. The accomplishments of these pioneers are best appreciated within the context of their own time rather than measured against that of their successors.

Jack Johnson was among the first of the "modern" stylists who perfected the art of hitting without being hit in return.

The late Nat Fleischer, founder of *The Ring* magazine, always insisted Johnson, who was nicknamed "Li'l Artha," qualified as the greatest heavyweight of all time. However, Johnson's exploits outside the ring tend to overshadow his fistic accomplishments.

As the first black fighter to wear the heavyweight crown, Johnson was a truly historic figure. And his flamboyant lifestyle, which included gold-studded teeth and the company of white women, made him one of the most controversial people of his time. The story of his exile from the United States due to conviction on a trumped-up charge under the Mann Act, which forbade the transportation of a woman across state lines for "immoral purposes," caused Johnson to be reviled as an "uppity black" or venerated as a tragic hero, a modern-day Othello.

Jack Johnson was indeed a larger-than-life individual. However, his era, which lasted from the mid–1900s to the mid–1910s, doesn't qualify as "great" under our criteria.

The period produced three great fighters: Johnson, Sam Langford, and Joe Jeannette, all of whom were black. It also marked the advent of the "White Hope" phenomenon, which originated in anti–Johnson hysteria to find a way, any way, to remove the crown from his smooth-shaven head.

Before he won the title, Johnson fought and won tough battles against Langford and Jeannette. After becoming champion, though, "Li'l Artha" preferred to take on white challengers of varying degrees of ineptitude, including Stanley Ketchel, the world middleweight champion.

The only black contender to gain a shot at Johnson's title was a hulking young man named Battling Jim Johnson, who held Jack to a ten-round draw in 1913. But Battling Jim was hardly in a class with Jeannette or Langford. Because of racial politics, some of the best potential matches of Johnson's era were simply never made.

Perhaps the biggest fight of Johnson's career occurred on July 4, 1910, when he took on ex-champion Jim Jeffries in Reno, Nevada. The 35-year-old Jeffries, who had retired five years earlier, was lured back into the ring by pride and a $100,000 purse — huge money for those days.

Spurred by the belief that no black fighter could beat him, Jeffries whipped his aging body into a semblance of shape, only to be beaten unmercifully by Johnson under a burning Nevada sun. The previously undefeated Jeffries collapsed in the fifteenth round. Former champion John L. Sullivan, who was covering the fight for the *New York Times*, wrote: "Seldom has there ever been a championship contest so one-sided."[1]

After that, Johnson reigned supreme. An example of his vast superiority over his opponents was his 1914 win over hard-hitting Frank Moran. Johnson was 36 years old then, and the fight lasted the full twenty rounds. Still, Moran's manager said afterward that "the only time Moran touched Johnson was when they shook hands."[2]

Many of Johnson's opponents lasted the distance; in 107 recorded bouts, he scored only 40 knockouts. He fought in a laid-back, defensive style, often taunting his opponents instead of hitting them. Before the Jeffries fight, Sullivan wrote in the *New York Times*: "Many good judges of boxing have maintained for years that the big negro seldom, if ever, extended himself, and was capable of striking harder blows than he has ever delivered in the ring. It appears to have been the general belief that Johnson was holding back."[3]

In other words, no fighter of Johnson's time was capable of forcing him to fight at a higher level. Langford, who was probably the best contender of his time, never got the chance to become Johnson's Joe Frazier.

Johnson finally lost his title in 1915, falling in twenty-six rounds to the fists of a 6'6" cowboy named Jess Willard. The belief that Johnson threw the fight in return for leniency on the Mann Act conviction remains common. The truth of the matter will never be known. As it was, twenty-two years would pass before another black man would receive a heavyweight title shot.

By our criteria, then, Johnson's era falls short of true greatness. And his successor, Willard, managed only one successful defense during the four years he sat on the title. In 1916, he plodded to a 10-round no-decision over an aging Frank Moran. Otherwise, Willard was content to make his money by roping steers in Wild West shows.

Let us now turn our attention to the period most old-timers refer to when they speak of the "Golden Age" of boxing: the 1920s, the era of Jack Dempsey, the "Manassa Mauler."

Like Johnson before him and Joe Louis after, Dempsey was unquestionably one of the greatest heavyweight champions. However, his reign, which stretched from 1919 to 1926, has to be considered the most overrated of all. The 1920s qualifies for greatness in only the first criterion: more than one outstanding fighter. Actually, there were three: Dempsey, Harry Wills, and Gene Tunney.

But Dempsey never fought Wills, and his two famous bouts against Tunney were fought when Jack had slipped past his prime. And Tunney had spent most of the decade as a 175-pounder.

Other than those three, the rest of the pack was so far behind that boxing expert Robert Ripley, editor of the *Everlast Record Book*, wrote in the 1925 edition: "Just at this present writing there is no one in the pugilistic horizon who is capable of giving Dempsey anything near a close fight." He went on to comment that the "Manassa Mauler" ruled over "a very mediocre gathering of contenders for his title."[4]

Criticism of Dempsey's era may be considered sacrilege by older fans. However, the facts speak for themselves. Let's go back to Toledo, Ohio, on the afternoon of July 4, 1919, the beginning of Dempsey's title tenure. The 24-year-old challenger, who stood 6'1" and weighed a lean 187 pounds, annihilated Willard in three brutal rounds. Willard went down seven times in the first round and was unable to answer the bell for the fourth.

To this day, the thrashing of Willard is considered one of Dempsey's two greatest accomplishments, the other being his climb back into the ring to stop Luis Firpo. However, the significance of the Willard fight has to be questioned.

Even in his prime, Big Jess was hardly great shakes, and by the time Dempsey got to him, Willard was 38 years old, had not fought in three years, and was noticeably out of shape. Dempsey was only one of many heavyweights who could have beaten Willard in 1919.

Leaping ahead momentarily, consider October 2, 1980, the day Larry Holmes forced an over-the-hill Muhammad Ali to quit in his corner after ten one-sided rounds. Like Willard, Ali was 38 years old and was coming off a long layoff. Yet Holmes's win over Ali is dismissed by boxing historians, while Dempsey's victory over an equally decrepit Willard is hailed as a major accomplishment.

Another shortcoming of Dempsey's era was the long lapses that occurred between his title defenses. During a seven-year reign, he managed only five successful defenses. Well over a year passed between the Willard fight and the first time Dempsey risked his laurels against Billy Miske on September 8, 1920, stopping him in three rounds. He then faced KO Bill Brennan on September 14 of the same year. Brennan went out in twelve. On July 2, 1921, he faced Frenchman Georges Carpentier in the first million-dollar gate in boxing history. Carpentier was stopped in four.

By the criteria we've established, these fights added little to Dempsey's resume. Miske was a competent enough fighter, but he was dying of Bright's disease when Dempsey fought him. Brennan had already lost to Dempsey in 1918, and in the rematch he hit the canvas so hard he broke an ankle. As well, he had previously lost to Miske, Bob Roper, and middleweight Harry Greb.

Carpentier was a slick boxer with a dangerous right hand. But he was also a light heavyweight, and at 172 pounds he simply wasn't strong enough to hold the "Manassa Mauler" off.

Two years passed before Dempsey met his next challenger, another light heavyweight named Tom Gibbons, in Shelby, Montana, on July 4, 1923. Gibbons lasted the full 15 rounds but lost the decision in a promotion that bankrupted the town that hosted it.

On September 14 of that year, Dempsey faced his biggest challenger to date, a 6'2", 216-pound Argentine named Luis Angel Firpo. Nicknamed the "Wild Bull of the Pampas," Firpo made up for a shortage of boxing skills with a pulverizing right-hand punch.

Dempsey–Firpo turned out to be the most exciting fight of the 1920s, if not of all time. Moments after the bell for Round One, the fight looked to be a replay of Dempsey–Willard as the Argentine crashed to the canvas again and again. Then, after pulling himself off the canvas for the fifth time, Firpo landed a desperate right that sent the champion flying out of the ring and onto the press table at ringside. Reporters pushed a dazed Dempsey back into the ring before the referee could count him out.

Jack managed to regain his senses and survive the round. In the second, he came out and dispatched his hulking foe. Then he followed up his sensational victory with a three-year layoff.

The reason for Dempsey's extended sabbaticals can be summed up in one word: Hollywood. His ring success made him a valuable commodity on the silver screen. Dempsey starred in silent serials like *Daredevil Jack*, and even had some cosmetic work done on his nose. He wasn't anxious to see the surgery undone by a well-placed blow to the face.

More relevant, though, was the clause in Dempsey's contract that stated that the deal was valid only as long as Jack remained champion. The easiest way to ensure his status was to stay out of the ring. Revile today's "alphabet organizations," if you will, but there is no way the WBA, WBC, or IBF would have allowed Dempsey to get away with putting his title in mothballs for three years.

Contemporary commentators didn't like what Dempsey was doing, either. Robert Ripley wrote in 1925 that the champion was hurting himself by not fighting on a regular basis.

"Inactivity," Ripley warned, "without question has robbed Dempsey of some of his vigorous strength, which characterized his climb from obscurity to the peak of the greatest fighting man in history."[5]

Not only was Dempsey wallowing in ring rust, he was also depriving his contenders of the title shots they deserved. Especially sad was the case of Harry Wills, the "Brown Panther," who had waited in the wings most of the decade.

The New Orleans–born Wills possessed impressive physical credentials even by today's standards. He stood 6'4", weighed 220 pounds, and had paid his dues by beating all the other fighters, black and white alike, who dared to face him.

Unfortunately for Harry, the memory of Jack Johnson remained fresh in many minds. The New York State Athletic Commission, which ruled American boxing along with the fledgling National Boxing Association, wasn't keen on having another black fighter challenge for the heavyweight title. Dempsey thus never came under official pressure to fight Wills, who was the #1 contender for the past four years.

Any champion has a moral obligation to defend against the best available contenders. But when Dempsey's manager, Jack "Doc" Kearns, was asked about prospective challengers after the Carpentier fight, Wills's name wasn't mentioned. Shockingly, the forty-year-old Jess Willard, who hadn't fought since Dempsey had butchered him in Toledo, was Kearns's first choice. Even welterweight champion Ted "Kid" Lewis's name came up.

Then, in 1923, Willard made a comeback and eventually signed to fight Firpo. Kearns announced that the Willard-Firpo winner would get the next shot at Dempsey, provided that winner looked impressive. Otherwise, Wills would get the call.

Firpo managed to stop the 42-year-old ex-champ in eight rounds. But he looked decidedly unspectacular in doing so. Nevertheless, Firpo, not Wills, went on to fight Dempsey.

After his battering by Dempsey, Firpo reeled off three impressive knockouts and clamored for another chance at the title. All he had to do to clinch the rematch was defeat Wills in a September 11, 1924, elimination match. Instead, Wills pounded the Argentine over 12 rounds. Although no decision was announced, the majority of fight reporters believed Wills won going away. In fact, Wills dropped Firpo in the second, but never seemed to press his advantage. Many insiders felt that the black man purposely held back on Firpo so as not to scare Dempsey away. If that was indeed his strategy, it made no difference. He never received a title shot, even though he remained the top contender.

When Dempsey finally decided to defend his crown in 1926, promoter Tex Rickard opted for Gene Tunney, the former United States light heavyweight champion. Nicknamed the "Fighting Marine" because of his service during World War I, Tunney had recently knocked out Georges Carpentier and Tom Gibbons. Those were worthy wins, but did they merit placing Tunney ahead of Wills?

Tunney didn't think so. Intelligent, fair-minded individual that he was, he felt that he should first meet Wills.

Promoter Tex Rickard, the 1920s equivalent of Don King and Bob Arum, would hear nothing of a Wills–Tunney eliminator that could jeopardize plans for Dempsey–Tunney. In fact, Rickard, who had promoted the Johnson–Jeffries fight, was very likely the one who shut the door on Wills. He didn't want to go down in history the promoter responsible for the coronation of two black kings.

Tunney signed to meet Dempsey on September 23, 1926, at Philadelphia's Sesquicentennial Stadium. The bout was scheduled for 10 rounds, the maximum distance allowed by Pennsylvania state law. Despite his age (31) and the three-year hiatus from competition, Dempsey was still the betting favorite. But Tunney, two years Jack's junior, was one of the brainiest boxers of all time. He had lost only one fight in his career, a bloody 15-round decision to Harry Greb, but he had then beaten Greb four times. In the midst of a driving rainstorm, Gene thoroughly outclassed Dempsey to win the title by decision.

Dempsey wasn't the only giant to be toppled in the fall of 1926. On October 12, Harry Wills lost on a 13th-round disqualification to a young ex-sailor from Boston named Jack Sharkey. By then, Wills was 37 years old and had fought more than 100 times during his 16-year career. He continued for a few more years, but was never again a factor in the division.

Thus died the dream of a Dempsey–Wills bout. It's a shame the boxing world was robbed of what surely would have been one of the truly great matches of all. Although Wills was six years older than Dempsey, both men peaked around the same time, 1918 to 1924. Their meeting would have been a classic boxer-vs.-slugger confrontation and probably would have been more competitive than the Dempsey–Tunney fights. The fact that the bout never came off is an indictment of the racism of the time, as well as a drawback to the era's greatness.

With Wills having fallen to the wayside, the "Manassa Mauler" still had battles to fight and money to make. To qualify for a rematch with Tunney, he took on young hotshot Jack Sharkey on July 21, 1927. Sharkey nearly kayoed Dempsey in the first round, but couldn't press his advantage. In the seventh, Sharkey turned to the referee to protest a low blow by Dempsey. Dempsey nailed him with a left hook, and Sharkey went down and out.

On September 22, Dempsey met Tunney at Soldier Field in Chicago. Again, the fight was scheduled for 10 rounds. And it began like a carbon copy of their first encounter, with Tunney picking Dempsey apart and winning every round. By the seventh, it looked as though Tunney was on his way to another lopsided victory.

Then Dempsey exploded a volley of crushing blows to the head, and Tunney crumpled to the canvas. But Dempsey didn't move to a neutral corner following the knockdown, and the referee delayed the count until the ex-champ did so. Tunney got up at "9," but estimates of the time he remained on the canvas vary from 13 to 17 seconds.

Dempsey's mistake cost him the fight and the title, as Tunney recovered and continued to outbox him over the remaining rounds. Tunney retained his title, but the bout went down in history as the "Battle of the Long Count."

The Tunney–Dempsey rematch was a superfight in every sense. It provided one of the most thrilling and definitely most controversial moments in sports history. The promotion was a monstrous financial success: 104,943 fans packed Soldier Field and paid a record gate of $2,858,660.[6]

Dempsey retired after his second loss to Tunney. Gene made one more title defense against a rugged New Zealander named Tom Heeney in July of 1928. Tunney dismantled Heeney over eleven one-sided rounds, then announced his retirement as undefeated champion.

Will Gould wrote in the 1929 *Everlast Record Book* that the Tunney–Heeney match was "a distinct flop in a financial way. Champion Gene Tunney and the challenger, Tom Heeney, did not appeal to the fans as a fight should and the gate amounted to less than $600,000. This was just about enough to meet the champion's guarantee."[7]

It was evident that without Dempsey, Tunney just couldn't draw big crowds. It is unfortunate that Gene never enjoyed the mass appeal Dempsey generated. Tunney was certainly an exemplary and deserving champion. However, in the 1920s even more so than today, the stereotype of a fighter was that of a flat-nosed, inarticulate pug. By contrast, Tunney was a fine-featured, intelligent, well-spoken man whose personality outside the ring seemed better suited to a poet than a prizefighter.

Consequently, Tunney wasn't well received by fight fans. As well, his classic, scientific boxing style wasn't nearly as popular as Dempsey's wild, relentless mode of mayhem.

Ironically, Dempsey's own popularity didn't reach its peak until after his first loss to Tunney. Tunney's own reputation suffered as a consequence.

At the end of the 1920s, the title remained vacant as promoters put on a marathon two-year tournament to determine Tunney's successor. The drawn-out process included almost every heavyweight of consequence. Jack Sharkey was on the list, as well as a promising German named Max Schmeling.

Otto von Porat and Knute Hansen represented the Scandinavian countries, and Spain provided Paolino Uzcudun. England weighed in with Phil Scott. American entries included Johnny Risko, Jim Maloney, Young Stribling, and Tommy Loughran. All these fighters' development had been stunted by Dempsey's inactivity and Tunney's short reign. The tournament would hopefully give them a chance to shine.

There was, however, one glaring exception. George Godfrey, who had succeeded Harry Wills as the best of the black heavies, found himself frozen out of the competition.

Like Wills, Godfrey was a big man, packing 245 muscular pounds onto a 6'2" frame. Nicknamed the "Leiperville Shadow," Godfrey first achieved prominence as one of the few sparring partners capable of surviving Jack Dempsey's ferocity. He rose from sparring work to top-ten contention, but he was never considered for participation in the tournament.

In 1928, Murray Lewin, a prominent boxing writer, published an article in the *New York Daily Mirror* that strongly criticized the drawing of the "color line" against Godfrey:

> It appears quite apparent that the entry list is open to all but colored fighters. Englishmen, Germans, Swedes, Australians, Spaniards or anyone representing the Latin race are eligible, yet an American-born warrior's name has been omitted.
>
> Until Godfrey is eligible to compete in the series, or until one of those entered in the tourney succeeds in eliminating him, we cannot take too much stock in the series.[8]

Despite Lewin's endorsement, Godfrey never fought in the tournament. George retired in 1937 with an impressive total of 76 knockout wins in 109 bouts.

In 1929, while the unwieldy tournament was still unfolding, boxing writer Sparrow McGann penned an article titled: "Where, Oh Where is the Puncher!" In it, he predicted that there would be no more million-dollar gates until another dynamic, hard-punching heavyweight emerged, someone like Dempsey.

Of the fighters who were vying for the vacant title, McGann wrote: "The fans will not give you a dime for the lot. Bring on the young man with the punch and then sit back and check the accelerated interest of the fans."[9]

The eliminations finally lurched to a close on June 12, 1930, with Sharkey and Schmeling facing off in the final. In Round Four, the bout ended with Schmeling writhing on the canvas and clutching his protective cup. The referee disqualified Sharkey for hitting low, and Schmeling became the new champion on a foul.

By our criteria, the 1920s were an improvement over the Johnson era. There were three great fighters, and three memorable fights: Dempsey–Firpo and two Dempsey–Tunneys. But any decade that features a grand total of eight heavyweight title bouts cannot qualify as a truly great one.

During the 1930–1937 period, McGann's prophecy appeared to be nothing but a pipe dream. Those years saw a succession of five heavyweight champions who managed a total of three successful title defenses among them.

Schmeling defended his title against Young Stribling in 1931, stopping his man in the 15th round. In a rematch against Sharkey a year later, the German lost a 15-round decision most ringsiders thought he'd won.

In 1933, Sharkey made his first defense against Primo Carnera, a 6'6", 260-pound behemoth from Italy. Despite his gargantuan size, Carnera wasn't much of a fighter. Yet he managed to stop Sharkey in six rounds.

Carnera defended his title twice, winning decisions over Paolino Uzcudun and Tommy Loughran. Loughran, an ex–light heavyweight champion, was outweighed by a whopping 86 pounds.

Then, in 1934, Primo risked his crown against Max Baer, a talented but erratic slugger with a dynamite right hand. Baer floored Carnera eleven times in eleven rounds to win the title.

Max, who was no midget at 6'2" and 210 pounds, was the most talented of the so-called "cheese champs" of the 1930s. But he never took the fight game seriously, and in his first defense he lost a 15-round decision to a washed-up Jim Braddock in one of the greatest upsets of all time. Braddock, who became known as the "Cinderella Man," was a likeable man who typified the "rags to riches" story. But he was also a limited fighter who kept the title on ice for two years before finally defending it against the "young man with a punch" who would fulfill Sparrow McGann's prediction.

That young man was Joe Louis, the "Brown Bomber."

Born in Alabama, Louis moved with his family to Detroit as part of the great black migration from the rural South to the urban North. When Louis turned pro in 1934, he gave the heavyweights a desperately needed shot in the arm even as he dispatched his opponents with short, well-placed shots to the jaw. Joe's methodical yet exciting boxing style and his carefully cultivated image outside the ring were so appealing that he singlehandedly shattered the racial barrier that had existed since the end of Jack Johnson's reign.

As the first major title threat since Harry Wills's downfall, Louis's life was subjected to the kind of scrutiny only presidential candidates have to endure today. And he passed all tests with flying colors. He was clean living, polite without being subservient, and his wife was black.

It is a commonly held belief that Johnson inadvertently did more damage to his people than any other black man in history. Joe Louis healed most of those wounds and opened the doors of opportunities for blacks in sports and many other endeavors.

Like Johnson, Louis's talent and accomplishments made him a legend whose influence transcended his sport. Unlike Johnson, the "Brown Bomber's" influence was unquestionably positive.

When it comes to discussions about the greatest heavyweights of all time, Louis's name is never omitted. His 11-year, eight-month reign and 25 successful defenses are records not only for the heavyweights but in every division to this day.

But his era, which lasted from 1937 to 1949, did not measure up to Joe's personal stature. At the risk of offending many of Louis's devoted fans, I would rate the "Brown Bomber's" reign as only slightly ahead of that of Larry Holmes. The challengers in Louis's famed "Bum of the Month" club would not have been out of place among the cut-rate contenders of the early 1980s.

Louis actually faced tougher competition during his march to the title than he did after he won it at age 23 by stopping Jim Braddock in eight rounds on June 23, 1937. Along the way, he had decimated the "cheese champs," flattening Primo Carnera in six rounds, Max Baer in four, and Jack Sharkey in three. His lone setback came at the hands of Max Schmeling, who scored an upset 12th-round stoppage of Louis in 1936. Due to the world and boxing politics of the time, it was Louis, not Schmeling, who received a shot at Braddock's title the following year.

After Louis won the title, Schmeling was thought to be the only fighter around with even a slight chance of beating him. The other contenders were competitive against each other, but Louis stood head and shoulders above them in talent.

In a 1938 article titled, "Oh! My Kingdom For A Good Heavyweight," Leslie Shoemaker of the *San Diego Sun* wrote: "It's worse than a good game of Blind Man's Bluff (and that's not a bad name for the big lugs masquerading as heavyweight fighters). If the coast prospects in the east are like those in the west, then a two-bit piece will bring you a money winner but not a champion; no, not even a threat."[10]

In the same year, W.D. McMillan of the *Savannah* (Georgia) *Morning News* commented that apart from ex-champs Braddock and Schmeling and British contender Tommy Farr, "those three are about all there is to the boxing game among the heavyweights, outside of champion Joseph Louis Barrow, and the up and coming youngsters are not getting far enough into the game to fan the customer's interest."[11]

An examination of the odds in Louis's title bouts provides another indication of what contemporary experts thought of his competition. With the exception of his 1938 rematch with Schmeling, in which Louis was only a slight 9-to-5 favorite, the odds for his other 24 defenses ranged from 13–5 to 20–1. No fewer than 13 of his challengers were 10–1 underdogs.[12]

Of course, odds makers aren't always right; remember the 42–1 odds against Buster Douglas vs. Tyson in 1990. Louis, on the other hand, made the odds makers look like geniuses. When Louis won the title, he didn't put it into suspended animation as had so many of the other champions before him. Only two months after beating Braddock, Joe defended against Tommy Farr, a light-hitting but rugged Welshman. Although Farr lost a unanimous 15-round decision, he won a moral victory by surviving on his feet.

At the start of 1938, Louis registered easy kayo victories over Nathan Mann and Harry Thomas, neither of whom offered much of a threat. Then, on June 22, one year to the day since he had won the title from Braddock, Louis defended his crown against Max Schmeling before a huge crowd at Yankee Stadium.

Schmeling, whose ring intelligence was second only to that of Gene Tunney, had beaten Joe in their first encounter by studying films of Louis's previous fights. As he watched reel after reel, Schmeling noticed that every time that Louis threw one of his patented left jabs, he would bring it back a little low. The German capitalized on this chink in Louis's armor by landing hard right leads over Joe's left.

However, on the night of June 22, 1938, the 32-year-old Schmeling faced a grimly determined Louis, who was bent on revenge. As well, Louis–Schmeling II was the most politically charged fight since Johnson–Jeffries in 1910. Although the fight did contain a racial element, that aspect was overshadowed by political ideology. Louis represented freedom and democracy; Schmeling inadvertently symbolized Adolf Hitler's Nazi dictatorship.

Louis struck a resounding blow for democracy and racial equality that night. In fact, Louis landed many blows, all of them exploding against the hapless Schmeling's head and body. Der Max went down three times and was counted out at 2:04 of the first round. This was the fight that cemented Louis's popularity in America and eradicated Jack Johnson's legacy once and for all.

After disposing of Schmeling, Joe took a well-deserved six-month rest. He returned to the ring in January of 1939 and knocked out light heavyweight champion John Henry Lewis in the first round. Three months later, he faced unheralded Jack Roper and also polished him off in one round. Just when it seemed that no challenger would be able to last even three minutes with the "Brown Bomber," along came "Two Ton" Tony Galento.

Galento, one of boxing's most memorable characters, began his career as a light heavyweight in 1929. As the years passed, his weight piled on; he carried an astounding 233 pounds on a 5'9" frame into the ring against Louis. Although Galento possessed a wicked left hook, he was given no serious chance of upsetting a champ of Louis's caliber. Undaunted, Galento vowed to "Moida da bum."

The champ was giving the tubby challenger a terrible drubbing, dropping him in the second round. Then, in the third, Galento landed one of his patented left hooks and deposited Louis on the canvas. More embarrassed than hurt, Louis picked himself off of the floor and administered a frightful beating, forcing the referee to mercifully halt matters in the fourth stanza.

Some experts believed that the knockdown along with his kayo loss to Schmeling proved that Louis's chin was suspect. Regardless, Louis stopped tough Bob Pastor in three frames three months later.

In 1940, Louis made four more successful title defenses, decisioning durable Chilean Arturo Godoy over 15 rounds, kayoing a petrified Johnny Paycheck in two, destroying Godoy in eight in a rematch, and then stopping Al McCoy in six.

From January till May of 1941, Louis disposed of his challengers at a clip of one every thirty days, giving rise to the famous "Bum of the Month" tag. Clarence "Red" Burman exited in three rounds in January. In February, Gus Dorazio went out in two. Abe Simon, a 6'4" 255-pounder, stubbornly hung in for thirteen rounds before the champ lowered the boom in March. Tony Musto put forth a surprising effort before succumbing in the ninth in April. In May, Buddy Baer, 6'7" brother of ex-champ Max, actually knocked Louis out of the ring in the first round. Joe regrouped and gave Baer a shellacking before the ref disqualified the challenger in the seventh.

In June, Louis faced what was supposed to be another soft touch: a light-hitting former light heavyweight champion named Billy Conn. In his own division, Conn is considered to be an all-time great. However, against Louis, Conn scaled 168 to the champ's rock-hard 200. Regardless, at the Polo Grounds on the night of June 18, 1941, that weight advantage meant nothing as the quicker Conn befuddled Louis with blinding hand and foot speed. With each ensuing round Conn added to his growing lead, actually hurting the champ in the twelfth round. With only three rounds remaining and the title virtually his, Conn made a fatal mistake: he decided to go for a knockout. Throwing caution to the wind, Conn left himself open and the sharp-shooting champ took full advantage. Louis flattened Billy Conn with only two seconds left in round thirteen. The first fight with Conn would prove to be Louis's most dramatic title defense.

Three months after his near brush with disaster, Louis dismantled the tough Lou Nova in six one-sided rounds. Negotiations were underway for a Louis–Conn rematch when the Japanese attacked Pearl Harbor on December 7, 1941, the event that brought America into World War II.

Louis enlisted in the U.S. Army, and his title was basically frozen from 1942 until 1946. The "Brown Bomber" made two successful defenses in 1942 against Buddy Baer and Abe Simon. Both men learned that Joe Louis was poison in rematches. On January 9, Louis blew Baer out in the first round, while Simon exited in the sixth on March 27. The champ donated the entirety of the purses to the Army and Navy Relief funds, a gesture that would enshrine him forever as an American hero. Throughout the course of the war Louis acted as a goodwill ambassador, entertaining Allied troops all over the world, as well as participating in promotional endeavors for War Bonds and recruiting.

In five years as champion, Louis had defended his crown an astounding 21 times, thoroughly cleaning out a relatively unimpressive heavyweight division. One year after the war had ended, Louis, then 32 years old and slipping badly, met Conn in a much-anticipated rematch. However, Conn, who had himself enlisted in the same capacity as Louis, had slipped even more. They met on June 19, 1946, and the rematch lacked the drama of their first encounter. Louis was never in any peril and stopped Conn in eight uneventful rounds.

After a one-round knockout of Tami Mauriello in 1946, Louis nearly lost his title when 10-to-1 underdog Jersey Joe Walcott dropped him twice, only to lose a highly disputed decision on December 5, 1947. Seven months later Louis knocked Walcott out in the eleventh round. Then on March 1, 1949, Louis announced his retirement. A year later, income tax problems forced him to make a return to the ring. On September 27, 1950, old Joe lost a lopsided 15-round decision to his successor, Ezzard Charles. Louis rebounded to reel off eight straight victories over decent competition until an eighth-round knockout at the hands of Rocky Marciano drove him into retirement permanently.

Louis's greatness as an individual fighter is beyond doubt. But his era provided only one truly great fight, Louis–Conn, and in that one Louis's opponent wasn't even a heavyweight. Louis–Schmeling II was great only in its build-up and political significance. To compare the reigns of Louis and Larry Holmes, then, is not so far-fetched as one may think. Holmes's career will be discussed at length in upcoming pages, but at this point it's fair to say that Larry, like Joe, thoroughly dominated his division and destroyed all opposition.

Yet because of Louis's stellar accomplishments outside of the ring, the quality of his accomplishments was overinflated. Holmes's reign, on the other hand, is undervalued because he followed not only Ali, but also the greatest era in heavyweight history. A daunting task indeed.

The 1949–1952 period was an interim during which two champions, Ezzard Charles and Jersey Joe Walcott, reigned in lackluster fashion. These two weren't bad fighters. In fact, Charles was pound-for-pound one of the best in history. Even though he weighed only around 180 pounds, Charles had beaten most of the best light heavy and heavyweights of the late 1940s.

When Louis retired, Charles was matched with Walcott for National Boxing Association recognition as champion. On June 22, 1949, Charles out-pointed Jersey Joe to capture the NBA version of the title. The New York State Commission withheld recognition until Ezzard decisioned the comebacking Louis on September 27, 1950. Unfortunately, Charles, like both Tunney and Holmes, had the misfortune of following a great and popular champion. There is always a general letdown after a great champion like Dempsey, Louis or Ali is either defeated or retires. The successor often endures a period of public indifference through no fault of his own.

Charles made the best of a bad situation and made eight successful title defenses in only two years. But the majority of his challengers were nonentities. Lee Oma, Pat Valentino, Nick Barone, Gus Lesnevich, Freddie Beshore and Joey Maxim were competent enough fighters, but there really wasn't much difference between them and Louis's "Bums of the Month."

In the end, only Walcott was left, and Charles had already beaten the old man twice: once to win the title, and again in a March 7, 1951, defense. When a Charles–Walcott III was arranged, the matchup generated little interest. James P. Dawson wrote in the *New York Times* that the fight was "a reflection on the current heavyweight situation."

However, the bout turned out to be the only exciting moment of the period when the

37-year-old Walcott, a 6-to-1 underdog, connected with a dynamite left hook to the jaw in the seventh round that left Charles an unconscious ex-champion. Jersey Joe became the oldest man to win the heavyweight title, a feat that remained unmatched until George Foreman knocked Michael Moorer out on November 5, 1994, at the age of 45.

Walcott outpointed Charles to retain his crown on June 5, 1952. Although Jersey Joe is rarely listed among the all-time greats of the division, he was an above-average fighter and a sentimental favorite for many fans. His long, slow rise from struggling club fighter to champion of the world was reminiscent of the "Cinderella Man" Jim Braddock. Unlike Braddock, though, Walcott defeated not only the odds in winning in his fifth attempt at the title, but also Father Time. His saga gave the little guy, the average Joe, a reason to look to the future with optimism. Unfortunately for Walcott, his own future proved to be a "Rocky" one.

Rocky Marciano and the Senior Citizens

At the time Walcott knocked the crown from Charles's brow, a dynamic young puncher named Rocky Marciano was busily battering his way up the rankings. And toward the end of 1952, the stocky (5'10", 185-pound) son of Italian immigrants had become the #1 contender, whose 42–0 record included 39 knockouts.

Known as the "Brockton Blockbuster" after his hometown in Massachusetts, Marciano was 29 years old and primed for his crack at Walcott's title. Public demand ensured that a Walcott—Marciano encounter would become reality. Because of his age, only four months short of his 39th birthday, the champ was installed as a decided 9-to-5 underdog. Yet Jersey Joe was probably the best-conditioned 38-year-old the sport had ever seen, and had twenty years of experience to draw on.

During the first few rounds of their epic September 23, 1952, war at Philadelphia's Municipal Stadium, Walcott's bravado proved prophetic. The old man floored Rocky in the first round, then proceeded to dish out a painful boxing lesson. But Marciano refused to take a backward step and slowly wore Walcott down. Still, after twelve rounds, Walcott was way ahead on points; all he had to do was stick and move for three more rounds.

Then, with only 43 seconds gone in the thirteenth round, lightning struck in the form of a short, powerful Marciano right hand. Walcott collapsed to the canvas and another legendary boxing era had dawned.

Marciano's reign produced some of the most thrilling and memorable moments in boxing history. Rocky's style, which featured thunderous power coupled with a total disregard for his own well-being, had been honed by Charley Goldman, one of the greatest trainers ever to work a corner. Although Marciano defended his title only six times in four years, some of those bouts were classic confrontations. The only problem was that Marciano's opponents did not measure up to the first of our criteria. The men he fought were outstanding, but none was in his prime by the time they challenged Marciano. Let us begin with Walcott. True, Jersey Joe fought the battle of his life the night he lost his crown to Marciano. But in their May 15, 1953, rematch, Walcott went out in the first round. Many boxing historians believe to this day that Walcott had no intention of undergoing another war of attrition with Marciano. At any rate, Walcott never fought again.

Prior to winning the title, Marciano had established his contender status by knocking Joe Louis into retirement. Louis was 37 at the time, but unlike his contemporary Walcott, the "Brown Bomber" looked ten years older than that. Even so, it took Marciano eight tough rounds to finish off what was left of Louis. Up to that point, Marciano hadn't fought many quality opponents. Two fights before he met Louis, "The Rock" took a 34–0 record with 31 knockouts into the ring against a big, rugged heavyweight from Utah named Rex Layne. Because of his superior previous opposition, Layne was installed as a 9-to-5 favorite over Marciano. As Joseph C. Nichols wrote in the *New York Times*, "The milk-fed Marciano was expected to be just another Layne victim."[13]

That didn't prove to be the case as Marciano left Layne battered, bleeding and unconscious by the sixth round. Still, the pre-fight odds provide an indication of what some boxing experts of the time thought of the quality of Marciano's opposition up to that point. In truth, Rocky was being carefully maneuvered by his crafty manager, Al Weill. Besides Layne, the only fighters of note that Marciano had faced were Carmine Vingo and Roland LaStarza. Vingo, a brawler in the Marciano mold, sustained career-ending injuries after six rounds of savage warfare in 1949. LaStarza, a stylish boxer who sported a college education, came closer than anyone else to beating Marciano, losing a 10-round split decision in 1950.

On the strength of his performance against Marciano in their first fight, LaStarza was granted the next shot at the title after Walcott's quick exit. With his championship on the line, Marciano bludgeoned LaStarza in eleven frames on September 24, 1953.

In 1954, Marciano fought a pair of grueling bouts against another aging ex-champ, Ezzard Charles. Unlike Walcott, Charles had not aged like fine wine. His once masterful skills had eroded substantially since his losses to Walcott. Charles had sustained back-to-back losses in 1953 to Nino Valdes and future light heavyweight king Harold Johnson. Subsequent kayos over Coley Wallace and Bob Satterfield had moved Charles into a shot at Marciano. Despite his erosion, the 1954 version of Ezzard Charles pushed Marciano to the limit twice.

In their first fight on June 17, Charles used every ounce of his boxing skill to force Rocky to go the full 15-round distance. The decision in Marciano's favor was unanimous and undisputed. But at times Ezzard made Marciano look foolish. The unexpectedly competitive showing earned Charles a rematch three months later. Like Louis, Marciano was always deadlier in rematches. The second fight proved to be more dramatic than the first. At the end of seven rounds, Charles had inflicted a grotesque gash on the champ's nose that threatened to stop the contest. With his title in peril, Marciano stormed from his corner at the start of the eighth round and knocked Charles out.

Following the second loss to Marciano, Charles would win only 10 of his remaining 23 contests. It must have been a shame to watch the ex-champ lose to fighters who wouldn't have been worthy of toting his water bucket a decade earlier. The question is, did Ezzard's downswing occur as a direct result of the Marciano wars? I believe the answer is twofold: Charles was already past his peak in 1954; Marciano merely hastened his decline.

After taking eight months off to recover from his wound, Marciano defended his title for the fifth time against Don Cockell, a British light heavy who had bloated up to 205 pounds. Although the champion finished Cockell in nine somewhat sloppy rounds, many observers wondered why he hadn't ended matters sooner.

In September of 1955, Marciano defended against the great light heavyweight champion, Archie Moore. Although Moore was 42 years old, he rated several cuts above Don Cockell. He didn't get his chance at the crown until 1952, when he was 39. Archie, who was nicknamed "The Old Mongoose," made the most of his opportunity by out-pointing Joey Maxim. Because Moore had always enjoyed success against heavyweights, he believed he stood at least an even chance of becoming the first man to defeat Marciano. On fight night he came close, flooring the champ with a sharp right hand in the second round. Marciano got up and inflicted a brutal beating that lasted until Archie went down and out in the ninth round.

The Moore fight turned out to be Marciano's last. Family pressure, a chronic back condition, and a disagreement with manager Al Weill combined to prompt Rocky to announce his retirement on April 27, 1956. He never came back, and remains to this day the only heavyweight king to retire undefeated with a perfect 49–0 record with 43 knockouts.

Marciano owed much of his unprecedented success to a nearly fanatical obsession to training. No fighter in history worked harder or longer in preparation for fights. He was a trainer's dream: a fighter who abstained like a monk and had to be chased out of the gym.

However, just before the Moore fight, the "Rock" began to show the first signs of weariness with the rigors and discipline of training. Marciano understood that if he didn't train with vigor, that he wouldn't hold his title for much longer. At age 33, he knew he couldn't allow himself to get out of condition.

Because of his retirement, Marciano never got around to fighting the younger men who came to age during the 1950s. It would have been interesting to see how Rocky would have fared against the likes of Floyd Patterson, Nino Valdes, Bob Baker, Eddie Machen, Zora Folley, Ingomar Johansson, and a young Sonny Liston.

In the aftermath of Marciano's retirement, a mini-tournament was set up to fill the vacant throne. In a classic youth-vs.-age encounter, Archie Moore was matched with Patterson, who was then only 21 years old. The trigger-fisted Patterson cut Moore down in five one-sided rounds to become the youngest man in history to claim the crown. Patterson's career will be discussed in detail in upcoming pages. At this point, suffice to say that his reign did not add much luster to the remaining years of the 1950s. Rocky Marciano notwithstanding, the decade does not come close to meeting our criteria for greatness.

The 1960s will also be discussed on their own, as that was the decade in which many of the fighters we'll be discussing were developed. And the 1970s, of course, is the subject of the bulk of this book. Thus, we will now fast-forward to the 1980s.

Mike Tyson and History

In general, the heavyweight situation of the 1980s can be split neatly between the first half of the decade, in which Larry Holmes ruled, and the second half, which was dominated by Mike Tyson.

Holmes's career spanned both the 1970s and '80s, and to a degree, the '90s. Like Louis, he was a great fighter who lacked credible opposition. Holmes had made 20 successful defenses by the time he was upset by Michael Spinks in September of 1985. Having won the WBC title in spectacular fashion from Ken Norton on June 9, 1978, Holmes had reigned supreme for seven years. Although Holmes never enjoyed an undisputed reign, his dominance was never in question. Despite his two close points losses to Michael Spinks, Holmes's place among the all-time greats was never in question. The biggest challenge to his supremacy turned out to be more of a promotional lark than an actual threat, when he dispatched Gerry Cooney in thirteen rounds on June 11, 1982. A frightening puncher in his own right, Cooney lacked the skills and chin to realistically challenge Holmes in his prime. By the time he stepped into the ring with an opponent of comparable talent, Tyson in 1988, Holmes was a washed-up 38-year-old, and was easily dispatched in four rounds.

At the beginning of 1985, when Holmes was on his last legs as champion, only a few boxing fans knew who Mike Tyson was. By the end of the year, the 19-year-old terror from Brownsville, New York, had become the hottest contender in the division. Not since the early days of Joe Louis had a young fighter progressed so rapidly.

By then, the division had deteriorated into a chaos of alphabet-organization titles and revolving-door champions. Holmes had been upset by light heavyweight king Spinks, who now claimed the IBF title. Pinklon Thomas held the WBC crown, while Tony Tubbs, a Pillsbury Doughboy, was the sixth WBA champ in six years. Tubbs lost the WBA title to former WBC champ Tim Witherspoon, who in turn lost to James "Bonecrusher" Smith. Thomas lost his crown to an erratic, transplanted Jamaican named Trevor Berbick.

If the fighters who held the title in the early 1930s were cheese champions, then these guys were Velveeta. Just as Louis saved the division in the '30s, Tyson was destined to save the entire sport in the 1980s. When Tyson, who was then 20, destroyed Berbick in two rounds to win the WBC title on November 22, 1986, he became the youngest fighter to ever win a piece of the heavyweight crown. Tyson was the breath of fresh air the division needed at the time.

"Iron Mike" took the public by storm, not so much for the quality of the opponents he faced as for the frightening ease with which he disposed of them. At 5'11" and 220 well-chiseled pounds, Tyson displayed a combination of speed and power in the ring that were a wonder to behold. As well, his story was appealing ... for a while, anyway. Accounts of his nightmarish youth in the streets of Brownsville, New York, and his rescue at the age of 13 from a juvenile detention center by Cus D'Amato, Floyd Patterson's former trainer and manager, were told and retold in the media. Tyson was embraced by the general public as an example of a bad boy who'd been made good.

D'Amato died early in Tyson's career, but co-manager Jim Jacobs, a noted collector of boxing films, and businessman Bill Cayton continued to guide the young fighter. In 1987, Mike unified the heavyweight title for the first time since Leon Spinks in 1978.

Tyson's ring performances that year were a bit erratic. On March 7, he won a sloppy 12-round decision over James "Bonecrusher" Smith to annex the WBA title. Then he battered former WBC king Pinklon Thomas into a sixth-round kayo defeat on May 30. Tyson then added the IBF crown with a surprisingly difficult 12-round decision over Tony Tucker. Tucker had won the title by stopping James "Buster" Douglas in a box-off after the IBF had stripped Michael Spinks. Despite the absence of a title from a sanctioning body, *Ring Magazine* and many fans still recognized Spinks as the true linear champion because of his two victories over Holmes.

Tyson finished 1987 with gusto by crushing 1984 Olympic gold medalist Tyrell Biggs in seven brutal rounds on October 16. He had gathered together all of the "alphabet organizations'" belts, but his claim to universal recognition was still disputed by Spinks.

"Iron Mike" started 1988 off with a bang when he dismissed comebacking ex-champ Larry Holmes in four rounds on January 22. Three months later, former WBA champ Tony Tubbs exited in two. By then, Tyson had married TV star Robin Givens and was looking forward to a multi-million-dollar showdown against Spinks that summer. As it was, he had decimated the fighters who had won titles before him as easily as Louis had dominated the "cheese champs" of the 1930s. Already, the 22-year-old was being compared to Louis, Ali, Marciano and Dempsey. After he smashed Spinks into retirement in a mere 91 seconds of the first round on June 27, Tyson's place in boxing history seemed assured. With his youth and incredible skill, a long Louis-like domination of the division seemed imminent.

But there was trouble in Tyson's paradise. Co-manager Jim Jacobs died of cancer, and his marriage hit some well-publicized rocks and ended in divorce. Tyson distanced himself from his other manager, Bill Cayton, fired longtime trainer Kevin Rooney, and gravitated more and more towards the flamboyant promoter Don King. Throughout the rest of 1988 and well into 1989, Tyson drifted like a ship without a rudder. Car crashes, street fights and rumors of mental disorders overshadowed the champion's ring performances.

After an eight-month layoff from the ring, if not from the headlines, Tyson stopped British champ Frank Bruno in five grueling rounds on February 25, 1989. On July 21, he flattened Carl "The Truth" Williams with a left hook in the first round. Williams claimed that referee Randy Neumann stopped the fight too soon after Carl got to his feet, but the result stuck.

Outside the ring, Tyson's troubles continued. King might have offered him guidance out of self-interest, but he couldn't take the place of Cus D'Amato, and Tyson went his own way. Tyson was like a bomb ready to explode. On February 11, 1990, in Tokyo, 42-to-1 underdog James "Buster" Douglas lit the fuse. Douglas picked himself up off the canvas to batter Tyson into a tenth-round kayo. The self-proclaimed "baddest man on the planet" was human after all.

Four months later, Tyson made a much-anticipated comeback, against 1984 Olympic heavyweight champion Henry Tillman. Tyson hung a first-round kayo on his old amateur nemesis, and then inflicted the same fate on Alex Stewart six months later. Two tough wins over Canadian champion Donovan "Razor" Ruddock in 1991 set the stage for Tyson to once again challenge for the title ... then the bottom dropped out. In a much-publicized trial, Tyson was accused of raping Desiree Washington, a contestant in the Miss Black America pageant. On February 11, 1992, two years to the day after losing his title to Douglas, Tyson was found guilty in an Indianapolis courtroom, and was sentenced to six years in prison.

Meanwhile, Buster Douglas, the new "Cinderella Man," was content to allow himself to become merely a footnote in heavyweight history. His first defense was scheduled against undefeated former cruiserweight king Evander "Real Deal" Holyfield. Douglas seemed as determined to lose his crown to Holyfield as he had been in winning it from Tyson. He put very little into training, which was evident at the scales; he'd ballooned from 231 for Tyson up to 246 for Evander. The writing was on the wall, and the hungry Holyfield easily knocked his man out with a single devastating right hand in the third. Douglas quickly faded into obscurity. He emerged from a six-year hiatus and racked up six wins over mediocre opposition before Lou Savarese starched him in one round on June 25, 1998. Two more inconsequential victories rounded out his career, and he retired in 1999. Still, regardless of Douglas's sorry performance against Holyfield, and the scorn that was heaped on him in the aftermath, we should always remember him as the man who put it all together and came off the floor to defeat Tyson.

Holyfield the Warrior

The next decade saw the comings and goings of many credible heavyweights, as well as some major disappointments. Through it all, Evander Holyfield proved time and again that his nom-de-guerre "The Real Deal" was well earned. His first three defenses did draw some criticism, as he fought two 42-year-olds and a last-minute substitute. Ex-champs George Foreman and Larry Holmes each gave the champ a decent challenge despite losing unanimous decisions. "Smokin'" Bert Cooper, a last-minute replacement, almost knocked Holyfield out before the champ came roaring back to halt his man in the seventh.

With Tyson's incarceration in 1992, the much anticipated Holyfield–Tyson went out the window, possibly forever. However, the early nineties did in fact produce some viable rivals. The first on Holyfield's horizon was 1988 Olympic silver medalist Riddick Bowe. The two met on December 13, 1992, and waged a twelve-round war. Bowe's size and strength were too much for Holyfield, who refused to take a backward step. In the end, "Big Daddy" Bowe won the decision and the undisputed title. However, when Bowe publicly dumped the WBC belt in the trash bin rather than sign a mandatory fight with former Olympic rival Lennox Lewis, he split the title that Tyson had unified in 1987.

After two easy defenses against over-the-hill Michael Dokes and Jesse Ferguson, Bowe lost the split title back to Holyfield on November 6, 1993. Although this would be the lone loss on Bowe's record, he would never again hold any title more significant than the bogus WBO crown. He would fight on with some success, even stopping Holyfield in their rubber match in 1995, though no title was at stake. Two bizarre disqualification wins over Poland's Andrew Golota and a host of personal problems seemed to take the fight out of "Big Daddy." It's a shame that Bowe couldn't maintain the seemingly limitless potential that he exhibited early in his career. A Bowe–Lewis and Bowe–Tyson fight would have undoubtedly added to the boxing scene in the 1990s.

Next on the radar for Holyfield was the undefeated Michael Moorer on April 24, 1994. Moorer was the hottest property in the light heavyweight division in the late eighties and early nineties, grabbing the WBO title before jumping up to the more lucrative heavies. At 6'2", Moorer had the frame to effectively carry the extra poundage. A wrecking machine at light heavyweight, Moorer managed to carry his knockout punch with him into the heavies. The former light heavyweight also proved resilient to a heavyweight punch, picking himself off of the canvas in the second to dominate Holyfield and capture the decision and the titles.

Moorer's chin wouldn't be so dependable in his first title defense against 45-year-old former champion George Foreman on November 5, 1994. Having boxed masterfully for nine rounds, Moorer let his guard down just long enough for Big George to slam through a pile-driver right hand, and separate him from his senses and his title in the tenth frame. Foreman's win was a moral victory for everyone over the age of forty, but realistically, we knew it would be a short ride. Soon enough, Foreman was stripped of his titles for failing to defend against credible opposition.

By the middle of 1995, attention was focused once again on Mike Tyson, who served only 3 years of his 6-year term. After only four fights he had reclaimed both the WBC and WBA crowns. This set the stage for the long-overdue Tyson versus Holyfield showdown. The general consensus was that Holyfield was a little too ring-worn to hold off a monster like Tyson for 12 rounds. On November 9, 1996, Holyfield fought the greatest fight of his illustrious career and stopped "Iron Mike" in eleven rounds.

Seven months later, on June 28, 1997, came the rematch, and the infamous ear-biting incident that did so much damage to Tyson's image and career. Despite his unstable nature and lack of a title, Tyson could still demand large purses whenever he fought. Six wins over a five-year period put Tyson in position to fight Lennox Lewis for the crown on June 8, 2002. The thrashing at the hands of Lewis ended Tyson's days as a contender. He kayoed

Clifford Ettiene and then was stopped in succession by nonentities Danny Williams and Kevin McBride before he retired. Mike Tyson's place among the all-time greats can never be disputed, and he was inducted into the Boxing Hall of Fame in June of 2011.

Michael Moorer rebounded from his loss to Foreman, and two fights later captured the vacant IBF title by decisioning Axel Schultz in Germany. After two successful defenses, Moorer found himself back in the ring with old nemesis Evander Holyfield. With Moorer holding the IBF title and Holyfield the WBA, the winner would hold two-thirds of the title. It was a much different Holyfield in this fight, as he dropped Moorer five times for a ninth-round TKO.

The Lennox Lewis Era

Along with Holyfield, the 1990s produced another heavyweight who will go down as a legend, Lennox Lewis. After stopping Riddick Bowe to win the super-heavyweight gold medal for Canada in 1988, Lewis moved back to his native Britain and turned professional. Lewis progressed quickly and carried a 21–0 record into the ring against Donovan "Razor" Ruddock on October 31, 1992. Ruddock, a frightening puncher with a solid chin, was to be Lewis's toughest test. Lennox's stock went through the roof with a stunning second-round blowout. After Bowe relinquished the WBC belt, Lewis was declared that group's champion on January 14, 1993.

Lewis made three defenses before he was shocked by unheralded Oliver McCall in two rounds. Five bouts later, Lewis again met McCall in what turned out to be one of the strangest title contests ever. On February 7, 1997, in the fifth round, McCall appeared to have some kind of an emotional breakdown and the bout was stopped, giving Lewis back his WBC belt. Lewis rolled over most of the top names in the division, and when he stopped Shannon Briggs in five frames on March 28, 1998, he became lineal champion, based on Briggs's victory over Foreman the year previous.

On March 13, 1999, Lewis's WBC and lineal titles were put up along with Holyfield's WBA and IBF belts to unify the championship. In a war of attrition, the two combatants fought to a 12-round draw that most experts believed Lewis should have won. Eight months later the two fighters met again, and this time Lennox's size and youth clearly earned him the victory. Lennox Lewis was finally the undisputed heavyweight champion of the world ... but not for long.

On April 29, 2000, the WBA stripped Lewis of their title for refusing to duel with John Ruiz. That action sent Ruiz and Holyfield into a three-bout juggling match over the WBA belt. The results of these fights had little impact on the question of dominance in the heavyweight division. Lewis had already proved he was the best big man on the planet. Lennox appeared to grow stronger with each fight, beating men like Michael Grant, Francois Botha and David Tua with relative ease. However, on April 22, 2001, lightning struck in the person of Hasim Rahman. As in the first McCall fight, Lewis was caught with one resounding shot that put him to sleep, and stripped him of his title. Like the other great fighters we've looked at, Lewis was always much tougher the second time around. Seven months after their first encounter, Lewis returned the favor and put Rahman away with one punch in the fourth. Lennox followed this up with the drubbing of Tyson. If Lewis's reign lacked the excitement of Holyfield's, it was only because he was so much better than the rest.

Lewis's next bout, the slugfest with Vitali Klitschko, proved to be his last. Unlike so many before him, Lennox Lewis announced his retirement following the win over Klitschko and stuck to his guns, never to return.

Unfortunately, the same cannot be said about Holyfield. Long after his skills and reflexes have abandoned him, Evander Holyfield struggles on. Lewis's retirement has ushered in the era of the Klitschko brothers, Wladimir and Vitali. In the years subsequent to Lewis's retirement the two Ukrainians have had a virtual stranglehold on a division void of any real competition. The question to this point remains: are the Klitschkos that good, or is the division that bad? I believe it's a little of both. Whatever the reason, the division is currently in the most abysmal state in its history. There is no competition to speak of, no rivalries, and the best two fighters in the division will never meet in the ring, for obvious reasons. The result is an all-time ambivalence towards the heavyweight division.

The 1970s are, of course, the topic of the rest of this book. In comparison to the other eras, that decade fulfills our criteria for greatness as no other ever has.

Great fighters? Try Muhammad Ali, Joe Frazier, George Foreman, and Larry Holmes. Ken Norton was a cut below the others, but his many accomplishments and contributions to the sport cannot be denied.

Memorable matchups? Try Ali–Frazier I, II, and III. Or Ali–Norton I, II and III. Or Ali–Foreman. Or Foreman–Frazier. Or Norton–Holmes. Indeed, the decade featured a total of ten fights among its top four heavyweights, Ali, Frazier, Foreman and Norton.

Quality contenders? Try Jerry Quarry. Or Ron Lyle. Or Earnie Shavers. Or Jimmy Young. Or Joe Bugner. Fighters such as these could conceivably have captured championships in another era, especially the 1980s or '90s, when titles proliferated like rabbits.

However, I wouldn't want to mislead anyone into believing that all 27 of the heavyweight title bouts of the 1970s were classics. Some were real stinkers that involved several of the most unworthy challengers in history. Still, the bottom line is that a great era leaves no major questions unanswered. In that respect, only the '70s measure up. As for the others: Would Dempsey have beaten Wills? Would Tunney have beaten a Dempsey who wasn't encumbered by three years of ring rust? Could Langford or Jeannette have dethroned Johnson? Could Louis have beaten a more prudent Conn in a rematch when both were in their primes? Could Marciano have beaten Louis, Charles or Walcott in their primes? Could Bowe have beaten Lewis or Tyson?

As you will see in the coming chapters, the '70s heavyweights answered virtually all the gripping questions of their time. That's why I call the 1970s the true "Golden Age" of the heavyweights. Now it's up to you, the reader, to judge for yourself.

Two

The 1960s

David and Goliath

To understand the circumstances that made the 1970s the greatest decade in heavyweight history, a detailed look at the previous ten years is necessary. For the 1960s, after all, had a mystique that was reflected in and out of the ring.

Floyd Patterson opened the '60s with a smashing 5th-round knockout of former conqueror Ingemar Johansson. Patterson thus became the first fighter in history to regain the heavyweight title. Legendary fighters like Corbett, Jeffries, Dempsey, and Louis had failed to do what Patterson did on the night of June 20, 1960.

Yet despite that brilliant accomplishment, Floyd's second reign was on shaky ground almost from the start. On the horizon loomed a fighter so strong, so fierce, and so intimidating that his cold stare could turn hardened professional pugs into quivering stacks of Jell-O. That fighter was Charles "Sonny" Liston.

Like a hungry lion, Liston chewed up the heavyweight division in the late 1950s and early '60s, flattening the likes of Cleveland Williams (twice), Zora Folley, Nino Valdes, Mike De John, and Howard King (twice). Liston even scared some heavyweights into quitting the division.

Willie Pastrano began his career as a successful heavyweight, rising to a top-ten rating. Then he pared down to 175 pounds and won the light-heavy title in 1963. Pastrano left the heavyweights because he didn't relish the prospect of facing Sonny Liston.

Although Liston was a big man and a powerful puncher, psychological warfare was also part of his arsenal. Most of his opponents were destroyed before the bell for the first round rang. Sonny's methods were quiet and subtle. No threats, no bantering; simply a malicious and menacing aura focused in a chilling, silent stare.

Liston's reputation spoke for itself. He was a violent man, both in and out of the squared circle. When Liston transfixed an opponent with one of his patented glares, the response was usually one of pure terror. For the opponent knew that Sonny's stare wasn't just a ploy; it was a true indication of the anger and hostility within.

Liston once said that in preparing himself for a match, he would make himself as evil as possible. In that respect, Sonny had no equal.

One example of the anguish Liston could inflict on a foe happened at the weigh-in for his fight against Albert Westphal of Germany in 1961. Liston's eyes drilled through Westphal as the latter stood on the scales. Finally, the visibly nervous German broke the silence.

"You can talk to me," he pleaded. "I'm your friend. Why you look so angry?"

"You'll find out tonight," Liston growled. After 118 seconds of the first round, the terrified Westphal hit the canvas and stayed there for a full six minutes.

Unfortunately, Sonny's "evil" ways weren't always restricted to the boxing ring. Consequently, he fought more than a few bouts with the law. The result of those confrontations was a pair of lengthy prison stretches and an arrest sheet as long as Sonny's 84-inch reach. For that reason, Liston was viewed with a prejudiced eye by those who felt he lacked the moral fiber to be heavyweight champion of the world.

Liston was thus faced with two hurdles on his way to the title when he got out of prison in 1957. One was the very capable crop of heavyweight contenders of the time. The other was the American public. The latter proved to be a far more formidable obstacle.

Suspensions from state boxing commissions and title sanctioning organizations hindered his career, usually due to his criminal record and mob connections. For example, his affiliation with Frank "Blinky" Palermo, a well-known underworld figure, led to a suspension from the National Boxing Association, which later became the World Boxing Association.

Most of the American public reacted favorably to the NBA's action. A sampling from a 1961 *Boxing Illustrated* magazine letter column titled "The Reader's Corner," in which Liston's NBA suspension was the topic, brought the following comments:

"If the NBA lifts its suspension in the year 2000, it will be too soon for me...."

"At a time when boxing desperately needs good, clean fighters, how you [*Boxing Illustrated*] support a thug like Liston is beyond me...."

Attitudes like those contained more than a touch of hypocrisy. Boxing is, without a doubt, a sport with a barbaric essence. Generally, the most successful fighters are those who are most adept at rendering their opponents unconscious for at least ten seconds.

The reason boxing is so popular all over the world is that it provides a release for one of our most basic animal instincts: physical violence. It vicariously satisfies our savage side, which in many cases is never all that far beneath the surface.

Yet even in the heat of a fight in the ring, we must set acceptable limits of brutality. We can cheer two men pounding each other into insensibility only as long as it's done without malice. Afterward, the fighters must shut off their vicious buttons and return to normal, accepted civilized behavior.

This control allows us to tolerate violence that would otherwise lead its perpetrators directly to a jail cell. The most popular fighters have been Jekyll–Hyde types who are quiet, soft-spoken gentlemen on the street and barbaric savages in the ring. Men like Joe Louis, Sugar Ray Robinson, Floyd Patterson, and Rocky Marciano possessed this dual quality, and were therefore well-loved champions. Liston didn't fit that mold. When he burst onto the fistic scene, he was viewed as a man burdened by a rough background and seedy affiliations. To many, he represented the darker side of human nature from which most of us try to disassociate.

Liston reminded us just how close to the surface our barbaric nature truly is. Unlike the Louises and the Pattersons, Sonny never felt it prudent to let his guard down long enough to shut off his vicious button.

To accept such an "animal," as many called him, would be to relegate boxing to the level of cockfighting, and deprive millions of fans of their only acceptable outlet for pent-up violent energy. But Liston was still the best fighter in the division, including the champion, Floyd Patterson.

The overwhelmingly negative public opinion of Liston and his poor standing with most boxing commissions accorded Patterson the luxury of avoiding Liston's challenge far longer than he should have. A proud man beset by inner demons, Patterson became involved in a political and emotional tug of war. Although anti–Liston sentiment was strong, there were also many fans and sportswriters who believed that Liston deserved his title opportunity. The heavyweight champion is, after all, the best fighter in the division, not the most popular or socially acceptable.

Patterson was torn between two extremes. On one side were those who were pressuring him into fighting Liston for the simple reason that Sonny was the most deserving contender. Others, such as the NAACP, advised Floyd to ignore Liston's challenge. The NAACP believed that Liston was a bad role model for American youth, and a detrimental representation of the black race at a very volatile time in their history.

In turn, Liston bore a lifelong grudge against the NAACP. When informed of the organization's opinion of him, he said they should all "get run over by a truck."

Despite his resentment of the civil rights leaders who disparaged him, Liston was not insensitive to the plight of his people. It's a little-known fact that he demanded the inclusion of a clause in the contract of his first fight with Muhammad Ali (then Cassius Clay) that prohibited segregation at all closed-circuit outlets for the fight. The clause stipulated that all locations must admit blacks, and that blacks not be relegated to back-row seats.

Liston said, "I felt that the color of my people's money is the same as anyone else's. They should get the same seats. If not, I don't want those places to have the fight."[1] Montgomery, Alabama; Waco, Texas; and New Orleans, Louisiana failed to comply with the clause and therefore lost the right to telecast the bout.

That happened after Liston won the title. And he won it only after Patterson overcame the final obstacle between him and his challenger.

Of all the voices that urged Floyd to bypass Liston, none cried louder than Patterson's cagey manager, Cus D'Amato. D'Amato was never one to overmatch his fighters; consequently he wanted nothing to do with Mr. Charles "Sonny" Liston.

Originally, D'Amato declared that Liston would never be granted a title shot as long as he remained under the management of "Pep" Barone, an associate of Blinky Palermo. Dutifully, Liston dropped Barone in favor of George Katz. But D'Amato reneged on his promise; Liston wasn't about to receive a crack at the title.

An exasperated Liston stormed into D'Amato's office one day and demanded his long-overdue opportunity. The feisty D'Amato, who had once faced down a Mafia hit man, refused to back down from the fearsome ex-convict, and Sonny departed more frustrated than ever.

The final decision was Patterson's. After searching his heart, Floyd realized that unless he risked his crown against the best available contender, he didn't deserve to be champion.

Against D'Amato's advice, Patterson gave Liston his shot at the title. For the first time, Patterson overruled his long-time mentor. "I will definitely give Sonny a chance at my title and, personally, I'd like it to be my next fight," Patterson declared.[2] Liston never dreamed the placid Patterson would defy D'Amato. Graciously Liston admitted that it would have been the best bet that he ever lost.

From the moment the contracts were signed, the fight took on a "good vs. evil" theme unparalleled since the Louis–Schmeling fight of 1938. At that time Louis, the champion, was given the task of crushing Nazi Germany in the persona of Schmeling. The lines were drawn just as clearly in 1962, with Patterson representing all that was righteous and good. Liston was viewed as the dragon, the beast from the underworld.

Although both fighters were black, Patterson was the "white knight." Even President John F. Kennedy got into the act, inviting Patterson to the White House to offer his encouragement. Franklin D. Roosevelt had done the same with Louis before the Schmeling fight.

Liston didn't mind his role as the villain. However, unlike in the movies, this bad guy didn't lose.

Indeed, Patterson was Liston's antithesis in every respect. He was a clean-living, polite, religious man who coveted his privacy and low-key lifestyle as much as he did the title he had won twice. As such, he was the nation's idea of what a champion should be, a Norman Rockwell type of character.

His popularity transcended the racial barriers that still existed in the 1960s. Like Louis, he was the crowd's favorite even when he fought "White Hopes." Fans who thought Floyd didn't stand a chance against Liston hoped he would win anyway. In the *New York Times*, Gay Talese wrote: "If Patterson loses, it would be a slam at the American ideal, a defeat for Our Way of Life."

Because of Liston's checkered past, many people continued to oppose the fight even after the contract was signed. The state of New York refused to lift its ban on Liston, and consequently Madison Square Garden, the Mecca of boxing, was ruled out as a site. The fight went to Chicago's Comiskey Park, and was scheduled for September 25, 1962.

Although the event brought the host city between 7 and 10 million dollars in revenue, many moralistic groups still called for boycotts. The *Chicago Tribune* printed an editorial on the fight titled "Not Wanted Here" in which, once again, Liston's suspect past was brought to the forefront. The piece concluded: "Chicago can do without this disgraceful spectacle."

The burden this fight placed on Patterson's shoulders was too much for one man to bear. To defeat Sonny Liston in 1962 was in itself a monumental undertaking. But the quick and skillful Patterson wasn't altogether incapable of pulling it off, even though he was thirty pounds lighter than Liston.

However, with additional pressure being exerted by everyone from Cus D'Amato to President Kennedy, plus the man on the street and the media, the fight's significance was inflated beyond all perspective.

Patterson entered the ring an emotional wreck. He left it three minutes later filled with a degree of shame he ought not have felt, even though he lost his title in devastating fashion.

Through his one-round knockout defeat at Liston's hands, Patterson believed he had let America down. He was so overcome by remorse that he wore a disguise as he left Comiskey Park.

Liston believed that once he had the heavyweight title in his possession, the public would more readily accept him. After the fight, the new champion said: "He [Patterson] told me if the public gives me a chance I can be a worthy champion, maybe a better champion than he was."

Unfortunately for Liston, the title did little to enhance his esteem in the eyes of the public. Shortly after his blowout of Patterson, a New York state legislator went so far as to say that Liston as champion "could spell the death knell for professional boxing in New York State" and "could result in outlawing the sport in the state."

Nevertheless, whether the public wanted him or not, Liston was the champion. And it appeared likely to retain the title for a long time, having cleaned out the division on his way to the top.

There was, however, one potentially interesting contender on the horizon, the 1960 Olympic light heavyweight gold medalist, Cassius Marcellus Clay Jr.

The Mouth That Roared

The interest young Cassius Clay generated stemmed more from his extroverted personality than any perceived threat to Sonny Liston's supremacy. The 22-year-old Kentuckian was simply the most flamboyant and quotable character to emerge on the boxing scene for many a year. And he was also the only contender Liston hadn't already demolished.

Clay began boxing at the age of 12 in Joe Martin's gym in Louisville, Kentucky. He enjoyed a successful amateur career that was capped by winning Olympic gold in Rome, Italy.

Upon his return to the United States, the talented 18-year-old was courted by a number of prospective managers, all trying to get his name on a contract. With his father carefully scrutinizing each offer, Clay eventually signed with the "Louisville Group," also known as the "Kentucky Millionaires."

The group was led by William Faversham Jr., vice-president of Brown Distilleries Corporation. Ten other prominent local businessmen comprised the remainder of the group.

According to Faversham, the arrangement would be good for Clay, boxing and Louisville. Little did he know what the future held in store for "Cass," boxing, Louisville, and the world.

The contract called for a 50–50 split between Clay and the group. Fifteen percent of all the fighter's purses would go into a pension fund that Clay couldn't touch until he turned 35 or quit boxing, whichever came first. He also received a $10,000 signing bonus.

Cassius Sr. turned down larger offers because, as Faversham put it, they were "unsound" and didn't present any long-term plans for the young fighter's future.

With his managerial team solidly behind him, Clay was ready for his professional debut as a heavyweight against Tunney Hunsaker on October 29, 1960. He won a six-round decision.

From there, the boxing prodigy progressed rapidly. In his sixth pro fight, he tangled with Lamar Clark, a knockout artist who had scored 46 stoppages in winning 49 fights.

After absorbing two of Clark's best shots, Clay finished him in the second round. Afterward, Clark's manager, Marv Jensen, said Clay was the fastest heavyweight he had ever seen.

Clay indeed possessed quick hands. Some said his hand speed was the fastest ever seen in a fighter of any weight division. Likewise, his feet moved with the grace of a dancer. To complete the package, his 6'3" frame gradually filled out to 210 well-proportioned pounds.

His ring style was unorthodox, to say the least. Gloves dangling by his hips, Clay appeared an easy target. Yet he constantly avoided punches by leaning or backpedalling out of range. Veteran trainers and other boxing purists shuddered at Clay's daredevil approach to defense.

However, it wasn't speed of hand or foot so much as speed of lip that gained Cassius his early fame and notoriety. His predictions, poetry, and pre-fight banter met with mixed reaction from fans and the press. Whether he was received favorably or otherwise wasn't so important to him as was the desire to evoke a reaction, any reaction.

The genesis of Clay's ring showmanship can be traced to a trip he took to Las Vegas as an amateur. Clay took in a wrestling show that featured the gregarious champion at the time, Gorgeous George. The wrestler bragged that he was "beautiful" and "unbeatable." The sellout crowd went crazy, rooting for his demise. Thus was the impetus for the rambunctious persona of young Cassius Clay.

Clay perfected Gorgeous George's techniques to a degree of success the wrestler could never have imagined. His cockiness became a bone of contention with many fans who came out in droves to witness the comeuppance of this loudmouthed braggart, who soon became known as the "Louisville Lip." Clay didn't care whether the fans loved him or hated him, so long as the filled the arenas.

Clay added some spark to a division otherwise dominated by the seemingly invincible Liston. His motor-mouth antics were entertaining, but he appeared to be playing court jester to King Sonny. Few experts considered him a bona fide title threat.

Boxing Illustrated was an early exception in its advocacy of Clay as a future champ. However, after Cassius scored an uninspired decision over veteran Alonzo Johnson on July 22, 1961, the magazine issued a public apology for ever "touting him in the past." *Boxing Illustrated* also predicted that if Clay fought the same way against his next opponent, Alex Miteff, "bouncy Cassius may be bounced into early retirement, and at 19 he may be looking for a job."

Instead, Clay bounced the dangerous Miteff in six rounds. Then he disposed of veteran Willi Besmanoff in seven.

Clay's 1962 campaign opened with a scare during his February 10 encounter with Sonny Banks. Banks, himself a hot prospect with a 10–2 record (8 KOs), floored Cassius with a solid left hook in the first round. Clay sprang to his feet and turned the tables on Banks, dropping him in the second. Banks also rose, but then absorbed a one-sided beating until the referee halted the fight in round four.

Clay then signed to fight "Ancient" Archie Moore, his first big-name opponent. At the start of Clay's pro career, the Louisville Group hired Moore to train their protégé in the fine points of boxing. A predictable personality clash ended the experiment. Angelo Dundee, a highly respected trainer, became Clay's chief corner man.

Now Clay and Moore would settle their philosophical differences in the ring. "Moore in four!" Clay bellowed to anyone who would listen, continuing his practice of predicting how many rounds his foes would last.

The 49-year-old Moore promised that he would teach the young upstart the finer points of boxing. Clay, on the other hand, promised to retire the Old Mongoose.

Once again, Clay's prediction came true as he dominated and then stopped Moore in the fourth round. He seemed to be as accomplished a prophet as he was a fighter.

Before the Moore fight, he had taken on tough Alejandro Lavorante of Argentina. Lavorante had been ranked as high as number four in the division by *The Ring* magazine, largely on the strength of his knockout win over perennial contender Zora Folley.

The Argentine came into the Clay fight at even money on the betting sheet. Cassius's prediction that he would stop Lavorante in five was not taken seriously. But a dozen blinding shots to the head laid Lavorante out in the fifth, just as Clay foretold.

But Clay could never have predicted the ups and downs that would come his way in 1963. He began the year in impressive fashion with a third-round blitz of Charlie Powell, a football player turned boxer. However, his next two fights raised doubts concerning his pugilistic future. On March 13, he met a capable contender named Doug Jones at Madison Square Garden. Clay unleashed his usual torrent of threats, insults, and predictions, but this time they fell on deaf ears because the *New York Times* staff was out on strike.

That was just as well for Cassius, for Jones proved a far tougher foe than Clay anticipated when he said the fight would end in six. Not only did he last the full ten rounds with Clay; in the eyes of many ringsiders he deserved the decision. The scorecards added up in Clay's favor. But his inability to floor Jones, who was a blown-up light heavyweight, raised questions about Clay's punching power.

Putting the near-setback behind him, he flew to London for a meeting with Henry Cooper. Cooper was the most beloved of all British fighters. His long quest for the heavyweight title was a matter of national concern. Small for a heavyweight at 6'1" and 186 pounds, Cooper had a big heart and a big left hook, which Britishers affectionately labeled "'Enery's 'Ammer."

But "'Enery" also had tissue-paper skin that tore open on contact. A confident Clay predicted that Cooper would fall in five. He also called the Englishman a "tramp, cripple, bum" and other uncomplimentary names to boost the gate.

The first three rounds of the fight were uneventful, with a slight advantage going to Clay. Then, in the fourth, Cooper caught Cassius against the ropes and delivered one of his patented left hooks. The blow landed flush on Clay's jaw, and down he went!

Clay rose on wobbly legs just as the bell sounded to end the round. In the corner, trainer Angelo Dundee noticed a slight rip in one of his fighter's gloves, and immediately called for a replacement.

The cagey Dundee had noticed the tear in the first round, and said nothing at the time. But after his warrior was so badly stunned in the fourth, Dundee admittedly stuck his finger in the tear to make it larger. This made it necessary to stop the fight until new gloves could be found.

After a frantic search, it was determined that there were no spare gloves available. Clay would have to make do with the split mitt. The delay allowed Cassius time to clear his head. When the bell for round five sounded, Clay came out fresh and opened a ferocious gash over Cooper's eye. As Clay worked the cut, buckets of gore spilled down Cooper's face, and the fight was halted once again in the round Clay had called.

Clay won, but there was no question that Dundee saved his bacon. Speculation as to what would have happened had the fight continued without the extra time between rounds continues to this day. The bottom line was that Clay had another victory in his column, bringing his record to 19–0. He was also the number-one contender for Sonny Liston's crown.

A month after Clay–Cooper, Liston fought Patterson in a rematch in Las Vegas. The only justification for the fight was a return-bout clause in the contract they signed before their first meeting. Once again, Liston overpowered Patterson in less than a round.

The events that occurred after Floyd was stopped drew more attention than the fight itself. Clay sprang into the ring and began to rant and rave, challenging the hulking champion. Liston accepted Clay's challenge with a confident, sinister grin.

"You're next, loudmouth," he said to the eager 22-year-old.

The Eclipse of the Sonny

Boxing Illustrated writer Bob Waters, covering the Liston–Patterson fight and Clay's subsequent challenge, stated: "Cassius Clay has brazened himself into a multi-million dollar fight.... But what are the chances of this fight being more of a contest than was the Las Vegas debacle of July 22? Slim."

The Ring magazine tended to agree. After Liston won the crown in 1962, they reviewed possible challengers. About Clay's chances, they said: "To send Cassius against Sonnyboy would be absolutely against the law."

And Arthur Daley of the *New York Times* wrote that Clay would "be seeing stars when Sonny hits him." Daley went on to say: "The irritatingly confident Cassius enters the bout with one trifling handicap. He can't fight as well as he can talk."[3]

Clay's army of detractors cited the Jones and Cooper fights as indications of the young contender's flaws. Liston himself thought Cassius was a joke. Asked about Clay's speed, Sonny shot back: "What speed? How fast is he? That fella in England, what's his name, Cooper? He's as slow as Christmas and he caught Clay and hit him."[4]

Asked if Clay could possibly give him more of a fight than did Patterson, Liston replied, "At least Patterson tried to fight back; will Clay? If he does, it might be quicker than Patterson."[5]

There were those who were sure that Clay's habit of leaning away from punches would prove suicidal against Sonny's 84-inch reach.

"He's got to be kidding! He can't be that bad," Joe Louis exclaimed after observing a Clay workout. "Liston will kill that boy if he keeps pulling back from punches and making a lot of other mistakes."[6]

But Cassius remained undaunted by the overwhelming odds against him and his growing host of detractors.

"This is going to be the biggest upset in the history of boxing," he crowed. "I'm actually tired of talking about it, I'm ready to shake up the world. Liston's not a champion, I am. He's got my job. He's too ugly to be champion."[7]

Labeling Liston as "the Big Ugly Bear," Clay predicted he would stop the champion in eight rounds. Virtually no one believed that prediction would come true. "Liston in one" was the call of most sports experts.

The February 25, 1964, confrontation in Miami, Florida, was not as large an attraction as promoters hoped it would be. There were three reasons for this relative lack of interest.

First, the fight was viewed as a gross mismatch. The only reason the 7-to-1 odds in Liston's favor were even that close was that five times as many people were betting on Clay's round of doom as were betting on the actual outcome.[8]

Second, two black fighters appearing in a main event was a tough sell in deep–South Miami in 1964.

Third, rumors were beginning to circulate that Clay had converted to a militant sect called the Black Muslims. In fact, the Clay–Muslim connection came close to causing the fight to be canceled.

Indeed, when his association with the Muslims became common knowledge, Clay's air of rambunctious innocence vanished. To most Americans, he now represented something far more menacing than Liston's criminal past ever did. And he lost the opportunity to play the "good guy" role against the champion.

When the fight finally occurred, Clay once again made good on his prediction. He shocked the world by forcing Liston to quit in his corner at the beginning of the seventh round. It was a result no one had anticipated.

The fight itself was unusual. Contrary to the experts' opinions, Clay's lean-away defense worked perfectly against Liston's ponderous swings. The challenger even survived a blinding foreign substance that mysteriously got into his eyes in the fifth round. In the next round, Ali peppered his bewildered challenger with rapid-fire blows. When the bell for the seventh round sounded, Liston remained on his stool, and Clay was the new champion.

Many observers thought it suspicious that Liston had given up so easily. In reality, after seven fast-paced rounds, Sonny was thoroughly beaten, bleeding, and exhausted.

He also suffered a torn tendon in his left bicep. If he couldn't catch Clay early in the fight while he was still fresh, he certainly wasn't about to do so in the later rounds. Liston surrendered his title with the knowledge that his return-bout contract guaranteed a rematch.

As Clay leaped ecstatically around the ring, a new era in sports dawned—an era in which even those who had no knowledge of sports knew who the heavyweight champion was. This new champion's persona transcended the world of sports and spread to many other areas of interest and controversy. Within a few years, his would become the most recognizable face and name on the planet. And that name was not the same one the fighter bore when he challenged Liston.

The day after the fight, Clay shocked the world a second time by verifying the rumors of his conversion to the Nation of Islam, more commonly known as the Black Muslims, a group known for its open hatred of whites. He announced that he was revoking his "slave name" of Cassius Clay and adopting the name "Cassius X." This interim name soon became Muhammad Ali. And the boxing world would never be the same.

In the public mind, the heavyweight champion of the world represents the epitome of manhood, the ultimate role model, the one adult male most men and boys strive to emulate. He wields a powerful influence in popular culture. When the heavyweight champ doesn't conform to society's expectations, society tends to shun him. The fate of Sonny Liston is a prime example of this process.

But Ali and the Muslims reversed the norm. Ali's embrace of the Nation of Islam served notice on White America that he didn't need its rules, guidance, or approval. Indeed, when his contract with the Louisville Group expired in 1966, Ali did not renew it. Instead, he opted to turn his career over to Herbert Muhammad, son of Nation of Islam leader Elijah Muhammad. He cut his ties with an America that was still half segregated, with blacks for the most part repressed both socially and economically.

Mainstream America's reaction was swift and emphatic.

"The delightful boy of 1960 has become a mixed up man," wrote Arthur Daley in 1967. "He has been so thoroughly brainwashed that he now believes what he says even if the words are put into his mouth by the Muslims."[9]

Daley voiced the majority opinion. Most Americans assumed that because the young champion chose to stop following the dictates of a society that viewed him as a second-class citizen, he must not be thinking with a clear mind. Many also assumed that the Muslims were taking advantage of an empty-headed, nationally visible young black man as a means of gaining publicity. This distrust was the result of ignorance and fear.

Without a doubt, there was widespread fear of the Muslims among white and black Americans alike. Their goals and directives were for the most part misunderstood. The Muslims were indeed radical in their beliefs. But they functioned quite well without the guiding influence of the white society they rejected.

Daley's view that the Muslims had brainwashed an impressionable young man was a fallacy. In reality, Ali was far wiser than commentators gave him credit for being. After representing his country in the 1960 Olympics, he returned home with a gold medal and the belief that his achievements would change his social standing in the segregated South. Of course, it did not.

After a week or so of hoopla, Cassius Clay became just another second-class citizen. From that point onward, the man who would become Ali was anything but naive. He realized that as a black man in America, his status would never rise above a certain level, even if he became heavyweight champion.

When Clay first heard the message of Elijah Muhammad, he was filled with a sense of purpose and direction. The Muslims had a maturing effect on Ali. No longer was he content to be the clown prince of pugilism; now he was a man of substance. This was a reality the pundits and commentators failed to take into consideration.

It isn't easy to nullify a champion's ring accomplishments by condemning his personal life in the court of public opinion. Still, it happened with Jack Johnson and Sonny Liston. Now it was Ali's turn.

Usually, a period of grace follows a "socially undesirable" champion's ascension to the throne. Sooner or later, he will slip up and a more acceptable challenger will end his reign, or so the detractors hope. However, in 1964, Ali and Liston were so far ahead of the rest of the pack that no one else posed a threat to either of them. Thus, the hopes of the anti–Ali crowd rested with none other than yesterday's "bad guy," Sonny Liston.

Their inevitable rematch was a fiasco from the outset. Soon after Ali won the title, the World Boxing Association decided that his return bout contract with Liston provided the perfect opportunity to erase both fighters from the heavyweight picture.

In an act of rare duplicity, the WBA stated that it disapproved of automatic championship rematches, and it would therefore withdraw recognition of Ali and suspend both men indefinitely if they went ahead with their bout. Never mind the fact no such action had been taken two years earlier, when Liston gave Patterson the opportunity to regain his crown, or two years before that, when Patterson granted a rematch to Ingemar Johansson.

Thus, Ali–Liston II lacked the WBA's sanction, which meant precious little to anyone other than the WBA. To all fair-minded and knowledgeable boxing people, the Ali–Liston encore matched the world's two best heavyweights. It also pitted a self-proclaimed Black Muslim against a man with a well-known criminal record and mob affiliations.

Out-of-the-ring activities aside, though, Ali–Liston II made sense. Many experts thought Liston hadn't taken Ali seriously in their first fight, and would do better the second time around. And the WBA didn't have much luck convincing the public that a heavyweight title fight without those two had any real credibility.

The rematch was scheduled for Boston during the fall of 1964. But it was canceled when Ali contracted a hernia. A comedy of errors followed, during which the fight was tossed like a hot potato from one location to the next, finally landing in tiny Lewiston, Maine, on May 25, 1965.

When it was over, the fight raised even more questions than the one in which Ali won the title. With only a minute gone in the first round, Liston suddenly went down from a punch half the spectators failed to see. Ali stood over him and yelled, "Get up and fight, you big bum!"

Finally the referee, former heavyweight champion Jersey Joe Walcott, forced Ali into a neutral corner and picked up the count. Liston got up, and the fight continued. Then the timekeeper convinced Walcott that Liston had been down more than 10 seconds. Walcott stopped the fight, declaring Ali the winner by a one-round knockout.

The spectators' cries of "Fake! Fake!" were echoed by many commentators, and the fight was the low point of heavyweight boxing in the 1960s. The cause of Liston's collapse remains a mystery.

Bringing Down a Champion

The WBA sifted through its ratings and matched a 6'6" string bean from Chicago named Ernie Terrell against a cagey albeit shopworn veteran named Eddie Machen for their now-vacant title on March 5, 1965. Terrell out-jabbed and out-grabbed Machen over fifteen sleep-inducing rounds to capture the artificial championship.

Ironically, Terrell was under investigation at the time for the same thing that had caused Liston's suspension in 1961: alleged mob affiliations.

Although Terrell was a talented fighter and a legitimate contender, his WBA "reign" was a thinly disguised joke. Over the next two years, Terrell managed two successful title defenses, decision wins over George Chuvalo and Doug Jones.

During the same time span, Ali defended the genuine title against Liston, Patterson, Chuvalo, Henry Cooper, Brian London, Karl Mildenberger, and Cleveland Williams. Ali's frequent and impressive championship performances made Terrell's already dubious title claim look even weaker. Consequently, public demand for the WBA to lift its ban on Ali and clean up the dual championship mess forced the association to sanction an Ali–Terrell unification bout.

On paper, the February 6, 1967, matchup appeared competitive. Terrell was the second-best fighter in the division, and his "spoiler" style figured to frustrate, if not defeat, the champion. Once the fighters met in a Houston ring, though, paper gave way to reality. Of the fifteen rounds the fight lasted, Terrell didn't win more than one.

In his bell-to-bell tormenting of Terrell, Ali exhibited an uncharacteristic cruel streak that had surfaced only once before, in his 1965 defense against Patterson. He tortured a helpless Patterson for twelve rounds before the referee stopped the fight.

Ali viewed both Patterson and Terrell with disdain because they lacked his strong social consciousness. In Ali's opinion, when a black man reached a high-profile position like world heavyweight champion, that man should use his status as a platform to speak out on his people's behalf. Neither Patterson nor Terrell did so, at least not to Ali's satisfaction.

Couple that "character flaw" with the fact that both men insisted on addressing Ali by his "slave name," Cassius Clay, and the result was one irritated champion. He abused Terrell and Patterson in much the same manner that Jack Johnson humiliated white fighters sixty years earlier.

The parallels between the reigns of Johnson and Ali don't end there. With his lopsided victory over Terrell, Ali was once again the undisputed champion. This obviously caused problems for those who wanted him gone, as Ali had now held the title three years. His grip on the championship belt was tightening with each successful defense.

As in Johnson's era, the hoped-for savior who would rid the sport of an undesirable champion never materialized. In 1910, former champion Jim Jeffries was lured out of retirement in hopes that he would smash Johnson from the throne. The hope was in vain; Johnson humiliated Jeffries before knocking him out in the fifteenth round.

When the next challenger, Fireman Jim Flynn, also failed to wrest the crown from Johnson's head, the establishment took matters into its own hands. Convicted of a trumped-up charge under the Mann Act, which forbade the transportation of a woman across state lines for immoral purposes, Johnson was forced to flee the United States. In his absence, boxing authorities fabricated a bogus "White Heavyweight Championship."

In a sense, Ali suffered a similar fate. By 1967, he had defeated every available challenger in the heavyweight division. And at age twenty-five, his best years were still ahead of him. A lengthy Ali reign seemed inevitable. He called himself "The Greatest," and no one could deny that claim.

As well, the social appeal of Muhammad Ali had far transcended boxing. He was the most high-profile young black man in America. The powers that be could ill afford such a radical black role model, especially during the already volatile mid–1960s. His period of grace had come to an end.

Since Ali could not be separated from his title in the ring, other means were sought. Like the Mann Act in Johnson's case, the Vietnam War presented a golden opportunity.

Originally classified by Selective Service as 1-Y, or unacceptable for the draft due to failure on the Army's intelligence test, Ali was mysteriously reclassified 1-A, which meant he was subject to immediate call-up for two years of military service. Ali protested, uttering the immortal line: "I ain't got nothin' against those Viet Congs."

For the remainder of 1967, the threat of the draft hung over Ali's head. On March 22, he stopped 34-year-old veteran Zora Folley in seven rounds. It was the ninth and final defense of Ali's first reign. He was ordered to report to his local draft board in Houston for induction into the U.S. Army.

New York attorney Hayden Covington stated that Ali devoted "160 hours a month to his ministerial duties. Boxing is an incidental sideline to him."[10]

However, all of his previous petitions for conscientious objector status had been denied by various legal bodies, including the U.S. Supreme Court. In a 67-page petition, sent three days before Ali's scheduled induction, District Judge Allen B. Hannay was asked to restrain Houston's Selective Service Office from reporting Ali as a delinquent if he refused induction. The letter told Hannay point-blank: "Clay has publicly declared and he alleges that he will not do as commanded on the 28th day of April, 1967, or any time thereafter."[11]

The petition was dismissed on April 27.

On April 26, Ali stated: "I don't want to go to jail, but I've got to live the life my conscience and my God tell me to. What does it profit me to be the wellest liked man in America who sold out to everybody?"[12]

Ali reiterated that he had no quarrel with the Viet Cong, and could not justify it within himself to go to war against them. His Muslim beliefs stated that a member of that faith could only take up arms in the cause of a jihad, or holy war.

As well as moral reservations, Ali and Herbert Muhammad saw a great danger to the champion in the army, especially from a "prejudiced soldier who thinks he's doing the country a favor." As Ali put it, "If the Viet Cong didn't get me, some Georgia cracker would."[13]

As expected, Ali refused to step forward on April 28, and was charged with draft evasion. Although indictment under the charge would take time, all boxing organizations immediately stripped the champion of his title. World Boxing Association President M. Robert Evans stated: "I feel that Muhammad Ali has defied the laws of the United States regarding selective service. His action today leaves me no alternative."[14]

Those sentiments were echoed by New York State Boxing Commissioner Edwin B. Dooley, who said: "His refusal to enter the service is regarded by the commission to be detrimental to the best interest of boxing."[15]

Ali had anticipated the actions taken by the boxing authorities, and had prepared a Xeroxed statement that read as follows:

> Regardless of the differences in my outlook, I insist upon my right to pursue my livelihood in accordance with the same rights granted to other men and women who have disagreed with the policies of whatever administration was in power at the time.
>
> I have the world heavyweight title not because it was "given" to me, not because of my race or religion, but because I won it in the ring through my own boxing ability.
>
> Those who want to "take it" and hold a series of auction-type bouts not only do me a disservice but actually disgrace themselves. I am certain that the sports fans and fair-minded people throughout America would never accept such a "titleholder."[16]

The WBA and other boxing bodies considered those words nothing more than typical Ali hot air. But stripping Ali of his title and banishing him from the ring didn't do so much to hinder as it did to enhance his popularity in many circles. In his exile, he became a sought-after speaker and a companion of many world leaders, not to mention a symbol of left-wing martyrdom.

With Ali gone, or so they thought, the WBA set about finding a replacement champion by staging an eight-man elimination tournament. The field consisted of previous Ali victims Ernie Terrell, Floyd Patterson, and Karl Mildenberger, plus talented newcomers Thad Spencer, Leotis Martin, Oscar Bonavena, Jerry Quarry, and Jimmy Ellis.

These men were all credible, ranked contenders. Still, the 1967–68 WBA extravaganza was only slightly less farcical than the coronation of a "White Heavyweight Champion" had been back in 1914. While the 1914 tournament was limited to Caucasian contenders, the 1967 version also purposely excluded a deserving fighter, Sonny Liston.

Liston hadn't lost a fight since the two Ali debacles. Yet the WBA refused to include him in its ratings. The suspension the organization slapped on Ali and Liston back in 1965 was lifted from Ali in 1967 to allow him to fight Terrell. In contrast, Liston carried his suspension the rest of his life.

"I didn't even sign that [rematch clause]," Liston complained in 1967. "That was an agreement between Clay's manager and mine, the hot dog salesman." (Liston's manager at the time was concessionaire Jack Nilon.)

"Clay got back fighting, and my man is still selling hot dogs. But me? I can't work."

Since most U.S. states came under WBA jurisdiction, Sonny was restricted to fighting in only a few locations. The separate New York State suspension imposed on Liston in 1962 remained in effect as well.

Liston would say with a shrug that the New York suspension didn't bother him any, but clearly it did. In 1967 New York City and Madison Square Garden were still prime boxing venues, and Liston's exile from them effectively squeezed him out of the spotlight. Consequently, he was relegated to fighting menial contests against opponents who did little to advance his standing. And he wasn't getting any younger. He was 35 when Ali was suspended, but some thought he was closer to 40.

Still, Liston remained a formidable presence among the heavyweights. After his title was taken away, Ali was asked who he thought was the next best heavyweight in the world. Without hesitation, he said it was his old foe Liston.

Ali was probably right. But Sonny would never again get the opportunity to prove it. He continued to slap down younger fighters who hoped to make their name by knocking off a former champion. None succeeded until a night in 1969, when age and frustration caught up with him and he was stopped in nine rounds by Leotis Martin.

Liston fought one more time, butchering Bayonne, New Jersey's Chuck Wepner in ten rounds. Six months later, Liston was found dead in his Las Vegas home by his wife, Geraldine.

The circumstances of Sonny's death remain as mysterious and clouded as his life and career. It was a sad, inglorious conclusion to the life of one of the greatest fighters in the history of the sport. Those who knew him best insisted that beneath the "Big Ugly Bear" facade, there existed a troubled, misunderstood man. Only in the past couple of decades is Liston finally receiving his due recognition.

The Search for a Successor

Sonny Liston wasn't the only noteworthy contender who didn't participate in the WBA's tournament. But Liston had no choice in the matter. 1964 Olympic heavyweight gold medalist Joe Frazier did.

Billy Joe Frazier was born in Beaufort, South Carolina, on January 12, 1944. He moved north to New York at the age of 15, and eventually ended up in Philadelphia with his new wife, Florence. Both bride and groom were only 16 years old.

Joe picked up a $100 a week job in a slaughterhouse. Always a stocky youth, his weight soon shot up to 235 pounds on a 5'11" frame. Interested in shedding some of that weight, young Joe began working out at the Police Athletic League (PAL) gym.

Always large for his age growing up in Beaufort, Joe rarely found himself in confrontations. His primary interest in going to the gym was the exercise.

Frazier may not have liked fighting, but his tenacity in the gym soon caught the attention of Yancey "Yank" Durham, who trained boxers at night after working all day as a railroad welder. Duke Dugent, another trainer at the PAL, also liked what he saw in the teenage Frazier.

Durham took to young Frazier from the start. Although Joe was lacking in skill, Yank instantly recognized and appreciated Joe's tenacity, work ethic and ability to take instructions.

Joe took many lumps in early sparring sessions against seasoned Philadelphia professionals like Leotis Martin and Bennie Briscoe. Durham said, "They banged the stuffing out of him but Joe never backed down or gave up."[17]

Every day he would return, eager to learn and improve at the sport that had gotten into his blood and helped him to train down to a lean and hard 205 pounds. As an amateur he gained quick success, winning Golden Gloves titles in 1962, 1963, and 1964. However, his amateur career appeared to end on a down note when he was defeated in the 1964 U.S. Olympic trials by Buster Mathis. However, when Mathis broke his hand in winning a second fight against Frazier, Joe went to the Tokyo Olympics as an alternate.

In Tokyo, Frazier knocked out his first two opponents, a Ugandan and an Australian, in a round each. The semifinal bout saw him stop Soviet fighter Vadim Yemelyanov in the second round, but not before breaking his left thumb. Frazier concealed the injury and went on to the final match against Hans Huber of West Germany. Fighting literally one-handed, Frazier won the decision and the gold medal.

Upon Frazier's return to Philadelphia, his success turned sour when it was discovered that his thumb would take six months to heal. He couldn't even perform his old duties at the slaughterhouse. By this time, Joe and Florence had two small children, and money was scarce. Frazier kept food on the table via a part-time janitorial job at his local church. There was no Louisville Group waiting to secure his financial future.

Once the hand was healed, Frazier and Durham decided it was past time to join the punch-for-pay ranks. On August 16, 1965, Frazier made his pro debut a short one, stopping Woody Goss in less than a round. In his next fight, he suffered a flash knockdown before stopping Mike Bruce in three rounds. Frazier rounded out 1965 with two more quick kayoes.

Durham was Frazier's manager, trainer, and financier through his first year as a pro. But he realized he needed big money to take his fighter to the top.

Eventually, Durham and Frazier met with Dr. F. Bruce Baldwin, a well-respected civic leader in Philadelphia and president of the Horn and Hardart Banking Co. Baldwin expressed interest in forming a syndicate to sponsor the young heavyweight. Thus, Baldwin became Frazier's Bill Faversham, and Cloverlay, Inc. was formed.

The name Cloverlay came from the mind of the organization's secretary. "Clover" represents good luck, and the dictionary defines "overlay" as "superbly favorable odds." Joe Frazier was Cloverlay's sole asset. Nonetheless, the organization was not a charity so much as a sound financial investment. Less than two years after the group's formation, Cloverlay stock rose an astounding 1,350 percent!

Frazier's deal with Cloverlay gave him 50 percent of all his purses and ancillary rights, with 35 percent going to the organization. Durham would take 15 percent and remain in control of all managerial decisions involving Frazier's career. As well, Joe received a $100 a week minimum salary.

With his financial worries a thing of the past, Frazier could now concentrate solely on his ring career. Cloverlay effectively saved Joe from his grueling job at the slaughterhouse. Not only was the work exhausting, it also wreaked havoc on the fighter's primary assets, his hands. Frazier had already lost the tip of his left pinky finger, and often sustained cuts to both hands.

Now the Philadelphian began his climb up the heavyweight ladder in earnest. His aggressive, left-hooking, caution-to-the-winds style was both crowd-pleasing and effective. He soon adopted the nom de guerre "Smokin' Joe," a nickname that became as distinctive to Frazier as the "Brown Bomber" tag was to Joe Louis.

Despite his in-your-face attack, Frazier proved deceptively hard to reach with head blows. Veteran contender Eddie Machen figured to easily exploit Joe's seemingly porous defense, but instead found his offense so overwhelming that it became a moot point.

Frazier's Cloverlay backers received their biggest scare on the night of September 21, 1966, when Argentine muscleman Oscar "Ringo" Bonavena floored Frazier twice in the second frame of their ten-rounder. A third knockdown in the round would have resulted in an automatic stoppage under New York rules. But Joe stayed on his feet and survived a further battering in the third round before finally taking control through the middle rounds.

Bonavena came back in the final two rounds, turning the fight into a "saloon brawl," as *New York Times* writer Robert Lipsyte put it. Frazier won a split decision.

Cloverlay had a banner year in 1967, with Frazier winning six fights, five by knockout. He also accomplished what had previously been considered impossible by becoming the first fighter to stop Canadian iron man George Chuvalo. He did it with a left hook that nearly knocked Chuvalo's eye out of its socket.

By the time the WBA put Ali's title up for grabs, Frazier had established himself as one of the hottest new attractions in the division. Needless to say, his participation would have given the tournament a touch of credibility. However, Frazier and Durham said "Thanks, but no thanks" to the WBA's invitation to participate. The action predictably annoyed the WBA and Sports, Inc., the group promoting the affair.

Frazier said the tournament was merely a money-grabbing extravaganza for promoters who weren't really concerned with the quality of its participants. Mark Malitz of Sports, Inc. stated that Frazier had made his decision and it was too late for him to change his mind even if he wanted to.

The WBA went so far as to demote Frazier from number one contender all the way down to number nine in their ratings. The action damaged the WBA's credibility more than Frazier's. Frazier remained undaunted by the WBA's action. Since he was the division's most dominant active fighter, Joe and Durham felt that they were in a strong position to thumb their noses at the WBA.

Several months after the WBA roadshow got underway, Frazier received an opportunity to take a shortcut to the title by fighting a one-bout elimination against old nemesis Buster Mathis. At stake was the heavyweight championship of the world, as recognized by the states of New York, Pennsylvania, Massachusetts, Illinois, and Maine.

Ironically, Pennsylvania was also a WBA state, which meant it would recognize the winner of that organization's tournament. Mathis, a two-time conqueror of Frazier in their amateur days, was undefeated as a pro. The 1964 edition of Mathis was a 6'3", 315-pound behemoth whose massive girth disguised a boxer with deceptive hand and foot speed.

At one time he was the top amateur heavyweight in the U.S., but Mathis's luck took a turn for the worse the day he broke his hand on Frazier's skull in the 1964 Olympic Trials. From that day onward, the fates of the two prospects unfolded in different directions. Frazier captured a gold medal that would in all likelihood have gone to Mathis.

In their professional careers, Frazier got off to the quicker start. By the time the rivals met in March 1968, Frazier had beaten proven contenders like Chuvalo, Bonavena, Machen and Doug Jones in compiling a 19–0 record with 17 knockouts. Mathis's slate stood at 23–0 with 17 stoppages.

But Mathis's competition was several cuts below that of Frazier. He began his career under the tutelage of Cus D'Amato, who was known for bringing his fighters along cautiously. While Frazier's opposition grew stiffer as his career progressed, so did Mathis's ... through rigor mortis.

Mathis's backers became dissatisfied with their fighter's slow progress under D'Amato, and they replaced him with Joe Fariello. The quality of his opposition rose a notch or two, and by March 1968, *The Ring* magazine ranked him #10. But that was a backhanded compliment. As the publication stated, Mathis's rating was due largely to the fact that "below the Michigan Mastodon is nobody worthy of a No. 10 location."

Frazier, by the way, was ranked #1 by the "Bible of Boxing." Contrary to other boxing authorities, *The Ring* continued to recognize Ali as champion, although editor Nat Fleischer continued to refer to him as "Cassius Clay."

Despite his amateur triumphs of over Frazier, Mathis went into the fight a 2-to-1 underdog. Buster remained confident, however. He had won more fights than Frazier, and had pared 70 pounds from his enormous frame since his amateur days. He still enjoyed a commanding size advantage over Frazier, coming in at 243½ pounds to Joe's 204½. Also, he didn't think much of Frazier as a fighter. He felt Joe was merely a left-hook artist, lacking any kind of right hand punch.

Frazier was guaranteed $175,000, while Mathis hauled in $75,000 for the first boxing program at the newest incarnation of Madison Square Garden.

The Garden's billing of the fight as a contest for the heavyweight championship of the world created no small stir. There was picketing planned outside the Garden for its presumption. Despite political and social protests, the fight came off.

Had the fight gone the three-round amateur distance, Mathis would have won as he had four years ago. But this was a fifteen-rounder, a route that allowed Frazier ample time to cut Buster down to size. At the 2:33 mark of round 11, Frazier became the first man since Ali to be hailed (by some) as the heavyweight champion of (part of) the world.

In the eyes of the rest of the world, Ali was still champion. After Frazier's triumph, Nat Fleishcer reiterated *Ring* magazine's support of the deposed champion: "No title was at stake in Frazier vs. Mathis. I repeat, Cassius Clay still is the world champion."

And what of the WBA's eight-man eliminations? While the tourney never provided anything that could be described as an epic battle, it did allow some of the division's top contenders to fight each other instead of Ali.

As Abe Glick, editor of *Boxing Illustrated*, wrote in the June 1967 issue, "This type of tournament could be the shot in the arm the ailing boxing business needs.... Consider what happens when Muhammad's giant shadow is removed from the scene. An entire new notion of competition emerges.... For openers a heavyweight elimination tourney would give a second chance to all who have fallen before the thunder of Ali's fists." Even so, Glick could never have predicted that of the seven bouts it took to crown the WBA's "champion," the favorite would be beaten in each contest!

The tournament kicked off on August 5, 1967, with a double-header televised from the Houston Astrodome.

In the first bout, former WBA titleholder Ernie Terrell took on Thad Spencer. Terrell was widely favored to win his second "paper" crown; Spencer, on the other hand, was a young prospect thought to be in over his head. The odds were 11 to 5 in Terrell's favor.

However, Terrell found himself on the canvas in the second round, courtesy of a Spencer right hand. Although he rose and later put Spencer on the deck, Ernie was unable to blunt the younger man's momentum. Spencer captured a unanimous 12-round decision.

Terrell's manager, George Hamid, said afterward that his fighter hadn't fully recuperated from the beating Ali had given him earlier in the year. After Terrell lost another decision to Mexico's Manuel Ramos two months later, Hamid persuaded Ernie to pack it in.

Unfortunately, like so many before and after him, Terrell couldn't resist the lure of the ring. In 1970, he mounted a comeback. He did well against second- and third-rate competition, and he even sprang an upset kayo win over highly touted prospect Jose Luis Garcia in 1971. But in 1973, Terrell suffered a devastating one-round knockout defeat at the hands of Jeff "Candy Slim" Merritt. That loss convinced him to retire for good.

The other half of the double-header matched Philadelphia's Leotis Martin with former Ali sparring partner Jimmy Ellis.

Martin was a dangerous puncher, with only one loss in 25 previous fights. Fourteen of his victories had come via the short route. Ellis, on the other hand, was an improbable participant in a heavyweight title eliminator. Only two years earlier, he had been a struggling middleweight with a spotty record.

Born and raised in Louisville, Kentucky, Ellis showed promise as an amateur, splitting a pair of fights with Cassius Clay, who was two years younger. However, it wasn't long after their youthful rivalry that their fistic fortunes diverged.

Clay gained Olympic gold and grew into a full-fledged heavyweight. Ellis turned pro as a middleweight without the financial backing or media hoopla that surrounded his friend. At the time, Ellis had a wife and several children to feed. Lacking the advantage of a sponsoring group, Ellis couldn't survive on the purses of a preliminary fighter. Like Frazier in his pre–Cloverlay days, Jimmy had no choice but to seek other employment.

Ellis worked long and hard hours in the concrete business and starved himself to keep his weight under 160 pounds, the middleweight limit. After losing three of four contests to contenders like Rubin "Hurricane" Carter and George Benton in 1964, his record stood at 15–5.

Believing he was better than that record indicated, Ellis sent a letter in 1965 to Angelo Dundee asking for help with his career. Dundee agreed not only to train Ellis but to manage him as well. Angelo would also use Jimmy as a sparring partner for Ali, to increase Muhammad's already considerable speed.

The shrewd Dundee knew Ellis was draining himself by fighting as a middleweight.

Beefing up to a more comfortable poundage for his 6'1" frame, Jimmy soon found himself competing with the big boys. As a heavyweight, he found immediate success, often fighting on Ali's under cards. His string of victories brought him credibility and international exposure.

On the Ali–Folley undercard, Ellis stopped slick-boxing Johnny Persol, who was a rated contender. It was his third consecutive first-round kayo and eighth straight victory since his rise in weight. After Ali toyed with Folley in the main event, he claimed that the only foreseeable challenge to his crown was his old friend, Jimmy Ellis.

Others didn't share that opinion, dismissing Ellis as a blown-up middleweight who lacked stamina. He was the final man chosen for the tournament, and few expected him to last more than a few rounds with Martin.

Ellis confounded his critics by maintaining a sustained attack through nine torrid rounds, giving Martin a thorough, bloody battering. Although Leotis never left his feet, the inside of his mouth was so badly lacerated that the referee had no choice other than to stop the fight.

Martin's career lasted two more years. His upset 1969 win over Sonny Liston vaulted him into the number-one contender's position. Unfortunately, a detached retina Leotis suffered during that fight forced him to retire.

Despite his overwhelming victory over Martin, Ellis's detractors remained unconvinced. His chances of advancing beyond the semifinals of the tournament were considered somewhere between slim and none, because his opponent was none other than the Argentine strongman, Oscar Bonavena.

A crude throwback to his countryman Luis Firpo, Bonavena had advanced to the semifinals by clubbing Karl Mildenberger to the canvas four times en route to a 12-round decision win in Mildenberger's German back yard. Incredibly, Mildenberger was the WBA's No. 1 contender at the time.

Against Bonavena, the frail-looking Ellis was once again the underdog. And, once again, he upset the odds. Not only did Ellis thoroughly outsmart his crude opponent over 12 rounds, he also decked him twice with sneaky right hands. Joe Frazier, considered a far more powerful puncher, couldn't floor Bonavena even once.

Now the ex–sparring partner was one step away from succeeding Muhammad Ali, at least in the eyes of the WBA. His opponent would be California hotshot Jerry Quarry.

The 22-year-old Quarry was the latest in a long line of "White Hope" heavyweights. Unlike most others, however, Quarry possessed genuine talent, even though his performances were sometimes erratic and inconsistent.

Quarry advanced to the final via a decision win over Floyd Patterson, who was by then becoming the elder statesman of the heavyweights, and a 12th-round stoppage of Spencer. The Patterson win was lackluster. But against the cocky Spencer, Quarry unveiled a potent combination of firepower and boxing skill. The beating Spencer took had lasting effects; although he continued his career until 1972, Thad never won another fight.

The impression Quarry made in his destruction of Spencer influenced odds makers' views of the tournament final, and the Californian was installed as a favorite over Ellis. But Ellis, with his experience and deceptive power, was a "live" underdog.

Although Quarry–Ellis had the potential to be a competitive, exciting matchup, the reality failed to live up to expectations. On April 27, 1968, Ellis won a dull, one-sided 15-round decision over an inexplicably passive Quarry.

The newly crowned Ellis now joined Joe Frazier in the category of heavyweight champion of an Ali-less world. Both men now had to fight their way out of Ali's shadow. Unless or until they fought each other, their title claims would be judged by the standard of comparative performance.

Over the next two years, Frazier clearly reinforced his cause by defending his five-state title four times. Two of those defenses were easy: a two-round stoppage of Manuel Ramos and a one-round taming of Dave "The Animal" Zyglewicz. The other two were tougher. Oscar Bonavena extended him over 15 grueling rounds in 1968. And in the summer of 1969, Frazier stopped a resurgent Jerry Quarry in seven of the most intensely contested rounds of the year.

Ellis didn't fare as well. Over the same time span, he made only one defense, a controversial and questionable decision win over persistent Floyd Patterson on September 14, 1968, in Stockholm, Sweden. The Patterson fight was very costly for Ellis. Not only did the disputed result give more ammunition to his detractors; he also sustained a severely broken nose that required a lengthy recovery period. Because of the injury and contractual problems, Ellis did not fight at all in 1969.

As the year and the decade drew to a close, Frazier and Ellis finally agreed to terms for a unification fight, slated for February 16, 1970.

A victory for either man would do much to bolster his claim to the title. But as long as Muhammad Ali remained alive and out of prison, both Frazier and Ellis knew they could never claim undisputed championship recognition.

The 3½ year period of exile from his profession Ali endured while his case dragged through the courts was both tragic and unjust. However, a look through the cold lens of objectivity indicates that his absence had a positive effect on the heavyweight division.

By the time the WBA and others stripped him of his title, Ali had eliminated virtually all of the older, established contenders. And he had done it in masterful fashion. During nine title defenses lasting a total of 74 rounds, he was never floored, cut, or even seriously hurt. And he won all but four or five of those rounds.

Already, some were calling Ali an all-time great, mentioning him in the same breath as Johnson, Dempsey, Louis, and Marciano. And, at 25, it seemed likely his peak years were still ahead of him, which was bad news for newcomers like Frazier, Ellis, Quarry, et al. If those young guns had fought an active Ali between 1967 and 1969, all of them, even Frazier, would have suffered one-sided drubbings.

Indeed, during a 1966 conversation between Ali and Frazier, Ali asked Joe how much he weighed. When Frazier responded that he weighed around 200 pounds, Ali suggested that Joe would be wise to pare himself down to light heavyweight to avoid an eventual thrashing. Presumably, Frazier's response was unprintable. But even Joe's manager, Yank Durham, admitted that his fighter wasn't yet ready to meet Ali in 1967.

As Tex Maule wrote in the July 10, 1967, *Sports Illustrated*: "When the intransigent Muhammad Ali lost a decision to the law of the land and was stripped of his heavyweight championship, he transformed a baker's dozen of potential victims into credible heavyweight contenders."

The effect of Ali's exile was to provide a three-year period of development for young, talented heavyweights to gain some experience and hone their skills. Had Ali been defending his title during that time, the division would have been denuded of talent by 1970. Instead, Ali's absence inadvertently created the conditions that gave rise to the most talented group of heavyweights of any one era.

Three

1970

And Then There Was One

The epochal year of 1970 began with three claimants to the world heavyweight championship, a situation unprecedented in boxing history. And each man's claim carried its own degree of legitimacy.

Jimmy Ellis held the WBA version by virtue of winning the 1967–68 tourney. But he had only defended his title once. Joe Frazier was recognized by five states and parts of South America, and he had notched four successful defenses. And the inactive Muhammad Ali, who had never been defeated in the ring, was recognized unofficially by a great many fans, and officially still by *The Ring* magazine.

The Ring had come under a great deal of pressure from almost every governing body to drop Ali from its pedestal and replace him with Frazier or Ellis. Some viewed the magazine's continued recognition of Ali as unpatriotic. Nat Loubet, *The Ring*'s managing editor and son-in-law of its venerable founder and editor Nat Fleischer, defended the action: "Boxing should stand up for its own and give a man who is its heavyweight champion the benefit of our due process system. That's the American way. While the litigation goes on to the Supreme Court, we have to wait to see if he is finally judged innocent or guilty. And if he's guilty, then see to it that he pays the price. That's justice."[1]

Ali was out of the boxing picture physically, pending a decision from the U.S. Supreme Court allowing him to fight. Verbally, however, Ali couldn't be repressed. He said in January that boxing had become dull with Ellis and Frazier as champions. Naturally, he felt he was the tonic needed to breathe life back into the sport.

But Muhammad Ali was not Smokin' Joe's immediate concern. Frazier was busy preparing himself for his February unification bout with Ellis at Madison Square Garden. The winner would receive undisputed recognition as heavyweight champion by all the governing bodies. Both men were guaranteed $150,000 against 30 percent of all ancillary rights.

As a potentially classic boxer-slugger confrontation, the Frazier–Ellis matchup generated a great deal of interest. Frazier was undefeated, powerful, and always single-minded in his mission to mangle all opposition. As Mark Kram wrote in a *Sports Illustrated* column prior to the fight, Joe's best weapon, "the one that is just as crippling as his bearlike swipes, is his rhythm; that pace is directed by a music he alone hears."[2]

Jimmy Ellis was hardly a slouch. Although he had five defeats on his record, they had all come when he was campaigning as an undersized middleweight. Since moving up in poundage, he was 12–0. "As a heavyweight," Dundee said optimistically, "Jimmy is as undefeated as Frazier is."[3]

Stylewise, Ellis was a superb boxer-puncher, with a quick jab and vastly underrated power in his right hand. He also had a great deal of heart. After suffering a fractured nose and a bruised hand early in his WBA title defense against Patterson, he hung in to capture a narrow decision.

Still, seventeen months had passed between that fight and his meeting with Frazier. Many observers wondered how Jimmy's nose would hold up against Frazier's left hook. He underwent reconstructive surgery only days after the Patterson fight. The surgeon, Dr. Julian Geoff, assured the media two days before the Frazier fight that there was "no weakness" in Ellis's nose. "Jimmy has more breathing space than he did before," Geoff said. "During the operation, I corrected his septum and also removed a piece of cartilage." Consequently, the doctor opined that Ellis's nose was "probably more resilient to a hard punch."[4]

Still, the nose problem had caused cancellations of several fights. But other woes plagued Ellis's attempts to defend his title. A proposed bout against Argentine stylist Gregorio Peralta, originally scheduled for December 1969, had fallen through for promotional reasons.

Consequently, when Ellis began training for Frazier on January 5, he was already in fine shape. In an unusual move, Dundee limited Ellis's sparring to almost nil 10 days prior to the fight so that Jimmy wouldn't be overtrained. Ellis was eager to spar, but he trusted his manager's judgment. "If they don't want me to box, I got to do what they say," Ellis stated.

What did Yank Durham think of Ellis's lack of sparring? "Every fighter's not trained alike," he said. I can't say the man's wrong. That's his fighter."[5] Meanwhile, Durham had Frazier sparring at least four rounds a day.

As fight day approached, Ellis seemed the looser of the two. He appeared confident and jocular as the moment of truth approached. Frazier, as was his norm, grew tense, serious, and cranky, anxious to get on with the business at hand. He had trained hard, and he looked superbly fit. Although he said he wasn't taking Ellis lightly, he believed the WBA champ's style was made to order for him.

"I don't think Ellis can move away from me as fast as I can move in on him," Frazier summarized.

"We'll see that Monday night," Ellis retorted. "How fast can he go, how fast can he come, we'll see. He talked about me running out. I'll be there Monday night."[6]

Ellis saw hope in the fact that Frazier had already been floored three times in his career. It proved to him that "Frazier will go if he's really hit."[7]

Dundee boasted that Ellis was the best one-punch knockout artist in the heavyweight division, and that Jimmy would "win, and win by a knockout. He will be a revelation."[8]

Durham also predicted a knockout. "There's no doubt in my mind that we'll knock him out. Anywhere from 1 to 15, you pick the round. We're going after him like we've gone after everybody else," he said.[9]

Ex-champion Muhammad Ali stated a few days before the bout that he had no desire to fight again, and that he'd recognize the winner as world champion. Ali also expressed his desire to present the winner with his championship belt, so that "all my fans and spectators will realize that I'm retired, and there's really a new champion to recognize."[10]

However, the New York State Athletic Commission refused to allow Ali into Madison Square Garden even to present the belt. "That doesn't make any difference," Ali said. "I'll give the winner my belt in the dressing room, or out on the sidewalk."

But Frazier and Ellis couldn't have cared less about Ali's belt. "Tell him to hang onto it," Frazier said prophetically. "He might get a license someday."[11]

Ellis was less optimistic about his old friend's fistic future. "He can keep the belt in a box," he said. "That man's not boxing anymore."[12]

Ring magazine honored Ali's retirement announcement and declared that it would recognize the Ellis–Frazier winner as the undisputed heavyweight champion.

Frazier was installed as a heavy 6-to-1 favorite in the eyes of the betting crowd. "Odds don't mean nothing to me," Ellis commented. "I'm a fighter, not a gambler.... The odds were against me against Martin, Bonavena and Quarry, and I won them all, and I expect to win this one."[13]

Ali, never one to mute his opinions, was understandably supportive of Ellis. He figured that his friend from Louisville possessed all of the tools necessary to knock Smokin' Joe out early. As for Frazier, Ali opined that the Philadelphia slugger had "no skills, no jab, no hook off the jab, no footwork, no timing."[14]

Jerry Quarry, who had fought both men, stated oddly enough that he considered Ellis the harder puncher, but found Frazier the more "damaging" hitter. When pressed for a prediction, Quarry said, "I dunno.... It should be a helluva fight."[15]

A large crowd of 18,079 curious fans filled the Garden on fight night, paying a whopping $647,997. Ellis, weighing a heavy 201 pounds, stepped into the ring wearing a gold satin robe with sparkling lapels. He danced around, throwing punches in Frazier's direction across the ring.

When the bell sounded, the WBA champ won the opening round, landing a few right-handers on the head of the bobbing and weaving slugger from Philadelphia. Frazier picked up the pace in round two and attacked Ellis. Ellis tried to hold him off with jabs, but Frazier walked through them and whacked away at whatever parts of Ellis he could reach.

In the third, Smokin' Joe staggered Ellis with a three-punch combination. Near the end of the round, Frazier cornered Ellis and was unleashing a barrage of blows when Jimmy suddenly caught him with a combination that momentarily backed him up.

Then, realizing he had just absorbed Ellis's best shots, Joe allowed an evil grin to crease his face.

"Sissy, you can't hit," he sneered. "I'm takin' everything you got, man, and you ain't hurtin' me."[16]

At the bell, the smile remained on Frazier's face. For all intents and purposes, the fight was over. All that remained was the mop-up.

Early in round four, a left-right combination from Frazier dropped Ellis for only the second time in his career. He rose at the count of nine. Then Frazier tore into his wounded prey and knocked him flat on his back with one of his patented left hooks. A glassy-eyed Ellis barely beat the ten count. The bell sounded before Frazier could continue the carnage.

In the corner, Dundee took one look at his battered warrior and refused to allow him out for the fifth round. Frazier had earned the undisputed championship.

Later, some criticized Dundee for being overprotective. Angelo was quick to defend his action.

"I know my fighter," he said. "I asked him questions and got no response. I slapped him on the thighs, poured water down his trunks, and he just sat there. He was feeling nothin' and I wasn't about to let him go on."

Ellis was asked if he heard the referee's count.

"I picked it up at the count of five," he replied.

"On which knockdown?"

"I was only knocked down once."

"That," said Dundee, "was why I stopped the fight."[17]

Ellis was also asked if the long layoff had affected his performance.

"If I'd have had four or five tune-up bouts and then got hit with that left hook, what difference would it have made?" Ellis responded.[18]

Although Dundee was duly impressed by Frazier's performance, he still believed Muhammad Ali could come back and beat him despite a three-year layoff, twice as long as Ellis's.

"He needs a couple of fights under his belt before he'd be ready for Frazier, but if they got together, Frazier would never lick Clay, never in a million years," Dundee stated.[19]

Speaking of Ali, the retired former champion viewed the bout at a closed-circuit outlet in Philadelphia. Forgetting his vow never to fight again and to recognize the winner as his successor, Ali jumped up and started to shadowbox.

"I want Frazier!" he shouted. "I'm starting my comeback now!"[20]

Ali was already becoming an annoyance to Frazier, who knew in his heart that he'd have to defeat the former champion to eliminate the last remnants of doubts concerning the legitimacy of his reign.

"I'm gonna wait until that other fella can fight me," Frazier said after his triumph over Ellis. "I'm gonna sing rock 'n' roll until that Muhammad Ali or Cassius Clay or whatever his name is can fight me."[21] Frazier insisted that he'd fight Ali, "even at Leavenworth, if they jail him."[22]

The quest to make an Ali–Frazier fight a reality was a top priority for 1970. Rumors of possible sites and dates dominated the sports pages throughout the year.

Less than a week after Frazier–Ellis, Ali reaffirmed his retirement. He told some 1,800 students at Michigan State University that he wouldn't return to the ring even though he believed he could easily whip "Smokin' Joe."

Despite Ali's repeated confirmations of his retirement, several elements were still pushing to bring him and Frazier together in a ring, any ring. However, the final decision on an Ali return to boxing was dependent on the bureaucratic whims of the various state commissions' sanctioning bodies.

Yank Durham said that if Ali somehow got his license back, Frazier would definitely fight him, but only in America. Nevertheless, by April negotiations for an Ali–Frazier fight were underway in Toronto, Canada. Harold Ballard, owner of the Toronto Maple Leafs hockey team and the Maple Leaf Gardens, said he was trying to arrange the fight in his building.

Ali's lawyer, Bob Arum, said of the proposed Toronto fight that it all depended on a motion by the courts that would allow the ex-champ to leave the country.

Predictably, the request was denied. Once again, Ali insisted he would never fight again.

In June, another rumor of a proposed Ali–Frazier showdown was leaked to the press. This time an anonymous source revealed that the fight would take place on September 21 in Detroit. Former Detroit mayor Jerome P. Cavanaugh was reportedly handling the negotiations. Arum reported that both fighters would receive a $1.5 million guarantee.

Michigan Boxing Commissioner Chuck Davey, once a leading welterweight contender during the 1950s, said he wasn't opposed to an Ali–Frazier fight in his state. But he hedged his position by adding he would need all the information first.

Ali, for one, was pessimistic about the rumored Detroit promotion. His skepticism was justified as the Detroit proposal fizzled out.

Despite repeated failures, the financial lure of Ali–Frazier could not be resisted. Seattle was the next entry in the race to stage the superfight. The promotion depended upon a pending decision by the Washington State Boxing Commission to grant Ali a license. It took the Commission only one day to refuse the request.

Toronto was still in the running, this time with a proposed date of October 18. However, the Fifth Circuit Federal Court again denied Ali permission to leave the United States.

Atlanta, Georgia, was also attempting to stage an Ali–Frazier fight, scheduled for October 26. Georgia State Senator Leroy R. Johnson stated that an Ali–Frazier fight was virtually assured. Johnson, the first black to be elected to the Georgia legislature in 92 years, joined forces with Atlanta businessman Harry Pett to form House of Sports, Inc., which would promote the fight.

Although Atlanta was considered the most liberal city in the South, many wondered if it was liberal enough to welcome Ali's return to the ring. Pett said yes.

Georgia Governor Lester Maddox said an Ali–Frazier fight couldn't be held in his state until Ali was ready to fight for his country. Maddox, a longtime opponent of racial integration, called on the people of Atlanta to boycott the proposed fight. But he couldn't do anything more than talk. Unlike most states, Georgia had no jurisdiction over boxing, leaving that responsibility to individual municipalities.

Despite Maddox's opposition, Atlanta gave the fight the green light. Mayor Sam Massell supported it fully, allowing Ali to be licensed to box. By September, several other U.S. cities had followed Atlanta's lead. Suddenly, the Dream Fight appeared ready to become reality.

However, amid all the rampant speculation and activity concerning the Atlanta Superfight, an important element had been overlooked. The Frazier camp had not yet been approached with the idea.

Sources close to Frazier revealed that there hadn't been any communication at all with the champion concerning an Ali fight. At the time, Frazier and Durham were in serious negotiations for a fall title defense against light heavyweight king Bob Foster. Ali would have to wait.

With the October 26 date still open, House of Sports decided to sponsor an unofficial Ali return to the ring in September. The former champion would fight three exhibition bouts against decidedly mediocre opposition. On fight day, Ali, weighing 221 pounds, boxed Rufus Brassell, Johnny Hudgins, and George Hill before an enthusiastic crowd of 2,700 at predominantly black Morehouse College in Atlanta.

"The Greatest" danced through two rounds with Brassell, landing quick, harmless jabs and combinations. Then Ali allowed Hudgins to hit him during the second two-round bout. Some of the spectators began to boo as Ali obviously held back. In the final bout, a four-rounder with Hill, Muhammad brought the crowd to its feet with flashes of his old brilliance. He landed lightning combinations, a 15-second flurry of blows, and performed his patented shuffle step.

Afterward, Ali said it would take about four weeks to whip himself into top fighting form.

Dundee was pleased by his fighter's performance. Before the exhibition, he had tried unsuccessfully to convince Ali to change the total number of rounds from eight to six. But he was still impressed with Ali's stamina over eight.

"It's all there," Dundee said. "Everything. He can still fake with the hip, the hand, and the shoulder. By October 26, he'll be a super heavyweight."[23]

On September 9, two major fights were announced. Frazier would defend his title against Foster on November 18 in Detroit. And Ali would make his official comeback on October 26, in Atlanta, against Jerry Quarry.

A skeptical Yank Durham said he doubted the Ali–Quarry fight would actually happen. But on September 10, the contracts were officially signed. Ali was guaranteed $200,000 plus 42½ percent of the closed-circuit revenue. Quarry, the number-one contender according to *The Ring*, would earn 150,000 plus 22½ percent. The promoters and both fighters agreed to donate $50,000 to fight drug abuse in Atlanta.[24]

Quarry vs. Quarry

Jerry Quarry was one of the greatest enigmas in the heavyweight division throughout the 1960s and '70s. As a competitor, he was a fixture in the rankings of the time. Yet he never really seemed to enjoy the sport at which he excelled until relatively late in his career.

Though Quarry's strength, talent, and courage were never in doubt, there was always a question of personal motivation. What was the driving force behind Jerry Quarry the fighter?

Probably it was the same force that drove Quarry the man: his ever-present family.

Jack Quarry, Jerry's father and even to an extent his mother, played a dominant role in his son's career. In a November 6, 1967, *Sports Illustrated* article titled "Waiting for Jerry," Mark Kram cited the Quarry family as the reason Jerry wasn't demonstrating the ring brilliance of which most observers thought he was capable.

The article called the family "insensitive," and in most respects they were. The interest Jerry's parents took in their son's career was not the typical, overprotective nurturing type of involvement one would normally expect. Somehow, they managed to detach themselves far enough to split Jerry the fighter and Jerry the son into two separate entities.

Jerry the fighter was viewed purely as a business asset. When Quarry suffered his first loss as a professional to the crafty Eddie Machen, Jack Quarry, who was his son's co-manager along with Johnny Flores, looked to unload Jerry's contract. "He's not going anywhere," Jack stated.[25]

Another indication of the Quarrys' ability to separate business from family occurred in Jerry's amateur career, during which he and his older brother James fought each other a total of seven times.

Jack Quarry first laced the gloves on Jerry when the boy was only three years old. Of Quarry's 128 amateur fights, he lost only seven. He capped his simon-pure stint by winning the 1965 National Golden Gloves heavyweight championship.

In his professional debut on May 7, 1965, the 20-year-old Quarry scored a four-round decision over Gene Hamilton in Los Angeles. From that time onward, he encountered the premature publicity and pressures that are the lot of a talented white heavyweight. Decades after the reign of Jack Johnson, the yearning for a "White Hope" was alive and well.

During the first year of his career, Quarry was a crude slugger. His style excited his local California fans, but it needed refinement if he hoped to compete at a higher level. Under the tutelage of trainer Teddy Bentham, Quarry evolved into an intelligent boxer. His trademarks became skillful counterpunching, a fierce body attack, and a solid chin.

Jerry was far from a pampered prospect. Early in his career, he was thrown in with demanding competition. He faced his first major hurdle only six months after his pro debut in the person of Tony Doyle.

Doyle, from Salt lake City, Utah, was another young white fighter with championship potential. He was only 21, with a record of 11–2 (9 KOs). Former heavyweight champion

Jack Dempsey described Doyle as "one of the best young heavyweights I've seen in years."

At 6'4" and 215 pounds, Doyle enjoyed all the physical advantages over the 6'0", 190-pound Quarry. Still, Quarry's 12–0 record prompted odds makers to make him a slight favorite. Quarry came away from the fight with a broken nose and a draw.

After three more victories, Quarry ran into another prospect, 26-year-old Tony Alongi. Alongi enjoyed a great edge in experience, as his 38–2–1 (22 KOs) record indicated. Quarry and Alongi met on March 4, 1966, in New York. Once again, Quarry had to be satisfied with a draw. They met again, and drew again. Quarry was still undefeated, but he wasn't racking up conclusive victories.

If Irish Jerry thought Alongi was an experienced foe, he was in for a real shock in his next fight, a crossroads contest against Eddie Machen.

Machen had compiled an excellent record of 48–8–3 against the top heavyweights of the 1950s and '60s. Bad luck more than lack of talent had frustrated the Redding, California, native's title hopes. Although his career was on the downswing when he faced Quarry, Machen had too much savvy for the younger man and took him to school, winning a lopsided decision.

It was around this time that former heavyweight champion Rocky Marciano began to consider investing in a young heavyweight. Acting on a tip about Quarry, he traveled to California to watch the Machen fight. After four rounds, Marciano walked out. Rocky felt that young Quarry lacked championship potential.

Perennial British contender Brian London concurred with Marciano's evaluation after losing a 10-round decision to Quarry in 1966. Using peculiar logic, London felt that if Jerry was a world class fighter that he would have "destroyed me."

Marciano and London were both wrong. Quarry did become a world-class fighter, even a potential champion. But he didn't seem to be operating up to his considerable capabilities. He was climbing the heavyweight ladder, but not in the spectacular manner of a Joe Frazier.

When the WBA lifted Ali's title in 1967, Quarry was matched with Floyd Patterson in the first round of that body's flawed elimination tournament. Quarry's performance conformed to his previous pattern, and Floyd held him to a draw. In a return match, Quarry won a disputed split decision. He managed to drop Patterson twice in each fight, and for the most part, that was all he did.

Most ringsiders felt that Floyd had outfought Quarry for most of both fights. However, the peculiar California scoring system gave Quarry enough points from the knockdowns to account for victory.

Afterward, Patterson summed up the mystery of Jerry Quarry: "He's terribly strong, and he takes an excellent punch. This makes Quarry's style even less comprehensible. He utilizes only 35 percent of his ability. Here you have a man who is either cheating himself or the public. Or both."[26]

Why wasn't Quarry "being all that he could be," to paraphrase a contemporary military recruitment ad? A 1967 *Sports Illustrated* article attempted to speculate: "It is almost certain that he never wanted to be a fighter in the first place, his mother supposedly shoved him into the ring.... But Quarry's real problem is himself.... He wants to be an individual, yet his family, which interests itself even in his marriage, holds a tight rein on him."[27]

Yet despite an apparent lack of deep personal motivation, Quarry fought on. And he fought well enough to break into the top ten in only two short years of competition. But, like a son trapped in a family business he despises, Quarry often trudged lethargically through his opposition. Sometimes glimmers of his true potential flashed through.

One such time came in the WBA tournament semifinal, in which he all but chased Thad Spencer out of the ring. Another came when he threw caution to the wind in his 1969 challenge of Joe Frazier. Although Quarry was stopped on cuts in the seventh round, the Frazier fight removed all doubts concerning Jerry's intestinal fortitude. He took and dished out heaps of punishment against the most feared fighter of the late '60s.

But then the "other" Quarry would show up in the ring. In the final of the WBA tournament, for example, the favored Quarry did almost nothing, practically giving the fight and the title to Jimmy Ellis.

Despite, or perhaps because of, his inconsistency, Quarry remained a crowd favorite. Part of his appeal was based on his pale Irish epidermis. Also, his true abilities surfaced often enough to keep hope alive in his long-suffering fans.

An appropriate title for the story of Quarry's career would be "The Fistic Phoenix." Every time it appeared his career was over, he managed to pull it out of the fire once more. Consequently, he found himself involved in more than a few crossroads fights.

After losing the heroic slugfest against Frazier, Quarry took on the "Canadian Chopping Block," George Chuvalo. Chuvalo was strong and almost inhumanly durable, but his skills were nowhere near a match for Quarry's. For Quarry, the fight was merely a way to mark time and stay in contention. Over the first six rounds, Quarry dominated his slower opponent, hitting Chuvalo with everything in his considerable arsenal. Then, late in round seven, Quarry leaned forward to deliver a right hand. Bang! Chuvalo stepped in with a vicious left hook that sent Quarry to the canvas.

He got up at the count of three. Then strangely, he went down again and took referee Zack Clayton's full count at 2:59 of the round. As Clayton waved the fight over, Quarry jumped up and protested vehemently, claiming that he hadn't heard the count. However, everyone else, including ringside reporters, heard the count quite clearly.

For the first time in his career, Quarry found himself written off as a has-been. Rumors even circulated that Jerry had "laid down" for Chuvalo. Even his courage and gameness were being questioned.

Two inconsequential wins early in 1970 led Quarry to yet another crossroads fight, this time against former Marine sergeant and Vietnam veteran Mac Foster. Most experts agreed that the hard-hitting Foster would knock Quarry, who was still only 25, out of contention once and for all.

For Foster, the fight would be his first against a major opponent. He wasn't being intentionally pampered; all the other contenders were ducking him. Quarry, on the other hand, ducked no one.

Again Quarry entered the fight at a physical disadvantage. Foster stood 6'3", and he weighed 214 muscular pounds. He also enjoyed a nine-inch edge in reach over Quarry. His record stood at 24–0, all knockouts. And he was ranked number one by both *The Ring* and the World Boxing Council, a dissident offshoot of the WBA. Imposing credentials, indeed.

Quarry's poor performance against Chuvalo made him an 8-to-5 underdog against Foster, whose fight plan was simple: put lots of pressure on his smaller opponent.

Quarry was well aware of the stakes involved. "If I lose this one, I'll be finished," he stated, as if he knew he was considered the final stepping stone on Foster's road to a challenge of Frazier.

But when the smoke cleared in Madison Square Garden on the night of June 17, 1970, Foster became the first rung on Quarry's climb back into contention.

Foster seemed in control early in the fight, winning the first three rounds on aggression. Then Quarry's counterpunching turned the tide in the fourth. The fifth frame saw Quarry take the offensive and batter the retreating Foster from pillar to post. In the sixth, Quarry kept up the punishment until Foster finally slumped to the canvas. Referee Johnny Lo Bianco stopped the fight without bothering to count. Once again, the "Phoenix" had resurrected his career from the flames. It wasn't the first or last time he would do so. But the Foster win was arguably the most important of Quarry's career.

Then came the call from Atlanta. Quarry had been chosen as Muhammad Ali's first opponent in his long-awaited comeback.

For Quarry, like so many other heavyweights of the 1960s, a confrontation with Ali was the ultimate goal. In a 1966 interview, Jerry said Ali was the one man he hoped to fight eventually. The interview occurred during the beginning of the champion's draft troubles. Quarry felt that Ali's politics outside of the ring shouldn't effect his status inside the ring.

Four years later, Quarry got his wish. But his fight with Ali was not for any recognized title. That belonged to Joe Frazier. Still, Ali was calling the Quarry match a title fight.

"The day they take my title in the ring, where I won it, then I'd say the next man is the champ. But not until," Ali declared.[28]

Quarry agreed: "I'm not fighting 15 rounds for nothing. I don't think anyone ever took the title away from him in the ring. There's always been an asterisk on Frazier's title. And if I win, I'm the champion."[29]

The Ali–Quarry fight was indeed scheduled for fifteen rounds, a distance usually reserved for championship bouts. As preparations for the fight progressed, Governor Maddox continued his protests. Calling the event a "travesty," he proclaimed that October 26 would be a day of mourning. Knowing he was unable to prevent the fight from being held, Maddox said he hoped Ali would get "beat in the first round by a count of 30."[30]

Ali was uncharacteristically subdued in the days that led up to this important fight. He realized his return to the ring would ruffle plenty of feathers, and he didn't want to say or do anything to jeopardize his comeback. Biting his tongue until it bled, Ali refused to answer any questions about his draft case or Governor Maddox. He used an indirect approach instead.

For example, when one reporter asked Ali what he thought of Maddox's statement that October 26 would be a "black day for Georgia," Ali replied: "Oh yeah, there'll be a lot of my folks there."[31]

Ali considered his reception in Atlanta friendlier than he had anticipated. However, there was one glaring incident that Ali revealed in his autobiography, *The Greatest*. According to Ali, a sniper took potshots at him and his entourage at Atlanta Deputy Mayor Maynard Johnson's cottage, which was serving as the ex-champ's Atlanta residence. Although the harrowing incident rattled some nerves, no one was hurt in the incident.

When Ali arrived in Miami to begin training for his comeback, he weighed a bulky 238 pounds. He trained diligently, laboring to shake off 3½ years of ring rust. Six weeks of hard work had remolded Ali's 28-year-old body to its pre-exile form. On October 26, he entered the ring at a rock-hard 213½ pounds.

But it was Ali's stamina, not his weight, that was the biggest question mark in the fight. It was scheduled for 15 rounds against an opponent who always showed up in great shape. Quarry saw conditioning as his ace in the hole.

"As the fight goes on, his [Ali's] physical problems will increase, I don't care what he says," Quarry predicted. "And mentally, he'll be wondering, can I take a chance this round? Am I going to have enough left in the next round? By comparison, I'm prepared to fight the fight of my life to beat him."[32]

Quarry's trainer, Teddy Bentham, also felt Ali's stamina would be the key to the fight. He believed that if Jerry could get through the first few rounds that he stood a good chance. Jack Quarry predicted that his son would stop Ali in the tenth.

Ali didn't think his conditioning would be a factor. "I can go 15 rounds, no trouble at all," he declared. "My legs, my lungs are great. Even if I had to go 15 rounds straight through without ringing the bell, I'd probably make it. To me, it's just another fight, hit and not be hit."[33]

Three weeks before the fight, Ali underwent an endurance test, sparring 14 torrid rounds with four different men. He was tagged hard and often throughout the session.

Still, Angelo Dundee exuded optimism about his fighter's chances. He admitted he couldn't really say how Ali would react under pressure, but he was confident Muhammad knew what it took to win.

He also said he and Ali couldn't have picked a tougher opponent than Quarry for a comeback fight. He felt that Quarry's style was ideally suited for Ali.

When asked if he had noticed any changes in his fighter since 1967, Dundee nervously conceded: "He's got the same old feints but now, instead of getting missed by a foot, he's getting missed by six inches. That's the difference between getting hit or not getting hit."[34] Ali said he was even better than before.

The odds makers also believed Ali couldn't be beaten, at least not by Jerry Quarry. "The Greatest" was installed as a 17–5 favorite. Dundee made his own quiet prediction in the dressing room prior to the fight, when he inscribed "Round 3" inside Ali's gloves.

Quarry entered the ring wearing a "bad to the bone" snarl, while Ali fixed his adversary with a vicious, penetrating stare.

"You're in trouble, boy," Ali threatened as referee Tony Perez recited his instructions.

"Shut up and fight," Quarry shot back.[35]

Ali came out for round one in vintage form, dancing and jabbing. It was as though no time had passed at all between 1967 and 1970. Quarry bobbed, weaved, and chased, but he failed to land a blow as Ali took full advantage of his 5½-inch reach advantage. The crowd, which was predominantly black, gave him a standing ovation at the end of the round.

The second round provided more of the same. Quarry, at a light 197½ pounds, did manage to dig a powerful left hook to the body, which Ali later described as painful. Ali was moving less as the round ended.

Midway through the third, Ali connected with a slashing right hand that tore through Quarry's left eyebrow. As the blood began to trickle down Jerry's face, Ali unloaded with both hands. Quarry didn't go down. But as he returned to his corner, his blood was flowing in gory quantities. Jack Quarry told his son he was stopping the fight.

Jerry protested bitterly, but Teddy Bentham supported the elder Quarry's decision. Bentham then asked Perez to halt the fight.

When Perez signaled the end of the proceedings, Quarry jumped up from his stool and appeared to storm toward Ali in an effort to renew the fighting. Perez caught him and calmed him down.

Bundini Brown, Ali's friend and assistant trainer, also stepped between Quarry and the victorious ex-champion. Brown then kissed Quarry on the cheek and told him, "The better man won, but we'll never really know because of the cut."[36] Ali also consoled the distraught Quarry.

By the time Quarry returned to his dressing room, he had regained his composure and accepted the reason for the stoppage.

"Teddy Bentham is working for me and he did the right thing," Quarry said.[37]

He went on to say he didn't realize how badly he was cut, and that was why he went into a rage and tried to rush at Ali.

"But then I felt the blood," Quarry admitted.[38]

The gash was so deep and severe, going almost to the bone, that it required eleven stitches. Many observers felt a cut that severe could only have been caused by a head butt. Quarry was quick to refute that notion, stating that it was from a right hand.

Bentham said it was "going to take a long time to heal and we'll have to wait a while before we think about any more fights."[39]

The briefness of the Ali–Quarry bout left many unanswered questions about Ali's stamina and durability. What if the cut hadn't occurred? Would Ali have been able to handle Quarry's pressure in the later rounds?

Quarry said he didn't feel he was beaten by "a better fighter." He believed if he could have taken control if the fight would have gone a couple of more rounds.

Ali disagreed. He felt that since he was doing the majority of the landing that he would have easily outlasted Quarry.

Dundee was enthusiastic about his fighter's performance. And felt that his man had returned to 1967 form. But was Ali really the same fighter he was before his exile? His timing appeared off, but only slightly. Surely more ring work would bring that back. There was one clearly visible difference, though. As Arthur Daly wrote in the *New York Times*, "The one item that caught my eye was the heavy handed way he delivered his punches. They appeared to crash with far more authority and damaging effect than in earlier and more carefree days when he could 'float like a butterfly, sting like a bee.' No longer is the sting a needle-like penetration. It's a gouge."

The former champion's new punching power should not have come as a surprise. The only difference in Ali's measurements since 1967 was a 1¼ inch gain in his biceps.

Joe Louis agreed that Ali's punching power had vastly improved, but at the cost of some of his lightning speed. However, on the basis of Ali's performance against Quarry, Louis said Muhammad was "not ready to meet Frazier."

Speaking of Frazier ... was he impressed by Ali's dismantling of Quarry, which took four rounds less than Joe's victory over the same fighter in 1969?

At the time of the fight, Frazier was in training for his upcoming bout with Bob Foster, and he opted to sleep instead of watching Ali in action.

Yank Durham didn't see the fight either. But he had a reliable source view it, then phone him with a blow-by-blow account. "From what I heard," Durham said, "I wasn't impressed with the things he [Ali] did."[40]

Durham went on to say he was disappointed in Quarry's performance, stating that he had expected Jerry to put up a stronger, more intelligent fight.

When asked what Frazier would do differently from Quarry's tactics, Durham revealed that the champ wouldn't let Ali move around, like Quarry had.

He said Frazier would be "delighted" to defend against Ali. "As soon as we get rid of Foster, we'll stay in camp and destroy Clay," Durham said, refusing to use Ali's Muslim name.[41]

Ali retorted that Frazier would be an easier fight for him than Quarry. He also declared that since he was once again a licensed fighter, he was the real champion of the world. He even went so far as to say that Frazier was now just another contender.

By now, public demand for Ali–Frazier was reaching monumental proportions. Two men had to power to derail what was already being touted as the "Fight of the Century": Foster and Ali's next comeback opponent, Oscar Bonavena.

Foster's Folly

Bob Foster would be battling more than Joe Frazier on November 18, 1970. He was also challenging history. At that time, no light heavyweight champion had ever moved up and taken a heavyweight king's crown. Old-timer Bob Fitzsimmons was the exception that proved the rule; the 167-pound slugger won the light heavy title after losing the heavyweight belt to Jim Jeffries.

Seven men had attempted the feat before Foster: Philadelphia Jack O'Brien, who fought a twenty-round draw with Tommy Burns and went six rounds to no decision against Jack Johnson; Georges Carpentier, who was stopped in four by Jack Dempsey; Tommy Loughran, who lost a fifteen-round decision to Primo Carnera; John Henry Lewis, who was bombed out in one by Joe Louis; Billy Conn, who challenged Louis twice and was stopped in thirteen and eight rounds; Joey Maxim, who lost a fifteen-round decision to Ezzard Charles; and Archie Moore, who was stopped in nine rounds by Rocky Marciano and five by Floyd Patterson.

Moore's 1956 attempt was the last time a light heavy king had attempted the impossible dream. But the failures of his predecessors didn't discourage Foster. He reasoned that there had to be a first time for everything. Foster declared his forthcoming victory to be a first, comparing it to the Apollo 11 astronauts on the moon.

This wasn't Foster's first venture into the land above 175 pounds. In fact, he had an 0–3 record against top-notch heavyweights going into the Frazier fight, although he did manage wins over trial horses like Bert Whitehurst, Willi Besmanoff, and Sonny Moore.

His last defeat as a professional came by decision against Zora Folley in 1965. Foster called Folley "the best heavyweight ever." But he refused to gave equal credit to his other major heavyweight conquerors, Ernie Terrell and Doug Jones. He took both of those fights on short notice with a minimum of training. For the Frazier fight, however, Foster had put in a full two months of training.

Foster was a 6' 3½" beanpole of a fighter who packed dynamite in both hands, especially the left. His limbs were long and sinewy, and boxing historian Barney Nagler compared Bob's physique to that of a praying mantis. Against Frazier, Foster would enjoy advantages of four inches in height and five and a half inches in reach. Frazier, of course, would be much the heavier man.

Born in Albuquerque, New Mexico, in 1938, Foster was a late bloomer. Early in his career, he fought fringe light heavyweight contenders for peanuts when he wasn't getting thrown in over his head against heavyweights. His problem was that he was a hard hitter who didn't have the financial backing necessary to lure the right opponents into the ring with him.

Because his boxing income was limited, Foster held a variety of jobs to support his family, at one point working in a bomb factory in York, Pennsylvania. He retired several times before manager Lou Viscusi finally put his career on track.

After years of frustration, Foster knocked Dick Tiger off the light heavy throne with a single left hook in 1968. He was now riding a string of 13 consecutive knockout wins. However, comparing those victims to Frazier was like comparing kittens to a tiger. His title opponents all weighed 175 pounds or less, and his nontitle foes were heavyweights in name only.

But Foster didn't acknowledge the difference. He was convinced that Frazier would crumble like the rest. He believed Frazier's success stemmed from the fact that all of his foes had fought him incorrectly. Unlike Joe's other opponents, who Foster claimed were stationary targets, he would be moving and banging his shorter foe with astounding results.

The most Foster had previously weighed for a fight, even against heavyweights, was a spindly 177 pounds. Bill Gore, Foster's trainer, said that for the Frazier fight they had utilized calisthenics and a proper diet to add some solid pounds to Bob's frame.

Gore revealed that Foster was drinking a food supplement used by many NFL football players to gain weight. And Foster indeed began to add a little bulk, something he had never been able to do before.

Although Foster still resembled a praying mantis, the extra weight made the light heavyweight king feel bigger and stronger. Gore said the added bulk gave his charge a "million pounds" of confidence.

However, not all of Foster's people were brimming with confidence. His manager, Viscusi, admitted: "I didn't want this fight, but Foster insisted."[42]

Why was Foster so intent on a match with Frazier? The answer could be summed up in one word: money.

As light heavyweight champion, Foster had never earned large purses. Few fighters in his division ever did, sandwiched as they were between the heavyweights and the middleweights. He hoped the heavyweight title would bring him the riches he thought he deserved.

He certainly wasn't going to make his fortune from the title opportunity itself. Frazier was guaranteed $150,000 or a percentage of the gate and TV revenue. Chuck Davey of the Michigan Boxing Commission stated that Foster would receive no guarantee and only a small percentage of the gate.

Considering Foster's training expenses, sparring partners, and other disbursements, he was literally fighting for nothing other than the opportunity to take Frazier's title.

Frazier couldn't foresee any serious threat from Foster. Bob's edge in height and reach was nothing new; nearly every other heavyweight had similar advantages over Smokin' Joe. Frazier simply turned their height advantage into a disadvantage by burrowing inside the other man's reach and hammering away at the body.

Frazier was also unfazed by Foster's reputation as a big puncher. He didn't believe a mere light heavyweight would ever be able to hurt him.

However, a week before the fight, Foster did manage to hurt the champ, not with a punch, but with a derogatory remark. In an interview, he called Frazier a "dumb fighter."

When the word got back the Frazier camp, Eddie Futch, Frazier's assistant trainer, commented that Joe was a "curious guy.... He never reveals his feelings. But that remark Foster made about his being dumb really got to him. He's too serious about his work to take a remark like that lightly ... and when an opponent's mouth gets to Joe, they are in trouble. They had better run like thieves."[43]

The odds makers couldn't have thought Frazier was too dumb. They installed him as a heavy 5-to-1 favorite. Foster's reputed punching power was the reason the odds for Frazier weren't higher.

Foster's facade of confidence began to crumble as fight day approached. A few hours before he left his hotel room to meet Frazier, he sat down and wrote a 32-line note. As Pat Putnam indicated later in *Sports Illustrated*, the consensus of those who read the note "was that the light heavyweight champion had penned his last will and testament."[44]

At the weigh-in, Yank Durham expressed displeasure with the scale. Frazier tipped in at a relatively heavy 209 pounds, while Foster weighed 188. Durham claimed the scale was off by five pounds. Either way, the champion enjoyed a 21-pound advantage.

The crowd at Frazier–Foster was a major disappointment. Fewer than 6300 spectators half-filled the 12,500 seats at Cobo Hall. Other than the Ali–Liston II fiasco in Lewiston, Maine, it was the smallest crowd in modern history to witness a heavyweight championship fight.

Some attributed the dismal turnout to the recently ended strike at General Motors. However, when the strike had been in full swing the month before, 9,103 fans had turned out at the Detroit's Olympia to see Ali–Quarry on closed circuit. Foster's shortcomings as a heavyweight probably had more to do with the turnout than Frazier's drawing power. Whatever the explanation, the poor gate guaranteed that Foster would be indeed be fighting for nothing but the title.

Many observers believed Foster's "dumb fighter" comment accounted for Frazier's poor performance in the first round. He seemed to be attempting to prove that he could box as well as slug. Consequently, Foster was able to land several hard rights to the head of Frazier, while Frazier seemed unable to work his way inside.

Joe said later: "Man, he was rattlin' my brain. Once he hit me so hard and so fast I didn't know if it was a left or a right."[45]

When the round ended, Frazier went back to his corner and asked Durham what he was doing wrong.

"You've got to get closer and put on more pressure," Yank instructed.[46]

Meanwhile, in Foster's corner, Gore instructed his fighter, "Just take your time."

Foster responded, "Take my time? It's kind of hard to take your time when you look up and see that big thing coming at you."[47]

Round two was only seconds old when Frazier delivered a short, crunching left hook over a Foster jab. The light heavyweight champ fell in a heap. He groggily pulled himself up at the count of nine.

Despite Foster's perilous condition, the referee allowed the fight to continue. Frazier pounced on his wounded foe like a starving animal, firing two more left hooks. The first one missed Foster's head and thudded into his shoulder. The second landed with a sickening smash on Foster's exposed chin, jarring his head in a grotesque, twisting motion. Foster fell like a puppet whose strings were suddenly cut. The fight was over at the 49-second mark of the round. Foster lay unconscious for about a minute, and needed a doctor's assistance to get back to his feet.

Frazier was concerned that Foster may have been seriously hurt. He seemed relieved when the challenger finally regained his senses.

Like Jimmy Ellis, Foster was surprised to learn he'd been knocked down more than once.

Despite Frazier's easy dismissal of his challenge, Foster refused to retract his "dumb fighter" comment, stating that he still believed it to be true.

"I'm dumb, huh?" Frazier responded. "Well he ain't so smart. He fought me, didn't he?"[48]

How did Foster think Ali would fare against Frazier? Never a big fan of Ali anyway, Foster prophesied Muhammad's demise. Foster didn't see any way that Ali could hold Frazier off.

The negative exchange between Foster and Ali was not surprising. The bad blood between them dated back to their amateur days. Eventually they would settle their accounts in the ring.

After Foster's near annihilation at the hands of Frazier, fifteen years passed before another light heavyweight champ would attempt to annex the heavyweight crown. On September 22, 1985, a beefed-up Michael Spinks made history by winning a unanimous 15-round decision over an aging Larry Holmes.

Ironically, the one former light heavyweight champion to whom Spinks was most frequently compared was none other than Bob Foster.

Ringo

Ali decided he needed one more test before tangling with Frazier. That test would be administered by the very durable Oscar Bonavena.

Bonavena was one of the most outlandish figures in boxing history. Born in Buenos Aires, Argentina, in 1942, he came to New York in 1964 to embark on a professional boxing career. Oscar's stocky frame was loaded with thick, heavy muscles that gave him an awkward, cumbersome appearance in the ring. He was generally considered the strongest man in the sport.

His father had worked as a motorman on a trolley in Buenos Aires. Part of his job was using a big iron bar to lever the tracks into alignment. Bonavena felt that he had inherited his father's strength from that iron bar.

However, an overabundance of muscle tissue wasn't the only reason for Bonavena's lack of fistic finesse. He also had flat feet, which caused him to be rejected for service in the Argentine army.

Nicknamed "Ringo" for a long-haired, Beatle-type role he had once played on Argentine television, Bonavena had Ali-like confidence in his own abilities, limited though they were. He would strut around with his head held high and his massive chest puffed out. His personality was almost theatrical, and he always evoked an extreme reaction. Many considered him arrogant and obnoxious.

Bonavena could be as obstinate outside the ring as in, especially in matters of money. Madison Square Garden promoter Harry Markson called him "an exasperating man when it came to financial negotiations."

When Oscar fought for Frazier's title in 1968, he finagled a $75,000 after-taxes purse, plus expenses, which amounted to a grand total of $115,000. He lost the fight, but came away with $10,000 more than Frazier. Bob Foster could have used Bonavena's financial expertise.

When Bonavena was scheduled to meet George Chuvalo on June 24, 1966, in Madison Square Garden, Oscar was to receive $7,500, plus $2,500 extra. On fight night he was a no-show as fight time approached. As panic ensued, matchmaker Teddy Brenner figured out where to find the AWOL contender. Brenner found the erratic boxer in his hotel room complaining of an upset stomach. "Having guessed the problem, Brenner reached into his pocket and pulled out 25 $100 bills. 'Better now?' Teddy said and handed over the bills. There was a smile from Bonavena. In five minutes he was dressed and ready to go."[49]

As a pro, Bonavena cannily acquired the training services of Charlie Goldman, who was famous for refining the rough edges of Rocky Marciano. In only his first year as a professional, Bonavena told Goldman he could beat Ali and Liston. The wizened old trainer was impressed by the young man's confidence and his guts.

One man who was as impressed with Bonavena as Bonavena was with himself was Dr. Marvin Goldberg, a well-known optometrist and New York State Athletic Commission boxing judge. After seeing one of Bonavena's early fights, Goldberg was sufficiently impressed to quit his position on the Commission and purchase Oscar's contract for a mere $3,000.

Bonavena's progress was swift. In only his sixth professional fight, on August 24, 1964, he stopped Tom McNeeley in five rounds. Less than three years earlier, McNeeley had fought Floyd Patterson for the world championship, losing by knockout in the fourth round.

This fine showing earned him a main event against Dick Wipperman at Madison Square Garden. No fighter in history had ever headlined at the Garden after only six fights. Wipperman, with a 26–3–1 record, was much more experienced than the young Argentine. That experience allowed him to become the first man to go the distance with Bonavena. But Bonavena won the decision.

In 1965, Oscar's reach exceeded his grasp when he was rushed into a fight with high-ranking contender Zora Folley. Folley beat Bonavena like a rug over 10 rounds; all Oscar was able to exhibit was his rock-like chin in dropping the decision.

Bonavena rebounded with 11 straight wins, 10 by knockout. He also captured the South American heavyweight title with a 12-round decision over countryman Gregorio Peralta.

His growing experience did not affect the basic crudity of his tactics. Indeed, his less-than-pinpoint accuracy often got him into trouble. On March 12, 1966, Bonavena's 11-bout winning streak came to an end when he was disqualified in the eighth round against an obscure fighter named Jose Georgetti.

Oscar's actions outside the ring were sometimes equally rank. In fact, Goldberg felt his fighter's talents and credentials had been unjustly overlooked because some critics didn't care for the content of his character. Goldberg was concerned that his fighter would be judged on etiquette and not his boxing skills.

Despite what American skeptics thought of him, Bonavena was a bona fide hero in his native Argentina. There, he could do no wrong, almost literally. He could park his car wherever he pleased and was under no obligation to obey speed limits. Why such lenience? Simply because he was Oscar Bonavena.

Back in New York, Ringo's fistic stock was about to skyrocket. A June 24, 1966, bout with Canadian champion George Chuvalo guaranteed the winner a chance at Olympic hot-shot Joe Frazier.

Bonavena–Chuvalo was far from a purist's delight. The two strongest, roughest men in the division waged a close, rough-and-tumble struggle that ended with a disputed decision in Bonavena's favor. Stories persist that Bonavena handed Chuvalo his only professional knockdown in that fight. But no knockdown was recorded by the referee.

Frazier, who was at ringside scouting his potential opponents, smiled in anticipation at the wide-open styles of both men.

But Frazier didn't smile later, when Bonavena floored him twice in a losing cause. Oscar won nine fights after that, and was invited to the WBA's 1967 tournament to replace Ali. He did well enough, winning a decision from Karl Mildenberger, then losing one to eventual champion Jimmy Ellis.

Seven more wins followed the Ellis defeat, the best ones coming against Leotis Martin and old nemesis Zora Folley. Then came his rematch with Frazier for the five-state championship. He didn't floor Smokin' Joe again, but he went the distance in a losing cause.

Bonavena's record for 1969 was 3–0–1, with the draw coming against Peralta, whose cunning style always frustrated him.

Oscar's 1970 campaign began disastrously, with a disqualification loss to Miguel Paez in Buenos Aires. Apparently Argentine referees were less lenient with him than the country's traffic cops. Bonavena rebounded by stopping Alberto Lovell for the second time in four months.

That win was followed by a series of early knockouts over fringe contenders Jose Menno, Manuel Ramos, James J. Woody, and Luis Pires. Then Ringo learned he was on tap as Ali's second comeback opponent. He was quick to accept the fight and its hefty $100,000 purse.

In choosing Bonavena as an opponent, Ali wasn't looking for an easy win. He was looking for someone who would test his endurance. "It's no tune-up," Ali assured reporters. "It's a serious fight."[50] He considered the Argentine "a strong, dangerous fighter, the toughest I've ever had to meet."[51]

Although Ali anticipated a tough fight from Bonavena in the ring, he couldn't have expected the crude brawler to beat him to the punch verbally. Even before the contracts were officially signed, Bonavena began to downgrade Ali's skills, saying that the former champion's talents were nothing but a "myth." In Oscar's opinion, Ali committed too many basic mistakes to ever beat him.

The fight was signed on November 5, and the very next day Bonavena stole Ali's thunder once again by predicting the round in which his opponent would fall. Oscar said Ali would go in the eleventh.

Ali was appalled at the Argentine's audacity. "He's talking too much," Ali said. Muhammad may have been the only person in the world who didn't appreciate the irony of that statement. "And I just don't like a fighter who talks too much," Ali continued. "I'm the onliest man who can do that. I can't let him predict on me."[52]

Ali put his own prediction into a poem:

> It's been a long time since I put my predictions into rhythm and rhyme,
> But it was Bonavena who started it all, getting out of line.
> He couldn't have been talking to some angel from Heaven,
> Now he has the nerve to predict I will fall in eleven.
> If this is his joke, it's at the wrong time,
> For being so rash, he must fall in nine.[53]

The ever-confident Bonavena insisted he would expose the flaws in Ali that other fighters couldn't exploit. He pointed out that he'd never been bothered by cuts, so there was no possibility of a fluke stoppage, an unflattering allusion to Ali's win over Quarry.

It was at the weigh-in, however, that Bonavena allowed his rhetoric to go beyond a downgrading of Ali's boxing skills. Ringo called Ali everything from a "black kangaroo" to a "maricon," which is Spanish slang for "homosexual." He even refused to allow Ali to come too close to him, stating that "The Greatest" smelled too bad.

For the first time in his career, Ali found the tables turned. He was losing a verbal battle, and to add insult to injury, he was losing it to a man whose English could be most charitably described as "broken." Visibly angry, Ali made a threatening gesture toward Bonavena.

Then Bonavena unleashed his knockout blow, bringing up Ali's refusal to be inducted into the military. Echoing the opinion of many Ali critics, Oscar asked: "Why you no go in army? You chicken? Cheep, cheep, cheep."[54]

By now, Ali was furious. He made another attempt to grab Bonavena. "Don't touch me," Bonavena threatened. "Or I kill now."[55]

Ali seethed with frustration. He had finally met an opponent whose ego matched his own, and the experience was far from pleasant. He confided later, "I've never wanted to whup a man so bad."[56]

He also promised to "punish" Bonavena in the ring. Fans who remembered the way Muhammad had "punished" Patterson and Terrell believed Bonavena would be earning his $100,000 the hard way.

Naturally, Frazier and Durham had a great deal of interest in the fight. Durham expressed some very definite opinions on Ali's chances against Bonavena.

"One thing you can be sure of is that Cassius Clay is gonna have more trouble with Bonavena than he expects," Yank opined. "That's what happened to Joe when he fought Bonavena, and Joe is a better fighter than Cassius.

"Before the seventh round of their second fight," Yank continued, "Joe told me in the corner that he was going to try for a knockout of Bonavena. 'You're not going to be able to do it,' I said. 'He's here to stay!' So Joe won a decision, and I'll admit quite frankly that Bonavena was stronger than Frazier at the end of 15 rounds."[57]

As fight day approached, Ali felt more confident in his conditioning than before the Quarry fight. Dundee agreed that Ali was better prepared for Bonavena. In fact, on his last day of training, Ali sparred an incredible 12 rounds. "Twelve rounds might be work for anyone else," Dundee marveled. "But it's enjoyment for him."[58]

However, Bonavena's new trainer, Gil Clancy, found encouragement for his fighter in Ali's spar-a-thon. "It's going to weaken him," Clancy said. "If Clay went 12 rounds, it means to me that he doesn't have any confidence in himself. I'm surprised Angelo let him."[59]

Clancy added that Ali had been lucky in his career up to this point. He believed almost all Ali's important fights featured "peculiar" endings. For examples, he cited the Quarry cut and the two bizarre encounters with Sonny Liston.

Agreeing with his fighter's assessment, Clancy predicted that Bonavena would show whether or not Ali really could fight. He was confident Oscar's crude, unorthodox "style" would confuse Ali, who looked best against classic boxers. "Oscar is far from classical," Clancy said. "He does the unexpected, and that could mix Clay up."[60]

Dundee didn't buy that. To him, Bonavena would be easy for Ali. "Bonavena runs into shots," he said. "You can nail him good."[61]

Concerning strength, which was Oscar's only asset, Dundee believed the added muscle Ali exhibited against Quarry would be the deciding factor against the Argentine. Ali still had his incredible speed and defensive skills, and these, coupled with his newfound strength, would in Dundee's mind allow his fighter to beat Bonavena in any situation.

Well aware of Bonavena's reputation as a strongman, Ali nicknamed him "The Bull." This was more flattering than some of his other labels for opponents, which included "The Rabbit" for Floyd Patterson and "The Washerwoman" for George Chuvalo.

"It'll be the matador against the bull," Ali said. "And you know who always wins in the bullring." Ali even broke from his traditional white trunks with black trim, opting instead for trunks that were crimson as a matador's cape. "Bulls don't like red," Ali explained.[62]

The day before the fight, both men continued their war of words. Ali reiterated his prediction of a ninth-round knockout.

He desperately wanted to do what Frazier was unable to accomplish in 25 brutal rounds against the Argentine. An Ali confidant told the press that Muhammad "relates everything to Frazier. That's why he wants a big knockout so bad."[63]

Bonavena predicted that Ali would probably retire after the terrible beating he was about to take. "Ali's bubble will explode when I beat him," Bonavena said. "His pride will be gone. He has to be the big shot."[64]

For all Bonavena's bombast, it was Ali who was issued a warning by New York State Athletic Commission Chairman Edwin B. Dooley of a possible $5,000 fine if he used any "vitriolic language" during the fight.

Bonavena, by the way, wasn't the only one to comment on Ali's draft problem. The very fact that Ali was fighting again while his case was still in court was anathema to some. However, the fight date, December 7, was Pearl Harbor Day. And that provoked the ire of many patriotic and moralistic groups. New York Republican State Assemblyman Neil W. Kelleher condemned the Ali–Bonavena bout as "a disgrace to the people of New York State ... to allow a draft dodger to perform in our state and in your city on the anniversary of the Japanese attack on Pearl Harbor."[65]

Despite protests and calls for a boycott, Ali–Bonavena drew a whopping crowd of 19,417 into Madison Square Garden. The spectators paid $615,401, a record for a non-title bout. Ali purchased $50,000 worth of tickets himself. Garden matchmaker Teddy Brenner said that Ali "put in a tremendous order for tickets to make sure that his special friends will have some to buy. The locations are scattered all over. When they cheer him, he wants the cheering to come from all over the building."

Like the Quarry fight, Ali–Bonavena was scheduled for the championship distance of 15 rounds. Ali was, of course, calling it a title fight. However, Dooley declared that Ali–Bonavena was not a title bout.

Ali scaled a sleek 212 compared to Bonavena's 204 pounds of "beeg muscles." At 6'3", Muhammad enjoyed a four-inch advantage in height. The odds makers favored Ali by a 6-to-1 margin. Still, most expected a good fight. One of the unanswered questions was whether Bonavena's pre-flight banter had affected Ali's composure.

The answer was evident from round one: it had. The opening frame looked more like a barroom brawl than a bout between two boxers. At one point, Ali threw Bonavena to the canvas. And, true to form, Oscar had the round taken away because of a pair of blatant low blows.

In the third round, Ali twice shoved Bonavena through the ropes. Bonavena bulled and roughhoused the taller man in close. Reporter Jimmy Meilleur said that round three "had the Marquis [sic] of Queensberry turning in his grave."

Even though he was fighting Bonavena's fight, Ali still clearly won rounds by remembering to use his whip-like left jab. But in round four, Bonavena reached him with a ponderous left hook. Ali was visibly shaken at the bell.

Despite Ali's flat-footed brawling, the fight was unfolding as he predicted. It was indeed the matador against the bull. But in this case, the bull was doing plenty of damage of his own. The normally elusive Ali was taking more punches than in any previous fight. Ringo was raking him with body shots and was reaching his head as well.

Nevertheless, Ali was far ahead on points going into the ninth round, the round in which he had predicted Bonavena's demise. The crowd stirred in anticipation, rising en masse as the round began. Determined to deliver on his promise, Ali moved toward Bonavena and rocked him with a heavy left hook.

Then, as Muhammad moved in to finish the job, Bonavena caught him with torrid right hand. Ali's legs wobbled. The two fighters spent the rest of the round pounding away, each staging momentary rallies before giving way to the other.

"In the ninth round," Ali said afterward, "I thought for a minute my prediction might be good for both of us. We both may go here."[66]

Ali coasted in the later rounds, outboxing Bonavena but looking very tired in the process. The crowd was not impressed with the performance. A chorus of boos erupted at the end of the fourteenth. Somehow, the graceful Ali of 1967 had been replaced by just another mauling, brawling heavyweight.

Hundreds of disgruntled fans began to file out of the building. They should have stayed three more minutes, because they missed what *Ring* magazine chose as "Round of the Year" for 1970.

Bonavena charged from his corner at the bell for the last round, and ran into a smashing Ali left hook. He had taken scores of Ali's punches without flinching, but this one spilled him like a sack of onions. He stumbled to his feet, only to be leveled again by a rapid-fire combination from Ali.

At that point, Oscar's corner threw in the towel. But referee Mark Conn didn't see it, and allowed the slaughter to continue. Ali, who had an underrated ability to finish off a hurt opponent, landed another flurry of blows that dropped the shell-shocked Argentine a third time. Under New York's three-knockdown rule, the fight was over at 2:03 of the fifteenth.

Had the fight gone the distance, Ali would have won anyway. Conn's scorecard had him ahead 12 rounds to 2. Judges Joe Eppy and Jack Gordon also favored Ali by scores of 10–3–1 and 8–5–1 respectively.

Afterward, Ali admitted he had somewhat underestimated Bonavena. "He's a better fighter than I thought," Ali said at the post-fight press conference. "And he was hard to reach with the left jab. He looks muscle-bound, but I found him fast and tricky."

And Bonavena had gained a great deal of respect for Ali through the course of the fight. "This is the champion," Ringo declared, pointing to Ali. "Frazier never win him."[67]

Bonavena also took the opportunity to apologize to Ali about his derogatory pre-fight remarks, especially the "black kangaroo" comment. Ali accepted the apology, and said that Bonavena's antics "helped build the gate." Bonavena could have said, "You ought to know, Ali." But he didn't.

Overall, Ali was pleased with his performance, summing it up as follows:

"I'm satisfied for three reasons. I proved I had the stamina to go 15 rounds against the toughest man I ever fought. I proved I can take a punch by taking more punches in one fight than I have in all my others. And I proved I could punch by stopping a man who'd never been stopped."[68]

Other than the electrifying fifteenth round, though, the Bonavena fight was a sub-par performance for Ali. The skills he would need to defeat Joe Frazier were hardly in evidence that night.

Frazier watched the bout on closed circuit TV and called it the "dullest" fight he'd ever seen. He was ready to walk out after round seven, but his brother persuaded him to stay. Frazier called Ali a dirty fighter, and promised Muhammad wouldn't "jive me the way he did Bonavena tonight."

Smokin' Joe said that he witnessed some major flaws in Ali that he had better correct before they met. Frazier was confident he could stop Ali in six rounds if their fight ever came off.

In his dressing room, Ali was asked how long it would take him to be ready for Frazier. "How long will it take Frazier to be ready for me?" Ali retorted.[69]

With Foster and Bonavena both out of the way, arrangements for Ali–Frazier could now begin in earnest. Early speculation saw the fight happening in February or March 1971 in either Madison Square Garden or the Houston Astrodome.

The Garden's matchmaker, Harry Markson, believed his venue was the front-runner, because New York could charge $100 a ticket.

On the other hand, Ali's lawyer, Bob Arum, said, "Right now, the Astrodome is leading.... The live gate at the Astrodome would be more than twice what the Garden could do. If there are 70,000 seats there, Ali will fill them with people."[70]

However, there was one obstacle working against Houston. As of December 8, the day after his win over Bonavena, Ali was not licensed to box in Texas.

According to Ali, Tommy Smith, director of the Texas Boxing Commission, had assured him of a license. Two days after Ali's statement, Smith denied having promised the ex-champ a license.

Ali had previously applied for a Texas license in 1969, and was turned down. He then went to court to overturn the refusal. In December 1970, a decision was still pending. Smith said Ali's lawsuit was the reason he couldn't issue a license.

On December 11, Smith received word that Ali's suit had been dropped. Ali then got his license, and the Astrodome was back in the running for the big fight.

Ali said on December 16 that he believed the Frazier fight would come off on February 23 in Houston. Ali also announced he would retire after his showdown with Frazier. As it turned out, neither statement proved true.

Although most boxing fans' attention was focused on the Ali–Frazier showdown, other heavyweights made news at the end of 1970.

On December 16, a bout between Bonavena and Floyd Patterson, who was still a ranked contender, was announced for Madison Square Garden on January 22, 1971. Later that same night, however, Bonavena phoned Markson and told him he couldn't fight until February. The reason: doctor's orders. Dr. Roberto Paladino, Bonavena's physician, said Oscar was exhausted after the war with Ali.

George Foreman, winner of the heavyweight gold medal in the 1968 Olympics, scored his 25th straight professional victory with a one-round kayo of trial horse Mel Turnbow. The 22-year-old, 219-pound Foreman was considered the hottest and hardest-hitting new fighter in the division.

And Ernie Terrell, who had retired back in 1967, returned to the ring to face another trial horse named Sonny Moore. Moore was filling in for Tony Doyle, who had done little since his mid–1960s draw with Jerry Quarry.

Terrell's objective was to get Ali in the ring again, as he believed Muhammad had used foul tactics in their title unification bout. Against Moore, though, Terrell showed copious quantities of ring rust. He managed to win the decision, but he faded in the later rounds.

Terrell and Foreman were background news, though. Ali–Frazier fever was sweeping the nation, and even the world. Late in December, Bruce Wright, a lawyer for Cloverlay, Inc., the organization backing Frazier, announced that an Ali–Frazier bout was set for March 8, 1971, at Madison Square Garden. Although no papers had been signed, Wright was confident of the date and location.

Harry Markson called Wright's announcement "premature." Until it was all in writing, nothing was certain.

Contracts were finally signed and the fight was officially announced on December 30 in New York. The event would be promoted by Jerry Perenchio and Jack Kent Cooke. Cooke chose the Garden over the Houston Astrodome, and the rumored date of March 8 turned out to be correct.

At the news conference announcing the fight, Perenchio put Ali–Frazier in perspective: "You've got to throw the book away on this fight. It's like *Gone with the Wind*. And that's why I'm involved. I don't think it takes any special talent to put a couple of guys in the ring. The trick is to merchandise them properly."[71]

Ali promised that if he lost to Frazier, he'd crawl across the ring and proclaim Joe "The Greatest."

Only one thing still threatened to block the "Fight of the Century." The United States Supreme Court had yet to rule on Ali's appeal of his 1967 draft evasion conviction. If the court ruled against Ali, he would be going to prison instead of Madison Square Garden.

Nevertheless, all parties concerned were moving full speed ahead in preparation for the phenomenon Ali called "the greatest event ever on the planet Earth!"

Four

1971

Anticipation

As 1971 began, the boxing world was in a state of climactic expectation, anxiously awaiting the March 8 encounter between Ali and Frazier. On January 11, the last hurdle was cleared when the Supreme Court granted Ali permission to go ahead with the fight, even though deliberations on his draft case were still pending.

"I am relieved," Ali responded. "I am happy, very happy that the Supreme Court has agreed to hear the case and eliminate any problem with the fight. Now I am going to show who the real champion of the world is."[1]

"The Fight," as it was billed, dominated not only the sports pages. The mass media in general took to the Ali–Frazier phenomenon like a duck to water.

Ali–Frazier was indeed an "Event" that transcended boxing. Indeed, Perenchio, who put the massive promotion together, had never been involved with the sport before. He was president of Chartwell Artists, Ltd., a Beverly Hills theatrical booking agency that boasted clients like actresses Jane Fonda and Elizabeth Taylor.

Just how did a theatrical agent who admittedly didn't "know the first thing about boxing" land the biggest boxing promotion in history?

It began with Ali's manager and agent Herbert Muhammad's search for a promoter for the fight. Both Madison Square Garden and a group from Houston were offering the fighters $1.25 million each. Neither offer was rejected, but the fighters' brain trusts were keeping an eye out for a better offer.

Herbert Muhammad was hoping to get as close to a $3 million guarantee as possible. He met with Chicago promoter Franklin Fried in December 1970. Fried then phoned Perenchio, who was London at the time, and explained Muhammad's quest for cash.

"I knew right away I wanted it," Perenchio said. "This was the sort of thing I'd been training 20 years for. I told Fried I'd put a pencil to it."[2]

It took Perenchio and his pencil only a few hours to come up with a deal. He called Fried and told him he would guarantee each fighter $2.5 million. Perenchio then proceeded to run up a $16,000 phone bill in a search for backers to put up the unprecedented $5,000,000 purse guarantee.

A persistent salesman, Perenchio approached seventy potential moneymen, including shipping magnate Aristotle Onassis. No one was willing to make a commitment. Upon his return to the United States, Perenchio made his seventy-first phone call, this time to Jack Kent Cooke.[3]

Cooke was a Canadian who had made his fortune in radio and TV. Then his interests turned to sports, and he bought the Los Angeles Lakers basketball franchise in 1961. Five years later he built the Inglewood Forum as a showcase for the team. In 1967, he established the Los Angeles Kings, an expansion National Hockey League franchise.

Unlike the other wheeler-dealers Perenchio approached, Cooke didn't see Ali–Frazier as a gamble. "It would have been if I'd gotten into it by a hunch or intuitive reckoning," he explained. "But it was based on facts. Numbers of seats are facts. My people had done their homework before Perenchio even approached me, and his figures agreed with mine. So we are in business."[4]

They were indeed, as Cooke gave Perenchio a starting bankroll of $4.5 million. The other $500,000 of the purse guarantee came from Madison Square Garden for the right to host the fight.

Perenchio set a goal of a $30 million gross, with half that amount coming from theater closed circuit television. In the United States alone, there would be 337 closed circuit sites. Outlets would also be available in 26 other countries.

The other $15 million would come from closed circuit commercials, a documentary on the fight to be shown at theaters at a later date, and an auction of the fighters' personal effects. As part of the contracts, Perenchio would claim the fighters' shoes, trunks, robes, and gloves following the fight. "If a movie studio can auction off Judy Garland's red slippers [from *The Wizard of Oz*]," Perenchio said, "these things ought to be worth something." Perenchio was hoping that any blood on the trunks would increase their value.[5]

The financial figures involved in the making of Ali–Frazier were staggering and unprecedented. *Ring* magazine's editor, Nat Fleischer, said that despite the outlandish promotional numbers and $150 ringside seats, he couldn't blame any of the participants. But he was still concerned about the long-term effect of the $2.5 million purses Ali and Frazier would receive. "Might not Joe and Cassius feel that a permanent financial standard has been set up?" Fleischer wondered.

Fleischer's concerns proved prophetic. The March 8 superfight did indeed set a precedent. Never again would two heavyweight stars square off in a major fight without hauling down multi-million-dollar purses.

Although the paydays of the early seventies were enormous by contemporary standards, they now look like pittances compared to the gargantuan quantities of cash hauled in by today's superstars. But every wealthy fighter since 1971 can thank Ali and Frazier for opening the door to the bank vaults.In reality, fighters only take home a fraction of the purses for their bouts. Ali and Frazier were not exceptions to that rule. A few weeks after the fight, Ali revealed that the money he'd earned was already gone. After paying $1.5 million in federal taxes and nearly $400,000 in state taxes, both men were left with a little over $600,000. Out of that they had to pay their trainers, sparring partners and all other expenses.

Ali then bought a new house, took care of his parents and brother, and donated money to the Muslims. And that accounted for the $2.5 million most people assumed he had pocketed.

Interest in the fight was, perhaps, even more inflated than the purses. Some commentators wondered why the spectacle of two men banging away at each other was becoming so significant. There were several reasons. Some were related to boxing; others involved broader issues.

First and foremost to boxing fans, the fight would determine the undisputed heavyweight champion of the world. For nearly four years, the title picture had been murky. Ali and Frazier both held legitimate claims, even though Ali had seemingly taken himself out of contention during his short-lived retirement. Frazier had won and defended his title in the ring, but Ali had never lost it there.

As an added attraction, Ali–Frazier marked the first time that two undefeated heavyweight champions had fought each other in a unification bout. But even if they'd been meeting in an ordinary ten-rounder on *ABC's Wide World of Sports*, the contrast in their ring styles would have guaranteed interest in the match.

Ali was probably the fastest big man of all time, with boxing skills reminiscent of a heavyweight Willie Pep. And Frazier, tabbed by some as the "Black Marciano," was a relentless slugger whose left hook was a thing of brutal perfection. Light heavyweight contender Ray Anderson, one of Frazier's main sparring partners, said that getting hit with Joe's hook was "like getting run over by a bus." Ali wasn't so impressed with the Frazier left hook, even though similar punches had accounted for the only knockdowns Muhammad had suffered to date.

When asked about Frazier's frightening destruction of Foster, Ali responded that he wouldn't even spar with a man that only scaled 188. The Greatest felt that more attention should be given to his knockout of Bonavena, considering the two tough battles that Ringo had given Frazier.

Physically, Ali enjoyed an advantage of four inches in height and eight inches in reach over Frazier. He was also as quick as a welterweight and elusive as a cat. Whatever raw speed he had lost during his exile was compensated by increased size and power, as he demonstrated during his manhandling of Bonavena.

Ali felt that with his newfound muscle, he didn't need to rely so much on floating like a butterfly. During his first reign, Ali admitted that men like Liston, Patterson and Mildenberger were physically stronger than he, so he had to rely on his blinding speed. With maturity and added strength, Ali now felt he had genuine punching power as well.

Yet the contrast in the participants' styles and the quality of their credentials could not explain the wave of anticipation sweeping the nation. An advertisement for Ali–Frazier in the *New York Times* shed light on the significance of the fight: "The Ali–Frazier 'Fight of the Century' is more than a fight. It's a confrontation of boxing styles and life styles, private philosophies and public images, attitudes and opinions."

The contrasts between Ali and Frazier extended beyond their boxing styles. Even the importance each man placed on the fight differed. Ali stated that Frazier had no cause to fight for; that Joe was only in it for the money. However, financial gain wasn't the only motivating factor for Smokin' Joe. He was a craftsman, a true professional who worked hard to hone his skills. Frazier believed he was the best fighter on the planet, to paraphrase a later champion's widely-quoted claim. He wanted to prove to the world, and himself, that he could beat anyone who dared to confront him. To Frazier, Ali represented the ultimate challenge. Beating him was Joe's primary career aim.

Much was made of Frazier's refusal to call Ali by his Muslim name. Many thought Frazier's motivation stemmed from rejection of the Black Muslim philosophy. But it was more psychological than political. Long after the fight, Frazier confided that he did it to make Ali angry.

Ali–Frazier was more than the best boxing matchup to come along in many a year. For some, it was a quiet, hardworking Christian family man against a loudmouthed, draft-dodging Black Muslim. For others, it was an oversimplified matter of good vs. evil, like Louis–Schmeling and Patterson–Liston.

Some even saw it as a political confrontation, with Ali representing the left wing and Frazier the right. In many cases, a person's political leanings could be determined by which fighter he was rooting for on March 8.

Oddly enough, the fight took on a racial overtone as well, with Ali standing for Black

America and Frazier for White America. A week before the fight, Ali said he "represented the [black] masses," while Frazier was "looked on by the eyes of the world as the American representative, as the white man's champion."[6]

That was a characterization Frazier deeply resented. It sparked within him a deep-seated hostility toward Ali that appears to have lingered until the day he died. He found the "Uncle Tom" label especially offensive.

For all his sincerity, though, Frazier simply could not compete with Ali's popularity, especially among blacks. Ali's importance to Black America, especially at that time, cannot be overstated. Regardless of their religion, or whether they appreciated his ring style or political viewpoints, a large segment of the black population regarded Ali as a hero because of his independence and intolerance for racial injustice. As well, his martyrdom and exile because of the draft issue made him a symbol of black resistance to racism. In their attempts to break Ali's spirit, to put him in his place, the establishment only made him stronger.

Ali didn't buckle under pressure. His visibility and outspoken attitude became a source of strength for the Black Consciousness movement of the late 1960s and early '70s.

Ali refused to be rendered invisible. And he definitely refused to be quiet. He believed it was his struggle to fight for Black Americans, while Frazier stood for nothing.

Frazier was always more low-profile than Ali. Then again, so was 99 percent of the rest of the world's population. It wasn't difficult for Ali to portray his foe as puppet of the white man, even though the accusation wasn't true, and was actually an unjust slur on a proud, strong man.

Although Frazier had his share of supporters in the black community, a majority of his people shunned him and echoed Ali's disparaging rhetoric. It bothered Frazier that Ali was also the favorite of fellow black celebrities like Bill Cosby and Coretta Scott King.

Even in matters other than the race issue, Ali still took every opportunity possible to degrade Frazier, to belittle his stature as an opponent and as a man.

"This ain't the biggest sports event in the history of all sports because of Joe Frazier," he said. "They're not coming to see Joe Frazier."[7]

Frazier wasn't the first opponent Ali abused verbally, and he wouldn't be the last. Still, Ali probably launched more vitriol at Frazier at any other foe. In the weeks before the fight, Ali degraded Frazier's boxing skills, looks, intelligence, and even his singing ability.

Ali was confident that his jab would win the fight for him. He figured that he would cut his shorter foe to ribbons by dancing and jabbing.

Frazier was no fool. He knew he'd have to wade through one of the sharpest and quickest jabs in history to reach Ali. He took extreme measures to prepare for the steady stream of jabs he would most assuredly have to withstand. Daily Joe would soak his head in rock salt and water to toughen the skin.

Brine facials weren't the only part of Joe's game plan. He intended to dig away at Ali's body hard and often. Frazier was a firm advocate of old-time fighter Sam Langford's theory of infighting: "Kill the body and the head will die." Indeed, Frazier had earned a reputation as one of the most feared body punchers in history. He told Ali that he need not worry about his "pretty face," that he intended to tear his kidneys apart.

Yank Durham had his own opinion of the way the fight would unfold: "When I fight Clay, I'm going to get him somewhere in the middle rounds."[8] Durham's reference to his fighter in the first person was a good indication of the relationship between the two men. When questioned about his reference to his fighter in the first person, Durham responded:

"I'm the boss when it comes to boxing. I decide who to fight and when. And now I'm the champ."

Frazier would laugh at his mentor's use of the first person. "When the bell rings, Yank goes down the steps. Then I'm the only I."[9]

Yank became as much a father figure to Joe as he was a manager and trainer. And Frazier respected Durham for his guidance, knowledge, and personal interest. He knew he owed everything he had to Durham.

Unlike the stereotypical boxing manager, Durham never viewed Frazier as simply a meal ticket. In fact, he said whether Frazier won or lost on March 8, he'd like to see the fighter retire.

"I think he's been at the game long enough," Durham said. "He's been monkeying around boxing for 12 years. He'd be the youngest heavyweight champion to retire."[10]

Yancey Durham's interest in boxing began when he went into it as an amateur in Camden, New Jersey, during the late 1930s. As a soldier in World War II, he suffered an accident in which his legs were run over by a Jeep during an air raid in England. The accident ended his boxing days. But then Yank never claimed he was a great boxer.

However, the forced ending of his ring days didn't diminish Durham's love for the sport. Working days as a welder for the Penn Central Railroad in Philadelphia, he spent his evenings training youngsters at the Police Athletic League. Like all trainers, he dreamed of discovering and molding a world champion.

At first glance, a chubby teenager named Billy Joe Frazier wasn't quite the stuff of Durham's dreams. However, when Frazier's developing skills and single-minded determination combined with Durham's knowledge and patience, the result was one of the game's all-time great boxer-trainer teams.

The only pair that could rival Durham and Frazier's success was Ali and Dundee. As far back as 1957, the then-amateur Ali knew that when he turned pro, Dundee was the trainer he wanted.

By the standards of the profession, Dundee was a progressive trainer. When he began working with the young Cassius Clay, he made no attempt to alter the fighter's unorthodox defensive techniques. Other trainers scorned Ali's seemingly suicidal practice of leaning away from punches, but Dundee was insightful enough to realize Muhammad possessed the reflexes needed to get away with it.

And Dundee was more than just a spectator to Ali's meteoric rise. Angelo's cunning and ring savvy saved his fighter's hide on more than one occasion. There was, of course, the famous "split glove" incident in Ali's first fight against Henry Cooper. Dundee was also the man of the hour when Ali upset Liston for the title.

Nearly blinded by a foreign substance that had found its way into his eyes during the fourth round, a panicking Ali was ready to quit when he returned to his corner. He told Dundee to cut off his gloves.

"This is for the championship," Dundee screamed. "You just got something in your eyes; it'll clear up. Just stay away from him until it goes."

"Cut 'em off!" Ali begged again.

"Get out there," Dundee ordered, shoving Ali off the stool as the bell for the fifth round rang. "Run until it clears up. Run, run!"[11]

A bleary-eyed Ali backpedaled as Liston went after him. But Sonny couldn't catch him. And by the end of the round, the substance flushed out. Ali battered Liston in the sixth, and the rest is history.

A trainer with less guts and faith in his fighter might have cut Ali's gloves off after that fourth round. And that action would have changed history. Now the two great trainers, Dundee and Durham, were doing whatever they felt necessary to ensure that their fighters would be ready on March 8.

Both Ali and Frazier were contractually obligated to spend their final two weeks of training in New York City in order to help build the gate, as if it needed any more buildup. However, Durham kept Frazier in Philadelphia, and Dundee made certain Ali never left Miami.

Even after the pre-fight physical on March 4, Dundee immediately whisked his fighter back to Florida. Ali wanted to remain in the Big Apple, but Angelo knew the city held far too many distractions.

"He loves New York, and he loves to get out among the people," Dundee explained.[12]

He went on to note that two of Ali's New York fights, against Doug Jones and Oscar Bonavena, resulted in poor showings because Muhammad was socializing too much beforehand. Angelo wasn't about to allow that to happen against Frazier.

Durham's biggest concern was that the New York State Commission might choose a referee who wouldn't be able to control Ali, who sometimes had a cavalier regard for the rules of the ring. One example was the rule that requires a fighter to go to a neutral corner after scoring a knockdown.

Ali had a Dempsey-like history of standing over a fallen foe. He did it against Liston and Cleveland Williams, and most recently against Bonavena. When asked if he was particularly concerned about Ali hovering over a knocked-down Frazier, Durham responded: "Knocked down with what? I want my man to go to a neutral corner, too. I just want the rules."[13]

Another rule Durham wanted enforced was the one stipulating that cornermen couldn't yell instructions to their fighters during the course of a bout. Durham believed Ali's assistant trainer, Drew "Bundini" Brown, was notorious for this infraction, and he wanted none of it March 8.

For all their predictable differences, both camps were in agreement on the subject of conditioning. Both realized it would be the key to victory. Frazier felt that Ali would have to be in better shape if the former champion were to stand a chance of winning. His reasoning was that Ali would have to do two things as the bout progressed: box and backpedal. "I only have to fight," Frazier said. "It's that simple."

Ali believed the media was placing too much emphasis on condition. He said he was in great shape. While Frazier had fought less than two rounds against Foster, Bonavena had extended Ali almost the full fifteen rounds.

The odds makers didn't share Ali's confidence in himself. They made Frazier a 7-to-5 favorite on March 3, just five days before the fight. The king of betting odds, Jimmy "The Greek" Schneider, said "The Fight" was a "pick-em" affair.

Ali said that he understood why he was the underdog: "I know why, they figure I'm shot because I didn't look so good in the Bonavena fight. They think I'm the same old Clay—I mean Ali. I'll show them. They picked Frazier, I'll open their eyes."[14]

By March 5, the odds had trimmed a shade to 6–5 for Frazier. However, in Britain the London bookmakers had established Ali as an 11-to-8 favorite.[15]

One indication of Ali–Frazier's enormousness as an event was the astronomical sums being wagered on the outcome. Las Vegas bookies indicated the fight was generating a staggering $1 billion in bets!

In the weeks leading up to the fight, both Frazier and Ali had been reluctant to issue any specific predictions on the outcome. "I don't want it to go beyond the first round if I can help it," Frazier joked. "I'll be at the party."

The "party" Joe referred to was a planned victory celebration to be held at the Sattler Hilton hotel after the fight. Music would be provided by Duke Ellington's band. Ticket prices ranged from $35 for "gold circle" to $15 for general admission.[16]

Ali was not impressed with Frazier's audacity in planning such an elaborate victory party. Ali promised that Frazier would be in no shape to attend his own party.

Frazier concluded his final day of sparring by pummeling light heavyweight Paul Cardoza. Durham hired smaller, quicker men to simulate Ali's speed.

Cardoza couldn't see how Ali could handle his boss. "I'm not Ali but I don't see how he can contend with the pressure Joe puts on you."[17]

Not all of Frazier's spar mates were as loyal as Cardoza. On February 25, eleven days before the fight, Don Warner, one of Frazier's regulars, was banned from the champ's camp for making nightly reports to Ali. Although he was criticized for paying Warner to spy on Frazier, Ali saw no harm in scouting an opponent. "Football and basketball teams send scouts to watch their opponents, don't they?"[18]

Frazier became involved in a far more serious situation on the day before the fight, when he received a letter warning him to "lose or else." The letter was followed by a bomb scare at the inn at which he was staying. Consequently, security at the fight was beefed up. Five hundred of New York's finest patrolled in and around the Garden on fight night.[19]

A crowd of 20,455 had paid $1,353,951 to see the clash of the champions. Scalpers had a field day, scoring as much as $450 for a $150 ringside ticket.[20]

Ali had sealed his prediction in an envelope to be opened just prior to the first bell on March 8. Always supremely confident, Ali prophesied that the world would be shocked at how easily he handled Frazier. He said that he would stop Joe in six and the world would know that he had been the true champion all along.

"The Fight"

Ali was the first fighter in the ring, dressed in red trunks with white trim. He came in at a svelte 215 and danced lightly around the ring, throwing quick combinations at the air.

A moment later, Frazier made his entrance. He weighed a solid 205½ pounds, his best fighting weight. Frazier's trunks and robe were green and spotted with gold flowers, resembling a pattern found on wallpaper or shower curtains. But Joe called the costume "regal, something that a king would wear."

As Ali pranced toward Frazier, he purposely bumped the smaller man. The two fighters continued to provoke each other during referee Arthur Mercante's instructions.

"Look out, nigger, I'm gonna kill ya," Ali said as the bell sounded. Undaunted by the threat, Frazier came out bobbing, weaving, and pursuing. Ali circled his foe at center ring. Frazier landed a hard left to Ali's jaw, but Muhammad clinched and shook his head "No" to assure the crowd that he wasn't hurt. Ali's jab found Frazier's face. Joe, in turn, found some success in herding Ali onto the ropes. The bell ended a fairly even first round. The two champions fought at a scorching pace in the second. Frazier continued to close in on Ali. Ali circled and jabbed. At one point, he snapped Joe's head back with a picturesque combination. As he had promised, Frazier attacked Ali's body every time he could catch him on the ropes.

Ali dominated the first half of round three, scoring well with combinations and staying out of harm's way. It was the Ali of old in the ring now, not the impostor who had wrestled with Bonavena. But Frazier simply kept on coming, throwing punches and connecting whenever he could.

Round four was a repeat of its predecessor, with Ali landing to the head and Frazier to the body. But a shift in momentum was beginning to appear. Ali was expending a great deal of energy, but he wasn't hurting or discouraging Frazier. And Joe was beginning to realize that he could walk through Ali's punches.

At the beginning of the fifth round, Ali stung Frazier with a three-punch combination. Frazier responded by dropping his guard and making a face, something no previous Ali opponent had ever done. Ali hit him again, then threw a flurry that Joe effortlessly bobbed and weaved around as he worked his way inside. A confident smile crept across Frazier's face as the round wore on. At the bell, Ali showed the first signs of fatigue when he plopped wearily onto his stool.

Frazier stayed right under Ali's nose throughout round six. Except for brief, inconsequential flurries, Ali spent the entire round with his back to the ropes, where Frazier buckled his knees with a succession of smashing hooks to the head. He also dug both hands to the body. Although Ali signaled to the crowd that he wasn't hurt, a pattern was beginning to emerge in the fight.

Frazier continued his body attack early in round seven before Ali made a successful counterattack off the ropes. His jabs continued to pop into Frazier's face, which was becoming visibly puffy. But he finished the round exactly where Frazier wanted him: on the ropes.

Muhammad approached round eight with more purpose, working his jab and combinations in a manner not seen in several rounds. Then, suddenly, Frazier appeared to "will" Ali onto the ropes without a struggle. On the ropes, Joe ripped powerful hooks to the body and head. Ali responded by clinching and throwing pitty-pat punches that would not have hurt a flyweight.

When Mercante separated the men, Ali waved Frazier back in to continue the assault. Frazier gladly accepted, and they exchanged a brief flurry. At the end of the round, Frazier was flailing away at Ali's body: "Kill the body and the head will die."

Ali spent the first part of round nine in his now-familiar position on the ropes, where Frazier shook him with a terrific left hook. Ali then moved the action to center ring, where he unleashed his best offense to that point. For the first time, Frazier backed up under Muhammad's two-fisted barrage. Ali's rights followed his lefts so quickly that they looked like one punch. It looked as though Ali had turned the tide back in his favor: "Sting like a bee."

By round ten, both men were showing signs of fatigue. Frazier uttered loud grunts as he threw his punches. Mercante had trouble separating the big men, and at times the action was rough for him as well as the fighters. At one point he inadvertently struck Frazier in the face with his right hand while separating the big men.

Neither Ali nor Mercante's punching power impressed Frazier. By the end of the round, he had regained the momentum he had lost in the ninth.

Ali hit the canvas early in the eleventh. But Mercante ruled it a slip. After backing into the ropes, Ali was nailed by a devastating left hook that shook him to his toes. Another Frazier hook had him wobbling and almost down. Although he was staggering like a drunk,

Ali still managed to make a face at his tormentor. Frazier landed another long left hook, and Ali retreated on rubbery legs. Somehow, he hung on to finish the round.

A fired-up Frazier tagged Ali early in round twelve. Muhammad appeared groggy; his legs were leaden and his arms were weary. Still, he managed to plant several combinations into Frazier's swollen features. Meanwhile, Frazier continued to mistreat Ali's sore ribs with powerhouse hooks. Incredibly, both men came out for the thirteenth as if it were round one. Ali danced the way he did before his exile, and his jabs seemed to whistle through the air. He snapped Frazier's head, and even fought well off the ropes. It was Ali's best round since the ninth. However, the right side of his jaw was swelling to abnormal proportions.

In the fourteenth, the fighters continued to show incredible stamina. Ali's blows continued to rearrange Frazier's features, which had become misshapen from the accumulation of punches Ali had landed. Lumps and bumps protruded "like a sack of potatoes," as artist Leroy Neiman put it. But Frazier kept chugging forward like a locomotive, and his hooks continued to thud into Ali's pain-wracked body.

The fight appeared even at that point. For most spectators, the final round would determine the winner, though no one knew how the judges were seeing it.

Mercante ordered the fighters to touch gloves at the start of round fifteen. Ali began by circling and pumping his jab at a crouching Frazier. Then it came: like a bolt of lightning, Joe sprang up from his crouch and exploded a left hook off Ali's swollen jaw.

Ali fell, landing flat on his back. He rose at four, and Mercante waved Frazier back in. Frazier crashed another hard left to the jaw, followed by a brutal two-fisted attack. Ali appeared helpless, about to fall again. But he remained upright as Frazier tried his best to finish him, slamming two more hooks into Ali's ballooning jaw. Then Ali dug down and mounted a desperate counteroffensive. The final bell must have sounded like sweet music to both the exhausted warriors.

The decision was almost anticlimactic. Referee Mercante scored it 8 rounds to 6, with one even. Judge Artie Aidala had it 9–6. Judge Bill Recht saw it at 11–4. All three officials had voted for Frazier. Smokin' Joe was now the undisputed heavyweight champion of the world, and he had beaten the man who had belittled him for so long.

When he heard the decision, an ecstatic Frazier yelled across the ring to Ali: "Who's the champ? Who's the champ?"

In Ali's corner, Bundini Brown burst into tears and grabbed Ali. "Don't worry, Champ," he cried. "You fought like a champ. You got nothing to be ashamed of."

"Don't hold me, Bundini," Ali responded. "Damn. I'm sore in the neck. I'm sore in the ribs."[21]

As the crowd roared in appreciation of a great fight, both men's handlers led them out of the ring.

Referee Mercante said afterward that it was a "tough fight to handle" because of the showy antics of both men. He felt the match was beautifully fought, but expressed surprise that "it went 15."

"I thought it would be more wide open on Ali's part," Mercante continued. "I was surprised to see him in close so much, slugging toe to toe."[22]

Mercante went on to say he had to stop the fighters from taunting each other throughout the contest. "They mumbled at each other something like, 'If that's your best shot, you don't have much.'"[23]

Frazier was a battered winner. Ice packs were applied to his grotesquely lumped face during the post-fight press conference. In his comments, Frazier gave generous praise to the loser. "I've got to give Clay credit, he takes some punches," Frazier said. "Oh my God, that shot I hit him with in the last round ... I went back home, back to the country for that one."[24]

Asked about Ali's performance, the champ said, "He must have been crazy, the way he stayed on those ropes. He thought I was flat footed. He knows better now."[25]

One reporter asked Frazier what he thought of Ali's "clowning."

"Clowning? Man, where were you?" Frazier shot back. "He wasn't clowning. He just couldn't move."[26]

Frazier was asked if Ali ever hurt him.

"A couple of times I felt his blows," Joe admitted. "You can't get hit by a man his size without hurting."[27]

Frazier made a brief appearance at the press conference but soon excused himself to "straighten up" his battered face before making a quick trip to the victory party.

Ali did not attend the conference. Reports indicated that he'd been taken to the hospital to have his swollen jaw X-rayed. After the X-rays were taken, Ali's personal physician, Dr. Ferdie Pacheco, advised the ex-champ to spend the night in the hospital. Ali refused. He didn't want to give the impression that Smokin' Joe put that kind of hurt on him.

Bundini showed up at the press conference in Ali's place. "We'll be back," he said. "And this time there won't be any three years between fights. You can't put a car in the garage for three years and expect it not to have a few kinks."[28]

On the subject of Frazier, Bundini was gracious.

"I always called Joe Frazier a turkey," he said. "But he's no turkey, he's no ordinary champion. He's a real champion. When we come back, we're gonna have to take the title away from the champion."[29]

The fight had some negative consequences for Bundini, when the New York State Athletic Commission slapped him with an indefinite suspension. The action was based on infractions of the type Yank Durham had alluded to before the fight.

First, Bundini had yelled advice to Ali during the course of several rounds. He had been warned about that prior to the fight. Second, Bundini had soaked a sponge and sprayed water from it toward Ali in an attempt to revive the fighter when he was on the canvas in the 15th round.

A Commission spokesman stated: "Chances are he [Bundini] would have been suspended for ignoring orders not to coach, but when an eye witness saw him throw the water, that was the last straw. The spray of water went all over, even into the lenses of some of the cameras ringside."[30]

"Trying to revive my soldier," Bundini protested. "My, you'd think I'd climbed into the ring to get Frazier with a baseball bat."[31]

Dundee said: "You can't forfeit a man for trying in that situation."[32]

Bundini, whose real name was Drew Brown, was as much a part of the Ali mystique as the phrase he had coined early in Muhammad's career: "Float like a butterfly, sting like a bee, rumble, young man, rumble!"

Brown began his association with boxing back in the 1950s, working with welterweight champion Johnny Bratton and the great Sugar Ray Robinson. He was introduced to Ali before the first Liston fight and, with the exception of a brief separation in the 1960s, he remained by the side of "The Greatest" throughout the rest of his career.

Bundini once explained that the reason he had approached the young Cassius Clay was to show him his self importance and keep him humble. Even Bundini couldn't induce

Ali to be humble. Otherwise, though, an almost mystical bond developed between him and the fighter. Bundini would often get physically ill before one of Ali's fights.

Brown's official title was "assistant trainer." Others recognized his status as much more than that. Jimmy Dundee once said that the only difference between Bundini and a witch doctor was the absence of a headdress.

Brown's life had been an adventure even before he hooked up with Ali. He'd been a "pillar-to-post baby," as he put it, never having any true roots. He joined the Navy at the age of 13, and served aboard three different ships during World War II. Eventually, he was discharged for attacking an officer with a meat cleaver.

Brown said the worst thing about the discharge was losing the Navy uniform. "Little girls like uniforms, and I was only 15," he said.

He then spent 12 years in the Merchant Marines. While he was on a trip to Beirut, Lebanon, a local family befriended him. When he left, his tearful Lebanese friends stood on the deck and cried, "Bundini! Bundini!" Though he didn't know what it meant, it became his handle.

And now he had a suspension.

Ali made himself available to the press the day after the fight. Contrary to some speculation, he didn't appear shattered by his first professional defeat.

Ali felt that he had done enough to capture the decision. "I know I won the most rounds, I think I won nine rounds. I caught a few shots and the knockdown made it exaggerating." Concerning the knockdown, Ali gave Frazier some credit: "When a man gets me going, when I'm wobbly, that's a punch. And when a man drops me, that was a helluva punch."[33]

Ali took the loss in stride and believed the experience would make him a better person. Now he just wanted to go home and spend time with his family.

He also repudiated his pre-fight pretense that Frazier was his enemy and an "Uncle Tom." He stated that Frazier was a nice man but vowed to beat him next time.

In fact, Ali waited only two days before calling for a rematch. The ex-champ said he and Frazier had a verbal agreement for a return go. "Any time he wants it," Frazier responded.

Ali insisted that for a rematch, he wanted a foreign referee and judges. He believed that his open repudiation of the war in Vietnam had destroyed his chances of receiving an unbiased decision in a close fight.

Thus ended the most anticipated fight in history, a fight that more than matched the hype and hoopla that surrounded it. Yet the closeness of the result created even more demand for a rematch. Ali–Frazier II became the most sought-after match in boxing over the next two years.

Ali impressed people with the way he was dealing with his first professional setback. In defeat, Ali had proven far more resilient than anyone could have guessed. Arthur Daley wrote the next day that Ali was "just too proud a man, too magnificent an athlete and too gutsy a warrior to let himself stay down."[34]

As the man who finally defeated Ali and temporarily buttoned the "Louisville Lip," Frazier finally dispelled the shadow that had hung over his claim to the title. After taking on a hectic schedule of engagements the week following the fight, Joe was admitted to St. Luke's Hospital in Philadelphia on March 16 for exhaustion and high blood pressure.

Rumors about Frazier's health ran rampant. Boxing writer Bob Waters reported that the champ was retiring due to pressure from his wife and Yank Durham. Frazier's physician, Dr. James Guiffre, stated that the champ possibly had a kidney ailment, but didn't think that it was a result of the fight because Ali landed so few body punches.

Despite that medical opinion, rumors continued to fly, the most extreme of which was that Frazier was dead or dying.

"Great, now they've killed him," an Associated Press reporter wrote in reference to the hearsay. "Getting him sick wasn't enough. What are they going to do when he leaves the hospital after three days?"[35]

When questioned about his possible retirement, Frazier didn't see why he should be pressured into making a hasty announcement. Dr. Guiffre didn't see any physical reasons for the champ to retire.

In fact, Frazier had no serious intention to retire. He simply needed a rest after one of the most grueling prizefights in modern boxing history. He won the battle. Yet he appeared to have paid a higher physical price than Ali. The March 8 fight was to be Frazier's last for 1971.

With the superfight over and the title in mothballs, interest in the heavyweights might easily have begun to wane. But Ali was showing interest in taking a few fights before the end of the year. And a young contender was beginning to attract a large following of his own.

Foreman to the Fore

By mid–1971, George Foreman was well on his way to becoming a new force in the heavyweight division. Many felt the 23-year-old strongman would be the one who would eventually knock Frazier and Ali out of the spotlight.

Foreman was a product of the "up-from-the-streets" background typical of most successful fighters. Born in Marshall, Texas, on January 22, 1948, and raised in a rough part of Houston, George was the seventh of nine children.

As a youth, Foreman had no difficulty finding trouble, or maybe it was the other way around. He dropped out of junior high school to pursue less constructive pastimes. He would hang out, smoking and drinking with a dangerous crowd in unseemly places.

George felt most comfortable in the streets of Houston's dangerous Fifth Ward community, where the powerful youth enjoyed the respect of those who knew of his incredible strength. Entire gangs of hard cases would take to their heels when they saw "Big George" strutting in their direction.

George was known to his gang as "Monkey," and former gang associate Don Thomas said in 1974, "When we started a fight, we'd look around to see if Monkey was there. You had two or three cats whipped if he was."[36]

Eventually George took a job washing dishes in a cafe. His pay was $15 a week, and that small amount was just enough to buy the cheap wine he liked to guzzle. Foreman was a young man with no ambition and, apparently, no future. And he soon found himself on the wrong side of the law.

One day George and his crew were picked up for breaking windows and ended up in juvenile court. At that point, George was encouraged to join the Job Corps, and was sent to Grant's Pass, Oregon, in 1965. It was a choice that changed his life.

For the first time in his life, Foreman experienced country air, regular chores, and discipline. He also learned productive skills like carpentry, electronics, and bricklaying. He even found enough motivation to earn a high school equivalency diploma.

In 1966, Foreman was transferred from Oregon to Pleasanton, California. From there, he returned to Houston with high hopes for employment and a fresh start in life. However, when no job was forthcoming, George returned to Pleasanton, where he was hired as a physical instructor at the local Parks Center.

It was during his second stay in Pleasanton that Foreman took up boxing. He once credited Muhammad Ali for sparking his interest in the sport. While listening to the Ali–Patterson fight on the radio, George began dancing around and mouthing off like the champ. Foreman maintained his love of boxing but soon dropped Ali's personality.

Foreman's amateur career lasted a mere 18 months, culminating in a position on the 1968 U.S. Olympic team. He won the heavyweight gold medal in Mexico City, and hoped his Olympic success would launch him to a world title as it had for Patterson, Ali, and Frazier.

It was at the Olympics that Foreman made his first major impression on the American public, not so much for the bullish way in which he handled his opponents as what he did following his gold medal–winning bout against a Soviet boxer named Ionis Chepulis.

As the triumphant Foreman paraded around the ring, he waved a tiny American flag at the crowd. Normally, such an action would have been viewed as just another display of patriotism. However, because he chose to do it in the wake of the highly controversial Tommie Smith–John Carlos fist-raising incident, Foreman's gesture of national pride was blown out of proportion.

During the medal ceremonies for the 200-meter dash, Smith and Carlos had bowed their heads and raised their fists in a Black Power salute as the American national anthem played. Their quiet act of protest brought an emotional reaction from the media and the public. Many viewed it as treason, an embarrassment to the nation. Others considered it a brave act of protest, a way of telling the world that the American Dream had not come true for everyone in the country, especially its black citizens.

Foreman's low-key gesture did a great deal to soothe the anger generated by those upraised, black-gloved fists. It also upset others who believed Foreman had acted as a tool of the white establishment by negating the impact of what Smith and Carlos had done.

In reality, however, Foreman's motivation was personal, not political. Later, he explained that he'd carried lucky beads and the American flag in the pocket of his robe. "I did it first because I'm an American, second, because I'm George Foreman, and third, because I was proud to represent my country."[37]

Indeed, strength and punching power rather than refined boxing skills were Foreman's trademarks from the beginning of his career. A massively built man with a ferocious left jab and a wrecking ball for a right hand, Foreman was compared to Sonny Liston even before the Olympics.

The similarity between the two was more than coincidental. George, who was only 20 years old, had an opportunity to train with Liston in 1968, before departing for his date with destiny in Mexico City. At that time, Liston was an aging ex-champion. But he retained his menacing demeanor.

Big George admitted to being scared the first time that he sparred with Liston. Foreman soon lost his stage fright, but never his respect for the ex-champ, whose picture still graces the wall of George's gym.

"Sonny was the only guy I could never back up," Foreman recalled years later. "I'd hit him with some monster shot and he'd just shake his head and say, 'No, son.'"

The two big hitters soon became close friends. In Foreman, Liston might have seen the son he never had. And young George found in Liston a role model more to his liking than Ali had been several years earlier. Fortunately, Foreman didn't adopt all of Sonny's surly ways outside the ring. But inside the ropes, he was Liston revisited, right down to the menacing pre-fight stare.

Although the young fighter was approached by hordes of potential managers after the Olympics, George chose the relatively obscure Dick Sadler. Sadler, a cousin of former featherweight champion Sandy Saddler, had worked in Liston's corner on a number of occasions. He was shocked and overjoyed when the Olympic champ picked him.

"I'm absolutely honored to have George choose me over everybody else. Simply flattered," Sadler said.[38]

Foreman made his professional debut on June 23, 1969, against Don Waldheim and he stopped his man in three rounds. Seven weeks and three fights later, he was headlining in Madison Square Garden against New Jersey tough guy Chuck Wepner. Utilizing a bludgeoning jab, Foreman shredded Werner's facial skin and stopped him in three bloody rounds. Three more knockout wins followed before Foreman was extended the full eight-round distance against a seasoned Peruvian named Roberto Davila. Three more lambs were led to the slaughter before George was once again forced to go the distance, this time against wellused trial horse Levi Forte in Miami Beach.

Foreman rounded out 1969 two days after the Forte fight with a one-round hammering of Gary "Hobo" Wiler on December 18 in Seattle, Washington. In the first six months of his professional career, the young contender had scored 13 wins.

He continued his rapid clip in January 1970, pounding out Charlie Polite in 4 rounds on the sixth of the month, then leveling 6'6" Jack O'Halloran in five frames twenty days later.

Then Foreman fought the toughest bout to that point of his career on the Frazier–Ellis undercard on February 16. His opponent was the tricky Argentine veteran Gregorio "Goyo" Peralta.

Although Peralta was only a blown-up light heavyweight with no punching power, he had an uncanny knack for defusing the bombs of heavyweight sluggers. Foreman was no exception to the rule. In the fifth round, the 197-pound Peralta opened a bad gash over George's right eye. Foreman, 213, stormed back at the end of the stanza and staggered Peralta with heavy shots to the head and body.

Foreman's jab became the controlling factor in the fight. But the experience Peralta had gleaned over 73 wins out of 86 professional fights kept him in the picture.

George pounded the smaller man along the ropes throughout most of round nine. Then "Goyo" valiantly fought his way off the ropes and engaged Foreman in a torrid toe-to-toe exchange at the bell. The crowd roared its approval as Peralta actually outpunched his stronger foe in the tenth.

Foreman captured a unanimous decision. This would be his last points victory until his comeback, which was then far in the future.

After the unexpectedly difficult Peralta fight, Foreman added the names of some of the division's most renowned stepping stones to his resume. Rufus Brassell exited in one. James J. Woody, touted early in his career but by then on the downslide, fell in three. Aaron Eastling went in four. The durable George "Scrapiron" Johnson, who had once gone the distance with Joe Frazier, lasted seven painful rounds against Foreman. And Roger Russell, once regarded as a hot prospect, folded in one, a result hardly surprising since Russell hadn't won a fight since 1967.

Even though his opposition was less than stellar, that kayo streak elevated Foreman to the number seven position in the WBA's ratings after only a year as a professional. Now he was ready to test his skills against stronger opposition. His camp, led by manager Dick Sadler, looked north to Canada to find the ideal foe. If Sadler, a cousin of the great featherweight champion Sandy Saddler, was looking for an opponent sturdy enough to gauge Foreman's power, he couldn't have found a more resilient character than Toronto-born George Chuvalo.

In boxing circles, Chuvalo's name had become synonymous with iron-jawed durability. Dave Anderson of the *New York Times* once wrote: "Forget Dick Butkus and all the toughies in the National Football League. The toughest guy anywhere in sports has to be Chuvalo."

Former heavyweight champion Rocky Marciano, who was an "iron man" in his own right, once commented, "If every fight was scheduled for twenty rounds, George Chuvalo would be heavyweight champion."[39]

Built like a block of granite, the Croatian-Canadian heavyweight seemed undaunted about being on the receiving end of abominable amounts of punishment.

His brawling, unorthodox and somewhat dirty tactics earned Chuvalo many victories but few friends among his opponents. In many ways, he was a heavyweight version of Gene Fullmer, the rugged middleweight champion of the late 1950s and early '60s. Like Fullmer, Chuvalo got into trouble with the officials on more than one occasion.

In 1961, for example, George was disqualified for butting in the fifth round of a fight with Joe Erskine of Wales. He complained that Erskine kept walking into his head.

Doing construction work as a young man helped George to develop the heavily muscled torso and thick, unwavering legs that were so valuable to him in the ring. Always big for his age, he was a full-fledged heavyweight by age 15. As an amateur, he captured the Canadian AAU title at 17. At 19, he turned pro, and on his first day in the punch-for-pay ranks he racked up an incredible four knockouts!

Chuvalo turned that trick while fighting in a Jack Dempsey Heavyweight Novice Tournament in Toronto in 1956. George won the tournament by pulverizing four foes in succession.

After that spectacular debut, Chuvalo wasted little time jumping into the ring with top-notch competition. Three fights after winning the Dempsey tournament, he faced an experienced warhorse named Howard King. King had tangled with the likes of Archie Moore, Zora Folley, Eddie Machen, and Roger Rischer. King won an eight-round decision. Nine fights later, Chuvalo knocked him out in two.

A first-round starching of James J. Parker in 1958 earned Chuvalo the Canadian heavyweight title. Then he jumped up in competition and went after top-ten contender Irish Pat McMurtry. The smooth-boxing McMurtry won a 10-round decision but said afterward that the wouldn't want to meet Chuvalo a year from now.

Chuvalo stopped Yvon Durelle in defense of his Canadian title, then lost his crown on a controversial 12-round decision to Robert Cleroux, a Montrealer who was just as rugged as George.

In a rematch three months later, Chuvalo reversed the outcome and regained his title. He followed up on that triumph with big wins over contenders Alex Miteff and Willi Besmanoff, who later served as cannon fodder for the young Cassius Clay.

At that point, Chuvalo's personal and professional lives went seriously awry. In a rubber match with Cleroux, he lost the decision and his title. Then came the disqualification against Erskine. Those reverses caused him to become disgruntled with boxing.

He didn't fight at all in 1962. But in 1963, he joined forces with Toronto businessman Irving Ungerman, and resumed his ring career.

Beginning his comeback in March of that year, Chuvalo reeled off four consecutive knockouts over so-so opposition. Then he took on highly rated contender Mike De John on short notice, filling in for an injured Ernie Terrell. An upset 10-round decision win over De John placed Chuvalo back into contention.

He almost suffered another setback on November 8, 1963, when the ring announcer pronounced him a loser to slick Tony Alongi in Miami Beach. The verdict was later changed to a draw when the boxing commission found an error on the scorecard of the referee.

In 1964, Chuvalo started on a down note, dropping a 10-round decision to master boxer Zora Folley on January 17. But Chuvalo didn't stay down long. His career was like a yo-yo. Every time he appeared to be out of the heavyweight picture, back he would come with a win over a worthy foe or a string of knockouts over non-entities.

The pattern continued after the Folley fight, as the Canadian racked up four consecutive kayo victories. The most impressive win in that set was an eleventh-round stoppage of Doug Jones. Highly regarded because of his near miss against Cassius Clay, Jones was the most important notch on Chuvalo's gun at that time.

Chuvalo was then matched with former heavyweight king Floyd Patterson to determine a challenger to the new champion, Muhammad Ali. George was given an excellent chance to defeat the supposedly washed-up Patterson.

But the boxing world discovered two things on the night of February 1, 1965. First, Patterson made it emphatically clear that he was far from washed up. Second, Chuvalo proved he could indeed handle himself respectably against a fighter of Floyd's high caliber. At the end of 12 grueling rounds, Patterson won the decision, and Chuvalo gained credibility.

After four more knockouts, Chuvalo found himself fighting for the heavyweight championship of the world, the WBA's version, held by Ernie Terrell. The November 1, 1965, bout turned into a 15-round exercise in boredom, with Terrell's jabbing and clinching tactics carrying him to a points victory.

Chuvalo looked listless in his next fight, an upset 10-round decision loss to a light-hitting Argentine named Eduardo Corletti. Despite (or perhaps because of) these back-to-back poor performances, Chuvalo secured another title shot, this time against the "real" champ, Muhammad Ali. The fight would take place in Chuvalo's home town of Toronto.

Ali labeled Chuvalo the "Old Washerwoman" in reference to the Canadian's pedestrian ring style. Although he was given no chance to win, Chuvalo mounted a courageous effort in dropping a 15-round decision to the champion.

Two fights later, George lost to Oscar Bonavena in a fight some thought should have gone to a finish, as in the old bare-knuckle days. He then reeled off fourteen straight knockouts over a collection of second-raters and walking heavy bags.

Then came the Frazier fight, in which Chuvalo stayed on his feet but almost lost an eye when Frazier's hook fractured George's right cheekbone and eye socket. Chuvalo stated that his eyeball swelled up like "a grapefruit." Surgery was required to save his eye and his career.

"Why?" Chuvalo's well-wishers asked. "Why continue?"

Chuvalo's answer was that he didn't think he'd reached the end of the line just yet, even though he was 31 years old. In fact, as he told one sportswriter, he didn't feel he'd reached his full potential as a fighter.

Among those calling for George's retirement was his wife. However, Chuvalo had nothing to fall back on other than fighting. He had to continue.

The extent of the injuries Frazier had inflicted kept Chuvalo out of action for the better part of a year. Once again, his career was at a low point.

Then, true to form, he roared back into serious contention with a sensational fifth-round knockout of Mexican hope Manuel Ramos on September 28, 1968. He cemented his position with a subsequent seventh-round icing of Italy's Dante Cane.

On February 3, 1969, the yo-yo dropped again. Chuvalo looked sluggish in losing a 12-round decision to Buster Mathis.

Although George rebounded from that defeat by flattening a pair of no-hopers named Stamford Harris and Leslie Borden, it appeared that his career had come to a standstill.

Time and again, he had proven his dominance over the lower echelon of heavyweights. But every time he attempted to reach a higher level, his efforts were thwarted. Few expected the yo-yo to rise when Chuvalo faced Jerry Quarry at Madison Square Garden on December 12, 1969. He vowed that a loss to Quarry would end his career.

His prophecy appeared to be coming true as Quarry totally outboxed him over six rounds. Indeed, Dr. A. Harry Kleiman of the New York State Athletic Commission contemplated stopping the fight after that round due to the eye injuries Chuvalo had sustained. Chuvalo and Ungerman begged for one more round. They got it, and Chuvalo went out and flattened Quarry for a ten count with only one second left in round seven.

The storybook finish salvaged Chuvalo's career one more time. Quarry was the best man Chuvalo had ever defeated, and the win put him into title contention once again. He was suggested as a challenger for Frazier after Joe whipped Jimmy Ellis to unify the title in 1970. To keep busy and retain his high ranking at little risk, George reeled off three quick knockouts against Billy Tiger, Gino Ricci, and Charlie Reno.

Then came to call to test yet another Olympic champion. Chuvalo was in his third decade of professional boxing, and never before had he come closer to the top. Only George Foreman stood in his way.

Because of his victory over Quarry, his proven durability, and his vast edge in experience, Chuvalo was given a good chance of upsetting the power-punching prospect. Still, by fight night on August 4, 1970, the odds favored Foreman by a slight 7-to-5 margin. The elder George would earn the lion's share of the purse: $50,000 to Foreman's $15,000.

Foreman, weighing 218 pounds to Chuvalo's 214½, controlled the action from the outset behind his thudding, Liston-like left jab. He scored well during the first two rounds, although Chuvalo managed to get in a few good shots of his own.

Shortly after the beginning of round three, Foreman delivered a hard left hook and Chuvalo staggered backwards into the ropes. The Canadian covered up in a protective shell as Foreman unloaded a succession of thunderous, unanswered blows from both hands. Foreman trapped Chuvalo in the latter's own corner and continued the bombardment until Ungerman leaped onto the ring apron.

Ungerman's action caused referee Arthur Mercante to step between the fighters and call a halt at 1:41 of the round. To his credit, Chuvalo never left his feet under what was perhaps the worst sustained beating he had taken to date. Still, Mercante may have been hasty in stopping the contest.

Foreman showed nothing but respect for Chuvalo after the fight. "That man's tough," he said in the understatement of the year. "You can't take chances with old George. That's why I was happy to have him out of there early."[40]

Chuvalo was equally generous in his assessment of his conqueror. "He's good, really good," Chuvalo said. "Right now, he's probably too much for just about anybody who's around right now. But he's a long way from being ready for Joe Frazier. Perhaps a year and a half of fighting steadily would do it."[41]

The win lifted Foreman another notch up the heavyweight ladder. As for Chuvalo, his yo-yo was on yet another downswing.

Naturally, the question of retirement was raised again. Asked in his dressing room following the fight if he planned to continue, George answered in the affirmative.

And retire he didn't. Only eleven days after the Foreman disaster, Chuvalo journeyed to his parents' hometown of Sarajevo, Yugoslavia. There, he knocked out American Mike Bruce in two rounds. Chuvalo insisted his easy destruction of Bruce, who had once floored Joe Frazier but also sported a record of 8 wins and 24 losses, showed he wasn't through as a fighter.

That was true, but only against competition of Bruce's low caliber. Chuvalo fought on for several more years, but he would never again be a serious title contender.

Foreman marched on in the opposite direction. In his next fight, he took on tough journeyman Lou Bailey. Bailey, who was cut in the "Scrapiron" Johnson mold, was a much-traveled pug who on most nights was booked as another win on the record of a more heralded rival. He rarely failed to play out his role.

However, unlike many other well-known "professional losers," Bailey always gave his all, and he didn't simply fold with the first hard punch an opponent landed. Showing enormous courage, Lou dragged himself off the canvas six times before Foreman finished him off in the third round.

On November 18, 1970, Foreman fought a fellow prospect, Seattle's Boone "Boom Boom" Kirkman. Since the mid–1960s Kirkman had been touted as a "White Hope," although Jerry Quarry tended to overshadow him in that category. An aggressive puncher with a solid 22–1 record (18 KOs), Boone was managed and trained by the legendary Jack Hurley.

Kirkman's only defeat had come on June 29, 1967, at the hands of a faded but still dangerous Doug Jones. Kirkman was ahead on points, but a badly cut eye forced a seventh-round stoppage. Six weeks later, Kirkman avenged the defeat by destroying Jones in six rounds. Going into the Foreman fight, Boone was rated in almost everybody's top ten.

But Foreman showed absolutely no respect for Kirkman, or for the Queensberry Rules. Rushing from his corner in the first round, he shoved the smaller man to the canvas. Moments later, Big George floored Kirkman with a clubbing right hand. Then referee Arthur Mercante took the round away from Foreman for once again pushing Kirkman to the mat.

The loss of the round made no difference, as Foreman came out in round two and crashed a right uppercut to Boone's chin. Kirkman landed flat on his back. He gamely arose at the count of four, but Foreman pinned him against the ropes and fired at will. Mercante halted the massacre at the 41-second mark of the round.

"I don't believe it," a stunned and disappointed Kirkman said later. "I just can't believe that happened to me. I expected Foreman to run, but not right at me."[42]

It was obvious that Kirkman's style was made to order for Foreman. He liked nothing better than a smaller, weaker opponent who had the audacity to try to outslug him.

Madison Square Garden boxing director Harry Markson said of Foreman, after the rout of Kirkman, that the young Olympian offered something beyond Ali and Frazier in the future.

Floyd Patterson? Yes, the man who had once been the youngest fighter to win the heavyweight title was now, at 36 years of age, the oldest contender in the top ten.

As for Foreman, he spent his next three fights squashing assorted tomato cans. Mel Turnbow and Charlie Boston said goodbye in a round apiece. Then Foreman faced Stamford Harris, a Joe Frazier look-alike. But the physical resemblance was all Harris had in common with the champ. Harris had been stopped in five of his last six fights and, as expected, Foreman took him out in two one-sided rounds.

Rumors of an impending Ali–Foreman confrontation were beginning to make the rounds, but nothing came of those speculations. In the meantime, George was preparing for his first "title" fight, a return match with Gregorio Peralta, with the vacant North American heavyweight championship at stake. Of course, Peralta was from South America, but details like that made no difference to the promoters.

Since the fight was billed as a championship event, a 15-round distance was scheduled. Although Peralta was 13 years older than Foreman, he believed the extra rounds would be a disadvantage for the younger man. He felt Foreman was the more fatigued fighter in the tenth round of their first encounter.

However, sound as Peralta's reasoning was in theory, in reality he was facing a much more seasoned Foreman. As the fight progressed, Peralta's clever moves were bothersome, but not nearly as effective as before. Foreman simply walked through Gregorio's punches and pummeled him along the ropes. The referee stopped the fight in the tenth, giving Foreman a TKO win and his first professional championship.

George scheduled two easier fights in September. The first was slated for the 17th in El Paso, Texas, against Al Banks. But Banks developed car trouble on the way to the fight and ended up stranded in New Mexico. A 218-pound substitute named Vic Scott was flown in from Los Angeles, and Foreman promptly blasted him out in less than a round. A week later, Foreman destroyed journeyman Leroy Caldwell in two.

On October 7, Big George administered a two-round shellacking to Ollie Wilson, finishing the job with a left hook to the ribs. He followed that victory with his first competitive matchup since the Peralta fight, an October 29 contest against Brazil's Luis Faustino Pires.

Pires was a big, strong puncher who, despite a spotty 19–7–1 record, was a legitimate foe for Foreman. The Brazilian had briefly claimed the South American heavyweight title in 1967 before losing it to Oscar Bonavena. In his two fights before meeting Foreman, Pires had stopped journeyman Willie Burton in seven rounds, and took eight rounds to dispatch a rugged Canadian named Bill Drover. Earlier in the year, Drover had held British prospect Joe Bugner to a draw.

Despite Foreman's superior skills and punching power, he could not drop the 6'4" Brazilian. Through four rounds, George pounded Pires all over the ring, with very little counterfire coming back. Pires suffered an arm injury in the second round, but Foreman still couldn't find the right punches to knock him down.

Referee Johnny Lo Bianco mercifully stopped fight before the bell for round five sounded. Dr. Edward Campbell of the New York State Athletic Commission said Pires had suffered a muscle hemorrhage in his left arm, as well as a possible hairline fracture. Still, many ringsiders booed Foreman's inability to floor his foe.

"What do they want of me?" Foreman asked. "I won, didn't I?"

Yes, he did. But in establishing his awesome reputation, Foreman had punched himself into a corner. When he fought, the fans expected him to produce nothing short of devastating, clear-cut knockouts. And they were also expecting Foreman to upgrade the quality of his opposition.

Despite the imposing 32–0 (29 knockouts) record he had compiled in only two and a half years as a pro, Foreman couldn't hope to challenge the popularity of Ali or Frazier without fighting better-known contenders like Quarry, Bonavena, Patterson, and Ellis.

Inevitable

By April, Ali was once again in high gear and was anxious to fight again. He was looking for a July date, and negotiations had already begun against a prospective opponent. This foe wasn't Frazier, Quarry, Foreman, or any of the other contenders. He wasn't even a professional boxer.

Instead, Ali was preparing to sign a $1 million contract to fight seven-foot one-inch basketball star Wilt "The Stilt" Chamberlain!

Jack O'Connell, executive director of the Houston Astrodome, believed there was a 50-50 chance that an Ali–Chamberlain bout would occur there on July 26. O'Connell stated that the 34-year-old basketball player had applied for a Texas boxing license.

Jack Kent Cooke, co-promoter of Ali–Frazier and owner of Chamberlain's current team, the Los Angeles Lakers, disapproved of even the possibility of such a bout. He felt Wilt would become part of a carnival show that could impair the basketball star forever.

Ali insisted that the proposed bout with Chamberlain was serious. When asked his prediction of the outcome, Ali quipped: "Timberrrr!"

Chamberlain's demand for a guaranteed $500,000 tax-free was rejected by the promoter because such a guarantee would have bumped Wilt's total purse up to $1.8 million. Still, Ali showed up for the April 22 contract signing. But Chamberlain wasn't there. He didn't want to reduce his financial demands. And he might have had second thoughts about his chances against Ali.

With the July 26 date still open at the Astrodome, further negotiations began to match Ali with a more credible opponent. By the end of May, the names most often mentioned were those of Jimmy Ellis and Jerry Quarry. On June 2, Ali and Ellis signed contracts, much to the chagrin of the Quarry family. Jack Quarry insisted Ali had told him he'd fight Jerry in July. The elder Quarry complained that Ali would rather tangle with his former sparring partner than with Jerry.

Quarry seemed to forget that Ellis, the "sparring partner," held a 15-round decision win over Jerry.

Still, the "sparring partner" label had stuck to Ellis despite Jimmy's solid accomplishments during his four years as a heavyweight. Dubious and disputed as Ellis's WBA title stint may have been, he had still defeated many of the best contenders of his time. Now he was an ex-champion. But he was still a top-rated contender.

Following the devastating loss to Frazier in 1970, Ellis remained inactive nearly nine months. Then he came back against a "safe" opponent, Peruvian trial horse Roberto Davila. During the bout, Ellis showed signs of ring rust and sustained a serious cut over his left eye. Bleeding profusely, the ex-champ unloaded a series of powerful right-hand blows to stop Davila late in the seventh round.

Ellis followed the Davila win with a tenth-round stoppage of used-up Tony Doyle.

Then he was matched with George Chuvalo in an attempt to find an opponent for either Ali or Frazier.

The bout was set for May 10, 1971, in Toronto. Both fighters were guaranteed $15,000. But the relatively paltry purses weren't the main point of interest. As Chuvalo's manager Irv Ungerman pointed out, the big prize for the winner was a shot at Frazier, and Ali would be the first step.

This was a golden opportunity for both fighters and each one trained as never before. This was Chuvalo's first big fight since his devastating loss to Foreman the year before. The 33-year-old Canadian put in 123 rounds of sparring for Ellis, and his chief sparring partner, Charlie Chase, said that he'd never seen Chuvalo in better shape.

Likewise, Ellis also announced he was in the best condition of his life. At a glance, Chuvalo's size advantage, 218½ pounds to Ellis's 191, appeared to give him overwhelming physical superiority. Joe Louis picked Chuvalo by a knockout for that very reason.

But Louis's track record as a predictor was questionable. He failed to take Ellis's superior speed and boxing skills into account, and he forgot that Oscar Bonavena had enjoyed a similar edge in size over Ellis four years before, and, of course, Bonavena was handily outpointed.

So was Chuvalo. Ellis utilized a quick left jab and a hard right hook to carry most of the action in the fight. He cut Chuvalo in the second round, and dominated the exchanges well enough to score a unanimous 10-round decision in front of Chuvalo's hometown fans.

The impressive victory breathed new life into Jimmy's career. He hoped it would bring him one step closer to a rematch with Frazier. But first, he had to get past an old, familiar obstacle that blocked his path, his "homie," Muhammad Ali.

Ali–Ellis was billed as "The Inevitable Fight." And inevitably caught in the middle was Angelo Dundee, who was Ali's trainer and also the manager-trainer of Ellis.

Dundee saw an Ali–Ellis clash as "inescapable" even before Ali fought Bonavena. He knew that if Ali beat Frazier, Ellis would want a shot at the title. And if Ali lost to Frazier, he would have to face Ellis to gain a rematch with Smokin' Joe.

When the Ali–Ellis fight became a reality, Angelo was forced to make a difficult decision. In his book *I Only Talk Winning*, Dundee wrote: "Simply it came down to this: with Muhammad I was the trainer, only part of the team; with Jimmy I was the team, and Jimmy paid me one-third of his purse, he was entitled to my services."

Ali performed for the press over Dundee's decision, but it was all in good fun. There were no hard feelings, and Ali would have Angelo in his corner for every fight thereafter, a show of the character and sportsmanship that was sometimes hidden beneath Ali's flamboyance.

Both Ali and Ellis hoped their fight would guarantee a rematch with Frazier. At that point, Frazier was the only man to have defeated both of the Louisville stylists. Ali had only the Frazier loss on his record; of Ellis's six losses, five had come during his ill-advised stint as a middleweight.

For Ellis, the Ali fight was much more than a stepping stone to Frazier. It was the only way he could escape the shadow Ali had cast over him since their boyhood.

Many observers, like Jack Quarry, regarded Ellis as second-rate despite his many accomplishments. Ellis's mission was to make the Jack Quarrys of the world eat their words.

Like Frazier before him, Ellis announced that beating Ali would be the climax of his pugilistic endeavors.

As for Ali, the former champ said that beating Jimmy Ellis had become a priority to him once his old friend had taken his vacated crown back in 1968. He claimed that Ellis had made some disparaging remarks about him and would pay dearly.

Ali promised he would be all business against Ellis. He felt that his fooling around in the Frazier fight cost him the decision.

As the number one contender, Ali was to earn 45 percent of the income against a guaranteed $450,000. Ellis, who was ranked number seven, would receive 30 percent of all income from the fight, including the live gate and closed circuit receipts.

Ali was in a very subdued state when he opened his training camp in Chicago on June 15. Sporting a lardy midriff after his post–Frazier period of inactivity, Ali realized he would have to work harder than ever to whip himself into form. He indicated that he would train seven days a week in Chicago before moving his camp to Houston on July 12.

Asked about his sparring sessions with Ellis, Ali remembered them as being spirited give-and-take affairs with little to choose between the two.

Ellis remembered things differently. He claimed that Ali had never hurt him, while he had decked the "Greatest" twice.

Important as "The Inevitable Fight" was to him, Ali had more than Jimmy Ellis to think about. The Supreme Court decision that would decide his fate on the draft case was due on June 28. Ali said it was all in Allah's hands.

On June 28 the Supreme Court, on an 8–0 vote, overturned Ali's conviction for draft evasion. The ruling stated that the Justice Department had erred in contending that Ali's refusal to be inducted was based on political opinion rather than the religious tenets Ali had expressed. The Court held that Ali's beliefs were strong and sincere, not unlike many previous conscientious objectors.

By then, Ali and Ellis were in the midst of their last two weeks of preparation in Houston. The two men taunted each other, no rarity in an Ali fight. Ali's flabby midriff provided Ellis with all kinds of verbal ammunition.

"He float like an elephant," Ellis joked. "After this fight, they gonna be a new saying about him, 'Buzz like a buzz saw, fall like a tree!' He got three speeds: slow, slower, and walk."

Although he would not be in Ali's corner this time, Dundee still sang Muhammad's praises. He recognized that Ali was the greatest thing to ever happen to boxing.

Ali's cornerman for this fight was Harry Wiley, one-time trainer of Sugar Ray Robinson. Ali said Wiley had made Sugar Ray "almost as great a champion as me."

Ali attempted to bring his weight down to about 212 pounds, while Ellis hoped to come in at 191, the same weight at which he had shellacked Chuvalo. Ali didn't even come close, coming into the ring at a career-high 220½. Ellis tipped the scale at a meager 189.

Despite the added poundage, Ali would put on a brilliant display of boxing in his best performance since his return to the ring. And he did it in front of an Astrodome crowd of 31,947, who paid $298,000 to witness the affair firsthand. An additional one million fans viewed the fight on closed circuit across the United States and Canada.

Ellis got off to his usual fast start, winning the first round by a shade and the third by a clear margin.

The advantage swung to Ali's favor in the fourth. Utilizing a spearing left jab and dazzling footwork, Muhammad seized the momentum from his smaller opponent. Then he caught Ellis flush with a lightning right hand. He managed to finish the round on instinct alone but admitted later that the right hand took most of the fight out of him.

Ellis faded noticeably after round six. Meanwhile, Ali continued to dance the way he had in his heyday.

Ellis was hurt again in the tenth, and once again barely managed to survive the round. In the twelfth and final frame, Ali came out looking to finish his man off. A vicious left uppercut followed by a jolting series of lefts and rights sent Ellis reeling against the ropes. Realizing that Jimmy was now defenseless, referee Jay Edson jumped in to save him from further punishment.

Muhammad was well ahead on points after eleven rounds. Judges Earl Keel and Earnie Taylor scored it 108–102 and 107–104 for Ali, while referee Edson favored Ali by a wide margin of 110–93.[43]

After the fight, Ellis insisted that Ali could come back to win the title. "All he needs is work," Jimmy said. "You can't lose 3½ years and have an easy time coming back."[44]

Work was exactly what Ali had in mind. "I can't let up now," he said. "I'll be running 4 to 6 miles again tomorrow. I'll be fighting again in 6 weeks."[45]

Although he wasn't 100 percent satisfied with his condition for the Ellis fight, Ali was pleased that he could dance and move for twelve rounds with a man of Jimmy's caliber.

"And you got to know, next to me Jimmy Ellis is the best heavyweight boxer in the world," Ali declared. "A much better boxer than Frazier. Ellis sings better than Frazier."[46]

Ali felt that the defeat wasn't the end of Ellis. "Anyone who fought like he fought will be around for a long time to come," he predicted. "He's not washed up."[47]

Maybe not, but the Ali fight marked the beginning of Ellis's downslide. He fought on for four more years, but never won another important bout. As for Ali, he had taken the first step on the long road back from the Frazier defeat. Before 1971 ended, he would take two more.

Mountain and a Blin

Ali's next fight, scheduled for November 17, brought him back to the Astrodome, this time to face the "Michigan Mastodon," Buster Mathis, over twelve rounds.

This was Buster's first fight in more than two and a half years, and he was given very little chance of upsetting "The Greatest." Still, Mathis's handlers, Peers Management of Grand Rapids, Michigan, must have had confidence in their fighter. Peers put up $200,000 of Ali's $500,000 purse to lure him into the ring with Mathis. Buster had to settle for a flat 15 percent of the gate.

It was an all-or-nothing gamble for a fighter whose career had not blossomed as expected. Following his loss to Frazier in 1968, Mathis had fallen into a period of seclusion and depression. With the help of a psychiatrist, he pulled himself out of the doldrums and began a comeback.

At first, he took on safe opponents like Mel Turnbow, Jim Beattie, Amos Lincoln, and Dick Wipperman. He said the Frazier loss had made him appreciate winning more. Still, he said of his failure to beat Frazier haunted him.

The loss and the layoff did little to detract from his potential in the eyes of knowledgeable boxing people. Cus D'Amato, Mathis's former trainer, said after the Frazier debacle that Buster still had all of the tools to one day ascend to the throne.

Charlie Goldman, former trainer of Rocky Marciano, was another Mathis supporter. He too believed that Mathis had the potential to win it all.

Mathis ended 1968 with a sixth-round knockout of James J. Woody. He started 1969 on the right note with an easy 12-round decision over George Chuvalo. Seven weeks later, however, Buster looked terrible in a decision loss to Jerry Quarry. He retired after the Quarry fight, turning his athletic efforts to semi-pro football.

Now cash flow problems were prompting Buster to return to the ring. Always one to balloon when he wasn't training, Mathis soared to 320 pounds during his two-year hiatus. However, by weigh-in time for the Ali fight, Mathis had managed to melt down to a more reasonable 256. Still, Buster was big enough to inspire billboards that proclaimed: "Be There When The Mountain Meets Muhammad."

For all the publicity surrounding Mathis' poundage, Ali was hardly a lightweight this time out, tipping the scales at a new career high of 227. He obviously wasn't very concerned about Mathis, since he invested only nine days in serious training for the fight. And "serious" might not have been the most appropriate adjective, as Muhammad resumed his pre-fight antics of old.

Both fighters were training at the Astrohall, which was located across from the Astrodome. After finishing a workout one day, Ali and a crowd of some two hundred waited to watch Mathis train. Never one to miss an opportunity to entertain a crowd, Ali decided to give his foe some unexpected exposure. As Buster lay stark naked on a rubdown table behind a small partition, Ali suddenly slammed a door, causing Mathis to leap up in surprise. Then Ali used a chair to topple the partition, thus displaying a shocked, blubbery Buster to an equally stunned audience.

On the day of the fight, Ali was such a prohibitive favorite that no betting line was established. Mathis didn't appear concerned by this lack of support from the bookmakers. He figured that he had a 50–50 shot. Mathis went on to say that he wasn't afraid of the possibility of losing so much as having people say, "I told you so."

What transpired in the ring turned out to be a less than awesome performance by Ali. Mathis was as agile as ever for a man of such enormous proportions, and he utilized fair movement against Ali in the early rounds. But he was ineffectual offensively, never coming close to hurting the ex-champ.

Action was minimal, and the crowd grew restless. Broadcaster Howard Cosell made the most accurate assessment of the evening: "They have been alternating those gal ushers in hot pants with the round cards, and that has been the most exciting thing that has happened here tonight."[48]

Ali played around during the first ten rounds, showing none of the brilliance he had displayed against Ellis. He finally caught fire in the eleventh and floored Buster with a short right hand. Up at six, Mathis crash-landed again near the end of the round. The bell saved him from further punishment.

Trainer Joe Fariello wasn't thrilled about allowing Mathis to go out for the twelfth. He agreed after a brief discussion with the referee. "I asked the referee to stop the fight if he saw Buster could not defend himself," Fariello said later.[49]

As the bell for round twelve rang, Mathis moved forward on shaky legs. Ali appeared to let up on him, but he still managed to floor him two more times with light punches. After the second knockdown, Dundee screamed, "Take him out, dammit!" But Ali permitted Mathis to finish the fight on his feet.

Although Ali won a lopsided unanimous decision, he was widely criticized for his failure to knock Mathis out when it was obvious he could have done so at any time during the final two rounds.

"I wouldn't kill a black man, or a white man, just to give some enjoyment to a crowd that comes out to pay a little money and see two men fighting," Ali said in his own defense.[50]

Then he turned the tables and did a little criticizing of his own. He argued that a fighter shouldn't bear the responsibility for deciding whether or not to seriously injure an already battered opponent. He said it was the job of the officials to intervene before matters reached that point. In reference to the Mathis fight, Ali believed it should have been stopped in the twelfth round.

Despite his third career loss, Mathis consoled himself with the conviction that he had put up a good effort despite his 2½ year layoff. "Nobody can call me a dog anymore," Mathis said. "I gave it all I had. I know I can fight, and someday I'm gonna be the champ."[51]

Mathis never came close to a title shot over the rest of his career. But he continued to give every fight "all he had."

On the undercard, by the way, George Chuvalo pounded out a decision win over a creaky, 38-year-old Cleveland Williams. Most observers agreed that Chuvalo–Williams was far more entertaining than the main event.

Both fights were telecast on ABC Sports three days later. After the show ended, Mathis and his management team threatened to sue ABC and in particular Howard Cosell for what they deemed unflattering and insulting characterizations of Buster. During the broadcast, special effects such as ballet music and cartoonish subtitles were dubbed in, especially when Mathis was on the receiving end of Ali's blows.

Jimmy Iselin, president of Peers Management, felt that ABC TV and Howard Cosell had made a mockery of Mathis and thus hurt his earning potential in the future. In the end, neither ABC nor Cosell issued any apology. But Cosell's performance in calling the bout wasn't much better than Ali's in fighting it.

Ali said he had used a new weapon, the "linger-on" punch, to defeat Mathis. He called it a "light stunner" that looked harmless but eventually left opponents delirious. He promised to use it on his next scheduled opponent, Jurgen Blin of West Germany. The fight was appropriately scheduled for December 26, "Boxing Day," at the Hallenstadion in Zurich, Switzerland.

Blin was a determined competitor who had established himself as one of the better European heavyweights. At 5'11" and 195 pounds, he wasn't particularly big. Nonetheless, he was the most durable heavyweight in Europe other than Joe Bugner. In compiling a respectable 29–8–6 record, Blin had never been stopped.

Coming into the Ali fight, Blin had just lost a 15-round decision to Bugner for the European heavyweight title. In defeat, Blin had given the highly touted Bugner fits and made him look less than stellar.

Still, Blin was given virtually no chance to defeat Ali. The German was entitled to a bit more confidence considering Ali's bland performance against Mathis. But he didn't appear to be entertaining any idea of springing the upset of the year. Instead, his ambition seemed to extend only to going the full twelve-round distance and putting up a credible effort while doing so.

A $45,000 guarantee was another good incentive for Blin to take his chances against the ex-champion. The promoter of the event, Hansurdi Jaggi, was not expected to do as well as Blin on the financial end. Jaggi, an eccentric 31-year-old Swiss with pink hair and an earring, realized he was likely to lose a bundle on the fight. But the possibility didn't seem to concern him.

Obviously, Jaggi was an extremely unlikely promoter for a pugilistic event, especially considering that he liked nothing about the sport. Nothing, that is, other than Ali. He stated that Ali was the biggest thing to happen to boxing in "500 years."

Despite Blin's limited credentials, Ali appeared to be taking the German more seriously than he had Mathis. He trained hard, and the spare tire around his waist diminished. Dundee said Ali's midsection was "beginning to mold. He has just got to keep working."

On fight night, only 7,000 fans paid their way into the 13,000-seat stadium. They saw a fight that was much better than the Mathis affair.

Ali came into the ring at 220 pounds, a weight his frame could carry comfortably. Surprisingly, Blin provided a spirited effort from the first bell. He tried with some success to push Ali's jabs aside or counter over them with hooks.

Later, Ali admitted that the German's tactics had hurt him twice, but he lacked the skill to follow it up.

After two fairly even rounds, Ali had figured Blin out. He then began to punish his smaller foe with a piston-like left jab Blin was no longer able to avoid. Ali stuck and moved in the fourth, leaving Blin with a face full of cuts, specifically, on both cheeks, his nose, and over his left eye.

In the sixth round, Ali rested and allowed Blin to expend the remainder of his energy in a futile attack. One round later, Muhammad lowered the boom, nailing the German with right hooks and crosses off the jab. As Blin sagged, Ali smashed home another right cross. That blow sent the battered, bloody Blin reeling into the ropes. Then he sank to the canvas, where the referee counted him out at 2:12 of the round.

For Blin, the Ali fight marked his single fleeting moment of international prominence. Although he failed in his quest to go the distance, he still fought bravely against a vastly superior ex-champion.

After Ali, the rest of Blin's career spanned a total of five fights over two years. He stopped Canadian journeyman Charlie Chase, then outgutted the Basque strongman Jose Urtain over 15 rounds to win the European heavyweight title. His reign lasted only four months before he was stopped in eight in a rematch with Joe Bugner.

Blin then scored an insignificant knockout over one Danny Machado early in 1973. Then he traveled to Denver, Colorado, to meet a formidable contender named Ron Lyle. The Lyle fight was Blin's 47th as a pro, and marked the first time he had left the friendly confines of Europe for a fight.

He probably wished he'd stayed home as the heavy-hitting Lyle clubbed him into defeat in only two rounds. At that point, Blin wisely decided to hang up his gloves.

As for Ali, he had now recorded three victories since March 8. Any residue of ring rust he might have carried into the Frazier fight was now chiseled away by 31 rounds of activity.

Although he was still an ex-champ, his frequent ring appearances had kept him in the public eye more than the inactive Frazier. Nevertheless, the significance of Frazier's win over Ali earned him the 1971 "Fighter of the Year" award from the Boxing Writers' Association.

As the year ended, the public was clamoring for an Ali–Frazier rematch. None of the other top heavyweights could excite the imagination the way these two natural rivals could.

However, other fighters besides Ali and Frazier could carry high hopes into 1972. George Foreman was ready to make a serious assault on the championship. Jerry Quarry had revamped his career with four wins. Floyd Patterson was still a credible contender. So were Oscar Bonavena, Jimmy Ellis, and Mac Foster.

Also, some new contenders were primed to shoulder aside the holdovers from the sixties. Foreman was the best of the new crop, but attention was also being paid to slick-boxing Larry Middleton, hard-hitting Ron Lyle, and promising British prospect Joe Bugner.

In 1972, some exciting matchups were promised. But for the most part, that promise was unfulfilled.

Five

1972

1972 Superfight II, Where Are You?

In the same manner as the previous year, 1972 began with the boxing world eagerly awaiting an Ali–Frazier fight. This time, though, it was a rematch between the two that fueled all the speculation and anticipation.

The moneyman behind the first fight, Jack Kent Cooke, had the market cornered on Ali–Frazier II. He was confident the two fighters would meet again in 1972. By June, however, the fight was still only a rumor. But Cooke continued to talk it up. He was confident that his Los Angeles Forum would host the extravaganza sometime in the fall of 1972.

Despite Cooke's repeated assurances that the rematch would be held in his building, neither Frazier nor Ali wanted to fight in Los Angeles. Ali favored the Houston Astrodome, while Frazier and Durham simply didn't want L.A.

According to the rumor mill, the reason for Frazier's aversion to Los Angeles was that he didn't think he could pass the California eye examination. Frazier was quick to deny that supposition. He said that Durham had some sort of issue with California state rules.

Actually, the rules represented only one of Durham's problems with California. A second beef involved Cooke and the Forum. Durham said that Cooke had offered Frazier a $3,000,000 purse for a rematch with Ali. But Durham wanted a guaranteed percentage instead of a purse. Yank figured that since figures of $20 million to $30 million were being tossed around, his fighter should get a bigger slice of the pie. Cooke felt that this was a matter of opinion.

As far as Durham and Frazier were concerned, the only opinions that mattered were their own. And if Cooke didn't agree with them, he wouldn't get the fight.

Durham was quite honest after the Ali fight when he said he was in no hurry to see Joe in the ring anytime soon. Still hoping that Frazier would retire as undefeated champion at the age of 27, Durham stated two days after the fight, "Even if he [Frazier] does decide to fight again, I don't think he'd fight before next year."[1]

Despite the haggling with Cooke, Frazier still opened 1972 in preparation for a title defense. The fight was scheduled for January 15 at New Orleans, and was timed to coincide with the National Football League's Super Bowl VI. However, this defense would feature an opponent light years away from Ali's class. In fact, there may never have been a less deserving challenger for heavyweight laurels than Terry Daniels.

Daniels wasn't even a likely candidate for a career in pugilism, let alone a title shot. Far from the "up from the streets" background most fighters came from, Terry was the son of a well-to-do Cleveland businessman. He attended Southern Methodist University, where he mixed his studies with football. His career as a defensive halfback came to an end when he injured a knee.

Daniels then turned to boxing. After a brief amateur career, he turned professional and racked up a string of knockout victories over second-rate opponents. Oddly enough, the 12-month period leading up to his title opportunity was the worst year of his career.

After opening 1971 with a knockout over Willis Earls, Daniels dropped a decision to used-up veteran Tony Doyle. Two insignificant victories followed. Then Daniels found himself facing comebacking former champion Floyd Patterson on May 26.

For Daniels, who had adopted Texas as his new home base, the Patterson fight was something of a homecoming to his Cleveland birthplace. A crowd of 6,000 turned out to witness what was intended to be the launching of Daniels as a serious contender. Instead, Terry became Patterson's 50th professional victim.

Two right uppercuts and a left hook decked Daniels in the third round, and he remained in desperate shape over the next few stanzas. He nailed Floyd with a hard right in the ninth, but Patterson responded with a left-right counter and Daniels was on the canvas again. He rose and fought back gamely, but he lost via a lopsided decision.

Bouncing back, Daniels scored two wins, one of them over a washed-up Manuel Ramos. Then he squared off against Jack "The Giant" O'Halloran. O'Halloran was a fighter whose appearance alone was enough to induce an involuntary bowel movement. At 6'6" in height and a muscular 260 pounds in weight, his intimidating demeanor was capped by one of the hardest-looking faces in professional sport.

However, Jack's record was far less impressive than his physiognomy. Despite beginning his career at 15–0–1, he had lost 12 of his last 17 fights, four by knockout. When he met Daniels on August 25, 1971, "The Giant" was riding a four-bout losing streak.

Daniels helped him to break that streak by falling in four rounds. Doug Lord, Daniels's manager, claimed that Terry's injured ribs were more responsible for the defeat than O'Halloran's punches. Regardless, Daniels hardly seemed suited for the Number 10 ranking the WBA had given him.

Other rating bodies disagreed with the WBA's assessment of Daniels's talents. *Ring* magazine left him out of its Top Ten, and *Boxing Illustrated* pegged him at a lowly 48 out of the 50 fighters it rated in the division. And the WBA didn't choose to elevate Daniels to the tenth spot until after he had signed to fight Frazier.

Nevertheless, the Frazier–Daniels mismatch at least marked an end to a ten-month championship hiatus. And even in the face of Daniels's questionable qualifications, Frazier was never one to take an opponent lightly. The champ had put in five solid weeks of training and even went as far as to predict that he'd be sharper for Daniels than he had been for Ali. His sparring partner, Ray Anderson, agreed that Frazier was sharper, and hitting harder than he was before the Ali fight.

Two weeks before the fight, Frazier had already sparred 130 rounds in preparation, as much as for any fight he'd ever had. The champ predicted he would enter the ring at about 207 pounds. But at the official weigh-in, he tipped the scales at a career-high 215½. At 191½, Daniels looked frail in comparison.

Joe doubted the accuracy of the Louisiana State Athletic Commission scales and stated that he had weighed 213 on his hotel's bathroom scale earlier that morning. Durham wasn't concerned about Frazier's extra poundage. He believed the weight gain was nothing more than a natural progression as Frazier matured. Smokin' Joe had turned 28 three days before the fight.

Also, this was Frazier's first fight since his period of hospitalization following the Ali war. Despite Daniels's feeble credentials as a challenger, some observers still questioned Frazier's physical condition.

Frazier had said the high blood pressure he suffered after the Ali fight was caused by excessive pounding from a 20-pound medicine ball during training, not Ali's punches. He vowed that for Daniels and all subsequent fights, he would switch to a 10-pound ball and use it less frequently.

Durham doubted the medicine ball could be blamed for the problem. He said Frazier had drunk champagne after the fight, taken a laxative, and then went outside in the rain. He blamed that combination of circumstances for throwing Joe's kidneys and blood pressure out of kilter.

Whatever the cause of his previous ailments, Frazier was pronounced fit for the Daniels fight, which was bad news for Daniels.

Despite the gargantuan task ahead of him, Daniels approached his opportunity with a positive attitude. He said that he wasn't in awe of Frazier and felt strong and confident.

In preparing for the fight, Daniels acquired the sparring services of Sonny Moore, a veteran fringe contender who possessed a straightforward style similar to Frazier's, although he employed it with considerably less success. In professional action, Daniels had fought Moore four times, winning three and drawing one. He felt the tactics he had used against Moore would also work against Frazier.

Despite his shaky credentials, Daniels possessed a certain savoir-faire that made him attractive to the public. As well, he was white, and the social and economic implications of a "White Hope" challenger were still relevant, regardless of how remote his chances may have been.

Daniels also had a reputation as a puncher with a crowd pleasing style. However, the quality that really set him apart was his education. He was the first college graduate to fight for the heavyweight title. Ron Fimrite of *Sports Illustrated* said of Daniels: "He may be the most articulate pug since Gene Tunney."[2]

Unfortunately for Daniels, he would be meeting Frazier in the ring, not a spelling bee. At first, the fight had no betting line at all. Later some bookmaking interest developed, with the odds settling at a hefty 15–1 in favor of Frazier.

In his own mind, Daniels had fought the Frazier match many times. Sometimes he'd win a decision, other times by knockout, but he always won.

Frazier found it freaky that the challenger showed no signs of being "uptight." Someone asked him if Daniels should be uptight. "If I was fighting somebody like me, I'd be uptight," Frazier quipped.

If Daniels wasn't uptight before the bout, Frazier gave him reason to be as soon as the bell for the first round rang. Daniels caught a left-right-left combination that dropped him face-first to the canvas. As Referee Herman Dutrieux counted, Daniels's manager Doug Lord leaped into the ring, thinking his man had been counted out. However, Dutrieux had only reached nine when the bell ended the round.

Showing gameness if nothing else, Daniels stayed on his feet as Frazier continued to shell him in the second. In the third, Terry was floored by a pair of brutal Frazier left hooks. He got up at nine, then crashed again for a seven count before the round ended.

In round four, Frazier landed yet another left hook, and Daniels went down yet another time. Incredibly, he dragged himself to his feet at the count of seven. As the sparse crowd of 7,500 called for a stoppage, the slaughter continued until Dutrieux finally called a halt at 1:45 of the round. Although Daniels finished the fight on his feet, he was lying helplessly on the ropes when the referee rescued him.

Upon returning to his dressing room, Daniels was told he should be proud of his courageous effort, and for refusing to stay down after hitting the canvas so many times. "I've got nothing to be proud of," Daniels wept. "It was just about the most one-sided fight in the history of boxing."[3]

To add insult to injury, Frazier felt that he had fought at only about 90 percent of his ability against Daniels. Nevertheless, Terry was impressed by that 90 percent.

Although dejected, Daniels retained his razor-sharp wit. "They needed a math major for a referee, he had to count so much."[4]

Later, the gracious loser came into Frazier's dressing room with two cups full of beer. He gave one to the champ, and they toasted each other.

Daniels stated that he had landed punches that were hard enough to have "kept a normal guy off me."

"What am I?" Frazier asked. "A gorilla?"

"I would have rather fought a gorilla," Daniels responded.[5]

Thus ended Daniels's one and only shot at the big time. He earned only $30,000 for his improbable title shot. Unfortunately, his massacre at Frazier's hands marked the beginning of a steep downward plummet.

He had challenged for the title with a deceptively promising record of 29–4–1. After the Frazier fight, he lost five in a row. He then pared himself down to light heavy, and met with modest success at that weight. With a second attempt to fight as a heavyweight, Daniels resumed his losing ways.

All told, Daniels fought 29 times after Frazier. Of those, he lost 23, including eight by knockout. In heavyweight history, he amounts to little more than a footnote.

Frazier–Daniels was the first world heavyweight title bout to be broadcast on home television since the Ali–Folley fight on March 22, 1967. Consequently, there were more spectators viewing Frazier live against Daniels than there had been when he fought Ali the year before.

After the fight, Durham declined to say who Frazier's next opponent would be. Obviously, everyone was hoping it would be Ali.

"I'll give Ali a fight," Durham jibed. "I'll give him a fight if he keeps winning, stops talking so much and comes down to earth."[6]

Frazier's next challenge came on May 25, and the opponent, Ron Stander, had only a touch more plausibility than Daniels.

Stander's name was barely a household word in his own household. Ron wasn't a terrible fighter; in fact, he was several notches above Daniels. However, to stand a chance against Frazier, a challenger needed to be a fistful of notches higher than either of those two latter-day "White Hopes."

Because Stander was a bigger man than Daniels, it was easier to sell him as a legitimate heavyweight. Indeed, the 218 pounds Stander carried on his 5'11" frame when he faced Frazier at Omaha, Nebraska, was a relatively svelte load. He had been known to come into the ring at 230 or more.

Ron's physique could be most charitably described as "stocky." Some of his supporters touted him as the second coming of "Two Ton" Tony Galento, the rotund, crowd-pleasing warrior of the 1930s who once floored the great Joe Louis. Their caution-to-the-winds styles were very similar. And, like Galento, Stander had a heart every bit as large as his midriff.

As a contender, Stander was not totally devoid of skills or credentials. As an amateur, he won the Midwest heavyweight title in 1968, and lost in the quarterfinals of the nationals.

In high school, Stander had excelled in wrestling and football, averaging two touchdowns a game in the latter sport. His gridiron career continued after high school, and he made the Metro Conference All-Star team. He stood a good chance of making it in the NFL, but with a wife and two small children to provide for, he decided to take advantage of the quicker money available in boxing.

He turned pro on July 31, 1969, stopping Bob Street in the first round. A native of Council Bluffs, Iowa, Stander adopted "Bluffs Butcher" as a nom de guerre.

In 1970, he scored what would eventually be considered his greatest victory. His opponent was 1969 AAU heavyweight champion Earnie Shavers, who, like Stander, had recently turned pro. Both men were undefeated, with a short string of knockout wins. The dynamite-punching Shavers was the favorite and looked the part from the opening bell. For two rounds, Stander stood up under a heavy bombardment of punches that bloodied his nose, mouth, and right eye. Welts and bruises appeared on his body, and his doom seemed only a matter of time.

Miraculously, Stander battled back in the third, dominated the fourth, and stopped Shavers at the 52-second mark of round five. The win established Ron as a prospect to watch.

He followed the Shavers triumph with a disappointing draw with Manuel Ramos, who had become a "must" opponent for up-and-coming heavyweights of the early 1970s. After an inconsequential knockout over Murphy Goodwin, Stander surprisingly announced his retirement in November 1970.

Although he cited weight, contractual, and hand problems as his reasons for hanging up his gloves, his wife Darlene was probably the major factor in his decision. She never bothered to conceal her distaste for her husband's chosen profession. Mrs. Stander wasn't exactly a "Stand By Your Man" kind of lady. Apparently Ron wasn't the boss of the Stander household.

Still, less than five months later, Stander came out of retirement, and 1971 was a good year for him. In April he beat a badly faded Thad Spencer. July saw him defeat Jack O'Halloran.

In August, he gained a measure of revenge over Manuel Ramos by battling his way to a clear-cut decision. The Ramos return drew a record Nebraska crowd of 8,821.

Spencer, O'Halloran and Ramos were credible stepping-stone opponents, but wins over them hardly qualified Stander for a title shot. To make matters worse, Stander lost his initial bout in 1972, blowing a 10-round decision to a part-time club fighter named Reco Brooks. Brooks had amassed a 3–1 record over a nine-year career.

Stander got back into the win column with decisions over a pair of trial horses named Mike Boswell and Johnny Mac. Now his record stood at 23–1–1. That was good enough to place him at number 15 in *The Ring*'s heavyweight ratings.

Still, anybody who could lose to Reco Brooks didn't belong in the ring with Joe Frazier. Odds makers agreed, listing the "Bluffs Butcher" as a 10–1 underdog.

Stander believed that if the fight were staged in an alley that he'd be the favorite. But that was wishful thinking. Against Frazier, Stander would have been an underdog even if he went into the ring armed with a baseball bat. No one, even his ever-supportive wife, gave Ron a snowball's chance in hell.

"I'm a realist," Darlene Stander told a reporter. "You don't enter a Volkswagen at Indy unless you know a helluva shortcut."[7]

Frazier came in heavy but fit at 217½. As could be expected when fighting such an inferior opponent, Frazier was being asked more questions about an Ali fight than he was about the battle at hand. Joe insisted he didn't want to talk about Ali, or "Clay," as he continued to call him. But somehow he always ended up doing just that. He claimed that after he took care of Stander that he'd be ready for "Clay."

On fight night, a pro–Stander crowd of 9,843 filled the Omaha Civic Auditorium and roared every time their hero so much as touched the champion. It was a fight in which Stander played Frazier's role as the bull-like aggressor. Joe respected Stander's considerable strength and ended up in the unfamiliar role of matador, a role he played to perfection.

On this night, it would be the "Butcher" who would be carved up by Frazier, who, after all, once worked in a slaughterhouse. "Smokin' Joe" ripped short hooks, uppercuts, and even jabs into Stander's face almost at will. To his credit, Ron never wavered and rarely took a backward step.

But his offense was limited to an occasional slapping blow or push punch, with a lot of wrestling inside. A volley of Frazier blows sent him staggering near the end of round two.

Nonetheless, Stander was once again the aggressor in the third. Frazier scored early in the round with a left hook that tore a gash across the bridge of Stander's nose. From that point on, nearly every blow Frazier landed appeared to inflict another cut or contusion.

The champ didn't miss many punches in the third or the fourth. Near the end of the fourth, Frazier had his foe reeling, though to his credit Stander never went down. When the bell sounded, ring doctor Jack Lewis brought the mismatch to an end. The Volkswagen hadn't found the shortcut.

The Stander camp raised no objection to the stoppage. Still, Ron was understandably heartbroken. He apologized for letting so many people down.

Frazier was considerate to his vanquished foe, saying that Stander was "a very tough opponent.... He was stronger than George [Chuvalo] or Oscar [Bonavena]."[8]

For his brave but futile effort, the 27-year-old Stander went home with $42,631, seventeen stitches, and a broken nose.

Like Daniels before him, his career took a nosedive after the Frazier loss. Over the next nine years, his record was 13–16–2 as he became one of the division's better-known stepping stones.

One of Stander's wins was a first-round blitz of Daniels in 1975, thus answering the trivia question, "Who was Joe Frazier's worst challenger in 1972?"

For his four-round workout, Frazier was guaranteed a mere $150,000 and donated half of that to the Sickle Cell Anemia Foundation, of which Yank Durham was founder and president.

Asked about his future plans, Frazier said: "Me and my title are going for a long rest on my plantation.... I'm not going to just sit and watch it, but I'm tired of all the hassle right now."[9]

Frazier–Stander would be the last heavyweight championship bout for the year. With the champ making two inconsequential defenses and not fighting past May, 1972 soon became known as the year of Muhammad Ali's fabulous "road show."

Ali's Magical Mystery Tour

Although a 1972 rematch with Frazier was not to be, Ali wasn't about to sit around gathering dust. He worked out a busy schedule for the year, bragging that while Frazier was fighting bums, he was taking on all the contenders.

Not only was his regular activity keeping the sport alive, Ali argued, it would also keep him sharp when the Frazier rematch finally materialized.

Frazier disagreed vehemently. He said that Ali was taking all of those fights purely for financial reasons. The champ didn't think that all of those matches would help Ali one bit once they hooked up for their rematch.

Whatever his reasons for keeping such a busy schedule, Ali was right. Champion or not, 1972 belonged to him, not Frazier. Ali fought six times that year, and that level of activity led many fans to label Ali the "People's Champion." It was a designation Muhammad was happy to accept.

The Ali roadshow's first stop was in Tokyo for an April 1 encounter with Mac Foster, a much-anticipated event in the island nation.

Promoter Yoshio Kou took on a major challenge when he decided to bring big-time heavyweight boxing to his homeland. His first task was to convince the Japanese Boxing Association to rescind a law prohibiting two foreign fighters from opposing each other on Japanese soil. The law had been enacted to protect the interests of Japanese boxers.

Kou managed to sell the JBA on the idea that Ali was the world's greatest boxer (notwithstanding his loss to Frazier), and that staging an Ali fight would bolster the image of boxing in Japan. The JBA agreed with Kou's reasoning and gave him the green light. Ali–Foster would be the first heavyweight fight ever held in the Orient.[10]

Foster had come back well after his devastating 1970 loss to Jerry Quarry. No one had beaten him since then, and he had stopped four opponents in a row leading up to Ali. In 28 wins, he had scored 28 knockouts.

A native of Fresno, California, MacArthur "Mac" Foster had served 6½ years in the United States Marine Corps, including 14 major operations during two stints in Vietnam. He achieved the rank of sergeant during his military career. It was while he was in the Marines that Mac took up boxing. He compiled an amateur record of 26–1, with 17 knockouts, and captured the following titles: two all-Marine, one all-service, and one AAU. After his release from the Marines, Foster turned pro under the management of Pat Di Furia.

Mac received a major scare during his pro debut on November 28, 1966, when he was dropped twice by 275-pound Jimmy Gilmore. Foster came back to put Gilmore to sleep for a full minute with a single right hand in round three.

In 1968, Foster gained prominence as a sparring partner for Sonny Liston. Liston was desperate for live bodies to punch in preparation for his crossroads bout with Henry Clark. Foster gladly accepted the job and succeeded in decking Sonny with a right hand during one session.

Once word of Mac's feat made the rounds, it became almost impossible for manager Di Furia to find any quality opposition for his fighter. The combination of Foster's reputation as a puncher and his intimidating physical appearance prompted most managers to keep their charges far away from the ex-Marine.

Reputable foes who did dare to cross gloves with him suffered the same fate as the stiffs. Ex-contender Thad Spencer fell in four, and Roger Rischer went out in one. But Foster's perfect 24–0, all-knockout winning streak came to an end when Quarry destroyed him in six rounds.

That setback didn't end Foster's title aspirations. Now he was about to face Muhammad Ali, the man Foster had wanted to fight since the day he turned pro. As a Marine and a Vietnam veteran, Foster considered Ali's antiwar stance unpatriotic.

At the beginning of his career, he announced that he would make the kicking of "Clay's" behind his top professional priority.

Strangely, that animosity never emerged once the contracts for the Tokyo bout were signed. It is ironic that a Vietnam vet and a conscientious objector to that war would choose an Asian country as the location for their fight.

Foster's arrival in Tokyo was something of a homecoming, as he had once been stationed at Yokosuka, an hour away from the big city. He arrived before Ali, and he received a great deal of coverage in the Japanese media. Outside of the sumo wrestling fraternity, a heavyweight is an anomaly in the land of the rising sun, and Foster stayed in the limelight until Ali came to town. After that, Mac was relegated to the status of the "other guy."

Despite Foster's record and reputation as a puncher, Ali was supremely confident in his ability to win. His weight was a slightly lardy 226, which indicated how seriously he took Foster's chances.

Japanese fans received the full Ali package, with pre-fight bantering and predictions thrown in free of charge. He paraded around Tokyo carrying a placard with the number 5, his forecast of the number of rounds Foster would last.

And that prediction wasn't based on whim or chance. Ali had several well-thought-out reasons for choosing the fifth frame.

"It shall be over not in round four or six," Ali declared, "but round five. I like the number five. I get up at five in the morning and I run for five miles. I eat five poached eggs for breakfast. I drink five glasses of orange juice and five glasses of ice water during the day. I take a nap at 5 P.M. My daughter is five years old. I have been married five years and I met my wife on June 5."[11]

Trusting in Ali's logic, Japanese fans fully expected Ali to carry out his prediction. But this was the Ali of 1972, not 1962. He had turned 30 the month before.

Ali wore an elaborate Japanese robe into the ring. It was the only sign of flash throughout the entire encounter, which commenced around noon, Tokyo time.

Although he was a slugger, Foster followed a defensive game plan, possibly to preserve his stamina. The bout was scheduled for 15 rounds, and Foster had never gone past eight complete rounds in his career.

Ali didn't expend much energy in the early going either. Presumably, he was holding back for the fifth. When the bell sounded to open that round, Ali sprang from his corner and threw everything but the kitchen sink at Foster. But Mac withstood the storm, and was still on his feet at the end of the round. Ali's prediction had failed, and the crowd erupted in a chorus of boos.

The fight dragged on for the full fifteen rounds. Ali won by a wide margin, but he disappointed the Tokyo fans with his inability to stop Foster. Except for a brief moment in round 11, Foster was never in any real danger of going down. Ali claimed that anyone who could survive 15 rounds with him must be "great."

But the "great" Foster was nothing more than a puffy-faced, one-sided loser at the end of the fight. This was Ali's poorest performance since the Mathis waltz the year before. A more aggressive showing from Foster might have made for an interesting contest, given Muhammad's power shortage that night.

Ali tried to make the best of a bad situation by saying that Foster was tougher than Frazier. Frazier must have laughed when he heard that.

Foster waited a year before stepping into the ring again. He stopped a ham-and-egger named Sam McGill in nine rounds. That would be Mac's last victory. After losing by

Five. 1972

decision to Bob Stallings, Joe Bugner, and Henry Clark, Foster hung up his gloves for good. His final record was a respectable 29–5, with all the wins coming by knockout.

The next stop on Ali's 1972 Grand Tour was Vancouver, British Columbia, Canada. His opponent there was former foe George Chuvalo, against whom Ali had defended the heavyweight title back on March 29, 1966.

Earlier in 1972, Ali and Chuvalo had appeared on the same January 27 card in Vancouver. Chuvalo retained his Canadian heavyweight title via a fifth-round stoppage of Montreal's Charlie Chase, while Ali delighted the fans with two exhibition bouts.

"You're the man I want to fight again," Ali told Chuvalo afterward. "You've never been knocked down, and all the greats have been knocked down. Jack Johnson, Sugar Ray Robinson, Joe Frazier, myself, we've all been knocked down."

Ali added, "You've been on one knee, haven't you?"

"Only in church," Chuvalo shot back.

The fight was set for May 1, only a month after the Ali–Foster yawner. Ali–Chuvalo was put together by a Vancouver promoter named Murray Pezim. To liven up the promotion, Pezim announced that a marathon 96-hour party would precede the fight.

The 34-year-old Chuvalo had tasted leather from just about every top-notch fighter of the past 16 years. Other than Jerry Quarry and Doug Jones, he had failed to defeat anyone in the upper echelon of the division. In his last two major fights, he had been stopped by George Foreman and decisioned by Jimmy Ellis.

Still, with 66 career victories and his reputation for absorbing punishment, George had kept his name in the ratings for the better part of fourteen years, an enviable span for a sport that doesn't encourage such longevity.

By 1972, however, Chuvalo's career was in an irreversible decline. The Ellis defeat had dropped him out of the top ten.

Regardless of his ranking, Chuvalo's most famous credential remained intact. In 85 professional fights, he had never been knocked off his feet. Ali said he would "consider it a defeat if Chuvalo isn't flat on his back." Chuvalo figured that if Ali couldn't stop him in 1966 that he'd never do it in 1972.

The buildup to this fight, like so many others in which Ali was involved, became a war of words. And this time Ali was not battling an unarmed man. Chuvalo could match repartee with the best of them. And Ali was definitely the best of them.

One aspect of Ali that hadn't changed was his sense of humor. Before the fight, Muhammad strode through the streets of Vancouver, wielding an axe and predicting that he would chop Chuvalo down once and for all.

But George wasn't intimidated by Ali's psychological ploys. "I'm not made of wood," he pointed out. "And he can't bring an axe into the ring."[12]

Another Ali prank a few days before the fight almost caused its postponement. Muhammad was doing his usual taunting and threatening routine outside Chuvalo's dressing room at the gym in which the Canadian champ was training. The dressing room door was split horizontally so that the top half could be opened independently of the bottom part.

Fed up with Ali's antics, Chuvalo pushed the door open and lunged forward, fist upraised. As Ali took off, George, forgetting about the bottom half of the door, crashed into it and bruised his ribs. The injury wasn't serious enough to force a postponement, but it was probably the hardest blow Chuvalo ever took to the body.

Another controversy that could have threatened the bout was a dispute over the size of the gloves to be used. Irving Ungerman, Chuvalo's manager, complained about a Vancouver Athletic Commission ruling calling for large 10-ounce gloves. The smaller gloves are to the benefit of the harder puncher, in this case Chuvalo.

Ali said the size of the gloves made no difference to him, but he asked that Chuvalo make a concession in return. He wanted the size of the ring expanded from a phone booth 16 × 16 feet to a roomier 18 × 18. Chuvalo agreed.

Muhammad refrained from making any prediction until the last few days before the fight. At that point he advised people to get to the theaters early. He said he had a strange premonition of an early kayo, much like before his rematch with Liston.

Ungerman's only prediction was that the fight would be dirty. For his part, Ali had always accused Chuvalo of bending the Marquess of Queensberry rules, and he even took the opportunity to both scold and warn the Canadian at the contract signing. Ali claimed that chuvalo hit him low "26 times" in their first fight. He warned that if Chuvalo attempted any dirty tactics in the rematch that he would reciprocate.

Chuvalo countered that Ali simply wore his trunks too high in their first fight. "It's just like those cartoons, where the rabbit pulls up his trunks until all you can see are his ears," Chuvalo quipped. "He's just trying to take away some of my best punches, to the solar plexus."

Chuvalo also said he was better prepared for Ali now than he had been in 1966. For their first fight, George had been a replacement for Ernie Terrell. Consequently, George had only 17 days to train for that fight. This time, however, George was in peak form.

Ali was also in excellent shape. He trained hard this time for three reasons: (1) He knew from experience that Chuvalo would be a tough opponent; (2) He wanted to look more impressive than he had against Foster the month before; (3) He desperately wanted to become the first fighter ever to floor the iron-jawed Canadian.

Consequently, by weigh-in time Ali's weight had dropped to 217½, 8½ pounds lighter than he'd scaled against Foster. At this weigh-in, Muhammad was uncharacteristically serious.

When asked why he wasn't up to his usual tricks, he replied: "There's $5 million at stake for me with the Frazier date. You watch those Wells Fargo guards when they unload a payroll. They look serious, too."[13]

From the opening bell, Ali erased the month-old memory of the sluggish, slow-moving heavyweight who had bored the fans in Tokyo. He danced the entire 12 rounds, peppering Chuvalo with jabs and combinations.

In round three, Chuvalo actually dropped his hands and invited Ali to try and knock him down. An odd invitation, considering that by then Chuvalo must have been painfully aware that Ali could hit him any time he wanted.

In the fourth, Chuvalo managed to get through with a crude combination topped by a left hook that drove Ali back against the ropes. Ali admitted later that the hook had hurt him. He shook it off, however, and quickly regained control of the fight.

At the end of the 12 rounds, the decision was pretty much a formality. One judge gave Ali every round.

Chuvalo emerged with a marked-up face, but Ali had never come close to decking him. A healthy $65,000 purse was further consolation.

In fact, promoter Pezim took it harder on the chin than Chuvalo. For him, the fight was a financial TKO. Of the 17,465 seats at the Pacific Coliseum, only half were filled. And his big 96-hour pre-fight blowout lasted only 23. Pezim's losses amounted to something in the neighborhood of $100,000.

The antagonists in the bout had nothing but praise for each other after it was over.

"I'd like to compliment Muhammad on a good, tough fight, which I enjoyed," Chuvalo said. "He surprised me because he seemed in the same good shape he showed against me in 1966."[14]

Ali likewise praised Chuvalo for his resiliency and clean tactics. "He threw only one low blow," Ali confided. "And that was on the side."[15]

The Ali fight was Chuvalo's last major ring appearance. He disappeared from the ratings, although his hold on the Canadian championship remained secure. Over the next few years, he displayed his fading skills against second-rate opposition. But even though his career was almost over, his fans still expected to see him in action against top contenders.

"What do they want me to do?" Chuvalo wondered. "I've already fought every top fighter you can name. Am I supposed to go back and fight all those guys all over again just to please the critics?"[16]

Yet Chuvalo had no immediate plans for retirement.

"When I think I can't function as well as I want to, and when I don't enjoy it anymore, I'll quit."[17]

He retired temporarily in 1975, then came back a year later to resume his position at the top of a sorry heap of Canadian heavyweights. His wars against competent countrymen like the long-retired Robert Cleroux were a thing of the past. Instead, he disposed of every creampuff opponent the promoters put in front of him.

Unfortunately, the Chuvalo of 1976–78 looked as though he'd feasted on too many creampuffs outside the ring as well. In his heyday, George was a solid block of muscle, a fighter who always stayed in shape. However, the comebacking Chuvalo jiggled like a white Buster Mathis as he knocked over the likes of Bob "Pretty Boy" Felstein and Earl McLeay in defense of the title he couldn't bear to part with.

Finally, Canadian boxing authorities stripped Chuvalo of the championship due to inactivity and, possibly, embarrassment. He never fought again.

The world title always seemed just beyond George Chuvalo's grasp. However, his record for durability has ensured his place in boxing history as the "King of the Iron Men." Today, he shows few effects from the many punches he took over his career, and he remains a national hero in Canada. Chuvalo has lost three of his four sons, one to suicide and two to drug overdoses, since his retirement from the ring. Amidst these tragedies, George also lost his wife to suicide. Since this unimaginable pain that Chuvalo has sustained, his image in Canada has escalated from sports hero to national treasure. As tough as Chuvalo proved to be throughout his 93-bout career, he has proven to be immeasurably more resilient to the pain life has thrown at him over the years. Instead of folding under the avalanche of tragedy, Chuvalo has instead dedicated himself to visiting Canadian schools, speaking of the evils and dangers of drugs. Because of his bravery both in and especially out of the ring, Chuvalo was rightfully honored with the Order of Canada in 1998.

Ali's next stop was Las Vegas, where he would settle accounts with another old foe, Jerry Quarry.

In the two years since their first meeting, Jack and Jerry Quarry had been pressing for a rematch with Ali. Jerry told everybody who would listen that the cut that undid him in Atlanta was a fluke, and he desperately wanted to show what he could have done to Ali had the fight been allowed to continue. On June 27, Quarry received his chance to avenge the heartbreaking loss.

Jerry's current ranking stood at number two, right behind Ali. And he had earned that position the old-fashioned way: he fought for it.

In 1971, he scored decisions over Rufus Brassell and old nemesis Tony Doyle, who had broken Quarry's nose en route to holding him to a draw back in 1965. Then came a November 16 showdown in London with newly crowned British, Commonwealth, and European heavyweight champion Jack Bodell.

Bodell had acquired that interesting array of titles by scoring an upset decision win over highly touted countryman Joe Bugner. He was rated eighth in the world, and he was practically guaranteed a shot at Frazier's title, provided he could get past Quarry.

As for Jerry, he was in the umpteenth "must win" situation of his career, even though he was only 27 years old. He vowed to quit if he couldn't beat Bodell.

Bodell should have known right then what was in store for him, considering what had happened every other time Quarry's back was against the wall. Despite a death threat he received while he was in England, Jerry flattened Bodell in only 64 seconds of the first round.

Quarry closed a successful 1971 campaign with a 10-round decision over Lou Bailey, a rock-jawed trial horse who lost only to quality competition. He continued his winning ways at the start of 1972 with a one-round demolition of Argentine Adonis Eduardo Corletti. In his next fight, against master boxer Larry Middleton, Quarry narrowly escaped with a split decision win. The Middleton bout took place in London; apparently British fans had forgiven him for his destruction of Bodell.

Despite Quarry's close call against the light-punching Middleton, there were some who questioned Ali's wisdom in taking him on when a rematch with Frazier was on the horizon. Ali was fully aware of the hazards involved in tangling with a fighter of Quarry's caliber.

But Ali would be well compensated for his gamble. A hefty guarantee of $500,000 was more than ample incentive to fight his most formidable opponent since Frazier. Quarry would receive $200,000 to even his record against the former champion.

The odds makers installed Ali as a healthy 4–1 favorite over the California Irishman. "Healthy" was also an appropriate word for Ali's physical appearance when he shed his robe on fight night. He weighed in at 216½, his lowest poundage in his last five fights. At 198, Quarry was also in excellent shape. What the 6,549 paying customers witnessed that night was Ali's best performance since his 1970 return to the ring. He fought flawlessly, hitting Quarry from every possible angle and position. He even outpunched Quarry while lying on the ropes.

Ali's defense was just as effective, leaving the frustrated Quarry unable to connect with any meaningful punches. The closest Jerry came to doing any damage was in the first round, when he jacked Ali up and held him several inches off the canvas. From that point onward, Muhammad owned the fight.

At first, he toyed with Quarry, making him miss and popping him with quick jabs. Gradually, Ali grew more serious. As methodical as a surgeon and cool as an assassin, he dispensed increasing amounts of punishment as each round passed.

After round five, Ali came down from his toes to add more leverage to his punches. Quarry's head was repeatedly snapped and jolted, but he stubbornly stayed on his feet. Finally, early in the seventh, Ali beckoned referee Mike Kaplan to stop the fight as Quarry had become literally defenseless. Kaplan wisely complied.

Over the six completed rounds, Ali had pitched a shutout on the cards of all three officials. Consummate as Ali's performance had been, it was magnified by Quarry's strange passivity. Ali himself said he couldn't understand why Quarry was so easy to defeat that night.

The reason for Quarry's apathy lay in the result of one of the undercard bouts. In that bout, Quarry's kid brother Mike challenged Bob Foster for the light heavyweight title. In fact, the double-header was billed as "The Quarry Brothers vs. The Soul Brothers."[18]

The younger Quarry did well until he ran into one of Foster's patented left hooks in the fourth round. Mike lay unconscious for several anxiety-producing minutes before finally being brought around with medical assistance.

"When I watched Mike, that did it," Jerry said later. "I wasn't in the mood for the fight after seeing Mike get beat. I wasn't defending myself. I really didn't give a damn."[19]

Even at his best, however, Quarry would have had a hard time doing anything with Ali that night. But other members of the Quarry clan were much more inspired to fight.

Quarry's brother-in-law went to jail for an outside-the-ring fracas that featured a racial slur followed by fisticuffs. Jerry and Mike's wives were also involved, but not charged. One witness claimed that the Quarry wives fought better that night than their husbands.

Jerry might not have agreed with that assessment, but he was so dissatisfied with his performance that he announced his retirement. He also changed his post-fight tune regarding Ali. After their 1970 fight, Quarry predicted that Ali would never beat Frazier. The second time around, he said that Ali's hand speed would be too much for Frazier at that point.

He went on to declare that his spectacular showing against Quarry was proof that he was now better than he had been prior to his 1967 exile.

Only three weeks later, Ali and his entourage packed their bags for a trip to Dublin, Ireland. There, on July 19, he would renew acquaintances with a former sparring partner named Al "Blue" Lewis.

Lewis had spent six years in prison for manslaughter before receiving an early parole as a reward for breaking up a prison riot. Blue explained that he did it not for the warden but to save the lives of his fellow inmates.

Although the 29-year-old convict turned social worker's boxing career had followed a somewhat erratic path, he enjoyed a solid reputation as a puncher. Ali had firsthand experience with the 6'5", 223-pound Lewis's power. Lewis almost derailed the first Ali–Quarry fight when he cracked Muhammad's ribs during a sparring session.

Despite the damage Lewis had done to Ali in training, few fans gave him much of a chance to defeat his former employer in real competition. Still, Al had a history of pulling off upsets.

In 1968, Lewis stepped into the ring as a tune-up for Eduardo Corletti, who was then ranked #2 by the WBA. Although Corletti was a native of Argentina, he was fighting out of London, where his handsome Latin looks earned him a large following among the "Mod" crowd. Unimpressed, Lewis flattened the Argentine in the second round.

Ali, of course, had much more going for him than good looks. But Lewis was still hopeful. He carried a 26–3 record with 16 knockouts into the Ali fight, and he was coming off a controversial seventh-round disqualification loss to Oscar Bonavena in Argentina. That result was an ironic role reversal for Oscar, who usually ended up on the short end of that type of outcome.

Pre-fight arrangements seemed to be moving along smoothly until a few days before the event. And then the proverbial brown matter collided with the proverbial fan.

The contract had called for a 20-foot ring that would give Ali plenty of room to maneuver. Only days before the fight, American promoter Harold Conrad discovered that there wasn't a 20-foot ring available "in the whole republic of Ireland!"

Then he located a man who said he knew of a ring up in Belfast that was "19 feet and a thread." Conrad's next job was to find someone brave or foolish enough to drive to Belfast to deliver the ring to Dublin. He found someone, the ring arrived safe and sound, and the problem appeared solved.

But appearances were deceiving. Once Conrad got to Croke Park he found that the ring was less than 16 feet! The promoter had to remove the 18-foot ring in Ali's training facility and set it up for the main event.

When the fight began, it was clear that Ali wasn't as sharp as he'd been against Quarry only a few weeks ago. His letdown could be partially explained by the effects of the severe head cold he had contracted. Also, Lewis fought a much more inspired battle than Quarry had managed. He was also the second tallest fighter Ali had faced, and a combination of that and his awkwardly effective style seemed to bother the former champ.

In round five, however, Muhammad nailed Lewis and the big man crashed heavily to the canvas. At this point, the gremlins or leprechauns afflicting the fight struck again.

Compared to the trouble involved in finding a decent ring, it would seem that timekeepers' watches would be a matter of little consequence. Wrong assumption! As Lewis reposed on the canvas, two of the watches stopped working. Not only that, but Ali once again failed to go to a neutral corner. Between the recalcitrant watches and Ali's flouting of the rules, Lewis received an 18-second rest before beating referee Lew Eskin's belated count.

Lewis survived that round, plus six more as Ali methodically wore him down. Referee Eskin finally stopped the fight in the eleventh, awarding Ali a TKO victory.

Lewis's career continued until November of the following year, but the Ali bout was his one and only shot at the big time. Reportedly, Lewis stopped along the side of the road to help a priest who was having car trouble. When battery acid sprayed into one of his eyes, he was unable to fight again.[20]

As for Ali, his campaign to steal the limelight from Frazier continued at full swing. The next stop on his road show would take him back to Las Vegas. His opponent would be another foe from his championship reign of the '60s, Floyd Patterson.

Farewell to Floyd, and Foster's Second Folly

By 1972, Floyd Patterson had become the Captain Ahab of the heavyweight division, a 37-year-old ex-champion obsessively seeking to regain the title he had lost ten years before.

Actually, Patterson was in the second year of a comeback. After his controversial loss to Jimmy Ellis in 1968, Floyd retired from boxing. But he couldn't stay away from the sport he loved, and in 1970 he resumed his career. His goal was clear: a shot at the title held by Joe Frazier.

"Let me stress that all of this might be a dream," Patterson said. "But what I want you to understand is that I'm going to enjoy trying. Whether or not I'm successful, I'm going to enjoy trying."[21]

Despite his age and the two-year layoff, Patterson had always kept himself in shape, and he returned to the ring with relative ease. His first step on the comeback trail took him to Madison Square Garden, where he fought a hard-hitting fringe contender named Charlie

"Devil" Green. Patterson was guaranteed $25,000 plus 32½ percent of the gate, while Green got only 15 percent and a chance to use Patterson as his stepping stone out of obscurity.

Green created a brief furor in the fifth when he opened a bad gash over Patterson's left eye. The cut had no effect on the outcome, as Floyd kayoed Green with a left hook in the 10th round.

Patterson made six ring appearances in 1971. On January 16, he met trial horse Levi Forte in Miami. The Forte go was a tune-up for a projected February meeting with Oscar Bonavena. However, Forte's manager, Mack Goodman, believed Patterson was underestimating his fighter, and that signing to fight Bonavena so soon afterward was a mistake.

Goodman insisted that Forte had "something special planned for Patterson." Whatever that something was, it wasn't special enough, as Floyd needed only two rounds to stop him.

Only three days after the fight, the Bonavena match was called off due to a hand injury Oscar had suffered in training. Bonavena's fragile left hand was a constant source of pain and frustration. He would injure and reinjure it several times over the next few years.

Consequently, the Patterson–Bonavena fight would be postponed for a year. In the meantime, Floyd remained active, following the Forte knockout with a ninth-round stoppage of oft-beaten Roger Russell. Next came his decision win over prospect Terry Daniels. Two more points wins followed, over veterans Charlie Polite and Vic Brown. Patterson finished 1971 with a one-sided thrashing of 218-pound Charlie "Emperor" Harris. A vintage Patterson combination in the sixth round stripped away the "Emperor's" new clothes.

On January 25, 1972, Patterson and Bonavena signed contracts for the fight they had planned on having the year before. It was scheduled for February 11, and the boxing world held its breath in hope that the matchup would come off without a hitch.

Three days before the fight, disaster of a deeper kind struck. Thomas Patterson, Floyd's father, passed away in Montefiore Hospital in the Bronx. Despite his grief over his father's death, Patterson announced that the fight would go on as scheduled.

Bonavena came into the fight rated #4 by both the WBA and *The Ring* magazine. Patterson had worked his way up to fifth in the WBA's ratings and sixth in *The Ring*'s. Both fighters were guaranteed $60,000.

Against their three common opponents, Patterson and Bonavena had achieved similar results. They had decisioned George Chuvalo, kayoed Tom McNeeley, and been stopped by Muhammad Ali.

Bonavena, however, had advantages in youth, durability, and size, weighing 206 pounds to Patterson's 191¾. For those reasons, odds makers installed Oscar as a 7-to-5 choice.

While nice guy Patterson played his customary role as sentimental favorite, Bonavena was cast in the villain's role. Oscar claimed that his intention wasn't to terminate Floyd's career, he simply wanted to win.

A crowd of 17,958 Madison Square Garden spectators paid $232,510 to witness a very close 10-rounder. There wasn't much action in the early going. Bonavena displayed his usual clumsy aggression, but he still managed to land several hard blows on an uninspired Patterson.

A wild shot from Bonavena sent Floyd face-first to the canvas in round four. Patterson bounced up immediately, but referee Johnny Lo Bianco ruled it a knockdown. As Lo Bianco gave him the mandatory eight count, Patterson smiled. The knockdown and the crowd's shouts of "Floyd! Floyd! Floyd!" acted as a wake-up call for the veteran ex-champ.

A rejuvenated Patterson picked up the momentum as the fight progressed. In the ninth, he stunned Bonavena with a series of shots to the head. He continued his assault through the tenth and last round.

Floyd's late rally had his fans hopeful as the officials added up their scorecards. Referee Lo Bianco scored it 5–4–1, Judge Tony Castellano 6–4, and Judge Bill Recht an amazing 7–2–1 ... all for Patterson.

Despite winning a unanimous decision over a tough opponent, Patterson carried no false pretenses regarding the quality of his work that night.

"I couldn't get started," he admitted. "I just could not get the momentum of my punches working. Maybe it was a lack of interest."[22]

He added that he hadn't slept well since his father's death, but he refused to utilize that as an excuse.

After the fight, it was revealed that Bonavena had once again broken his left hand. However, like Patterson, Oscar offered no excuses. He didn't think he had to.

"I did not lose," Bonavena insisted. "I did everything I was supposed to do. But I had predicted a knockout, and I didn't accomplish that. He [Patterson] was the sentimental favorite of the people, that's why he won."[23]

Many observers agreed with that assessment, including the Associated Press, which scored the fight 6 rounds to 4 in favor of Bonavena.

Patterson said he was still aiming for a shot at Frazier, though he was aware that his performance against Bonavena didn't speak well for his chances against the champion. "I'd have to be a lot better than I was tonight," he said.[24]

The bottom line, however, was that Patterson had defeated a high-ranking contender. Accordingly, the ratings the WBA released on February 28 pushed Patterson up to the #3 slot. George Foreman was demoted to #4 due to lack of activity against rated opposition.

For Patterson, a long awaited rematch with Ali was a natural step along the road to Frazier. The two ex-champs signed for a September 20 meeting at Madison Square Garden. While Ali had tuned up against "Blue" Lewis in Dublin, Patterson chose to sharpen his tools on a 24-year-old prospect named Pedro Agosto.

A native of Puerto Rico, Agosto carried a record of 24–3 into the Patterson match. Unimpressed, Floyd pitched a shutout over six rounds before referee Arthur Mercante came to Agosto's rescue. Patterson was satisfied with his performance, and said he was getting better with age.

He went so far as to predict that he would reach his peak in two years, at age 39! He figured by then that he would have completely mastered the sport. He also believed he would be better prepared both mentally and physically for Ali than he had been for their first fight.

Ali–Patterson II was a much more cordial affair than their 1965 encounter. This time, they displayed a greater degree of respect for each other.

In 1965, Patterson had said that "the image of a Black Muslim" as champion was a "disgrace" to boxing and to America. Now, he kept his opinion of the Muslim religion to himself.

Likewise, in 1972 Ali wasn't as overtly offended by Patterson's insistence on calling him "Clay." But he still damned Floyd with faint praise by commenting:

"He's what you call a white house boy. He's a good American, that's all, a real good American Negro. He don't bother nobody, just a nice fellow. But he's very behind for a black man. He's not wrapped up in no kind of black man's freedom. He ain't a bad fellow. He's just neutral."

Those words weren't exactly a ringing endorsement of Patterson, but they were kinder than the accusations of "Uncle Tom" and "White Man's Champion" Ali had hurled at Floyd back in 1965.

Not only was Ali–Patterson II less hostile than their first fight, it was also more competitive, even though Ali weighed in 218 to Patterson's 188½. The weight gap didn't worry Patterson. "I'm a full-fledged heavyweight," he said. After 20 years of successful competition against bigger men, size differences weren't about to bother him now.

On fight night, Patterson's efforts against Ali were far more effective than they had been seven years earlier. This time, Floyd wasn't handicapped by the back injury that had made him vulnerable to Ali's punishment. His quick hands got through Ali's defense on more than a few occasions.

Still, Floyd's best efforts weren't good enough to defeat his stronger, faster foe. Ali hit Patterson at will, and damaged Floyd's left eye so badly that the fight was stopped in the seventh round.

Although Patterson never officially announced his retirement, the second Ali fight would be his last. He went on to become New York State Athletic Commissioner, and he then trained his son Tracy Harris Patterson to two world titles in the 1990s.

Patterson later suffered from Alzheimer's disease and prostate cancer. He passed away on May 11, 2006. Although Patterson could never be considered one of the greatest heavyweight champions of all time, he is one of the most beloved and respected ex-title holders.

As for Ali, his 1972 campaign came to an end in Stateline, Nevada, on November 21. His opponent was a man who had wanted to get him into the ring since their amateur days, Bob Foster, who was in the fourth year of his reign as world light heavyweight champion.

The buildup for Ali–Bob Foster began immediately after the two had annihilated the Quarry brothers on the same card back in June. At that time, Foster told the press he had all the necessary tools to beat Ali.

Foster's belief in his superiority over Ali was long standing, dating back to 1958. He claimed to have twice beaten Ali as an amateur.

Both Foster and then 16-year-old Cassius Clay were candidates for the team that would go to the 1958 Pan American Games. Bob revealed that young Cassius Clay was an annoyance even back then.

Needless to say, Foster wasn't Ali's biggest fan. In fact, his contempt for Ali would remain long after their 1972 matchup. And Ali didn't much care for Foster, either.

Despite the alleged 1958 knockdowns, few experts gave Foster much of a chance against the current edition of Ali. Still, the promoters argued that the thinner air at Tahoe's 6200-foot altitude wouldn't affect Foster as much as it would Ali. Foster was from Albuquerque, which sits at an altitude of 4953 feet.

If that kind of altitude weren't enough, the promoters also pointed out that Foster stood half an inch taller than Ali's 6'3". Some Foster partisans went so far as to say their man would retire Muhammad.

However, the Foster supporters failed to take one very obvious factor into account: Ali's 41-pound weight advantage. Ali possessed several other edges as well. His reach was longer than Foster's, and he was three years younger. Also, Foster had never beaten a top heavyweight, his most recent failure being the 1970 loss to Frazier.

Still, Foster had nothing to lose by fighting Ali. If he lost, he still had his light heavy title to defend. If he won, he would be in a position to claim the elusive pot of gold he always thought he deserved.

Indeed, Foster's purse for the Ali fight would be $125,000, a far cry from the financial beating he took when he challenged Frazier.

Ali became uncharacteristically taciturn as fight day approached. "I'm not excited about fighting any more," he said. "You people are the ones who're excited, not me.... It's just another night to jump up and down and beat up somebody."[25]

Regarding Foster's prospects, Ali said he expected Bob to give him a few rounds of trouble, and added that Foster "has to rely on a lucky punch to win."[26] Muhammad predicted that he would finish Foster in five, the same round in which another Foster named Mac was supposed to have fallen.

The fight drew a sparse crowd of 1,941 to the High Sierra Theatre. This was the smallest crowd ever to witness Ali as a professional. Despite the poor attendance and the obvious disparity in size, the fight was not devoid of exciting moments. Ali did little offensively through the first few rounds, and Foster was actually out-jabbing him. At the end of round four, Muhammad returned to his corner with a nasty purple welt under his left eye. Picking up the pace in the fifth, Ali sent Foster to the canvas four times. But he couldn't keep him there, and Foster added to the intrigue by opening a cut over Ali's left eye. It was the first blood Ali had shed during his professional career.

Over the next round, Ali was content to stay away and flick jabs at Foster. Then he went on the attack in the seventh, flooring Foster two more times. Foster responded by landing three hard rights to the head that buckled Ali's knees. Ali lowered the boom in the eighth, decking Foster for the seventh and last time at the 40-second mark of the round.

The courageous Foster had nothing to be ashamed of; he had carried himself better than most had expected. Ali had nothing but praise for him after the fight, noting that Foster had been the first to cut him.

Begrudgingly, Foster praised Ali's speed. He said the speed rather than the weight differential was the deciding factor. "A guy who weighs 221 pounds isn't supposed to have hands that fast," Foster said.

But that was as far as Foster's compliments went. Having fought both Ali and Frazier, Bob felt that Smokin' Joe was the better fighter.

"Clay can't punch hard enough to knock out Joe Frazier," he emphasized. "Clay will never beat him."[27]

Never one to have anything good to say about Ali, Foster was appreciative of the purse: "He made me more money in one night than I ever made in my life."[28]

Foster returned to the light heavyweight division, where he defended his title three more times before announcing his retirement on September 16, 1974. He was 35 years old, and his skills were rapidly declining.

However, like so many other "retired" champions, Foster couldn't resist the lure of money and glory, and he returned to the ring a year later. He fought semi-successfully for two years, knocking over opponents of a caliber that did nothing to push him back into the big time.

A pair of knockout defeats in 1978 ended Foster's career for good, just shy of his 40th birthday. He will be remembered as one of the greatest light heavyweight champions of all time, racking up a record 14 successful title defenses. It's a shame he couldn't have come along a decade or so later, when fighters in divisions below heavyweight began to earn huge paydays.

As for Ali, the cut, which required five stitches, was a sore point in more ways than one. He had always prided himself on his good looks, and he had never received so much as a nick throughout his extensive career. As he always said, "I am the greatest and the prettiest!"

Ali's vanity was probably the reason some sportswriters read more into the cut than was really necessary. In its March 1973 issue, *World Boxing* magazine declared: "The cut Bob Foster opened in the corner of Ali's left eye was far more symbolic than most. It ended an era."

The article went on to say that since Ali's perfect ring record came to an end at the hands of Joe Frazier 20 months earlier, the only thing Ali had left to brag about was his unscathed face. Now, they argued, this too had passed.

In reality, the cut proved nothing other than the fact that Ali was as human as the rest of us. "Now people know he's got blood," Angelo Dundee said. It was as simple as that.[29]

By the end of 1972, there was a logjam at the top of the heavyweight division. Frazier was still champion, but he had had defended the title only twice against challengers with suspect credentials. Ali's six victories against credible opposition had cemented his position as the #1 contender.

Ali reiterated his contention that he was fighting on a regular basis not just for himself, but for the good of boxing.

Opinions varied as to who would win an Ali–Frazier rematch. However, nearly everyone in the world of boxing fans and commentators agreed that the fight was long overdue.

Of the other contenders, only a few made significant progress during the year. George Foreman had fallen into an inexplicable rut, scoring five consecutive two-round kayoes over opponents who couldn't carry Ron Stander's jockstrap. Sixties holdovers like Quarry, Patterson, Bonavena, Ellis, and Chuvalo were on their way out.

Of the newcomers, Joe Bugner was not living up to the promise he'd shown earlier in his career. Larry Middleton's rise was only slightly impeded by his close defeat by Quarry, but a knockout loss to ex-con Ron Lyle put Larry's prospects in doubt. Lyle out–Foremanned Foreman by scoring eight knockouts in eight 1972 fights. And a once-beaten California body beautiful named Ken Norton was beginning to attract some attention.

Still, Ali–Frazier II was the only matchup the public wanted. But instead, Frazier had signed to defend his title against an untested George Foreman in January of 1973.

The heavyweight logjam was about to be broken with a vengeance.

Six

1973

Sunshine Showdown

At the beginning of 1973, the twenty-two months that had passed since the classic 1971 superfight between Joe Frazier and Muhammad Ali could be summed up in three words: activity, isolation, and frustration. Ali provided the activity with his globe-trotting fistic roadshow. Frazier provided the isolation by putting his hard-won championship on ice. And the frustration was caused by the apparent futility of attempts to arrange a rematch between the two best heavyweights in the world.

However, within three amazing months, the division exploded, transforming from a two-man duet to a full chorus of contenders. The true greatness of the 1970s was about to begin.

On New Year's Day, only three fighters in the heavyweight Top 10 could boast undefeated records: Frazier, George Foreman, and Ron Lyle. Barring a draw, that number would drop to two on January 22, when Foreman challenged Frazier for the title in Kingston, Jamaica.

Despite both men's unsullied slates, there was no comparison between Frazier and Foreman when it came to the quality of the competition each had faced. Besides common opponent George Chuvalo, the only noteworthy fighters on Foreman's resume were fringe contenders Boone Kirkman and Gregorio Peralta.

Although George had compiled a commendable 37–0 record with 34 knockouts in four short years, there was serious doubt over the extent to which his skills had been advanced by his most recent efforts. In preparation for Frazier, Foreman had dug deep into what can best be described as the sediment of the pugilistic talent pool. If George's 1972 campaign were a movie, it would have been titled *The Year of Living Cautiously*.

On February 29, Foreman destroyed Murphy Goodwin in two rounds in Austin, Texas. One week later, Clarence Boone suffered the same fate in Beaumont. Neither of those fighters was within walking distance of respectability, let alone title contention.

At this point, the fans were beginning to lose patience with the quality of Foreman's opponents, and they weren't about to part with their hard-earned cash to witness the execution of another stiff. Thus, when Foreman fought Ted Gullick on April 10 in Los Angeles, he would do so for a less than princely sum.

The contract called for Big George to collect 27½ percent of the live gate, while Gullick, a failed prospect, was to receive a flat rate fee of $2,000. Fewer than 1,500 fans showed up to view the debacle, and they paid under $6000. Ironically, Gullick ended up getting paid more than Foreman. Considering the punishment he absorbed during the two rounds the fight lasted, Ted probably earned those extra bucks.

It wasn't as though Foreman's manager, Dick Sadler, didn't have bigger things in mind for his tiger. Sadler believed Foreman could handle Frazier, and he also insisted it was time George was given his chance to prove it. He complained, as others had, that Daniels and

Stander were undeserving challengers in 1972. Sadler claimed that Stander had jumped from #49 in the ratings all the way to #10, just so he could fight Frazier.

Continuing his talk-big, fight-small strategy, Sadler next matched Foreman with Miguel Angel Paez, a 32-year-old, shaven-skulled Kojak look-alike from Argentina. Although he was not a ranked contender, Paez had been considered as a challenger for Frazier's title in 1971. However, as Smokin' Joe's last two opponents indicated, world-class credentials were no longer a requirement for a title shot.

Regardless of Paez's unimpressive standing, Sadler believed a victory over the Argentine would lead to a fight with Frazier. He stated that if Foreman won he would pressure the WBA and WBC to give him a title shot.

Predictably, the fight was no contest. Foreman dropped the 191-pound Paez twice in the first round, then floored him for a nine count in round two. Miguel arose only to be pinned in a corner, where Foreman worked him over until the referee stopped the so-called contest. Foreman rounded out 1972 in Salt Lake City, Utah, against one Terry Sorrels on October 10. The fight provided little competitive action, and the end came at 1:05 of the second round. Disgusted fans booed and tossed debris into the ring. Perhaps they remembered that Sorrels had been knocked out by Terry Daniels two years earlier.

Now Foreman's opposition was about to take a quantum leap forward in the person of Joe Frazier in a fight billed as "The Sunshine Showdown."

Frazier's 1972 competition had been only slightly better than Foreman's. However, his ledger also boasted victories over the likes of Chuvalo, Mathis, Ellis, Bonavena, and Bob Foster. And he was the only man to hold a professional win over the great Muhammad Ali. Consequently, there was a widespread perception that Foreman was in over his head against Smokin' Joe, even though George was the bigger man.

In the November issue of *The Ring* magazine, Dan Daniel commented on what he called the "Foreman Controversy." Citing Foreman's untested skills and stamina, Daniel concluded: "The general belief is that Foreman is far from ready to fight Joe Frazier.... It would appear that in signing with Frazier, Foreman would be laying his career on the line."[1]

Daniel wasn't alone in his assumptions. The odds, 3½ to 1 in Frazier's favor, were an indication of the uncertainty concerning Foreman.

Regardless of the experts' doubts, Foreman arrived in Kingston for the "Sunshine Showdown" in a mood that was both serious and confident. For one thing, he believed the law of averages was on his side. Foreman figured that since most heavyweight champs rarely reign for more than two or three years, Smokin' Joe had exceeded his shelf life.

The Foreman camp went to extreme lengths to prevent outside distractions from impeding the fighter's concentration. He left his wife and two-week-old daughter (whom he had not yet seen) at home, and would make no further contact with them until the fight was over. The emotions one feels when holding an infant would not have been helpful to Foreman in the ring.

Frazier, on the other hand, appeared to be placing too much credence in the opinions of the experts and odds makers. While Foreman left his wife and newborn child stateside, Joe brought his spouse and five children along for a Caribbean holiday.

Despite the tropical temperatures, however, the champion received a chilly reception in Jamaica. The people came out in droves, sometimes as many as 2,500, to boo Frazier at his open sparring sessions. Foreman, on the other hand, was the object of cheers and ovations. The locals had no special attachment to George, they merely resented Frazier for beating Ali.

Frazier claimed to be unaffected by the heckling. Inside, though, Frazier must have been hurt and angry by the way Jamaican fans were treating him. If he were planning to take that anger out on Foreman, the challenger would be in serious trouble indeed.

Yet despite the common belief that Foreman had bitten off more than he could chew, there was one factor that could not be overlooked: the pair of H-bombs Big George carried in his boxing gloves.

Despite Foreman's power, there were those who questioned whether the challenger had the speed to actually nail the deceptively elusive champion. Frazier's chief sparring partner and friend Ken Norton was in Jamaica for the fight and felt that Big George posed no threat to Smokin' Joe. "As far as his [Foreman's] big punches, you can pack a lunch before they get there."[2]

If nothing else, the challenger had to be given a puncher's chance. Consequently, some observers were fearful that Foreman could jeopardize the lucrative and long-anticipated Frazier–Ali sequel. Frazier tried to lay that notion to rest two days before the fight. He claimed that he was in great shape and wouldn't let Foreman impede his rematch with "Clay."

One man Frazier couldn't reassure was Angelo Dundee, who was in Jamaica to witness the bout firsthand. Ali was too busy training for a February 14 bout with Joe Bugner to attend the Sunshine Showdown. In his absence, he sent Dundee and Bundini Brown with strict orders: "Make sure nothin' happens to Frazier."

The day before the fight, Dundee was so nervous he had no appetite. "Who can eat?" he moaned. "Frazier loses and there's no fight with Ali. He's throwing away millions. Believe me, this kid [Foreman] can punch. What is Frazier trying to prove?"[3]

Quite a lot, as it turned out. Although Frazier was still the undisputed champion, he was not a happy man. He was far from satisfied with the way events had progressed since his victory over Ali. Frazier had fought his heart out to win the decision, and with it recognition as the world's best fighter. But Ali's popularity had soared over the past two years, while the champ was becoming just another guy named "Joe."

Frazier was understandably disillusioned and angered at the purses and publicity Ali was receiving. As undisputed, undefeated champion, Frazier believed he was entitled to the fruits of victory. Instead, he was quickly discovering that Joe Frazier minus Muhammad Ali equaled obscurity and short money.

Point in fact: For his first post–Ali title defense, Frazier received only $250,000 for mugging Terry Daniels. To add insult to injury, the champ's purse was cut to $200,000, with the additional $50,000 coming only if the promoter made sufficient profit. For his other defense, against Ron Stander, Frazier was guaranteed a mere $150,000.

Ali, on the other hand, earned $450,000 for his first fight after Frazier, the 12th-round TKO over Jimmy Ellis. Then came $300,000 for the Mathis waltz; $300,000 for Jurgen Blin; $200,000 for Mac Foster; $200,000 for Chuvalo; $500,000 for Quarry; $200,000 for Al "Blue" Lewis; $250,000 for Patterson; and $250,000 for Bob Foster. The loser of the 1971 superfight was obviously emerging as a winner at the bank.[4]

As it was, there were those who believed Frazier should have been grateful to have received any money at all for fighting the likes of Daniels and Stander. For those undemanding defenses, manager Yank Durham offered no apologies. He reasoned that if they could get $250,000 for fighting a Daniels or Stander, then why not?

Still, Frazier was a proud man, and the criticism of his choice of opponents was beginning to get under his skin. He was also desperate to prove that he could earn a big payday with an opponent other than Ali. He demanded that Durham get him a fight with Foreman, the only other major name in the division.

Legend has it that Durham refused the request, fearing that Foreman might derail the multi-million dollar rematch with Ali. Driven by the same never-say-die determination that enabled him to defeat Ali, Frazier initiated negotiations himself. Surely a win over the young, undefeated power puncher would shut the critic's mouths, if not Ali's.

Frazier–Foreman generated much interest among American venues, including the Houston Astrodome and Madison Square Garden. In the end, however, it was National Sports, Ltd., a promotional group owned primarily by the Jamaican government, that clinched the deal. Frazier was guaranteed a respectable purse of $850,000. And Foreman's $375,000 far exceeded any of his previous paydays.

Joe considered his $850,000 to be easy money. To him, it was inconceivable that an upstart like Foreman could cope with his particular brand of aggression, or "smokin'."

Joe Louis was in Jamaica as a member of Foreman's entourage, along with Archie Moore and Sandy Saddler. Louis, a great former champion but a notoriously poor prognosticator, nevertheless offered some sound insights into the upcoming fight.

Louis believed that if Foreman's left hand was as effective as it had appeared to be against weaker opposition, he would have an excellent chance against Frazier. The Brown Bomber admitted he had only seen Foreman fight on TV.

"But I know that he is five years younger than Frazier, that he's four inches taller, and has a five inch longer reach. He's proved he can hit and he's never lost a fight as a pro," Louis summarized.

Louis also believed Foreman's lack of experience against high-caliber opposition would not be a factor. "You don't need experience to beat Frazier," Louis observed. "He's always there in front of you.... You don't have to worry about out-thinking him the way you would Cassius Clay.... But you've got to be in condition. You've got to be ready to go three minutes every round."[5]

Although Frazier's stamina was beyond question, Foreman's remained a mystery because only four of his opponents had lasted more than five rounds. Frazier was the type of fighter who grew stronger as a bout wore on. What was overlooked by many analysts was Joe's vulnerability during the early rounds, the time during which Foreman had always been at his devastating best.

The late Sonny Liston, Foreman's idol and mentor as well as the fighter to whom George was most frequently compared, said in 1968 that he dearly wanted to fight Frazier. "I don't have to chase him," Liston said. "It'll be like shooting fish in a barrel."

Sonny proved to be something of a prophet, given the way his fight-alike protégé handled Frazier five years later.

Frazier weighed in at 214 pounds, Foreman a rock-hard 217. Although the weight difference was only three pounds, Foreman dwarfed the champion as the fighters stared at each other during referee Arthur Mercante's instructions.

The 36,000 fans in attendance at Kingston's National Stadium didn't have to wait long for the action to heat up as both men charged from their corners at the first bell. Frazier landed a sweeping left hook that snapped Foreman's head sideways, then another that grazed George's chin. And that was the extent of Frazier's effective offense as Foreman, having tasted his opponent's power, decided it was time to launch some chin-seeking missiles of his own.

George's strategy had been well planned by his brain trust, and he executed it to perfection. After Frazier landed those first few hooks, Foreman simply extended his arms and pushed the champ back every time he attempted to burrow his way inside. Then he ripped his own hooks to Joe's head and body, forcing Frazier to fight defensively.

The pushing tactic was unorthodox, and possibly even illegal, although the referee never intervened. Bottom line: it worked. Never before had Frazier's rhythm been disrupted the way it was against Foreman.

As the round continued, George continued to push and punch. A sharp uppercut hurt Frazier. Then, to the shock of viewers everywhere, a jab and a sweeping right dumped Frazier on the seat of his trunks.

Howard Cosell, who was doing the television commentary, went berserk, screaming into the microphone: "Down goes Frazier! Down goes Frazier! Down goes Frazier!"

More embarrassed than hurt, Joe got up with a surprised and angry expression on his face. Much as he had when Oscar Bonavena decked him back in 1966, Frazier rushed straight at his tormentor. Bad move! Foreman had forgotten more about finishing an opponent than Bonavena ever knew.

George greeted Frazier with a pile-driver right to the ribcage. Frazier groaned aloud and backed up. Foreman trapped him on the ropes and fired away with both hands as Joe tried to bob and weave his way out of trouble.

Still, even though he was half dazed and in deep trouble, Frazier's instincts still led him to swing back. But Foreman clubbed him to the canvas again with three successive right-hand blows. Frazier rose from the second knockdown like a man in a drunken stupor.

"When a fighter takes the count, he usually looks for his opponent in the neutral corner," Mercante said after the fight. "But after the second knockdown, Frazier couldn't even find Foreman."[6]

Foreman didn't have any trouble finding Frazier. Another combination dropped Joe for a third time. There was no three-knockdown rule; otherwise Foreman would have won the fight in the first round. As it was, the bell saved Joe from the second-worst three minutes of his professional life. The worst would come one minute later, when he answered the bell for round two.

Durham had worked frantically to revive Frazier during the interval, but Joe was like a jukebox with only one tune on the turntable. When the second round started, he moved forward, still groggy but intent on taking Foreman out with a left hook. Foreman easily herded him onto the ropes for more punishment. Frazier staggered aimlessly away, momentarily turning his back on Foreman. Taking advantage of the opening, George tossed a right over Joe's left shoulder. The blow landed flush on the side of Frazier's face, and sent the champion down for the fourth time.

Somehow, Frazier managed to rise again. His eyes were completely vacant, but Mercante allowed the massacre to continue. Foreman walked in, landed a left uppercut, missed a right, then scored with another left uppercut to the jaw. Down went Frazier for the fifth time.

Drawing from a deep well of courage, Frazier pulled himself to his feet yet again. By now he was using all his remaining energy simply to stay upright. Yet he still tried to land a left hook on Foreman, hoping the punch that carried him to the top of the heap would save his title for him now.

It was not to be. Foreman, an engine of destruction, walked through Joe's hook and bombarded him with wide, roundhouse haymakers, most of which landed. The coup de grace was a right hand that thudded into the side of Frazier's head, lifted him several inches off the canvas, and deposited him in a heap.

Incredibly, Frazier beat Mercante's count. Joe had always insisted that the man who took his title would have to kill him to beat him. And to Mercante, it appeared as though Foreman was in the process of doing exactly that. So Mercante finally stopped the slaughter, and the heavyweight championship changed hands.

Glassy-eyed, blood and saliva hanging from his mouthpiece, Frazier stumbled back to his corner. His title was gone, but in defeat his championship heart beat stronger than ever.

Recognizing the courage of his foe, Foreman pushed his way to Frazier's corner and found him slumped on his stool.

"I respect you more than any man in modern boxing," George told the battered, bleeding Frazier. "You were a great champion."

"Right on," Frazier muttered in reply.[7]

Then a horde of jubilant Jamaican fans carried the triumphant new champion out of the ring.

In a post-fight press conference, Frazier faced a barrage of questions from reporters, and he made an honest attempt to explain his defeat.

"George clobbered me," Frazier said, shaking his head after viewing a TV replay of the fight. "My hands were down, like some old man. I got hit with a wicked shot, and my old hot head took over. Instead of stepping back and clearing my head, I went after him. I got hit and hit and hit. George might've knocked me down six more times, but I would have kept getting up and trying."[8]

Frazier wasn't the only one in a state of shock over his upset loss. So were Angelo Dundee and Bundini Brown; their worst nightmare had come true. In less than six minutes, the millions of dollars Ali–Frazier II would have earned had sprouted wings and flown off into the Jamaican sunset.

And suddenly, the much-maligned Dick Sadler was looking like a genius. As always, when an underdog upsets the odds and ascends to the heavyweight throne, the public undergoes a get-acquainted period with the new king. Media experts must backtrack and determine why their predictions and evaluations went awry, especially when the underdog demolishes the favorite.

The first Clay–Liston fight had caused that kind of reaction, but Foreman–Frazier was even more bewildering. Never in modern heavyweight history had an underdog slaughtered a defending champion so quickly or easily. Joe Frazier, the man who defeated Ali, had been reduced to the level of Ted Gullick, Terry Sorrels, and the other journeymen Foreman had blown away in two rounds apiece the year before.

Before Foreman–Frazier, the heavyweight scene consisted of two stars, Frazier and Ali, and a collection of lesser lights glimmering in the background. Now a new star was born, and the future of the division had altered in a radical way.

Because Foreman's victory was so one-sided, the prospect of an immediate rematch with Frazier aroused little interest. Indeed, serious questions now arose concerning Frazier. Many wondered if the grueling Ali fight had sapped Joe's skills and resilience. Was Frazier finished?

Not necessarily. The real story of Foreman–Frazier was more a matter of styles than any deterioration on Frazier's part. Joe was a straightforward, aggressive, but predictable fighter. Foreman was a bigger, stronger slugger who feasted on opponents who rushed straight at him. If Frazier was a rock, then Foreman was a rock crusher.

As long as their styles stayed consistent, Smokin' Joe seemed as custom-made for Foreman as Floyd Patterson had been for Sonny Liston. Thus, Frazier's chances of regaining the title from Big George appeared to lie somewhere between slim and none.

His awesome performance notwithstanding, there were also some lingering misgivings about Foreman. The primary question fans and experts asked each other was: "Is Foreman that good, or has Frazier slipped that far?"

And the most popular answer was: "Let's see how Foreman does in his next fight."

The public likes to see a new champion in action quickly after he wins his title, especially when he does so in spectacular fashion. If he's a fluke, then he'll be exposed and eliminated. If he's for real, then his reputation can begin to build.

Ultimately, the questions about Foreman could only be answered in a title defense against the best available contender. And that contender was, of course, Muhammad Ali. The clamor for Ali–Frazier II had died in Jamaica.

Foreman–Ali was now the fight that excited the public. Could Foreman snuff out the other star that lit the early '70s? Millions of fans were willing to pay big money to find out. But Foreman wasn't about to go begging for a fight with Ali. He figured that, since he was the new champ, Ali should challenge him.

For his part, Ali wasn't concerned about George just yet. He said that Foreman was just out of the Olympics and wasn't ready for him yet. Ali was conveniently forgetting that Foreman had won his Olympic gold medal in the 1968 Olympics, not 1972. Foreman–Frazier, by the way, marked the first time two Olympic heavyweight gold medal winners had faced each other for the professional title. Ali's gold medal came in the light heavy class.

Despite Ali's professed lack of interest, his lawyer and promoter, Bob Arum, spent the next two months scanning various offers to finance and host an Ali–Foreman title bout.

Arum revealed in March that there were three proposals that he viewed as serious. Those offers ranged from $3.25 million to a mind-boggling $5 million per fighter. Arum said he expected confirmation on them as early as April.

In the meantime, Ali had other fish to fry, specifically a large British kipper named Joe Bugner.

The British Are Coming

Since Ali–Bugner was scheduled for February 14, Muhammad promptly dubbed it the "St. Valentine's Day Massacre," in reference to the bloody gangland slayings in Chicago back in 1929. Although Ali didn't plan on emulating the extremes of Al Capone, he did predict a seventh-round knockout victory.

At the tender age of 22, Joe Bugner was far from a novice. Leading up to the Ali match, he had compiled an impressive 42–4–1 dossier. By contrast, Ali had engaged in only 19 bouts at a similar stage in his career, and even now he had six fewer fights than his youthful opponent.

Born in Hungary in 1950, Bugner fled to England along with his mother and sisters during the 1956 uprising in that country. The refugee family found new roots in Bedford. Bugner had become interested in boxing at the age of 13 after watching a Lazlo Papp fight on television. Papp was a three-time Olympic gold medalist and the greatest fighter Hungary ever produced.

Blessed with plenty of natural athletic ability (he had excelled in track and discus throwing in school), the tall, blond youth enjoyed a successful amateur boxing career. When he moved to St. Ives, he was taken in hand by a small-time trainer/manager named Andy Smith.

Under Smith's guidance, Bugner began his professional career at the age of 17. He was matched with a transplanted Jamaican named Paul Brown on a hotel card. Young Joe floored Brown twice in the second round and was administering a one-sided shellacking when a Brown right came out of the blue and flattened the teenager for the full count.

Despite that disastrous beginning, fifteen more years would pass before Bugner would again fail to finish a fight. Undaunted by his debutant disaster, Joe gained his vengeance by stopping Brown twice in the following year.

Early in his career, Bugner made a name for himself as a sparring partner for then contender Thad Spencer, who was in England to fight Eduardo Corletti. During training sessions, the youngster banged Spencer's eye so badly the Corletti fight had to be postponed.

Bugner was heartbroken when a Jamaican fighter named Ulric Regis collapsed and died after losing a decision to Joe in 1969. However, like so many others before him, Bugner continued his career. As the '70s began, he methodically pounded out wins over less than formidable opposition, the same fistic roadkill that appeared on the records of every other prospect of that time. His more notable victims included Jack O'Halloran, Charlie Polite, Johnny Prescott, Eduardo Corletti, Brian London, Scrap Iron Johnson, and Chuck Wepner.

On paper, Joe Bugner was a potential superstar. He was a good-looking, big (6'4", 220 pounds), well-built, well-spoken, clean-living young heavyweight with a solid chin, a winning record, a sterling future, and, as Ali always put it, the "complexion with the connections."

He had it all, except for the one thing he wanted more than anything else: the unalloyed admiration of British boxing fans and media. Bugner had plenty of supporters, but they were always outnumbered by his critics.

Why didn't Bugner achieve greater popularity in his adopted country? A number of explanations may be advanced. One factor working against him was his foreign background. At that time, the British weren't quite ready to accept an immigrant hero, especially one from a Communist country.

Bugner's style worked against him as well. Despite his size and sculpted muscles, he was a boxer, not a puncher. And then there was Joe's obvious lack of passion for the sport. He once said that boxing was something he happened to be very good at, not something he particularly enjoyed. The death of Ulric Regis may have contributed to that attitude.

Even without the kind of desire that burned in a Joe Frazier, natural ability and stringent conditioning were sufficient to carry Bugner to victory over opponents on the lower and middle rungs of the heavyweight ladder. But his lack of fire and ferocity hampered his relationship with the British public.

British boxing fans are a different breed from those on the other side of the Atlantic. Both British and American aficionados love a winner. However, British fans seem to take more stock in gritty determination than actual victory. This attitude came about through decade after decade of watching their best fighters getting chewed up and spat out by "bleedin' Yanks." Eventually, any British heavyweight who managed to look respectable in defeat, as did Tommy Farr against Joe Louis, became a national hero.

Now, in Bugner, the Brits had the most complete package of a heavyweight fighter most had ever seen. But he appeared to lack the requisite spirit. Some of the more extreme fans almost blamed God for having squandered such extravagant physical potential on a lad who didn't know what to do with it. Most fans' feelings for him were summed up in his nickname: "The Bug."

Then, in March of 1971, Bugner committed the ultimate sin by hammering the final nail into the pugilistic coffin of the islands' most beloved fighter, Henry Cooper. Never did Joe's popularity sink so low as on the night he won a squeaker of a decision over the 37-year-old three-time British champion. Bugner was only 21 and outweighed Cooper by 23¼ pounds, yet he came within an eyelash of losing the 15-round verdict to old "'Enery."

Now Bugner occupied the same unenviable position as fighters like Gene Tunney and Ezzard Charles, both of whom succeeded extremely popular champions. Great fighters in their own right, Tunney and Charles never achieved the level of adulation enjoyed by their predecessors, Jack Dempsey and Joe Louis. In England, Cooper was as adored as Dempsey and Louis, and that spelled trouble for Bugner.

When the decision in Bugner's favor was announced, a rain of garbage flew into the ring, hardly a glorious coronation. Nevertheless, Joe now reigned as champion of Britain, the Commonwealth, and Europe. In terms of significance, with those titles and a dime he could make a phone call.

Cooper announced his retirement after the Bugner fight. He remained one of the most beloved public figures in the United Kingdom. In contrast, Bugner's career fell into a tailspin. The rejection he experienced gnawed at the young champion, and its effects showed in his performance. Two months after the Cooper fight, he defended his European title with a lackluster decision over Jurgen Blin. Then, on September 27, Bugner hit rock bottom.

His triple-title defense against the awkward Jack Bodell was supposed to be easy. Bugner had more talent in his little finger than Bodell had in his entire 6'2" frame. Yet Bugner fought as though he were sleepwalking, and allowed Bodell to walk away with the decision and the titles.

Bugner rebounded slightly by out-pointing American trial horse Mike Boswell. Then he lost another decision, this time to Baltimore stylist Larry Middleton. The Middleton verdict was so close and controversial, even Bugner's detractors decried the scoring. *London Times* writer Neil Allen, who rated himself "among the most severe critics of Bugner," believed Joe had been robbed.

At this point, Bugner appeared to be just another prospect who had failed to live up to his potential. But he managed to pull himself together and score eight consecutive wins in 1972.

The streak included seven knockouts, the sweetest being a seven-round stoppage of Blin that enabled Joe to regain the European crown. That crown must have been tarnished with fingerprints, having passed from Bugner to Bodell to Jose Urtain to Blin, then back to Bugner, all in a mere 13 months.

Joe opened 1973 with a routine 15-round decision over a durable Dutchman named Rudi Lubbers in defense of the European title. Less than a month later, he was in Las Vegas, facing the legendary Muhammad Ali.

The Ali–Bugner fight had been in jeopardy almost from the moment it was proposed. When Bugner inked the contract on December 8, 1972, he did so despite threats from the British Boxing Board of Control. Ray Clarke, BBBC Secretary, said Bugner had been told that he was forbidden to sign the contract.

The BBBC's opposition to the fight was based on purely economic grounds. They wanted the bout to be held in Britain, where they could take a percentage of the gate. On December 14, after a lengthy interview with Bugner, the BBBC reversed its stance. Bugner would be allowed to fight Ali in America.

Ali was guaranteed $275,000 for his efforts, while Bugner stood to earn a reported $125,000, mainly from British closed circuit rights.

This fight had something of a different angle in that Bugner was a well-known Ali fan, unlike most of the rest of Muhammad's opponents. In fact, Bugner's 10-rounder with Mike Boswell had occurred on the undercard of the Ali–Buster Mathis fight in Houston. Ali and Bugner had sparred 20 rounds with each other in preparation for their respective bouts, and Bugner was suitably impressed by the experience.

Joe told the media he wanted to dispose of Boswell quickly so he could shower up and get back to the arena in time to watch Ali take on Mathis.

Unfortunately, Boswell spoiled Bugner's plans by lasting the full distance. But then the Ali–Mathis square dance wasn't worth watching, anyway.

Now the situation was different. Bugner needed to put his hero-worship aside and do his best to defeat Ali in a 12-round bout appropriately billed as "The British Are Coming."

The odds makers tabbed Bugner an 8–1 underdog, but the young contender remained undaunted. He reasoned that his credentials as European title holder meant that he was "champion of half the world" already, and was by no means out of Ali's league.

Also, Bugner had by now sparred a total of forty rounds with the ex-champ over the past two years. With that kind of experience under his belt, Joe assured the press that Ali didn't frighten him.

Still, Ali made a monumental effort to unnerve Bugner from the moment Joe set foot on American soil. Not since his bombastic Cassius Clay days had Ali been so determined to psych out an opponent. Ego might have motivated Ali's ire. For the first time, he was facing a much younger man, and his return to the Clay persona could have been an attempt to recapture his carefree youth.

Both men trained at the same facility for promotional purposes and there were those who felt that this would be detrimental to Bugner's psyche, especially when Ali tried to accuse Bugner of calling him a "nigger." But Bugner took it well: "I've heard it all before. When I've sparred with him. He has to have a crowd around him and when the black Americans come in he naturally turns it on even more. He makes his own rules and breaks all the normal ones — like saying I called him a nigger. Can you imagine me saying such a thing? ... But I treat Ali just like another good turn in the Las Vegas show business program."[9]

Ali later said he regretted having made the unfounded allegation. But he had dropped several notches in Bugner's estimation.

Instead of attempting to escape or ignore Ali's taunts, Smith and Bugner preferred to meet the "Louisville Lip" head-on. In fact, Bugner regularly attended Ali's sparring sessions at Caesars Palace. Naturally, Ali would spot Bugner in the crowd and would immediately bombard him with threats and insults. The majority of Bugner's fans believed Smith shouldn't have subjected his fighter to so much contact with Ali. Bugner disagreed. He figured that it was better to know up front what Ali was up to rather than lie in bed and fret about what he might be doing.

Ali's frustration at his inability to rattle his opponent became increasingly obvious. After fifteen minutes of ranting at the weigh-in, the most he could get out of the cool Briton was a grin. Afterward, Ali admitted that he'd been frustrated in his inability to goad his young opponent.

Besides his out-of-the-ring shenanigans, Ali's training regimen also recalled earlier days. He worked harder for Bugner than he had for any other opponent since Frazier. He sparred a full 67 rounds in the week preceding the fight. In fact, the day before the contest, when most fighters would be resting, Ali put in six rounds of sparring. He trained diligently because he expected Bugner to be a difficult opponent.

He also said that during his sparring experiences with Bugner, he found the Briton difficult to reach. Ali conceded that he hadn't trained hard enough for his fights with Blue Lewis, Floyd Patterson, and Bob Foster.

Many believed the embarrassment of being cut by Foster in his most recent fight had spurred Ali to become more serious in training, and any concern about Bugner's skills was more apparent than real.

At any rate, that appeared to be the consensus among British fans, who didn't appear to fancy their boy's chances against "The Greatest." Still, more than 1,500 Brits poured into Las Vegas to witness the event.

Likewise, the hyper-critical British press did not hesitate to take a few more swipes at Bugner. In reference to a statement Ali had made about Bugner's being a "spoiler, like George Foreman," *London Times* boxing writer Neil Allen penned a rather disparaging retort: "That comparison, which some might feel is almost blasphemous, is a measure of how hard Ali, one of the best publicity experts in the world, is trying to boost next Wednesday's 12 round bout between 'the greatest' and our sometimes lackluster European heavyweight champion."

In another article a few days before the fight, Allen wrote: "I hope he [Bugner] can rise to his best form against Ali though I have no doubt he will be beaten."

On fight day, Ali stepped into the ring wearing a $2,000, jewel-sparkled robe with the label "The People's Champion" emblazoned on the back. The garment was a gift from another celebrity superstar, Elvis Presley.

Beneath the robe, the fruits of Ali's rigorous training were revealed: a sleek 217½-pound form. But Bugner's physique matched Ali's ripple for ripple.

Not long after the opening bell, Ali opened a severe cut over Bugner's left eye. Because of the wound, Bugner fought cautiously, and Ali was cast in the unfamiliar role of aggressor. Over the next few rounds, Ali pursued while Bugner back-pedaled in an attempt to protect the cut. An occasional flurry from Bugner prevented Ali from launching an attempt to knock him out.

Ali coasted a bit in the fifth and sixth rounds. Many observers thought he was easing up in order to go all-out to put Bugner away in the seventh, as predicted. That didn't happen, but Ali did appear intent on finishing his man in the tenth.

In that frame Ali opened up and raked Bugner with a series of lefts and rights that left the younger man's face a bloody mask. Bugner's corner did a fantastic job of cleaning their fighter up between rounds. However, Ali's jab repeatedly speared the cut over the next two rounds, and the former champ appeared to have won a lopsided decision.

However, the judges' scoring was surprisingly close. On a five-point system, Roland Dakin had it 57–54; Ralph Mosa 57–52; and Lou Talbot 56–53, all for Ali.

Still, Bugner had performed better than most had believed possible. He demonstrated a good left jab, a sturdy chin, courage under fire, and a great deal of potential. Above all, he proved he wasn't just another "horizontal heavyweight" from Jolly Olde England.

Ali predicted a bright future for Britain's "Golden Boy." "I should be out of this thing in 1½ to two years."

Ali said, providing an intimation of mortality. "I'll give him two years, and he'll be the world's heavyweight champion with no trouble."[10]

Ali also said Bugner was three times better than he'd been during their sparring sessions a year or two earlier. He even indicated that if he hadn't trained so industriously, Bugner might possibly have won the fight. Others took issue with that assessment, believing that Ali had overtrained, and had he been a little sharper, he would have stopped the Briton.

Overall, though, Ali was pleased with his performance. Having bested a man nine years his junior, the Greatest was looking for better things in 1973.

But Ali, like Frazier a few weeks earlier, was about to learn that "pride goeth before a fall."

The Jawbreaker

In the wake of Foreman's upset of Frazier, Ali had the choice of either continuing his active ring schedule or taking a break while his management negotiated a title bout with the new champion. Ali opted to remain active and risk his status as the #1 contender for Foreman's crown.

The next stop on Muhammad's schedule was San Diego, where he would meet Ken Norton on March 31. Although Norton was ranked #7, he was considered nothing more than an easy way for Ali to pick up a six-figure paycheck.

However, circumstances few foresaw would conspire to make this one of the most memorable fights of the 1970s. First, the Ali who stepped into the ring with Norton was in much worse shape than the one who had fought Bugner only six weeks earlier. Second, Kenny Norton, always in peak physical condition, had no intention of becoming just another anonymous Ali foil. Third, Norton possessed a ring style that was uncommonly effective against Ali. Fourth, Norton's trainer, the wily Eddie Futch, knew exactly how to employ that style to maximum advantage.

Ken Norton was not a stranger to Muhammad Ali. Ken had once served as Ali's sparring partner. However, he was better known as Joe Frazier's chief sparmate over the past three years. During the course of their gym wars, Frazier and Norton became such good friends that they turned down several lucrative offers to fight each other in earnest.

Norton's style was awkward and low-key. Futch felt that his fighter didn't have any one great attribute, but did everything well enough.

Also, he was exceptionally quick for a man whose physique appeared better suited for a bodybuilding competition than a boxing match. He adopted Archie Moore's crossed-arm "armadillo" defense, and he would stalk his opponents around the ring, dragging his right leg behind him. His offense consisted of a deceptively effective jab followed by a strong left hook and overhand right.

Conditioning was another Norton trademark. His greatest flaw, which had thus far been exposed only once, was his inability to fight backing up. Only the big punchers could take advantage of that weakness, however. And Ali had never been a big puncher.

Norton also possessed one other outstanding trait: an incredible ability to withstand physical damage outside the ring. His first brush with death occurred at the age of 8, when the high-spirited youngster lost a race to a railroad crossing. Kenny was riding a bike; the winner was a train.

His second defeat on a bicycle happened when he was 14. This time, the winner was a lumber truck. Young Norton escaped serious injury on both occasions, although the bicycles weren't so lucky.[11]

At age 17, Norton got into a dispute with another young man and suffered a quick and one-sided defeat, resulting in a broken collarbone. The other guy happened to be driving a 1960 convertible at the time. Norton also narrowly escaped death while he was in college, when a car he was driving smashed through a bridge railing and teetered fifty feet above a lake.[12]

More recently, Norton miraculously survived a 1988 automobile crash that turned his magnificent body into a twisted, broken travesty. Barely able to speak or walk, Norton had battled back from his injuries with the same spirit he displayed in his ring encounters.

Although he was always secretive about his age, the record books indicate that Norton was born on August 9, 1943, in Jacksonville, Illinois. As a youth, Ken displayed tremendous athletic gifts, starring in football, basketball and track. Of several scholarship offers he received, he chose Northwest Missouri State. However, he dropped out near the end of his sophomore year and joined the U.S. Marine Corps.

Norton played football in the Marines, but then he realized that members of the gridiron squad were regularly being sent off to Vietnam, but the men on the boxing team weren't. Ken decided boxing was his game, and at the age of 21 he put on the gloves for the first time.

He learned quickly, becoming the All Marine champion three years in a row from 1965 to 1967. In 1967, he beat highly touted Forest Ward to earn the heavyweight spot on the U.S. Pan American Games team. But Ward was given the spot instead. The reason? Ward apparently possessed a more "international" style. Ward went on to win the gold medal. He turned pro, but failed to live up to the hype and hoopla of his amateur career.

One week before his discharge from the Marines, Norton was offered a professional contract by managers Bob Biron and Art Rivkin. He departed the amateurs with a record of 24–2 (19 KOs).

In his November 1967 professional debut, Norton scored a 9th-round knockout over one Grady Brazell.

Norton found himself on the canvas in his third professional fight, courtesy of Harold Dutra. Norton got up and put Dutra away in the third round. In his thirteenth go, Norton was floored again, this time by Aaron Eastling. Again, Norton rose and blasted his foe out in the second round. Ken won his first 16 fights, 15 by knockout, and he became the hottest new attraction on the West Coast.

For his next fight, on July 2, 1970, Norton was rather cocky as he looked across the ring at his opponent, a 6'4", 187-pound Venezuelan string bean named Jose Luis Garcia. Garcia looked far from intimidating to the muscular, 210-pound ex–Marine. And the 6–1 odds in his favor further inflated Norton's confidence.

However, in the first round the string bean deposited Norton on the seat of his pants. Unlike Dutra and Eastling, Garcia had more than enough ability to follow up on his advantage. Norton survived the round, but he never fully recovered.

Garcia continued to dominate the action and flattened Norton again in the eighth. Norton got up, absorbed a fearsome beating, and retired on his stool at the end of the round.

Thus it was Garcia, not Norton, who broke into the Top Ten. After the fight, the Venezuelan said he was never intimidated by Norton's muscles or his reputation. The fight was televised, and Garcia was determined to make a good impression before an American audience.

"Norton would have to kill me to knock me out," Garcia said. Instead, he nearly killed

Norton. Garcia would enjoy only a brief period in the heavyweight limelight. Several years later, he would fight Norton again under vastly different circumstances.

As for Norton, his career and his confidence had run into a major roadblock. But he was determined to fight his way back into contention, and he went undefeated through 1971 and 1972.

In 1971, Ken had been offered a bout with Ali. At that time, though, Futch didn't think his fighter was ready. When they were approached for the March 1973 date, however, both fighter and trainer agreed that the time was right.

Ali was hardly worried. He approached the fight in a rather lackadaisical fashion, perhaps believing that a fighter who could be kayoed by the likes of Garcia posed no threat to him. Those close to the former champ revealed that he was doing roadwork one day and gym work the next, but never both on the same day.

When asked about his preparations prior to the fight, Ali admitted that he hadn't done any serious training since before the Bugner fight. Nevertheless, Ali assured all concerned that losing to Kenny Norton was an impossibility.

Then came a rumor of an ankle injury the week prior to the fight. Dr. Paul Woodward of San Diego disclosed after the fight that he had X-rayed Ali's ankle on March 25 and diagnosed a minor sprain. Woodward said Ali had sustained the injury while "horsing around on the golf course."

Despite the injury, Ali refused to postpone the fight. He believed he could beat Norton even in sub-par condition. His overconfidence was understandable, given the lopsided 5–1 betting odds in his favor. As well, Norton's 30–1 record was considered deceptive because none of his opponents were household names even in their own households.

One of the reasons for the lack of big-name fighters on Norton's resume was their unwillingness to fight him even after the Garcia disaster. Quarry, Lyle, Chuvalo, and Mac Foster had all turned down offers to face Norton.

Eddie Futch told *Ebony* magazine: "We tried every one of the ranking heavyweights prior to this, and they all turned us down. We were willing to give them 50 percent of the purse with a guarantee of from $12,000 to $25,000 from our end. But those in boxing know Norton's ability."[13]

Norton approached the Ali fight with as much confidence as did the former champion. The difference was that while Ali's belief in himself was as much a part of him as his hair and fingernails, Norton's was a recent acquisition.

After suffering the knockout loss to Garcia, Norton sought the help of a hypnotist named Dr. Michael Dean. Ken had caught Dean's hypnotic act in a night club after the Garcia fight, and he believed the doctor's services could be an asset to him. Dean agreed to work with the fighter.

In the three years that had passed since Norton and Dean's association, Ken had reeled off 13 consecutive victories and developed what Dean called a "killer instinct," as well as a more receptive attitude to Futch's instructions. "The biggest thing he's done for me was to teach me the difference between cockiness and self confidence," Norton said.[14]

It's not difficult to imagine the amount of verbal ammunition Ali gleaned from Norton's alliance with a hypnotist. When the former champ spotted Dean at one of his workouts, he jumped out of the ring and tried to stare the hypnotist down. Dean stared back and placed his hand on Ali's face. Ali responded with a loud kissing noise on Dean's hand, which delighted the crowd of fans that had come to see him train.

Once he was in the ring, however, Ali soon realized the seriousness of his situation.

Eddie Futch, who had worked in Frazier's corner during the March 1971 superfight, had instilled a fight plan that Norton carried out to perfection.

In Dave Anderson's book *In the Corner*, Futch revealed what he told Norton during training: "You're not going to hit Ali by slipping or pulling back or dropping underneath or parrying. You have to hit him when he's punching. When he starts to jab, you punch with him. Keep your right hand high. His jab will pop into the middle of your glove and then your jab will come right down the pipe into the middle of his face."

Although there appeared to be little decisive action in the first two rounds, when the second frame ended Ali returned to his corner with his mouthpiece filled with blood. He told Dundee he thought his jaw might be broken. Dundee and Ferdie Pacheco agreed with Ali's diagnosis and asked him if he wanted to continue. Muhammad insisted he wasn't in any pain, and all three men believed he could still knock Norton out.

Futch always maintained Ali's jaw was broken in the eleventh round, not the second. Whenever the injury occurred, Ali didn't come close to stopping the determined Norton, although he still managed to fight well enough to be even on points going into the 12th and final round. In that round, Norton staged an assault that nearly ran Ali out of the ring.

"I beat you, sucker!" Norton yelled at Ali when the final bell rang. The judges' scorecards bore out Ken's confidence. He had earned a split decision victory and become only the second man to defeat Ali in the professional ranks.

Norton deserved full credit for the win, but Ali showed tremendous courage in lasting the distance despite going into the fight with a sprained ankle and finishing it with a broken jaw and a bruised right hand.

Still, Norton had scored the second major heavyweight upset of the first three months of 1973. In the course of 36 minutes of hard fighting, Ken launched himself from obscurity to celebrity. Foreman now had some company at the top of the heavyweight heap.

After the fight, Dundee acknowledged that fighting Norton in his hometown of San Diego had been a definite mistake. He added that Norton had fought an inspired fight because "Ali always brings out the best in a man."

Despite Ken's noteworthy performance, Dundee still felt Ali had done enough to win. With sarcasm dripping from his voice, he stated that he wanted to "compliment the California officials on being such great mathematicians."

For once in his life, Ali wasn't talking. Immediately after the fight, he underwent an hour-and-a-half operation on his jaw. Dr. William Lundeen, the surgeon who performed the operation, said afterward: "I can't fathom how he could fight. The lower left jawbone was broken clear through."[15]

Thankfully, the operation was a success. Although Ali's jaw would have to be wired shut for six weeks, Lundeen said the ex-champ's career would not be hampered by the injury. In fact, the jaw would probably be stronger than ever after it healed.

Ali felt that there was a logical reason for losing to Norton: "I lost because of two reasons. One is that I didn't train like I should have. Another is that I have not been faithful to Almighty Allah or to the Honorable Elijah Muhammad. No more joking or fooling around for me. I'm gonna take every fight seriously from now on."[16]

Always able to overcome adversity and to turn any situation into a verbal shot at Frazier, Ali told the press, "Joe Frazier never could have fought a big, hard-hittin', 210-pound man for 10 rounds with a broken jaw."[17]

All verbiage aside, however, for the first time in the '70s, both Ali and Frazier had been forced to step away from the spotlight. Now it was Foreman and Norton's turn to reap the benefits of heavyweight hype.

Norton's victory had naturally brought the Foreman–Ali negotiations to an abrupt halt. Bob Biron, Norton's co-manager, revealed that serious talks had begun regarding a Foreman–Norton matchup. He figured that contracts would be signed within a week or not at all.

It turned out to be the latter. Foreman's manager, Dick Sadler, offered Norton a $250,000 guarantee to challenge George for the title sometime in 1973. No promoter or location was named, only a set of conditions that were bizarre, to say the least. In exchange for the title opportunity, Norton would have to surrender 5 percent of all future purses and a considerable chunk of any future ancillary rights.[18]

Norton's other co-manager, Art Rivkin, said he would never agree to such a ludicrous arrangement. "I'll just say it was an unlivable offer, one we would never acquiesce to," Rivkin stated emphatically.[19]

Just as some had written Frazier off after his devastating loss to Foreman, others were now writing Ali's fistic obituary, saying that boxing may have seen the last of Muhammad and his shattered jaw. Conventional wisdom also held that the departure of Ali would mean the end of the multimillion dollar matches as well.

In the April 16, 1973, issue of *Newsweek*, Philadelphia promoter J. Russell Peltz said: "I'm not interested in seeing Ali fight anybody. And I always liked him more than Frazier. I don't think people will break down doors to see Norton, either."

Peltz's was not an isolated opinion. Many thought that Ali was finished, regardless of how well his jaw healed. But Ali had other plans. He said he intended to come back and stop Norton in four, Frazier in six, and Foreman in thirteen. At the time, few experts took those predictions seriously. But Ali had proven the experts wrong many times before.

The first step on Ali's agenda was a rematch with Norton. He wasted little time in signing a contract. On April 26, Ali signed to meet Norton on September 10 at the Inglewood Forum. The sequel made sense for both fighters. Ali needed to prove that Norton's win was a fluke. And, with the Foreman negotiations going nowhere, a second fight with Ali would be a major money maker for Norton.

Ken's second Ali contract was far more lucrative than the first. Although the $50,000 he hauled down for the first fight was well above his previous career high of $8,000, he was guaranteed $200,000 for the rematch, which was billed as "The Battle of Broken Jaw."

Norton's last fight before the first Ali fight was a $300 purse for beating Charlie Reno. "Those were the desperate years. Life was a monster. Once I even planned on robbing a liquor store.... But I could never rob anyone."[20]

With full medical assurance that the jaw in question was indeed stronger than ever, odds makers installed Ali as a 5-to-2 favorite in the rematch.

Joe Louis said he was picking Norton to repeat because Futch was in his corner. Louis and Futch were old friends, having trained together as teenagers in Detroit's Brewster Center. The Brown Bomber gave Futch the highest of compliments, comparing him to the great Jack "Chappie" Blackburn, the man who had molded Louis into one of the greatest fighting machines of all time.

Futch was a worthy heir to Blackburn's mantle. He knew Norton was in for the fight of his life because Ali would be approaching the rematch with far more serious intentions. And he knew Ali would train like he never had before.

Eddie Futch knew by Ali's weight and condition before the first fight that the former champion had underestimated his charge.

Consequently, Futch was aware that if his fighter were to repeat his victory over Ali, he, too, would have to be in the best shape of his life. Norton said his ideal fighting weight was 205 pounds. He knew he couldn't afford to carry any excess weight against a fit Ali. Although his fat percentage had always been low, Norton said he understood that he too would have to train like never before.

Ali immersed himself in his training at his camp in Deer Lake, Pennsylvania, a beautiful $200,000 facility known as "Fighter's Heaven." There, he embarked on a regimen that molded his body back to what it had been during his pre-exile days. Painfully aware of the mistakes he had made in March, Ali was determined not to repeat them.

"What happened," Ali said analytically, "is that Muhammad Ali ate a lot of ice cream and cake, he didn't do his running, he didn't punch the heavy bag ... if he hadn't been clowning around with his mouth open and got hisself hit with an uppercut, he would have beaten Norton that first time."[21]

Ali revealed, "I became soft and slow because I ate white man's food."[22]

Another reason Ali advanced for his poor performance was that he'd become lackadaisical in his religious practices. He had fallen into disfavor with the Muslims at that point, and those closest to him recognized the effect that estrangement would have on his morale.

Ferdie Pacheco was one of the first to bring this theory up after the Norton loss, and Herbert Muhammad agreed wholeheartedly. In a very basic sense, a strong, practicing Muslim lives a lifestyle of restraint. Had he stuck to that lifestyle, Ali would have entered the ring in the best of shape. In the months that followed the Norton setback, Ali set about mending not just his jaw, but also the rift between himself and the Nation of Islam.

In all, Muhammad spent 14 weeks at Deer Lake, far longer than for any previous fight in his career. Up every morning at 4:30, he ran four miles through the mountains in an effort to regain the bounce and stamina of his youth. After a healthy breakfast, he would chop down oak trees, building strength in his hands, arms, and shoulders.

In the gym, Ali's reflexes remained lightning-fast as he attacked the heavy and speed bags. As for sparring, he put that off until the final few weeks to ensure his jaw would be totally healed. When he commenced his ring work, he did so without headgear, leaving the jaw unprotected.

"Look," he said. "No headgear. No protection. Nobody tellin' sparring partners to hold back. If it's gonna happen, I want it to happen here."[23]

By September 10, Ali weighed a svelte 212, his lowest weight since the beginning of his comeback. He had never been more serious about a fight in his life, "not even for the first one with Liston," observed Harold Conrad, a promoter who had known Ali for years.[24]

In Ali's career, which eventually spanned 61 fights, there were many turning points: the Liston fights, the comeback debut against Quarry, the trilogy against Frazier, and of course his battle against Foreman. However, no single bout was as pivotal to the continuation of his career as the second Norton fight.

A repeat win by Norton would have ended Ali's career and robbed the world of another half decade of excitement. Ali realized the gravity of the task he faced, but he also enjoyed the international attention the question of his professional survival generated.

"Is he through, or is he not?" Ali asked rhetorically. "Is he still the fastest and most beautiful man in the world, or is he growing old and slow? Well, it shows you what they think of Ali that the question would come up."[25]

Norton knew the significance of the fight as well. The difference was, Norton's future wasn't on the line. If Ali beat him, it would only even the score. Ken was well aware that Ali would be in far better mental and physical condition the second time around. But he was also confident that his style and strategy would prove just as troublesome for the ex-champ.

Norton promised that whether the fight ended in a knockout or decision, he would repeat his victory over Ali. However, because Norton could only manage s split decision over a subpar Ali, most experts didn't share his optimism. Against the "real Ali," the conventional wisdom held that Ken didn't have a chance.

In the early rounds of the fight, the conventional wisdom appeared correct. Norton charged in recklessly, and Ali simply stood out of range and popped away with his left. Ali even hurt Norton a few times, and he swept nearly all the first six rounds.

Then, despite his heroic efforts at conditioning, Ali began to slow down. And Norton reverted to Futch's fight plan. Now Ken was doing the pitching, and Ali the catching. Round after round, Norton chipped away at Ali's points advantage.

As in the first fight, the scorecards were virtually deadlocked after eleven rounds of interesting, if not spectacular action. Angelo Dundee shouted at Ali before the start of the twelfth that he needed the round to win. Ali already knew this.

"I knew the man who finished strongest in the end would probably take the fight," Ali said later. "My work was cut out for me."[26]

The fate of the greatest career in boxing had come down to three short, or long, minutes. Both men fought their hearts out in that final round, but it was Ali who summoned up the energy for an eye-catching flurry in the final seconds.

Now Muhammad's future hung in the balance as the officials added up their scorecards. Judge John Thomas called it 6–5–1 for Ali. Judge George Latka also came up with a 6–5–1 score, but his tally was in Norton's favor. Judge Dick Young cast the deciding ballot: 7–5 for Ali.

The split decision victory saved Ali's career, and didn't do all that much harm to Norton's. Although Ali pulled it out in the end, he wasn't thrilled by his performance.

"But I'm still the greatest," he consoled himself. "Because Ken Norton is better than all those other guys I beat when I was young. He's better than Sonny Liston, Henry Cooper, Ernie Terrell, Floyd Patterson and George Chuvalo. He's the best man I ever fought, and that includes Joe Frazier!"[27]

Carried away by his own hyperbole, Ali even claimed that the Cassius Clay who humiliated Sonny Liston would not have beaten Norton. He said his experience allowed him to overcome his stubborn 1973 foe.

Now that he had evened the score with Norton, Ali was asked about a possible shot at Foreman. Muhammad claimed that Foreman would be "easier" than Norton.

Experts disagreed. Dave Anderson of the *New York Times* predicted the following Foreman–Ali scenario: "For a few rounds, Ali might be able to escape Foreman's sledgehammer strength. But not for 15 rounds. Sooner or later, the new heavyweight champion will land one of his sledgehammer punches. For the first time in his career, Muhammad Ali will be counted out."

Considering Ali's two life-and-death struggles against Norton, that scenario seemed sensible.

Distant Shores

After his soul-stirring triumph over Muhammad Ali in 1971, Joe Frazier had found life as the undisputed heavyweight champion a bittersweet experience. Now, in the wake of his disastrous loss to Foreman, Joe was learning that the life of an ex-champ was just plain bitter. For Frazier, the months that followed the "Sunshine Showdown" can best be described as a winter of discontent.

During that time, Frazier regrouped and recuperated while his manager, Yank Durham, tried to secure a rematch with Foreman. More than anything else, Frazier wanted to pay George back for the humiliating defeat the new champion had inflicted. But Foreman was dealing with problems outside the ring, and consequently wasn't available.

When the Foreman rematch failed to materialize, Durham decided to send his fighter back into action against lesser game. Yank could have set Joe up with a designated victim or two to restore Smokin' Joe's confidence. Instead, he signed his man up for a crossroads bout against a young, hungry contender. On July 2, 1973, Frazier stepped into the ring for his comeback bout, a 12-rounder against Joe Bugner, who had put up a brave battle against Ali five months earlier. The location was London, and Frazier, the ex-title holder, was going in as a substitute for another fighter.

Originally, Bugner was scheduled to take on British and Commonwealth champion Danny McAlinden in a triple-title affair, with Bugner's European crown up for grabs as well. However, that applecart was upset on May 14 by a little-known Omaha, Nebraska, heavyweight named Morris Jackson. McAlinden was a crowd-pleasing knockout artist of whom great things were expected, but those expectations took a beating when Jackson flattened the Irishman in the third round.

Although McAlinden was now unavailable, the July 2 date remained open. London matchmaker Mickey Duff pulled off a promotional coup by securing Frazier's services. However, the canny Durham made certain the contract contained a release clause that would allow Frazier to withdraw from the fight if he were offered a Foreman rematch before June 14.

June 14 came and went with no Foreman bout in sight. Thus, Smokin' Joe set his sights on British Joe.

The Bugner fight was as pivotal for Frazier's future as the Norton sequel had been for Ali's. In the wake of his shocking annihilation by Foreman, he realized his effort against Bugner would be thoroughly scrutinized by fans and critics alike. Like Ali, Frazier was determined to squelch any notion that he was finished.

During the course of their careers, Frazier and Bugner had both defeated Charlie Polite, Manuel Ramos, and Scrap Iron Johnson. However, their most respectable common opponent was Ali, who flew to London to watch the fight. Ali predicted a Bugner victory, provided the Briton fought Frazier at the same level of intensity he had displayed against Muhammad in February.

Despite Bugner's respectable showing against Ali, his customary army of detractors was once again out in full cry. Not only did they doubt Bugner's ability to handle a pressure fighter like Frazier, they also pointed out their countryman's history of trouble against shorter fighters.

After winning a dull 15-round decision over 5'11" Rudi Lubbers, Bugner himself conceded that he never looked impressive against smaller opponents. Jurgen Blin and Scrap Iron Johnson were two other sawed-off heavies who had bothered Bugner. Frazier's listed height of 5'11" was often considered generous, but of course he operated at a much higher level than Euro-pugs like Lubbers and Blin.

The pre-flight consensus was that Bugner wouldn't be able to withstand Frazier's non-stop attack. However, when the two Joes met in the ring, Bugner revealed a side of himself British fans had long since despaired of ever witnessing.

Afterward, he said he had trained for Frazier with a new determination, and he "felt good mentally and physically." That confidence showed in his performance.

When the fight started, Bugner made good on his promise to come out fast against Frazier, looking to see if the ex-champ truly was finished, as the rumors would have it. He quickly discovered that Frazier was far from "gone." Smokin' Joe stayed right in front of him, winging left hooks to the head and body.

Although Bugner was as big as Foreman, he was nowhere near George's class as a puncher. Therefore, Frazier was able to work his way inside and fire at will.

The two men fought on fairly even terms over the first few rounds, with Frazier attacking and Bugner counterpunching.

Then Frazier stepped up the pace. In the sixth and seventh, Frazier surged, ripping away at Bugner's midsection. By the eighth, Bugner was bleeding from the nose and cuts over both eyes. And Frazier's features weren't unscathed; his left eye was showing signs of puffiness.

Then came a tenth round that qualified as the most dramatic three minutes of the year. Frazier crashed one of his patented left hooks into Bugner's skull. The Briton crumpled in a heap near a neutral corner.

Frazier thought the Brit was finished. But Bugner proved tougher than Frazier anticipated.

Bugner glanced at his cornermen, who advised him to stay down a few seconds longer. At the count of 9, he rose on legs that were surprisingly steady. Immediately, Frazier pounced in for the kill. But Bugner withstood the punishment.

Then, out of nowhere, Bugner fired two hard rights to the head of Frazier. Smokin' Joe's knees buckled, and the roar of 15,000 spectators was so loud that no one, including the fighters and referee Harry Gibbs, heard the bell that ended the round. Andy Smith, Bugner's manager, had to jump into the ring and inform all three men that the round was indeed over.

The next two frames were anticlimactic, with neither fighter able to finish the other. At the end of the 12th and final round, Frazier sported a closed left eye, and Bugner bore multiple scars of battle.

Referee Gibbs, the only scoring official, awarded the decision to Frazier by 59¼ to 58½ points under the old British scoring system. That score translated to 6–3–3 in rounds, a fair assessment, although some of the partisan crowd greeted it with boos.

After the fight, both men felt they'd been within one good punch of a knockout win in the wild and woolly tenth frame.

In the end, Frazier–Bugner was something of a moral victory for both fighters. Frazier had proven that the Foreman beating hadn't ended his career. And Bugner had, for the moment, at least, erased longstanding doubts that he was capable of waging a blood-and-guts war against a fighter of Frazier's caliber. Despite back-to-back losses to Frazier and Ali, Bugner's fistic stock was rising, as was his approval in the eyes of British fans. "The Bug" had finally displayed "bottom," British term meaning "intestinal fortitude."

Still, some skeptics claimed that the closeness of the fight was explainable more in terms of Frazier's decline than Bugner's prowess. However, in his *London Times* column, long-time Bug-basher Neil Allen wrote: "It would be unfair to Bugner, the man who has at last revealed the flame in his heart, to suggest that the British boxer was fighting a has been."[28]

Bugner came out of the fight with a great deal of admiration for Frazier. He was surprised not only by Smokin' Joe's condition but also the fearsome power of his patented left hook.

On a sadder note, the Bugner fight would be the last time Yank Durham would be in Frazier's corner. The veteran manager/trainer died of a stroke in late August, and the boxing world joined Frazier in mourning. Durham will always be remembered as the man who molded a chubby Philadelphia teenager into the one of the greatest heavyweight champions of all time.

Despite the tragedy of Durham's death, Frazier had fought his way back into the chase for Foreman's title. And Bugner had established himself as a world-class contender. He had gone the distance with both Frazier and Ali, a feat no other fighter would ever accomplish.

But the fire Bugner had shown against the two ex-champs proved only temporary. In his two subsequent 1973 outings, he reverted to his previous dull but effective style, winning decisions over Italian Bepi Ros and a still useful Mac Foster.

Frazier didn't fight again that year. He wanted Foreman or Ali; no one else was worth his while.

As for Ali, he desperately wanted to even matters with Frazier before going after Foreman. But before facing Smokin' Joe again, Muhammad embarked on a foreign excursion of his own.

On October 20, he squared off with Dutchman Rudi Lubbers in Jakarta, Indonesia. The fight had been signed well before the second Norton battle, so Ali was obligated to go through with it only a month after his draining struggle in Los Angeles.

The odds of 4 to 1 in Ali's favor were surprisingly close, given the decidedly modest credentials Lubbers carried into the bout. The odds makers may have believed the Norton wars had exhausted Ali's gas tank. After all, the first Norton fight had come only six weeks after 12 fast rounds with Bugner. And Norton had been a bigger underdog than Lubbers.

Ali paid no attention to the skeptics. Although none of his predictions had come true of late, the former champion couldn't resist the impulse to say he planned on stopping Lubbers in the fifth round.

Despite the havoc indifferent preparation had caused him in the first Norton fight, Ali admitted he was once again having difficulty motivating himself to train. He said he'd put in only 10 days of training for the Dutch champion.

Lubbers, whose only loss in twenty fights had come in January at the hands of Joe Bugner, had been training nine months for Ali. Although he was a durable scrapper, his ring record read more like a "who's that" than a "who's who." The only "name" opponent he had faced was Bugner, who had decisioned him in January.

At 5'11" and 196 pounds, Lubbers posed little physical threat to Ali. Muhammad came in at 217½, five pounds heavier than for Norton, but still a good weight for him.

Despite Lubbers's questionable credibility, Ali as always took the opportunity to build up a weaker opponent and tear down Joe Frazier. In Rudi's defense, Ali guessed that the Dutchman must be good because he was handsome, unlike Frazier and Foreman, whom Ali regarded as "ugly."

And the Ali–Lubbers fight was ugly, too. The predominantly Muslim crowd in Jakarta was understandably pro–Ali, but what they witnessed was more an extended sparring session than a serious fight. As expected, Muhammad pleased his partisans by dominating the action from start to finish. He bloodied Lubbers's nose and banged up his right eye. But the Dutchman lasted the full twelve rounds, marking the third consecutive bout in which Ali had failed to score a knockdown, let alone a stoppage.

Still, Muhammad had won virtually every round, and was so comfortably ahead on points between the tenth and eleventh rounds that he actually leaned over the ropes and gave a short interview to reporters at ringside.

After the unanimous decision in Ali's favor was announced, the ex-champ praised Lubbers's grit and claimed he'd tried his best to knock the Dutchman out. "I'll admit Lubbers was much tougher than I thought he would be," Ali said.[29] Rudi said he'd fought as best as he could, and believed Ali had done the same.

The Ali fight constituted Lubbers's fifteen minutes of fame. He returned to obscurity on the European circuit, losing as many fights as he won.

Despite the ease with which he'd dominated Lubbers, Ali had fought almost one-handed, using his right hand only sparingly throughout the uneven contest. Had he unleashed the right more often, chances are he would have stopped his overmatched opponent.

When asked why he'd relied so heavily on his left, Ali clenched his right fist and said, "I have to save this for Joe Frazier."[30]

But a possible Ali–Frazier sequel, while still intriguing, was no longer the only heavyweight fight the public longed to see. Speculation now focused on George Foreman vs. anybody in the top ten.

Although both ex-champs had recovered a great deal of the ground they'd lost in 1973, they were not the dominant figures they had been at the beginning of the year. Now, they were part of a large crowd of contenders lining up for a shot at Foreman's crown.

That crowd included a not-so-young prospect on the rise and a familiar face embarking on yet another comeback.

The Meteor and the Phoenix

"Is Ron Lyle for real?"

That's the question many boxing fans asked themselves in early 1973 whenever conversation drifted away from Foreman's upset of Frazier. In only two years of professional action, Lyle had blasted his way into just about everyone's top ten.

Although Foreman was often considered the second coming of Sonny Liston, Lyle's early life also paralleled that of the "Big Ugly Bear." Born February 11, 1942, Ron was the third of nineteen children. Although Liston's father, who sired 25 offspring from two marriages, was always depicted as a low-life, Lyle's dad was a Pentecostal minister in Denver, Colorado.

Two of Lyle's brothers followed their father into the ministry. Of all the Lyle children, only Ron got into trouble with the law. At the age of 20, he participated in a gang fight during which a man was shot fatally. Lyle was convicted and sentenced to 15 to 25 years in the Colorado State Penitentiary on a charge of second-degree murder.[31]

The state pen wasn't Lyle's first exposure to institutional life. As a teenager, he spent nine months in a reformatory for burglarizing an ice cream stand.

Lyle's life came close to a tragic ending while he was in prison. In the midst of a fight with a fellow inmate, he was stabbed in the stomach with a rat-tail file. A team of surgeons operated for 7½ harrowing hours, at one point deeming it necessary to remove Lyle's intestines. He was declared clinically dead twice, and 35 pints of blood were needed to save his life.[32]

The grim brush with death proved a blessing in disguise. Lyle emerged from the ordeal with a newfound respect for a man who would ultimately point him in a positive direction.

For some time Clifford Mattux, the prison's recreation director, had attempted to befriend Lyle, but to no avail. Lyle was a gifted, 6'3", 215-pound athlete who had excelled in basketball, baseball, and especially football. Despite his obvious interest in sports, Lyle shunned Mattux as just another "screw," the convicts' derisive term for guards and administrators.

But when Lyle woke up from his operation, the first face he saw at his bedside belonged to Mattux. Lyle was moved to the point of tears. "Mattux was white, and he wore a badge, but he really cared," Ron recalled later. "Right then I decided to be a success."[33]

As Lyle regained his strength, Mattux introduced him to boxing. He mastered its skills as easily as he had every other sport he'd taken up. From the beginning, it was clear that his greatest asset was his punching power.

In 1969, Lyle became eligible for parole. But he was refused on the grounds that boxing was not a viable career choice. Fortunately for Lyle, an organization called the International Boxing League had a local franchise known as the "Denver Rocks." Bill Daniels, chief sponsor of the Rocks, heard about the talented prison heavyweight and took steps to acquire Lyle's services.

When Daniels offered Lyle a side job as a welder, the parole board reversed its decision and Lyle was released on November 9, 1969.[34]

Lyle left prison with a definite mission in mind: to become heavyweight champion of the world. The chances of a fighter embarking on a boxing career in his late twenties and making it to the top were slim at best. But Rocky Marciano had done it in the 1950s, and Lyle was confident he could do it as well. He had already overcome great odds just to reach a point where he had an opportunity to make the attempt.

He enjoyed a short but sweet amateur career, capturing the AAU, IBL, and North American heavyweight titles en route to compiling a 29–4 record.

On April 23, 1971, Lyle made his pro debut, knocking out A.J. Staples in the second round. From there, his rise was nothing short of meteoric. By the end of 1972, Lyle had catapulted his way into contention with an 18–0 record (16 KOs).

The quality of Lyle's opposition was a cut above what one usually finds at the beginning of a prospect's career.

Whereas Foreman had been criticized for feasting on ham-and-egg fighters, Lyle fought tougher foes. He had no choice; unlike the youthful Foreman, Lyle didn't enjoy the luxury of time. He was 29 when he made his debut in a sport known for the brevity of its participants' careers.

Still, some of Lyle's fans thought he was being rushed by his manager, Bill Daniels. In his eighth fight, which occurred only five months into his career, Lyle took on tough Mexican contender Manuel Ramos, who had shaken Joe Frazier during an unsuccessful title challenge back in 1968. Despite the Mexican's edge in experience, Lyle won an easy 10-round decision.

Besides Ramos, the only other man to go the distance with Lyle at this point was veteran trial horse Leroy Caldwell, in Ron's fifth pro outing.

Lyle finished his first year as a pro by demolishing Jack O'Halloran in four rounds and Bill Drover in two. Earlier, Drover had held Joe Bugner to a draw.

In his second fight in 1972, Lyle took on journeyman George "Scrap Iron" Johnson. With 235 pounds packed loosely onto a 5'9" frame, Scrap Iron wasn't much of a physical specimen. But he was a stubborn, durable opponent. Although his humble 16–15–3 record didn't boast any significant victories, Johnson had crossed gloves with many of the best heavyweights of the 1960s and '70s.

Through defeat after defeat, Scrap Iron displayed a champion's heart in a body capable of only mediocre boxing skills. He had gone the distance with the likes of Frazier, Quarry, and Bugner, and lasted into the seventh round before falling to Foreman.

The experts thought Scrap Iron would test Lyle's stamina. But Lyle starched him in three rounds. Following that win, Ron waded through a couple of the usual suspect opponents. Mel Turnbow crashed in seven rounds; Mike Boswell lasted only four. Lyle then flattened former WBA light heavyweight king Vicente Rondon in two.

Then Lyle's first major test came in the person of Buster Mathis. At the time, Mathis had lost only to Frazier, Ali, and Quarry, and many observers believed he would be too talented and experienced for the hard-punching newcomer. But Lyle deposited the 263-pound Mathis on the canvas at 2:58 of the second round, prompting the "Michigan Mastodon" to hang up his gloves for good. In his next fight, Lyle flattened Brazilian Luis Pires in three rounds. It was the first time Pires had ever taken a 10 count.

In his final 1972 outing, Lyle registered his finest victory to date by stopping Larry Middleton in three. With a record of 20–2–1, Middleton was a bona fide contender, ranked #7 by *The Ring*. He had just lost a narrow, controversial decision to Quarry. Before that loss, Larry had ridden a 19-bout winning streak over foes like Joe Bugner, Roy Williams, Bob Stallings, Tony Doyle, and Danny McAlinden.

The three quick and brutal kayo wins over Mathis, Pires, and Middleton opened the eyes of those who hadn't taken the 30-year-old Lyle's chances seriously. As well, Ron had become a celebrity in his hometown of Denver, the site of many of his bouts.

After the Mathis fight, an article in *Sports Illustrated* stated: "In Denver ... Ron Lyle is a living monument to the perfectibility of man.... Among Denverites, he can do no wrong, and it is a foregone conclusion that Frazier's days as champion are numbered."[35]

Through boxing, Lyle, once a bitter, scowling loner with a chip on his shoulder, had blossomed into an outgoing, civic-minded individual. He was chairman of the 1972 Colorado March of Dimes Walkathon, and also worked with a group called "Pardners," which spent time befriending problem children.

In a way, Lyle was following in Sonny Liston's footsteps. For a short time in the mid–1960s, Liston had found solace in Denver. In fact, one of Sonny's best-known quotes was: "I'd rather be a lamppost in Denver than the mayor of Philadelphia."[36]

Lyle was much more than a lamppost in Denver. His seven straight knockout wins in 1972 earned him the World Boxing Association's recognition as "Fighter of the Year."

Now, early in 1973, Lyle was poised to join Foreman, Frazier, and Ali in the division's elite. The only obstacle in his path was Jerry Quarry, whom he was scheduled to fight on February 9.

Although he was only 27, four years younger than Lyle, Quarry seemed to have been around forever. One month after his one-sided 1972 loss to Ali, a discontented Quarry had announced his retirement from boxing. He said he'd lost his desire to fight after seeing his younger brother Mike's frightening knockout defeat at the hands of Bob Foster.

Although Quarry's problems originated far from the ring, his workplace was where they had manifested themselves over the years. An overbearing family and an unhappy marriage weighed heavily on him and affected his performance.

Although his retirement lasted only six months, Jerry used the time profitably, clearing up some of the difficulties that had hindered him in the past. He divorced his wife, and then, in the wisest decision of his professional career, he acquired the training services of Gil Clancy. Quarry also switched his home base from California to New York.

Quarry believed that Gil Clancy was the man who could finally tap his gold mine of talent. He'd felt unfulfilled as a boxer until the partnership with Clancy.

He also said in a January 1973 interview that during his retirement, most of the "hangers-on" in his life had fallen by the wayside. Now his mind was clear. "When my head is clear, nobody can beat me," Quarry stated flatly. Those words were far from an idle boast. Jerry was about to enjoy the most successful year of his professional career.

His first stop on the comeback trail took him to Madison Square Garden, where he met Cliffside Park, New Jersey's Randy Neumann on January 5, 1973. Neumann, the former New Jersey state heavyweight king, was a clever fellow in and out of the ring. Besides sporting a 22–2 pro record, the 23-year-old prospect was also a straight-A student at Farleigh Dickinson University.

So what was a nice, well-educated, middle-class young man like Neumann doing in boxing? Surely a safer, better-paying career was his for the asking.

"To me," Neumann said by way of explanation in 1972, "death is a 9-to-5 job."

Then why bother to pursue a college degree?

The quick-witted Neumann responded that he'd take his diploma and "hang it on the ring post to intimidate my opponents."

Although he didn't pack much of a punch, Neumann was a rugged, resourceful boxer who had recorded wins over Chuck Wepner and a then-unknown Jimmy Young. If trends and omens were to be believed, Neumann should have been a sure-fire pick over Quarry. Both men had made five appearances at the Garden. Quarry's record there stood at 2–2–1, while Neumann had scored a perfect 5–0 mark at boxing's Mecca.

Weighing a sluggish 209 pounds for his return, Quarry lost the first two rounds to the quicker, 197½-pound Neumann. In round three, Jerry shook off the ring rust and started to take control of the fight.

But Neumann kept trying, and it wasn't until the seventh round that Quarry finally caught up with him and unleashed a deadly two-handed attack. As a result, Neumann sustained several deep cuts over his left eye. Ring physician Dr. Edward Campbell advised referee Tony Perez not to allow Neumann to answer the bell for the eighth round, giving Quarry a TKO victory. Although Quarry didn't look like a title threat in his comeback bout, he was pleased to get in the ring time — and to be back in the win column.

Now the way was clear for the Quarry–Lyle showdown. As the date for the bout approached, the similarities between Lyle and former Quarry foe Mac Foster became apparent. Before fighting Quarry, both men possessed big punches, undefeated records, and major media build-ups. Both were also favored to defeat Quarry, and perhaps even end his career.

Jerry had made mincemeat out of Foster in 1970, and he foresaw a similar fate in store for Lyle. Quarry felt that once Lyle realized his big bombs were ineffective, Ron would cave in. He also cited "Garden jitters," a nervous condition that affected some fighters when they appeared at boxing's most hallowed venue. Finally, Quarry believed that Lyle was underestimating his opponent's punching power.

Quarry's assessment looked sound on paper. Still, the odds makers favored Lyle by a slight 7-to-5 margin. The odds makers had not yet realized that 1973 would be a bad year to bet against Jerry Quarry. This time, the "Phoenix" would rise higher than ever from the fire.

From the moment the first bell sounded, Quarry stayed close to Lyle, nullifying the bigger man's punching power. He also hurt Lyle on several occasions, although he never floored him. Lyle was never able to get his offense going, and he hardly laid a glove on Quarry.

"I made a defensive fighter out of him," Quarry said later. "You give me a defensive fighter and I'll pound him."[37]

Jerry pounded Lyle throughout the 12-round affair, exposing Ron's lack of experience in the process. In the end, the decision in Quarry's favor was a mere formality. His comparison of Lyle to Mac Foster was, for the most part, correct. Like Foster before him, Lyle was in over his head against Quarry at this stage of his career.

In another way, though, Lyle was a cut above Foster. Where Foster quickly folded under Quarry's bombardment, Lyle stood up for 12 one-sided rounds. Consequently, few experts wrote him off as a contender. In defeat, he proved himself durable and determined, although his skills clearly needed refinement.

Another encouraging sign was the way Lyle handled his first pro loss. Many fighters who start their careers on winning streaks become devastated psychologically by defeat. Not so with Lyle. Although he was terribly disappointed, it was inconceivable that a lost prize fight compared in any way with his near-death experience on a prison operating table.

In defeat, Lyle displayed a rare graciousness. After the fight, he acknowledged Quarry's masterful performance.

Lyle was back in action two months later, winning a 10-round decision over journeyman Bob Stallings. His next three bouts ended in points victories as well, over Gregorio Peralta, Wendell Newton, and Lou Bailey. Had Lyle's punch deserted him in the wake of the Quarry setback? Ron insisted it hadn't, explaining that he needed the rounds to hone his skills at jabbing and counterpunching.

In his next two 1973 bouts, Lyle returned to his devastating norm, icing Jose Luis Garcia in three rounds and Jurgen Blin in two. He ended the year with a points win over Larry Middleton and a disputed draw with Peralta. Lyle was still a genuine contender. But Quarry had stripped away his aura of invincibility.

As Lyle went back to the drawing board, Quarry paid a visit to the chopping block in his next fight, disposing of James J. Woody in two rounds. Woody was a talented prospect in the mid–1960s, but was near the bottom of his downhill slide when Quarry got around to him on August 31, 1973.

Ten days later, Jerry was in the ring again, this time facing old rival Tony Doyle on the Ali–Norton II undercard. Doyle and Quarry had both been Irish hopes on the rise when they first fought each other in 1965. That time, they drew over 10 rounds. In 1971, Quarry won a decision over Doyle. Since then, Quarry had remained near the top of the ratings while Doyle settled into the role of journeyman.

Now, Quarry wanted a knockout win to prove once and for all that he was the better Irishman. In his third try over eight years, Quarry finally stopped Doyle in four rounds.

Had fate not intervened, Quarry's next opponent would have been one-time conqueror

Jimmy Ellis. Like Quarry, Ellis had gone into semi-retirement after losing to Ali in 1971. Ten months later, the ex–WBA champ returned to the ring. He then spent eight fights plowing through some of the more notorious residents of Palooka City, i.e., Charlie "Emperor" Harris, Reco Brooks, Richie Gosha, and so on. Now it was time to raise the quality of his opposition.

A victory over a balding 27-year-old Earnie Shavers on June 18 would virtually guarantee a Quarry–Ellis fight later in 1973. This was a pivotal fight for both men. Although Shavers was riding a 30-bout unbeaten streak, the Warren, Ohio, slugger hadn't beaten anyone of Ellis's caliber. And Ellis needed to prove he could still beat quality fighters. If he beat Shavers, Quarry would be next. And if he got past Quarry a second time, a shot at Foreman's title beckoned.

Jimmy entered Madison Square Garden in excellent trim, weighing in at 190¾. He hoped to add Shavers's name to his list of early knockout victims. Although he was known more as a boxer than a puncher, Ellis had still scored nine first-round knockouts. But Shavers's credentials in that category were even more impressive. His 45–2 log included 44 knockouts, 15 of them coming in the first round.

Given those staggering statistics, few analysts expected Ellis–Shavers to last very long. A press release from the Madison Square Garden publicity office stated: "The advance word for boxing fans from fight experts on the 12-round heavyweight elimination bout between Earnie Shavers and Jimmy Ellis is get there early and don't turn your head."

The fighters didn't let the experts down. Two minutes into round one, the fistic fireworks exploded. Ellis nailed Shavers with one of his patented short right-hand blows. Earnie retreated to the ropes. Ellis smashed two lefts into Shavers's face, and the Ohioan's legs turned to rubber.

Earnie then managed to spin away from the ropes and stumble to center ring. Ellis charged after him to finish him off. Then Shavers came up with a right uppercut that caught Ellis flush on the chin. The powerful blow sent Jimmy to the canvas for 10 seconds of shuteye. The 10 count came at 2:39 of the round.

The stunning knockout of Ellis established Shavers as a solid entry in the 1973 heavyweight sweepstakes. Fans who loved knockouts were salivating at the very prospect of a nuclear war between Shavers and Foreman. However, Shavers needed a few more wins over top-notch opposition to qualify for a title challenge.

Among the contenders ranked ahead of him, Shavers liked his chances against Quarry. With other contenders tied up in other deals, the match made sense for both men; indeed, tentative contracts had already been signed before the Shavers–Quarry fight. Quarry was to receive $25,000 for the fight, and Shavers $12,000.

However, on the strength of Ernie's one-round blitz of Ellis, the pot was sweetened considerably. Now Quarry would be guaranteed $60,000 against 30 percent of the gate, and Shavers would haul down $40,000 against 27½ percent.

The bout was originally scheduled for July 25, but it had to be postponed when Shavers's jaw was broken in training by sparmate Jeff "Candy Slim" Merritt, a thunderous puncher in his own right. The injury occurred only ten days before the original scheduled date. Shavers's manager, a fellow named Don King, blamed the trainer, Archie Moore, for "putting in his man with a puncher like Merritt with the big fight so close."[38]

Moore, writing an article for *Ring* magazine, revealed that after Merritt landed the blow, "Earnie's lower mandible was laying [*sic*] nearly on his chest, being cracked in two places." Earnie's jaw healed, just as Ali's had, and the fight was rescheduled for December

13. Because both fighters were well established hitters, their encounter was billed as "the shortest 12 round fight in history."[39]

Again, much was at stake for both men. Shavers, who was now ranked #6, needed to prove his win over Ellis was more than just the product of a lucky punch. His manager, a big-talking Clevelander named Don King, said, "If we lose this fight, we go from obscurity to oblivion."[40]

Quarry, on the other hand, had reestablished his credentials for the umpteenth time. In the past, his pattern was to rise to a certain point, only to be knocked back down the ladder. Shavers promised to repeat the pattern.

But Quarry shrewdly predicted that Shavers's wide-open attack would be made to order for a good counterpuncher. "My hands are much faster than his," Jerry said. "I don't profess to be the greatest puncher, but I can hit."

The odds makers agreed with Quarry. For once, the Irishman was installed as the favorite in a crossroads bout, with bookies taking bets on him at 11–5.

A crowd of 14,962 filed into Madison Square Garden to watch a fight guaranteed to be a barn burner regardless of the winner.

Once again, Shavers participated in a one-round shootout. This time, however, Earnie was the one who bit the dust.

Gil Clancy had instructed Quarry to box Shavers. But when the "Black Destroyer" came out bombing, Quarry elected to slug it out.

"He gave me no chance to box," Quarry said later. "Hell, I had to fight him."[41]

Halfway through round one, Quarry hammered eight consecutive shots to Shavers's head. Earnie sagged against the ropes, then staggered in the direction of Quarry's corner. At that point in the Ellis fight, Shavers had fired a magic bullet that rescued him from disaster. This time, though, his guns were empty.

Quarry drove in another combination that dropped Shavers. Although Shavers struggled to his feet before the count of 10, Quarry was on him like a shark on a piece of bloody meat. Although Earnie didn't go down again, referee Arthur Mercante called a halt to the slaughter.

A heartbroken Shavers announced his retirement after the fight. Like countless other fighters before him, including Quarry, he couldn't resist the lure of the ring. He returned five months later to begin a long climb back to respectability.

Quarry had now reached the pinnacle of his career. The "new" Jerry Quarry appeared to be the best Quarry of all. His decisive wins over Lyle and Shavers had overshadowed Frazier and Ali's erratic 1973 performances. He was now in an eminent position to challenge George Foreman.

But Foreman had other things on his mind. For the new champion, life at the top had become one big headache.

Roman Holiday

During his three-and-a-half-year march to the title, George Foreman had fought 37 times, an average of almost a fight a month. But in the seven months that followed his crushing victory over Frazier, Foreman's battles had taken place in the courtroom, not the ring.

Foreman's current troubles had originated back in 1971, when manager Dick Sadler decided it was time to earn some big bucks fast. Accordingly, Sadler struck a deal with Marty Erlichman. Erlichman was the manager of superstar singer/actress Barbra Streisand, and he was also apparently a keen judge of boxing talent.

Erlichman offered Sadler a $500,000 promotional deal. Foreman would receive $100,000 upon signing, then $100,000 in 1972, followed by $25,000 annually for the ensuing 10 years. Some small benefits were included as well, such as personal public appearances with Streisand. In return, Foreman would grant Erlichman half of all ancillary rights for his fights over the next 10 years.[42]

Erlichman was gambling that Foreman was indeed a future champion. Sadler, so it seemed, was gambling that he wasn't. How else could an agreement so disadvantageous to his fighter be explained?

"The deal was made before I knew it was in existence," Foreman said in 1973. "I never wanted to sign that contract. But Dick believed in it so much that even before he told me about it, he had an agreement and took some money. I told him I didn't want to sign, but he said he had accepted the man's money. He was so determined, that I signed. I think that Marty Erlichman just promoted Dick Sadler."[43]

Once Foreman signed to meet Frazier, he demanded a revision of the contract. When the consequent legal wrangling reached a point of absurdity, a disgusted Foreman threatened to forego the title shot and quit boxing altogether.

After some last-minute persuasion by an old friend and advisor named Colonel Barney Oldfield, Foreman decided to go through with the Frazier fight. He also accepted a compromise agreement that would give Erlichman 25 percent of all rights instead of the original 50 percent. After winning the title, however, Foreman went to court in an effort to get the entire Erlichman contract nullified.

Meanwhile, the title-winning triumph in Jamaica had opened a second can of worms for the new champ. It seemed that in order to get the Frazier fight, Sadler had agreed that should Foreman win, he would make his first defense under the promotional banner of Mrs. Ludene Gilliam of Houston. Gilliam wanted a Foreman–Frazier rematch as George's initial defense. An enraged Foreman swore he had no recollection of any such agreement. But Gilliam was able to produce signed contracts.

Thus, no matter who he fought in his first defense, Foreman was legally bound to fight for Gilliam. While the Gilliam and Erlichman cases wound their way through the court system, Foreman's title sat in suspended animation in the same way Frazier's had in 1971, though not for the same reason.

In an eerie parallel to his idol, Sonny Liston, Foreman possessed the biggest money-making title in all professional sports, but wasn't able to squeeze a dime out of it. Liston had fought Patterson for short money, only to see his purses tied up in liens and escrow. "It's not anything like I thought it would be," Foreman lamented. "I'm the champion, but I can't get any fights."[44]

With his career in a shambles due to Sadler's inept management, Foreman refused to renew his contract with his mentor when their agreement expired in the summer of 1973.

"I'll never sign another contract with anyone," Foreman declared. "Dick will always be in my corner. But our agreement will be verbal."[45]

Despite all the legal entanglements, rumors of names, dates, locations, and purses for a Foreman title defense persisted throughout the spring and summer. First there was Ali, then Norton after he upset "The Greatest." Then the names of Quarry and Bugner were mentioned. But nothing came of any of the rumors, and the title remained on ice.

As well, interest in the new champion began to wane. Foreman's behavior didn't help matters. He wasn't an extroverted showman like Ali, but then, who was? On the other hand, Foreman didn't come across as a solid family man like Frazier. Soon after he won the title, Foreman divorced his wife and began an epic round of carousing and womanizing.

Although he was personable at first, Foreman's financial and contractual problems caused him to retreat into surly silence. His hopes of becoming a popular champion were not being realized.

Once the leading contenders lost hope for an immediate title shot, they set about making money and jockeying for position in fights against each other. Ali and Norton signed contracts, and as well Ali had the Lubbers contract in his pocket far in advance of their fight date. Bugner signed with Frazier, and Quarry with Lyle and Shavers.

By the time Foreman emerged from his legal battles, his best opposition was already busy. But Foreman needed money, if not ring action. His legal fees and his expanded championship lifestyle required a heavy cash flow. Foreman had purchased the requisite clothes, cars, and a ranch in Texas where the livestock consisted of lions and tigers, rather than cattle. He needed to fight someone, anyone, soon.

Finally, Sadler announced that unless unforeseen circumstances intervened, Big George's first defense would occur in Tokyo on September 1, against little-known Puerto Rican champion Jose "King" Roman.

Roman wasn't a Murphy Goodwin or Clarence Boone, to name two of the sorrier opponents Foreman had fought before meeting Frazier. But he wasn't a Frazier, either. Despite a credible 43–7–1 record, Roman was at best only a fringe contender, with no wins over rated heavyweights on his resume.

Beginning his career as a light heavyweight in New York City, Roman eventually moved back to his native Puerto Rico and built himself up to 190 pounds. But in the post–Patterson era, any heavyweight who weighed under 200 was "livin' small." Still, Roman was skillful enough to outpoint some of the division's dinosaurs, including 6'6", 250-pound Jack O'Halloran and 6'5", 225-pound Chuck Wepner.

Never one to kill himself training, Roman was a fun-loving, personable sort who, as Frank Iwama wrote in *Sports Illustrated*, "broke training rules at the drop of a glass."

However, after an upset win over Basque strongman Jose Urtain in 1972, Roman realized his career could indeed go somewhere. Accordingly, he became more serious. "He's hungry now," trainer Al Braverman told anyone who would listen.

A pair of quick knockouts over cannon-fodder opponents Charlie Polite and Tony Ventura led Roman to a more important bout against former title challenger Terry Daniels. Daniels had lost three consecutive fights since the Frazier disaster. Roman extended that slide to four with a 10-round decision on November 21, 1972.

A June 28, 1973, knockout of an unknown Elmo Brown lifted Roman to the position of challenging Foreman for the title.

Incredibly, Roman had been on the brink of a title shot before. His manager, Bill Daly, said they had been approached to fight Frazier for the championship in late 1972, but they turned it down on the money issue.

Given massive public interest in such summer spectaculars as Ali–Norton II and Frazier–Bugner, enthusiasm for Foreman–Roman was understandably low. In fact, the WBA refused to sanction the bout because they considered Roman an unworthy opponent.

The WBC, on the other hand, bumped the "King" up to the #10 position in its ratings, supposedly on the strength of Roman's wins over Urtain and Daniels. But neither Urtain nor Daniels was anywhere near the top ten, so Jose's victories over them were scant grounds for advancement.

The ruling by then–WBC President Ramon Velasquez that shoehorned Roman into the top ten was reminiscent of Daniels's great leap upward the year before. As such, it met with internal and external disfavor.

Madison Square Garden matchmaker Teddy Brenner called the decision "Terrible!" He went on to say, "They can rate anybody they want, sanction a fight in a foreign country and then take a trip, with the tab picked up. Just a paid vacation. What do you expect from a bunch of politicians?"[46]

Likewise, Bob Turley, chairman of the WBC ratings committee, put in his two cents' worth. He, too, felt that the WBC president raised Roman into title contention simply to get a free trip to Tokyo.

Others, however, were happy simply to see Foreman in action again, regardless of the identity or quality of his opposition. "I don't care if Foreman's fighting a one-armed Sumo wrestler," Miami promoter Chris Dundee said. "Watch the interest in boxing boom."[47] As if the Ali–Norton rivalry, Frazier's comeback, and the resurgence of Quarry weren't "boom" enough.

Because his contractual problems still hadn't been ironed out, Foreman was taking a legal if not a professional risk in fighting Roman. Ludene Gilliam actually filed an injunction in an attempt to stop the Tokyo title defense. Sadler said he and Foreman would ignore the injunction and go ahead with the fight.

Tokyo fans had been burned by foreign heavyweights once before, when Muhammad Ali and Mac Foster waltzed for 15 rounds in 1972. With Foreman–Roman, they would be burned again, this time with merciful quickness.

Roman and Braverman came into the fight with a sound game plan. Jose would use his superior speed to keep away from Foreman in the early rounds, then strike hard in the late going once the big man had worn himself out. That plan had worked well against Wepner and O'Halloran.

Unfortunately for Roman, Foreman was light years ahead of those two, who were, ironically enough, common opponents for both the title contestants. Roman had outsmarted Wepner and O'Halloran to win decisions. Foreman simply punched their lights out.

Although Roman's weight of 196½ was heavy by his standards, he appeared puny alongside the 219½-pound champion. As the fight commenced, it became painfully apparent that Roman had no business being in the same country as Foreman, never mind the same ring.

Big George wasted little time getting Roman against the ropes, where he unleashed his customary brand of mayhem. Roman hit the canvas at about 1:10 of the first round. Then, inadvertently or not, Foreman hit the challenger while he was still down, a clear violation of the Marquess of Queensberry Rules.

Braverman yelled protests concerning the obvious foul. But the thought of Jose Roman winning the heavyweight title via disqualification never crossed Referee Jay Edson's mind; Foreman wasn't even given a warning. Edson took heat from the crowd and Daly for not penalizing the champ for his infraction. "It's hard to stop a punch once you have started it unless you're a magician or something," Edson reasoned. "It was not a foul."[48]

The groggy Roman struggled to his feet, only to be floored again 20 seconds later. He got up again, and promptly dropped again under Foreman's furious assault. This time, he stayed down for the 10 count, which came at the 2:00 mark of the round.

Afterward, the customary excuses flowed from the loser's camp. In this case, however,

Roman's people had a legitimate grievance. Foreman did hit Roman when he was down the first time. "That's what put him on queer street," Bill Daly complained. "He had dead aim at him with a hook."[49]

Daly was overlooking what was obvious to everyone else: even without the extra punch, Roman would have been annihilated anyway. The Puerto Rican simply didn't possess the endurance necessary to survive Foreman's early-rounds offense.

Roman recovered from the beating and went on to a busy career as a trial horse. Foreman, who stood to earn the easiest million dollars of his career for disposing of Roman, soon learned that his purse would be tied up by the Ludene Gilliam lawsuit. The title he had won so convincingly from Frazier had become a millstone around Big George's neck.

At the end of 1973, there was no shortage of legitimate challengers eager to relieve Foreman of his burden. Seldom had there ever been a year of such intense competition among the top fighters in the division. In the end, however, only two had been eliminated as title threats: Ellis and Shavers.

Jerry Quarry clearly enjoyed the best year of all. His manager, Gil Clancy, made dogged and persistent attempts to secure a title shot for his fighter. At every opportunity, he badgered Foreman and Sadler, hoping to embarrass them into signing a contract. But the Foreman team's assurances were only verbal.

Frazier had shown he was still a formidable fighter. But his victory over Bugner did little to indicate that he could regain his title from Foreman.

Although Ali was able to avenge his defeat at the hands of Ken Norton, it was becoming painfully clear that the skills and reflexes that had carried him to the top in the 1960s were beginning to decline. If he had to struggle to beat Norton, what were his chances against a dreadnought like Foreman?

Norton's two split-decision contests with Ali had established his position in the front ranks of the division. But there were some who continued to question the quality of his chin, an essential asset for any Foreman challenger.

Lyle was still in the running, but the Quarry fight had shown that he had a lot to learn in a short amount of time. He had a puncher's chance against anyone. But he had difficulty landing decisive blows against fighters with any knowledge of defense.

Bugner had done well against Ali and Frazier, but the bottom line was that he'd lost both fights. He was still the youngest fighter in the top ten, though, and had plenty of time to continue his development.

The queue of deserving, competitive contenders was long and restless. In 1974, Foreman would have to fight or get off the pot.

Seven

1974

The Skirmish in the Studio

If 1973 was a year of upsets, transitions, and the emergence of new contenders among the heavyweights, 1974 would be a year of superfights. Over twelve tumultuous months, the division's top five fighters engaged in what amounted to an elimination tournament that left fans gasping for breath by December 31. And on one occasion, a serious altercation occurred outside the ring.

The first of the 1974 star wars was none other than the long-awaited rematch between Muhammad Ali and Joe Frazier. But the sequel to their historic battle of March 8, 1971, had lost much of its earlier significance. Upset losses to Foreman and Norton had cut Frazier and Ali down to size; they no longer stood head and shoulders above the rest of the division.

Both ex-champs had managed to regain credibility by the end of 1973. And they were both legitimate challengers to the crown Foreman wore. But the Ali–Frazier rivalry had a mystique all its own, and when the contracts for their second meeting were finalized, boxing fans rejoiced.

Jack Kent Cooke, who had held the promotional option on an Ali–Frazier rematch since 1971, put together the extravaganza that was billed as "Superfight II" in association with Bob Arum and Madison Square Garden. The depth of Arum's involvement in the promotion was of great interest to many observers. Because Arum was Ali's attorney as well as co-promoter of the fight, the New York State Athletic Commission raised the issue of conflict of interest. One top official stated that it was unethical for anyone to have a stake in both a fighter and a promotion.

Arum did admit to being on the Ali payroll, but contended that it was simply a "fee" arrangement for legal services. He further contended that he had "merely a lawyer-client relationship" with Ali. However, Arum was also president of Top Rank, Inc., and though he was careful not to list Top Rank as the official promoter of Ali–Frazier II, the organization controlled the closed-circuit telecast of the fight. That arrangement automatically linked Top Rank to the promotion.

Arum's role behind the scenes of Superfight II was thought to encompass much more than just the closed-circuit rights. On paper, however, Cooke and the Garden controlled the live fight. Arum carefully kept his name out of the top billing, and made certain that Top Rank was never officially involved in the arena promotion.

Regardless of the overt or covert identity of the promoters, their job was simplified by the very nature of the product they were offering the public. Like their first encounter, Ali–Frazier II virtually sold itself.

Beyond the money they would earn and the satisfaction victory would bring, the two ex-champs were fighting for a virtually guaranteed shot at Foreman's title. Neither man, however, could have been accused of looking ahead to Foreman while they were preparing to fight each other.

There was probably no one on the planet Joe Frazier would have hated to lose to more than Muhammad Ali. As for Ali, he wanted more than anything else to avenge the defeat he had suffered at Frazier's hands. "I lost so much prestige the first time," Ali admitted. "I didn't realize until later what I had lost. Now I want to get it back."[1] Beating Frazier meant as much to Ali as regaining the title that had now been out of his hands for seven years. "I want Joe Frazier," he insisted. "I want to get even with Joe Frazier. If I can fight Frazier, I can quit and feel satisfied. I don't need Foreman."[2]

Professional survival was also on the line. If Ali lost, it would mean the end of his career. He couldn't withstand another setback hard on the heels of his struggles against Norton, and he was well aware of that reality. As for Frazier, a loss would definitely hinder his drive to regain the title. But it wouldn't necessarily spell the end of his career. An Ali win would only square the series; a Frazier win would forever establish Joe's supremacy over the man who called himself "The Greatest."

To Frazier, the second Ali fight was simply a means to an end. His sights were set on the title, and aside from another opportunity to serve Ali another smorgasbord of left hooks, Joe's greatest desire was to get Foreman into the ring again. A win over Ali would guarantee a chance to prove that the slaughter in Jamaica had been a fluke.

For fight fans in general, Ali–Frazier II took on the tone of a sentimental journey. After the upset losses both men had suffered in 1973, few believed they would ever meet in the ring again. Now they were the position of contenders at the crossroads. Most believed that the loser of Superfight II would retire, while the winner would go on to be slaughtered by Foreman.

The conventional wisdom held that on January 28, 1974, the world would witness the magic of an Ali–Frazier grudge match for the last time. By that token, boxing columnist Red Smith described Superfight II as "Auld Lang Syne, and money."

And Smith wasn't the only pessimist. Dave Anderson dismissed the rematch as an "Old-Timer's Night," even though Ali was only 32 and Frazier 30. Comparing the fighters to their 1971 incarnations, Anderson stated: "Their bodies haven't been the same since. And their spirits never again will soar, as they did before the $20 million extravaganza."[3]

Neither Smith nor Anderson doubted the public's genuine interest in Superfight II. However, Anderson attempted to place the widespread appeal of the rematch in perspective, saying that "heavyweights of the stature of Frazier and Ali are almost an endangered species. What they once were is enough to create another multi-million dollar promotion."[4]

Even though the fight didn't match two undefeated heavyweight champions, and even though both fighters had slipped past their peaks, most experts believed their rate of depreciation was fairly even. Thus, despite the cynicism of observers like Anderson, Ali–Frazier II promised to be as intense and competitive as their first unforgettable collision.

Superfight I had earned each participant $2.5 million. For the rematch, the purse guarantees came to only $850,000 apiece. At first glace, that appears to be a substantial drop in revenue. However, both fighters were also guaranteed 32 percent of the closed-circuit income. Once the percentage figures were tallied up, Arum announced that Frazier and Ali had pulled down a whopping $2.6 million each, which totaled $100,000 higher than their 1971 take.

Strategically, the second fight contained just as many intriguing elements as the first. Neither man's style had altered over the intervening years. Ali did promise to increase his work rate the second time around. If nothing else, he had learned that against Frazier, extended periods of inactivity along the ropes would prove both costly and painful.

"I fought his fight last time," Ali admitted. "This time, I'm gonna move, I'm gonna dance."[5] He added, "Sure, I wasted a few rounds in the '71 fight, clowning around, but I won't waste a minute this time."[6]

Frazier saw no reason to change the tactics that brought him success in 1971. "Stay on him, keep him moving back, don't give him the big punch," Joe said in summation of his fight plan.[7]

But Superfight II would mark the first time Frazier had ever stepped into the ring without his mentor and chief tactician, Yank Durham, in his corner. Durham had passed away the previous year. Obviously, Joe would miss Yank's guidance. The question was, would Durham's absence have any bearing on Frazier's preparation or performance?

The answer was an emphatic "No." For anyone who knew boxing, the identity of Frazier's new trainer was a virtual guarantee that Smokin' Joe's career would still be in good hands.

Eddie Futch was one of the most widely respected men ever to be connected with the fight game. Frazier's confidence in Futch was complete, and he was certain that with Eddie's help, he would repeat his victory over Ali.

Of course, Futch and Frazier weren't exactly strangers. Eddie had been working with Frazier and Durham off and on since 1966. And Durham had always told Futch he wanted Eddie to handle Joe's career if Durham passed on. Although he was saddened by the loss of his friend, Futch welcomed the opportunity to work with Frazier full time. In Dave Anderson's book *In the Corner*, Futch called Frazier "the easiest fighter I ever had. When you asked Joe to do something, he did it."

Futch had helped Durham work out the strategy that enabled Frazier to beat Ali in 1971. He also orchestrated Ken Norton's 1973 winning effort against Ali. More than any fighter Ali ever faced, Eddie Futch may have been Muhammad's greatest professional nemesis.

With Futch in his corner, Frazier had good reason to feel confident as the date for the rematch approached. Not only did Smokin' Joe predict another victory; he also vowed: "This time I'll knock him out."[8]

As for Ali, he wasn't about to abandon his trademark on pre-fight verbal warfare. This time, though, his attacks on Frazier didn't have the social and political overtones that marked his 1971 "Uncle Tom" rhetoric. But he continued to maintain, at the top of his lungs, that he was superior to Frazier in skill, speed, looks, and any other quality one could name. Though Ali's criticisms carried less sting in 1974, they still elicited a volatile response from Frazier. Like a tick on a dog, Ali had worked his way under Frazier's skin during the buildup for their first fight. Now, virtually any negative comment Ali might direct Frazier's way was more than enough to heat Joe's blood to the boiling point.

Peter Axthelm of *Newsweek* wrote, in reference to Ali's verbal abuse of Frazier: "Frazier never asked for his uncomfortable role as a foil to the mercurial Ali. He sympathized with Ali when the champion was unfairly exiled from the ring by boxing authorities, and he long endured Ali's doggerel taunts with poise and restraint. Above all, he has always rejected the implication that he should be the white man's standard-bearer against his loud-mouthed Muslim adversary."[9]

With Frazier's tolerance for Ali's antics at an all-time low, the stage was set for a serious, and even dangerous, out-of-the-ring confrontation, courtesy of Howard Cosell and ABC Sports.

As part of the pre-fight hype, ABC set aside an hour-long segment on its weekly *Wide World of Sports* telecast to promote Superfight II. The centerpiece of the segment involved a replay of Ali–Frazier I, complete with running in-studio commentary by Cosell, Frazier, and Ali.

Eddie Futch was opposed to the whole idea. He saw it as nothing more than a golden opportunity for Ali to engage in his usual psychological warfare. Cosell assured Futch that he would be able to defuse any potentially volatile situations. He also promised that Frazier would not be subjected to any verbal abuse from any members of Ali's entourage.

Given Cosell's assurances and Frazier's willingness to participate, Futch grudgingly consented to ABC's proposal. After all, Ali could be adversely affected by having a national TV audience witness his defeat at Frazier's hands.

Still, the wily trainer's initial instinct proved well founded. His misgivings were borne out almost from the beginning of the broadcast.

Instead of creating a cordial atmosphere for the encounter, Cosell appeared to be setting the stage for a confrontation. Rather than sitting between the fighters like a referee, Cosell perched on the extreme right, placing Frazier in the middle and Ali on the left. As well, the promised security was virtually nonexistent. From the background, Ali's brother Rahaman needled Frazier throughout the broadcast of the fight.

Frazier was already inflamed by Rahaman's taunts, so the fuse on Frazier's temper was primed for ignition by Ali. As the tenth round of Superfight I came up on the monitor, the discussion turned to the swelling that had arisen on Ali's cheek. Frazier then made reference to Ali's trip to the hospital after the fight.

"I went to the hospital for ten minutes," Ali shot back. "You went for a month."[10]

Frazier said he was hospitalized only because he needed some rest.

"That shows how dumb you are," Ali sneered. "People don't go to the hospital to rest. See how ignorant you are."[11]

For once in his life, Ali must have wanted to bite his tongue. At that point, like a tidal wave, years of pent-up resentment, anger, and hatred came crashing to the surface. Frazier always detested any negative reference to his intelligence, and when the word "ignorant" spilled out of the mouth of the man he despised above all others, his self-control slipped away. He sprang from his seat and stood over Ali, fists clenched and teeth bared.

"Why you think I'm ignorant?" Frazier growled. "I'm tired of you calling me ignorant all the time. I'm not ignorant."[12]

Ali sat wide-eyed and speechless. If he had intended to rile Frazier, he obviously hadn't counted on such an explosive reaction.

"Why you think I'm ignorant?" Frazier repeated, as if he expected a reply. "Stand up, man...."[13]

Frazier was clearly inviting much more than a discussion. At that moment, Rahaman Ali burst onto the scene. When Frazier turned to see what was happening, Ali lunged from his seat and grabbed Joe's arms. The two men crashed to the floor and wrestled until they were forcibly separated. Then Frazier left the studio.

This was no pre-fight gimmick, at least on Frazier's part. Smokin' Joe was sincerely and royally infuriated. Whether he got in the first blow or the last word, he intended to put Ali in his place once and for all.

"His eyes meant it," Ali said shortly after Frazier had been whisked away. "When he was standing over me, I didn't know what he was going to do. If he landed a hand on me, he could have broken my jaw. I had to get up and hold him."[14]

In Frazier's absence, Ali had no difficulty carrying the rest of the telecast on his own. He even hinted that he may have intentionally provoked a staged imbroglio with Frazier. "It was just the way we rehearsed it," Ali declared. "The code word was 'ignorant.'"[15]

Be that as it may, no one who saw the impromptu wrestling match believed it was rehearsed or staged. Intentionally or unintentionally, Ali had goaded Frazier one time too many. After more than three years of systematically demeaning Frazier, Ali was like a master chemist who knew exactly which ingredients he needed to set Joe off. This time, however, the mixture blew up in his face.

If Ali was the mad scientist responsible for the nationally televised fiasco, then Howard Cosell played the role of an Igor-like assistant. Futch blamed Cosell for the entire incident, and cursed at the broadcaster on the way out of the studio. Most of those in the know concurred with Futch's assessment. The next day, Dave Anderson wrote: "In retrospect, it was all Howard Cosell's fault."[16]

After the dust settled, Ali believed he had gained a psychological edge over Frazier. Others disagreed, saying that the embarrassment Frazier had suffered would harden his attitude, leading to a situation similar to the pre-fight bitterness that had driven Emile Griffith into a merciless rage against Benny "Kid" Paret during their 1962 welterweight title bout. Paret died from the savage beating Griffith inflicted that night.

Speculation and theory aside, the donnybrook in the ABC studio demonstrated beyond the shadow of a doubt that the grudge between Frazier and Ali was genuine. Now a new dimension had been added to the Ali–Frazier mystique. Although their first fight stirred plenty of political passion, their personal animosity was sometimes questioned. This time, the emotions the fighters displayed on *Wide World of Sports* were unmistakable.

Whether or not an advantage was gained one way or the other, Ali was certain the results would be positive at the closed-circuit venues. "Every theater that isn't sold out is selling now," he grinned.[17]

Ticket sales notwithstanding, the incident at ABC had repercussions for both fighters the next day. The scrap had been taped on a Wednesday, and wasn't scheduled to be aired until the following Saturday. Nonetheless, with only newspaper reports as evidence, Edwin B. Dooley and the New York State Athletic Commission fined the fighters $5,000 apiece.[18]

In response to the fines, Red Smith wrote: "Somebody ought to explain to Messrs. Edwin B. Dooley, Manuel A. Gonzalez, and Kenneth N. Sherwood that actors don't get fined for playing a role in New York."[19]

Whether either party intended to pay the fine or not, no more fireworks issued from Ali or Frazier until fight night.

"The Fight," Part Two

As if any more promotional shenanigans were necessary to hype an Ali–Frazier battle, Bob Arum moved the official weigh-in from the morning of the fight, which was on a Monday, to the preceding Sunday afternoon. His strategy was to have the weigh-in televised so that the few remaining fence sitters could be swayed into buying a closed-circuit ticket.

However, the show operated under a bit of a handicap. To avoid a repeat of the disaster at ABC, the fighters were weighed separately. Consequently, the atmosphere made for rather serene television. "It is doubtful," wrote Red Smith, "that the network weigh-in sent customers off buckety-buckety to the theater outlets. Captain Kangaroo delivers better entertainment five days a week."[20]

Despite the blandness of the circumstances, the condition of the two finely-tuned athletes spoke louder than words. Even the critics who believed both fighters' better days were behind them couldn't deny the effects hard training had produced.

Ali scaled a lean 212 pounds, and Angelo Dundee was positively giddy over the shape Muhammad was in. "It's 1964 all over again," Dundee crowed. "The champ's at his old weight...."[21]

As he had for the second Norton fight, Ali had secluded himself in his "Fighter's Heaven" training quarters at Deer Lake, Pennsylvania. There, he lived a Spartan life devoid of the frills readily available to those of his economic means. He chopped down trees, ate fresh food, and ran up and down the mountains, breathing clean country air as he went.

Even his water came fresh out of a pump. "I've been drinking well water," Ali stated. "Frazier's been drinking chlorine."[22]

Frazier had indeed remained in the city. But he made his own sacrifices as well. In his Philadelphia gym, Smokin' Joe trained as never before in an effort to excise a tick called Ali once and for all. The results of his labors were revealed when he shed his robe and displayed a physique that matched the 209 pounds of muscle he carried into the ring on March 8, 1971. At the weigh-in, he was solemn yet sincere in his desire to knock Ali out.

Ali wanted a knockout, too. He wasn't predicting a round, but he did declare it was his patriotic duty to stop Frazier early. Facetiously, he said: "We have an energy crisis. I got a call from Washington to cut this fight short to kind of help things out."[23]

Bettors wagering on Superfight II had several factors to consider. Almost everyone agreed that both fighters were past their prime, with neither further "gone" than the other. In Ali's favor was the matter of activity. In the three years since their initial meeting, Frazier had gone to the post only four times, while Ali had seen action on 13 occasions. Frazier doubted that Ali's busy schedule would be of benefit, though it was generally acknowledged that a busy fighter was a sharp fighter.

The downside was that Ali's high volume of fighting and training were having a detrimental effect on the fighter's hands. Rumors concerning the fragility of Ali's right hand had been running rampant for quite some time, and had intensified following Ali's sparing use of the right against Rudi Lubbers.

As well, his nominal use of the hand during his preparation for Superfight II had caught the media's attention. Another detail that hadn't escaped the watchful eyes of the press was the Theraffin Ali smeared on his hands before wrapping them each day in the gym. Theraffin is a waxy substance commonly used to relieve inflammation.

Dundee tried to dispel the concerns about Ali's use of the right in training: "Oh, the champ's the worst gym fighter in the world. What's he got to use his right for? He's been doing this 20 years. He knows what he can do."[24]

Dr. Edwin Campbell, a physician with the New York State Athletic Commission, seemed surprised when he caught wind of Ali's Theraffin treatments. He characterized Theraffin as "an astringent. It's supposed to be used to stop inflammation. I know that Ali's had problems before with the cartilage around his right knuckle, but I hadn't heard of anything lately."[25]

Campbell vowed to X-ray Ali's right hand at the pre-fight physical. The rumor mill's theory was that Ali had injured his right hand during the second Norton fight. In reality, however, Ali had been experiencing pain in both hands since the period leading up to the first Frazier fight.

Ali insisted he could handle Frazier with one hand, his left. Now a new element of intrigue piqued observers' interest. If Ali's right hand was indeed as delicate as reports indicated, it was doubtful he could hold off Frazier one-handed. Good as Ali was, history had yet to produce a heavyweight capable of a one-handed victory over Smokin' Joe. Even Foreman needed both hands to club Frazier into submission.

Were Ali's hand problems fact or fiction? Muhammad wasn't about to reveal the answer to that riddle. He believed the questions concerning his hand added an interesting twist to the fight.

"The mystery hand," he intoned. "Can it hold up? Is it really injured? That's the surprise. A big, colorful production."[26]

As for Campbell's promised X-ray, it showed nothing, although it was suspected Ali was suffering from bursitis.

Despite the speculation the Ali's hand stimulated, odds makers installed Ali as a 7-to-5 favorite in Superfight II. In the first fight, Frazier had been the favorite. As expected, the rematch generated enough interest to have long since sold out the Garden: 20,748 fans paid $1,053,688, a record gate for an indoor, non-title bout.[27]

As the moment of truth approached, pride dictated something of a standoff as to which fighter would be first to enter the ring. Generally, the champion enters the ring last, thus allowing the honor of a grand, regal arrival. Also, the last man in the ring generally enjoys a psychological advantage, forcing his opponent to sweat it out until he deigns to emerge from the dressing room.

It is doubtful, however, that professionals of the caliber of Ali and Frazier would be affected by such a ploy. For the rematch, both were ex–world champs, so the protocol of ring entrance shouldn't have applied. However, Ali did hold the North American Boxing Federation title, which he had won after stopping Jimmy Ellis in 1971. He lost and regained that title in his two 1973 battles against Norton, and it was at stake in the second Frazier fight.

Still, each fighter's prestige was so immense that the NABF belt was reduced to insignificance. Because Frazier won their first fight and had held the world title more recently, he was given the honor of entering the ring last.

The slight, such as it was, had little apparent effect on Ali as he climbed between the ropes. Through Frazier's entrance, the introductions of celebrities, and the instructions of Referee Tony Perez, "The Greatest" focused completely on the task at hand. His serious demeanor contrasted markedly with his 1971 antics.

When the first bell rang, both fighters moved directly toward each other. The blueprint of the fight was established in its first few moments. Ali fulfilled his promise to stay on the move, and Frazier quickly jumped into his role as the aggressor. This time, though, he found his foe to be much more elusive. Ali danced from side to side, circling the ring and firing rapid combinations at the ever-pursuing Frazier.

On the rare occasions that Frazier worked his way inside, Ali grabbed Joe behind the neck and pulled him in closer, thus nullifying the shorter man's offense. The tactic wasn't pretty, but it worked.

In the second round, Frazier tagged Ali with a left hook. Muhammad came back with a chopping right hand to the head, and Frazier stumbled backward. In a flash, Ali unleashed a flurry of blows that drove Frazier against the ropes. Joe was more hurt at that moment than he'd been during the entire fifteen rounds of Superfight I. Then Perez stepped between the fighters to signal the end of the round.

Although no bell had sounded, Perez believed he had heard someone at ringside shout "Time." The fighters were on their way back to their corners before Perez realized the round wasn't really over. He then waved Ali and Frazier back into a few more seconds of action; then the bell rang.

Perez's miscue had gotten Joe off the hook. Given Frazier's proven ability to absorb anything Ali could dish out, it was doubtful that he was in any serious danger.

Still, if Ali could have landed a few more punches, ...

Over the next two stanzas, Ali continued to stick and move. Frazier dutifully absorbed Ali's long-range sniping and continued to move forward, never allowing the bigger man a chance to rest. Although Joe did manage to connect occasionally, Ali was clearly outscoring him. Undaunted, Frazier maintained the pressure, hoping it would pay off in later rounds.

By the end of the fourth, both men had proven the critics wrong. Superfight II was far from an "Old-Timer's Night." So far, the level of action and intensity was on a par with that of their first encounter, keeping everyone in the Madison Square Garden crowd at the edge of their seats.

Well, almost everyone. During the interval between the fourth and fifth rounds, a massive, well-dressed spectator rose from his ringside seat and departed the building. When asked why he was leaving, the spectator, whose name was George Foreman, responded, "Because I was bored."[28]

George should have stuck around; he might have learned something.

In the fifth round, Frazier switched tactics. Unable to reach Ali's head, he began digging to the body. Ali continued to hold. Both Frazier and Futch complained to Perez about Ali's clutching and grabbing, but to no avail. Still, Frazier was slowing Ali down and smothering the quicker man's offense.

By the seventh, Frazier had closed the gap in points. He opened the round with a thudding hook to Ali's jaw. Joe seemed the fresher of the two at this stage, and he decided to steal a page from Ali's book. Dropping his hands, he taunted Ali, daring him to take a swing. Ali obliged. Frazier, however, came back with harder shots of his own.

The eighth was also a good round for Frazier. Ali was now a much more stationary target. But he had learned his lesson from the first fight. Instead of clowning or throwing pitty-pat punches, Muhammad held on whenever he could. His clinching saved him from the kind of damage that left him vulnerable back in 1971.

Before the end of the eighth, the action heated up when Ali bombarded Frazier with a combination in center ring. Joe lashed back with a rare overhand right that landed flush on Ali's jaw. The unexpected blow sent Ali spinning into the ropes as the bell ended the round. With only four frames remaining, it was anybody's fight. But the momentum appeared to be all Frazier's.

Joe was now supremely confident, grinning and bouncing in his corner as he awaited the bell for round nine. He should have remembered that the ninth was Ali's best round in their first fight. A series of rapid-fire combinations from Ali quickly wiped the sneer from Frazier's face. The sheer volume of Ali's punches prevented Frazier from getting inside.

Although Frazier weathered the storm, Ali had regained control of the fight. And Joe's face was beginning to display the effects of the myriad of blows Ali landed.

Ali fought flat-footed in the tenth, but still managed to stay out of danger. But Frazier took the round on two of the judges' cards on the strength of a solid left hook and a late barrage of body blows.

Despite the intensity of the combat, both fighters found their second wind in the eleventh. In the first fight, this was the round in which Ali was almost knocked out. This time, Muhammad absorbed Frazier's body punches, then riveted his own shots to Joe's face.

Going into the 12th and final round, Ali appeared to have edged ahead on points. Still, Dundee sent Ali into the fray saying that he needed a knockout.

Undoubtedly, Frazier was thinking the same thing. The rivals met in mid-ring like a pair of barbarians. Frazier trapped Ali on the ropes and went to work like a lumberjack cutting down an oak tree. Muhammad wasn't about to take that kind of punishment, and he managed to move back to center ring.

Still pursuing, Frazier crashed a left hook off Ali's chin, then resumed his body attack. Moving away, Ali summoned up the energy to shoot stinging blows to Frazier's swollen features. Finally, the bell ended their second confrontation.

When they separated, the rivals stared at each other for a moment. Then they turned and walked back to their corners. There was no embrace between them; no kind words; no gentlemanly slap on the back.

Their professional respect for one another had undoubtedly been enhanced by the twelve grueling rounds they had just endured. Yet neither was at a point where he could drop his guard and approach the other with a gesture of friendship.

As the fighters and the crowd awaited the decision, most were aware of the degree of subjectivity involved in judging a close contest between a boxer and a slugger. Those who favored aggression would vote for Frazier, who rarely took a backward step and appeared to have landed the harder punches. And Ali had the vote of those who were more impressed by sheer volume of punches landed. To make matters more difficult for the judges, Ali-Frazier II featured several shifts in momentum, with no single dramatic moments like the knockdown that occurred in the fifteenth round of the first fight.

On this night, the scoring of Judges Tony Castellano and Jack Gordon, along with that of Referee Perez, was unanimous in favor of Ali. Perez, the man closest to the action, gave Ali his vote by a hair, scoring it 6–5–1.

Perez became the focus of a storm of post-fight criticism. Generally, the "phantom bell" incident in the second round was written off as human error. Still, many critics, including Eddie Futch, weren't so understanding when it came to Perez's failure to prevent Ali from holding Frazier behind the head. In explanation of his handling of the fight, Perez said, "The only violation is if you hold and hit at the same time. Ali was holding, but he wasn't hitting."[29]

For Ali, the taste of victory was doubly sweet because he had vindicated himself over his arch-rival. He could now boast that he had beaten every man that he'd ever faced.

Indeed, the career many had proclaimed finished when Ali lost to Norton 10 months earlier had undergone a remarkable rejuvenation. Regardless, the nay-sayers couldn't be silenced.

Failing to appreciate the arduous pace the fighters had set throughout the twelve rounds, many in the media considered the fight competitive but stale. They claimed the rematch lacked the ferocity of the first fight, and cited the deterioration of the participants' skills as the reason.

On the surface, that observation had some validity. The fight did lack the blood-and-thunder fervor of the initial meeting. But the reason for the change had little to do with any erosion of skills or talent. The rematch was tamer because Ali fought a more intelligent, defensive battle. Unlike the first fight, in which he needlessly soaked up punishment from Frazier, Ali avoided danger in the rematch by utilizing steady movement and clinching whenever Frazier pressed in.

Those tactics neutralized much of Frazier's offense and resulted in a match that in many ways substituted strategy for excitement. Yet the constant changes in momentum created uncertainty once the judges added up their scorecards.

At ringside, Red Smith and Dave Anderson both believed Smokin' Joe deserved the nod. The pro–Frazier observers felt that Joe's aggression should have carried the day.

Naturally, Frazier felt he had won. But he refused to make any excuses.

Judging solely on the basis of the combatants' appearance at the post-fight press conference, Frazier looked like a one-sided loser. Dark glasses couldn't hide the huge lump that protruded from the right side of his face, stretching from forehead to hairline. His eye was virtually closed and his face seemed painfully sore.

Joe's wife, Florence, was hoping her husband would retire, but her pleas fell on deaf ears. Frazier felt satisfied with his showing, if not the decision, and saw no reason to hang up his gloves just yet.

Frazier fought well against Ali, even though he didn't win the fight. In fact, he had now lost two of his last three ring encounters. Now he was eager to avenge both those defeats. Not only did he continue to seek a rematch with Foreman; now he wanted a third crack at Ali.

"I want him again," he said of his rival. "One more time."[30]

Some promotional interest was expressed in an immediate rubber match. But Foreman–Ali was the fight Joe Public really wanted to see. As the wheels for that promotion began to turn, Joe Frazier's career was left in a temporary state of limbo.

The Fracas in Caracas

Superfight II started the year in grand style. Now it was time for George Foreman to remind boxing fans who the heavyweight champion really was. March 26 marked the date of Big George's first legitimate title defense. His opponent: Kenny "The Jawbreaker" Norton. If George got past Norton's challenge, a mega-bucks fight with Ali beckoned on the horizon.

The most fascinating aspect of Foreman–Norton was that it was the first major heavyweight title fight of the 1970s that didn't include either Frazier or Ali (Foreman–Roman doesn't count). By now, though, Foreman and Norton were superstars in their own right, and their pairing generated as much public interest as the Ali–Frazier reprise.

In his short title tenure, Foreman had become the Magellan of boxing, winning his title from Frazier in Jamaica and defending it against Jose Roman in Japan. Now he was set to tangle with Norton in Caracas, Venezuela.

Foreman wasn't necessarily a globe-trotter by inclination. He was simply avoiding the web of contractual disputes that would ensnare him if he defended his title in the United States. As it was, Foreman still hadn't received a penny of the purse he had earned in the Roman fight. Financially, he would have been better off hocking his championship belt at a pawn shop.

The contractual mess Dick Sadler had led him into was the principal reason behind Foreman's inactivity. Considering his bleak fiscal outlook, a healthy payday he could get his hands on was imperative. But scarcity of cash wasn't his only motivation for accepting the Norton fight. Foreman was coming under increasing pressure from boxing's governing bodies to defend his title against a legitimate challenger. He had been champion more than a year, but had racked up only one defense.

Because the World Boxing Association refused to sanction the Roman fight, in that organization's eyes Foreman had not yet defended his title. So the WBA issued an ultimatum. "They sent me a letter," Foreman revealed, "stating that action would be taken unless serious negotiations began immediately toward the defense of my crown."[31]

Accordingly, in December 1973 the Foreman team began to look for a qualified challenger to face their dreadnought early in 1974. With Frazier and Ali tied up in Superfight II, only two logical and lucrative options remained: Jerry Quarry and Ken Norton.

Foreman chose Norton, much to the indignation of Quarry and his manager, Gil Clancy. The feisty Clancy issued written complaints, arguing that since Quarry had beaten Ron Lyle and Earnie Shavers while Norton had lost to Ali, Jerry was the more qualified contender.

Still, Norton's performance in his two fights with Ali had earned him more than sufficient credentials for a title challenge. As well, Clancy conveniently forgot that Norton's record against Ali was 1–1, with both fights ending in split decisions. In contrast, Quarry's Ali log stood at 0–2, both losses coming by stoppage.

Although some fighters lose their competitive drive or hunger once they become champion, Foreman's financial difficulties had given him a different perspective. The richest title in sports had yet to parlay itself into bundles of cash, but Big George was still determined to hold on to it.

For all his bumbling outside the ring, Dick Sadler also knew the value of the title, and he took every precaution to ensure that Foreman would hold onto it as long as possible. Once the Foreman entourage arrived in Venezuela, Sadler demanded an American referee for the Norton fight.

His reasoning was straightforward. Foreman's success depended partly upon his ability to shove his opponents into ideal punching range, as he did in the Frazier fight. Sadler believed an American referee would be more lenient toward the champ's roughhouse tactics. After the inadvertent swipe George took at Roman while he was down, Sadler was determined not to risk a loss on a foul at the hands of some narrow-minded referee who might interpret the Marquess of Queensberry Rules too strictly.

However, the Venezuelan boxing commission proved just as stubborn as Sadler, and refused to bend on their demand for a local referee. The impasse continued until the morning of the fight, when Foreman suddenly began to limp along the streets of Caracas and complain of a pinched nerve in his knee. The "injury" threatened to scuttle the fight and sink the promoters' investments.

Catching the true cause of Foreman's mysterious malady, the Venezuelans engaged the services of Jimmy Rondeau, an American referee who happened to be in town at the time. Then, miracle of miracles, Foreman's knee healed and he was ready to fight.

Like Frazier–Foreman the year before, Foreman–Norton looked interesting on paper. A matchup of two of the biggest, strongest, hardest-hitting heavyweights in modern boxing history should have yielded action at least on a par with the crowd-pleasing performance Ali and Frazier had recently provided.

In the buildup to the bout, Norton talked a good fight, saying that if Foreman used his pushing tactics on him, Ken would put a dent in Big George's protective cup. However, like his old buddy Frazier, Norton represented another example of the wrong style at the wrong time. Against a back-pedaling boxer like Ali, the naturally aggressive Norton was in his element. As long as Norton could move forward, he could comfortably and effectively control the pace of a fight.

But a strong puncher, even one as frail-looking as Jose Luis Garcia, who had the ability to back Norton up, could nullify Ken's offense. Not only was Foreman a strong puncher; he was also one of the few fighters in the division who could out-brawn the muscular Norton.

To most observers, the Garcia loss was a fluke rather than an indicator of a chink in Norton's armor. Based on his performances against Ali, Ken was given an excellent chance to dethrone the untested champion. All Norton had to do was make it past the first two rounds.

Ali, for one, fully expected Norton to win. In fact, only hours before Norton entered the ring in Caracas, Ali received confirmation that if Ken pulled off an upset, he would replace Foreman in a proposed multi-million dollar September showdown against Muhammad.

Ali was in Caracas as part of the broadcast team for the fight. The moment he heard the news, he scurried to Norton's hotel to let Ken know what was going on. Unfortunately, Norton had already departed for the stadium.

In his book *The Greatest*, Ali contended that if Norton had found out about the big payday that awaited him, he would have fought a much more focused fight against Foreman. "I still think if he had known earlier, I would have fought Norton, not Foreman, in Zaire," Ali wrote.

Ali's speculations aside, it is doubtful that news of any kind would have helped Norton in the ring against Foreman. Ken was a world-class contender, but he didn't possess the style or the chin to stand up to a wrecking machine like Foreman.

As Norton stepped into the ring, it was obvious that he was tense. But no one knew just how nervous he was until opening bell clanged.

As Foreman treated Norton to a Liston-like glare during Rondeau's instructions, the physical disparity between the fighters was startling. Norton's well-chiseled 212¾-pound physique actually looked puny next to Foreman's 224¾-pound, fat-free bulk.

From the opening bell, Foreman stalked his prey with the patience of a hunter. Norton moved and landed the occasional left jab, but he looked tight and his punches lacked snap. Midway through the round, Big George picked up the pace and began to attack Norton's well-defined abdominal muscles. Ken continued to retreat, but it was obvious that he couldn't "float like a butterfly."

As awkward as Norton looked when he was on the attack, he appeared positively clumsy moving away from Foreman. The stiff right leg that anchored his offense was now impeding his backward motion, making him an easy target for Foreman's pile-driver blows.

To an idle observer, nothing much was established in the first round other than the fact that Norton stayed on his feet. To Foreman, however, the first round told him everything he needed to know about Ken Norton.

In the second round, Foreman marched forward like a man on a mission. He effectively cut off the ring and began to muscle Norton into the ropes. As Ken tried to get away, Foreman hauled off and hit him with a long, sweeping right hook. The moment that blow detonated against Norton's jaw, the fight was over, for all practical purposes.

Ken's legs wobbled and his eyes took on a glassy look. Foreman, the consummate finisher, blasted him with three more rights to the head. Norton fell backward, landing on the bottom rope. Referee Rondeau gave him a standing eight count, then Foreman rushed in with a right to the body and a right to the head. Once again, Norton bounced off the bottom rope.

Amazingly, the dazed Norton got up so quickly that Rondeau didn't bother to issue a count. The referee actually pushed Norton back into action. This time, Foreman met him with two left hooks and a shattering right uppercut. As the defenseless Norton teetered, Foreman caught him with another right. Then a short left came close to tearing Norton's head off.

Ken fell a third time. Valiantly, he attempted to pull himself up for more punishment. But his knees had turned to Jell-O, and Rondeau wisely called a ceasefire to spare Norton from certain annihilation.

The drubbing Norton took did as much damage to his professional reputation as it did to his body. For the entire Norton team, the fight had turned into a disaster from every conceivable standpoint. A matchup that was supposed to have been competitive had turned into just another early-round rout by Foreman. It didn't seem to matter whether a top fighter or a mediocre one challenged Big George; the outcome remained the same.

"The fight was awfully disappointing," Norton's co-manager, Art Rivkin, admitted. "Kenny didn't do much of anything."[32]

But the worst wasn't over yet. When the fighters and their entourages went to the Caracas airport to fly home, they were forcibly detained until they paid an 18 percent non-residence tax on their purses. Promoter Hank Schwartz had already returned to New York and couldn't be reached.

Both camps were miffed at Schwartz, who had assured them that the Venezuelan government had waived the tax as an incentive to lure the promotion to Caracas. However, in the period between the agreement and the fight date, a new government had taken power. And the new government refused to honor the waiver agreed to by its predecessor.

As a result, Norton was stripped of $85,000, and Foreman was forced to hand over an astounding $241,000! Both fighters were detained in Caracas until they coughed up every last dime.[33]

The widely-traveled Foreman said that he'd never been treated so shabbily in any other country. As Foreman's entourage was turned away from the airport, the champ felt that they were in serious danger of being shot. Although Big George had looked like a Superman in the ring against Norton, he knew he was far from bulletproof.

Norton's team suffered a further indignity when co-manager Bob Biron was left with a $4,000 hotel bill, an indemnity that is customarily taken care of by the promoter. "No doubt about it," an angry Biron fumed. "We were railroaded! This whole thing was a story of broken promises and unpaid bills."[34]

Eventually, both fighters made it home in one piece. Norton wanted to forget the Caracas experience altogether. As for Big George, although he left South America a little lighter in the wallet than he had anticipated, his aura of invincibility now shone brighter than ever. He had chewed up the only two men to defeat Muhammad Ali and spat them out in two rounds apiece.

Since Foreman was only 26, and heavyweights tend to mature later than fighters in lighter divisions, a title reign spanning the rest of the decade didn't seem out of the question. Some boxing purists scoffed at Foreman's brutish tactics. But no one could dispute the results: a 40–0 record with 37 knockouts.

Dick Sadler summed up the boxing world's opinion of Foreman when he boasted: "I have created a monster!"[35] Foreman wasn't loath to embellish his menacing mystique. When asked what nickname he thought he might like to go by, Foreman issued a deadpan reply: "The Executioner."

Now it was Ali's turn to try to bring the monster down. Not many people thought he could do it, but they were certainly willing to pay through the nose to see him make the attempt.

Foreman–Ali was the fight the public wanted to see. Many millions of dollars sat ready for the taking. Big Question #1 was, where would the next superfight occur? And Big Question #2 was, who would promote it?

The answers to both those questions were as unexpected as the outcome of the fight.

Up in Smoke

Following Superfight II, the conventional wisdom decreed that Joe Frazier was on his way out, regardless of the narrow margin by which Muhammad Ali had defeated him. Many observers believed that the internal fires that kept Joe "smokin'" earlier in his career had diminished to an ember. At the early age of 30, it seemed that the undisputed, unstoppable champion was on the verge of becoming a big-name "opponent" for the division's younger guns.

Many of Frazier's admirers hoped he would avoid such a sad fate. In an article titled "The End of the Road," *Newsweek* sportswriter Pete Axthelm paid tribute to Frazier, but also urged Smokin' Joe to retire. "For the sting is gone from Joe's once-savage left hook and the smoking speed has deserted his fists," Axthelm wrote poetically. "Now he is left with only his fierce fighting courage and a personal dignity that has grown even more striking in defeat.... It is time for Joe Frazier to take his considerable fortune and his hard-used 30-year-old body and walk away."

Axthelm's view was echoed by many who believed Frazier had given too much of himself in both the Ali fights, and had too much taken out in the Foreman debacle. While Axthelm and other experts were busy penning Frazier's professional obituary, others waxed enthusiastic over the resurrection of another holdover from the 1960s: Jerry Quarry.

Quarry's storybook 1973 comeback had convinced his army of supporters that a title was close at hand. In his wins over Neumann, Lyle, and Shavers, the Irishman had displayed a degree of desire and conviction that was conspicuously absent earlier in his career. With the shackles of a bad marriage and a domineering family finally cast aside, Quarry had rampaged through his opposition like a man possessed. Now he had firmly established himself as a prime contender for Foreman's crown.

But then it seemed Quarry had always been a contender for *somebody's* crown.

James Tuite described the "new" Quarry as a "renascent Californian purged of his Freudian restraints." Others were satisfied merely to say Quarry was a damn good fighter.

With his career cruising in high gear, Quarry and Gil Clancy believed they deserved an early 1974 shot at the title. But Foreman signed to fight Norton in March, and Ali's win over Frazier had set up a title fight for "The Greatest" later in the year.

Those moves convinced Quarry and Clancy that they were being frozen out of the title picture. Clancy had verbally assaulted Foreman the year before, accusing him of "ducking" Quarry. There was also a story going around that Quarry had beaten the stuffing out of Foreman during a sparring session that occurred in 1968, long before George turned pro. Since then, Foreman had supposedly vowed to steer clear of Quarry.

Although the truth of the sparring story may never be known, it is doubtful that a man who had scored a total of nine knockdowns against Frazier and Norton and come to believe in his own myth of invincibility would feel intimidated by Quarry. As an amateur, Foreman had also sparred with Sonny Liston and suffered no long-term psychological effects from the experience.

Opinion on the outcome of a Foreman–Quarry fight swung between two extremes. On the one hand, it was thought that Jerry was just too small to stand up to the kind of bombardment Big George was certain to unload. However, Quarry's greatest victories had come against huge, hard-hitting sluggers like Mac Foster and Ron Lyle, not to mention Shavers, who was thought to be a better puncher than Foreman. Quarry had taken the best those giants had to offer, then came back to destroy them.

Could he have done the same to Foreman? It was beginning to look as though the answer to that question would never be known, much to Quarry's chagrin.

With Foreman tied up for the foreseeable future, a frustrated Quarry turned his sights on Ali. He insisted that Muhammad had an obligation to fight the "new" Quarry, with the winner to get the shot at Foreman. Although his rationale was shaky at best, Quarry continued to hound Ali for a third match.

Never one to duck the chance to pick up a few hundred grand against a fighter he had already beaten twice, Ali accepted Jerry's challenge and set Bob Arum to work on securing the promotion. The grapevine soon indicated that Ali–Quarry III was set for May 6, 1974, at Madison Square Garden.

Unfortunately for Quarry, the grapevine's information proved faulty. The fight fell through because Ali's brain trust did not want him to jeopardize a guaranteed title bout against Foreman. Left in the lurch again, Quarry bitterly complained to anyone who would listen that the top heavyweights were intentionally avoiding him.

Some of the seamier elements among Quarry's fans even raised the specter of "reverse racism," conjuring up a conspiracy among black contenders to keep the title out of the "White Hope's" hands. Quarry himself believed he was being squeezed out. "I say it's a black conspiracy," Quarry declared. "They're trying to keep me away from the title, from making a decent payday. I'm talking about three black fighters—George Foreman, Ken Norton and Muhammad Ali!"[36]

Anyone who understood the economics of boxing dismissed that theory out of hand, knowing that a good white heavyweight was a highly marketable commodity. It was circumstance, not color, that stymied Quarry's mid-'70s title aspirations.

Then Quarry's old friend Joe Frazier stepped into the breach. After a quick round of negotiations, the two camps agreed on a June crossroads bout at Madison Square Garden. The winner would be guaranteed a shot at the Foreman–Ali victor. And the loser would have to seriously contemplate retirement.

Since Quarry had injured his hand during his December 1973 blitz of Earnie Shavers, he hadn't stepped into the ring for several months. Therefore, a tune-up bout seemed advisable to prime Jerry for the Frazier fight, which was certain to be a war regardless of the winner.

Quarry's sacrificial lamb turned out to be a native New Yorker named Joe Alexander. A virtual novice with a sparse 7–3 record, Alexander at least offered punching power. In his last fight, he had starched a slipping Jose Luis Garcia in one round.

When the pair met in Uniondale, New York, on May 8, Alexander came within seconds of scoring an amazing upset. When the bell for the first round sounded, Alexander stormed out of his corner and quickly deposited Quarry on the seat of his shorts. More shocked than hurt, Quarry got up and weathered the storm over the rest of the round. Realizing that the New Yorker was too dangerous to play around with, Jerry coolly dispatched Alexander in the second round.

After his brief flirtation with fame, Joe Alexander returned to the obscurity from which he had come.

Now the stage was set for Frazier–Quarry II, the third of 1974's superfights. For the first time in his career, Frazier was facing a make-or-break situation. A loss to Quarry would undoubtedly end Joe's days as a title threat. Frazier was well aware of the seriousness of his position.

Frazier already held a victory over Quarry, stopping him in seven furious rounds back in 1969. Despite the decisiveness of that win, and despite the jarring spectacle of Quarry's trip to the canvas via Joe Alexander's less than competent hands, the momentum still appeared to be on the Irishman's side. The odds makers agreed, tabbing Quarry as a 6–5 favorite over Smokin' Joe, the second time in a row Frazier played the unfamiliar role of underdog.

With his personal, emotional, and professional problems well behind him, the Jerry Quarry who stepped into the ring against Frazier on June 17 was expected to be at his pugilistic peak. Consequently, Jerry realized he would have no excuses to offer if he lost to Frazier a second time.

Both fighters came in at good fighting weights: 212 for Frazier and 197½ for Quarry. Ironically, the 14,611 fans at the Garden saved their loudest ovation for the bout's referee, who was none other than the Brown Bomber himself, Joe Louis.

For most of the fans, this was the first time they had seen the 60-year-old Louis in a ring since 1951, when he was knocked out by Rocky Marciano. The crowd remained attentive to Louis until the first bell rang; from that point forward the evening became the Joe Frazier Show.

Frazier quickly moved onto the offensive, which was far from unusual for him. This time, though, he displayed a repertoire of strategies he had never shown before. A machine-gun jab and a thundering right hand were the weapons Smokin' Joe had added to his arsenal, and the "new" Quarry didn't know how to cope with a "new" Frazier.

Despite Frazier's novel tactics, Quarry managed to stick and move during the first round. But he had a hard time avoiding Frazier's blows, and Joe's bobbing and weaving defense caused Quarry to miss more punches than he landed.

One punch Quarry didn't miss in that first round was a body shot that strayed south of the border of Frazier's trunks. Groaning in agony, Frazier turned away and began to jog in an attempt to shake off the ill effects of the low blow. Quarry immediately attempted to apologize, but Frazier wasn't interested.

"I'm gonna kill you," Frazier grunted a moment before digging a left hook into Quarry's protective cup. Joe made his point; from then on the fight remained intense, but clean.

By the third round, the writing was on the wall for Quarry. Frazier had found his rhythm, and Jerry had no answer for Joe's two-handed barrages. Still, Quarry gritted his teeth and fired back whenever he could. But his bursts of activity became less frequent as the rounds progressed. At the bell ending the third stanza, Quarry trudged wearily back to his corner while Frazier bounced confidently back to his own stool on legs that looked fresh and strong.

By the fourth round, Quarry's back was glued against the ropes. His face was badly battered, and his pace had slowed to a crawl. Frazier, on the other hand, was growing stronger as the fight progressed. Quarry's counterpunches weren't bothering him at all.

Toward the end of the round, Frazier reverted to his favorite weapon, the left hook. The blow caromed off Quarry's jaw. Jerry was stunned, but somehow he remained on his feet. Then Frazier took his hook downstairs, driving it deep into Quarry's rib cage. Quarry's lungs emptied, and he sank to one knee. The bell saved Quarry, but the look on his face indicated that the fight wouldn't go on much longer.

Frazier had also seen that look. At the beginning of the fifth, he charged out of his corner like a pit bull. A jab popped into Quarry's haggard features. Then a right hand sent Jerry staggering into the ropes. At that point, Quarry raised his hands in a gesture of surrender. Frazier looked at Louis and asked the Brown Bomber to stop the fight.

"I asked Joe to stop the fight but what could I do? I wasn't gonna turn and look at his [Quarry's] corner. Eddie [Futch] was tellin' me to go back out there. He couldn't see how bad Jerry was cut, but I did."[37]

Inexplicably, Louis refused and ordered Frazier to continue. Frazier moved in and pounded away at the defenseless Irishman until Louis had no choice other than to call a halt to the battering. Once again, the Phoenix had been singed by Smokin' Joe's flames.

The one-sided nature of Frazier's victory impressed most observers, including the ones who had written him off after the second Ali fight. Despite the beating he had taken, Quarry was no fraud. He was every bit as good as the odds makers made him out to be. But Frazier had his "number," and chances are if they had fought ten times, Smokin' Joe would have won them all.

In destroying Quarry's title hopes, Frazier exhibited a ferocity that had been missing since the first Ali fight. He had recognized the urgency of the moment, and risen to the occasion, another testimony to his greatness.

Quarry's facial injuries, which included a 15-stitch gash over his right eye, amply attested to the intensity that continued to blaze inside Smokin' Joe.

Frazier said that he felt stronger and hit harder than ever before. His new-found right hand seemed almost as dangerous as his already lethal left.

Indeed, with the exception of his gesture of compassion in the final round, Frazier had seemed almost out of control, like a runaway locomotive. Once his emotions had cooled down, he seemed a little embarrassed about his threat to kill Quarry in the first round. Joe chalked it up to a reflex response to the low blow Jerry had landed. He knew Quarry hadn't meant to hit him below the belt; the two fighters respected each other too much to engage in deliberately foul tactics.

At the post-fight press conference, Garden official John Condon introduced the winner: "Gentlemen, the former heavyweight champion of the world and, if he fights the way he did tonight, probably the next heavyweight champion of the world, Joe Frazier."

Frazier's fans hadn't had such an occasion to celebrate since his 1971 win over Ali. Now, even the harshest Frazier critic had to agree that Frazier had looked awesome against a Quarry who was at the top of his game. Now the boxing world was forced to look at Frazier in a new light, and also to reassess the significance of Superfight II.

One reason many thought Frazier was a "has-been" going into the Quarry fight was that Joe had just lost to another supposed "has-been" in Ali. After the mauling Frazier had administered to Quarry, it appeared that the doomsayers had spoken prematurely. If Frazier was still as fierce and dangerous as ever, then Ali, who had beaten him, however disputed the decision may have been, must also have had much more left than had previously been supposed.

Was that enough to beat Foreman? Boxing fans the world over were eager to find out.

In the meantime, Frazier stood ready to challenge the winner of Foreman–Ali. And for Quarry, his up-and-down career had gone down again, possibly for the last time. His parting comment on his career echoes now as a grim prophecy: "The man who beats me from here on in is gonna have to practically kill me!"[38]

The King of Zaire

On September 30, 1971, Inmate #6178 was released on parole from the Marion Correctional Institute in Ohio.[39] Formerly in the numbers game, an illegal lottery popular in the black community, the inmate had just completed a sentence for manslaughter. Three years later, the ex-convict who walked out of those prison gates would become the first black man to promote a world heavyweight championship bout. His name: Don King.

Before King began his incredible journey in the boxing world, most of Muhammad Ali's fights had been promoted by his lawyer, Bob Arum. Arum was also president of Top Rank, Inc. Through Top Rank, Arum controlled closed-circuit rights to most of the fights that featured Ali, the top drawing card in boxing.

Until January 1974, Arum's hold on closed-circuit was virtually a monopoly. But then a fledgling promoter from Cleveland dared to dispute Arum's control over the telecast of Ali–Frazier II in Ohio. This conflict marked the first of many to come between Arum and Don King.

In 1975, King called Arum his "greatest foe and nemesis, completely devoid of principle and character."[40] Before then, though, King had made up his mind to snatch the Foreman–Ali fight away from Arum. His task was daunting, and his chances of success improbable. In 1974, King was still a small fish swimming in a sea full of sharks. And Arum was the biggest shark of all.

Although King managed heavyweight contenders Earnie Shavers and Jeff Merritt, he had yet to prove himself at a major level. In fact, his main meal ticket, Shavers, had flopped against Jerry Quarry in 1973. It seemed highly unlikely that a nobody like King could upstage the established, well-connected Arum.

However, the world would soon discover that Don King was, and is, a unique individual, blessed with an abundance of skill and talent, and a burning ambition to succeed at all costs. The small fish was about to become a bona fide shark.

Steven Ende, editor of *World Boxing* magazine, said in the January 1974 issue that King was "not a technical boxing expert." "King's value," Ende went on to say, "is in promotion. There he is mostly a self-made man, combining the dynamics of a hell-raising Baptist preacher, the willingness to take risks of a riverboat gambler, and the street knowledge of someone who has done time. King calls it a 'gift from God.' But he improved on that gift."

As Arum was about to find out, the manner in which King applied his talents has caused many to wonder where they really came from. Naturally, King would prefer to give credit to the man upstairs.

The not-so-humble King also placed himself in select company in the history of the fine art of promotion. "There's been only three really great promoters in our lifetime," he once declared. "There's Michael Todd and P.T. Barnum and yours truly."[41]

King developed his gift or knack on the gritty streets of Cleveland and polished it in prison. Ironically, his background appeared more typical of a fighter than a promoter. And King was indeed a fighter, but not in the ring.

As a child, King lost his father on December 7, 1941, the day the Japanese bombed Pearl Harbor and drew the Americans into World War II. Don's dad didn't die at Pearl Harbor; he lost his life in an industrial accident in Cleveland.[42]

The family received a $10,000 insurance settlement, and Mrs. King used the money to move her children to a better neighborhood. To supplement their small income, the Kings would peddle homemade pies and roasted peanuts on the streets. It didn't take young Don long to seek out a more adventurous and profitable way to make a living.

At an early age, King became involved in the numbers racket. Numbers running was illegal, and primarily confined to inner-city communities. King often reflected that the concept behind the numbers game, or "policy" as it was sometimes called, was misunderstood by white society.

"What we recognize," King once mused, "is that whites were going to church playing bingo, they were going to their bookmakers placing their bets and nobody was bothering them, so why did they bother us when we had policy?"[43]

In 1975, King insisted he had never been involved in more sordid underworld activities like prostitution, drugs, or robbery. But he freely admitted to having had his hand in gambling. "I rationalize it all in a naive manner," he explained. "That if gambling was such a predominant factor that they set aside a whole state of Nevada to gamble in and 75 percent of the country gambles, then it couldn't be all bad."[44]

The young gamesman quickly became known as Don "The Kid" King, numbers baron of Cleveland. In 1967, he extended a helping hand to a young ex-convict named Sam Garrett. He brought Garrett into his organization and trusted him to keep his hand out of the cookie jar.

Before long, the relationship soured, with King suspecting Garrett of siphoning money from the "policy." When King voiced his suspicions, Garrett became enraged. As King was getting into his car one day, Garrett attacked him and a vicious street scuffle ensued.

In the heat of battle, Garrett's head cracked against the concrete and he died eight days later. King was charged and convicted of manslaughter, and sentenced to prison.

Once he was behind bars, King could have succumbed to self-pity. Instead, he put his period of incarceration to good use. "I had one of the most delightful times, if I may say, under desperate conditions," King later said.[45]

In prison, King began a lifelong love affair with books, which opened a whole new world for the young hustler. He also took correspondence courses in business law, economics, English, and political science from Ohio University. Letters of recommendation from King's professors were partly responsible for securing his parole after only four years.

Upon his release, King decided to get into the boxing business. As a manager, he specialized in heavyweights, guiding the careers of Shavers, Merritt, and a fledgling pro from Pennsylvania named Larry Holmes.

After Shavers's disappointing loss to Quarry, King left the managerial ranks to try his hand at promoting. His first break came when Hank Schwartz of Video Techniques, Inc., hired him to work on the ill-fated Foreman–Norton fight in Caracas.

At first, King was essentially a "black interface dealing only with blacks," in other words, a figurehead. Within a year, though, the tables turned and Schwartz found himself working as executive director of Don King Productions, Inc. Perhaps King needed a "white interface."

Well before Foreman–Norton, King had envisioned an Ali–Foreman showdown sometime in 1974. He first approached Ali with the idea in 1973, but Muhammad told King he was "crazy." Eventually, King convinced both Ali and Foreman that he was sane, capable, and audacious.

In his dealings with the two fighters, King played an unprecedented angle. For the first time in history, it was possible for a black promoter to use his complexion to advantage in competition with a white one. As performers, blacks had long since begun to dominate the sport in the higher weight divisions. And managers like Julian Black, who handled Joe Louis, and George Gainford, who guided Sugar Ray Robinson, had made inroads. But the major promoters, from Tex Rickard to Mike Jacobs to Jim Norris to Bob Arum, had all been white.

To paraphrase former Los Angeles Dodgers official Al Campanis, it was thought that blacks did not have the "necessities" to handle big-money promotions. Don King was about to knock that theory into a cocked hat once and for all.

King's appeal to Ali and Foreman was uncomplicated: "Give your black brother a chance." First he appealed to Ali and Herbert Muhammad, arguing that it was time for a black man to get a shot at the kind of position held by privileged white folks, i.e., Bob Arum. After several weeks of discussion, the Ali camp gave King the go-ahead.

It took only a matter of hours to convince Foreman. Foreman liked the idea of a black promoter, although given the monumental purse King was offering, George probably wouldn't have cared if Don were polka-dot. In a gamble even P.T. Barnum might have shied away from, King promised the fighters an unprecedented guarantee of $5,000,000 each, twice the amount Ali and Frazier had received for Superfight I.

As an added incentive, King agreed to reimburse the champion for the Venezuelans' unexpected tax grab after the Norton fight. "I would jump out of an airplane and fight 20 Alis for $5 million," beamed Foreman, who was finally getting an opportunity to cash in on his title.

Although he was confident he could defeat Ali, the champion still considered the proposed purse a victory in itself. It's a big jump from fighting on street corners in Houston in 1965 to competing in Zaire for $5 million in 1974.

Once rumors of King's coup in-the-making began to circulate in the boxing world, several questions came to mind:

Did King have the $10 million on hand? No.

Did he have any collateral? No.

Did he have a site? No.

Did he have the "cojones" of a brass monkey? Yes.

And exactly where was Kinshasa, anyway?

The world was about to find out.

King, who was once described by Red Smith as having "no especial gift for silence," had talked his way into what was then the biggest boxing promotion in history. All he had to do now was put $10 million where his mouth was.

In the unlikely location of Zaire, formerly the Belgian Congo, King found a site, the money, and a kindred spirit. Zairean President Mobutu Sese Seko, who had seized power during a 1960 military coup, had already expressed interest in staging the fight. King convinced Mobutu that Foreman–Ali would cast a positive light on Zaire, a light that would be seen by 500 million pairs of eyes on worldwide closed-circuit television.

For that kind of image enhancement, $10 million was a bargain, especially for a dictator who controlled the purse strings of an entire nation. Mobutu ran a one-party government, and what he said went. Like it or not, Zaireans were going to expend their limited resources on an event few of them could have afforded to view on closed-circuit.

Before Mobutu came into the picture, Madison Square Garden had been approached to stage Foreman–Ali. But the Mecca of Boxing was unable to meet the fighters' astronomical financial demands. Tough New York state and city tax laws were another factor that eliminated the Garden from consideration. Ali, for one, remembered how quickly the state had seized its share of the purses from Superfight I. And Mobutu had agreed to waive all taxes on Foreman–Ali.

Given his experience in Caracas, Foreman might have viewed that promise with justifiable skepticism. Still, Big George trusted King, if not Mobutu.

Suddenly, Madison Square Garden found itself sitting on the big-time boxing sidelines. Garden Director Teddy Brenner said that Madison Square Garden was initially offered the fight, but because of New York's heavy taxes, it priced itself out of the running. Foreman and Ali would save $700,000 each by fighting in Africa.

Indeed, the loss of Ali–Foreman signaled the beginning of a decline in Garden and the Big Apple's influence on the major boxing scene. Foreign countries and gambling casinos eventually filled the gap the Garden left.

Besides the guaranteed bankroll from Mobutu, King also received $1.5 million from Hemdale Leisure Corporation, headed by John Daly. The British corporation managed the careers of recording stars like Elton John, and also had interests in betting shops, film studios, and a merchant bank in London.

A self-congratulatory King took pride in the fact that a "poor product of the black ghetto in Cleveland" had put together the financing for Foreman–Ali, and double the amount of the total purse Jerry Perenchio had raised for the first Ali–Frazier fight. King also said his goal was to become a shining role model for underprivileged youth.

In the future, race ("The brothers gotta stick together!") and patriotism ("Only in America!") would become Don King's calling cards. King's value as a role model is certainly open to debate. However, his success in his chosen field cannot be denied. The Foreman–Ali extravaganza entrenched him in his position, and he has placed a unique stamp on the boxing world ever since.

Although some fans expressed skepticism about Zaire as a site for the most anticipated fight since Ali–Frazier I, it seemed somehow appropriate that the two most famous black athletes in the world would be performing in a contest staged by a black promoter in an African nation.

Ali promised that the fight would be a "Rumble in the Jungle," and that phrase became its billing logo.

Once the Zaire location was confirmed, President Mobutu organized a campaign to beautify the capital city of Kinshasa in anticipation of a massive influx of foreigners. The city underwent a complete face lift, and accommodations for media and fans were prepared. And the 20 Mai (May 20, Zaire's independence day) was practically rebuilt, expanding from a 38,000-seat capacity to a mammoth 120,000.

Mobutu's motivation in hosting the fight was twofold. Not only did he hope to showcase his emerging nation on an international stage; he also viewed the event as an opportunity to unify his people via a common undertaking. Zaire is a vast nation geographically, and in 1974 its population stood at 23 million.

However, within the country's borders, the Zaireans or Zairois consisted of 200 varied and distinct ethnic groups. With many of these groups having virtually nothing in common other than their color, Mobutu believed the Ali–Foreman fight would foster a sense of national pride in his people. To him, the fight would be a gift to Zaire, perhaps the only one he ever gave to the country he would dominate over the next two decades.

Superhype

Once the contracts for Foreman–Ali were signed and the initial incredulity over Zaire as a site for a superfight had passed, it was time for the hype and anticipation to begin. The intensity of the buildup for Foreman–Ali eventually matched that of Ali–Frazier I, albeit for different reasons.

At first glance, the story of Foreman–Ali seemed fairly straightforward. Some called it Ali's last hurrah, as a loss to Foreman, especially by knockout, would probably have ended Muhammad's storied career. The facts of the fight seemed to speak for themselves. A 32-year-old ex-champ who was past his prime and had recently engaged in life-and-death struggles against Ken Norton and Joe Frazier challenges a 26-year-old champion who had flattened the selfsame Norton and Frazier like pancakes: didn't the outcome of such a matchup appear inevitable? Couldn't everyone read the handwriting on the wall?

Not necessarily. For all Foreman's advantages in youth and power, for all his chilling efficiency in dispatching Frazier and Norton, there were still some question marks surrounding the self-styled executioner.

Question #1: How would Foreman react to the pressure of a major superfight? The Frazier and Norton bouts were important, but nothing Foreman had experienced in his short career could possibly have prepared him for the stress involved in media extravaganza like the one unfolding in Zaire.

Ali, of course, thrived on media attention. Indeed, he controlled the tempo of the pre-fight hoopla, and almost seemed to gain strength from burdens that would have broken other men. Ali was the spoon that stirred the stew, to paraphrase a later quote by baseball star Reggie Jackson. As far as superfights went, Ali would play veteran to Foreman's novice.

Question #2: How would Foreman cope with Ali's trademark psychological warfare? "He has never fought anybody like me," Ali proclaimed. True enough. Ali had rattled the cages of many past opponents long before he laid a glove on them.

And Foreman was susceptible to the kind of tricks Ali had up his sleeve. In the light of more recent impressions Foreman made during his late 1980s–1990s comeback, it's sometimes difficult to remember him as he was in 1974.

Back then, Big George didn't project the fun-loving, extroverted persona we now know. The 1974 edition, although well-spoken, was also an introverted, brooding young man who cherished his privacy. Like Floyd Patterson before him, Foreman accepted the limelight as a price he had to pay for being champion. But he often blinked in its merciless glare.

While the Foreman of today would have been an even match with Ali in a verbal sparring session, in 1974 he was grossly outmatched. And he was intelligent enough to know it. He said he had seen Ali infuriate Frazier far too many times to allow the same thing to happen to him.

Besides, unlike Frazier, Foreman claimed he had nothing negative to say about his rival anyway. "Two men you can't say anything bad about are John Wayne and Muhammad Ali," Foreman said.[46]

That bonhomie didn't last long. Regardless of his efforts to remain above Ali's antics and shenanigans, he would be drawn into them like an iron filing to a magnet.

A New York banquet honoring Foreman as "Fighter of the Year" provided Ali the perfect opportunity to crack George's bland veneer. During the course of the festivities, the two fighters engaged in some playful physical jousting that soon turned serious.

Push came to shove, and Ali tore Foreman's coat. Once the fighters were separated, they continued to swing at each other, with plates and glasses flying in the direction of ducking dignitaries before order was finally restored. It was the ABC studio war with Frazier all over again, the difference being that this time, Ali knew exactly what he was doing.

While most observers believed the incident was staged, Ali insisted it wasn't. "If that kind of thing was staged," he said, "I wouldn't have gone along with it and I am a pretty cooperative guy."[47]

Madison Square Garden Publicity Director John Condon's view concurred with Ali's. "The hell he's kidding!" Condon snorted. Of Ali, he said, "I've seen enough of these things to know when he's kidding."[48]

Unlike the one-fall wrestling match with Frazier, the Ali–Foreman imbroglio was viewed only as a minor incident. Although Big George was embarrassed, he couldn't seem to bring himself to hate his tormenter. How could he hate a man who was about to make him $5,000,000 richer?

The relative lack of personal and political conflict between the participants marked a major difference between Foreman–Ali and Ali–Frazier I. Superfight I wasn't just a boxing match; it was also a clash of conflicting social, political, and religious viewpoints.

The conservative Frazier supporters considered Ali a draft-dodging, loud-mouthed black militant infidel opposed to everything America stood for. At the same time, Ali's left-of-center army painted Frazier as an Uncle Tom, a cheese champ only too happy to wear the white man's crown. And Ali himself was instrumental in creating that false impression of Frazier. For that reason, Ali–Frazier I was the most political heavyweight championship bout since the second Joe Louis–Max Schmeling bout in 1938.

In Foreman–Ali, though, left- vs. right-wing politics remained in the background. Ali's politics hadn't changed, but he kept whatever misgivings he had about Foreman to himself. The reason for his silence was that Ali had changed in other ways since Superfight I. And so had his country.

In 1971, Ali had been cleared of all the draft evasion charges initially laid against him in 1967. By 1974, the war in which he had refused to participate was over, for the United States, at least. American troops had been withdrawn from the conflict, leaving the South Vietnamese to fend for themselves. In effect, the United States had lost a war for the first time in its history.

By the time of Foreman–Ali, a long period of national introspection had begun. Americans were taking a long, objective, and painful look at the war that had needlessly sacrificed young men in Vietnam and had come close to tearing the United States apart. Many who had initially despised Ali for his antiwar stand in the 1960s now forgave, forgot, understood, or simply kept quiet about the ex-champion's past.

Civil rights was another '60s cause that had wound down by 1974. Federal legislation had been enacted, the inner cities were quiet, and racial volatility had cooled, on the surface, at least. For the most part, Americans appeared ready for a period of social complacency which soon became known as the "Me Decade."

Ali became a prime beneficiary of this mellowing process. Although there would always be those who disliked him and continued to refer to him as "Cassius Clay," it was no longer kosher to openly oppose him. One reason for that change in attitude was a mellowing that in turn occurred within Ali.

With his conversion to Islam in 1964, the yappy, rhyming, carefree kid named Cassius Marcellus Clay had transformed into a mature young man known as Muhammad Ali. Ten years later, Ali remained steadfast in his Muslim beliefs. But now he expressed religion in a more circumspect manner.

Not that such restraint was necessary, since the period of anti–"Black Muslim" paranoia had long since passed. The Nation of Islam had toned down its anti-white rhetoric over the years, and by 1974 the Muslims were actually receiving good publicity for its programs in drug rehabilitation, youth centers, and efforts at neighborhood improvement.

The new acceptance of Ali encompassed the fistic fraternity as well. Many old-guard fight fans and ex-pugs of the flat-nosed persuasion who had scorned Ali's balletic fighting style and questioned his intestinal fortitude found their attitudes changing after they watched Muhammad absorb inordinate amounts of punishment from Frazier and Norton. Anyone with that much courage can't be all bad, the cauliflower-ear crowd reasoned, even if he is a Muslim and a draft dodger.

Thus, by the time Ali signed to fight Foreman, his legion of fans had reached an all-time high. His supporters encompassed every race, religion, and walk of life. Many of the people who hated his guts in the 1960s now found themselves pulling for him to regain his title.

A man who truly loves people, Ali reveled in the tide of adulation that now washed over him. He wasn't about to suppress his personal belief in social equality for all, but he wasn't looking for trouble, either.

Had he engaged in the same bitterly personal rhetoric that had marked the buildup to Superfight I, Ali would have seriously damaged the good relationship with the American public he had developed over the past three years. Choosing a more diplomatic approach, he kept his verbal assaults against Foreman on a professional level. He ridiculed Foreman as a fighter, calling him "The Mummy" because of his slow, plodding style.

It is highly likely that Ali found Foreman's politics any more palatable than he had Frazier's. Foreman's flag-waving gesture during the 1968 Olympics had been viewed as a commendable outburst of national pride by the same people who supported Frazier over Ali. Others, who would also have been Ali supporters, thought Foreman was consciously countering the raised-fist protest of Tommie Smith and John Carlos.

For that reason, many black activists still resented Foreman and called him a flag-waving Uncle Tom, even though Foreman had always denied any intention to demean Smith and Carlos. Evidence that Ali shared the activists' opinion can be found in Ali's autobiography, *The Greatest*, in which Muhammad reproduces a tape-recorded conversation he had with Frazier in August of 1970. Along with a host of other topics, the fighters discussed Foreman. About the flag-waving incident, Ali said: "George Foreman carried that flag 'cause he was a brainwashed black super patriot."

The Ali of 1971 would have skewered Foreman mercilessly on ideological grounds. The Ali of 1974 opted to remain silent. However, an inkling of his true feelings was revealed at the New York luncheon scuffle when Ali was heard to tell Foreman he was going to "beat your Christian tail, you flag-waver!"

But that religious reference would have been lost on Foreman. The preacher we know today was a confirmed hedonist in 1974. In the July 1981 issue of *The Ring*, Foreman told Steve Marantz: "I remember in Africa, Ali called me a Christian, and I didn't even know what that was. I thought it was some kind of nationality."

Indeed, in Zaire Ali did play the racial card, though not nearly as heavily as he had against Frazier. Starting with Sonny Liston, Ali had always attempted to "out-black" his black opponents. With Foreman, he went so far as to claim that Africa was Muhammad's ancestral home, but not George's. He depicted himself as the emblem of African post-colonial freedom. And, whether he liked it or not (and he didn't), Foreman became the symbol of white oppression.

Ali was dedicating this fight to all Africans who were fighting for their independence. He went so far as to compare Foreman to the Belgian oppressors who had once ruled Zaire.

It was hard to imagine anyone mistaking George Foreman for a "Belgian oppressor." Thus, for the most part, Ali's were taken as lightly as intended. Other Ali comments, however, resulted in a much graver, and unintended, impact.

In an attempt to indicate that he had the support of the African people, Ali said he was going to make a voodoo doll of George. On another occasion, he warned a reporter that he'd better be careful or "my brothers in Africa will put you in a pot!"[49] Those references to voodoo and cannibalism, along with Ali's constant allusions to Zaire as "the jungle," not only insulted the Zairois, it also threatened to harm the promotion.

One of the main reasons Mobutu accepted the fight was to demonstrate to the world that his nation was a civilized, modern country that was perfectly capable of staging a major international event. He was hoping to shatter the stereotypes Ali was reinforcing. Because they really did like Ali, the Zarois gave him the benefit of the doubt.

Don King wasn't so forgiving. The promoter had put together a package deal that included a return flight, accommodations, and tickets to the fight for a total of about $2500. But he wasn't getting as many takers as he thought he would, and for that he partially blamed Ali. King claimed that Ali's banter about voodoo dolls and the jungle were scaring Westerners away. Eventually, prices for the superfight package had to be reduced from $2500 to $1500.

As well, rumors of substandard accommodations in university dormitories had reached the U.S. Still, King believed Ali's jungle talk was more damaging. "Kinshasa is a city like any other big city," King said. "We're bringing in buses. We're bringing in food. We'll show everyone a black nation can run things perfectly. But we need white people. And white people have been turned off because of what Ali says."

Despite the derogatory nature of his comments, Ali's own magic continued to work on the Zairois people. One reason they were able to forgive his ignorance was that they'd followed his career for years, and knew where he stood on many black issues. Another reason was that they didn't know George Foreman from Adam.

One Zairois official said that the public was being educated about the combatants. The education included the fact that Foreman, not Ali, was the champion. As in the USA, not everyone in Zaire bought Ali's act. The same official revealed that about 20 percent of the population was rooting for Foreman, the "Belgian oppressor."

An Unkind Cut

As fight day drew closer, experts, odds makers, and the average fan in the street evaluated the attributes of both participants to determine which of them was more likely to win. The assessment wasn't an easy one; each fighter was remarkable in his own right.

In his 1964–1967 reign as heavyweight champion, Ali had established himself as one of the all-time greats, if not "The Greatest." As a comebacking contender, he had held his own against the best fighters of a newer generation. Although he wasn't the physical phenomenon he'd been in his younger days, Ali's skills and experience still made him a fighter to be reckoned with.

Foreman, on the other hand, was power personified. His punching ability had already become legendary, his knockout percentage stood higher than that of any other heavyweight king, including such legendary hitters as Joe Louis, Jack Dempsey, and Rocky Marciano. The effects of Foreman's blows were frighteningly destructive and, as the old boxing saying goes, when he hit you, you "stayed hit." Big George was a wonder even to himself. "I think I'm blessed," he said after his annihilation of Norton. "I hit a man and it's magic. He falls to the floor."[50]

Here was a monster who could launch 214-pound Joe Frazier completely off the canvas with a single mighty uppercut, break the arm of 215-pound Luis Pires with bone-splintering force, and make the muscular 212-pound Ken Norton look like a 97-pound weakling. "Anything George hits he's gonna hurt," bragged Dick Sadler.[51]

Coupled with his innate ability to render a man unconscious with a single blow was Foreman's intimidating demeanor, which was comparable only to that of George's idol, Sonny Liston. In the same way Liston unnerved opponents with his icy, deadpan stare, Foreman also developed a psychological edge over most of the men who faced him. Ken Norton was a prime example of a foe who came unglued under Big George's menacing glare.

Like Liston, though, Foreman would discover that Ali wasn't vulnerable to glowering intimidation. "Everybody Foreman has fought before has been scared of him when they got in the ring," Ali observed. "I ain't scared of nobody or nothin' in this world, so there is no reason why I should be scared of Foreman."[52]

However, some observers claimed there were signs Ali might be whistling past the graveyard in his denials of fear or, at least, serious misgivings. After his victory over Frazier in January, Ali had said he didn't "need" Foreman, even though Foreman held the title.

Concerning that attitude, Dave Anderson stated in the *New York Times*: "The suspicion is that Ali realizes he doesn't need his career ended."

Anderson was certain a huge purse guarantee would change Ali's mind about a showdown with Foreman. "When the match with Foreman can't be avoided any longer, Ali will take the money and run until he's counted out," Anderson predicted.

Others called attention to Ali's continuous claims that the Foreman fight would be his finale. The promise to retire win or lose was interpreted as a sign of shaky confidence on Ali's part. Was he unconsciously foreseeing his own doom beneath the sledgehammer fists of the champion?

And then there was Ali's relative lack of verbal pyrotechnics other than the incident at the New York banquet. Considering the significance of the fight, Foreman was getting off easily. One possible inference was that Ali didn't want to dig too deeply for fear of angering his opponent. And that definitely wasn't the Ali of old.

Still, the "Ali is scared" crowd failed to take one important fact into account. If a wet-behind-the-ears kid like Cassius Clay refused to be intimidated by Liston in 1964, the mature 32-year-old Ali of 1974 could hardly be expected to cringe at the thought of facing Foreman.

The ghost of Liston seemed to haunt the "Affair in Zaire." Never before had the analogy between Foreman and his mentor seemed more appropriate. Ten years earlier, Ali, as a young, fresh, undefeated challenger, had dazzled and defeated a battle-worn Liston, who was 32 going on 40. In Kinshasa, the tables would be turned. Ali was the old man now; Foreman the young Turk.

Ironically, a past-his-prime Ali would be facing a bigger, younger, stronger, and harder-hitting edition of Liston. The speed demon of 1964 might have run rings around Foreman, but the slower, more hittable Ali of 1974 appeared to have bitten off more than he could chew.

Foreman was confident that was the case. He said he intended to score a quick knockout so "nobody'll get hurt."

Given the demolition job he had performed on Ali's only two conquerors, George's confidence appeared well-founded. Not since the first Liston fight had Ali been such an underdog in the eyes of both the odds makers and the public.

Foreman appeared to have legitimate answers to any questions concerning his ability to handle Ali. When asked how he would deal with Muhammad's speed and defensive skills, Foreman responded: "I believe that a man, once he gets in the ring, he does what I let him do. How would I stop Ali from running? By knocking him out, that's how."[53]

Indeed, Foreman was riding a 24-bout knockout streak, and his last eight victims had been cut down in less than two rounds. The last fighter to last as long as four rounds with him was Pires, back in October of 1971.

Ali, by contrast, hadn't stopped anyone since his eight-knockdown blowout of Bob Foster in 1972. Although Muhammad was never a powder-puff puncher, as some of his critics claimed, he also wasn't a banger. The conventional wisdom held that if Ali were to stand any chance against Foreman at all, he would have to stick and move for 15 rounds. And few believed Ali's 32-year-old legs could keep him out of trouble that long.

Most experts pointed to Foreman's string of quickie kayoes as evidence of his superiority over Ali. Yet Foreman had his critics as well as admirers. And the critics believed the champion's lack of competition could prove his undoing. Because Foreman had always controlled the action in the ring, no one knew how he would react to unexpected adversity. In reference to Foreman, Joe Louis said: "Those one and two round knockouts really aren't helping him learn...."[54]

Ali, on the other hand, had skated close to the edge time and again, and had proven himself capable of handling dire situations even in losing causes.

As another boxing adage goes, "Great fights make great fighters." A fighter needs to be extended every now and then to test his courage and polish his skills. Foreman had been extended only once, in his first fight against Gregorio Peralta. He'd passed that test. But Peralta was not Ali. Not by a long shot.

Louis, by the way, was also asked what he thought of Ali's chances, given Foreman's lack of big fight experience. "There is no way Muhammad Ali can beat George Foreman," Louis declared. He believed Foreman was simply too strong, and that Ali's legs wouldn't hold up over the distance.[55]

But then, Louis had been wrong before.

Speculation about Ali's legs aside, one of the major question marks about Foreman was his stamina. He had never been tested in that department since he'd stopped Peralta in the tenth round of their rematch. In Ali, George would be meeting the cleverest boxer of his time, and if anyone could force Foreman to fight beyond his customary two-round limit, Muhammad was the man.

"Now," Ali said, "I've never seen George Foreman tired yet. George Foreman lately hasn't heard the man say, 'Round four,' 'Round seven,' 'Round nine,' 'Round thirteen,' 'Last round.' I can't take nothing away from George, but I haven't seen George in a good scuffle yet."[56]

Foreman, however, wasn't very concerned about the prospect of going 15 rounds. He had trained for fifteen rounds and figured that youth and strength were on his side.

Doubts concerning Foreman's stamina and reaction to adversity were merely hypothetical at this point. However, Ali's supporters could point to some tangible advantages "The Greatest" held over the champion.

First, Ali enjoyed a distinct edge in reach. On paper, the difference was only 1½ inches (80" over 78½). But in strategic terms, the advantage meant something because Ali threw straight punches while George's were almost always thrown in looping fashion.

Second, Ali's hand speed was much greater than Foreman's. He wasn't as quick as he'd been in his heyday, but his hands were still the quickest in the division. Even Foreman's most ardent supporters had to concede that their man's punches were delivered ponderously.

So far, though, "ponderous" had worked well. Foreman himself said, "Some people say I'm slow, but I get the job done, sometimes quicker than most people. So maybe I'm fast." George's logic might have been questionable, but his undefeated record spoke for itself.

As the "September Showdown" approached, a third factor that went largely ignored by the general public was susceptibility to cuts. But the boxing media showed more interest in that matter. In a pre-fight analysis in *Boxing Yearbook 1974* that indicated how Ali and Foreman stacked up in 20 different categories, both fighters received a rating of 4.5 out of 5 in "Resistance to Cuts."

During his entire career, Ali had received only a pair of minor abrasions at the hands of Norton and Bob Foster. Foreman had also proved resistant to cuts. Although a close gaze at Big George's face would reveal several small scars, those marks were souvenirs of teenage battles that had not occurred under the auspices of Marquess of Queensberry rules.

Then, with only a week remaining before the fighters would step into the ring, the unimaginable happened. In his final days of sparring, Foreman received a severe gash over his right eye. After George had hammered the daylights out of sparmate Henry Clark, Dick Sadler tossed in Bill McMurray, a 38-year-old ex-heavyweight turned truck driver. McMurray's role in the training camp was to mimic Ali's style and get mauled by Foreman in the process.

Fate often casts people in unexpected roles. McMurray probably never dreamed that he would come close to causing the cancellation of what was then the biggest fight in history.

Like most fighters, McMurray must have entertained dreams of glory at the beginning of his career; dreams of winning the world title and enjoying all the benefits that go with it. But McMurray's dream had turned into the mundane reality of a .500 record over 80 pro fights.

Now he was reduced to playing punching bag for one of the hardest hitters of all time. After pounding the pulp out of McMurray for two rounds, Foreman advanced in the third, still throwing bombs.

"I was taking a shellacking," McMurray said afterward, "and raised my left arm to protect myself."

As he lifted his arm, McMurray inadvertently rammed his elbow into George's forehead. The skin above the champion's right eyebrow split, and blood spurted from a large gash.

The injury proved serious enough to force a month-long postponement of the fight. Given all the variables King and Mobutu had been forced to juggle to secure the event, including scheduling the fight in advance of Zaire's rainy season, the mishap couldn't have occurred at a worse time.

Naturally, McMurray regretted the damage he had done. But Foreman wasn't angry, "just disappointed."

Had Foreman's brain trust dug deeper into McMurray's background, they would have discovered that Bill had slashed more victims during his career than Jack the Ripper. Inadvertently or otherwise, McMurray had a knack for inflicting cuts on superior opponents.

In a 1966 bout with promising contender Thad Spencer, McMurray was well behind on points when a head butt opened a bloody wound on Thad's face. The bout was stopped, and McMurray was awarded a TKO victory.

Like Foreman, perennial "White Hope" Boone Kirkman suffered a bout-postponing injury at McMurray's hands during a sparring session. A lesser "White Hope" of the late 1960s, Dave Zyglewicz, also had his problems with McMurray.

A year before his 1969 challenge of Joe Frazier, Zyglewicz tangled with "Razorhands" McMurray and a memorable bloodbath ensued. Though behind on points, Bill managed to slice a cut over Ziggy's eye in the sixth round. Then the fighters banged heads in the eighth, and both sustained gashes. Reports stated that ringsiders were spattered with blood over the final two rounds. Zyglewicz won the decision, but came away with some nasty scars. "I must've lost three quarts of blood," Ziggy complained later. Thirty stitches were required to close his wounds.

McMurray was probably #1 on the enemies list of the Red Cross. By some unwritten law of boxing, he never shared a ring with notorious bleeders Henry Cooper and Chuck Wepner. Undistinguished though his career may have been, McMurray's claim to fame, or infamy, remains the cut his elbow inflicted on Foreman in Zaire.

Needless to say, Ali was displeased by the postponement. He was certain Foreman would use the cut as an excuse to get out of the fight altogether. However, Zairean officials saw no reason to call it off. Local co-promoter Bula Mandunga felt that the cut was overdramatized. But Foreman's personal physician stated that the cut could easily tear open a week later if not properly healed.

With the stakes as high as they were, who could blame the Foreman camp for accepting a postponement? The African promoters attempted to reduce the delay to a week. But Sadler insisted the cut would take at least four weeks to heal properly.President Mobutu, who had a great deal of personal prestige invested in the promotion, demanded a guarantee that the contest was merely postponed, not canceled altogether. As part of that guarantee, neither fighter would be permitted to leave Zaire before the rescheduled fight date, October 30. Considering his experience in Venezuela, Foreman couldn't have been happy to have heard that news.

Because of a wide difference in time zones, the fight would be held at 4 A.M. Zaire time to allow American viewers to catch it at a reasonable time on closed circuit. Neither fighter seemed concerned about the odd starting time of the bout. Big George claimed to have had numerous battles on the streets of Houston at 4 in the morning.

For all Big George's nonchalance, the ramifications of his cut eye went far beyond just the postponement of the fight. It also exposed a chink in the champion's armor of invincibility.

Like those of so many devastating punchers before him, Foreman's reputation had grown with each one-sided victory. The possibility of defeat became harder to imagine. Foreman was beginning to look unstoppable, perhaps even superhuman.

It took a freak accident at the hands of an aging sparmate to remind boxing fans that Foreman was made of flesh and bone, not iron and steel. When his skin was sliced,

Foreman bled, just like the rest of us. And that led to the plausibility of an Ali TKO victory on cuts.

Throughout his career, Ali had demonstrated an ability to deliver slashing, scalpel-like blows capable of cutting even thick-skinned opponents. Sonny Liston, for example, had never bled in the ring before the fists of young Cassius Clay performed fistic surgery on the Big Ugly Bear's face.

If Foreman, who was Liston's pugilistic heir apparent, was prone to cuts, that weakness would be made to order for Ali's pin-point punching. As the additional month the postponement caused wore on for the fight crowd that remained in Zaire, a Foreman victory no longer seemed such a foregone conclusion.

Rope-a-Dope

During October, everyone concerned with the "Rumble in the Jungle" prayed that no further mishaps would arise to endanger the fight. One more screw-up would surely have canceled it, at least in Zaire.

Three weeks before the rescheduled date, an incident did occur that took several years off the promoters' lives. Foreman was involved in a car crash that resulted in minor injuries to several members of his camp. Fortunately for the fight, Big George emerged without a scratch.

Fight day arrived without any further difficulties. The collective sigh of relief breathed by all parties concerned was almost, but not quite, strong enough to dissipate the rain clouds gathering in the sky.

At the weigh-in, both fighters appeared in excellent condition. The extra baggage Foreman reportedly carried a month earlier was gone; the champion scaled 220 bone-crunching pounds. At 216½, Ali was in peak form. He had trained full-out since June, and Angelo Dundee claimed that his fighter was better prepared for Foreman than he'd been for the second Norton and Frazier fights.

In anticipation of Foreman's thunderous body blows, Ali had put himself through a phenomenally difficult regimen of abdominal exercises. Both Frazier, who favored Foreman, and Norton, who picked Ali, stated that Muhammad was vulnerable to a body attack. If that was the case, it was a weakness Ali was determined to remedy.

Dick Sadler scoffed at Ali's conditioning techniques, saying all the training in the world wouldn't make any difference. In Sadler's mind, nothing Ali could do would save him against his "monster."

After the weigh-in, the fighters rested until it was time to step into the ring. In the meantime, the 20 Mai Stadium began to fill, as did closed-circuit outlets all over the world. Whether the multitude of spectators realized it or not, the fight they were about to see meant much more than merely Foreman's retention of the title or Ali's professional survival. At stake was a prize of a far more eternal nature than a current claim to the championship.

Both Ali and Foreman were on the verge of legendary status.

Ali, of course, had already staked his claim to greatness during his 1960s title reign. To regain the crown ten years after he had first won it would secure Muhammad a spot next to the likes of Johnson, Dempsey, and Louis.

As for Foreman, a win over Ali would launch him into a reign of Louis-like longevity, as none of the other contenders appeared remotely capable of beating him. He would also stand better than even odds of breaking Rocky Marciano's record of 49 bouts without a defeat. As well, decisive victories over Ali and Frazier, the two best heavyweights of the past ten years, would be a magnificent accomplishment in its own right.

Greatness beckoned Foreman. To get there, he would have to button the Louisville Lip. By a 4-to-1 margin, the odds makers believed George would do just that.

Ali had no problems with those odds, and he was pleased that most members of the press were predicting his downfall. Of course, his relations with the press had always been adversarial, dating back to his pre–Liston days. Proving the pessimists wrong had always been a great inspiration to Ali.

Before the Foreman fight, Muhammad had already served notice on his press-corps sparring partners. "Now listen up," he growled, "because you'll have to write different columns after I teach you the ways of boxing and show you how dumb you are."[57] The boxing scribes recorded Ali's words dutifully, knowing that this could be the last stop on the ex-champion's roadshow.

As the challenger, Ali was first to arrive in the ring at the pre-dawn hour of the fight. The moment he climbed through the ropes, the ex-champion began to stir up a crowd he already knew was partisan in his favor. The 20 Mai Stadium shook with the roar of "Ali bomaye," which in the Lingala language means, "Ali, kill him!"

Foreman took longer than usual to emerge from his dressing room. For many the spectators viewing the fight live and on closed-circuit, the sight of Ali performing his usual prefight routine brought on a sense of melancholy. His dancing and shadow-boxing routine might well be the last the world would see of the vintage Ali.

Finally, Foreman's brain trust decided they'd kept Ali waiting long enough, and the champion made his way to the ring. The crowd gave him a polite reception. There were no chants of "George bomaye," but there weren't any boos, either. Obviously, Ali had not been able to convince the Zairois that Foreman was a Belgian with a deep tan.

As the champion entered the ring, Ali shook in mock horror. When Referee Zack Clayton called the fighters to center ring, Foreman applied his updated version of the Sonny Liston stare. Although both fighters were listed as the same height, 6'3", Foreman looked at least an inch taller than Ali. Ali talked to Foreman throughout Clayton's instructions. Tension mounted as the clang of the first bell cut through the warm African air. The fighters came right at each other, and Ali scored with a snapping right-hand lead. That blow raised the hopes of the pro–Ali crowd. Then Foreman drove a left at Ali's head, and forced the ex-champ into the ropes.

To the horror of the spectators, not to mention Angelo Dundee, Ali remained on the ropes as Foreman flailed away with both hands. Some of George's body shots landed, but he had less success when he brought his attack upward. Ali managed to score with some sharp blows, but he wasn't moving away from Foreman. Instead, he stayed on the ropes.

Muhammad's legions of followers stared in disbelief as Ali again took to the ropes in the second. In 1974, it was thought that there were two sure methods to commit suicide: (1) step in front of a truck, and (2) let George Foreman catch you on the ropes. And here was Ali, apparently choosing Method 2.

"Get off the ropes!" Dundee screamed as Foreman belabored Ali. The ropes had been of concern to him earlier, as they had appeared far too loose. Dundee had tightened them, but had never expected to see Ali use them to deliberately squander the only advantage he had over the champion: mobility.

The ropes would later become a bone of contention as Foreman accused Dundee of loosening the ropes earlier in the day, not tightening them. When Angelo arrived at 20 Mai Stadium, he found the ring to be in abominable shape. Photos clearly showed the ropes to be "as loose as a clothesline," in Dundee's memorable phrase.

The problem was that 24 feet of rope had been allotted for a 20-foot ring. Dundee and publicist Bobby Goodman worked on the ring from 10 A.M. to 3:30 P.M., tightening the ropes, balancing the surface, and sweeping resin onto the slippery canvas.

At the time, though, Big George couldn't believe his eyes. Here was the legendary dancing master sitting stationary, almost inviting a beating. Not needing any further encouragement, Foreman waded in and fired away.

Ali, however, knew what he was doing. The slack ropes allowed him to lean farther back, thus diminishing some of the force of Foreman's blows. Also, Ali was catching many of George's punches on his gloves and elbows and counter-punching effectively. His success went unnoticed, though. To most spectators, it looked as though Ali was facing imminent destruction.

Still, he made it through the round. When the bell for the third session rang, Foreman entered territory he hadn't explored for more than three years: the seventh minute of a fight.

Before the third round started, Ali brazenly leaned over the ropes and spoke to reporters at the press table. "He don't hurt me," Ali said. "I told you he's got no punch." He said the same thing to Dundee, who still wasn't convinced.[58]

In the third, Ali continued to fight with the ropes at his back. As Foreman unloaded his bombs, Ali taunted him, calling him a "sissy" and saying George's punches didn't hurt.

The man closest to the action, Zack Clayton, believed Ali's gibes were really getting to the champion. "Foreman got so mad that he blew himself up to where he might as well have weighed 400 pounds," Clayton recalled.

A pinprick of doubt began to work its way into Foreman's psyche. The punches that had leveled Frazier and Norton appeared to be having no effect on a fighter who was supposed to be washed up. Indeed, Ali seemed impervious to pain.

"You can't hurt me, sucker!"[59] Ali informed his frustrated opponent. Although no one, probably not even Ali, knew it at the time, the spectators at the Foreman fight were witnessing the birth of a new technique that would soon become known as the "Rope-a-Dope."

Ali soaked up more of the champion's shots in the fourth, but also landed some stinging jabs and combinations. At times, Foreman looked amateurish, waving his gloves as though he were swatting at mosquitoes. Still, he managed to rock Ali near the end of the round. Muhammad later admitted: "I could feel my toes shaking."[60]

Nevertheless, despite pleas from his corner, Ali returned to the ropes in the fifth. Foreman was beginning to breathe hard, puffing like a locomotive as he drove punch after punch into Ali's cast-iron midsection. Late in the round, Ali sprang off the ropes and tattooed Foreman with a blazing flurry of blows. George stumbled backward, but survived the round.

The champion looked to be in bad shape as he lurched out for the sixth round. His face was beginning to show the effects of Ali's crisp punches. His lungs were burning, and the world he had dominated was beginning to fall apart. Ali was even outmuscling Foreman now, reaching behind the bigger man's neck and pulling his head down.

Still, Foreman kept trying, and Ali kept playing the ropes, using their slack to disperse the force of Foreman's punches. Not knowing anything else to do, Big George continued to sling blows at Ali's head and body. But the punches were visibly losing steam.

Clayton remembers the words Ali used to express his awareness of Foreman's fatigue.

"This is the worst place to get tired, young fella," Ali taunted. "You're here all by yourself and the referee can't help you."

At that point, Foreman must have experienced a deep sense of foreboding. He had been deceived by his own reputation. For six rounds, he had emptied his guns on a stationary target. And that target was still standing, still talking, still punching. For the first time in his career, Foreman was the prey, not the predator. Now he knew how his mentor, Sonny Liston, must have felt in that Miami Beach ring ten years ago. As Ali would say later, "I took the heart right out of him."

Unlike Liston, though, Foreman wasn't going to quit on his stool. If it was his fate to go down, he would go down fighting.

By now, Ali's corner understood the strategy their man had improvised. Between rounds, Dundee said that Foreman was "sleepwalking," and implored Ali to finish him off in the seventh. But Ali knew Foreman was still dangerous, and needed another round's worth of attrition.

Once again, Muhammad assumed his station on the ropes. As Foreman lumbered toward him, Ali led the crowd in a booming chorus of "Ali bomaye!" Poor Foreman was being psyched out in stereo.

George's massive arms were now almost too heavy for him to lift. Yet he continued to throw slow, snapless punches that could not have hurt a welterweight. And Ali continued to pick them off, one by one, until the round ended.

As he awaited the bell for the eighth, Ali told Dundee and Bundini that Foreman was ready to go. His cornermen concurred heartily. Yet when the round began, Big George piled into Ali with a resurgent fury. Had the champion found his second wind?

No, he hadn't. The blows Foreman landed were little more than taps. As Ali backed against the ropes one more time, he knew Foreman was finished.

Moving off the ropes, Ali launched a series of straight, hard blows to Foreman's head. The big man staggered like a drunk. Ali fired again. A left, then a right crashed full into Foreman's puffy face.

As Ali circled, fists cocked to deliver more blows if necessary, Foreman did a clumsy pirouette that ended on the canvas. Flat on his back, Sadler's "monster" stared vacant-eyed at his conqueror, then at Dick Sadler and Archie Moore. Somehow, Foreman dragged himself to his feet just as Clayton completed his 10 count.

The announcement that Ali was "winner and new champion" was drowned out by the sustained roar of the crowd. Not long after the end of the fight, the clouds finally released a torrent of rain.

Immediately, shock waves rumbled through the boxing world. The one outcome nobody expected had just occurred. Muhammad Ali had accomplished the "impossible" again. He had destroyed another destroyer, and added weight to his claim as "the greatest of all time." Satisfying as the victory in Africa had been, Ali would have preferred to regain his title in the USA, because that's where most of his critics were.

Recognizing the magnitude of Ali's feat — he was only the second fighter to regain the heavyweight title — the sporting world applauded Ali and honored him with countless awards and ceremonies. Perhaps the most prestigious accolade he received was the 1974 "Athlete of the Year" award. To win it, he beat out Hank Aaron, who had broken Babe Ruth's all-time home run record.

As another indication of the cooling of the political climate, Ali received an invitation to the White House. In the 1960s, such an invitation would have been unthinkable. Now

Ali, the "draft-dodger," toured the White House with President Gerald Ford, both men apparently enjoying the occasion.

With the title securely in his grasp, and with widespread public approval as well, it appeared that Ali was finally the "People's Champion" in every sense. He had worked long and hard to achieve his second reign, and it would prove to be much more enjoyable for him than his first one.

And his victory couldn't have come at a better time. Had Foreman won in Zaire, the heavyweight division would have stagnated over the rest of the decade. There wouldn't have been a worthwhile contender that Foreman hadn't already knocked kicking.

Now, with Ali at the helm, new life would infuse boxing's flagship division. All kinds of challengers loomed on Ali's horizon. And fight fans would pay plenty to watch Ali turn back those challenges.

The vanquished Foreman was young enough to mount a credible comeback, especially if he matured in defeat, as Ali had following his losses to Frazier and Norton. One thing was certain: Foreman's myth of invincibility had been laid to rest. Never again would he intimidate an opponent simply by stepping into the ring.

Ken Norton, with a style that always gave Ali fits, saw his championship hopes flicker back to life for the first time since his debacle against Foreman in Caracas. He had held Ali virtually even over 24 rounds. Given 15 more, he might well take the title.

Ron Lyle had re-established himself as a leading contender and was optimistic he would receive a title shot in 1975. Since he was the same age as Ali, Lyle knew time wasn't on his side. At least Lyle possessed proven stamina, a quality Foreman seemed to lack.

Rounding out Ali's hit list was Smokin' Joe Frazier. At the beginning of the year, many critics had dismissed Superfight II as a contest for bragging rights between a pair of has-beens. With Frazier's annihilation of Jerry Quarry and Ali's upset of Foreman, the critics were now swallowing their words.

By the end of 1974, Ali and Frazier had proven beyond a doubt that they were still two of the greatest heavyweights in history. The stage was now set for a final confrontation between the two rivals, with the title once again at stake.

The new order thought to have been established in 1973 turned out to be a short-lived phenomenon. Now the old order was back. And boxing fans licked their chops in anticipation of Superfight III, the battle that would once and for all settle the question of superiority between Ali and Frazier.

Eight

1975

The Bayonne Bleeder

During his first championship reign, Muhammad Ali maintained a busy schedule, defending his title against the best available contenders. Of course, he wasn't above taking a "breather" every now and then, as attested by his title fight against an undeserving Brian London. The first year of Ali's second reign promised to bring boxing fans more of the same, as the champ spoke of squeezing four defenses into 1975.

Along with the obvious financial advantages an active reign would bring, Ali also believed he needed the work to maintain his skills. He turned 33 in January, an advanced age in the demanding sport of boxing.

On paper, Muhammad's first 1975 challenger appeared to be a soft touch: Chuck Wepner, a ring-worn 34-year-old veteran from Bayonne, New Jersey. Wepner, whose father Charlie fought as a heavyweight in the 1930s, was known primarily for his big heart and tender skin.

Chuck's courage and resiliency were on a par with that of Canadian iron man George Chuvalo. Unlike Chuvalo, however, Wepner suffered from a bad case of boxing hemophilia. His tendency to suffer cuts at the slightest contact between leather and skin bordered on the gruesome. In that regard, Wepner was an American counterpart to that notorious blood-shedder from Britain, Henry Cooper.

By the time he signed to fight Ali on March 24, 1975, at the Cleveland Coliseum, Wepner, nicknamed the "Bayonne Bleeder," had accumulated more than 300 stitches in compiling a modest 30–9–2 record. Six of his losses were due to the cuts those sutures closed.

But Wepner wasn't one to become squeamish at the sight of his own blood. "Chuck's a sadist for stitches," Wepner's manager Al Braverman once said. "He loves 'em."

Braverman wasn't much bothered by his charge's gore, either. In fact, as long as Chuck's battered head was still attached to his body, Braverman rarely found reason to stop a fight. It was always the referee or ring doctor who came to Wepner's rescue; like Chuvalo, Chuck had always finished his fights on his feet.

Wepner first met Braverman when he came to the latter's aid at a time when Al was having a physical discourse with three opponents. That chance encounter resulted in a partnership that lasted 16 years. Fighter and manager maintained a mutual understanding concerning the incredible amount of punishment Wepner was willing to absorb to pursue his career.

"My motto," Wepner said in a 1987 interview, "was you don't ever stop a fight unless I tell you to. I don't give a damn if I lose a quart of blood and I'm dead on my feet and look like I've been hit by a bus. If I can't go anymore, I'll tell you. And I never said I can't go anymore. I never quit."[1]

When he was stopped on cuts by Joe Bugner in 1970, an angry Wepner complained: "I had worse cuts shaving." In the Bugner fight, noted British referee Harry Gibbs halted the bloodbath because he claimed Wepner's cut was six inches long. Braverman suggested that Gibbs should have brought a tape measure.

For Wepner and Braverman alike, any injury would have seemed superficial subsequent to the bludgeoning Chuck received at the hands of Sonny Liston on June 29, 1970. When the fight was stopped at the end of nine rounds, Wepner had suffered a broken nose, broken left cheekbone, and cuts that required an incredible 72 stitches to repair.

Still, Braverman screamed, "Don't you dare stop it!" at ringside doctor Reginald Farrar when Farrar decided to end the bloodbath. New Jersey Athletic Commissioner Abe J. Greene had restrained Farrar from examining Wepner after rounds three and six. Greene explained later that Wepner had made a plea before the fight that the contest not be stopped due to superficial cuts.

Whether it was pride or stupidity that drove Wepner on, one had to admire Wepner's sheer, stubborn fortitude that night. In an out-of-character gesture, Liston visited Chuck's dressing room after the fight. Sonny congratulated Wepner on his durability and asked him why he didn't fall down. Wepner told Liston that he'd never had the practice.

Asked later if Wepner was the bravest man he'd ever met, Liston responded, "No, his manager is."[2]

A year earlier, Chuck had served as a trial horse for Liston's protégé, George Foreman. It was only George's fourth professional fight, and Wepner learned what many foes after him would discover: Foreman's left jab was one of the heaviest in boxing history.

At the 54-second mark of round three, the fight ended when Foreman's jab broke open a 14-stitch gash over Wepner's left eye. Naturally, Wepner and Braverman protested the stoppage.

Still, Wepner's career wasn't totally unsuccessful. Several bright moments managed to shine through the bloodstains. As an amateur, Chuck accumulated a perfect record of 65–0, including AAU and Golden Gloves titles. As a pro, he developed a reputation as a spoiler when he upset 1967 Pan-American Games gold medalist Forest Ward in 1968. Ward was touted as championship material until the less heralded Wepner stopped him in seven rounds. The following year, Wepner overcame 12-to-5 odds to gain a close decision over another hot prospect, Peru's Roberto Davila.

The biggest name to grace Chuck's win column was former WBA champion Ernie Terrell. However, the storm of controversy that surrounded Wepner's 12-round decision in 1973 diminished the thrill of victory. Held in Atlantic City, the bout had been sanctioned for something called the United States Heavyweight Championship, but the furor over the decision became so intense that no title was awarded.

Referee Harold Valan held the only scorecard, and he gave the fight to Wepner by a margin of 7 rounds to 5. But a poll of reporters at ringside gave Chuck no more than two of the twelve rounds. Commissioner Greene also felt Terrell deserved the nod.

Terrell and his manager, George Hamid Jr., understandably believed they had been robbed. Hamid went so far as to charge at Valan with a pair of scissors in his hand when the decision was announced. In a subsequent investigation, Valan told Greene he favored Wepner as the aggressor. Also, he alleged that Terrell had engaged in foul tactics.

This wasn't the first time a Valan decision had drawn fire. As the sole official in the 1968 Jimmy Ellis–Floyd Patterson WBA title bout, Valan had given the nod to Ellis when virtually everyone at ringside thought Patterson had won the fight.

Regardless of how it came about, Wepner could now claim a victory over a former world champion. Well, at least a partial world champion. The United States title was withheld pending a rematch that never occurred. As a final footnote to Wepner–Terrell, Chuck bled throughout the contest.

At the time, Wepner was already a titleholder of sorts by virtue of an April 15, 1972, victory over arch-rival Randy Neumann. The title at stake was the New Jersey state heavyweight championship. The 12-round verdict evened Wepner's score against Neumann; Randy had gained a decision over Wepner four months earlier.

The Jersey rivals settled their differences once and for all in a rubber match on March 8, 1974. Wepner ended the series decisively with a seventh-round stoppage of the smaller Neumann.

In September of that year, Wepner finally got his hands on the United States belt when he kayoed prospect Terry Hinke in eleven rounds. Hinke was also one of George Foreman's chief sparring partners, which said something for Terry's resiliency, as sparring partners didn't last long in Foreman's camp.

Foreman was said to have offered Wepner a title shot that was contingent on Big George's emerging triumphant in Zaire. When Ali upset Foreman, the Wepner camp put its title hopes on hold.

According to the fistic grapevine, Ali was negotiating to defend his title against Ron Lyle. Then, early in 1975, Ali created a stir by announcing that he would fight a tune-up against Wepner in March, then take Lyle on in May or June. Wepner gladly accepted his long-shot chance to win the title.

Many boxing people doubted Wepner's credibility as a title challenger. Joe Frazier was one of the first to speak out. He claimed that Wepner was an unworthy challenger, and as champion, Ali should be defending against men closer to his own ability.

New York Times writer Dave Anderson gave Frazier a justified slap on the wrist for that statement. "Frazier conveniently forgot that three years ago he defended the title against Terry Daniels and Ron Stander, neither of whom could carry Chuck Wepner's Band-Aid," Anderson commented.

In truth, Wepner was not an undeserving challenger. Through hard work and persistence, he had risen from journeyman to the Top Ten. He hadn't lost a fight in well over three years, and was ranked #8 in the world.

Wepner was growing weary of the critics questioning his viability as a title challenger. "I've worked for this shot. Ali wanted to fight someone white who was ranked. Well, I'm ranked no. 8, and I'm about as white as you can get."[3]

One skeptic sneered that if Wepner was #8, then a punching bag must be #7. Others pointed out that Wepner had been defeated by both George Foreman and Jose "King" Roman.

Madison Square Garden had originally been approached to host Ali–Wepner, but the Mecca of Boxing declined the honor. Matchmaker Teddy Brenner claimed that Wepner had never beaten a worthy opponent in the Garden. As well, Brenner complained that Chuck was always bleeding ... no kidding.

Contracts were signed on February 10, and the fight was slated for March 24 in Cleveland, Don King's home town. Although the fight was billed as a heavyweight title bout, it didn't receive the sanction of the World Boxing Council. WBC President Ramon Velasquez stated that the fight would be such a mismatch that it "could end in a tragedy."[4] This was, of course, the same Velasquez who bumped Jose Roman up to #10 in the WBC ratings so he could challenge Foreman back in 1973.

Ali's pre-fight commentary didn't do much to boost the Bayonne Bleeder's credentials. Indeed, Ali considered himself so superior to his opponent that Chuck's tender skin would not be a factor in the outcome. He claimed that he could whup Wepner without hitting him in the face.

The champ was finding it hard to motivate himself to train hard for Chuck. "I'm getting paid $1.5 million to fight this pug and it's fool's gold. I won't suffer for Wepner. I want to fight for ten more years, and so I can't go all-out for every fight. This sucker is a cinch."

Asked if he considered Wepner a "White Hope," Ali replied, "That's the only hope he's got."[5] In his unique way, Ali was right. Wepner received none of the buildup from which white American title challengers usually benefited. White fans who cared about such matters were not eager to invest their hopes and dreams in an obscure, unglamorous 34-year-old like Wepner. Even if Wepner did somehow manage to pull off a miracle upset of Ali, what other top heavyweight did he stand a chance of beating? Foreman? Frazier? Norton? Quarry?

Not likely.

For the most part, the media appeared to be more interested in mocking Wepner than in building him up as a blue-collar underdog. Some of the more satirical sportswriters had a field day ridiculing the challenger's susceptibility to cuts.

Robert Lipsyte provided a typical example of the scarlet prose that marked much of the Ali–Wepner coverage. "Muhammad Ali's first defense in his second hitch as heavyweight champion is the kind of entertainment that will attract Medical Center and Marcus Welby fans," Lipsyte wrote. He also suggested that Ali be required to present a large percentage of his $1.6 million purse to the Red Cross Blood Bank.[6]

At the contract signing, Ali had announced that he would indeed donate portions of his future ring earnings to worthy charities. Dave Anderson commented that for $1.6 million, Ali shouldn't be fighting hopeless challengers. "Perhaps that's why, tortured by guilt, Ali has discovered charity," Anderson commented cynically. But Anderson also made a statement that proved prophetic: "Sometimes the fights that appear easy turn out to be difficult."[7]

Wepner was determined to make this fight, billed as "Chance of a Lifetime," as difficult for Ali as possible. Although he wasn't operating under any false illusions concerning the vast difference between Ali's ability and his own, Wepner was banking on Ali's taking him too lightly. Chuck also realized that the only possible advantage he could carry into the ring was conditioning.

If Ali wasn't training very seriously, Wepner was. The "Bayonne Bleeder" abstained from alcohol, fatty foods, and his greatest temptation: women. A noted ladies' man, Wepner found enforced chastity a bitter pill to swallow. As the date for the fight approached, Wepner said his six weeks of abstinence provided ample incentive for him to knock Ali's head off once he got him in the ring.

The rigorous training paid off. Wepner weighed in at a trim 225 pounds. At 6'5", Chuck enjoyed a 2" height advantage over Ali. He often joked that he used to be 6'2", but all the uppercuts he'd caught had stretched him three inches taller.[8]

Ali came in at a sloppy 223½, an accurate reflection of his indifferent preparation. By taking Wepner so lightly, Ali appeared to be agreeing with the media's low opinion of Chuck's chances. The champion also put a great deal of stock in his superior performances against their common opponents.

Both fighters had taken on Foreman, Liston, Terrell, Buster Mathis, and Joe Bugner. Ali defeated them all, while Wepner could only claim a highly disputed decision over Terrell. The rest had stopped him.

Braverman was quick to point out that Wepner's TKO losses had come on cuts and that no one, not even Liston or Foreman, had been able to knock Chuck off his feet. Braverman promised that even Ali's slashing fists wouldn't be able to cut his warrior.

At first glance, Braverman's statement smacked of blind faith in his fighter. However, during training the wily manager had administered a secret ointment designed to toughen Wepner's skin. Al said the concoction had been handed down to him by Jack "Doc" Kearns, the man who had guided Jack Dempsey to the title almost sixty years before.

Wishful thinking or not, Wepner and Braverman seemed to think they had all the bases covered. But what about the "Rope-a-Dope," the strength-sapping technique Ali had utilized to weaken Foreman, a man eight years younger than Wepner? Chuck vowed that unlike Foreman, his arms wouldn't drop after a few rounds.

For all Wepner's confidence, only his loyal fans from Bayonne appeared to be giving him much of a chance. The Bayonne contingent was strongly represented in Cleveland on fight night, and their support was vociferous and, in some cases, eccentric. "I've been cleaning the blood out of his robe since he started and I'm still doing it," boasted a fan named Mrs. Barresi. Mrs. Barresi owned a dry cleaning store in Bayonne.

Once the bell for the first round rang, Ali soon discovered that Wepner was more than just a bleeder. Over the course of his career, the Jersey brawler had acquired an extensive repertoire of unsavory tactics. Wepner's Bayonne cronies were confident his roughhouse techniques could do some damage to the stylish Ali.

One Bayonne supporter who was familiar with Chuck's roughhouse tactics declared that if they left the referee home that their man could beat Ali, Frazier and Foreman at the same time.

Wepner himself once bragged that he could whip any man in the world, provided that the fight was held in a phone booth. Against Ali, he wasted little time implementing some non–Queensberry moves, and eventually managed to induce the champion to emulate him.

Wepner's repeated rabbit punches, or illegal blows to the back of the head, went unnoticed by Referee Tony Perez despite Ali's frequent complaints. Finally, Ali fought fire with fire. Holding Wepner with one hand, Muhammad administered a rapid-fire series of rabbit punches with the other.

That caught Perez's attention and he issued a warning to an incredulous Ali. But Ali shouldn't have been surprised by Perez's actions. In the aftermath of Superfight II against Joe Frazier, Ali had accused Perez of robbing him of a knockout in the second round. Did Perez see the Wepner fight as payback time?

As the rounds wore on, Wepner switched his attack from the back of Ali's head to his kidneys. The innocuous looking blows took their toll on the champion. Ali's physician, Dr. Ferdie Pacheco, estimated that Wepner landed 300 blows to Muhammad's kidneys. The resulting discomfort gave him considerable trouble over the next couple of months.

During the fight, however, Ali was handling Wepner easily, if not spectacularly. One television commentator cracked that Ali was paying more attention to Perez than he was to Wepner.

Then, in Round 9, came the greatest single moment in the Bayonne Bleeder's career.

As Ali was retreating, Wepner landed a thudding right hand under the champion's heart. Down went Ali, for only the fourth time in his career. More embarrassed than hurt, he got up immediately. As the crowd screeched in disbelief, Perez sent Wepner to a neutral corner and issued a mandatory eight count to Ali.

Later, Ali would protest that the knockdown wasn't legitimate because Wepner had stepped on the champion's foot before landing the telling blow. But Perez had ruled it a knockdown, and that's the way it stands in the record books.

Unhurt but still angry, Ali began to fight with more purpose, and that spelled an end to any hope Wepner had entertained of pulling off a miraculous upset. The champ went to work on Wepner's left eye, which had been cut in the seventh round. From the knockdown on, Ali landed innumerable jabs and combinations to Wepner's battered features, slowly turning the Bayonne hope into ground Chuck.

To Wepner's credit, he hung in and tried to fight back, but he couldn't match Ali's hand speed. Still, by the fifteenth round, it looked as though Wepner was on his way to a moral victory, going the distance against "The Greatest."

Toward the end of the round, though, Ali blasted Wepner with a brutal combination. Chuck reeled into the ropes, then sagged to the canvas, a victim of fatigue and too many punches. He rose at the count of "9," but he could barely stay on his feet. Perez called a halt at 2:41.

Braverman practically had to drag his defeated gladiator back to his corner. Still, the feisty manager denounced the stoppage.

Wepner echoed his manager's sentiments. The valiant warrior said that he could have continued. He declared that he fell because he was tired, not hurt. On the whole, however, Wepner was satisfied with his performance and happy that he received "only 23 stitches" for his pains.

Ali seemed tired, too, actually collapsing in the ring after the fight was over. He said later that he was "weak, not tired."

Of his battered but unbowed opponent, Ali said, "There's no other human being in the world that can go 15 rounds like that."[9] But he also continued to dispute the knockdown, insisting he had been tripped.

Naturally, Braverman disagreed. "The guy was going down anyway," he claimed. "He got hit a good right under the heart, and was on his way backwards and down when Chuck stepped on his foot. Having his foot stepped on had nothing to do with getting knocked down, believe me."[10]

And so Wepner joined the ranks of Sonny Banks, Henry Cooper, and Joe Frazier as the only men ever to have dropped Muhammad Ali. Wepner would be also the last man to accomplish that feat. As such, his days as a fistic nobody had come to an end.

In the immediate aftermath of the fight, Wepner's gutsy effort made him an instant celebrity and an inspiration to many other underdogs. Dave Anderson wrote: "Most people probably can identify with Chuck Wepner quicker than with any of Ali's other opponents whether those people be white, black, or polka dot."[11]

Anderson theorized that Wepner's performance touched millions of people because Chuck was basically an average guy. He wasn't "pretty" like Ali, and he worked a 9-to-5 job as a liquor salesman. He wasn't exceptionally talented, and when he got hit in the face he bled profusely, just like the majority of the population.

Ironically, the characteristics that had earned him ridicule before the fight caused the media to jump on Wepner's bandwagon after his never-say-die effort. And, although no one knew it at the time, Wepner's courageous stand also inspired the creation of one of the most popular film characters of the next two decades.

A talented but out-of-work actor and writer named Sylvester Stallone had watched the

Ali–Wepner bout on closed-circuit TV. Impressed by Wepner's grit, Stallone later sat down and wrote the script that later became the hit movie *Rocky*.

Wepner's silver-screen counterpart, Rocky Balboa, eventually won the world title. In real life, Chuck never came close to another title shot. However, he did collect some sizeable purses over the rest of his career. After he retired, he slipped out of the public eye until he was arrested for selling cocaine in the late 1980s. Having paid his debt to society, he is still remembered by ardent fight fans for his night of gore and glory in 1975.

Ali–Wepner wasn't the only major heavyweight bout held on March 24. On the same night, two of the top contenders, Ken Norton and Jerry Quarry, met in a crossroads bout at Madison Square Garden. It was a crucial meeting for both men. In their last significant bouts, each had suffered a one-sided drubbing: Quarry by Frazier, and Norton by Foreman.

The fighters were well aware that their careers hung in the balance. Quarry, who was no stranger to the fistic tightrope, stated before the fight that a loss to Norton would end his career. Norton, who was already beginning to eye a Hollywood career, figured a win would gain him a shot at Ali, while a loss would make him a full-time actor.

Both men had begun their careers in California, and Norton said he had been trying to arrange a fight with Quarry for several years. Now that he had the opportunity, he was determined to make the best of it.

Quarry was 29, and so was Norton, depending on which birth certificate one chose to accept. Although Norton had only been in the limelight since 1973, Quarry had been in the public eye for the better part of a decade. Now he was beginning to consider what life after boxing had to offer. He indicated that even if he beat Norton, he would still retire at the end of 1975.

The fighters received healthy purses; Norton pulled down $100,000 while Quarry, a long-time Garden favorite, earned $175,000.

Norton enjoyed all the physical advantages: three inches in height, seven inches in reach, and 11½ pounds in weight. But Quarry had fought and beaten bigger men before. And he was a big puncher, which had always been Norton's downfall.

Both fighters promised a war, and 15,397 paying customers took them at their word. And the spectators were far from disappointed.

The fireworks started at the first bell. Norton controlled the early action with a rapid and accurate left jab. Then he hurt Quarry with a short right hand. Jerry responded by driving Norton into the ropes with a whirlwind attack.

Round two was marked by frequent and lethal exchanges. Early in the third, Norton opened a cut over Quarry's left eye. Ken followed up with powerful combinations as the flow of blood began to hamper the Irishman's vision.

Sensing that the fight might be stopped, Quarry attacked like a wild man, forcing Norton against the ropes and ripping away with both hands. Jerry was desperate for a knockout, but he didn't get one. Late in the round, Norton came off the ropes and stabbed away at the cut over Quarry's eye.

The ring physician checked Quarry between rounds and permitted him to come out for the fourth. The round was all Norton. Ken nailed Quarry time and again with short, chopping uppercuts. Still, Quarry attempted to close in on Norton, who was having a field day.

By the fifth, Quarry was exhausted and his head was snapping back with each shot Norton landed. Still, Jerry never went down and he never stopped trying to land a knockout blow. But Norton caught most of Quarry's punches on his gloves and arms, and the few that got through lacked steam.

Norton's pace had also slowed, but he was still landing at will on an almost stationary target. A final succession of blows topped by a jarring left hook prompted Referee Johnny Lo Bianco to jump between the fighters to save Quarry from further punishment.

Examining his bloody brow after the fight, Quarry declared that it was his final cut from boxing. He held to his word and retired, as he had threatened to do before each of his many crossroads bouts. From start to finish, Quarry's saga had been by turns promising, disappointing and always well publicized. The Phoenix had always risen from the ashes, but against Norton, Quarry's wings had failed him. He knew the time had come to call it a career.

As in so many other fighters before and since, the flicker of hope failed to die completely, and Quarry made a comeback in November of 1977. Fighting on the undercard of Norton's 15-rounder against Jimmy Young, Jerry took on Lorenzo Zanon, a slick but feather-fisted boxer from Italy.

For eight rounds, Zanon made a fool of an out-of-shape, ring-worn, frustrated Quarry. The Italian's jab tattooed Quarry's face, leaving it bumpy and bleeding. In the ninth round, Quarry's power punches finally connected with Zanon's fragile chin, and it was lights out for Lorenzo. Embarrassed by his poor performance, Quarry retired again.

In 1983, due to financial woes, Jerry chased money the best way he knew how: he tried another comeback, this time in the newly created cruiserweight division. Although the 190-pound class was better suited to a fighter of Quarry's size, at 38 he was too old, and already exhibiting signs of pugilistica dementia. After two inconsequential wins in 1983, Quarry slipped back into retirement, this time until 1992. Despite the fact that Quarry had earned in the neighborhood of $5 million in his career, by 1990 he was on Social Security. His mental and physical decline accelerated after 1983. Although most states wouldn't allow him to fight, he managed to nail down a match on October 30, 1992, in Colorado against a cruiserweight 16 years his junior. Resilient till the end, Quarry remained on his feet despite losing a six-round nod. He never fought again. He declined rapidly after that, and required constant care from his brother Jimmy, needing to be both fed and dressed. Jimmy was also caring for brother Mike, another former light heavyweight contender who also suffered from pugilistica dementia.

Jerry Quarry was hospitalized with pneumonia on December 28, 1998, and soon succumbed to cardiac arrest. He passed away on January 3, 1999, at the age of 53. Mike died on June 11, 2006.

Jerry lived long enough to see himself inducted into the World Boxing Hall of Fame in 1995; it was quite a feat for a man who had never won a world title. He left boxing with a remarkable record of 53–9–4 (32 KOs) against some of the greatest fighters in history. His incredible durability was not only his legacy, but unfortunately his undoing. Quarry's skill and heart would have earned him a championship in many other eras; however, to his great misfortune, he peaked in the same period as Ali, Frazier Foreman and Norton.

As for Norton, he had once again established himself as a legitimate contender. But the lineup for a million-dollar payday against Ali was a long one.

Mirage

Less than two months after his unexpected struggle against Wepner, Ali was once again in the ring. It was as though he were repeating his roadshow of 1972, this time as champion.

This time out, he would be facing a recognized, legitimate contender: Ron Lyle, who boasted much more impressive credentials than Wepner.

Since the setback he had suffered at Quarry's hands two years before, Lyle had rebounded well, running up an impressive string of victories and re-establishing himself as a contender. However, in his first four fights after the Quarry loss, Lyle's punching power appeared to have deserted him.

His initial comeback victory came against a well-used trial horse named Bob Stallings. A 5'10", 220-pound fireplug of a fighter, Stallings was a "spoiler" in the truest sense of the word. By the time he met Lyle, Stallings had compiled a lackluster 15–22 record. But the numbers were deceptive, as he had managed wins over the likes of Al "Blue" Lewis and Chuck Wepner.

Stallings lost, as expected, to Lyle, but he won a moral victory by going the 10-round distance. Over 22 more fights, Stallings won 15, including upsets over Mac Foster and the ever-dangerous Earnie Shavers. He finished his career with an even slate of 30 wins and 30 losses.

Lyle's next foe was the clever and elusive Gregorio Peralta, the Argentine slickster who had given Foreman fits half a decade earlier. The aging Peralta proved just as difficult for Lyle. They met twice in 1973, with Lyle winning a decision the first time, then having to settle for a controversial draw in their second encounter. The second fight was held in Peralta's adopted home town of Frankfurt, West Germany, and even the Germans believed Lyle deserved the victory.

Distance wins over shopworn Lou Bailey and one-time prospect Wendell Newton caused boxing fans to seriously question Lyle's punching prowess, which was once considered on a par with Foreman's. Had the beating he'd taken from Quarry inhibited Lyle from going all-out on offense?

Ron soon dismissed those doubts with a pair of devastating stoppages of Jose Luis Garcia and Jurgen Blin. Garcia, the one-time conqueror of Ken Norton, crashed in three rounds. Blin lasted only two, and retired immediately thereafter.

Lyle's next opponent was Larry Middleton, whom he had blasted out in three rounds a year earlier. On October 31, 1973, however, Middleton fought to survive rather than win and lasted the full ten rounds. Lyle captured the decision.

March 19, 1974, marked Ron's biggest test since the Quarry fight. His opponent was another holdover from the 1960s: Oscar "Ringo" Bonavena. Bonavena's best days were well behind him, but he remained in the bottom half of the Top Ten on the strength of his previous accomplishments.

The fight, like so many of Bonavena's 1970s encounters, had been postponed due to hand injuries. Once it got underway in Lyle's hometown of Denver, the bout looked to be a replay of the Quarry disaster. "Ringo," who was aging but still dangerous, dominated the first three rounds, applying constant pressure and landing his awkward bombs on Lyle's head and body. Lyle seemed confused by Oscar's wild aggression.

In the fourth, Lyle showed the boxing skills he had lacked against Quarry. Finally finding his range, he tagged the onrushing Bonavena with accurate counterpunches and took the momentum into his own hands. Bonavena was still the aggressor, but Lyle was now meeting him blow for blow.

Lyle sent Oscar's mouthpiece flying in the sixth and had him hurt in the eighth. The only round Ron lost after that was the tenth, and that was only because he'd been penalized a point for hitting Oscar below the belt — poetic justice, considering Bonavena's reputation for fouling.

The Argentine dropped to his knees and was given a minute to recover. Oscar's brother thought the fight should have ended in a disqualification, and he threw a towel at the referee in protest when the bout continued.

In the end, nearly 11,000 joyous Denver fans cheered as their hometown hope won a unanimous 12-round decision. But Lyle didn't share his supporters' satisfaction with his performance. He said he had trained himself to peak condition earlier in the year; then, because of the performance, he had to train himself down.

The Denver Boxing Club was also high on the local hero. Its members went so far as to offer then-champion Foreman $750,000 tax-free to defend his title against Lyle in Denver. But Foreman wasn't about to fight in the U.S. until his contractual problems were solved, and besides, $750,000 was peanuts compared to what Foreman would earn by fighting Ali.

Lyle rounded out 1974 with three more victories. On July 16, he gained a unanimous 12-round decision over former WBA champion Jimmy Ellis. An eighth-round knockout of Boone Kirkman and a fifth-round disposal of Memphis Al Jones propelled Lyle to the #3 spot in the ratings, even though Kirkman was a has-been and Jones a never-was.

After Ali regained the title from Foreman, negotiations began for a spring 1975 Ali–Lyle fight. To tune up for the bout, Lyle traveled to Honolulu in February. His opponent was a Philadelphian named Jimmy Young. Handicapped by a punch that couldn't have broken an egg, Young was regarded as a safe workout for a fighter with Lyle's strength and durability.

What Lyle's camp neglected to take into account was the fact that Young's power shortage was compensated by what were arguably the finest boxing skills in the division, other than Ali's. A fighter who couldn't punch needed to develop such skills simply to survive the notorious Philly gym wars. Jimmy demonstrated the art of hitting without being hit in return on a befuddled Lyle and came away with a lopsided ten-round decision.

Lyle returned to the mainland with his second career loss and a seriously compromised reputation. As he had demonstrated after the Quarry fight, Ron was not a sore loser. He was accustomed to overcoming adversity and remained optimistic about his chances of challenging Ali. "Maybe he won't be so afraid of me after he reads about the [Young] fight," Lyle said.[12]

Sure enough, it was Lyle, not Young, who was penciled in to fight Ali on May 16, 1975, in Las Vegas. Although Lyle got his chance despite the loss to Young, both he and Ali suffered a financial setback. They were originally scheduled to fight at Madison Square Garden on June 2, but the Garden backed out after Young's win.

Ali was to have collected $2.2 million for fighting Lyle in New York. Now he was guaranteed only $1 million. And Lyle's purse dropped from $325,000 to $110,000. As well, their fight was originally slated for live telecast on closed-circuit. But Lyle's loss to Young ended interest in that kind of financial risk.

The fight was, however, available on home TV, courtesy of ABC. It was the first live Ali title fight on "free" TV since 1966. The prospect of appearing on a live broadcast pleased Ali. With typical humility, "The Greatest" went on to predict that the streets would be empty that Friday night because everybody would be indoors watching him fight Lyle. The champ said that he would allow Lyle to last at least eight rounds so ABC could get some commercials in.

Ali planned to wear Lyle down through use of the Rope-a-Dope. He was confident that Lyle, whose style was similar to Foreman's, would fall into the same trap. But Lyle was no fool. He had already publicly proclaimed that he wouldn't be lured by the Rope-a-Dope.

His trainer, Chickie Ferrara, promised that Lyle would pace the action to avoid falling victim to a late-round onslaught.

Both Ali and Lyle came into the fight heavier than usual. Although Lyle weighed in at a career-high 219 pounds, he looked extremely fit. By contrast, Ali scaled 224½ and sported a slight case of midriff bulge. He blamed his waist expansion more on age than conditioning.

But Lyle was the same age as Ali: 33. And Ron's abdomen was as hard as Ali's was soft. Still, the rugged ex-con's intimidating physical appearance did little to sway the opinion of the bettors. A combination of Ali's past greatness and Lyle's loss to Young caused the odds makers to lean heavily toward the champ. In fact, the only Las Vegas odds on the fight were on whether or not Lyle could last eleven rounds.

Despite the overwhelming consensus in Ali's favor, Lyle remained confident. After all, he was no stranger to Ali, having sparred with "The Greatest" a few years earlier. At the time, Lyle was still an amateur.

As if fighting for the title weren't enough pressure, though, Lyle went into the ring with a huge psychological millstone hanging from his neck. He was embroiled in two lawsuits involving domestic violence. In the first, he allegedly shot at his wife, and in the second he threatened her with his fist. The fist of a professional fighter is considered a dangerous weapon which must be registered by law, and a boxer who lands a punch outside the ring can be charged with assault with a deadly weapon.

With legal difficulties like that weighing on Lyle's mind, the gambling crowd felt more confident than ever in their choice of Ali.

Then, on fight night, Ali proceeded to put on one of the worst performances of his career. Lyle did exactly what he said he would. Every time Ali attempted the Rope-a-Dope, Lyle would simply stand back and stare at him. Ali then had to come off the ropes; otherwise there wouldn't have been a fight for the spectators to watch.

Had Lyle and Ferrara outsmarted Ali? Hardly. Ever resourceful, Ali invented a new tactic which became known as the "Mirage." Quite simply, the Mirage was the Rope-a-Dope without the ropes. Now Ali stood in center ring with his hands held high and allowed Lyle to swing to his heart's content.

The Mirage did induce Lyle to throw punches. The problem was, Ali wasn't firing many jabs or counters in return. As the rounds dragged on, Lyle built a lead on points through his steady, workmanlike aggression. Although Ali was never visibly hurt, he also appeared to be clowning his title away.

Ali's cornermen, as well as manager Herbert Muhammad, grew more concerned with each passing round. Angelo Dundee implored Ali to get going. But the champion continued to sacrifice rounds in an attempt to drain Lyle's stamina.

And his strategy was working, although nobody knew it other than Ali himself. For all Lyle's domination of the first ten rounds and refusal to go along with the Rope-a-Dope, he was beginning to wear down, though nowhere near as quickly and dramatically as Foreman had.

Going into the eleventh round, Lyle was ahead on two of the judges' scorecards. The third official had the fight even. Sensing that the time was right to break out of his defensive shell, Ali opened up on Lyle and staggered him with a jarring right to the head. As Lyle floundered against the ropes, Ali bombarded him with both hands.

Lyle reeled from one side of the ring to the other as Ali pursued him. The champion's punches came in so quickly and accurately that Lyle couldn't even defend himself, much less mount an effective counterattack. Although he somehow remained upright, the challenger's dream ended when Referee Fred Hernandez halted the fight at the 1:08 mark.

An angry Lyle bitterly protested the stoppage, claiming that Hernandez's action was premature. "I wasn't hurt," Lyle protested.

Ali disagreed. "I told the ref to come and get him. I could see he was hurt. I can't kill a man. I did the same thing with Quarry and Ellis, same way."[13]

Observers who were less biased than Lyle were split in their opinions. Some believed Hernandez had stopped the bout at the right time, as Lyle appeared defenseless and in serious danger of getting hurt. Others, citing Ali's lack of punching power, believed Lyle could have weathered the storm.

Ali was satisfied with the result. He believed the Mirage had worked, sapping Lyle's strength and making him susceptible to the eleventh round blitz. He concluded that although the Wepner fight was tougher, overall Lyle was a much more polished fighter than the "Bayonne Bleeder."

The question most boxing fans asked was, "Who's next for Ali?" The logical choices were rematches against Foreman and Frazier. And Ali's next match was indeed a rematch, but not against either of the two former champions.

Pacific Heights

After his 1974 triumph over Quarry, Joe Frazier took a long rest before resuming his campaign to regain the title. The opponent he chose for his first 1975 battle was old foe Jimmy Ellis, whom he had beaten decisively in 1970 to unify the heavyweight title. Their second meeting was set for March 1 in Melbourne, Australia.

While Frazier–Ellis II lacked the significance of their first encounter, the fighters were still two of the division's better known contenders. By now, though, they were headed in opposite directions. Frazier's destruction of Quarry had placed him back in the thick of title contention. At 35 years of age, Ellis was on a downhill slide that was picking up speed as time went on.

Since his one-round embalming by Earnie Shavers in 1973, the former WBA titleholder had tasted victory only once in five fights. In his first fight after Shavers, Ellis stopped habitual loser Memphis Al Jones in seven rounds.

He then took on Renton, Washington's Boone Kirkman in Seattle on December 12, 1973. Kirkman, a capable, hard-hitting battler, had shown promise in the 1960s, but had fallen short of big-time contention. However, he still attracted a degree of attention because he was a white fighter in a division dominated by blacks. Regarded by some as a poor man's Jerry Quarry, Kirkman carried an eight-bout winning streak into his encounter with Ellis.

The Ellis–Kirkman fight was action-packed from beginning to end. In the third round, Boone found himself on the seat of his pants. He got up and had Ellis in bad shape in the next stanza. The 28-year-old Kirkman kept the pressure on Ellis throughout the rest of the bout, with the exception of the tenth round. At that time, Ellis staged a last-ditch rally that left its mark on Kirkman's physiognomy.

In the end, Kirkman won what could arguably be called a hometown decision. Ironically, four months later, Boone was knocked out in three rounds by none other than Memphis Al Jones!

Ellis's next stop was in Landover, Maryland, where he took on another local hero,

Larry Middleton. Although Ellis appeared to control most of the action, the ring-wise Middleton fought in eye-catching flurries and had Ellis hurt in the last round.

Although the former champion sustained a considerable amount of facial damage, he still did enough to win in the opinion of everybody except the judges. On the scorecards, the fight came out a draw.

From Ellis's viewpoint, the Kirkman and Middleton affairs were debatable. However, Jimmy's next two losses were decisive.

Ron Lyle and Joe Bugner, both younger and bigger men, found Ellis a cagey and challenging opponent. Angelo Dundee, who was still Ellis's manager and trainer, said his charge was still a viable contender.

However, Ellis's once remarkable hand and foot speed had diminished considerably, and he lost control of both fights after the first few rounds. Only the wealth of experience he'd accumulated over 15 years saved him from being knocked out by a pair of young lions eager to add his name to their lists of victims. Even Ellis couldn't argue with the scorecards that made him a loser to Lyle and Bugner.

Because of his losing streak, Ellis dropped precipitously in the ratings, and his hopes of getting another title shot were growing dim. But a victory over Frazier would not only enhance his standing, it would also avenge the mauling Joe had inflicted in their first fight.

In a ring on the other side of the world, the two ex-champs went at it hammer and tongs. Although Ellis had faded much more than Frazier, he put up a much better fight the second time around. Making full use of his remaining boxing skills, Jimmy actually dominated the first three rounds. Then Frazier took over, utilizing the same overhand right that had dismantled Quarry.

Smokin' Joe tore open a five-stitch gash over Ellis's eye in the seventh round. He continued to attack his rapidly tiring foe over the next two rounds. To his credit, Ellis stayed on his feet, but he was a thoroughly beaten man when Referee Bob Foster, who had recently retired as light heavyweight champion, called a halt 59 seconds into the ninth.

Ellis had one more fight, a one-round blowout of a Jamaican journeyman named Carl Baker. After that, he wisely ended his career on a winning note.

Unlike most of his contemporaries, Ellis never tried a comeback. He remained in Ali's camp as a sparring partner for a couple of years, and was unfortunately blinded in one eye during a sparring accident with another fighter.

Frazier now believed he was ready for a title shot against Ali. But Ali wasn't yet ready for Frazier. The fighter he did feel ready for was another Joe named Bugner.

On July 1, Ali made his third title defense in less than one hundred days against Bugner in the exotic locale of Kuala Lumpur, Malaysia. The promoter in the Southeast Asian nation was Dato Harun Indris, whose official title was chief minister, a position equivalent to a governor in the U.S. He said his prime objective was to "project Malaysia to the world," a motivation similar to that of Zaire's President Mobutu.

Most of the people close to Ali refused to take Indris's proposal very seriously. Then the Malaysian deposited $1.5 million in the champion's bank account and $500,000 in the challengers'. At that point, Mr. Indris was taken very seriously indeed.

In an echo of the hype for Ali–Wepner, Ali–Bugner II was billed as "The Fight of a Lifetime." But Bugner, who still held the European heavyweight championship, stood several notches above Wepner in terms of talent and credibility. Since his back-to-back losses to Ali and Frazier in 1973, the Briton had gone undefeated in eight fights. Mac Foster, Pat Duncan, Jimmy Ellis, and Jose Luis Garcia were among his victims.

Going into the Ali rematch, Bugner was rated third by the WBC, the highest that organization had ever placed a British heavyweight. As such, he was probably the best title hope the British could boast thus far in the 20th century.

Bugner possessed none of the weaknesses that had hampered the past crop of challengers from the UK. Unlike his predecessors, he enjoyed the luxury of solid heavyweight dimensions at 6'4" and 230 pounds. Don Cockell, who had lost to Rocky Marciano in nine rounds, was little more than a beefed-up light heavyweight.

Also, Bugner wasn't plagued by delicate skin, as was Henry Cooper. Like Tommy Farr, who went 15 rounds with the great Joe Louis, Bugner was blessed with a dependable chin. Unlike Farr, Joe could punch when he wanted to.

Given his youth, boxing skills, and physical advantages, Bugner approached his title opportunity with a great deal of optimism. He viewed his career as a seven-year apprenticeship that prepared him for the day he would ascend the heavyweight throne. He believed the time was right for him to topple Ali.

Bugner firmly believed that his edge in youth, 25 to Ali's 33, would be a huge advantage in dealing with Kuala Lumpur's stifling heat. The furnace-like summer climate of Malaysia would indeed be a factor in the fight, and had to be taken into consideration during the fighters' training. Bugner prepared himself for the extreme heat and humidity by training in a special chamber at the Royal Air Force Institute of Aviation. Wearing a getup that resembled a space suit, Bugner rode a stationary bike under conditions of 110 degrees Fahrenheit and 70 percent humidity.

Out of respect for both his opponent and the heat, Ali paid more attention to training for Bugner than he had for Wepner or Lyle. Although there were some mornings when the champ simply rolled over and went back to sleep instead of rising for his roadwork, he made up for it with marathon sparring sessions.

On June 18 he alternated between Jimmy Ellis and Levi Forte, fighting ten brisk rounds and punishing both men in the process. Then, on June 27, just four days before the fight, Ali sparred an incredible 15 rounds, once again alternating opponents and doing without the customary one-minute rest between stanzas. Ali had neglected his roadwork that morning and, on impulse at the breakfast table, decided to do something "unique in the history of boxing!"

The mere fact that he attempted and completed such an unorthodox stunt so close to fight day was made all the more amazing by the impressive fashion in which he executed it, dancing and moving throughout. Who needed further proof that the champ could easily adapt to the demanding climate in Kuala Lumpur?

Still, Ali weighed in at 224½, his heaviest to date for a title fight. But the extra weight was part of the game plan. Dundee wanted his fighter to have some additional padding to burn off during the course of the fight.

At 230, Bugner was his usual statuesque self. Still, his recent sparring sessions often left something to be desired. His final performance was widely attended by both the British and American press, and the observers were unanimous in their belief that the Briton looked fit, but lacked mental focus.

He looked mechanical and ineffective against sparmates Pat Duncan and Bjorn Rudi, a Norwegian prospect. One British writer likened Bugner to a windup robot. Then again, the British press had always been hard on the local boy.

In the weeks leading up to the fight, British fans wondered aloud which Bugner would appear in the ring on July 1: the pit bull who had thrown caution to the wind against Frazier, or the all-too-familiar underachiever who seemed in need of a heart transplant.

Three days before the fight, Neil Allen wrote: "I believe the best we can hope for Bugner and quite possibly the best he subconsciously hopes for himself is that he will go the full 15 rounds against Ali on Tuesday morning and end up a much admired loser on points."[14]

In other words, a replay of their first encounter.

Despite the poor impression he made in his sparring, Bugner appeared confident on the surface. He even engaged in some verbal exchanges with Ali, something he hadn't attempted in 1973.

One reason for Joe's feistiness was that he was no longer in awe of "The Greatest." In their first fight, the youthful contender was star-struck; after all, he was fighting his ring idol. Bugner bore much less respect for Ali the second time around.

In fact, Bugner went so far as to say that every notion he had of Ali was shattered in their first encounter. When Ali failed to deliver on his seventh-round prediction, Joe re-evaluated just how great the "Greatest" really was.

Even on a personal level, Bugner thought less of Ali. In the buildup for their 1973 fight, Muhammad had falsely accused Bugner of calling him a "nigger." In the face of Bugner's protests, Ali had retracted the remark and apologized. Then he turned around and repeated the accusation prior to the second fight. Instead of becoming upset or attempting to deny the allegation, Bugner simply gave in.

While Andy Smith grew increasingly annoyed at Ali's tirades, Bugner handled himself quite well. He even shot a few zingers at Ali. "In this tropical heat," he quipped, "Muhammad Ali would soon be reduced to a lightweight. He will need a stick to walk, but maybe I'll help him around."

Not all of Bugner's rhetoric was playful. Still bitter over Ali's unfounded racial allegations, Bugner questioned Ali's self-proclaimed position as a "liberator" of the poor and oppressed.

Ever since he won the title the first time, the champion had been a fervent fighter for the rights of his people, and often spoke out against the injustices of poverty and the ghetto.

At the contract signing, however, Bugner pointed out to Ali that the champion had never lived in a ghetto. Bugner also pointed out that as a Hungarian he had personal knowledge of oppression and poverty. He could still remember the way Russian tanks crushed the 1956 revolt in his native Budapest, and his family's desperate escape from Soviet vengeance. Young Joe spent 14 months of his childhood in a refugee camp in Yugoslavia. When the Bugners arrived in Britain, there were times that the family struggled just to put bread on the table.

In London, Ali was installed as an 11–5 favorite, indicating that some British bettors were willing to take a chance on the local hope. Meanwhile, in Kuala Lumpur the odds makers favored the champ by a much wider 4-to-1 margin.

Ali was the favorite in Malaysia in other ways as well. When he arrived at Kuala Lumpur, the crowd that greeted him was five times larger than the one that had turned out for Bugner a few days earlier. Although this would have been the case almost anywhere in the world, the Malaysians, like the Indonesians back in 1973, had a special place in their hearts for the champion.

Because Malaysia was a predominantly Muslim nation, the populace looked upon Ali as one of their own, not a foreigner. And Ali, out of sincere feelings of kinship, promotional opportunities, or a combination of the two, went to great lengths to stress the bout's Islamic importance.

He revealed to the Malaysian press that he fought not for money, but for the liberation of the Islamic people. He went so far as to say that Allah would help him conquer Joe Bugner.

It's likely Ali was well aware that he wouldn't need divine intervention to handle Joe Bugner. In fact, he was predicting a knockout victory, a tall order considering Bugner hadn't been stopped since his pro debut seven years and 56 fights earlier. However, men like Foreman, Bonavena and Lyle had never been stopped either, until they met Ali.

During his last few fights, Ali had created techniques like the Rope-a-Dope and the Mirage to befuddle his opponents. For Bugner, he promised to unveil two new additions to his bag of tricks. The "Russian Tank," which may have been a subtle dig at Bugner's Iron Curtain origins, was yet another derivation of the Rope-a-Dope. It called for Ali to cross his arms in front of his face and allow the challenger to blast away. With his chin thus protected, Ali reasoned that Bugner would grow weary punching at nothing but arms and elbows.

Plan "B" was dubbed the "Malaysian Waltz." As the name implied, Ali would tie Bugner up and "waltz" him around the ring. With his ability to float like a butterfly and sting like a bee sapped by age, it seemed Ali had switched to soaking up punishment like a sponge and clinging like a octopus.

Bugner was certain he could easily counter any and all of Ali's ploys. In fact, he boldly proclaimed that he would stop Ali within six rounds.

However, when the bell rang and Bugner's opportunity of a lifetime materialized, he failed to rise to the occasion. What unfolded under the hot Malaysian sun was fifteen of the dullest, most one-sided rounds in heavyweight title history.

Bugner fought like a mannequin, looking stiff and confused from the outset. As the "fight" progressed, it became evident that the heat was having a greater effect on the younger man.

But it wasn't just the heat. Bugner was totally passive, allowing Ali to do whatever he pleased. Even though Ali wasn't doing much in the way of visible damage, Bugner looked as though he wished he were back in England. He even flinched when Ali feinted a blow. Only Joe's chin and youthful resilience saved him from a knockout defeat, as Ali dominated virtually every minute of the bout.

The decision was a mere formality, with only one judge giving Bugner as many as three of the 15 rounds. Although Ali's praise for his opponent was overgenerous, as once again he predicted Bugner would succeed him as champion, the reaction of the British press and fans was predictably scornful.

Surrounded in his dressing room by the critical British press, Bugner was questioned about his inept showing. A frustrated Joe blurted out, "Get me Jesus Christ, I'll fight him tomorrow." To which Hugh McIllvaney of the *London Observer* retorted, "Ah, Joe, you're only saying that because you know He's got bad hands." Those were kind words compared to the comments others, such as former British champion Henry Cooper, were throwing around. "It looked to me as if Joe was quite content to go the distance with Ali. I'm sure that the British fans would rather have seen him have a go, even if he had not managed the distance, than just last out the 15 rounds."[15]

Neil Allen called the fight "memorably boring." Of Bugner's character, Allen added, "I don't think he was afraid — rare but not unknown in boxing. He just does not possess a personality which can reach violently for victory."[16]

In Kuala Lumpur, the real news wasn't Ali's easy victory. It was the announcement of

Ali–Frazier III. Rumors of a rubber match between the two greatest rivals of the 1970s had run rampant during the past few months. Just as it appeared that both parties were on the verge of signing contracts, however, Ali made an announcement that was shocking even by his standards.

A week before the Bugner fight, a mysterious cloud of gloom suddenly dampened the champion's mood. He hinted that he intended to retire once he had finished his business with the Briton. As the days passed, he became more specific, saying he was going to hang up his gloves, and would formalize his decision immediately after the fight.

"This will be my last fight," he warned. "As soon as I finish annihilating Joe Bugner, as soon as I finish giving him the whupping of his life, I'm done with boxing."[17]

Coming from one of the most colossal egos of all time, those words were almost unbelievable. But there was more to come. Muhammad complained about the rigors of training, the time spent away from his family, and the burdens of celebrity status.

Tears formed in Angelo Dundee's eyes when he was asked about the future of boxing without Ali. "I think it's going to be dull for everyone," he sighed.

However downbeat Ali may have appeared, few of those close to him expected his retirement plans to stick. And Joe Frazier, who only wanted to be close to Ali in the ring, flew to Malaysia the moment he heard what the champ was saying.

Sure enough, as Ali was about to leave his corner for the start of the fifteenth round against Bugner, Ali leaned over the ropes and hollered to Frazier at ringside, "You're next!"

"I'll be waitin', Clay!"[18]

When asked why he changed his mind about retiring, Ali stated: "I don't want anybody to say I'm afraid of Frazier or George Foreman. They doubted Moses and some still doubt that I'm the greatest."[19]

Later, Don King removed all doubts concerning Superfight III when he announced from Malaysia that Ali and Frazier would meet one more time on September 30 in Manila, capital of the Philippines.

The Thrilla in Manila

Like their two previous encounters, the third fight between Ali and Frazier took on a unique flavor from the outset. Their 1971 encounter transcended boxing; not only was it a contest between fighters of different style and temperament, the fight also spotlighted social and political conflicts outside the ring. It was radical vs. conservative, left wing vs. right wing, pro–Vietnam War vs. anti–Vietnam war, and black vs. white. As well, Ali was fighting to regain the title he'd never lost in the ring, while Frazier fought to overcome the last obstacle between himself and undisputed recognition as champion.

Ali–Frazier II, on the other hand, was a battle for survival between a pair of ex-champions struggling to save their careers. And their third fight was something else again. This time, ideology and politics sat in the cheap seats.

Ali–Frazier III would be fought on much more basic terms. Both fighters were past their primes, but still the best in the division.

Ali wanted to keep his title. Frazier wanted to take it. That constituted all the motivation anyone needed to be eager to witness the third installment in one of the greatest boxing rivalries of all time.

Like its predecessors, Superfight III was a promoter's dream, a license to print money.

However, Madison Square Garden, the site of the first two battles, once again found itself priced out of the picture, losing out to the Philippine Islands.

In the same fashion as Zaire and Malaysia, the Philippines were quick to seize the opportunity to gain the international exposure a heavyweight superfight would provide. President Ferdinand Marcos and his wife Imelda claimed to be building the "New Society" in the island nation: a compatible blend of ancient Eastern traditions and modern Western technology. But Marcos's "New Society" was really nothing more than an old-fashioned dictatorship.

Nevertheless, the Ali–Frazier fight would present Marcos the opportunity to showcase his nation to the world. Even as he worked behind the scenes to make the fight a reality, Marcos never could have guessed the extent to which the name of his nation's capital would become part of boxing lore. Ali called the fight a "Thrilla in Manila," and that's the way it will always be remembered. However, the fight was actually held at the Araneta Coliseum in Quezon City.

While Ali once again took every opportunity to belittle Frazier before the fight, he refrained from calling Joe an "Uncle Tom." Frazier never was a "Tom," and if Ali believed that to be the case in 1971, by 1975 the political climate had changed. If Muhammad had merely been attempting to build up the gate for their first fight by smearing Frazier's reputation, there was no need to do so for the "Thrilla in Manila." Ali and Frazier had become such natural gate attractions that the fight would have been a sell-out even if they'd sworn eternal brotherhood on a stack of Bibles live on *Wide World of Sports*.

Of course, the chances of that happening were virtually nil. Ali's promise to make Frazier "more ugly than you is" was met by Joe's vow to "whup you like you stole something."

The fighters continued to downgrade each other, and the enmity between them was real, especially on Frazier's part. Although Ali had toned down his rhetoric, Frazier could neither forgive nor forget the slander he had endured over the years. Whereas it appeared that, beneath the surface, Ali actually liked Smokin' Joe, Frazier's disdain for the champion was genuine and well-founded.

"What is Frazier mad at me for?" Ali once asked in mock bewilderment. "I have made him the world's second most famous athlete."

Comments like that couldn't fail to raise Joe's blood pressure. Still, he made a strong effort to control his temper. He didn't want to embarrass himself the way he did at the ABC studio before the second fight. This time, Joe kept his cool during Ali's verbal pyrotechnics. But his loathing of Ali was sincere. A confidante revealed in January 1974, "Joe really hates him [Ali]. In the years when Joe could have put him down, he never did. He showed respect for Ali's beliefs, but now Ali doesn't have any respect for him. That's why Joe despises him."[20]

As if Superfight III weren't intriguing enough, a rumor began to circulate that the fighters had agreed to a private million-dollar wager on the outcome. This arrangement was reminiscent of the old bareknuckle days, when the combatants often fought not only for the prearranged purse but also for a "side bet" provided by the fighters themselves.

Whether or not the Ali–Frazier "side bet" was authentic remains a mystery. At the time, though, it piqued further public interest in what was shaping up as an epic battle. Both fighters, and their fans as well, were aware that their third fight would be the culmination of their careers.

Ali–Frazier III was likely to be the final meeting between the two antagonists, the definitive answer to the question of which man was the better fighter. As well, the result would go a long way toward determining each fighter's ultimate standing among the all-time greats.

While Frazier had an added incentive of intense dislike of Ali, both men realized their personal prestige was at stake.

Ali's true feelings for Frazier made no difference; his persistent verbal campaign against Frazier had made Joe his arch-enemy.

Frazier wasn't about to accept all those years of serving as Ali's public whipping boy for without satisfaction. The rubber match would provide him an opportunity to prove that the media and public had been wrong to cast him as the supporting player in the Ali–Frazier show.

And Ali had not fanned Frazier's flames only to be burnt once they stepped into the ring. A second defeat at Smokin' Joe's hands would be to bitter a pill for Ali's ego to swallow.

Conditioning, heart, motivation: there was no question that both fighters possessed those qualities in abundance. Thus the odds makers were forced to scrutinize other factors in their efforts to predict the outcome. As in the second fight, the activity factor appeared to favor Ali. Since January 1974, Frazier had made only two ring appearances, against Quarry and Ellis. Ali had gone to the post five times.

However, Frazier's manager Eddie Futch pointed out that his fighter had been on a two-fights-a-year schedule since 1969, and always came in strong after an intermission of five to seven months. Since Joe had stopped Ellis six months earlier, in Futch's estimation he was right on schedule.

By contrast, Futch believed Ali's hectic schedule in and out of the ring since regaining the title would drain the champion's physical resources. "I feel that with the extra weight and all the running around Ali is doing, personal appearances and exhibitions as well as the fights, he is wearing himself out," the wily manager/trainer observed.[21]

A factor in Frazier's favor was his new-found right hand. Futch had worked tirelessly to help Frazier to become an effective right-hand puncher, and the results were evident in Joe's one-sided defeats of Quarry and Ellis. If Ali had been hard pressed by a Frazier who relied solely on his left hook, how would he cope with a fighter who could "smoke" with both hands?

Futch also made it clear he would not tolerate a referee who allowed Ali to get away with his holding tactics. In the second fight, Tony Perez had allowed Ali to continually clutch the back of Frazier's head every time the shorter man bulled his way inside. Futch wasn't the only observer who believed that trick nullified Frazier's offense and cost him the decision.

Of course, Futch didn't agree with the decision. But he wasn't about to let Frazier lose that way again.

Just as Futch believed Frazier deserved the nod in Superfight II, Ali's trainer Angelo Dundee insisted Ali should have won their first encounter. Dundee indicated that for the third fight, he would bring Ali in at a weight somewhere between 220 and 225 pounds.

True to his trainer's word, the champion weighed in at 224½. This time, that weight looked solid on his frame; the spare tire he usually carried was gone. Dundee believed the extra muscle would make Ali stronger, and indeed the champion looked more powerful than ever before.

But Dundee probably got carried away when he proclaimed that Ali "hits as hard as Frazier, maybe even harder when he sets himself to punch."[22]

Frazier came in at 214½, every pound of which looked as hard as granite.

In the end, as in all fights, the speculation and anticipation mean nothing once the combatants face each other in the ring. When Ali and Frazier climbed through the ropes in Manila on October 1, 1975 (Manila time; it was still September 30 in the Western Hemisphere), the tension was high. This was it. Ali and Frazier were about to write the conclusion to a tremendous ring story. Both men had decidedly contrasting ideas as to how that story would end, and the entire sporting world breathlessly awaited the first bell.

Ali had already stolen the show during the pre-fight ceremonies, when Philippine officials displayed the huge trophy that would be awarded to the winner. Ali promptly ran out, grabbed the trophy, and carried it back to his corner!

That stunt marked the end of the foolishness. Once the bell for the first round clanged, the rivals confronted each other in deadly earnest. And the fight that followed unfolded like a three-act drama.

In Act I, Ali looked strong and confident as he stood in the center of the ring and delivered his blows with solid force. A bobbing, weaving Frazier appeared intent on reaching his opponent's body. Ali knew exactly what Frazier was trying to do, but that knowledge didn't lessen Smokin' Joe's intensity. He managed to pin Ali against the ropes a few times in the first round, but couldn't keep him there.

Toward the end of the round, Ali actually turned the tables and forced Frazier against the ropes. To the amusement of the crowd, Joe retaliated by pinching Ali's backside as the fighters returned to their corners after the bell.

At the beginning of round two, Ali attempted to hold Frazier behind the neck. Referee Carlos Padilla quickly intervened and issued a warning to the champion. It was evident that Padilla had listened to Eddie Futch, who had insisted he would not tolerate a repeat of the tactic.

As it turned out, Ali didn't need to hold Frazier, at least not over the first four rounds. The speed and volume of his punches dominated the action, though not by much. Ali remained flat-footed, catching his persistent challenger coming in. The spacious 21 × 21 foot ring afforded the champion plenty of room to maneuver, although he wasn't doing any dancing.

Yet for all the punishment Ali was dishing out, Frazier remained relentless. Muhammad found that he was simply unable to halt Smokin' Joe's advance. A few times, Ali tried to buy a few moments' rest with the Rope-a-Dope, but he quickly thought better of it. Unlike Foreman's roundhouse swipes, Frazier's punches were short, crunching, and quick. Against Frazier, the ropes were the last place Ali wanted to be.

Most dangerous to Ali was the realization that Frazier could "smoke" all night long. The champ's only breather would come during the sixty-second intervals between rounds.

In round five, the curtain began to rise on Act II of the "Thrilla." Ali began to show the first signs of fatigue even though he held the edge during the first half of the round. Then Frazier trapped him on the ropes, and this time Ali couldn't punch his way out of trouble. A head-snapping left hook by Frazier marked the beginning of a turn in the tide.

During the middle rounds, Ali's early zest appeared to be waning, and he found it increasingly difficult to keep Frazier away. Fighting like a man obsessed, Joe managed to slip into a higher gear that Ali couldn't match. Time and again, Frazier herded Ali onto the ropes and ripped away at the champ's head and body. It was beginning to look like a repeat of Superfight I, minus any clowning from Ali. Ali punched back, but he spent an alarming amount of time taking punches in a bent-over, arthritic position.

In the tenth round, Ali mounted an offensive, continually bouncing jabs and combinations off Frazier's skull. Frazier bobbed, weaved, and dug in the occasional body shot.

They ended the round trading heavy leather on the ropes. Frazier got in the last blow, a looping hook that wobbled the champion.

When Ali returned to his corner, he looked like a discouraged and apparently beaten fighter. Exhausted as much from the inhuman pace Frazier set as from the body blows he had absorbed, Ali told Dundee he wasn't sure he could go on.

Amazingly, both men came out for the eleventh as if it were the first. Aside from the welts and abrasions that marked the fighters' faces, they appeared remarkably fresh, given the demanding tempo of the first ten rounds.

Ali, who was ready to quit before the bell sounded, found enough energy to pepper Frazier with lightning combinations. He had learned through painful experience that the only way to keep Frazier off him was to hit him repeatedly. Ali was determined to do just that, and round eleven became the beginning of the third and final act of the "Thrilla."

The equally determined challenger soaked up punches like a sponge. But he never lost sight of his task, and he continued to march steadily forward. However, Frazier's face was beginning to puff up as it had in the previous two Superfights.

Ali carried his newfound momentum into round twelve. Frazier managed to back him against the ropes, but Ali scored heavily in retreat. Eventually, Frazier worked his way inside and connected well to the body and head. Neither man was willing to yield to the other.

After a dozen brutal rounds, the fight appeared too close to call. However, there were telltale signs that indicated an advantage to Ali. The steady diet of head shots Frazier had gobbled up since round one was beginning to take its toll. The puffiness around his eyes that had started a few rounds earlier had now blossomed into huge lumps that were a serious impediment to Frazier's vision. As well, Frazier's punches were beginning to lose steam, and he was no longer hurting Ali the way he had during the middle rounds.

In round 13, it became evident that Frazier was having trouble seeing Ali's punches coming, thus nullifying the bob and weave the champion found so frustrating. A smashing right by Ali sent Frazier's mouthpiece sailing several rows into the screaming crowd early in the round.

Summoning up his remaining strength, Ali blasted Frazier with both hands, sending the challenger stumbling backward. Miraculously, Frazier not only stayed on his feet, he actually charged forward again. The power in his punches was gone, but his spirit would not be denied. Just as he continued to rise from the floor against Foreman, Frazier would continue to attack Ali.

Still, Ali finished the round landing virtually every punch he threw. After the bell, Frazier slumped on his stool. His eyes were now mere slits, the left side of his forehead was grotesquely distended, and his mouth was filled with blood. But there was no quit in Frazier, and he came out for the fourteenth bent on forcing Ali into the ropes.

Ali was dancing now, and he easily avoided the half-blind bull in front of him. Then Muhammad stood flat-footed and machine-gunned Frazier with combinations to the head. Once again, Joe defied logic by staying on his feet for the entire three minutes.

As the round ended, the outcome seemed a foregone conclusion. Smokin' Joe couldn't win. Ali was ahead on all three scorecards, and Frazier would need a last-round stoppage to pull out a victory. By that point, though, he couldn't see well enough to avoid Ali's punches, let alone land any of his own. For all Frazier could tell, Referee Padilla could have been the one hitting him, not Ali.

Sensing the futility of three more minutes of punishment and not willing to risk his fighter's well-being, Eddie Futch performed the ultimate act of compassion when he informed Padilla that he wasn't going to allow Frazier to answer the bell for the final stanza.

Frazier protested, but Futch stood by his instincts. Ironically, Ali himself was at the point of collapse and would have had to struggle to answer the bell.

The fight was over. After fourteen rounds, all three judges had Ali comfortably ahead. But the Associated Press scored it even at 66–66 on a 5-point scoring system.

In vanquishing Frazier so decisively after looking as though he were going down to defeat himself, Ali had secured his position among the greatest heavyweight champions of all time. And Frazier's blood-and-guts effort against Ali in three fights earned him a niche of his own in boxing's annals of renown.

As well, the fighters were finally able to acknowledge each other's greatness.

"Don't nobody say nothin' bad about Joe Frazier," Ali said after the fight. He added that Frazier was "the toughest fighter I ever fought." In what was probably his most telling comment, he said the middle rounds of the fight were "the closest thing to death."[23]

Ali even said the words no one ever thought he would say, calling Frazier "great, he is greater than I thought."[24]

Frazier returned the compliment, saying that Ali "had to be great. Man, I hit him with shots that could have knocked down a wall."

Still, Ali had to get in the last word. "No other man tonight could have beaten Joe," he said. "Except for me, he is the toughest man in the world."[25]

Ali and Frazier would never become friends in the way Jack Dempsey and Gene Tunney did after their intense competition in the 1920s. But they had finally earned each other's respect, so much so on Frazier's part that he now addresses his rival as "Ali" rather than "Clay."

For all the accolades both fighters received after their titanic battle, Eddie Futch was also the object of praise for his humane action in stopping the fight. Dundee said Futch made the correct decision and that he would have done the same thing.

Before the post-fight press conference ended, Ali paid Frazier the highest compliment of all, back-handed though it may have sounded. "I'll never have to fight him again," the champion said, his relief obvious to all.[26]

Ali may have been relieved, but for the boxing world the aftermath of Superfight III struck a sad note. The Ali–Frazier rivalry, one of the greatest ongoing conflicts in the history of sport, had come to an end.

Ali ended 1975 with still sitting on the champion's throne. But the enormous effort he had expended in Superfight III had taken so much out of him that many of his friends were urging him to retire. Others believed Ali would never be the same again, and that his title was ready to be taken in 1976.

But who would do it? Frazier had tried his utmost and failed. Now he, too, was contemplating retirement.

Ron Lyle? Not likely. His losses to Ali and Jimmy Young had dropped him into the bottom half of the Top Ten.

How about Young, then? The Philadelphian was an excellent ring technician, but his safety-first style did little to inspire boxing fans' enthusiasm.

Ken Norton, with his smashing victory over Jerry Quarry, appeared to have the inside track on a 1976 title shot at Ali. Considering the trouble the muscular Californian had given Muhammad during two fights in 1973, Norton had to rate at least an even chance to win the title in a third meeting.

And what about George Foreman? Not so long ago, Foreman had stood at the top of the boxing world. Throughout much of 1975, though, Big George appeared to be lost in a world of his own.

Nine

1976

Superbrawl

The year 1976 promised to be a spectacular twelve months for the American public. Not only was it an Olympic year, it also marked the 200th anniversary of the Declaration of Independence. With patriotic fervor running at fever pitch, the Bicentennial provided a promoter's dream, filled with endless possibilities.

Don King, the promoter's promoter, hoped to capitalize on the Bicentennial by staging a July 4 superfight between Muhammad Ali and Ken Norton somewhere in the United States. King said he'd been offered more money to hold the fight in various foreign venues, but he declined, claiming that as patriots they wanted the fight in America.

King could wave the flag until his arm fell off, but the final decision as to the when and where of a third Norton fight was up to Ali. The champion envisioned another busy year, though few expected him to match the heroics of the Thrilla in Manila. He was, however, expected to make easy money against some soft touches before meeting Norton again.

While the public awaited Ali's next appearance, the excitement caused by the third Frazier fight had not yet faded. It was difficult to imagine the possibility of a fight of equal brutality occurring anytime soon. As it turned out, fight fans had to wait only until January 24 to be treated to one of the greatest pure slugfests in modern boxing history. The combatants were former champion George Foreman and perennial contender Ron Lyle.

At the beginning of 1976, Foreman's career was in a perilous state. Since he had lost the title to Ali fifteen months before, Big George had lived the life of a pugilistic hermit. Although he emerged physically intact from his defeat at Ali's hands, he was devastated psychologically. George had made the fatal mistake of believing his own press notices.

"Invincible," they called him. Going into the ring in Zaire, Foreman saw no way he could lose to a "washed-up" Ali. But he did lose, and in humiliating fashion. With his self-image still lying on the canvas, Foreman lashed out blindly, seeking someone, anyone, to blame besides himself.

He fired his brain trust, Dick Sadler, Archie Moore, and Sandy Saddler, because he believed they had failed to prepare him for Ali's trickery. Then he contended he'd been drugged by people who had a stake in an Ali victory.

For months, Foreman wrapped a cloak of pity around himself and showed no interest in making an effort to regain his title. When that cloak became too stifling, he began to contemplate a return to the ring. Unfortunately, the initial step on his comeback trail turned out to be a sad circus in Toronto on April 26, 1975, billed as "Foreman Against Five." In a live, televised exhibition, Foreman fought five successive opponents of inferior quality. A crowd of 10,700 gathered at the Maple Leaf Gardens to watch Foreman take on Terry Daniels, Charlie Polite, Jerry Judge, Alonzo Johnson, and Boone Kirkman in three rounds (or less) apiece.

Two of the five, Polite and Kirkman, had faced George in legitimate bouts earlier in his career, and both had been knocked out in short order. Ironically, in the Toronto exhibition they each lasted the full three rounds.

At the time, Kirkman was still a fringe contender and was by far the best of the five. As the last of the five to face Foreman, he did well, although he received a nasty cut and was knocked down once.

Polite, on the other hand, had won only two of his last 16 fights and was expected to make a quick exit. Perhaps he disrupted Foreman's "fight plan" by kissing him on the chin during the pre-flight instructions; at any rate, Polite was the only one of the five not to hit the canvas.

The other three went out in two rounds each. Johnson, a 40-year-old one-time contender who had been inactive over the past 10 years, crashed to the canvas twice. Daniels, who had fought Joe Frazier for the title in 1972, came out aggressively and paid dearly for his efforts. Foreman actually asked the referee to intervene for Daniels's own good, then cracked Terry again for mouthing off.

Judge, a one-time prospect, hit George with the hardest punch any of the five landed. Foreman repaid his temerity by flattening him with a right hand. When the exhibition ended, Foreman leaped up, kicked his heels in the air, and and almost fell on his face when he came back down.

The glorified workout session earned him $100,000. But if he hoped it would increase his popularity, he was sadly mistaken. He received a great deal of abuse from press and fans alike. To add insult to injury, his conqueror, Muhammad Ali, was in the audience, and the spectators began to shout "Ali, Ali, Ali." When Foreman tried to clown by dancing around the ring and toying with his opponents, the fans booed him unmercifully.

However, the boos were an accurate indication of the low esteem into which Foreman had fallen due to his inactivity and excuses. Stung by the criticism, he went back into seclusion for another seven months.

On November 26, he returned for another exhibition. In the interim, Foreman had acquired the services of veteran trainer Gil Clancy. Less than two years earlier, Clancy had pressed Foreman to grant Jerry Quarry a title shot. With Quarry retired, Clancy decided to undertake the challenge of guiding Foreman back to the title. Hiring Clancy was the first positive move Foreman had made since he lost his title. The opponent for his November exhibition was Jodie Ballard, a heavyweight prospect with a decent 22–3 record. Although the bout was scheduled for ten rounds, an odd length for an exhibition, Foreman blasted Ballard in two heats.

By then, Foreman had signed to fight Lyle for Jerry Perenchio, the man who promoted Ali–Frazier I. Clancy arranged one more tune-up for his fighter, another exhibition against a journeyman named Eddie Brooks in San Francisco on December 17. Brooks managed to last four rounds before Big George lowered the boom.

Foreman had fought nothing but exhibitions in 1975. Now it was time for him to face a real test against Lyle, who was a ranking heavyweight.

Crossroads fights were nothing new to Lyle. Following his defeats at the hands of Ali and Jimmy Young, he needed a big win in 1975 to remain in serious title contention. To that end, he chose a dangerous foe in the person of Earnie Shavers.

Shavers was still the most terrifying puncher in the division, and when Lyle faced him in Denver on September 13, he found out why most of the other contenders gave Earnie a wide berth.

A crunching left hook from Shavers in round two put Lyle on the canvas for the first time in his career. Ron rose at the count of eight and shook off the effects of the blow. Over the next three rounds, the fighters took turns dishing out punishment. After five rounds, the fight was virtually deadlocked.

At the clang of the bell for round six, Lyle charged from his corner, forced Shavers against the ropes, and smashed five consecutive rights hands to Earnie's head. Shavers pitched forward and was counted out face-down on the canvas. Had it not been for Ali–Frazier III, Lyle–Shavers would have been the heavyweight fight of the year.

In the aftermath, Lyle received a 10-minute standing ovation from the Denver fans. Shavers remained incoherent for about six of those minutes.

When he recovered his senses, Shavers complained that Lyle benefited from a hometown advantage in the second round knockdown. He said the Colorado State Athletic Commission had allowed Lyle too much time during the mandatory eight count. He also suggested Lyle had received an extra minute's rest between the second and third rounds. Whatever the circumstances, Lyle had survived the onslaught of one of the division's all-time great hitters to turn defeat into victory and save his career.

After the fight, Lyle seemed undeterred by his first trip to the canvas. The ability to rise from a knockdown and come back fighting was an important attribute for anyone who was about to tangle with Foreman, the only fighter in the division whose punch compared to Shavers's. But then Lyle had shown that he was no slouch as a hitter in his own right.

Because Foreman–Lyle was a gamble for both fighters, it was fitting that their encounter was held in Las Vegas. In Lyle, Foreman was meeting one of the few men in the division who could match him in size, strength, and power. Indeed, a showdown between the two big men had been anticipated since the beginning of the decade.

Despite the age difference (34 to Foreman's 27), there were several factors in Lyle's favor that odds makers needed to take into consideration. For starters, Foreman hadn't fought a serious bout in more than a year. During that same time span, Lyle had met some of the best fighters in the division.

As well, the Ali fight had exposed several flaws in
Foreman's fistic makeup. To be specific:

- George could be outboxed.
- George lacked stamina past the first few rounds.
- George did not know how to handle adversity.
- George could be knocked out.
- Maybe, just maybe, George lacked heart.

In short, Lyle knew he wasn't going into the ring against Superman. Still, his game plan was to outbox Foreman. Although he was known as a slugger, Ron did possess good boxing skills, and he intended to use those skills to extend George into the later rounds.

After adding all those factors into their equations, the odds makers still installed Foreman as a 4-to-1 favorite.

At the weigh-in, both fighters were on the heavy side, with Foreman scaling 226 and Lyle 220. But Lyle and Foreman each had the frame to carry that kind of weight comfortably, and given the kind of fight they were about to put on, they had to have been in good shape.

In the opening moments of the first round, there was little indication that the fight would live up to its billing as the "Superbrawl in Vegas." After missing with an amateurish right, Lyle settled into his game plan, circling and jabbing. Foreman followed suit. Each man was wary of the other's power.

Then Lyle snapped Foreman's head back with a solid jab. Although Foreman seemed unaffected by the blow, Lyle became more aggressive. With less than thirty seconds remaining in the round, Ron connected with a thunderous right that shook Foreman. Lyle went after him, but George managed to clinch and maul his way to survival.

Lyle's success in the first round seduced him into abandoning his fight plan. "He was so easy to hit with the right," Ron said later, "I thought I could take him out, so I went after him."[1]

As Lyle pressed his attack in the second, both men jabbed, shoved, and landed looping blows on even terms until Foreman crashed a left hook under Ron's guard. Lyle stumbled backward into the ropes. George trapped him in a corner and probed for an opening. Lyle did a fair imitation of Ali's Rope-a-Dope, but he was still fortunate when a malfunction in the timekeeper's watch ended the round a minute early.

The third round unfolded on a fairly even basis, with Lyle scoring with the right and Foreman pummeling him against the ropes. They fought at a brisk pace for big men, and it didn't seem possible the bout would go the scheduled 12 rounds.

Then came the fourth, the round that was every major boxing publication's choice as "Round of the Year." Lyle seized the momentum early, nailing Foreman with a solid right to the jaw. He followed with a right to the body and a left to the head that sent Foreman floundering across the ring.

Lyle continued to land blockbusters, and suddenly George was on the canvas. The ex-champ appeared more surprised than hurt, and rose to take the mandatory eight count. Trying to buy some time, Foreman wrestled Lyle to center ring. There, both men dug in and exchanged haymakers. Foreman reached down to his ankles for three successive left hooks, and it was Lyle's turn to stagger.

Then a clubbing left-right combination floored Lyle. Ron rolled onto his back, then rose in time to beat the count. But his legs looked unsteady as Big George barreled in to finish him off. Once again, Lyle's back was against the ropes.

Just when it looked as though Lyle was through, he fired a succession of blows that made Foreman back up. With Lyle safely off the ropes, the fatigued warriors threw punches on instinct alone. In the midst of an exchange, a torrid right from Lyle sent Foreman down again and the Las Vegas crowd yelled itself hoarse.

This time, George landed face first. By the time he pulled himself to his feet, the bell had sounded.

"When I got knocked down the second time," Foreman said later, "I felt like I'd paid my dues. I actually thought, I swear it, 'Joe Louis got up, so I can get up and win.' I felt embarrassed and angry, and it gave me more energy."[2]

Foreman credited Clancy with excellent motivational techniques during the crucial minute between rounds four and five. "He's hurt and you're hurt," Clancy told his fighter. "The one who's gonna win this fight is the one who wants it the most. Do you want it more than he does?"

Foreman said he did.

"Then go out and get it!"[3]

Shortly after the bell rang, Foreman went out and got hit with two left hooks by Lyle. Ron had come out shaky but determined to capitalize on the advantage he's gained in the preceding round.

Foreman staggered forward. Lyle delivered an uppercut and a solid combination, but Foreman defied gravity by remaining upright. He tried to keep Lyle away with a left jab.

Unimpressed, Lyle regained control with a brutal right-left-right combination to the head. Foreman teetered again, but miraculously stayed on his feet, finally displaying the heart his critics had accused him of lacking.

By now, Lyle's gas tank was running low. Foreman dug deep and launched a counteroffensive. He landed three ponderous combinations, and Lyle was once again on the ropes. Then George blasted away with about twenty unanswered punches. The force of Foreman's blows actually prevented Lyle from going down until the ex-champ stepped back.

Lyle dropped like a felled tree, and he remained on the canvas as Referee Charlie Roth counted ten.

In the aftermath, many observers compared Foreman–Lyle to the famous 1923 war between Jack Dempsey and Luis Firpo. Boxing purists may have cringed at the crudity of the free-swinging sluggers, but most fans applauded the non-stop action and courage Lyle and Foreman had displayed. Red Smith appropriately called the "Superbrawl" a "dreadfully two-sided fight."

Don King stated, "It was a bad fight. But it was the best bad fight in history."[4]

Paying tribute to his opponent, Foreman said, "It was most definitely the toughest fight I've ever had."[5]

Lyle gave Foreman due credit. But he also had an excuse. He complained that he'd split his mouthpiece earlier in the week and didn't have time to replace it. Consequently, the Denver heavyweight claimed he had trouble breathing throughout the fight.

Be that as it may, it was probably Lyle's decision to slug rather than box that cost him the fight. His abandonment of his fight plan was improvident, but it did provide fans an incredible spectacle. Since that 1976 afternoon, Foreman–Lyle has become the yardstick by which action fights have been measured.

At the time, though, many critics thought Foreman's performance hadn't measured up, even though he won the fight. Foreman was still the unrefined, straight-ahead slugger he'd always been. The shortened punches and new boxing skills Clancy claimed to have taught him were not in evidence against Lyle.

However, Foreman had come through with flying colors in other areas. His determination and desire in the face of adversity could no longer be questioned. Big George was definitely back. His goal was another shot at Ali. And woe betide anyone who dared to stand in his way.

In defeat, Lyle had done himself proud. Twice within a twelve-month period, he had come close to defeating the world's two top heavyweights and stopped the division's hardest hitter. Still, he had lost three of his last four fights, two by knockout.

At 34, Lyle had displayed every quality a fighter would need to win a title. But luck was against him, and time was running out. He clamored for a rematch with Foreman, but circumstances, and perhaps discretion on the part of Foreman and Clancy, prevented that fight from occurring. Lyle fought only twice more in 1976, stopping Kevin Isaac in seven rounds and losing a 12-round decision in a rematch against Jimmy Young.

The Lion and the Dove

Foreman and Lyle had inaugurated the 1976 heavyweight season with a reverberating roar. On February 20, Muhammad Ali would return to the ring for the first time since the Thrilla in Manila. And the Superbrawl had given him a tough act to follow.

The main question in most fans' minds was how much the grueling battle against Joe Frazier had taken out of the champion. But the fight he planned for February was hardly intended to provide an answer. Ali reached all the way across the Atlantic to that hotbed of fistiana, Belgium, and tapped the unsuspecting Jean Pierre Coopman to stand in the opposite corner for the fifth defense of his second reign.

Coopman, nicknamed the "Lion of Flanders," was a 29-year-old stone sculptor who had compiled a 24–3 record with 16 knockouts. However, his opposition was mediocre even by European standards.

Turning pro in 1972, he won his first four bouts. Then, in 1973, he lost a decision to light heavyweight Harald Skog and was knocked out in two rounds by one Ireno Werleman. He reversed the Werleman defeat in 1974 via one-round kayo. Three months later, he dropped a decision to Holland's Rudi Lubbers, who had gone the distance with Ali.

Undaunted, Coopman bounced back with a string of eleven victories, including a revenge win over Lubbers, an eighth-round stoppage of American Charlie "Devil" Green, and a seventh-round disqualification over Terry Daniels. Daniels was penalized for butting after putting Coopman on the deck in the second round.

A couple more victories moved the Belgian to #17 in *The Ring*'s ratings. And that rating somehow earned him a choice of two major title opportunities.

At that time, Coopman and Britain's Richard Dunn occupied the two top contenders' slots for the vacant European heavyweight championship. After his pathetic performance against Ali, Joe Bugner had retired and left his title up for grabs. The European Boxing Union (EBU) was setting up a match between Coopman and Dunn when the Belgian received his unexpected call from Ali's management.

The chance of a $100,000 guarantee to fight for the world title made Coopman's choice to meet Ali obvious. Still, the EBU felt slighted. The organization also believed that Coopman's chances of putting up a good fight, never mind winning, were so slight that the credibility of European boxing would suffer were Coopman to step into the ring with Ali. Accordingly, the EBU threatened to bar Coopman from challenging for the European title for two years if he went through with the Ali fight. EBU Secretary-General Piero Pini issued the following statement: "The decision was unanimously taken by the Union's general ruling council as a result of Coopman's open contempt for the interests of others and his detrimental conduct for European boxing. Coopman and his manager acted in open contempt of the European title for the sake of money."[6]

Correct though the EBU may have been in principle, who could blame Coopman and his manager, Karl de Jaeger, for reaching out to grab the brass ring? Boxing careers tend to be short-lived, and there's no guarantee a title opportunity will ever arise, especially for a fighter of Coopman's modest abilities. The $100,000 he would make against Ali in one fight was more than he could hope to earn in the rest of his ring lifetime.

The European scene, in which Coopman was competitive, would always be there for him. American soil, on the other hand, was dangerous territory. The only U.S. fighters he had faced were the limited Green and Daniels, and they had given him all he could handle. It was unlikely Coopman could have beaten many of the 16 contenders *The Ring* rated above him. Yet now he was being offered a shortcut to the championship of the world.

Is it any wonder, then, that Coopman ignored the EBU's self-righteous edicts? As it was, he and his manager believed he had a legitimate shot at upsetting the champion. Coopman fancied himself another Joe Frazier, and every boxing fan knew the trouble Frazier had given Ali.

Through an interpreter, the "Lion of Flanders" said: "Ali cannot fight for three minutes. I will keep the pressure on him like Frazier did."[7]

Red Smith commented on the comparison to Frazier in his column after the fight: "In the publicity buildup for this disaster Jean Pierre's style had been compared favorably to Joe Frazier's. If Joe decides to sue he can get witnesses."[8]

If Frazier had drained enough out of Ali in Superfight III ... if Coopman could mount a reasonable facsimile of Smokin' Joe's style ... if Ali took his opponent lightly and didn't train ... maybe, just maybe, Coopman stood an outside chance to go the distance.

The bookmakers didn't believe the Lion had much of a bite; consequently, no odds were offered on the fight. WBC President Jose Sulaiman went so far as to withhold his organization's sanction because "bizarre mismatches that are a fraud to the fans cannot be tolerated."[9] The WBA accepted the match as a title bout.

When questioned about Coopman's qualifications, Angelo Dundee replied that he hoped that Coopman was as inferior as everyone was saying. The trainer said that the "nobodies" had often presented problems in the past.

He cited Wepner, Norton, and Karl Mildenberger as examples. But if Dundee was taking Coopman seriously, Ali certainly wasn't. The champion's nonchalance was evident in the 226 pounds he carried into the ring at the Roberto Clemente Coliseum in San Juan, Puerto Rico, on fight night, compared to the Belgian's 206. Ali was only a pound and a half heavier than he'd been against Frazier, but his physique looked softer.

Muhammad's verbal insouciance had taken a vacation as well. He remained uncharacteristically subdued during the buildup to the fight, probably because he knew his sharp tongue would have no effect on an opponent who didn't understand English. "I can't get mad at Coopman, anything I say he just smiles and smiles."[10]

Ali was trying to find a moniker to hang on the Belgian the way that he had on so many other opponents, but he couldn't come up with one. When someone informed Ali that Coopman was already known as the Lion of Flanders, Ali responded, "He's not a lion, he's a pussycat."[11]

Ali's nonchalance in preparing for Coopman carried into the ring when the bell for the first round rang. Coopman didn't exactly come out smokin', and it quickly became clear that the challenger simply did not possess the strength or skill necessary to take advantage of Ali's sub-par condition.

The only reason the "fight" lasted more than one round is that Ali allowed it to. For four dreary frames, he jabbed, sparred, danced, mugged, and toyed with his hapless opponent. On one occasion, he even spanked Coopman's backside. The crowd soon became restive at the sad spectacle Ali was forcing it to witness.

After the fourth round, Ali's manager, Herbert Muhammad, threatened to leave the building if the champion didn't soon end the farce. Ali came out deadly serious in the fifth. He came down off his toes, put some weight behind his punches, and by 2:46 of the round, Coopman was down and out.

To his credit, Jean Pierre had struggled valiantly to beat the count. "I felt like 500 pounds were falling on me and I fell down," he said later.[12]

Coopman proved so ineffectual he didn't win a round on any of the judges' scorecards. Dave Anderson commented that the taming of the "Lion of Flanders" was easy, "as if Ali had used a whip and chair."[13]

In fact, Ali hadn't even worked up sufficient perspiration to require a post-fight shower. For this "no sweat" performance, he pocketed the easiest $1.1 million of his career.

As for Coopman, the EBU followed through on its threat to ban him from challenging for its title. As well, his manager was suspended for allowing Coopman to "play the part of sparring partner for Ali before an international audience."

One year later, the EBU lifted its suspension of Coopman, who immediately kayoed Spain's Jose Urtain in four rounds to win the European heavyweight championship. But Jean Pierre's reign lasted only 57 days. Frenchman Lucien Rodriguez relieved Coopman of the crown via 15-round decision.

Later in 1977, Coopman was blasted out in one round by Spanish-Uruguayan prospect Alfredo Evangelista. And the Belgian's slide into oblivion continued as he lost eight of the remaining 13 fights in his career.

Still, he can tell his grandchildren he once fought for the heavyweight championship of the world. Whether or not he tells them how futile his challenge turned out to be is up to him.

In the meantime, Ali took plenty of heat for fighting such a soft touch. He became openly annoyed at his critics, feeling that after the epic against Frazier he deserved a breather, especially with Norton and Foreman looming on the horizon.

Before making any demanding defenses, Ali intended to mark time and make money. After Coopman, he signed for two fights within a 24-day period, an indication of the low esteem in which he held the prospective opponents. Richard Dunn of Britain was inked for May 24. Then Ali decided to take on Jimmy Young on April 30 in Landover, Maryland.

Interestingly, the Young fight would be promoted by Don King, while the Dunn date was being put together by King's arch-rival, Bob Arum. Asked if he thought the Young fight would jeopardize the Dunn promotion, Arum replied that Young was a "joke," and posed no threat to Ali or his promotion.

Arum wasn't alone in his estimation of Young. On paper, Jimmy wasn't much, an extremely light hitter with a record that was unexceptional other than his upset victory over Ron Lyle. And in his last outing, on the undercard of Ali–Coopman, Young had unspectacularly outpointed ringworn Jose "King" Roman in ten rounds. After the fight, one commentator quipped: "Young can't take anybody out. Hell, he can't even take his wife out to dinner."[14]

However, as Lyle discovered, there was more to Jimmy Young than met the eye. He was from Philadelphia, but he wasn't a "Philadelphia Fighter," which is defined in the fistic lexicon as a left-hooking slugger who shows little concern about defense. Prime examples of "Philadelphia Fighters" include Joe Frazier, middleweight Bennie Briscoe, and light heavyweight Matthew Saad Muhammad. Their careers tended to be spectacular, and short.

Hellraisers like these had conditioned Philly boxing fans to expect all-out war every time a local fighter stepped into the ring. Defensive specialists like Young were never appreciated in the City of Brotherly Love. Still, fighters who don't get hit tend to enjoy longer careers. As *Sports Illustrated* boxing writer Pat Putnam put it, "If he [Young] was a foot soldier, he'd live forever."[15]

Longevity was part of Jimmy's game plan. After his conquest of Lyle, the loser said: "Never underrate Jimmy Young again, not until he's 40 years old."[16]

Young's beginnings in boxing were similar to those of a young Cassius Clay. At the age of 14 Young was robbed of his transistor radio by three local toughs. Determined to get his radio back, Young was going after them with a butcher knife and a wrench. His father intercepted him and suggested boxing lessons at the local PAL.

As an amateur, Young had compiled a fair 15–6 record and captured two Golden

Gloves titles. He turned pro in 1969. Married and raising a family, Jimmy toiled at various day jobs and trained on the side. Consequently, his early years in the punch-for-pay ranks were dotted with losses. Clay Hodges, a former amateur sensation, Roy Williams, an above-average fringe contender, and the intellectual Randy Neumann all defeated the part-time heavyweight.

Then came a devastating loss to Earnie Shavers that ironically turned Young's career around. At that point in his career, Young was in over his head against the Ohio slugger. In three years, Young had managed to fight only eight times. By contrast, Shavers sported a 40–2 log and hadn't lost in three years.

Predictably, Earnie stopped Young in three rounds. But even without the benefit of full-time training, Jimmy still showed some potential during the short time the fight lasted. He also displayed amazing courage by rising from knockdowns in the first and third rounds.

Referee John Fitzpatrick stopped the fight with Young on his feet. But before Shavers launched his final assault, Jimmy had shown flashes of elusiveness and actually landed more punches than Shavers.

Few observers detected any signs of a future contender in the aftermath of the fight. Jack Fried of the *Philadelphia Bulletin* said the next day that Young "didn't belong in the same ring with Shavers." Furthermore, he commented that Shavers's record included "many knockouts over similarly unqualified opponents."[17]

Young came out of the experience determined to become more than just another "unqualified opponent." He sat down and examined his style and his ability, and concluded that some changes were in order. He would capitalize on his defensive skills and leave the slugging to fighters like Shavers. "I realized that standing there and letting the other guy pound me wasn't the answer. I had the brains, I decided to use them."[18]

Young studied the slicksters like Sugar Ray Robinson and Billy Conn and recreated his style. His career turned around immediately.

As time passed, Young became a master boxer, a technician who could out-move, out-stick, and outsmart opponents of greater size and strength. This style did not endear him to the Philly fight crowd, but that made no difference to Young.

Although he stood 6'2" and weighed more than 200 pounds, Young had no illusions about his size. He realized his success would have to be based on brains, not brawn.

"The key to victory," he said, "is to out-think the other man. Whether it's in combat, craps, or playing chess. And there's no heavyweight alive that I can't out-think. No matter how strong a man is, and a lot are stronger than me, well, I always say there isn't a horse that can't be broken or a man that can't be thrown."[19]

So much for the Jimmy Young philosophy of boxing. However, theory alone wasn't enough; Young needed to apply his skills on a more regular basis. His disaster against Shavers had occurred after a year of inactivity.

He made three more ring appearances in 1973, scoring two wins and a draw. It was the first time in his career that he'd gone three fights without a loss. A modest beginning, but a beginning nonetheless.

Young had a banner year in 1974. He opened with a rare kayo win in London over Richard Dunn, his current companion on Ali's hit list. Two fights later, he returned to London and outpointed a prospect named Les Stevens. The globe-trotting Philadelphian next landed in Caracas, Venezuela, where he decisioned former contender Jose Luis Garcia.

He rounded out 1974 with a much-anticipated rematch against Shavers. Earnie couldn't touch the "new" Jimmy Young, who appeared a clear points winner after ten rounds of slipping and sliding. But the judges declared it a draw. Still, it was a moral victory for Young.

Then came the February 11, 1975, Honolulu meeting with Ron Lyle. Lyle viewed Young as a routine tune-up before his scheduled title shot. The "tune-up" almost jeopardized the proposed Ali–Lyle fight. "Some tune-up," said Angelo Dundee at the time. "I knew Lyle had goofed. I'd seen Young work before. I knew who was going to get tuned up."[20]

Lyle came in at an intimidating 218½ pounds, compared to Young's 204. At 26, Young was six years younger than his foe. And, although he didn't come close to Ron's punching power, he was undoubtedly the superior boxer. "When you box like Jimmy, you don't need to have power," Young's manager, Frank Gelb, said.[21]

But Lyle appeared to belie those words as he concentrated on Young's body in the early rounds. Then Young turned the momentum to his favor by utilizing hit-and-run tactics. The slower Lyle found himself unable to reach his smaller, swifter foe.

Lyle did manage to stagger Young with a left hook in the seventh. Jimmy was able to hang on. Then he resumed control and thoroughly outboxed Lyle over the final three rounds. He won by unanimous decision and lifted himself out of anonymity. Young explained his upset triumph as simply "a matter of styles." He said he had mapped out a battle plan for Lyle and followed it to perfection.

Unfortunately, the win over Lyle caused Young to be stereotyped as a "spoiler." In boxing parlance, a "spoiler" is a fighter who makes his opponent look bad, win or lose. The worst kind of spoiler is the one who seldom wins a big fight, but is still capable of pulling off an upset.

Young spent the next two years fighting his reputation as well as his opponents. He scored two more wins in 1975, knockouts over unknown Robert Lloyd and a Memphis Al Jones who was so faded he was practically invisible.

Entering 1976, Young was a rated contender and his name was mentioned as a possible opponent for Ali. His fight against Jose "King" Roman on the Ali–Coopman undercard was intended to showcase Young's skills. Ali, hyping his prospective challenger, shouted "You're next!" whenever he saw the Philadelphian in San Juan. "Get the contract ready," Ali bellowed. "You're next!"[22]

Young's "showcase" against Roman backfired as the faded Puerto Rican played the role of spoiler. Young won an easy decision, but Roman's survivalist tactics negated Jimmy's counterpunching style.

Ali wasn't impressed by Young's performance. He assessed the Philadelphian as "a decent fighter ... but he don't have the hittin' power."[23] Interestingly, that's the way some experts had assessed a young contender named Cassius Clay a decade and a half earlier.

For Young, who had never earned more than $7,500 for a fight, the shot at Ali proved a financial boon and the opportunity for more. "I don't even own a car. To me this fight means the heavyweight championship, it means being on top, and most of all it means money. The cash —$85,000."[24]

Although Young was ranked as high as #2 by *The Ring*, his chances of pulling off an upset were regarded as slim at best, an opinion reflected in the high 15–1 odds against him. Still, he was approaching the biggest moment of his career with surprising confidence. The challenger was hardly intimidated by Ali's victory over Coopman.

The challenger appeared quite confident as he prepared for his opportunity of a lifetime. Young prepared for the fight in Joe Frazier's gym in Philly. Frazier advised Young and told him that "after five rounds, Ali doesn't hit as hard as he does in the early rounds. Not that you can take him for granted then."[25]

"I'm just layin' here in the background, really cool," he explained. "No one has any idea how capable I really am."[26]

Ali certainly didn't. Consequently, he couldn't quite motivate himself to train hard for a punchless challenger. In the past, whenever Ali slacked off, Dundee would remind him what happened the last time he went into a fight unprepared.

One morning, Dundee banged on Ali's door to wake him for his morning roadwork. "No, not today," the groggy champ grumbled.

"Remember San Diego," Dundee said, referring to the first fight against Ken Norton. "I'll be right down," Ali said.[27]

But Ali didn't answer Dundee's call often enough. On fight day, he entered the ring at a blubbery 230 pounds, his highest yet. At 211, Young was also heavier than usual. But he looked small next to "The Greatest."

Ali said that he was happier with the extra pounds, because he had the fight coming up in 24 days with Richard Dunn and had to have something to play with. The champ claimed the extra weight made him stronger.

The champ came out playfully in the first round. He obviously felt Young would pose no problem. Frazier and Norton had out-punched Ali to hand him his only two losses, but he had never, ever been outboxed.

Ali kept his hands high in the "Mirage" defense he employed against Lyle. But Young was moving backward, not forward, and Ali found himself cast in the unfamiliar role of pursuer. Young scored with pitty-pat jabs. Ali hardly punched at all, and when he did, Young evaded most of the blows.

The pattern continued through the next two rounds. Although Young was anything but aggressive, he was landing effectively if not hurtfully. Ali's lack of training was woefully obvious; his timing was way off, and sharp timing was a necessity against an opponent as elusive as Young.

A smattering of boos greeted Ali when he returned to his corner at the end of the third. At ringside, Herbert Muhammad shared the crowd's sentiments and hoped that Young would hit Ali hard enough to wake him up.

An aroused Ali decided to take charge in the fourth. He threw enough punches to take the round on aggression. But more of them missed their mark than ever before in his career.

When he came out for the fifth, Ali looked concerned for the first time. Although he had picked up the pace in the last round, he wasn't in control of the fight. Young was still in front of him, pecking away with pesky fleabites of punches. At last Ali realized he was in a legitimate fight, a fight for which he wasn't prepared.

As always, the champ gritted his teeth and did what he could to win. In the sixth, he managed to trap Young on the ropes. Then he threw a Foreman-like barrage of punches which Young easily evaded. Jimmy bobbed, weaved, ducked, and blocked every blow the champion threw. Incredibly, Ali was being beaten at his own game.

The seventh round featured more of the same. Young's confidence grew in direct proportion to Ali's frustration. In the eighth, the challenger became sufficiently bold to land a stinging combination to Ali's face.

In the ninth, Ali tried to turn back the hands of time by getting up on his toes. He jabbed and danced in vintage fashion, but his jabs fell short of the mark. Young's didn't. Late in the round, Young stopped Ali in his tracks with a jarring right hand. Then Jimmy let his hands go in a rare burst of offense.

When the bell rang, Young strolled back to his corner with both arms raised in a gesture of victory. And the crowd, sensing an incredible upset in the making, cheered.

Young caught Ali on the ropes in the tenth. Knowing it was too late to squander any more rounds, the champ fought back. Whatever options remained to him to save his title, the Rope-a-Dope wasn't one of them. By now, the effort he had expended chasing Young was catching up with him. He looked lethargic during the eleventh and twelfth rounds, throwing few punches and landing fewer. Young was busier, but he wasn't displaying the "go for it" spirit of a man trying to win a world title.

Not only was Young unassertive, at times he even appeared passive. Some of his defensive moves were downright bizarre. Five times during the fight, he actually slipped his upper body between the ropes to avoid Ali's attacks. He did it once in the seventh round, once in the twelfth, twice in the thirteenth, and once in the fifteenth.

The tactic bewildered Referee Tom Kelly, who didn't know how to respond to it. In the twelfth, he actually started counting as though a knockdown had been scored. At one point, Ali became so irritated by the maneuver that he leaned over the top rope and punched Jimmy in the back. The ploy may have stymied Ali's sputtering offense, but it also may have alienated the judges.

At the beginning of the last round, the crowd sensed that Ali's hold on the title was in jeopardy. His fans began the familiar chant of "Ali, Ali, Ali" in an attempt to spur their hero to a storybook finish. Ali tried, but he couldn't pull it off. When the final bell rang, Young's jubilant cornermen poured into the ring and mobbed the man who had apparently dethroned the champion. Ali's corner was a study in sobriety.

As the officials tallied their scorecards, the crowd and the TV audience sat on the edge of their seats. Few had expected the fight to go the distance, and fewer guessed that Young could possibly win. However, after 15 rounds that were paradoxically harrowing and dull at the same time, the decision that was about to be announced was potentially the most dramatic since Jim Braddock upset Max Baer back in 1935.

And the decision was indeed shocking. Ali was declared the winner by margins of 70–68, 72–65, and 71–64 on a five-point system.

Young's wasn't the only mouth to drop open in utter disbelief. Although the fight was close enough that it was possible Ali won by a hair, no one could understand the wide margin of victory on the last two scorecards.

"I figured I'd win by split decision," the distraught challenger told the press afterwards. To a large extent, the media agreed with him. The Associated Press, for example, scored the fight 69 to 66 in favor of Young. Dick Young of the *New York Times* felt that Young won by a "comfortable margin" of 11–4.[28]

Of course, the scoring of any fight is a highly subjective endeavor. One judge may favor aggressiveness and harder punching, while another might be more appreciative of a fighter's defensive skills. Some judges are impressed by a high quantity of punches, others look at the quality of the blows a fighter lands. Fortunately for Ali, the officials on the night of April 30, 1976, appeared more impressed by his aggression, ineffective though it may have been.

Young was in shock when the decision was announced. "I thought I'd win by split decision."[29]

Although not exactly overjoyed by his showing, Ali still felt he deserved the victory. "I thought I won," he said. He also had high praise for his challenger. "I would like to say that I underestimated Jimmy Young, that I didn't know Jimmy Young would be so awkward, that he was so hard to hit, that he was so fast. I didn't worry about him. I took him lightly."[30]

"Everybody rated him a 15–1 underdog, but he didn't fight like one. I almost lost the fight," Ali admitted.[31]

Ali revealed that Young hit much harder than anticipated, and was hard to land a glove on. "Look at him," Ali said at the post-fight press conference. "Not a mark on him."

With his usual candor, Ali said he could "feel my weight. I could feel my age. I could feel his youth. That used to be me, the young guy, poppin' around like that."[32]

Dundee was quick to label the Young fight as the worst in Ali's career. And he was right. Muhammad looked fat, slow, and uncoordinated. Why, then, didn't Young get the decision?

There were two factors involved in the fight's outcome. The first was the mystique that had grown around the Ali name over the past two decades, a mystique that might have clouded the judges' vision. Ali's reputation may have given him a lead in the scoring before the first bell rang, which meant that Young had an uphill battle from the start.

The second factor was Young's inability to take charge of the fight. Regardless of how well he may have boxed, no one can expect to win a title by fighting like a conscientious objector. The referee would have been within his rights to award the fight to Ali by TKO or disqualification every time Young leaned through the ropes to avoid punishment.

Whether or not the victory was a gift from the officials, Ali had still chalked up another successful title defense. Young's showing gained him a great deal of credibility, and over the next two years he became a major force in the division.

Although Ali–Young was hardly "Fight of the Year" material, it did show that an out-of-shape, 34-year-old Ali was still capable of defeating the best pure boxer in the division. Ken Norton, who was at ringside, said of Ali's performance: "That's not the guy I'll have to fight. I wish it was, but it won't be. He'll be ready for me."[33]

Norton was already guaranteed the next shot at Ali's title. But Ali still had to fulfill his already signed contract to fight Richard Dunn before settling accounts with the Jawbreaker.

A Dunn Deal

Ali had only twenty-four days to recover from his fifteen frustrating rounds with Young. As well, he would have to travel to Munich in what was then West Germany to take on Richard Dunn, who on paper appeared closer to Coopman in quality than to Young. Indeed, the light-hitting Young had managed to kayo the big Englishman.

Young's feat hardly qualified as a fluke. Dunn was far from a stranger to the canvas, having been knocked out nine times in a career that began in 1969. Those losses had come against such run-of-the-mill heavyweights as Billy Aird, Ngozika Ekwelum, Bunny Johnson, Rocky Campbell, Jose Urtain, and Danny McAlinden.

Even though Dunn had won 33 fights to offset those kayo losses, he still fit nicely into the stereotype of the horizontal British heavyweight. He looked like a fighter, with stony features that unfortunately ended in a chin of Delftware china. Ironically, the crook in his nose came as a result of a rugby injury rather than the punches he had absorbed in the ring.

On the positive side, Dunn had a heart as big as his 6'4", 215-pound body. But his face-first style and limited skills meant that his success would be confined to the level of competition Britain and Europe had to offer.

"I'm no Fancy Dan," Dunn once said. "I'm just a fighter."[34]

Truer words were never spoken. British journalist Neil Allen once wrote that Dunn "is often as awkward and ineffective as a jammed revolving door."

Despite his uncooperative chin, Dunn's internal toughness often drove him past great adversity. In 1970, Dunn broke his left hand, yet could not afford to give up boxing while it healed. He literally fought Billy Whynter and Obie Hepburn with one hand.

Lack of financial backing not only kept Dunn in the fight game, it also deprived him of some of the basics of the trade. He couldn't train full-time; by day he worked as a scaffolder. Trained by his father-in-law, Jimmy Devanney, in a reconstructed farmhouse, Richard underwent preparations that included running, hitting the bag, and shadow boxing. Sparring partners were a luxury the Dunn camp could never afford. At that time, there weren't many heavyweights in Britain, and the few who were active demanded cash on the line in exchange for sparring services.

Consequently, Dunn went into most of his fights without so much as one round of sparring under his belt. He struggled through the first six years of his career, incurring several disappointing losses along the way. At one point, he wanted to toss his fistic ambitions into the rubbish heap. A good tongue-lashing from his wife, Janet, caused him to change his mind.

Janet Dunn was the antithesis of Darlene Stander, who deplored boxing and belittled her husband Ron's ability. Dunn's wife was born into a boxing environment. She not only loved the sport, she also understood the many sacrifices and hardships a fighter faced. She became Richard's staunchest and most outspoken supporter.

It was Janet who encouraged Richard to approach manager George Biddles, who had guided Nigerian Hogan "Kid" Bassey to the world featherweight title back in 1957. In Dunn, Biddles saw untapped potential that could be developed with the right training.

Dunn's assets included size, punching power, conditioning, and courage. As well, he was a southpaw, and southpaws often confused orthodox fighters. Ali always said the toughest defense of his first title reign was the one against German left-hander Karl Mildenberger. Biddles became Dunn's first bona fide manager. Now Richard could train full-time, with good sparring partners, proper facilities, and even a hypnotist named Romark who was hired to bolster the fighter's confidence.

In short order, Biddles' gamble paid off. On October 1, 1975, Dunn was matched against Bunny Johnson for the British and Commonwealth heavyweight titles. The two had met twice before, with Dunn taking an 8-round decision in 1971 and Johnson coming back to score a 10th-round stoppage in 1973. This time Dunn swept the final six rounds to prevail by a 15-round nod.

In his first defense of his titles, Dunn reversed another defeat by dispatching Danny McAlinden in two rounds. He followed the McAlinden win by crushing Germany's Berndt August in three rounds to add the vacant European heavyweight championship to his collection. The victory earned Dunn a #12 ranking by *The Ring* and a shot at Ali's world title.

The twelve-month period that had passed since Dunn and Biddles had joined forces must have seemed like a storybook tale of success for both men. And a win over Ali would have eclipsed even Sylvester Stallone's *Rocky* as a triumph for underdogs everywhere.

Not everyone had the vision to foresee a Dunn victory. Neil Allen weighed Dunn's chances in the May 24, 1976, *London Times*, quoting a middle-aged cockney who said,

"Dunn's got less chance in Munich than Chamberlain did." Allen went on to predict: "I expect him [Ali] to become the sixth man, and much the best known, to knock out Richard Dunn."

Biddles believed he and Dunn were fortunate to be getting to Ali at this point in the champion's career. "Do not be surprised," Biddles advised, "if the fight here on May 24 brings the greatest sensation in modern boxing history. Ali is a 34-year-old ageing multimillionaire presently in poor form. If he fights against Richard like he did against Jimmy Young ... then he'll lose."[35]

Aside from Biddles, however, few boxing people could be found who thought Ali had gone downhill far enough to lose to Dunn. Still, Dunn was thought to be at least a cut above the Coopmans and Terry Daniels level of credibility. He was on a winning streak, and held three titles. Nonetheless, Dunn was still considered nothing more than a tune-up for Ali's fall showdown against Ken Norton. For credibility's sake, Ali needed a convincing win to erase the memory of his sorry performance against Young.

As an added incentive, the champion would be pulling down a guaranteed $1,650,000. And Dunn would receive a career-high $125,000. Given the one-sided caliber of the matchup, these were amazing figures. In fact, the event nearly fizzled before it got off the ground.

The bout was being co-promoted by Bob Arum's Top Rank, Inc., and a group of West Germans, and came close to being scrubbed altogether when the Germans failed to come up with the final $225,000 they owed Top Rank.

Early ticket sales were so dismal that Dunn and his entire entourage were at one point in danger of being evicted from the Munich Hilton Hotel because the promoter hadn't paid the bill. The fact that the bout was being held at 3:30 A.M. Munich time to accommodate American television probably didn't help its box office.

The promotion hit another snag when Dunn and his crew threatened to leave Munich two weeks before the event unless they were accommodated with better training facilities. The first location didn't even have a heavy bag. "I meant what I said, too," Dunn declared. "Ali would never have accepted what they offered me."[36]

In the end, Arum decided to absorb the financial loss and put on the fight anyway. Ali helped out by purchasing $100,000 worth of tickets for U.S. servicemen stationed in West Germany. This was quite a generous gesture, given Ali's earlier stand against the Vietnam War.

True to his word, Ali approached Dunn much more seriously than he had Young. He lost ten pounds in less than a month. Still, at the weigh-in in Munich, the day before the fight, Ali and several others crashed through the stage upon which the scales had been set. Although the champ and the others fell six feet onto broken wooden planks, no one was hurt.

Dunn, like every other Ali opponent, came in at peak form for his encounter with "The Greatest." In fact, the Britisher actually had to suspend training a week before the fight because he was losing too much weight. He had been running eight miles a day, which dropped his poundage from 211 to 202.

Ali thought Dunn's decision to halt training for a couple of days was a wise one. He said he had done the same thing in the past, as had some of his opponents. Joe Bugner was one example he cited as an overtrained challenger.

The comparisons to Bugner's ill-fated title shot were unavoidable in the days leading up to the fight, especially in the British press. UK sportswriters were still shaking their heads at Bugner's lack of effort in Kuala Lumpur. Biddles took a poke at Bugner when he declared that Dunn was "not here to set any survival records against Ali. He is here to win."[37]

With Bugner's premature retirement in January 1976, Dunn had become, in the words of London-based poet/author Ulick O'Connor, "the last bottle of beer on the wall for British boxing."

And that last bottle promised to have plenty of bite as Dunn made it clear he would be coming out aggressively. "You can only beat him if you are aggressive, like Joe Frazier was," he said, not explaining how he planned to duplicate Frazier's smokin' style.[38]

Successful or not, he intended to go down fighting. Most people admired Dunn's grit, but the odds of 9 to 1 in Ali's favor seemed rather generous to the Englishman. Dunn remained undaunted in the face of widespread skepticism.

"I know I can do it, even if the rest of them outside this room and outside the family doesn't give me a chance at all, when I fly back home, I'll be world champion, never fear." Biddles believed in his fighter's chances, especially after seeing the Ali–Young fandango.[39]

Ali engaged in his usual pre-fight carnival routine to boost lagging ticket sales. He labeled Dunn "Frankenstein," and took every opportunity to needle his foe. "Come on, Frank, didn't Igor get you a new body?" Ali taunted. "I understand I can't kill you. But I can knock you out."[40]

Dunn responded with a page from Ali's poetry book:

> Ali fights for money, Ali fights for fun.
> But he'll be fighting for survival
> When he fights Richard Dunn.[41]

When the bell sounded for the first round, Dunn lived up to his vow to take the fight to the champion. Moving forward on stiff legs, he landed southpaw jabs on Ali's face. The challenger continued to pressure Ali throughout the first three rounds. Although Dunn possessed surprising hand speed, he wasn't hurting the champ.

Except for a some brief interludes of dancing, Ali fought Dunn flat-footed. In an attempt to compensate for his opponent's southpaw stance, the champ fired right-hand leads that proved increasingly effective as the bout progressed. Dunn had carried himself well so far, fighting at a level above his usual ability. Then Ali ended Richard's hopes with a single right-hand lead in round four. Dunn looked as if he'd been struck by lightning; his red hair stood on end and he quivered before crashing to the canvas.

Incredibly, the Englishman tottered to his feet and came storming back at Ali, who met him with a salvo of right hands. Dunn stood at center ring and tried to cover up as Ali fired away. Ferdie Pacheco later compared Dunn to "a man charging madly into a threshing machine."

Finally, Ali once again found the "sweet spot" on Dunn's jaw. The challenger stumbled two steps backward, arms grasping madly for some invisible handle that would keep him on his feet. He found it, and the instant he realized he wasn't going down, he rushed Ali into the ropes.

Ali brought the action back to center ring, and unleashed a right that nearly decapitated the Englishman. Dunn went down hard and groped blindly for ropes that were a good eight feet away. Somehow he got to his feet, and practically pushed the referee aside in an effort to get at Ali.

But Ali got to him with another right-hand lead that sent Dunn down for the third time. Dunn actually tried to throw a counterpunch while he was still on his knees. He rose just as the bell ended the round.

Before the bell for the fifth sounded, Ali pointed to Dunn, then to the canvas. Unfazed, the challenger came out swinging, a testament to the arduous training he had endured. Ali laid back and picked off Dunn's punches. Midway through the round, Muhammad dropped him with a solid right cross. Amazingly, Dunn got up again. Ali, who had been windmilling his right arm during the mandatory eight count, unloaded a three-punch combination that sent Dunn to the canvas for the fifth time.

Dunn got up, and he might still be getting up had the referee not ended a slaughter that had gone on too long.

For Ali, the Dunn fight put a temporary end to whispers that he was finished. But he knew only too well that his next fight, against Ken Norton, promised to be his toughest since the Thrilla in Manila.

Dunn came out of the fight with an enhanced reputation, much as Chuck Wepner had a year earlier. It was raw courage, not any particular boxing skill, that won Dunn the respect of fans all over the world after the fight was over. And nowhere was he respected more than in his home country.

If Joe Bugner was annoyed by detractors before Dunn's challenge of Ali, he must have maddened by the flood of unfavorable comparison's between Dunn's effort and his own. As Dick Young (an American) wrote, "Dunn's determination to try and make of fight of it makes Bugner's showing against Ali look very sad. Sure, Dunn has a glass jaw, but he showed guts by the way he kept coming back."[42]

Obviously fed up by the scorn he endured from press and fans alike, Bugner lashed back by pointing out that guts or no guts, Dunn still suffered a one-sided thrashing. Bugner, on the other hand, had gone the distance. "Dunn put up a great show as far as his capability was concerned," Bugner told the press, "but I thought it was a mismatch from round one, as soon as Ali teed him up with a right hand.... Although Dunn is European champion, he didn't have the experience to fight Ali."[43]

Dunn's fans replied that Bugner had fought only to survive, while Richard had fought to win. The verbal sniping made a Dunn–Bugner showdown a British promoter's dream, a true grudge match. Predictably, Bugner announced on July 4, 1976, that he was coming out of retirement to secure a shot at Dunn's three titles. "I have to prove to myself that I can beat Richard Dunn," Bugner declared.[44]

Promoter Harry Levene signed the fighters to a contract and scheduled the fight for October 12 at Wembley Stadium. The animosity between Bugner and Dunn was sincere, and more than the British, Commonwealth, and Empire titles would be at stake when they met in the ring.

For the first time, Bugner displayed Ali-like verbal pugnacity before a fight. Some observers thought he was trying to psych himself into an aggressive mood; others thought he was merely attempting to hype the confrontation. While the fight generated enormous interest in the UK, there were some who criticized Levene for exaggerating its overall importance.However, as Neil Allen wrote: "These two big men, whether or not they stir your blood, are the best we have around...."

On fight night, Bugner entered the ring to a chorus of boos that could have made the *Guinness Book of World Records.* Dunn, the hero of the day, was cheered mightily. But those cheers quickly turned to gasps of shock when Bugner nailed Dunn only seven seconds into the first round. By the 2:14 mark, Bugner, who was miles ahead of Dunn in ability, had floored his rival three times and taken back the titles he had walked away from. The crowd applauded; Bugner had finally showed them the tiger beneath his calm exterior.

As Bugner received the Lonsdale Belt from British Boxing Board of Control chairman Alexander Elliott, the latter whispered to the stunned Bugner, clearly taken aback by the cheers, to smile.

Bugner was elated by the public's response to his inspired performance. "I think the public has always wanted to support me. Now, I've learned that you can't please people all the time. You've got to plod along and persevere."[45]

Indeed, never before had British fans shown so much affection for their prodigal heavyweight, not even after Bugner's 1973 war against Joe Frazier. At 26, it seemed that he had finally grown into his talent. With Ali going downhill, all Bugner needed was a couple of wins over credible opposition to be back in the title picture.

The promoter of the event, Harry Levene, thought, based on his performance, that "Bugner can still fight his way to the heavyweight championship of the world."

Bugner's manager, Andy Smith, agreed: "This is the fight he found himself. You saw a new Joe Bugner. In this form and mood nothing is beyond his capabilities."[46]

But the Bugner who showed up to fight an over-the-hill Ron Lyle in Las Vegas on March 20, 1977, was the irresolute ring Hamlet of old rather than the dynamic destroyer of Dunn. After piling up a point lead, Bugner passively allowed Lyle to walk away with a split decision win.

Bugner promptly re-retired, then made a moderately successful comeback in the 1980s after emigrating to Australia. In the end, Bugner's was a story of unlimited potential coupled with limited desire.

As for Dunn, after the fight, Biddles persuaded him to hang up his gloves. But the boxing bug bit him again, and he staged a brief, sad comeback before finally retiring for good. Now, Dunn is part of boxing history, the last fighter to be kayoed by Ali.

The Gladiators

Through most of 1976, Ali appeared to be testing the limits of his credibility as a champion and a celebrity. When he fought Jean Pierre Coopman, he proved that he could take on a challenger who would have lost to the most inept member of Joe Louis's "Bum of the Month" club and still retain his popularity. Against Jimmy Young, he proved that he could go into a fight completely out of shape and still manage to win. Against Richard Dunn, he showed that he still possessed some of his old firepower.

But what was he trying to prove with his bizarre June 25 boxer vs. wrestler showdown against Antonio Inoki in Tokyo?

Did he intend to prove that he could stage a superior circus to the "Foreman vs. Five" farce? Or did he really believe the Inoke exhibition would, as billed, answer once and for all the burning question of superiority between a champion boxer and a champion wrestler? Or was it the $6,000,000 guarantee, more money than Ali had ever made in a legitimate boxing match? You figure it out.

Ali–Inoki wasn't the first boxer-wrestler confrontation. In the early 1900s, wrestling champion Frank Gotch seriously considered challenging Jim Jeffries and later Jack Johnson for the heavyweight boxing title. But Gotch would have gone into the ring as a gloved fighter, not a wrestler.

In 1913, Johnson kayoed a Russian wrestler named Al Sproul in a Paris exhibition. Twenty-seven years later, Jack Dempsey did the same thing to one Cowboy Lutrell. As wrestling transformed from a sport to a type of performance art, speculation about boxer-wrestler confrontations faded.

Still, the 1976 matchup received a great deal of hype as a "World Martial Arts Championship," a modern-day gladiatorial combat without parallel. But many boxing purists viewed it as a corruption of the heavyweight title.

Ferdie Pacheco was among those who were skeptical. "Any wrestler giving an honest effort is very dangerous for a boxer and I'm talking about bone-breaking dangerous," he said. "When a wrestler gets you down on the mat, you're in his ball game, his trenches."[47]

The "Fight Doctor" need not have worried, as the rules for the match were stacked in Ali's favor. Inoki would be banned from executing such standard wrestling moves as the flying drop-kick and the karate chop. The "fight" would consist of 15 three-minute rounds. Ali would wear gloves and fight according to the Queensberry Rules. Inoki, who was similar to Ali in size and bore a striking resemblance to Oscar Bonavena, was allowed to use both his hands and his feet.

As drama, Ali–Inoki proved only slightly less exciting than watching grass grow. Muhammad had floored more than his share of opponents, but he'd never encountered a foe who hit the canvas voluntarily and remained there for forty-five excruciatingly boring minutes.

The wrestler's strategy appeared to be to keep his back on the floor while kicking at Ali's legs. It was impossible for Ali to punch a supine opponent. Inoki did manage to pull Ali to the canvas in the sixth, and administer a head butt to the groin in the 13th.

Other than that, the "action" consisted of several kicks to the legs by Inoki and perhaps half a dozen harmless punches from Ali, which worked out to a million bucks a blow. Inoki, by the way, made $4 million for lying down on the job.

The final verdict, for anyone who cared, was a draw. On an "undercard" event at Madison Square Garden, 7'4", 450-pound wrestler Andre the Giant shot-putted Chuck Wepner into the front seats.

The only conclusive result of the Ali–Inoki spectacle was that such an event should never be repeated. However, such sideshows were somewhat of a precursor to our current, and very popular, mixed martial arts shows. Who could have guessed, in 1976, following the Ali–Inoki debacle, that similar events would actually one day surpass boxing in popularity?

Ten days before the farce in Tokyo, a pair of ex-heavyweight champions engaged in a gladiatorial showdown of their own. In the wake of his rock-'em sock-'em win over Ron Lyle, George Foreman demanded a rematch with Ali. But Ali had already penciled in Ken Norton's name for a September superfight at Yankee Stadium. To stay active and to keep his name at the top of the contenders' list, Foreman signed to meet Joe Frazier in Uniondale, New York.

Frazier, who had considered retiring after the Thrilla in Manila, jumped at the chance to erase the memory of the humiliating defeat Big George had inflicted in 1973. The promoter for Foreman–Frazier II was Jerry Perenchio. Perenchio guaranteed both fighters $1 million.

For once, though, Perenchio's instincts misled him. Fan interest in a Foreman–Frazier rematch was minimal, most likely due to the ease with which George had extinguished Smokin' Joe the first time. Eventually, Perenchio resorted to desperate measures to breathe life into his promotion.

Billing it "The Battle of the Gladiators," Perenchio had the principals photographed in full Roman arena regalia for fight posters. A similar gimmick, which featured Frazier and Ali in bareknuckle tights for the Superfight I poster, had worked well. But in studs and leather, Joe and George looked a little silly.

That didn't deter Perenchio from persuading Frazier to dress up in a Betsy Ross costume and suggest that Foreman would soon be seeing stars!

Despite such indignities, the Foreman–Frazier rematch did have some intriguing elements. The title wasn't at stake, but the stakes were still high for both men: professional survival. The curtain would surely come down on one of their careers. The victor, on the other hand, would be in an excellent position to challenge the winner of the Ali–Norton fight.

Regardless of the six-knockdown bludgeoning Foreman had inflicted in Jamaica, there were some who gave Frazier a good chance of evening the score. The Ali fight, and to an extent the Lyle war, had exposed George's lack of stamina. Those fights had also shown how easy to hit Foreman was, provided he didn't hit you first, of course.

Frazier's stamina was unquestioned. And his left hook remained a potent weapon. He had taken Foreman lightly the first time; now that he knew what to expect, he was certain to fight more defensively. Frazier's supporters believed that if he could survive the early rounds, he would ultimately wear Foreman down and defeat him.

Objective opinion held that the Foreman–Frazier matchup would always be a matter of styles. Neither fighter's technique had changed since 1973. Frazier's straight-ahead style would always play into Foreman's dynamite-laden hands, stamina or no stamina. According to that reasoning, Frazier could fight Foreman ten times and lose on each occasion.

Eddie Futch, one of the greatest strategists in boxing history, felt that a few adjustments could drastically alter the outcome from their 1973 encounter. Futch indicated he had no intention of attempting to change Smokin' Joe's style. At 32, Frazier was too entrenched in his ways to learn a new way of fighting. Futch only wanted to alter a few specific aspects, adding techniques he believed would be effective against Foreman.

Big George still carried all the advantages, though. He had youth, strength, size, and the memory of the beating he had laid on Frazier. As well, this would be Joe's first outing since the epic battle he had waged with Ali. Since then, Ali had shown signs of declining. It was certainly reasonable to assume that Frazier, the loser in that fight, would also have depreciated physically.

Despite Foreman's superiority on paper, there were still enough sentimental Frazier supporters to give George only an 8–5 edge in the odds.

Neither Perenchio's antics nor the reputation of the fighters helped the promotion. On fight night, only 11,000 of the 17,000 available seats had been sold. The fans who did show up were treated to some interesting surprises.

Actually, Frazier had already provided an unexpected moment at the weigh-in. He scaled 224½ pounds, the same as Foreman. The weight looked good on George, but Frazier appeared more fat than fit. The extra weight, which was nine pounds more than Joe's previous high, was intended to provide some extra anchorage should Foreman attempt the shoving tactic that had proved so successful during their first fight.

Surprise #2 was unveiled when Frazier climbed into the ring and pulled back the hood that covered his head. Lo and behold, Frazier's skull was shaved bald as a cueball! Also missing was Joe's characteristic moustache and beard. He had shorn himself on impulse only hours before the fight.

Perhaps the biggest surprise of all came after the bell for the first round. Frazier, who had never voluntarily taken a backward step in his entire 12-year career, opted to backpedal against Foreman. He and Futch both knew a straight-ahead rush would be suicidal. Frazier's new fight plan was to stay away; Joe would go on the offensive and take Foreman out in the late rounds.

Sound though it may have been in theory, the strategy Futch had devised only delayed the inevitable. Using a powerful left jab and strength-sapping body shots, Foreman controlled the first three rounds. At the end of the third, though, George appeared to be showing early signs of fatigue. Frazier was still fresh.

In the fourth, the crowd began to chant "Joe! Joe! Joe!" as Frazier crashed home several of his patented left hooks. Asked later if any of those blows had hurt him, Foreman said: "You don't say 'oops' when Joe Frazier hits you, you say 'Oh Lord!'"[48]

Frazier's flash of success in the fourth injected hope in the hearts of his fans. The fifth round was the time Foreman usually began to fade. If Smokin' Joe could only last three more minutes, anything could happen....

It didn't take Big George long to dash those hopes. Early in the round, he pinned Frazier against the ropes and proceeded to unload his bombs. Joe tried and failed to emulate Ali's Rope-a-Dope as Foreman's blows crashed thunderously against his head and body. Finally, Frazier slid to the canvas.

When he climbed to his feet, Frazier sported a badly torn right eyebrow. Foreman resumed his assault and dropped Frazier with a left hook. Frazier got up at the count of seven, but Futch called for a halt to the proceedings. Joe protested, but referee Harold Valan agreed with Futch and waved an end to the fight at the 2:26 mark.

Later, Futch said the fight plan had worked perfectly until Frazier became "careless in the fifth and got himself caught on the ropes."[49] But no fight plan in the world could have given Frazier the physical attributes he needed to stand a chance against Foreman.

Foreman's second victory over Frazier solidified his position in the upper echelons of the ratings. Because Ali was committed to fight Norton in September, Foreman rounded out 1976 by taking on a pair of young white prospects, Scott Ledoux and John "Dino" Dennis. Ledoux, who could best be described as Chuck Wepner without the blood, lasted three rounds. Dennis, a stylish boxer with plenty of potential, exited in four. At the end of the year, Big George was in an ideal position to challenge the winner of Ali–Norton III.

As expected, the proud but vanquished Frazier announced his retirement soon after the Foreman fight. With a record of 32–4 (27 knockouts), his place among the all-time greats of the division was assured.

It took that final, futile effort against Foreman to gain Frazier the fan support he always believed Ali had stolen from him. For the first time in his career, Smokin' Joe had gone into the ring as a sentimental favorite. Never before had the fans been so unanimously and emotionally supportive of him. And when he went down to defeat, the boxing world respected Frazier's wisdom in admitting he was through. No one wanted to see him take any more beatings.

Joe Frazier's importance to the greatness of heavyweight boxing during the 1970s cannot be overstated. Although he could never escape the shadow of Ali, it was Frazier who forced his nemesis to reach deep inside himself to summon qualities no other opponent could demand from him.

The Ali fights earned Frazier millions of dollars and raised his stature to heights he never could have dreamed of back when he was chopping beef in a slaughterhouse by day and training in a rough Philly gym at night. Without Ali, Frazier might have gone down in history as a footnote, an interim "cheese" champion who got lucky when Muhammad's career was cut short by his draft troubles. Because of Ali, Joe's name is written in the record books in capital letters.

Ali, on the other hand, would have earned the money anyway, and he had already achieved his own level of celebrity before Frazier arrived on the scene. Still, it was the Frazier fights that finally earned him the respect of the die-hard boxing fans who had always questioned his courage. The savage beating Ali took from Frazier in the first fight convinced the critics that he was much more than just a fancy-dancing "pretty boy."

The Ali–Frazier trilogy became the cornerstone of both men's careers. Ali's 2-to-1 edge in the series was arguably the foremost of his many pugilistic accomplishments. And Frazier's greatest achievement was his victory in Superfight I. Because they brought out the finest in each other, their names will be forever linked in the annals of fistiana.

Ironically, the intensity of their rivalry also resulted in physical depreciation for both men. They left many pieces of themselves in Madison Square Garden and Manila, pieces that could never be recovered. In hindsight, they both should have retired after the Thrilla in Manila.

Frazier's exit after the "Battle of the Gladiators" struck a melancholy chord among fight fans. After spending the better part of a decade playing the supporting role in the Ali–Frazier show, Smokin' Joe sat alone at a press conference and proclaimed an end to his career, and an era. For even though Ali was still active, he couldn't evade Father Time much longer.

Nor could he avoid Ken Norton.

If Norton believed he was destined to win the title in 1976, his confidence was well justified. Since his decisive win over Jerry Quarry the year before, Ken had kept busy and solidified his position as the #1 contender. After disposing of Quarry, Norton had traveled to St. Paul, Minnesota, to even an old score. On August 14, 1975, he fought a rematch with Jose Luis Garcia, the man who had handed him his first career loss five years earlier.

The win over Norton, combined with follow-up victories over names like Thad Spencer, James J. Woody, Alberto Lovell, and Florida Al Jones, had lifted the Venezuelan stringbean to the #3 slot in some ratings. But in 1972, he was derailed by a comebacking Ernie Terrell.

Trouble often comes in threes, and Garcia's track record proved no exception to that rule. After losing to Terrell, Garcia was knocked out by Joe Alexander and Ron Lyle. With his credibility rapidly fading, Garcia regrouped by taking on some of the division's most notorious record-padders. He defeated Charlie Polite, Bob Mashburn, Charles Atlas and Charlie James before dropping two in a row to Jimmy Young and Joe Bugner. A pair of wins against middling opposition did nothing to advance his status.

In two short years, Garcia had slipped from contender to journeyman. But that didn't matter to Norton, who wanted only to wipe out the humiliation of the thrashing the Venezuelan had inflicted. He hammered Garcia into submission in five rounds, and Jose Luis wisely called it quits afterward. Ironically, Norton had provided both the high point and the termination of Garcia's career.

The Venezuelan retired with a respectable 28–2–1 record. Although he is largely forgotten now, Garcia was for a short time a serious contender during the Golden Decade of the heavyweights, and he can say with pride that he accomplished a feat that eluded Ali: a kayo victory over Norton.

Norton's next opponent was another South American: Argentine medical student and knockout artist Pedro Lovell. Lovell, the tall, lanky son of an Olympic gold medal winner, had caused quite a stir through the early 1970s. He turned pro on November 13, 1970, with a first-round knockout of Ron Howard (no, not the actor who played Richie Cunningham on *Happy Days*).

Since then, Lovell had amassed an 18–1–1 record with 14 kayoes. The draw came against Charlie James, and the loss was a freak knockout by Terry Krueger. Krueger, a rugged but limited slugger out of San Antonio, Texas, boasted 15 first-round kayoes, including a streak of five in a row.

However, five of Terry's six defeats had also come by knockout as well. Lovell was heavily favored to win, but he went into the fight suffering from the flu and Krueger stopped him in four rounds. Less than three months later, a healthy Lovell starched Krueger in the first stanza.

After four more wins, two by knockout, the Argentine's chance to break into the ratings came when he signed to fight Norton on January 3, 1976. Although Norton had faced much better opposition during his career, Pedro was given a puncher's chance. Norton's weakness had always been heavy hitters who could back him up. However, Lovell simply didn't possess the tools to handle Norton, who stopped him in five one-sided rounds. Lovell continued his career, but never fulfilled his early promise.

Ken's next fight was on the undercard of Ali–Young in Landover, Maryland. His opponent: Ron Stander, the "Bluffs Butcher" who had fought so heroically in a losing challenge of Joe Frazier in 1972. Stander had gone to the post a dozen times since then, and was batting .500, fantastic for a baseball player, but terrible for a boxer.

Stander wasn't expected to give Norton much trouble, and he satisfied those expectations in full. The chunky 229-pound Stander did manage an occasional shot to Norton's head, but for the most part the muscular ex–Marine pummeled him from pillar to post. Ken's sharp, accurate punches turned Stander's face into a sieve, with blood spurting from half a dozen cuts. Referee Harry Chechini stepped in at the 1:19 mark of round five to rescue Stander, who resembled a character from a B-grade slasher movie.

To keep his edge for the upcoming Ali fight, Norton signed to fight Oscar Bonavena in June. However, a terrible tragedy canceled the fight and robbed the boxing game of one of its most colorful and controversial characters.

After his disputed loss to Floyd Patterson in 1972, Bonavena began a slow but steady slide out of the limelight. His recurring hand problems kept him out of action for nearly eighteen months. When he returned to the ring, he knocked over trial horses Leroy Caldwell and Cookie Wallace.

Oscar was then approached by a promoter named Mike Hayes, who intended to match him with Ron Lyle. At the time, Hayes was putting together the Lyle–Jose Luis Garcia fight in Denver, and wanted to put Bonavena on the undercard against a veteran named Lou Bailey. Bonavena's promoter, Loren Cassina, was well aware of Oscar's colossal ego and he told Hayes he would agree, provided Bonavena–Bailey was billed as a co-main event with Lyle–Garcia.

Hayes agreed, and Bonavena signed the contract. Bailey should have been easy pickings, but his hard head proved to be a dangerous obstacle for Oscar's brittle hands. Bonavena escaped with a decision that proved costly. He needed three months to rest his sore hands before testing them on Terry Sorrells, who went out in two rounds.

His next fight was the hard-fought loss to Lyle in 1974. That would be the last defeat in Oscar's storied career. Six victories over mediocre competition over the next two years kept his name in the ratings, but he was never seriously considered as a title opponent.

By 1976, "Ringo" was fighting under the managerial banner of Joe Conforte, owner of the Mustang Ranch, a legal brothel in Reno, Nevada. Cassina, who still promoted Bonavena's fights, hoped to get him a bout that would put him back in title contention. A televised slugfest with Earnie Shavers loomed as a serious possibility.

However, Bonavena's sluggish performance against a spoiler named Billy Joiner on February 26 clearly indicated that he was in no condition to take on an opponent as dangerous as Shavers. Instead, Shavers fought and beat Henry Clark, and Bonavena was left to sharpen his diminishing skills for the proposed bout with Norton.

Cassina had no trouble selling CBS on the idea of a televised Norton tune-up against a big-name opponent like Bonavena. However, Oscar was having problems of a different kind in his new location in Reno.

With his wife and children still in Argentina, Bonavena began an affair with the spouse of his manager, Conforte. Conforte responded by banning Bonavena from the ranch. In a related incident, Oscar's trailer was broken into and several items, including his passport, were destroyed.

Mrs. Bonavena later said Oscar had told her he was receiving telephoned death threats and indicated he was thinking of returning to Argentina. If he had followed that impulse, Bonavena might still be alive today.

The complete story surrounding the events of May 22, 1976, may never be uncovered. What's known is that Bonavena attempted to confront Conforte at 6:00 A.M. at the Mustang Ranch. Two of the brothel's security guards approached the fighter, and Oscar ended up with a bullet in his chest. He died instantly. Because a pistol was found hidden in Bonavena's boot, the man who pulled the trigger received a minor two-year prison term.

Unlike so many other fighters, Bonavena didn't die penniless. He owned a clothing store, a restaurant, a night club, and a barber shop in Argentina. Although his days as a title threat were long behind him, Bonavena's tragic demise was a terrible blow to the fistic fraternity. He was given a hero's burial in Buenos Aires.

With Bonavena gone, Norton looked elsewhere for a last tune-up before his showdown with Ali. He finally settled on Larry Middleton. Middleton's once-promising career had seen him score victories over Joe Bugner, Tony Doyle, Danny McAlinden, Roy Williams, and Bob Stallings. He had also fought a draw with Jimmy Ellis and gone the distance with the ever-dangerous Jerry Quarry. Now, though, Middleton was on the downslide.

Since the draw with Ellis two years earlier, Larry had lost four of his last five fights. He dropped decisions to Bonavena as well as Scott Ledoux and touted newcomer Duane Bobick. Hard-hitting Howard "KO" Smith of California put Larry away in five. Middleton did manage to stop journeyman Rochell Norris in nine.

Now he was rapidly settling into the role of speed bump on younger fighters' road to title contention. He was the type of opponent who could take a prospect to school without hurting him in the process. What Norton hoped to gain from fighting Middleton was a competitive, risk-free workout that would hone his skills for Ali, whose style was similar to Middleton's. What he got was ten tough rounds of action before Middleton finally succumbed.

Larry took only one more fight after Norton, a ten-round decision win over Roger Russell. Far better than he 23–9–2 record indicated, Middleton fought the best in the division and was probably one of the best contenders nobody knew about. Today he works as a trainer in the Baltimore area.

Although Norton's win over Middleton wasn't exactly awe-inspiring, the closeness of the outcome pleased trainer Bill Slayton. He figured it was a good wake-up call and would drive Norton even harder in his preparations for Ali.

One look at Norton's Herculean physique provided ample evidence of his dedication to training. Still, his work in preparation for his third fight with Ali surpassed all previous standards. Other than Joe Frazier, no one knew the champion inside the ring as well as Norton did. He well understood that it would take a career-best effort to displace Ali from the heavyweight title throne. And that was an effort Ken was more than capable of giving.

Intimations of Mortality

Norton's intense desire to win the title from Ali drove him to new heights in his pre-fight preparations. He sparred an astounding eight rounds daily and followed up with 10 rounds of floor work. The single-minded manner in which Ken attacked his training did much to dispel a popular notion that he was more interested in acting than boxing.

Norton had already played the lead in two successful movies: *Mandingo* and *Drum*. Although originally chosen for those vehicles because of his handsome face and bulging muscles, Norton proved quite adept at delivering his lines. He made no secret of his plans to pursue the bright lights and big bucks of Hollywood stardom.

That ambition brought skepticism and derision from the denizens of "Bash Boulevard," who believed that fighting and acting just didn't mix. The oldest of them remembered that Jack Dempsey was never the same fighter after he got his nose reconstructed so he could star in silent movies, and they predicted that Norton would become overly protective of his matinee idol looks in the ring. Norton himself admitted that he was wary of shots to the face during sparring sessions. But when it came to actual combat, he threw caution to the winds. Asked about possible ring hazards to his physiognomy, Norton joked that he could "always make horror movies."

Ali, always on the lookout for verbal ammunition to use against an opponent, jumped at the opportunity to ridicule Ken's Hollywood aspirations. He figured that after he got through with Norton he'd be lucky to get a role in a Lassie movie.

Norton absorbed Ali's antics without breaking stride. Having defeated Ali once and losing by only a split decision in their second encounter, Norton was not susceptible to the champ's psychological ploys. Once you've broken a man's jaw, there isn't much he can say or do to intimidate you.

Although Norton was Ali's greatest rival now that Joe Frazier had retired, their competition was far less volatile at the personal level. Ali and Frazier were practically born to be antagonists, and the tension between them had begun long before they ever met in the ring. In contrast, the Norton rivalry arrived out of the blue in San Diego in March of 1973.

As well, the Ali–Frazier conflict encompassed not only the ring, but also the political and social arenas. Ali–Norton was strictly a boxing rivalry. Consequently, Ali's pre-fight badgering of Norton was far less cutting and personal than his anti–Frazier rhetoric. He confined himself to chanting "Norton must fall!" every chance he got.

For that reason, Norton bore Ali none of the bitterness and animosity that Frazier carries to this day. Norton realized that Ali, more than anyone else, took him from rags to riches.

Norton's visit to Ali in the hospital after the jaw-breaking incident in their first fight was an indication of the esteem in which he held "The Greatest." Ken also paid a call on Ali when the latter was hospitalized for leg injuries incurred during the Inoki fiasco.

For this fight, however, Norton placed his respect for Ali on the shelf. He knew that the only way he could take Ali's title was to either knock him out or outpoint him so decisively that even the judges who scored the Jimmy Young fight would have to give him the decision. He also knew that when he fought Ali, he would be fighting history as well. The champion was at the height of his popularity, and that popularity was bound to influence both the crowd and the judges.

After the courage he displayed in his 1971 loss to Frazier, Ali had enjoyed overwhelming crowd support wherever he fought. From New York to Las Vegas, from Malaysia to Zaire, Muhammad was the favorite of the fans. As heavyweight contender Randy Neumann noted while moonlighting as a writer for the *New York Times*, "Ali is a hometown favorite wherever he fights; the world is his backyard."

Ali thus had an advantage with the officials, an advantage of which the officials themselves were probably unaware. Norton, having sweated through two close decisions against "The Greatest," was well aware of that factor. Norton acknowledged that he was behind the eight ball going into the fight with Ali. To win, he knew he must do so decisively.

But Ali believed he was the one who would win decisively. "Norton must fall" was more than mere rhetoric; Ali and Dundee both thought Ken would not last the full fifteen rounds in their rubber match.

Their rationale for that belief wasn't clear. True, the Ali of 1976 was bigger and stronger than the Ali of 1973, but so was Norton. Ken retained his well-chiseled musculature, but his body had also become thicker, more mature, and definitely more powerful, as demonstrated by the seven straight knockouts he had scored leading up to the Ali fight.

Yet Ali was convinced he was a harder hitter than he'd been in 1973. For one thing, he was spending far less time on his toes, and a flat-footed fighter can deliver more telling blows than one who is constantly on the move.

Another advantage the 1976 Ali held over the 1973 edition was stronger hands. For much of the 1972–1974 period, his hands were so fragile that landing a solid blow was a source of agony. During the first two Norton fights, he needed Novocain shots in both hands to ease the pain punching caused. According to Ali, his hands were so bad he couldn't hit the heavy bag during training. For the rubber match, however, his hands were fine, and he believed that would cause a major improvement in his performance.

One reason Ali cited for the strengthening of his hands was the use of a different kind of heavy bag. As opposed to the old sand-filled bags that had virtually no give, Ali opted for a softer bag packed with rags. The champ had been utilizing the bag since the second Frazier fight and the improvement in his hands was nothing short of miraculous. Ali brought the bag with him to Zaire, Indonesia and Manila. With the improvement to his hands, Ali was setting himself and punching much harder. This, he vowed, would spell disaster for Ken Norton.

Norton was indeed vulnerable to a hard hitter, as his destruction at the hands of Foreman amply demonstrated. So if Ali had indeed turned puncher, it wasn't beyond the realm of possibility that he could stop Norton. After all, he'd kayoed Foreman, hadn't he?

Dundee predicted that Ali would finish Norton inside ten rounds. He felt that the Ali who had stopped both Foreman and Frazier was far more dangerous than the one who had struggled 24 rounds with Norton in 1973.

Angelo's reasoning was fine in theory. But if the guy Norton was fighting turned out to be the one who fought Jimmy Young, then the title could possibly change hands.

On fight night, though, Ali appeared to be in excellent condition at 221 pounds. Norton weighed in at 217½. The odds favored Ali, but only by an 8-to-5 margin based on the closeness of their first two battles.

The temperature at Yankee Stadium that night was only 55, but the elements could not dampen the fervor of the 30,298 fans who piled into the ball yard that had hosted such classics as Joe Louis vs. Max Schmeling II, Joe Louis vs. Billy Conn I, and Rocky Marciano vs. Archie Moore.

Norton proved correct in his assumption that the crowd would be predominantly pro-Ali. When the champion entered the ring, he received a thunderous ovation. Then he led the masses in a repetitive chant of his theme for the fight, "Norton must fall!"

He taunted Ken during Referee Arthur Mercante's instructions and swung his right arm in windmill fashion as he waited for hostilities to commence. And that was Ali's high point for the night.

The crowd and the closed-circuit spectators from around the globe were expecting one more miracle from Ali, one more brilliant performance to stand beside the Foreman and Frazier fights. Instead, they saw a pugilistic equivalent of the picture of Dorian Gray, aging before the spectators' incredulous eyes, round by round.

In the first, the champion came out as he'd promised, feet planted firmly on the canvas and spread wide apart in an attempt to generate more power. He controlled the round as Norton did little more than stand in front of him and analyze the situation. What he learned was that Ali couldn't hurt him.

Although Norton lost the first round on all three scorecards, he fought with more purpose in the second and increased his momentum over the next five rounds. He won the second through the sixth on at least two of the three judges' tallies.

Ali had intended to force Norton to back up, realizing that Ken was almost completely ineffective when he retreated. Instead, Norton continually bulled Ali into the ropes and whacked away at his head and body. Muhammad tried a new twist on the Rope-a-Dope, contemptuously shimmying his rear end as Norton attacked. But his clowning wasn't earning him any points.

Prior to the sixth round, Dundee reminded Ali that he shouldn't give any ground to Norton. Muhammad hadn't lost sight of his fight plan; the difficulty was in the execution. His body was betraying him; the blows that were supposed to detonate like bombs were having no more effect than rubber bullets. Ali landed plenty of flicking left jabs and an occasional slapping right hand, but Norton was walking right through the punches.

The challenger accelerated his attack in the sixth, landing several hard overhand rights to Ali's head as the champion continued to fight off the ropes. Then he dug a hard left under Ali's right elbow. The blow crashed with sledgehammer force against the champ's rib cage. Ali winced and staggered; the bell saved him from further punishment.

The crowd murmured in astonishment as Ali appeared to be taking a flat-out beating. But the man who rallied against Frazier in Manila wasn't about to go down without a fight in the Bronx. Sensing the desperation of his situation, Ali came alive and captured the next three rounds through sheer volume of punches thrown. The comeback ate up much of Norton's early lead on the scorecards.

Both fighters came out cautiously in the twelfth, fatigue having taken an obvious toll. They spent the first part of the round circling each other without throwing any punches.

Norton broke the holding pattern and opened up on Ali, forcing the champ into his accustomed position on the ropes. He landed some telling blows. Toward the end of the round, Ali retaliated with a flurry that was more show than substance.

One of the blows, however, caught Ken in the right eye. The challenger clutched his glove to his face and fell back against the ropes. At the end of the round, he pawed at his eye as he went back to his corner. Later, he claimed Ali had thumbed him.

The injury wasn't serious. And, after twelve hard-fought but unspectacular rounds, two of the judges had Norton ahead 7 rounds to 5. All Ken needed to do was capture just one of the remaining three stanzas on those two judges' cards and the title would be his!

Knowing his hold on the crown was becoming precarious, Ali showed some aggression in the thirteenth. Norton was still able to force Ali into the ropes, but this time Ali punched back every step of the way. This exchange, the first major one of the fight, brought an ovation from the action-starved crowd. All three judges gave the thirteenth to Ali.

Round 14 became a bone of contention for Norton supporters who believed their man won it by a wide margin. Ali appeared to be fading while Norton surged. But on the scorecards, only Mercante gave the round to the challenger. Judges Smith and Lederman both favored Ali.

Thus, as in their previous two encounters, the outcome of Ali–Norton III came down to the final round.

"I want you to turn tiger," Dundee implored Ali during the final one-minute rest period. "Take him out if you can."

The champ didn't come out like Foreman. But he did come out up on his toes, dancing like the Ali of the 1960s. The champ circled the challenger, flicking jabs and controlling the action.

Despite his sub-par performance throughout the fight, Ali somehow summoned the energy to stick and move, to float like a butterfly even though he was feeling every one of his 34 years. It was an amazing testament to his heart and resiliency, but was it enough to save his title.

Strangely, Norton suddenly reduced himself to a supporting role as he passively followed Ali around the ring. During the last minute of the round, he finally broke out of his shell and crashed two hard blows to Ali's head. The champion came down from his toes and backed into the ropes. They fought on even terms the rest of the round, though Norton seemed to be coming on in the final seconds.

When the final bell rang, Norton removed his mouthpiece and shouted taunts at the quiet champion. His cornermen lifted him into the air and he raised his arms in triumph. For the short time between the end of the round and the announcement of the decision, Ken Norton truly believed he had become the new heavyweight champion of the world.

Ali and his corner seemed to believe that as well. His side of the ring was as solemn as the other was jubilant. Then the verdict was announced: a unanimous decision for Ali!

Upon hearing the decision, a distraught Norton dropped to his knees in shock and disbelief. Then he burst into tears.

Although the announcement drew a smattering of boos from the crowd, most of the spectators sat silent and stunned. Some couldn't believe what they'd heard. Others weighed the fighters' performance against the final outcome. Still others shook their heads over the obvious end of an era, regardless of the decision.

Ali had mixed emotions. He was obviously relieved that he hadn't lost the title. But he was also displeased at his subpar performance.

Hours after the fight, however, Ali was able to look at the contest from a more positive perspective. At the post-fight press conference, he stated: "Great race horses come through by a nose. I came through by a nose."[50]

Ali's confidence had been boosted in the comfort and security of his dressing room. His entourage of leeches and hangers-on had reassured him he was still "The Greatest" and had defeated Norton decisively. Their reassurance applied as much to themselves as the champ; they knew that once Ali retired or lost the title in the ring, their free ride would come to an end.

Outside the warm embrace of his entourage, however, reality greeted Ali like a harsh winter wind. The press was almost unanimous in its support for Norton. All Ali would admit to was the closeness of the fight. "The three judges had it just about right," he said.

He even went so far as to claim, "For my age and all I've been through, and the shape he was in, and he's younger than me, it was a perfect performance tonight."[51]

That statement seemed designed to convince Ali more than anyone else. It certainly didn't convince Ken Norton.

Before the fight, Norton had indicated that he needed to win convincingly to take the title, and in his mind he had done exactly that. "I thought I won big," Norton said. "If it was a close fight and they gave it to him, that's cool. If he won decisively, that's cool. But to take it away from me like they did, I don't go for that. To me, boxing's gone sour in my mouth."[52]

Norton's assistant trainer, the colorful Pat O'Grady, had some choice words for the press. "You prejudice people into watching one fighter all the time," he complained. "And then the people aren't watching the other guy; they're only watching Ali. He gives you all the psyche before the fight and it builds up to the point you think he's invincible. You don't believe what your eyes tell you, that he's being beat."[53]

Sportswriter Red Smith agreed with O'Grady that Norton had been victimized by officials who were "so dazzled by the man's mystique that they can't believe their eyes when they see him losing."[54] Smith even implied that Ali was given the decision as a gift. "Muhammad Ali has given boxing a lot. This time he got something back."[55]

Those comments were perceptive. But the fight was close. Therefore the outcome would have been controversial regardless of the winner. In the end, it wasn't so much a matter of Ali's being "given" the decision as it was Norton's failure to "take" it.

Covering the fight for *Newsweek*, Pete Axthelm scored it narrowly in favor of Norton. But he qualified his unofficial verdict with one of the most pertinent and accurate commentaries from anyone in the media:

> I gave Norton the fight, seven rounds to six with two even. But I don't agree with the bitter, tearful challenger that he was "robbed" when all three officials gave eight rounds to Ali. Many rounds, including the decisive fifteenth, were so uneventful they could have been scored for either man. It is a long-standing custom to give the champion the benefit of such doubts, and if Norton and the people in his corner were naive enough to think that Ken could coast to narrow victory, they will have to live with that crucial mistake.[56]

Indeed, it was that crucial fifteenth round that cost Norton the fight, or, to be more precise, the first two and a half minutes of that round. Had he kept up the pressure instead of falling for Ali's dance-and-jab act, Norton would have taken the round and the title.

Regardless, Norton's manager, Bob Biron, lodged an official protest against the decision with New York State Athletic Commission Chairman James A. Farley Jr. The appeal was turned down. A disgruntled Norton threatened to retire unless he was granted an immediate rematch.

Ali also spoke of hanging up his gloves. At the post-fight press conference, he declared he had "nothing left to prove." Three days later, he announced his retirement while visiting Turkey. "I declare I am quitting fighting as of now and from now on I will join the struggle for the Islamic cause."[57]

Although Ali seemed sincere about leaving boxing, very few insiders took him very seriously. Thus, neither the WBA nor the WBC made any arrangements to seek a successor to the throne. Like the boy who cried "wolf," Ali had tossed out too many retirement announcements in the past.

Ring magazine editor Nat Loubet wrote in the January 1977 edition that *The Ring*'s recognition, which had always carried more credibility than the WBA or the WBC, would continue to list Ali as heavyweight king until he was 100 percent sure. Loubet: "To give Ali time to ponder, *The Ring* will give him sixty days in which to make his final decision. If at the end of that period Ali still maintains that he is in retirement, we will consider his announcement as final and his title vacant."[58]

The bottom line was that it was unlikely Ali would retire as long as big money and continued fame loomed on the horizon. He indeed had "nothing left to prove." But he couldn't stand the thought of stepping out of the limelight.

Although his love for the training and combat involved in boxing had long since faded, for Ali the sport remained a necessary evil. Only through the ring could he keep his face on the television screens and his name in print. He was addicted to fame and money; for that reason he wasn't going to do the sensible thing and retire as champion.

But his days as champion appeared to be coming to an end. The handwriting was on the wall, written plainly by the fists of Ken Norton and Jimmy Young. But Ali, like so many before him, turned a blind eye to the obvious deterioration of the skills that had carried him to such dizzying heights. It seemed as though only a terrible beating in the ring would make him understand what even the most casual observer could see.

At the end of 1976, Muhammad Ali was still champion. But he was also a pugilistic time bomb. The year had provided mixed blessings. Financially, it was one of the most successful 12 months of his career. In fistic terms, however, it was a year marred by poor performances, dubious decisions, and constant controversy.

Ferdie Pacheco, who had been with Ali since the first Sonny Liston fight, heard the ticking of the bomb and disassociated himself from the champ's corner after repeatedly advising him to stick to his retirement plans.

But Don King, who understood what was driving Ali better than almost anyone else, dangled the lure of another megabucks showdown in front of Muhammad's eyes, a rematch with the resurgent George Foreman. King was throwing around a potential figure of $10,000,000 for the extravaganza.

Pacheco was telling Ali what he needed to hear. But King told him what he wanted to hear. It was no contest. As expected, Ali reneged on his retirement and spoke of a defense against Foreman sometime in 1977. Whether or not he would actually follow through on that plan, and he had ten million reasons to do so, didn't matter. What mattered was that he did intend to fight again. And in the now wide-open heavyweight division, the brass ring of the title was ready to be taken by any fighter bold enough to give it his best shot.

Foreman, Norton, and Young were the cream of the crop of contenders going into 1977. Most of the rest were either dubious, like the aging Ron Lyle, or untested, like the much-ballyhooed Duane Bobick. But that didn't really matter. The consensus on the "Sock

Exchange" was that Ali's special skills were vanishing day by day, and even a tune-up defense against a "no-name" challenger could prove risky.

It seemed almost inconceivable that the gap between "The Greatest" and the rest of the heavyweight pack had narrowed so quickly. Fighters who at one time couldn't carry Ali's shoes were now being hyped as future champions.

In sum, 1976 came in like a lion with the Foreman–Lyle slugfest and went out like a lamb with the disputed Ali–Norton III decision.

What lay ahead for 1977?

Ten

1977

San Juan Surprise

The onset of 1977 brought a great deal of speculation concerning the future of Muhammad Ali. After a listless 1976, no one but Ali himself could doubt that he had entered his fistic twilight. His interest in the rigors of his profession was waning, and his second reign as champion was skating toward the thinnest of ice. It seemed certain that he, at 35, would lose his title in 1977, either voluntarily through retirement or involuntarily at the hands of one of the host of worthy, hungry young contenders.

Four fighters stood at the top of the heap at the beginning of 1977: the embittered Ken Norton, the unappreciated Jimmy Young, the untested Duane Bobick, and the resurgent George Foreman. All of these fighters deserved a shot at Ali's title during 1977; none of them received one.

For the first time in his career, Ali appeared to be ducking worthwhile competition. However, a potentially disastrous year was saved as the top contenders fought each other in an effort to bolster their credibility and force a showdown with Ali. Thus, 1977 became the first year of the decade in which Ali failed to dominate the division's agenda.

Foreman was odds-on favorite to win the Ali succession sweepstakes. At 29, he was still in his prime, and his crowd-pleasing performances in his four 1976 comeback bouts had restored his reputation. Experts believed Foreman's youth and strength would prove too much for an Ali who wasn't half the fighter who had mystified Big George in Zaire.

George began 1977 with a four-round blowout of a badly overmatched Pedro Agosto on January 22. His next fight, scheduled for March 17 in San Juan, Puerto Rico, pitted him against Jimmy Young. The winner of Foreman–Young would take a giant step toward a title bout.

Young had risen high in the ratings on the strength of his performances against Ali and Ron Lyle. Since his heartbreaking loss to Ali, Jimmy had fought three times. His first two opponents, Lou Rogan and Mike Boswell, became only the sixth and seventh kayo victims on his record.

Rogan, a 193-pounder from West Virginia, exited at 2:09 of the second round at the Philadelphia Arena on September 3, 1976. Ten days later, Young tangled with Boswell on a nationally televised doubleheader that also featured Ron Lyle against Kevin Isaac. The card was meant to provide a tune-up for the Lyle–Young rematch scheduled for November 5.

Isaac, a 21-year-old prospect from Brooklyn, gave Lyle a good test until the older man's strength and experience began to prevail. Ron ended matters in the seventh. Isaac went on to become an above-average journeyman.

Boswell didn't provide any test at all for Young. The 204-pound native of Youngstown, Ohio, had once been a prospect, but was now riding a 17-bout losing streak. Young made it 18 straight when the fight was mercifully halted in the fourth frame. Now Young and Lyle could safely prepare for their second encounter.

Lyle–Young II was of much greater significance than their first fight. At that time, Young had gone in as a "safe" tune-up opponent, and their purses reflected the lack of esteem the promoters bore for the Philadelphian. Lyle had made only $10,000 for his pains, and Young had pulled down even less. But Jimmy's upset win had upped his market value. For the rematch, both men earned $40,000.

During the course of the 12 rounds, the old adage "styles make fights" was borne out once again. Young proved too quick for the ponderous Lyle, and he came away with another decision win. Afterward, Jimmy said the rematch had been one of his toughest fights, and he warned that Lyle was still "no pushover for anybody." Still, Ron was 34, and he appeared to be close to the end of the line.

However, Lyle was a survivor in and out of the ring. Four months after the Young loss, he bounced back to out-will Joe Bugner in a crossroads fight. Behind on points, he rallied in the late rounds to snatch victory from defeat. Lyle went undefeated for three years following the second loss to Young. Victories over credible foes like Stan Ward and Scott Ledoux kept Lyle's name in the ratings. But his days as a major force in the division were over, as his contractual and legal problems kept him out of some lucrative bouts.

While Ron waited, the clock ticked relentlessly. Finally, on December 12, 1979, Lyle ran into an inspired puncher named Lynn Ball, who knocked him out in two shocking rounds. The 38-year-old Lyle kept going with a pair of inconsequential wins. Then, in 1980, he signed up for a clash with the newest white hope, Gerry Cooney.

At that time, Cooney's managerial team was looking to pad the prospect's record with wins over sliding superstars. And the 1980 version of Lyle fit the bill perfectly. Now a mere shadow of the destroyer of the early '70s, Ron was blasted out of the ring by a Cooney left hook in less than a round. Had Cooney faced the Lyle of 1972–75, the result would probably have been different.

After that fight, Lyle retired to become a trainer and a security guard. In an interesting twist of fate, he played the role of Sonny Liston in an *Unsolved Mysteries* segment about the strange circumstances surrounding Sonny's death.

As for Young, upon beating Lyle again, he had upped his record to 20–5–2, and enhanced his standing as a contender. Yet Jimmy continued to be dogged by his reputation as a "spoiler." A win over Foreman would do much to dispel that reputation. But few observers believed that the Philadelphian possessed the physical necessities to offset Foreman's immense advantages in strength and punching power.

Foreman's confidence was no secret. He stated that he hadn't seen any improvement in Young over the years. "Jimmy Young two years ago is Jimmy Young today," George said dismissively.

To an extent, that was true. Young's safety-first style remained unvarying and predictable. But it was also effective, especially against sluggers like Foreman.

Foreman and his manager, Gil Clancy, should have remembered that George hadn't changed that much, either. Foreman was still a home-run hitter who swung for the fences with each punch. His stamina and boxing skills had shown no appreciable improvement despite Clancy's tutelage.

If styles made fights, Jimmy Young was the last opponent Foreman should have picked to act as a stepping stone to the title. Young had done well against Earnie Shavers and Ron Lyle, the two fighters in the division whose styles most closely resembled Foreman's. Their strengths were Foreman's strengths; their vulnerabilities Foreman's vulnerabilities. The fight shaped up as the purest boxer-slugger confrontation since the "Rumble in the Jungle."

Knowing that, Young was hardly in awe of Big George. As Ali had labeled Foreman "The Mummy" in 1974, Young took the comparison a step further and called him "The Dummy." "He's got two arms, two legs and one head, but only uses the arms and legs," Young quipped.

Foreman probably realized it would be difficult to look good against Young. Still, he needed the work and the money. A $700,000 purse guarantee was ample inducement for Foreman to face Young, who would be making $250,000. And, based on their performances against common opponent Jose "King" Roman, Foreman was confident he would win. Young had struggled to a 10-round decision over Roman; Foreman had annihilated the Puerto Rican in less than a round.

On the other hand, though, Young had gone the distance with Ali, who had knocked Big George out....

As the two fighters faced each other in the ring at Roberto Clemente Stadium on a Puerto Rican St. Patrick's Day, Foreman's size advantage appeared much greater than the 16 pounds and two inches in height revealed by the "Tale of the Tape." It looked more like a heavyweight looming over a middleweight. Nonetheless, Young appeared unfazed by the monumental task ahead of him.

In the early rounds, Foreman set out to impose his strength on Young any way he could, legally or illegally. He roughed Young up in the clinches, hit him behind the head, and tossed him around like a rag doll. Growing tired of Foreman's barroom tactics, Referee Waldemar Schmidt penalized him a point in round three.

Over the first six rounds, Young had picked up enough points to earn a deadlock on the scorecards. With the oppressive Puerto Rican heat rapidly draining his gas tank, Foreman knew the time had come to unload his bombs and obliterate the pest from Philadelphia.

Fifteen seconds into the seventh, Foreman stunned Young with a heavy left hook. Suddenly the "unhittable" Young was shaky and vulnerable. With nearly three minutes left on the clock, Big George apparently had Jimmy exactly where he wanted him.

Foreman chased and swung and banged and pushed. But Young bobbed and weaved and ran and clinched. At the end of the round, Young was miraculously still on his feet. Foreman went back to his corner with his massive chest pumping like a bellows.

Well aware that Foreman had spent nearly all his stamina, Young took control of the fight as the rounds wore on. One of his more unusual tactics was to take a little stroll from one side of the ring to the other, with Foreman following him like a dog on a leash. Sensing the likelihood of an upset, the San Juan crowd adopted the underdog as their own, and began to chant "Jeemy Yooung, Jeemy Yooung!" Foreman must have heard maddening echoes of "Ali bomaye."

As the twelfth and final round began, Foreman lumbered toward Young like an old, toothless bear. As in the eighth round of the Ali fight, George was reduced to a caricature of a fighter, unable to mount a threat to anyone of even modest ability. Totally disdainful of Foreman's slow-motion swings, Young stung him repeatedly with sharp one-two combinations. Foreman reeled like a drunk, a victim of the heat, fatigue, and Young's incessant tattoo of blows. Then the incredible happened. Jimmy stepped inside with a solid combination and Big George toppled to the canvas!

As the crowd roared in disbelief, Foreman rose immediately and had to be restrained by Referee Schmidt from going after Young before the mandatory eight count was completed.

The fight went the distance, but now the outcome was sealed, or so Young hoped. Once before, he had stood in seeming triumph, only to have the judges snatch away the victory he thought he had earned.

This time, he needn't have worried. With scores of 118–111, 116–112, and 115–113, Young captured the unanimous decision. He had proved once and for all that he was a contender, not a "spoiler." The upset win over Foreman represented the pinnacle of Jimmy Young's career.

For Foreman, the night of March 17, 1977, represented the end of his career, for ten years, at least. In his dressing room after the fight, Foreman collapsed from heat exhaustion. During that ordeal, he claimed to have seen a vision of the Lord that changed the course of his life.

After a brief stay in a local hospital, Foreman vowed to follow up on his experience and retire from the ring to become a preacher. He founded a church in his native Texas and dropped out of the boxing scene. At first, few believed he would stick to his retirement plans. Despite the setback to Young, Foreman was still one of the biggest attractions in the division. With a new string of knockout wins over limited opposition, he could have remained a serious contender for the rest of the decade, and he might have won the title again.

Don King, for one, predicted that Foreman would return to the ring. The flamboyant promoter hoped to have Foreman back in action before the end of 1977. But Foreman confined his action to the pulpit. Despite repeated rumors of an imminent comeback over the next few years, Foreman showed no inclination to fight again, and he eventually became part of heavyweight history.

Then, in 1987, ten years after the Young debacle, Foreman came back. He cited the financial needs of his church and community center as the motivation for his unlikely return to action. At 39 years of age, he had shaved his head and eliminated the bristling moustache from his upper lip. He had also added 50 pounds to his huge frame, and in his first comeback effort, a four-round stoppage of journeyman Steve Zouski, he looked like a joke come to life.

Indeed, Foreman told quite a few jokes during his comeback, most of them at his own expense. Having reached middle age, he had left the surly, arrogant side of himself behind, and he became more popular during his comeback than he had ever been as champion. In 1991, a 43-year-old Foreman amazed the boxing world by lasting the full 12-round distance with a young, fit, and determined heavyweight champion named Evander Holyfield. The feat provided a true indication of the greatness of the 1970s, in that a fighter who wasn't the best of that era was able to leapfrog a generation to hold his own against the champion of a new era.

Foreman's comeback, initially viewed as a joke or a nostalgic glance back at the seventies, was now looked at with a different eye. George proved in his stellar performance against Holyfield that he was still a force to be reckoned with. Not only had he maintained his power and durability, but "Big George" had added something new to his ring arsenal: stamina. For whatever reason, the "new" Foreman seemed to be able to pace himself far better he had in his first career. On November 5, 1994, three and a half years after his loss to Holyfield, Foreman was given another title opportunity, against Michael Moorer. Twenty years and six days after running out of gas in the eighth round versus Ali, a 45-year-old Foreman knocked Moorer out in the tenth round!

But in the '70s, even though the Young defeat had once again exposed his weaknesses,

Foreman's departure left a major void in the heavyweight scene. Masterful a boxer as Jimmy Young was, he could not begin to fill Foreman's shoes as a gate attraction.

But Foreman's weren't the shoes Young wanted to try on for size. He was ready to try once again to dethrone "The Greatest."

The Great Black Hope?

By 1977, Duane Bobick had become a serious contestant for heavyweight title honors. On May 11, he was scheduled to meet Ken Norton in another of the year's unofficial elimination contests to determine a challenger for Ali.

Born and raised in the hamlet of Bowlus, Minnesota, Bobick was the first major white heavyweight hopeful since Joe Bugner. The division had been dominated by black fighters for more than two decades. In the '60s, however, the ratings were loaded with solid white fighters like Jerry Quarry, George Chuvalo, Henry Cooper, Oscar Bonavena, and even Karl Mildenberger. Given different circumstances, such as the absence of Ali and Frazier, any one of those fighters could have won the title during the second half of the decade.

In the early 1970s, only Quarry remained as a white representative at the top of the heavyweight ladder. Bugner, Randy Neumann, and Chuck Wepner were above average, but they just couldn't cut it against the likes of Ali, Frazier, Foreman, Norton, Lyle, and Young. At mid-decade, credible white heavyweights had become as scarce as hen's teeth. From that point onward, the contract of any white fighter over 200 pounds who showed a degree of talent became the equivalent of a license to print money. The reasons for that state of affairs were rooted in race and economics.

In racial terms, blacks had held the heavyweight title for thirty-five of the forty years that had passed since Joe Louis dethroned Jim Braddock in 1937. Of the ten men who were undisputed champions during that period, only two were white: the great Rocky Marciano and the mediocre Ingemar Johansson.

Johansson was the last white heavyweight champion, and he had lost his title back in 1960. After nearly two decades in the wilderness, some white fans were hungry to see one of their own wear the championship belt.

Of course, there were others who couldn't care less what color the champion was, but their voices tended to be overlooked whenever White Hope hysteria hit. For far too many people, black and white alike, race did make a difference, in the ring and out. And that repugnant difference spelled big box office, just as it did in the days of Jack Johnson.

In terms of supply and demand, the fewer white heavyweights there were in the Top Ten, the more attention, and money, each one received. During the 1976–1977 period, Bobick stood virtually alone in the ratings, especially after Bugner lost to Lyle. He thus received a lion's share of media attention. And the decades-old mantle of the "White Hope" was draped over his broad shoulders, whether he liked it or not. And he didn't like it. In fact, Bobick stated repeatedly that he loathed the "White Hope" label and everything attached to it. He knew the association would be inevitable. Still, his reaction was: "I don't like it. Unfortunately, there's too much prejudice in the world. I know white people will come to see me win and black people will come to see me lose."[1]

In reality, Bobick was trained and managed by black men, Eddie Futch and Joe Frazier. He also employed a host of black sparring partners in his training camp. He often jokingly referred to himself as the "Great Black Hope."[2]

Some of the baser elements in the "White Hope" crowd didn't share Duane's sense of humor. The day before the Norton fight, Ken received an envelope that contained what he described as a "one way ticket back to Africa, to return to my people."[3]

The envelope was reportedly sent by the Ku Klux Klan.

Not all white heavyweights disdained the racial angle, as did Bobick. In boxing's earlier days, ethnicity and nationality were often as important as race. Irish, Jewish, and Italian fighters engaged in rivalries as intense as any black-white confrontation. Randy Neumann even billed himself as the "Great Jewish Hope" for a time, until it was discovered that he wasn't Jewish at all. Like Max Baer, Neumann was of German background.

It's easy to see that Neumann majored in business in college, and he was well aware of the financial benefits his complexion could bring. Neumann, like Bobick, was anything but a racist (his boyhood idol was Sonny Liston); however, he understood the financial benefits of being a "White Hope" heavyweight. "Boxing has always been ethnic ... it's just a term to put on a side of beef these days ... it's not really a racial term."[4]

Going back to Bobick, the knock against him was the quality of his opposition. When it came to securing opponents, Duane's backers left no rock unturned. The sparkling 38–0 record Bobick would carry into his big test against Norton included a substantial proportion of Palooka City's population. He had flattened enough tomato cans to overload a landfill site.

Thus, Bobick remained a question mark even in his supporters' minds. Despite his high rating, he had yet to fight a top-notch contender. As a result, he lacked the experience under fire that was necessary to handle a fighter of Norton's caliber. After five years of treading shallow water, Bobick was about to be pushed into the deep end of the pool.

Things were different before he turned pro. Young Duane went into the 1972 Olympic Games in Munich, West Germany, as one of the most celebrated amateur fighters in history. He was on a roll of 61 fights without a defeat against the best competition the world had to offer. His record stood at 92–9 overall, and included the gold medal in the 1971 Pan-American Games and the 1972 National Golden Gloves championship. He also captured a shipload of Naval and All-Service titles while serving a four-year hitch in the U.S. Navy. Bobick was understandably touted as the favorite to win a gold medal at Munich. The Olympics had become a breeding ground for future heavyweight champions, even when they fought in lighter divisions at the time. The 1956 Games produced Floyd Patterson; 1960 launched Muhammad Ali, then known as Cassius Clay; 1964 gave us Joe Frazier; and in 1968 it was George Foreman's turn. If Bobick had followed that trend, his gold medal would have paved the way for a lucrative launch into the professional ranks.

Since he was the most highly touted amateur in American history going into Munich, big things were expected from Bobick. U.S. Coach Pappy Gault stated: "I think the kid'll do as great as Muhammad Ali in bringing in money for the promoters. He's got a good jab, a good right, a good heart and a wonderful personality. He's way ahead of George Foreman at a similar stage of his career."[5]

Understandably, Bobick's ego became inflated by all the adoration. "With all the attention I was getting, I began to feel unbeatable," he admitted.[6]

Before he departed for Munich, Duane received a call from a potential benefactor in Georgia. "This guy's name was Jenkins and he said 'I've got $500,000 for you, Duane.' I said, 'Fine, see me after Munich.' After Munich, I never heard from him."[7]

The reason Bobick's telephone remained silent after Munich was that during the preliminary rounds he met a young Cuban sensation named Teofilo Stevenson. Because Bobick had beaten Stevenson during the Pan-American Games the year before, he wasn't expected to have much difficulty with the Cuban at the Olympics.

But Stevenson's right hand separated Bobick from his senses in the third round of their fight. Teofilo went on to win the gold medal; Bobick didn't even get a chance to win a bronze.

Eventually, the passage of time would show that it was no disgrace to lose to Stevenson, who became the only fighter to win heavyweight gold in three successive Olympics. At the time, though, the loss was considered a major upset, and Bobick's fistic stock took a sudden nose dive.

Rumors about Bobick's future ran rampant during the five-month sabbatical he took after the Olympics. Some reports indicated he was contemplating a career in professional wrestling. To the relief of most boxing fans, Bobick announced on February 1, 1973, that he would be entering the punch-for-pay ranks.

Although the loss to Stevenson had dimmed his luster as a prospect, Duane was astute enough to realize he could easily regain his hold on the public's imagination.

Bobick was still an easy guy to sell to the American public. As Iring Rudd, spokesman for Top Rank, Inc., stated: "Being white, personable, with a middle–America image and shoulders like coat hangers helps."[8]

He turned pro under the management of Bill Daniels, who also handled Ron Lyle. A well-developed 6'3", 215-pounder, Bobick made his professional debut on April 10, 1973. The designated victim: a Canadian named Tommy Burns, no relation to the heavyweight champion of 1906–1908. Burns said goodnight in one round.

Bobick went on to record 19 consecutive knockout wins over opponents only marginally superior to Burns. In 1975, Daniels sold Duane's contract to Eddie Futch and Joe Frazier. At the time of the transaction Bobick wasn't happy with Daniels. He found that Daniels focused too much on Ron Lyle and that his own career wasn't progressing quickly enough. Daniels was sorry to lose Duane: "I didn't want to lose him. But when athletes get unhappy, they don't perform. I thought he would be the heavyweight champ and I still think so."[9]

Under the tutelage of Frazier and Futch, Bobick slowly became a more complete fighter. Smokin' Joe taught him the brutal art of body punching, and Duane proved an apt pupil.

Bobick was happy with his connection to Frazier and Futch: "My attitude improved because I was with people who knew a lot about boxing. Futch is the top trainer around and just sparring with Frazier has to teach a boxer something about self preservation."[10]

The quality of his opposition also increased. Now he was fighting and beating the likes of Randy Neumann, Young Sanford, Larry Middleton, and Chuck Wepner. However, Bobick was still benefiting from shrewd matchmaking. His opponents of 1975 and 1976 were recognizable names, but they were also fairly safe. Neumann, Middleton, and Wepner were all past their prime, and Sanford was a prospect who never panned out.

Consequently, Bobick received more than his share of media criticism. Even his hometown fans in Minnesota questioned his credentials. Don Riley of the *St. Paul Pioneer Press* wrote that Duane had gained his high ranking "by beating old ladies, round-heeled has-beens, and clowns moonlighting in the Shrine Circus."[11]

In all fairness, however, it must be noted that George Foreman faced similar disapproval before he challenged Joe Frazier in 1973. Foreman had passed his test against Frazier with flying colors, Bobick's supporters argued, so why shouldn't Duane pass the exam Norton would provide?

A $300,000 guarantee was more than enough inducement for Bobick to take a giant step up in class. His highest previous purse was the $50,000 he received for chopping Chuck Wepner in six rounds. Norton was guaranteed $500,000.

Fed up with media carping at the quality of Bobick's opposition, Eddie Futch argued that Norton's credentials weren't all that impressive. Bad blood had existed between the two men since Futch left Norton to take over Frazier's career in 1974, and it showed in Futch's commentary.

"When people think of Norton," Futch said, "they think of the three fights he had with Ali, but he had the style to beat Ali and I knew it. That's why I put him in with Ali back in 1973 when he broke Ali's jaw. Norton looked best when he knocked out Quarry two years ago but Quarry was shot."

One common opponent of Norton and Bobick, Middleton, felt that their upcoming encounter would be an "interesting fight." He said Bobick was mechanical but strong. Although Duane lacked speed, Middleton still found him an effective infighter.

Larry was less impressed with Norton, even though Ken knocked him out while Bobick was forced to go the distance. Despite the difference in results, Middleton didn't consider Norton "world class." His conclusion: "With what's around today, he [Bobick] can very well become champ."[12]

Norton, who was one of the top two contenders, had been relegated to "what's around today" because he hadn't fought since his loss to Ali, and he appeared to have become totally disillusioned with boxing. Speculation about Norton's Hollywood ambitions began to supersede discussions of his title hopes.

Yet the odds makers still installed Ken as a 12–5 favorite. The reason for those lopsided odds? Whatever his flaws, Norton was a proven contender, while Bobick remained a fistic enigma.

Despite his underdog status, a Bobick victory would not have shaken up the world. In the days leading up to the fight, Norton seemed uninspired during his training sessions. But that may have been due to the fact that he didn't think Bobick was in his class as a fighter; therefore he felt he didn't need to extend himself in training.

Some believed Ken was repeating the mistake Ali had made before facing Norton for the first time in 1973. Norton couldn't afford to take Bobick too lightly; the Minnesotan's straightforward, hard-hitting brand of offense was similar to (if not as effective as) Foreman's, and may well produce the same result.

Based on his extensive experience with both men, Futch concluded that Norton couldn't handle Bobick's pressure. He said Norton had always been overly cautious about getting hit in the face. According to Futch's fight plan, Bobick would work the body in the early rounds, then go upstairs once Ken's hands came down. A good plan, for Joe Frazier, not necessarily Duane Bobick.

Interest in Norton–Bobick was manifested by a network television audience of nearly 42 million viewers on fight day. Few of that 42 million could have expected Norton to come out as aggressively as he did. But Norton, like many others, believed that if the fight went the distance and was at all close, Bobick would get the decision. He didn't think the judges would favor him over a young, undefeated white contender. In the wake of what he still considered "robbery" in his third fight with Ali, Norton swore he would never again leave a fight in the hands of the judges if he could help it.

Only seconds after the opening bell, an overhand right from Norton crunched into the side of Bobick's jaw and throat. As Bobick wobbled, Norton was on him in a flash, firing a volley of uppercuts and hooks.

Dazed and disoriented, Duane staggered into his own corner. There, Norton unloaded five successive rights to the head. Bobick crashed to the canvas. Showing courage, if little else, he pulled himself to his feet before the referee reached the count of ten. But he was clearly in no condition to continue, and the fight was over in a mere 58 seconds.

Later, Norton said he never dreamed he would hurt Bobick so badly with just one blow early in the fight. In a strangled voice, Bobick explained that the blow to the throat had momentarily choked him and caused his eyes to water. He was virtually helpless in the face of Norton's subsequent assault.

Norton, who could afford to be generous, predicted that Bobick would have no trouble bouncing back from the defeat. Futch agreed, saying that his fighter had been blitzed before he could get untracked.

"If he had been outclassed for four or five rounds and then knocked out, that would have been a different story," Futch said. "A one-round knockout? I've seen too many guys who have been knocked out in the first round come back. We'll be back for some big paydays."[13]

Futch and Norton proved to be poor prophets. Bobick continued to make headlines, but he never made much of an impression as a contender.

Having emphatically eliminated Bobick from title consideration, Norton was now ready for Ali. But Ali wasn't exactly ready for Norton.

Thirty Rounds

During his two championship reigns, Ali had always maintained a busy schedule, often defending his title four times a year. After the Norton fight, however, he waited eight months before making his next ring appearance. It was his longest period of inactivity since his return from exile in 1970.

On May 16, Ali opened his 1977 campaign in Landover, Maryland, the site of his near disaster against Jimmy Young. His opponent was Alfredo Evangelista, a 22-year-old Spaniard by way of Uruguay. And what credentials did Evangelista possess to entitle him to a shot at the most coveted prize in sports?

In a word, none.

A pro for only a year and a half, Evangelista had never faced an American opponent, or anyone else in the WBC's top 30. And he had never fought beyond eight rounds.

Born to a family of poor laborers in Montevideo, Uruguay, young Alfredo took up amateur boxing and compiled a 25–0 record. He caught the attention of a local manager who in turn contacted Kid Tunero, a retired Cuban middleweight who was now training fighters in Madrid. Tunero, who was one of the greatest fighters Cuba ever produced, liked what he saw in the young South American. Within a year, Alfredo and his family had emigrated to Spain.

Evangelista made his pro debut on October 10, 1975, stopping one Angelo Visini in one round. By the end of 1976, he had racked up a record of 14–0–1, with 12 KOs. His list of victims comprised an array of washed-up European fighters like Bepi Ros, Jose Urtain, Mario Baruzzi and Rudi Lubbers. He also boasted a knockout win over fellow Euro-prospect Lucien Rodriguez.

But 1977 began on a sour note for Alfredo, as he lost an eight-round decision to Lorenzo Zanon, who was Italy's answer to Jimmy Young. Then, in a scenario stranger than anything Hollywood could devise, Evangelista found himself fighting for the heavyweight championship of the world.

Evangelista was strictly a tune-up for Ali, and tune-ups are as much a part of boxing as superfights. When a champion fights and defeats the best available contenders, as Ali had done, he is entitled to an occasional breather.

The acceptability of such "soft" defenses is a matter of degree. A case could be made for the legitimacy of blue-collar fighters like Chuck Wepner and Richard Dunn, who could at least be counted on to put up a good fight in a losing cause. But Evangelista, who held neither a national nor a European title; had not yet fought past eight rounds; had never fought anyone even resembling a world-class contender; and had lost his last fight to feather-fisted Lorenzo Zanon, had no business challenging Ali that night.

Why, then, was the match accepted by the title sanctioning bodies and the general public? For one thing, the nation was still under the spell of "Rockymania." Sylvester Stallone's movie about a washed-up club fighter named Rocky Balboa who comes close to winning the world title was such a smash hit in theaters that the idea of a real-life *Rocky* piqued public interest.

Second, Ali's uneven performances in 1976 underscored the fact that an upset was possible. As *Ring* editor Nat Loubet wrote in his July 1977 editorial, "At Ali's time of life as a boxer one can no longer go by his past ability because if he continues to fight, some humpty dumpty will knock his block off in what was supposed to be another workout."

Third, so little was known about Evangelista on this side of the Atlantic that an element of mystery intrigued some fans. Could Evangelista be another Ingemar Johansson, who was a non-entity before he defeated Floyd Patterson in 1959?

Finally, you could put the scarecrow from *The Wizard of Oz* in the ring with Ali, and the fight would still draw spectators simply because Ali was part of it.

Even so, promoter Don King was still worried about the fight's credibility. Although he had a contract with ABC to televise the bout, King was concerned that the network might renege because of Evangelista's questionable credentials. Another iffy element was the scandal surrounding King, ABC, and the defunct United States Boxing championships.

Fortunately for King, ABC made good on its promise to televise Ali–Evangelista. The rationale provided by one ABC executive was: "It's just that Ali is near the end of his career; any fight could be his last."[14]

King was relieved. Knowing the game as he did, though, he could see the wry side of the Evangelista challenge.

"You know what the big story of this fight is? It's that I got $2.7 million for Ali to fight a name in a book," King quipped.[15]

A promoter's job is simple when the fight he's trying to sell matches stars like Ali and Frazier. But when one of the opponents is "a name in the book," the work becomes much more difficult. For Ali–Evangelista, King received a great deal of help from Dundee and Ali, both of whom shamelessly boosted the challenger.

Dundee said he'd been scouting Evangelista and found him to be "pretty cute" with "good hands." Ali added that a fighter's anonymity was no reason to take him lightly: "Last year people were saying, 'Who is Jimmy Young?' and then the next day they were telling me that I was beaten by Jimmy Young. Four years ago, they were saying 'Who is Ken Norton?' Now they say 'Who is Alfredo Evangelista?' He's a good fighter. We don't want to underestimate anybody with two hands."[16]

Ali's words were a far cry from his "They all must fall in the round I call!" heyday during the 1960s.

Another rationalization from those who sought to legitimize the fight was that Evangelista was a better fighter than Jean Pierre Coopman. Evangelista's advisor, Dr. Edward Mafuz, stated that his man was far more capable than the Belgian. And WBC President Jose Sulaiman, who had generously bumped Alfredo to the #10 position in his organization's ratings and sanctioned the fight, chimed in by saying Evangelista was "definitely better than Jean Pierre Coopman."[17]

Angelo Dundee unwittingly put that comparison in its proper perspective when he remarked that Evangelista was "easier to find information on than was Coopman."

Evangelista was better than Coopman, all right, but so were two or three dozen other heavyweights in the world.

Another Evangelista question mark was his loss to Zanon. Indeed, many wondered why the Italian wasn't given the title opportunity instead of Alfredo. The answer was that Zanon's defensive style would have produced a boring fight and made Ali look bad. If nothing else, Evangelista fought aggressively.

Mafuz, by the way, did have an alibi for his fighter's poor performance against Zanon. It seems Alfredo had recently married, and his mind was on more enjoyable pursuits than training.

As for the *Rocky* angle, the network and public picked up on it to some extent, but those who were closer to reality left it alone. Dundee, who grasped at any straw to help the promotion, said: "This kid's no Rocky. Rocky couldn't fight...."[18]

Mafuz added that unlike the fictional Rocky, Alfredo was "not going to just try and last the distance. He's a bit more optimistic than Rocky. He thinks he can win."[19]

On fight night, Evangelista did last the distance. And he carried himself far better than most fans expected. Unlike the movie, however, there was no blood, neither man was hurt, and no one in the crowd was on the edge of their seat awaiting the decision, which was unanimous for Ali.

Despite lasting the distance with the champion, Evangelista didn't gain much standing. The reason was that it was Ali's lack of interest rather than Evangelista's talent that allowed the Spaniard to survive 15 lackluster rounds.

In most evaluations of Ali's career, the Evangelista fight is considered one of his sorriest performances. He clowned, made faces, Rope-a-Doped, but did little offensively. His lack of effort wasn't a matter of physical incapacity, as he came in at a relatively fit 221½ lbs. It was more a matter of taking a vacation while he was supposed to be working.

Ali's heart simply wasn't in the fight. He went through the motions, but Evangelista didn't have the skills necessary to take advantage of the situation. After the fight, Ali offered his usual high praise for an overmatched foe.

"I tried to knock him down but I couldn't do it," Ali said. "Don't tell me he was a bum. He was good."[20]

For his part, Evangelista expressed surprise that Ali had survived the whole fifteen rounds! Evangelista actually believed he had done enough to win. Through an interpreter, Alfredo contended that if the fight had been held in Spain, he would have garnered the decision and the title.

And if wishes had wings, pigs would fly....

Ali also said Evangelista was a better fighter than Duane Bobick. That comment was probably intended as a jab at Bobick's conqueror, Ken Norton.

Although Ali's half-hearted effort was good enough to take the decision, it was also poor enough to cost him one of his most valuable professional efforts: Dr. Ferdie Pacheco.

Pacheco had been Ali's physician throughout most of his career, and had stood by him through all its ups and downs. Now, the "Fight Doctor" had seen enough. After the Evangelista fight, Pacheco stated publicly that Ali should retire.

"Ali is now at that dangerous mental point where his heart and mind are no longer in it," Pacheco said. "Like this fight [Evangelista], it's just a payday. Ali, to be Ali, has to have a super challenge. Not even Ken Norton creates that kind of challenge. Norton's style is such that Ali can't get up because he knows he can't look good."[21]

Pacheco's assessment provided a good indication of the direction of Ali's career. He was still champion, but there was now doubt that he was the best fighter in the division. *World Boxing* magazine actually rated Norton ahead of Ali in its Top Ten. "Being champion does not necessarily mean a fighter is the best in the world in his weight class," the magazine explained.

With Evangelista out of the way, Ali now faced the unpleasant prospect of defending his title against Norton or Young, or perhaps both. Instead, his second and last challenger of 1977 was Earnie Shavers, the hard-hitting but limited battler from Warren, Ohio. The bout was scheduled for September 29.

Shavers's eight-year road to a title shot was paved with several truckloads of quick knockout victories. That road also included several deep potholes.

Earnie's punching power was arguably the best in the division during the 1970s, with the possible exception of George Foreman's. Even in comparison to Foreman, some experts thought Shavers to be the better one-punch knockout artist.

It was other factors that prevented the 33-year-old Shavers from gaining a title opportunity well before 1977. One of those factors was a suspect chin, a trait he shared with such storied sluggers from the past as Cleveland Williams and Bob Satterfield. Kayo losses to Ron Stander, Jerry Quarry, and Ron Lyle tended to confirm that doubt.

In his own defense, Shavers blamed his style for those defeats. He said he was never relaxed in the ring because he was always looking to land a knockout blow. A tense fighter doesn't absorb a punch as well and is therefore more susceptible to a kayo.

Another Shavers question mark was his stamina. Like most big bombers who end their fights early, Earnie had rarely been called upon to demonstrate his powers of endurance. Thus, when an opponent managed to survive the first few rounds, Shavers usually found himself in trouble. His losses to Stander and Lyle, for example, came when he ran out of gas after having both those fighters on the verge of stoppage.

Even in victory, Earnie's shallow gas tank was evident. A March 28, 1976, decision win over wily veteran Henry Clark saw Shavers drained of energy in the final round. Later that year, he knocked out Roy Williams in the 10th round, but was so fatigued that he nearly became a knockout victim himself.

Between that pair of grueling battles, Shavers met Clark in a rematch on the undercard of Ali–Norton III. This time, Clark couldn't escape Shavers's early assault. In less than two rounds, Earnie had notched another quick win.

Still seeking that elusive shot at the title, Shavers opened 1977 with a crossroads outing against another big puncher, Howard "KO" Smith, holder of the California state heavyweight title. In only 19 contests, Smith had established himself as one of the division's fastest-rising young stars. His lone pro defeat had come in his fourth fight, a six-round decision awarded to one Henry Culpepper.

Over the next five years, Smith went undefeated against mid-range opposition, including Mike Weaver, Jack O'Halloran, Tony Doyle, and Larry Middleton. Going into the

Shavers fight, Howard had scored back-to-back decision wins over fellow prospect Johnny "Black Knight" Boudreaux and an over-the-hill Henry Clark. The win over Boudreaux, who had been touted as a "new Ali," did more to establish Smith's status than any other fight in his career.

Because he possessed youth and stamina to go along with his punching power, many experts believed Smith would write the "finis" to Shavers's storied career. However, Smith suicidally elected to slug it out with Earnie and paid the price as Shavers crushed him in two one-sided rounds.

Although there was no shame in losing to Shavers, Howard made only one more ring appearance afterward, a tenth-round kayo over trial horse Charlie James. Smith then retired.

The emphatic dismissal of one of the division's "comers" earned Shavers his September chance at the title. The fight would be held at Madison Square Garden, which hadn't hosted a heavyweight title bout since Ali–Frazier I.

Despite Shavers's awesome record of 52 knockouts in 54 wins (he had also lost five and drawn one), Ali viewed his opponent as nothing more than a $3 million payday to be taken only slightly more seriously than the Evangelista walkabout. With the exception of his superfights with Frazier and Norton, Ali had not burdened himself with arduous training during his second title reign. But that didn't seem to matter; Ali won anyway.

Sure, Shavers was miles ahead of Evangelista as a contender. But Ali was still Ali. The champion had firmly established his supremacy in 1974 and 1975, and he still held the title despite an uneven 1976. The Ali–Shavers matchup did stir interest among fight fans, who are always fascinated by fighters like the Ohioan who live or die by the sword. A heavyweight who is capable of ending a fight with a single, sleep-producing blow will always attract a following, even if his boxing skills are minimal, his defense porous, and his chin pure glass.

Shavers' limitations weren't that extreme. Still, as a fighter he was something like a Saturday Night Special, which will either hit the target or blow up in your face once you pull the trigger.

Against almost any champion other than Ali, Shavers would have been given a better-than-average puncher's chance to pull off an upset. Even the great Joe Louis couldn't escape a shadow of uncertainty that resulted from his early career knockout by Max Schmeling and his deckings at the hands of Jim Braddock, Tony Galento, and Buddy Baer. The image of the Brown Bomber's crashes to the canvas recurred every time Louis accepted the challenge of a big puncher.

As usual, though, Ali was different. Since 1960, fight fans had seen him defeat every fighter of consequence in his division. He had pulled himself off the canvas to finish his first fight with Joe Frazier; he had fought eleven rounds with a shattered jaw; he had offered his body as a punching bag for Foreman and Frazier; and he had avenged the only two defeats of his career.

But he had never been knocked out. And the chances of anyone performing that feat, even a bomber like Shavers, seemed remote. Ali's proven durability appeared to more than offset Shavers's proven power.

As well, Earnie's reputation for fading as a fight progressed had to have boosted Ali's confidence. Few fighters in the business had Ali's ability even at the age of 35, to turn it on in the late rounds. Given Ali's repertoire of strength-sapping tactics, Shavers seemed certain to be a sitting duck by the middle rounds.

Indeed, the champ predicted a seventh-round knockout over the "Acorn," a label that referred to Shavers's hairless pate. "It's September, and the acorns are fallin'!" Ali roared.[22]

Shavers told the press that Ali "can't tell the difference between an acorn and a mighty oak."[23]

As did most Ali opponents, Shavers trained harder than ever before. A chance to make history by defeating "The Greatest" was a strong motivating factor. When Ali met his opponents in the ring, they were usually far superior to the versions of themselves the champ may have studied on videotape.

Nonetheless, Ali placed little stock in Shavers's preparations or even his punching power. After all, hadn't Muhammad already defused the bombs of the two hardest-hitting champions in recent history, Sonny Liston and George Foreman?

In the six weeks prior to the fight, Ali had reportedly taken an 11-day hiatus from training. The champ became testy as reporters badgered him with questions concerning his lackadaisical preparation. He said he'd been training for fights since age 12, so he knew what he was doing. Still, many sportswriters speculated about how the dangerous combination of age and complacency might affect Ali's performance against Shavers.

An early indication of vulnerability surfaced eight days before the fight when Ali was floored twice in a sparring session with Jimmy Ellis. Explaining the knockdowns, Ali said: "I was pressing too hard. I worked out too much on the floor before going into the ring."[24]

Shavers had to have been encouraged by the fact that Ellis, who was 37 and had been retired for two years, could put Ali on the canvas. When questioned about the incident, however, Shavers laughed it off. He reasoned that Ali was practicing how to hit the canvas for September 29.

Despite persistent reports of poor conditioning, Dr. Kleiman of the New York State Athletic Commission said he'd never seen Ali in better shape physically or mentally. At the weigh-in, Ali scaled a respectable 225, while Shavers hit the beam at a hard 211¼. Ali had a three-inch height advantage over the 6-foot Shavers, but their reach was measured at an identical 80 inches, incredibly long for a man Earnie's height.

When the fighters swung into action in the Madison Square Garden ring, they provided a spectacle far more dramatic than anyone had anticipated. Not much happened in the first round. Then, in the second, Shavers hit Ali with what was probably the hardest single shot anyone had ever landed on him. For a split second, the champ was out on his feet. But he was able to "con" Shavers into thinking he wasn't hurt, and the moment passed.

Over the next several rounds, Ali alternated between Rope-a-Doping and firing flurries of curious side-arm punches. Shavers plodded forward, hoping to land another home run shot. Halfway through, the fight was virtually deadlocked. Ali appeared to be holding back, while Shavers opted to use his lethal left hand as a shield to guard against Ali's right.

Ali wasn't exactly dazzling in the ninth through twelfth stanzas. Still, he did enough to win those rounds on most of the judges' scorecards. Shavers was fighting conservatively in an effort to pace himself. Also, he and his corner believed the fight was going in his favor and saw no reason to apply more pressure just yet.

But there was no need for either corner to speculate. In an experimental move, NBC, the network that broadcast the fight, flashed the officials' scoring on the screen between each round.

Because NBC had publicized its intention to do so well in advance, the canny Angelo Dundee had an associate watch the TV monitors and relay the scoring information to him. Thus, he knew Ali was so far ahead on points after twelve rounds that Shavers needed a knockout to win.

Shavers's trainer, Frank Luca, chose to remain in the dark about the scoring. He felt that they might have overreacted had they known the scores.

This oversight may well have cost Shavers the title. He waited until the 13th and 14th rounds to unleash his full offense, and by then it was too late. He rocked Ali several times and brought the crowd to its feet during those rounds, but under the New York round-by-round scoring system, his effort wasn't enough to make up the lost ground.

Going into the 15th, Dundee knew Ali had the fight won. Luca, on the other hand, was unaware that Shavers's only chance lay in a stoppage. Not wanting Ali to become complacent, Dundee never told him how the scoring was going. He implored Ali to win the final round.

As the bell sounded, both fighters thought they needed a big round to capture the decision. Thus, the final frame provided the most exciting action of the evening.

Early in the round, Shavers pursued Ali and landed several hard rights. Both men were near exhaustion, but it was Ali who found the last ounce of strength needed to turn the fight his way. Late in the round, he broke Shavers's momentum with a sudden, snapping combination. Shavers stopped dead in his tracks and backed into the ropes as Ali tattooed him with a machine-gun blast of leather.

The crowd roared as Shavers looked ready to fall. But when the bell ended the fight, the challenger was still on his feet.

When the decision was announced, Ali retained his title by unanimous decision, winning nine rounds on all three scorecards. Most observers felt Ali had edged out a victory that was closer than the scorecards indicated. The *New York Times* even called it a draw at 7–7–1.[25]

Unofficial opinions aside, though, Ali was still champion. But, given his condition after the fight, his hold on the title appeared shakier than ever. He was so fatigued that it took him an hour to summon up sufficient energy to meet the press. Later, he said the Shavers fight had been almost as demanding physically as the "Thrilla in Manila."

"I'm living by the skin of my teeth," Ali admitted candidly.[26]

Ali had displayed conditioning and courage in holding off the challenge of an inspired Shavers. The question was, how many more times could the champ go to the well?

Although Shavers lost the decision, in defeat he exploded most of the myths concerning his courage and stamina. Not only did he last the fifteen rounds, he won two of the last three of them. And he withstood Ali's last-minute barrage.

At age 33, Earnie had finally arrived as a legitimate title threat rather than a one-dimensional bomber. With Foreman retired, Shavers was now the undisputed king of the heavyweight punchers, even though he wasn't the champion. For the remainder of the decade, he was the man fans looked to for the spectacular knockout.

Boxing Politics

Throughout the summer of 1977, the Norton and Young camps had angled for a shot at the title. The day after Norton–Bobick, California, promoter Ben Thompson said he had the inside track on an October Ali–Norton fight in Rio de Janeiro, Brazil.

Norton and his management were certainly interested in the deal. Mysteriously, Young's manager, Jack Levin, had turned down the same offer. His refusal may have been due to the fact that Young had signed a promotional contract with Don King.

Thompson said he was prepared to offer Ali an unprecedented $12 million for a "Rumble in Rio." But Ali and Herbert Muhammad said, "No, thanks." Setting themselves up as unofficial matchmakers, the Ali team said they wanted Norton and Young to face each other in an elimination contest. Ali would then defend his title against the winner.

"There are a lot of people who think Norton beat me and a lot who think Young beat me, and I'm too old to go around fighting everybody to prove it all, so I will fight the winner of the two fighters I have mentioned," the champ said.[27]

"I'm not getting any younger either," an impatient Norton groused to reporters after Ali's statement.

Nonetheless, Norton's options were limited despite his win over Bobick. He could either fight Young or stay on the sidelines and risk losing his rating. If Norton beat Young, Ali would have no choice: he would have to fight Norton a fourth time.

Negotiations began for a Norton–Young meeting in November. The winner would be the "undisputed" #1 contender. Ali would have to commit to a 1978 defense against that contender, or risk having his title taken away by one, or both, of boxing's sanctioning bodies.

On September 14, two weeks prior to Ali–Shavers, Don King promoted a nationally televised, all-heavyweight card from Las Vegas that matched Norton, Young, Ron Lyle, Larry Holmes, and Leroy Jones against relatively safe opponents. King's purpose for putting the show on prime time was twofold. First, he wanted to showcase Norton and Young in an attempt to build the gate for their November meeting. Second, the card provided the opportunity to introduce his latest protégés, Holmes and Jones, to the television audience.

The results were mixed. Jones, a Buster Mathis look-alike, plodded to a boring 10-round decision over Greg Johnson. Lyle gave up-and-coming Stan Ward a boxing lesson en route to a decision victory of his own. The talented Holmes stopped Young Sanford in seven rounds.

Of much more importance, naturally, were the performances of Young and Norton. Young's mark for the night was Houston native Jody Ballard, a small heavyweight with modest skills. At age 26, the 206-pound Ballard once showed promise, but he had never been the same after suffering a two-round stoppage at the hands of George Foreman in a November 1975 exhibition.

Now Ballard made his living as a journeyman and sparring partner. Needless to say, Jody wasn't given much of a chance of upsetting the second-ranked Young. But the Texan came to Las Vegas determined to make the most of his opportunity.

Over the first three rounds, Ballard fought with surprising grit and inspiration. However, Young took control away from his less-skilled opponent in the fourth. Over the rest of the fight, Ballard was unable to land anything significant, while Young virtually hit him at will. To his credit, Jody went the distance in an obvious losing cause. The announcement of Young's decision win was a formality.

Norton's opponent, Italy's Lorenzo Zanon, was expected to provide Ken a preview of what to expect from Young in November. The Italian, whose chief claim to fame was his win over Alfredo Evangelista earlier in the year, was a gifted boxer with excellent hand and foot speed. His only problem was that he couldn't hit hard enough to scare a welterweight, and his chin should have had a "Fragile" sticker taped across it.

Over the first four rounds, Zanon actually embarrassed Norton, holding him off with movement and a pitty-pat jab. Norton didn't seem to be able to land any heavy blows, but perhaps he wasn't really trying.

In the fifth, however, Ken decided enough was enough. A sizzling overhand right sent Zanon crashing to the canvas. The Italian got up on legs that were about as sturdy as wet spaghetti. Norton stepped in with a left-right combination that sent Lorenzo down for the count.

In reference to an insignificant scratch over his right eye, Norton cried out "I'm cut, I'm cut!" in mock horror after the fight.

The respective performances of the two top contenders provided ammunition for detractors on either side. The anti–Young crowd pointed to Jimmy's inability to stop or even hurt a limited opponent like Ballard. They doubted Young's powder-puff punches would be sufficient to hold off the stronger, harder-hitting Norton.

Norton's critics pointed out that prior to the knockout, Zanon was boxing circles around Ken. Sure, Zanon went to sleep once Norton lowered the boom. But Young, who had absorbed the best shots of Foreman, Lyle, and Shavers, wasn't likely to crumple under Norton's blows. And the thinking was that Norton would need a knockout to beat a master boxer like Young.

Because there were so many negatives involved, Norton–Young was a difficult fight to pick. The odds, which ended up 7 to 5 in Norton's favor, reflected the lack of clear-cut advantages for either man. Eddie Futch predicted that Young would defeat Norton. He recalled using Young as a sparmate for Ken in preparation for the second Ali fight in 1973.

"I never let Young go more than two rounds with Kenny because he gave Norton fits even in those days,"[28] said Futch, who could always be counted on to offer a few bad words about his former pupil.

It bothered Norton that Futch was always against him. Bob Biron said: "Futch and that crack about being an amateur really got Norton motivated in camp. The only time I've ever seen him work harder in camp was for an Ali fight. And for Bobick. Futch also said that Bobick would win. Anything Futch says bothers Ken; they used to be very close. If I could pay Futch $100,000 to pick against Ken every fight it would be a sound investment."[29]

For Young, the Norton fight was a financial victory from the outset. His $1,000,000 guarantee quadrupled his previous high purse, which he had received for the Foreman fight. But the fight's significance transcended financial considerations. The winner would be guaranteed a mandatory shot at Ali's title.

World Boxing Council President Jose Sulaiman provided further significance to what was already shaping up to be one of the year's most important fights when he declared that Ali must sign by January 5 to meet the winner.

Ali wasn't fazed by Sulaiman's threat. "I am boxing. Jose Sulaiman doesn't tell me what to do — I tell him what to do. I made boxing. Tell him 800 million people saw me fight Earnie Shavers. I'm the king of the ring."[30]

It was no coincidence that Norton–Young was scheduled for 15 rounds, a distance usually reserved for championship contests. Sulaiman, obviously under a tremendous amount of pressure from all sides, insisted he was serious in his intention to strip Ali of WBC recognition if he refused to comply with the directive. Asked if the public would accept Young or Norton as champion instead of Ali, Sulaiman shrugged his shoulders and admitted: "That is a good question."

In contrast, the World Boxing Association, having learned their lesson the hard way on two previous occasions, stated openly that it had no intention of stripping Ali. And *The Ring* magazine, the "Bible of Boxing," agreed with the WBA. In his editorial for the February 1978 issue, editor and publisher Nat Loubet wrote the following:

In the days gone by if a champ fought once or twice a year in defense of his title he was considered well within his rights. Now we are beginning to tell the heavyweight champion whom he will fight and when. That may be fair if a heavyweight champ were ducking one or more of the logical and dangerous opponents, but in Ali's case he has been fighting them all and is certainly entitled to meet a few men who can be considered as breathers in between the hard ones.

Whether Ali complied with the WBC's January 5 deadline or not, it was commonly accepted that he would live up to his word and fight the winner of Norton–Young. But the situation became muddled when Ali's manager, Herbert Muhammad, said that Ali would indeed fight the Norton–Young victor, so long as Young was the winner.

Ali himself chucked another handful of manure into the fan of controversy when he announced that his next title defense would take place in Las Vegas on February 15, 1978, against the winner of an upcoming bout. However, Ali wasn't talking about Norton–Young. Instead, he planned to risk his title against the winner of a November 18 contest between Italian prospect Alfio Righetti and Leon Spinks, the 1976 Olympic gold medalist in the 178-pound class who had turned pro as a small heavyweight less than a year before.

Ali's choice of opponent was in open defiance of the WBC's edict. However, the champion let Sulaiman off the hook by promising to accept the challenge of the Norton–Young winner, whomever he may be, immediately following his fight with the Spinks–Righetti victor.

Ali's assurance satisfied those who were beginning to wonder about his willingness to fight the most deserving contenders. Let Muhammad have his "breather" against Righetti or Spinks, the conventional wisdom held. Then one last big fight against Norton or Young. Then, win or lose, retirement would beckon.

Norton–Young thus became the most significant fight of the year because it would determine Ali's next, and perhaps final, major challenger. And there was the possibility it would split the heavyweight title for the first time in 10 years if the WBC changed its mind and followed through on its threat to strip Ali. Several publicity photos showed Young and Norton grasping a crown.

As the fight began, Ali, who really was tired of fighting Norton, cheered openly for Young. So did many of the other 5,000 spectators at Caesars Palace. They were rooting for the underdog in much the same way that fans in San Juan had cheered Young on against Foreman earlier in the year.

Although Norton–Young was much closer and more competitive than Foreman–Young, it lacked much of the emotional impact of the latter contest. Neither fighter was on the canvas or even seriously hurt. It was a physical chess match, with each man sticking meticulously to his fight plan.

Norton's goal was to attack Young's midsection in an effort to slow him up. He knew that trying to tag Jimmy on the jaw was like trying to hit a fly without a swatter. Young was content to elude the stronger man's blows and counter to the head to pile up points. Throughout the 15 rounds, both fighters executed their plans with varying degrees of success. Neither Norton nor Young created any sustained momentum, and at the end one could have flipped a coin to determine the winner.

Judging a fight is an art, not a science. Certain officials favor the aggressor; others give high marks for defense. The Norton–Young fight, in which aggression and defense played equal roles, was so hard to score that the three judges agreed on only 5 of the 15 rounds.

When the scorecards were finally tallied, Norton came out the winner via split decision.

The two judges who voted for him, Raymond Aldeyou of France and Jimmy Rondeau of Washington, D.C., scored five and six rounds even. Judge Art Lurie gave it to Young. The fight was so close it could justifiably have gone either way.

Despite the narrow margin of victory, the boxing world seemed relieved that Ali now had a single mandatory challenger. Only the champion's upcoming defense against the Righetti–Spinks winner stood in the way of Ali–Norton IV.

Norton had done his job. Now he needed only to wait and train for what he believed to be his date with destiny sometime in 1978.

Young, on the other hand, was far from encouraged by his performance against Norton. Instead of increasing Jimmy's determination to do better next time, the defeat snuffed out that all-important flame that separates hungry, ambitious fighters from complacent journeymen.

Once again discouraged by losing a questionable decision, Young and his management felt they might have been better off if the Blinky Palermo rumors had been true. Jack Levin stated, "I'm beginning to think that we would have won the fight if we were really connected to him."[31]

Over a three-year period, Young had defeated Lyle and Foreman, and held Ali and Norton to virtual standstills, great accomplishments during the heavyweights' golden decade. Yet the razor-thin loss to Norton sent this talented craftsman on the road to oblivion.

"Do I think I won the fight?" Jimmy asked rhetorically at the post-fight press conference. "Of course I do. I disagree with the whole scoring, but what can I do about it?"[32]

For a light hitter who has to leave most of his fights in the hands of the judges, the close calls against Norton and Ali must have been discouraging in the extreme. If the officials weren't willing to give him credit for what he did best, what was the point in trying?

In his next two fights, an out-of-shape Young lost back-to-back decisions to an unheralded Puerto Rican named Osvaldo "Jaws" Ocasio. Over the next ten years, he gradually declined from contender to trail horse. His name became a "must" for the records of young contenders on their way up the ladder.

Young usually lasted the distance because he always retained his exceptional defensive skills. But without conditioning or desire, he couldn't put forth the sustained effort needed to get back into title contention.

Today, Jimmy Young's name rarely comes up in discussions of the great heavyweights of the '70s. But he should be remembered as a fine defensive technician who twice came within a hair's breadth of becoming champion. His last recorded fight was on August 13, 1988, a 10th-round TKO over a fellow named Frank Lux in Missouri. Young's final record stood at 34–19–2 (11 KOs). Jimmy was already showing the effects of pugilistica dementia. There were also rumors of drug and alcohol abuse that quickly dragged Young down both mentally and physically.

Tragically, Jimmy Young suffered a heart attack in January of 2005 and passed away on February 20, at the age of 56. It was a sad conclusion to the life of one of the greatest ring tacticians of all time.

In the aftermath of Norton–Young, few paid particular attention to the Leon Spinks–Alfio Righetti affair. Fighting as a pro for only the seventh time, Leon won a difficult 10-round decision over the Italian. The victory put him next in line for a heavyweight title shot, but it was treated as little more than a footnote, barely warranting more than a few lines in *The Ring*.

Despite Ali's continuing decline, 1977 proved to be an interesting year. It had provided the biggest shakeup in the division since 1973. The top of the heap had grown smaller. Foreman was gone, Bobick had returned to the drawing board, and Young was about to drop out of the picture. Ron Lyle was still hanging in, but he was no longer a title threat. Earnie Shavers had proven himself, but the title seemed out of his reach.

Among the new generation of heavyweights who had turned pro in the early 1970s, few generated much interest other than Larry Holmes, who had still not fought a ranked contender.

All in all, it appeared that 1978 would belong to the champion in waiting, Ken Norton. Few regarded the upcoming Ali–Spinks fight as anything other than a farce.

Eleven

1978

Neon Leon

With its series of ups, downs, transitions and surprises, 1978 rivaled 1973 as the most tumultuous year of the decade. Once again, Muhammad Ali was forced to share the limelight. And his companion in the headlines was one of the most unlikely characters ever to fight for the world heavyweight championship: Leon Spinks Jr., also known as "Neon Leon."

Before he turned professional, Spinks was a member of the 1976 United States Olympic boxing squad, possibly the most talented and successful team of amateurs ever assembled. It produced five gold medal winners, four of whom went on to win professional championships. Ironically, Howard Davis, recipient of the Val Barker Award as outstanding boxer at the Montreal Olympics, never won a title in the punch-for-pay ranks.

Davis's disappointment was more than compensated for by the success of his teammates. Sugar Ray Leonard held six titles in five weight divisions. Michael Spinks won the world light heavyweight title, then became the first reigning light heavy king to ascend to the heavyweight throne. Actually, three members of the 1976 team became heavyweight champions. And Leo Randolph's brief professional career included a reign as WBA junior featherweight king.

However, it was Leon Spinks, who with Michael became the first brothers to win gold medals in the same Olympics, who became the first member of the Class of '76 to receive a crack at a world title.

Even as an amateur, Spinks was a perennial underdog. Going into the Montreal Olympics, his credentials consisted of a bronze medal from the 1974 World Championships in Cuba and a silver from the 1975 Pan-American Games in Mexico City. Sixto Soria of Cuba was the odds-on favorite to take Olympic gold in the 178-pound class, but Leon stunned the experts and Soria with a one-sided drubbing that was mercifully halted in the third round.

Fans who were seeing Spinks for the first time fell in love with his aggressive, whirlwind style. His lack of finesse was more than compensated by the ferocity of a wolverine. Former Olympian George Foreman offered this summation of Leon's performance: "Spinks isn't a boxer, but he is the best street fighter I've ever seen."

Spinks's connection with boxing began during his childhood in the notorious Pruitt-Igoe housing project in St. Louis. Unlike Foreman, who took up boxing to channel his aggression, or Joe Frazier, who was only trying to lose weight, Spinks looked to the sweet science as the key to his survival on the inner city streets. The oldest of seven children, young Leon was a frail, sickly child who quickly became an easy target for the hoodlums to be found on every corner. He soon acquired a nickname: "Mess over," because of the ease with which he could be intimidated. Encounters with bullies cost Leon his front teeth and much of his self-esteem.

His parents separated when he was young, but that didn't prevent Leon's father from continuing to abuse him. Leon Spinks Sr. would belittle his eldest son to his face as well as behind his back. In the old man's estimation, his offspring was destined to amount to nothing. One of Leon Jr.'s most painful memories was the time his father punished him by hanging him up on a nail and hitting him in the face with a cord. The experience left lasting physical and emotional scars.

Instead of allowing his degradation at his father's hands to defeat him, Spinks turned it into inspiration.

For a youth of Leon's background and physical disabilities, the road to self-respect ran straight uphill. When he first tried his hand at boxing, he was 15 years old and weighed a mere 118 pounds. He persisted, and began to pick up weight and a few ring skills. Those skills made the streets a less intimidating environment. His "Mess over" days had come to an end. Now Leon was one of the tough guys. Education had never been a high priority for him, and he dropped out of school in the tenth grade. He was, however, smart enough to realize that street life invariably led to a dead end. When he saw that his friends were beginning to wind up in prisons and graveyards, Leon joined the United States Marine Corps as a way to build character and a future.

Unfortunately, Spinks didn't adapt well to the rigors of military discipline. His rough background was poor preparation for a regimented life. Because he knocked out several superior officers and NCOs, Leon was forced to repeat boot camp. Only his success on the USMC boxing team prevented an early and unceremonious discharge.

Seven years and 195 fights after his amateur debut, Leon Spinks Jr. stood proudly on the podium in Montreal. A gold medal hung from his neck, and the band was playing the American national anthem in his honor. His younger brother, Michael, had taken the gold in the middleweight class. Both young men had come a long way from Pruitt–Igoe.

They lent each other tremendous emotional support throughout their amateur and professional careers. But growing up, the Spinks boys weren't always so loving. They engaged in their share of sibling scraps, and, according to Michael, "fought like madmen." Michael once received a gash on the cheek courtesy of a curtain rod during a fight with Leon over ownership of a bologna sandwich. With Olympic gold medals in their possession, though, the Spinks brothers were about to begin fighting for a lot more than bologna....

Leon didn't wait long to sign a professional contract. The day after he won his medal, he inked a contract that designated St. Louis Teamster official Millard "Mitt" Barnes as his manager. Barnes owned the gym in which Leon had trained as an amateur. The contract guaranteed Barnes 30 percent of Leon's earnings over the next three years.

Having chosen a manager, the neophyte pro also needed a promoter. Don King had clawed his way to the top of the promotional ranks, but Bob Arum wasn't far behind. Arum also had an ally in Butch Lewis. Lewis was a newcomer to the fight game, but he had an "in" with the Spinks brothers.

The Lewis connection was one factor that led Leon and Barnes to choose Arum as their promoter. They were also impressed by the way Arum had handled Ali–Norton III in Yankee Stadium.

Now Spinks had both a manager and a promoter. However, he also had an obligation to the USMC. He took care of that by applying for and receiving an early discharge late in 1976.

Because so many TV viewers had witnessed Leon's wild and woolly battle against Soria in the Olympic finals, his professional debut became a much-anticipated event. Spinks, like

Muhammad Ali before him, had moved up from light heavy to heavyweight as a pro. On January 15, 1977, he overwhelmed "Lightning" Bob Smith in five rounds. But Leon failed to impress with an undisciplined display of flailing, chasing, and wrestling. He threw a boatload of punches, but missed far too many of them.

Still, a win was a win. And like so many other prospects before and since, Spinks would build his record by mistreating the fistically handicapped. In his second and third bouts, he snuffed out a pair of non-entities named Peter Freeman and Jerry McIntyre in one round each.

Fight four pitted the newcomer against a "name" opponent, Pedro Agosto, the heavyweight champion of Puerto Rico. Agosto's record stood at 25–7–1, decent for a journeyman. But he had lost his last three fights, with George Foreman and Duane Bobick stopping him in four and three rounds respectively, and Boone Kirkman outpointing him in 10. Still, Agosto was a respectable opponent for a fighter of Spinks's limited experience.

Leon belted him out in one round, his third consecutive abbreviated victory. He was beginning to attract attention, but only as a promising prospect.

For his fifth fight, Spinks returned to Montreal, the site of his Olympic heroics. When his Canadian opponent arrived at the weigh-in in a state of total intoxication, the promoters frantically searched for a replacement. They found one in Bruce Scott, a ham-and-egger who happened to be in the right place at the right time.

Although Scott was ill-prepared and minimally talented, he put up an effort that showed how rough around the edges Leon was. Spinks charged after the substitute, but couldn't land any meaningful blows. Frustrated, the ex–Marine wrestled Scott to the canvas twice in the second round. In the third the referee warned him for roughhouse tactics.

Spinks finally pulled himself together and smothered his opponent with one of his trademark whirlwind assaults. The referee rescued Scott late in the third.

Then came the fight that nearly derailed Leon's progress. On October 22, 1977, he faced Minneapolis native Scott Ledoux in a matchup that seemed much too demanding for a five-fight newcomer like Spinks.

Nicknamed the "Fighting Frenchman," Ledoux was a classic fringe contender. Although he did manage to make it to #9 in the ratings, he spent most of his career just outside the top ten. He was not a gifted boxer, but with 220 beefy pounds packed onto a six-foot frame, he won on durability and determination. "I'm not a great fighter," he once admitted, "but I'll give anyone a good fight."[1]

Turning pro early in 1974, Ledoux fought in the shadow of another Minnesota heavyweight, Duane Bobick. To add insult to injury, Scott was also overshadowed by Duane's younger brother, Rodney. Minnesota wasn't big enough for three "White Hopes," but Ledoux stubbornly refused to relocate and he constantly challenged the Bobick brothers to meet him in the ring to settle their intrastate rivalry.

Eventually he received his wish. At the start of his career, though, Ledoux won a dozen fights over the usual no-names. Fight thirteen turned out to be unlucky as trial horse Roy "Cookie" Wallace stopped him in the second round.

Ledoux rebounded well from the setback. In his very next fight, he pounded out a ten-round decision over Rodney Bobick. He then took on a pair of former Joe Frazier challengers, Terry Daniels and Ron Stander. Daniels fell in six, and Stander came out on the short end of a ten-round decision.

Ledoux started out well in 1976. He stopped Bill Carson in nine rounds, then won an important 10-rounder from Larry Middleton. Then, on April 22, he finally got Duane

Bobick into a Minneapolis ring to settle their differences once and for all. Bobick, who was much more talented, won the decision. The crowd of 14,130 that attended the event remains a state boxing gate record.

Two months later, Ledoux was outpointed by another rising white fighter, John "Dino" Dennis. Then came his three-round annihilation at the hands of George Foreman. A string of defeats like that might have induced another fighter to find another way to make a living. If nothing else, though, Scott was determined. He rounded out the year with a two-round kayo over a warm body named Junior Bentley.

In 1977, the fight for which Ledoux is best known occurred. Competing in the Don King/ABC Television United States Championship tournament, Ledoux was matched in the preliminary round against Johnny "Black Knight" Boudreaux, a hot prospect who was favored to win the heavyweight section of the tournament. The bout was nationally televised from Annapolis, Maryland. Ledoux fought an inspired battle and appeared to have won handily when the final bell sounded.

But when the scorecards were added up, Boudreaux was declared the winner. Ledoux went berserk and attacked Boudreaux while Johnny was being interviewed by Howard Cosell. One of Scott's wild blows sent Cosell's hairpiece sailing out of the ring.

In the aftermath, the Maryland State Athletic Commission laid a six-month suspension on Ledoux for what it termed "profane language and ungentlemanly conduct." Despite the suspension and the loss, the outcome turned out well for Ledoux. He had performed well on television, and gained fan recognition as "the man who kayoed Cosell's hairpiece."

The apparent injustice done to Ledoux helped to focus attention on the shadier side of the tournament. It was soon revealed that many of the entrants were under contract to Don King, and others had been forced to sign with him in order to participate. Even worse, some of the fighters had improper ratings and phony records. The tournament was suspended, but King survived the scandal.

As for Ledoux, he fought on, taking a clear-cut decision over once-promising Pedro Soto. He then stopped durable journeyman Tom Prater in seven. With his professional status somewhat restored, Scott jumped at the opportunity to even the score with Duane Bobick.

Bobick, who had recently been humiliated by Ken Norton, was considered vulnerable to the resurgent Ledoux's momentum. But Bobick was determined to prove that he was still a contender, and he stopped Ledoux in eight rounds.

That defeat turned Ledoux into a trial horse, and the Spinks brain trust considered him little more than a stepping stone for their young tiger. Yet there was plenty of evidence to indicate that they were taking the Minnesotan far too lightly.

Ledoux wasn't an Agosto type who was still hanging on for a few extra paydays. He was a hungry fighter who still had enough pride left to resent being viewed as just another notch on Leon's gun. He also had a vast edge on Spinks in professional experience against credible opponents, with more than thirty fights to his credit.

Another factor in Scott's favor was sheer size. Spinks was taller at 6'1", but he weighed only 194 pounds — puny in the era of the big heavyweight. Ledoux's 224 pounds were solid, if not well-sculpted. Spinks's blows had proved devastating thus far to fighters close to his own size. But how effective would they be against a true heavyweight like Ledoux?

The Ledoux fight would serve as a yardstick for Spinks's development thus far. When the bell ending the tenth and final round rang, Leon hadn't measured up very well.

Ledoux failed to crumple in the face of Spinks's maniacal onslaughts. Not only was the Minnesotan hard to hurt, he also knew most of the lower points of the trade. When he "accidentally" butted Spinks and chipped one of his precious teeth, Leon plaintively asked: "Why you got to cheat to win?"

Ledoux told him that was how he earned a living.

As the rounds rolled by, Spinks threw his usual multitude of punches. A high percentage of the blows missed their large target. Ledoux used his weight advantage to bully the novice and keep him off balance. He also did a lot of body work. The fight was close enough to be ruled a draw by the officials, an outcome that confirmed Ledoux's status as a fringe contender and actually moved Spinks closer to a title shot.

After his life-and-death struggle against Earnie Shavers, Ali had been fishing for a soft opponent to fight before his mandatory defense against Ken Norton.

Spinks's name was mentioned, among others. At first Ali wrote Leon off, considering him too green to sell as a legitimate challenger. After watching the Spinks–Ledoux struggle, the champion had a change of heart. Not only did he consider Spinks eminently beatable; he also saw a promotional angle in the fact that this would be the first time two Olympic light heavyweight gold medalists would face each other for the heavyweight title.

The only problem was that Leon wasn't rated in anybody's top ten. That problem was rectified by putting him in a Las Vegas ring with a rated contender for his next fight, only three weeks after his war with Ledoux. His opponent was an undefeated young Italian named Alfio Righetti. At age 25, Righetti held the Italian heavyweight title and had won 26 straight fights. But he had never fought an established opponent, and the Spinks bout would be his first showing outside his homeland.

Ali had already announced that he would take on the winner of Spinks–Righetti in his next defense. In the ring prior to the contest, the champ announced that he would fight the winner.

The financial terms of Spinks–Righetti were unusual. Leon was guaranteed $30,000, with $300,000 to come if he became Ali's challenger. Righetti would get $10,000 for fighting Spinks, plus a $90,000 bonus if he won. His purse for facing Ali would come to $120,000.

As usual, Spinks entered the ring at a physical disadvantage, weighing 201 pounds to Righetti's 217. The Italian also had the upper hand in height and reach.

Not intimidated, Spinks charged out at the opening bell and fired bombs at Righetti. Somewhat taken aback by his opponent's recklessness, Alfio held on and fought defensively. His offense picked up steam as the fight went on, and by the middle rounds, Leon appeared to be tiring.

The seasoned Italian took full advantage of the situation and pounded away at Spinks. In the seventh round, he landed a pair of rights that sent Leon spinning across the ring.

Going into the last two rounds, the fight was a virtual dead heat. Spinks caught his second wind and outpunched Righetti to eke out a narrow points win on the officials' scorecards.

Righetti had still managed to impress American fight fans with his spirited performance. As well, he seemed unaffected by Spinks's rain of punches, which prompted *The Ring*'s John Ort to observe: "Either he [Righetti] takes a hell of a punch or Spinks' power is overrated."[2]

However, Righetti never cashed in on the recognition he achieved. He went back to Italy, fought nine more times, then was shockingly kayoed in one round by an American journeyman named Terry Mims.

Spinks, on the other hand, was now in the WBA's ratings and was about to become a world title challenger in only his eighth professional fight.

As for Ken Norton, his victory over Jimmy Young two weeks earlier had earned him little more than a longer wait for his fourth crack at Ali. His manager, Bob Biron, was disgusted that the WBC was allowing Ali to fight Spinks in the first place. The WBC's failure to follow through on its threat to strip Ali of the title grated on both men's nerves. Biron openly accused the WBC of being afraid of Ali.

Ali was guaranteed $3.7 million for what many anticipated to be nothing more than a high-priced gym workout. Spinks's inexperience, combined with his less-than-stellar showings against Ledoux and Righetti, spelled "mismatch." ABC and NBC showed no interest in televising Ali–Spinks. CBS, which through Bob Arum held promotional rights to Spinks, decided to broadcast what promised to be a nonevent.

Fight or Farce?

Now the promoters of Ali–Spinks faced the unenviable task of trying to hype the fight to a skeptical public. Ali had fought undeserving challengers before: the names Coopman, Dunn, and Evangelista came readily to mind. The main difference between them and Spinks was the recognition factor. Spinks had been on view in the Olympics and on network TV; the others were totally unknown. Still, even the casual boxing fan knew that Spinks had no business being in the same ring as a legend like Ali.

For the most part the media belittled the fight. In the February 6 *New York Times*, Peter Maas wrote that the real question wasn't whether or not Ali would beat Spinks; it was whether the champion, "starring on CBS, can outpoint *Charlie's Angels* in the Nielsen network ratings."

The promotion was made all the more difficult by some out-of-character behavior from Ali. To the astonishment of all, he went into a two-month period of silence. The most media-accessible champion of all time suddenly refused to speak to or be interviewed by the press. Many theories were advanced to explain this anomalous behavior. Don King, angry over being beaten out on the promotion by archrival Bob Arum, assumed that Ali was too embarrassed to try to "ballyhoo" such an inferior opponent.

Another hypothesis held that Ali was angry with the press for its constant trashing of the Spinks bout. His lack of lip would rob the fourth estate of its primary source of quotable material.

Ali's former physician, Ferdie Pacheco, felt that the silence indicated that the champion had become bored with boxing. Others thought he was ducking questions about a fourth fight with Norton.

The champ himself told a confidante that he was staying quiet "to give his words more impact" when he did decide to talk.

Not only wasn't Ali doing much talking; he wasn't doing much training, either. At age 36, he was finding it increasingly difficult to apply himself to the rigors of proper preparation. His minimal effort leading to the February fight indicated that he shared the common belief that Spinks's chances of pulling off an upset were minimal.

Regardless of Ali's conditioning, or lack thereof, few believed he could come into the ring in sorry enough shape to lose to Leon. Besides, even at the tender age of 24, Spinks was hardly a Spartan in the gym. In fact, his unique approach to training nearly cost him his place on the Olympic team. Although he intended to fight in the 178-pound class, Spinks reported to the Olympic camp weighing 191. Because of Leon's refusal to conform to the team's training standards, Coach Pat Nappi came close to telling him to take a hike.

Another Olympic coach, Sarge Johnson, said that coaxing Leon to train was always an uphill battle. Johnson often had to pry Spinks out of bed for early morning runs with the other team members. Sometimes Leon splashed water on himself to simulate sweat in an effort to convince the coaches that he'd completed his roadwork. To some observers, Spinks's gold medal in the Olympic was less surprising than the fact that he stayed on the team.

As a pro, Spinks came under the wing of veteran Sam Solomon. Solomon, a robust 62-year-old who had been through the wars as a boxer and a cornerman, and had also played in the old Negro baseball leagues, jumped at the chance to mold a wild man into a polished professional.

Solomon brought Spinks to Philadelphia and worked with him in Joe Frazier's gym. He was knowledgeable, but also easygoing, and the latter trait wasn't what the undisciplined Spinks needed. Leon's adherence to Sam's training proved selective. He frequently ignored his trainer's advice about the use of the jab and the need to pace oneself.

Well aware of Spinks's penchant for breaking training, Solomon tried to keep a close eye on his charge. Still, Leon managed to sneak away for days at a time.

The kind-hearted Solomon described Spinks as "a kid, a happy kid." And like any happy kid, Leon loved to play. When it came to a choice between partying and punching the heavy bag, partying always won hands down. In Montreal for the Bruce Scott fight, Spinks slipped his short leash and went on a three-day tour of the local nightclub scene. That may have accounted for his erratic performance when he made it into the ring.

Prior to the Ledoux fight, it appeared that Spinks had consciously avoided the gym. Two weeks before the fight, Leon went to St. Louis for a benefit exhibition. He arrived in horrid shape and put on a poor demonstration of the sweet science.

Ledoux's trainer, Joe Dazkiewicz, drew encouragement from the exhibition as well as rumors that Solomon was overworking the fighter in an attempt to make up for lost ground. Twenty-four hours before fight day, a time most fighters use for relaxation, Solomon was still putting Leon through his paces.

Spinks's less than rigorous work ethic showed during his moments of fatigue in both the Ledoux and Righetti bouts. For a fighter who relied on sheer volume of punches the way Spinks did, lack of conditioning was a major flaw.

The combination of Leon's inexperience and his apparent stamina problems were probably the main selling points in Ali's selection of him as a challenger. At this stage in his career, the champion hardly relished any more do-or-die 15-round dramas like the one he had endured against Earnie Shavers.

Ali believed Spinks would punch himself out by the middle rounds, allowing Muhammad to stand back and pick him apart. His view of the Spinks–Righetti fight confirmed his thinking. But Leon fooled Ali, as well as everyone else who knew him. This time, he took his training seriously. Except for one isolated incident when he took off to spread his wings, Spinks focused on the mammoth task ahead of him and worked as he never had before.

Then Fate threw a monkey wrench into Spinks's efforts. With only ten days to go before the big night, Spinks sparred with a huge heavyweight named Roy "Tiger" Williams. Like Ledoux, Williams was a blue-collar fighter who hung just below the rated contenders.

At 6'5" and 230 pounds, Williams had a solid chin, exceptional strength, and a good punch. His 25–6 record included 16 knockouts, seven in the first round. All his losses came at the hands of name opponents, and only Earnie Shavers ever managed to stop him.

Williams's main problem was inconsistency. He gave Shavers a scare before Earnie stopped him. But Roy also had the nerve to drop a decision to Richard Dunn.

In the gym, however, Williams lived up to his nickname. With Spinks, his job was to mimic Ali's holding tactics so Leon could learn to adjust. At one point, Williams held and hit, landing a hard left to Spinks's rib cage.

As a result, Leon experienced great discomfort whenever he tried to move his right arm. Now Solomon was in a real bind. If a two-fisted Spinks was thought to be in over his head against Ali, what was he going to do with only one hand? Postponement was out of the question. As it was, Ali had stretched the tolerance of the WBC by fighting Spinks in the first place. Any delay of a fight already condemned as a ludicrous mismatch would have meant outright cancellation.

Spinks's people decided to inject a painkiller into the fighter's side before each workout, and once again immediately before the fight. The procedure worked. Leon was once again a two-handed fighter, with no one the wiser.

Even without knowledge of the rib injury, however, few observers gave Spinks so much as an outside chance of winning. Only Pete Rademacher, whose professional debut had been a challenge of Floyd Patterson, had gone into a title bout with less experience. And Leon hadn't even won all his few fights.

Ali was a veteran of 57 professional bouts. Spinks had fought only 31 professional rounds. Spinks's only assets, youth and enthusiasm, were greatly overshadowed by Ali's array of advantages. In size, Ali was taller, had a longer reach, and his 27-pound pull in weight was the greatest disparity he had ever held over a challenger. Along with size came the obvious advantage of strength. If Ali could manhandle a fighter like George Foreman, he could easily outmuscle a sub-200-pounder like Spinks.

Nor did Spinks's 12-year gap in the youth department appear to make much difference. Even a faded Ali was believed to possess enough skill and class to polish Leon off without much trouble. After all, the challenger's wide-open style seemed tailor-made for Ali's pinpoint punches, especially the left.

Ledoux had commented that Spinks "eats the jab real good." And Ali dished out jabs the way McDonalds' served hamburgers.

Punching power was also a non-factor. Despite the first-round kayoes he had scored, Spinks had failed to floor or even hurt Ledoux and Righetti. Ali, on the other hand, had absorbed the best shots of punchers like Foreman, Frazier, Norton, Shavers, and Liston. How, then, could he be troubled by the blows of a fighter only one year removed from the light heavyweights?

Finally, there was the question of stamina. Even in less than peak condition, Ali had sailed through the 15-round distance on more than one occasion. Spinks had gone ten rounds twice, but had flagged badly each time.

An aging Ali might have been ripe for the taking in 1978. But the consensus of opinion was that Leon Spinks wasn't the right man for the job. Most Vegas bookmakers weren't even bothering to declare a betting line. Those who did tabbed Ali an 8-to-1 favorite, and those odds seemed unduly generous to Spinks.

Still, there were some intangibles that were overlooked in the general atmosphere of ridicule that surrounded the fight. One of those intangibles was Spinks's hunger. He wasn't that far removed from his experiences in the St. Louis ghetto, and bad memories still burned deep within him. He had known extreme poverty and degradation, and those who were close to him reminded him that a return to that existence was only a loss away.

Indeed, Ledoux's trainer said that the day before his man fought Spinks, he passed Leon's hotel room and overheard Butch Lewis screaming at his fighter that if he lost he'd end up back in the ghetto.

Although Lewis denied using those words, it wouldn't have been the first or last time he used them as a motivating tool. Throughout the Ledoux fight, whenever Spinks began to tire, someone in his corner would start yelling about the ghetto. Spinks's reaction was Pavlovian: he would start swinging as though he were fighting for his life.

Against Ali, this reaction could only be intensified. Because Spinks was given virtually no chance, he had nothing to lose. So the pressure a more deserving challenger might have felt was no burden to him. Leon's mother Kay told the press that her son didn't really expect to win.

And the possibility that something could "happen" wasn't that far-fetched. Since the "Thrilla in Manila," Ali had not produced a good performance in the ring, never mind a great one. Even Angelo Dundee admitted that it was only a matter of time until the Ali circus came to an end.

Still, Dundee didn't think Leon would be the one to burst Ali's bubble. He assumed that the magnitude of the situation would overwhelm the young challenger.

Logically, Dundee was right, and so were all the pugilistic pundits who predicted an easy night's work for Ali on February 15. But Leon Spinks didn't know anything about logic.

"I'm the Latest!"

On fight night, Spinks entered the ring with surprising composure considering the monumental task ahead of him. One contributing factor was Ali's moratorium on pre-fight shenanigans. Even after he began to speak in public again, the champion refrained from his usual repertoire of gibes and insults.

As he entered the ring to the strains of "Pomp and Circumstance," Ali didn't speak to, joke with, or even look at Spinks. It was as though the underdog challenger were beneath his notice.

Most of the fans were there to see the ring persona Ali had constructed back when he was Cassius Clay. They wanted to watch him float like a butterfly and sting like a bee. And some had paid for the pleasure of seeing him make a fool of his inept challenger.

Consequently, as the early rounds dragged on with Spinks swinging earnestly and Ali doing nothing, some of the patrons began to boo. Ali's intentions were clear: he was going to allow Spinks to tire himself out, then take him out in the late rounds. Despite Spinks's energy, the process was as exciting as watching paint dry. It was Rope-a-Dope revisited for the umpteenth time, and Ali appeared to be just as bored as the paying customers.

But keener observers were noticing a difference between this fight and the one against Foreman in Zaire. Although Ali was staying on the ropes, Spinks was landing far more punches than Big George had managed. Spinks's power was hardly in Foreman's class, but his blows were rapid, regular, and point-scoring.

By the time the middle rounds began, Ali had handed Spinks a sizeable lead on the scorecards. And he had also boosted the challenger's confidence. Not only had Spinks out-punched a legend, he had also drawn blood from Ali's mouth.

As for Ali, the realization slowly began to dawn on him that he was in for a difficult evening. The few times he had attempted some offense had been unsuccessful. His punches were sloppy, his timing was off, and Spinks was punching like a perpetual motion machine.

Late in the ninth round, Ali woke the crowd up with a flurry off the ropes. The bell cut his rally short, but for the first time, Spinks was forced on the defensive.

Ali picked up where he left off in the tenth. As Spinks showed signs of fatigue, Ali pinned him against the ropes and launched a fusillade of hard blows with both hands. Instinct more than experience enabled Leon to roll and weave to lessen the effects of the punches. Not only did Spinks survive Ali's first full-scale attack; he managed to come back to control the final moments of the round.

Despite Leon's rally, it still seemed that Ali had taken control of the fight. Spinks had done better than anyone could have expected. But he was now going into what was for him an undiscovered country: the eleventh round. The time had come for Ali to close the show.

But Ali knew something the crowd didn't. Spinks had found his second wind, and Ali's own gas tank was running dangerously low. The champ sensed that his gamble of giving away the early rounds was about to backfire. His cakewalk defense had suddenly turned into a stroll through quicksand.

In short, Ali realized that his title was in jeopardy, and if he didn't do something soon, he would suffer the ignominy of losing his title to a seven-fight greenhorn. Over the next few rounds, Muhammad threw flat-footed bombs at his challenger.

But the blows had little effect, either missing their target entirely or landing with little authority. In the meantime, Spinks just kept on punching, no matter what.

The crowd's boredom had long since disappeared. Some pulled for Ali to put the upstart in his place; others rooted for the underdog in hopes of witnessing sports history firsthand.

Going into the fourteenth round, Ali had become desperate. His fight plan was failing and so were the weapons that had always come through for him before. Still, he attempted to recapture his past by dancing and jabbing. But a miraculously fresh Spinks simply herded him into the ropes and blasted away. Ali could do nothing but try to weave away from the punches. Spinks captured the round by a wide margin.

The spectators hung on the edge of their seats as the final round began. Could Spinks keep it together for three more minutes? Or would Ali pull off one more miracle?

Spinks came out like a buzz saw, knowing he had to keep the pressure on the champion. Ali tried to match the younger man's workrate, but he simply couldn't move his hands quickly enough.

Leon caught Ali on the ropes, but Ali managed to spin him around and trap him in a corner. Then the champ threw everything but the kitchen sink at Spinks, to no avail. Surviving the assault, Leon landed a combination that staggered Ali. The champ was in real trouble, but he still came back with a flurry of soft punches.

Disdaining Ali's toothless offense, Spinks caught Ali with a slashing right hand. Then he drove home a smashing left uppercut that set Ali back on his heels.

By now, both fighters were calling on their last reserves of stamina. But Ali's indifference to training betrayed him; he couldn't land anything significant. He could only sag against the ropes as Leon teed off with a three-punch combination just before the bell.

Before the echoes of the final bell died down, Spinks's cornermen were practically climbing over each other to embrace their fighter. Ali's entourage looked somber as the scorecards were tallied. Finally, the ring announcer went to the microphone.

"Ladies and gentlemen, we have a split decision," he said.

The crowd erupted in boos. Was Ali going to be given another gift a la Jimmy Young and Ken Norton? The booing intensified when Judge Art Lurie's card favored Ali by a 143–142 margin. Judge Harold Buck scored it for Spinks, 144–141. Now the crowd was silent. What would the third scorecard say?

"Judge Lou Talbot calls it 145–140 for the winner and new heavyweight champion of the world, Leon Spinks!"

The crowd, boxing fans, and the world in general reacted with shock and disbelief. Spinks's win constituted the biggest upset since a brash kid named Cassius Clay wrested the title from Sonny Liston in 1964.

After the fight, a swollen but gracious Ali admitted that he'd been undone by Spinks's stamina and determination. Though bitterly disappointed by the loss, he at least gained a measure of solace from the fact that Spinks had done something he himself had always taken pleasure in doing: making hash out of the experts' opinion.

"I know all you press people were surprised, and I'm glad he proved you all wrong. I was surprised myself and I was right there in the ring."[3]

As for Spinks, he was understandably ecstatic. But he also showed class in paying tribute to the man he had beaten. "I'm the latest, but he's the greatest," Leon said, looking at Ali.[4]

Latest or not, it was difficult to say the words "Leon Spinks" and "heavyweight champion" in the same breath. And he wasn't given much time to savor his improbable but well-earned victory. Before the smoke had cleared from the upset of the decade, the agreement both fighters had signed to fight Ken Norton next became the focal point of the heavyweight division's greatest controversy since Ali was stripped of his title in 1967.

Norton and his manager, Bob Biron, were anxious to see Spinks live up to the agreement. As far as they were concerned, Spinks was eminently beatable.

However, despite his defeat, Ali also believed he could beat Spinks. As the bruises to his face and pride healed, the ex-champ mounted a campaign to convince the public, and Spinks, that he deserved an immediate rematch. To undercut Norton, Ali asked a rhetorical question: "Who is more deserving of a shot at the world championship, Ken Norton or Muhammad Ali?" Ali went on to proclaim himself "the number one contender in the eyes of the people."

Behind the scenes, the promoters maneuvered to make the best of an unexpected situation. Bob Arum and Don King both had a great deal at stake. Norton was under contract to fight for King, and the frizzle-haired dealmaker saw Ken as his ticket to regaining control of the heavyweight title. And Arum, who promoted Spinks, wanted to keep the title as far away from King's hands as possible.

And, as usual, the WBA and WBC only added to the confusion. The WBA had no interest in whether Spinks fought Norton or Ali. Their only demand was that the new champ defend against someone in the organization's top ten in his next fight. Within a year, though, Spinks would have to accept the challenge of the WBA's #1 contender, whoever that might be.

The WBC's options were much more limited. Because of the agreement both Ali and Spinks had signed, Jose Sulaiman indicated that by April 7, Spinks had to sign to fight Norton within 90 days of that date. Failure to comply would end the WBC's recognition of Spinks as champion.

Arum didn't take Sulaiman's ruling seriously. He called him a "joke" and declared that Spinks would make one defense of his title and then give Ali a rematch.

Then Arum decided to snooker Norton and King. He agreed to offer Norton the first crack at Spinks, provided Ken was willing to accept some Byzantine contractual arrangements.

The contract that linked Spinks, Top Rank, and CBS called for the network to carry Leon's first three title defenses as long as they were against anyone other than Ali. CBS would pay $1.5 million for each fight. From that kitty, Spinks would get $1 million, plus $300,000 for expenses. The challenger would receive the remaining $200,000.

Arum thus okayed a Norton fight, knowing that if Ken chose to be one of the first three challengers, he would get only two hundred grand, chump change for a fighter of Norton's stature. It wouldn't even cover his training expenses.

Norton and his brain trust knew exactly what Arum was trying to do. And they surprised him by accepting the offer. Norton was so hungry for another crack at the title, and he was so certain that he could beat Leon, that he took Arum's bait. Biron called the $200,000 figure "insulting," but agreed with Norton that the title would be the key to a considerable fortune in the future.

Norton's acceptance of the offer backed Arum into a very tight corner. He had no intention of letting Spinks anywhere near Norton, and he made that clear by ignoring Ken's consent and forging ahead with plans for the Ali–Spinks rematch.

Now it was time for the WBC to put up or shut up. The organization and its president were in a very precarious position. Ali had scoffed at its edicts and done what he pleased. But Sulaiman was astute enough to realize that Ali was bigger than boxing, and the WBC would have lost public support if it had taken his title away.

Now Spinks also chose to defy the WBC. The organization could not afford to have its authority undermined again. And Spinks, unlike Ali, was hardly bigger than boxing. Thus, the moment Ali–Spinks II was announced, the WBC withdrew its recognition of Spinks and handed the title to Norton on the basis of his 15-round victory over Jimmy Young.

Norton made history by becoming the first man to become heavyweight champion without winning the title in the ring. It is unfortunate that a fighter of his ability and character had to ascend the throne in such an inglorious manner.

As for Spinks, only one month into his title reign, he found his domain cut in half at the stroke of a pen. To make matters worse, during the Machiavellian events that unfolded during ensuing months, Leon's hard-earned title was reduced to the status of a pawn in a promotional chess match.

Sulaiman's title-stripping gambit was probably less an effort to remove the WBC crown from Spinks's hands than to make certain it didn't return to Ali's. It was obvious that Ali would never consent to a fourth fight with Norton. Therefore, if Ali regained the title in a rematch with Spinks, the WBC would find itself right back where it had been in 1977.

Spinks's decision to fight Ali again allowed Sulaiman to indirectly lock WBC recognition away from the ex-champ and throw away the key. Even better, he could do it without risking a loss of public support. Any criticism over stripping Spinks of the title could be, and was, brushed aside.

The WBA, on the other hand, was quick to reaffirm its recognition of Spinks as champion. Thus, for the first time since 1970, two fighters presented themselves as world titleholders. The result was a moral tug of war in which fans and press debated over who the rightful, legitimate champion should be, Ken Norton or Leon Spinks.

Most observers believed Spinks had the stronger claim. After all, he had won his title in the ring, not on paper. As well, many fans believed that as a long-time, two-reign champion, Ali deserved an immediate chance to win the title for an unprecedented third time.

At the same time, though, there were some who argued that Norton deserved some compensation for the shafting he had received over the past two years. Indeed, the common consensus was that Norton could beat both the faded Ali and the inexperienced Spinks. Where, then, was the justice in freezing the best fighter in the division out of a title shot for another year?

Norton had no illusions about the legitimacy of the title belt the WBC had strapped around his waist. He knew he could only gain acceptance by proving himself in the ring. He promised to be a "fighting champion," and even went so far as to say he was still willing to take Arum's $200,000 offer to challenge Spinks. Naturally, Arum ignored Norton's counterploy.

Ken bore no animosity toward the WBA champ, saying that he actually "kind of liked" Leon. However, he felt Spinks was being misguided.

With Spinks and Ali tied up in their up in their rematch, Norton had to look elsewhere for a credible challenger. And Don King was more than willing to help him find one.

Through his promotional ties to Norton, King had regained a foothold at the top of the heavyweight heap. And he intended to maintain his hold on the WBC portion of the title. His strategy was to ensure that Norton's first title defense would be against a King-controlled fighter.

Thus, on March 25, 1978, a 12-round elimination bout was held to determine Norton's challenger. The bout matched the WBC's #3 contender, Earnie Shavers, against fourth-ranked Larry Holmes. Both fighters had promotional ties with King.

Shavers's reputation as a puncher had already been firmly established, and his excellent showing against Ali six months earlier was still fresh in the public's mind. Holmes was 28 years old and had a perfect 26–0 record. Yet he remained a mystery man to most boxing fans.

The Easton Assassin

Born in Cuthbert, Georgia, on November 3, 1949, Larry Holmes moved at a young age with his family to Easton, Pennsylvania, joining the great migration of blacks from south to north. Because of his close association with that town, his ring nickname became "The Easton Assassin."

Before he turned to boxing, though, young Larry appeared to be on the road to becoming an "Easton Statistic." Life in the gritty Pennsylvania town was no picnic for his family. Holmes was one of 12 children, and his parents parted company when he was still a boy.

Like all too many poor black youths, Larry quit school in the seventh grade and immediately joined the work force. His first job was a dollar-an-hour car wash gig. Although he was a tough kid, Holmes possessed an admirable work ethic. Unlike most of his friends who viewed minimum-wage labor as a chump's game, Larry believed it was his duty to help his mother, Flossie, and his many brothers and sisters. During his teenage years, he toiled as a garbage man, sandblaster, steelworker, and quarry worker, among other jobs.

He also found his fair share of trouble. A bad attitude backed up by quick fists led to more than a few scrapes with the law. Still, Larry Holmes refused to give in to despair. He was presented with every opportunity to fall into a pernicious and endless cycle leading from the streets to jail and back again. But a sense of destiny burned inside him, and like many impoverished youths all over the world, he saw boxing as his ticket to the top.

As Holmes told *Sports Illustrated* in 1978: "When I dropped out of school, I had to go to work. Then one day I said, what the hell, I might as well be a fighter. You don't have to go to school to be a fighter, you don't have to go to college. All you have to do is know how to fight and how not to get hurt."[5]

At the relatively advanced age of 19, Holmes began to train at the Easton PAL gym. During a two-year amateur career, he compiled a 19–3 record. After losing to Duane Bobick at the 1972 U.S. Olympic box-offs, he decided it was time to start getting paid for his efforts.

The young heavyweight received his initial tutelage from Ernie Butler, a former welterweight and fellow resident of Easton. Butler guided Larry through the amateur ranks as well as the first six fights of Holmes's pro career. After that, the two parted company because Holmes felt Butler wasn't moving him along quickly enough.

Holmes then hooked up with Don King as manager and Richie Giachetti as trainer. King remained in the picture through the early part of Holmes's career, but as Giachetti stated in 1978, he and Larry carried the load. "[I]t was always Larry and me," Giachetti insisted. "We were the ones sacrificing, sharing the same bad hotel room eating the same lousy food, taking the lesser fights."[6]

Holmes may not have needed to go to college to become a fighter, but he did go to school in the training camps of most of the 1970s' best talent, including Muhammad Ali's famous headquarters at Deer Lake, Pennsylvania. Ali agreed to hire Holmes as a sparring partner, and Larry remained part of Ali's entourage well into 1975.

His stint with "The Greatest" proved valuable in more ways than one. Ali paid his sparmates generously, but the skills and polish Holmes gained through boxing hundreds of rounds with the champ were worth more than money. In a way, Holmes did go to college after all.

Like every fighter who begins a pro career, Holmes wanted to become champion one day. But his road to the title wouldn't be an easy one. He didn't have an Olympic gold medal to trade on, nor did he have the financial support some of the other '70s success stories enjoyed. He paid hard dues, fighting on Ali's undercards and headlining in small towns and out-of-the-way arenas. He took any fight he could get and won them all.

Yet as he prepared to meet Shavers, there were many who questioned Holmes's credentials as a contender. Despite his unblemished record and steady climb upward in the ratings, Holmes had not yet ventured into the ring with a world-class opponent. In the early stages of his career, which began on March 21, 1973, with a four-round decision over Rodell Dupree, he had taken on the usual assortment of record-building foes. One of them, Kevin Isaac, had decked Holmes before falling in three rounds. After that near-disaster, Larry had reeled off a nine-fight knockout streak in venues ranging from Cleveland to Toronto to Honolulu.

He also gained a minor degree of exposure by appearing on the undercards of three Ali title defenses. According to Giachetti, that was Don King's "idea of a break." And it might have been, had someone else been fighting in the main event. However, as Giachetti observed, no one else got much attention when Ali was around.

Nevertheless, Holmes faced his first major test on the undercard of the "Thrilla in Manila." His opponent was Rodney Bobick, the younger, larger, and less publicized brother of Duane. Although he didn't have a high-profile amateur career like Duane, Rodney was the first of the two to turn pro.

Rodney carried a strong 18–5 amateur record into professional ranks. Growing up in a family that included nine other brothers provided plenty of experience in fighting outside the ring, and when brothers Duane and Leroy began training as amateurs, they'd come home looking to practice their newfound skills on Rodney. He had to take up boxing himself just to survive around the house.

On March 8, 1972, Bobick launched his pro career by stopping one Mickey Shannon in two rounds. He then proceeded to build an impressive 10–0 record. An active fighter, he went to the post 17 times in 1973, winning 14.

In 1974, Rodney had his best year as a pro. He went undefeated in nine bouts, including a three-round stoppage of former WBA light heavyweight champion Vicente Rondon and a decision over future WBA heavyweight champ Mike Weaver. He also reversed one of his 1973 losses by beating Argentina's Raul Gorosito.

At that point Bobick's manager, a businessman named Mike Hayden, decided it was time to give his fighter the added polish needed to break into the big time. Hayden contacted Angelo Dundee and proposed that the veteran trainer work with the 23-year-old prospect.

Dundee went to Minnesota to work Rodney's corner in a fight against former contender Ron Stander. Dundee was impressed even before the 6'3" 230-pounder stepped into the ring. Rodney had just been attacked outside of a Dairy Queen by four thugs, and despite being whacked in the head by a tire iron, managed to destroy his attackers.

Obviously, durability was Bobick's greatest asset. With six stitches in his head from the Dairy Queen encounter, Rodney easily defeated Stander over ten rounds. He rounded out 1974 with a 10th-round stoppage of the very capable Pat Duncan.

Rodney soon became part of Dundee's vast array of fighters. He sparred regularly with Ali, helping him to prepare for the Foreman and Wepner fights. As well, Rodney worked with Jimmy Ellis. Both champions admired the Minnesotan's strength and durability and touted his potential as a contender.

Bobick's first fight of 1975 saw him dismantle hard-hitting Terry Krueger in one round. The victory pushed him into the #13 slot in *The Ring*'s heavyweight ratings. Some observers began to wonder if the wrong Bobick was getting all the publicity. Duane was still undefeated at that point, but Rodney had been in with tougher competition.

Unfortunately, Rodney disappointed his partisans over the remainder of the year. Houston's Jody Ballard decisioned him in 10. He beat Pedro Agosto, then lost to Scott Ledoux. After a win over trial horse Cookie Wallace, Rodney went to Manila to try to end Holmes's unbeaten streak.

Holmes proved miles ahead of Bobick in boxing skill, and he battered the Minnesotan into a sixth-round TKO defeat. Only Bobick's iron chin kept him on his feet at the time of the stoppage. It was a key victory for Larry, who could now look forward to bigger paydays in 1976. Of his nine bouts in 1975, Holmes only earned in the neighborhood of $18,000.

Bobick never fully rebounded from the defeat. By 1977, both his career and his life had come to an end. He fought only four more times, winning three. On June 5, less than a month after decisioning Walter White, Rodney was killed in a car crash outside his native Bowlus, Minnesota.

His final record stood at a respectable 38–7. Had he lived, he might have pulled his career together and risen higher in the division.

As for Holmes, he racked up four more knockouts over opponents of the cannon-fodder variety. Then he fought big Roy Williams on the Ali–Young undercard at Landover,

Maryland. Williams was a notorious spoiler, but Holmes punched out a unanimous 10-round decision.

However, Larry paid a high price for the win. He broke his right hand, and it would be nine months before he entered the ring again. Despite the costly layoff, however, Holmes didn't sit around sulking. Instead, he continued to train, using only his left hand. His sabbatical thus gave him the opportunity to hone what may have been the most punishing left jab in heavyweight history.

"I just worked with the left," he said. "The left hand is probably 100 percent better right now than my right."[7]

Holmes's jab became likened to both a meat tenderizer and Chinese water torture. Its metronomic repetitiveness coupled with a crisp, snapping delivery spelled disaster for anyone who faced it. Larry's left was not as quick as Ali's, but it packed more power. If Ali's jab was a rapier, Holmes' was more like a spear.

Unlike other fighters who relied heavily on their jabs, Holmes complemented the weapon with a quick, underrated right hand. In terms of ring talent, he was best of the many prospects who emerged during the mid–1970s. Because he was overshadowed by Ali, though, few fans paid much attention to him.

By the time Larry's hand healed, Don King's ill-fated U.S. Championships were in full swing. Holmes entered the heavyweight competition, and his first fight was against Indianapolis's Tom Prater. Although Prater was a respectable fringe contender with an 18–3–1 record, few expected him to give Holmes much trouble.

But Prater fooled the experts by extending Holmes the full 8-round distance. Holmes won a unanimous decision, but he looked ordinary in the process. The layoff probably accounted for his sub-par performance, but the skeptics believed their doubts were justified.

Two months later, Holmes stopped Horace "Big City" Robinson on the Foreman–Young undercard in San Juan, Puerto Rico. Despite the win, Holmes was criticized for failing to floor his less-than-talented opponent.

Then, on September 14, 1977, Holmes appeared on King's *Night of the Heavyweights* TV extravaganza. His opponent was another prospect named Fred "Young Sanford" Houpe.

Houpe, managed by actor/comedian Redd Foxx, had turned pro in 1974 after a sensational amateur career that saw him score a win over Ron Lyle. (Lyle passed away November 23, 2011, of a stomach ailment.) The Oakland, California, native quickly tallied a 12–0 professional slate with eleven knockouts. One victim was former title challenger Jose "King" Roman.

Young Sanford's 13th fight proved unlucky, for he was matched with former amateur foe Duane Bobick. Although both fighters were considered comers, Houpe was giving away experience as well as 19 pounds in weight. At 195 pounds, Houpe was a small fighter by '70s heavyweight standards.

However, the Californian did better than expected in the early rounds, thoroughly out-boxing Bobick. In the middle rounds, he lost momentum due to a swollen left eye and a body attack by Bobick. At the end, Houpe finished strong but still lost a close decision.

Because of his showing against Bobick and the publicity the Redd Foxx connection gave him, Houpe was Larry Holmes's first "name" opponent. And Holmes had plenty to prove as he stared coldly across the ring at Young Sanford. He wanted to do what old amateur rival Bobick had failed to accomplish. He wanted to knock Houpe out.

The 211-pound Holmes seemed to dwarf Houpe, who came in at 199. But it was skill, not weight, that enabled Larry to dominate his opponent. To his credit, Houpe climbed off the canvas in the third round, only to soak up a terrible beating as the fight went on. Finally, in the seventh, Young Sanford was belatedly rescued by the referee.

Houpe was never again a factor among the heavyweights after that debacle. Unfortunately, he was born too soon for the cruiserweight division, which wasn't established until 1980.

Holmes had now regained some of the ground he had lost after his poor showing against Prater. Next on his hit list was a tough white fighter named Dale "Ibar" Arrington. Like Rodney Bobick, Arrington's most notable attributes were strength and an uncanny ability to absorb punishment. Otherwise, as one of his opponents, Randy Neumann, said, "The guy can't fight." Nonetheless, Arrington stopped Neumann on a cut the latter claimed had been inflicted by an elbow to the eyebrow.

At 23, Ibar was considered a prospect who had gone about as far as he could, which was fringe contender. He was expected to extend Holmes a few rounds without posing much of a problem. And he performed as expected, surviving a one-sided battering until the fight was stopped in the tenth round.

Although the win didn't raise Larry's fistic stock, he did become the first man ever to stop the durable Arrington. Still, Holmes was regarded by many as an unproven commodity.

Al Bernstein, who became the regular boxing commentator for the ESPN sports network, was a young journalist in 1977. In a story on the Holmes–Arrington fight published in *Boxing Illustrated*, Bernstein criticized the quality of Larry's recent opposition. "At the age of 28," Bernstein wrote, "Holmes is at the crossroads. He doesn't need anybody else to 'beat up,' he needs some top notch competition to tell the boxing world, and Larry himself, whether his high ranking is justified."

The criticism concerning his sub-par opposition had become a thorn in Larry's side: "What can I do? Nobody will fight me. None of the contenders will have anything to do with me. All I can do is stay active and hope for my big chance."[8]

With the Shavers fight, Holmes was finally ready to prove himself once and for all. *Boxing Illustrated* editor Reg Noble accurately called the Shavers showdown Holmes's "acid test." This was Larry's chance to back up what he'd been saying for years: that he was "the baddest fighter alive."

His critics took the opposite view, saying that Holmes hadn't fought anyone, didn't have a knockout punch, and lacked heart. If any of that was true, Shavers's explosive fists would expose Larry's deficiencies quickly enough.

And Holmes's doubters were not confined to the media. "Even one of my own uncles bet $1,000 on Shavers," Holmes told Pat Putnam in 1978. "And later I learned that Don King had already given Shavers $25,000 front money for his next fight after he beat me."[9]

Holmes and Shavers were hardly strangers. As they were both members of King's stable, they had done a great deal of sparring together. In fact, they were good friends outside the ring. Still, they put their careers first and when the fight was proposed, both readily accepted.

Although Shavers's dangerous punch was always a factor, Holmes was the one who rose to the occasion. As the fight went the distance, Larry pitched a virtual shutout, winning all twelve rounds on two judges' scorecards and eleven on the third. The fight was Holmes's "coming-out" party as he displayed fast hands, quick feet, good defense, and the jab that was soon to become famous. On the few occasions that Shavers was able to land a solid blow, Holmes never wavered. In the last round, he came close to stopping Shavers, but Earnie exhibited tremendous courage by remaining on his feet.

Holmes exhibited all the heart and skill anyone could hope for, and a bit more as well. In the second round of the fight, the back seam in his trunks split, and by the fourth he was on the verge of "mooning" a national television audience. His trunks were changed in his corner between the fourth and fifth frames.

The lopsided victory over Shavers certified his status as the best of the '70s newcomers, Spinks's win over Ali notwithstanding. Next loomed a chance at Norton's WBC crown.

The Changing of the Guard

Although they would be fighting for a title still considered bogus by at least 50 percent of boxing fans and media, Norton–Holmes was still an important event for all parties concerned. For Norton, a decisive win over Holmes was a must. As far as he was concerned, anything less would diminish not only his credibility, but also that of Jose Sulaiman.

Sulaiman had taken a major gamble in unilaterally proclaiming Norton as WBC champion. If the Norton–Holmes fight turned out to be a dud, the WBC would end up with egg on its face.

Don King also had a great deal riding on Norton–Holmes. The two fighters represented his only connection to the heavyweight title. Consequently, his influence would only be as strong as the credibility of the WBA's title, and that credibility hinged on the quality of Norton's first defense.

Whether it was for a legitimate title or not, Norton–Holmes still stirred a great deal of interest. Norton's credentials were already established. Now Holmes had finally shaken the "unproven" label and some observers regarded him as the fighter who would carry the division into the 1980s.

Even Norton, who was hardly a Holmes fan, was impressed by the latter's easy win over Shavers. He realized that he had underestimated his nemesis from Easton.

The pre-fight odds, a slim 13 to 10 in favor of Norton, accurately indicated how widely split the experts were over the outcome. Norton's advantages were experience, punching power, and determination; Holmes's were youth, speed, and boxing skill.

Along with the fight's obvious importance to the future of the division, another intriguing aspect surfaced. It seemed the fighters would be carrying some personal animosities into the ring.

Holmes confessed to a distaste for Norton that went "way back." Part of it was that Holmes felt Norton, along with most of the other top heavyweights, had ducked him while he was on the way up.

However, his specific grudge against Norton apparently dated back to the Ali–Frazier III fight in Manila. Holmes was there to do battle with Rodney Bobick on the undercard; Norton was there to do TV commentary on the main event.

As usual, Norton attracted a great deal of attention from members of the opposite sex. Holmes apparently made a "God's gift to women" remark to Norton. Ken reportedly retorted: "It wasn't my fault the ladies weren't hanging around Holmes, it wasn't be kind to animals week."

From that moment on, Holmes's feelings for Norton paralleled the way Joe Frazier regarded Muhammad Ali: at best, resentment; at worst, pure hatred. And Norton didn't much care for Holmes, either. Neither man made any attempt to mask his animosity as they prepared for their confrontation, which was scheduled for June 9 in Las Vegas.

Holmes declared: "I don't like the man. He's said some bad things about me, and I intend to make him pay for them. He's going to get a whupping he'll never forget."[10]

Norton's sentiments towards Holmes were no warmer. "I don't just want to beat Holmes, I want to hurt him."[11]

Holmes continually attacked Norton's "pretty boy" image. He constantly referred to him as "that movie star," and promised to rearrange Norton's features on fight night. Holmes vowed to throw 80 to 90 pinches a round and planned to aim 70 of them at Norton's handsome face.

On June 6, Norton and Holmes almost started their fight ahead of schedule. They shared the same training facilities at Caesars Palace, to be used, of course, at different times. On the 6th, those times inadvertently overlapped and the fighters found themselves in the same room at the same time.

Holmes initiated a verbal attack. When Norton moved closer to him, Larry pushed the WBC champ back several feet. Ken flew into a rage and the fighters had to be physically restrained from settling their differences street-style.

Norton's show of anger seemed out of character. In the past, Ken had projected a gentlemanly, almost docile demeanor. But his manager, Bob Biron, was pleased that Norton's blood was boiling. He said Ken had disliked only one other opponent: Jerry Quarry. And that was mild compared to his disdain for Holmes. Biron had always wanted his fighter to exhibit more killer instinct. Against Holmes, Biron anticipated Norton to be a tiger.

Norton's trainer, Bill Slayton, considered Holmes's behavior "childish." Many believed the "Easton Assassin" was attempting to mimic Ali's vintage pre-fight routine. According to Slayton, if that was Larry's goal, he had failed miserably.

Norton accused Holmes of copying Ali's ring style as well as his personality. "Why don't you do something original?" Norton asked. Although Holmes admired Ali, he resented the charge of ring plagiarism, especially coming from Norton. He went on a personal campaign, telling everyone who would listen that he and Ali were two different fighters.

As for the charge that he had appropriated Ali's pre-fight banter, Holmes insisted that he "was always loud and very arrogant" before he'd ever met "The Greatest." Still, Holmes gave Norton an Ali-like nickname: "The Mummy." Ken claimed that Ali had originally dubbed him that back in 1975. Norton referred to Holmes simply as "Pinhead."

Because the tension between the fighters was so high, they were weighed in separately. Norton was a heavy 220, but he maintained his sculpted physique. Holmes scaled a light 209.

Both men predicted a knockout victory, which was to be expected considering how they felt about each other. However, some believed a knockout was the only way Norton could win because Don King was rumored to have both promotional and managerial connections with Holmes. If that rumor was true, a Holmes win would be of more benefit to King than would a Norton triumph. When asked about that possibility, Norton said that King had always been fair with him, but admitted to being concerned.

Regardless of the rumors, Norton was convinced that his style, which had proven so detrimental to Ali, would spell disaster for a fighter he considered nothing more than a watered-down version of the original. And for a career-high purse of $2.3 million, he was willing to risk any back-room shenanigans. Holmes, by the way, would be getting $500,000, which was his own career high at that point.

On fight night, Holmes was the first to enter the steamy ring at Caesars Palace. When Norton made his entrance and the fighters met at center ring to receive their instructions,

Holmes attempted a Liston-like staredown. Norton refused to cooperate, looking away from Holmes as though the challenger were beneath his notice.

In the fight's early stages, Holmes quickly established his jab as the dominating factor. Staying on the outside, the challenger rammed straight left after straight left through Norton's crossed-gloves defense. From time to time, Holmes varied his attack by nailing Ken with right crosses.

Norton seemed to have no answer to the lance Holmes carried in his left hand. He simply followed his opponent around the ring, swinging every now and then, mostly missing. Through his uncharacteristic passivity, Norton virtually gave away the first third of the fight.

By round six, Ken's face was red and puffy from the steady tattoo of jabs he had absorbed. Whatever his fight play may have been, it wasn't working. Holmes was handling him as easily as he had Earnie Shavers.

Sensing that the fight was slipping out of his grasp, Norton began to assert himself in the seventh. He began to throw his own jab, disrupting Holmes's rhythm for the first time. Gaining in confidence, Ken notched his pace upward in the eighth as Holmes appeared to be tiring. Norton drove home several jabs to Holmes's head, and after one exchange the challenger emerged with blood pouring from his mouth.

As the crowd cheered what was becoming a classic, both men inflicted damage in the ninth. Holmes took the tenth by virtue of his piston-like jab, but Norton regained his momentum in the eleventh, trapping the younger man against the ropes and raking him with crushing hooks to the body and head.

Round twelve saw both men on the brink of exhaustion from a combination of the heat and the intense pace they had set. Holmes had slowed considerably, and the nauseating effects of swallowing his own blood were taking their toll. His jab was no longer keeping Norton off him.

Just as it appeared that Ken had gained control of the fight, Holmes swung the momentum back in his favor in the thirteenth. Forcing Norton against the ropes, Larry propped him with his left, then smashed literally dozens of rights into Ken's "God's gift to women" face. Somehow, Norton stayed on his feet, but his eyes were glazed when the bell rescued him.

Then, in the fourteenth, it was Norton's turn to launch an all-out offensive. Ken's intense pressure forced Holmes to abandon his scientific approach and slug it out toe to toe. He ended up on the losing end of the exchanges, so much so that commentator Howard Cosell said Norton was "wiping the floor" with his opponent.

Then came round fifteen. Drained and battered, both men were operating on pride alone. Norton was in a familiar position. In his fights against Ali and Jimmy Young, the outcome hinged on the final round. And he intended to make these three minutes the best three he'd ever fought. His only problem was, so did Holmes.

The crowd stood on its feet and howled in a frenzy as the two warriors teed off on each other. Norton struck first, wobbling Holmes with a short right to the head. Larry, whose white trunks were stained with his own blood, retreated behind his reliable jab.

Norton went after him, and after a fierce exchange Holmes once again backed up. Larry's mouthpiece dropped to the canvas courtesy of a Norton uppercut. Just when it appeared Holmes was about to succumb to Norton's attack, he stormed back with a two-fisted attack of his own. When the bell ended the fight, Holmes was doing the pitching and Norton's face was doing the catching. A hoarse Cosell said, "I've never seen a guy put on a gutsier stand at the end of a fight than did Larry Holmes."[12]

One of the most vicious battles in heavyweight history was over. The crowd gave both fighters a well-deserved standing ovation.

It was a great fight, and a close one. Had Holmes's early round advantage held up over 15 rounds? Or did Norton's late rounds rally carry him to victory? Opinions varied, but the only ones that mattered were those of the three judges. And the crucial round was the fifteenth.

Two judges gave Holmes that round, and that was the margin of victory in a split decision. Harold Buck and Joe Swessel favored Holmes by a paper-thin margin of 143–142. Lou Talbot's card also tallied to 143–142, but he voted for Norton.

An ecstatic Holmes took the WBC championship belt and dove with it into the Caesars Palace swimming pool. Two hours passed before he was ready to meet the press as new champion. When he did, he expressed plenty of respect for Norton, saying Ken was stronger and more determined than he had anticipated.

And the new champion expressed no interest in granting Norton an immediate rematch, as Spinks had Ali.

Norton wasn't loath to talk about the fight, even though he loss meant that he was the only heavyweight champion who never won a title bout. As Arthur Harris wrote in the March 1980 issue of *Boxing Digest*, "You might say he [Norton] was the Gerald Ford of heavyweight champions." Harris was referring to America's unelected president.

Naturally, Ken thought he'd won this one. But he conceded the fight was close enough that the judges could have picked Holmes. Consequently, he wasn't as distraught as with the Ali fight in 1976.

Ironically, Norton's losing effort was probably the most inspired performance of his career. The desire to legitimize his half of the crown drove him to a level he had never achieved before, not even against Ali.

At the time, the common belief was that an aging Norton had valiantly succumbed to a younger fighter who happened to have been in the right place at the right time. However, Holmes subsequently proved to be one of the greatest heavyweights of all time. And it was the Norton fight that provided the first glimpse of that greatness, as Holmes had to battle back from the brink of defeat to win by the narrowest possible margin.

Holmes wasn't the only winner that night. The public's overwhelming response to the fight bestowed instant credibility to the WBC championship. Dave Anderson called Norton–Holmes "the best fight since Manila," and he wasn't the only observer to make that comparison. Holmes–Norton was voted fight of the year by *The Ring*.

Jose Sulaiman said Holmes and Norton were "definitely the best heavyweights in the world." He was probably right. At any rate, his gamble in stripping Spinks had paid off handsomely.

The full impact of the fight encompassed a far greater scope than the WBC/WBA turf war, however. For the entire decade of the '70s, the division's attraction had been based on the exploits of Ali, Joe Frazier, and George Foreman, and, to a lesser extent, Norton. Now Frazier and Foreman had retired, Norton had lost his brief hold on the WBC title, and Ali's fistic finale appeared imminent.

Most fans believed that Ali's departure would signal an end to interest in the heavyweight division, as well as boxing as a whole. However, Holmes–Norton attracted a viewing audience of 40 million, proof that the heavyweights could still provide ring thrills even in Ali's absence.

But Ali wasn't gone yet. The busy year of 1978 had one more major fight to offer: the

Spinks–Ali rematch. Could Ali regain his title, and his reputation, from the St. Louis upstart? That was the question on boxing fans' minds after the smoke from Norton–Holmes had cleared.

Ali Again, Naturally

Going into his September 15 superfight against Ali in New Orleans, Leon Spinks was the unhappiest heavyweight champion since Sonny Liston. Instead of the glory that usually accompanies a title win, Spinks had experienced nothing but upheaval in both his professional and personal lives.

Professionally, he was the Rodney Dangerfield of the ring: he received "no respect" for accomplishing what other fighters had failed to do. As an underdog who toppled a legend, he was viewed more as a fluke than a phenomenon. After all, he had barely outpointed a lethargic, 36-year-old champion who hadn't taken him seriously. By contrast, the last heavy underdog to win the title, George Foreman, had bounced Joe Frazier all over the canvas in a one-sided win.

Hordes of critics attributed Spinks's victory more to Ali's lack of interest than to any extraordinary abilities on Leon's part. Few believed Spinks could defeat a well-conditioned ex-champ who was determined to regain his title. Early odds favored Ali at a 12–5 margin.

In the meantime, Leon's legitimacy as champion took a constant beating in the media. One boxing magazine went so far as to headline a cover story with the question: "Is There Anyone Who Cannot Beat Leon Spinks?"[13] The magazine's conclusion was that there weren't too many top contenders who couldn't knock Leon off his half of the heavyweight throne. Ironically, one of the ones thought to have no chance against Spinks was Larry Holmes.

Of course, that was before the epic Holmes–Norton battle. Even before that, most observers thought Norton would destroy Spinks. Because of the wide gap between Norton's and Spinks's accomplishments and credentials, Ken's otherwise questionable claim to the title received greater credibility. And when Holmes shut out Shavers and put on a performance for the ages against Norton, his own claim to championship glory outstripped Spinks's.

Leon admitted that it irked him to have his accomplishment belittled and scoffed at. However, given his troubles outside the ring, it was obvious something was messing his head up. In an endless succession of headlines, Leon was arrested for drunk driving and driving without a license, sued by old landlords, hit with paternity suits, and tried on drug charges. Within a few months of winning the title, Leon Spinks had become a national joke, courtesy of a combination of his own behavior and a media feeding frenzy.

Indeed, a large sector of the press corps appeared to be targeting Spinks for some major muckraking. And Leon, a confused and misguided individual whose philosophy of life was "I party, therefore I am," presented a target too vulnerable to be overlooked.

In time, Spinks developed a predictable resentment for the army of reporters that dogged his heels. Beyond the headlines, it was easy to feel sorry for Leon Spinks. Boxing politics had cut his championship domain in half, and instead of acclaim, all he seemed to be getting was ridicule and character assassination. He had always wanted to "be somebody," but not this way.

With his mind in disarray and his life in turmoil, the WBA champion tried to prepare himself to defend a title that had turned into a nightmare. Promoter Bob Arum commented later that "he [Spinks] wasn't mentally ready at the time to assume the responsibilities of the championship.... Leon was so confused, so screwed up."[14]

But Leon wasn't the only one facing difficulties in getting ready for the rematch. The 36-year-old Ali, who had been fighting since he was 12 years old, had grown weary of the demands hard training placed on his mind and body. And the prospect of another fight against Spinks didn't in itself turn him on, even though it meant regaining the title and his reputation. Still, Ali agreed with the general consensus that if he trained properly, he would easily defeat a crude novice like Spinks. And that consensus may have had the wrong effect on Ali's contrary ego. Not only did he enjoy winning, he enjoyed proving the experts wrong as well.

In his earlier effort to win the title from George Foreman, Ali had thrown himself wholeheartedly into training. He was inspired not only by the desire to win, but also by the wish to destroy the invincible-appearing Foreman in front of all the critics who had predicted his downfall.

He'd gone into the Foreman fight as a 4–1 underdog, a strong motivating factor. But the bettors had made him the favorite in the Spinks rematch, and that made it difficult for him to push himself.

An additional problem was Ali's age. At 36, his body simply did not respond as quickly or favorably to the rigors of training. Still, he slogged on. This time, his motivation had to come from within. He would be fighting history, not Spinks. He wouldn't be fighting to turn the experts' opinions upside down. This time, he was fighting for Muhammad Ali.

With one last mountain to climb, Ali took his first step on his comeback by staging a series of exhibition bouts in the Soviet Union. On an ambassadorial level, the tour was a rousing success. Ali was known and loved by everyone from the comrade on the street all the way up to President Leonid Brezhnev. One of the highlights of the trip was a 35-minute meeting between Ali and Brezhnev, a moment the former champion called "the biggest honor of my life."

So enthralled were the Soviets by Ali's persona that the Kremlin authorized the broadcast of Ali–Spinks II on Soviet television. In a country that participated enthusiastically in amateur boxing but disdained the professional game, that decision was unprecedented.

From a boxing standpoint, however, Ali's Soviet visit exposed some signs that seemed dangerous. He looked overweight and sloppy in his exhibitions against a group of Russian amateurs, and his showing caused some to wonder if Ali–Spinks II might be only a replay of the first fight. Apparently, the task of proper preparation for September 15 would prove an uphill battle.

Despite both fighters' problems, Ali–Spinks II was understandably an easier sell than their first meeting. The fight would be of historical significance for many reasons. First, Ali had the opportunity to become the first three-time heavyweight champion, even though he was fighting to regain only a partial title. Second, it was widely believed that win, lose or draw, this would be Ali's final ring appearance. Third, it would provide Spinks a chance to prove that he really was "The Latest," not "The Luckiest." Television networks engaged in a bidding war for the fight. ABC, which wouldn't touch Ali–Spinks I, emerged victorious with a bid of $5,150,000. The network's investment paid off: the Ali–Spinks rematch attracted a whopping 46.7 percent in the Nielsen ratings, the highest for any sporting event at that time.

Arrangements for the rematch had begun as early as March. Incredibly, early negotiations proposed the recently created South African "homeland" of Bophuthatswana as a site. South Africa had granted Bophuthatswana "independence" in 1977, but most of the world regarded that independence as a sham designed to maintain the system of apartheid. South Africa was the only nation that recognized the phony nation it had created.

To add insult to injury, one of the proposed financiers of the bout would be a South African company called Southern Sun Hotels Corporation. The fight would have been held in Sun City, a Las Vegas–style enclave in the heart of the poverty-stricken "homeland."

The very thought of Ali and Spinks fighting in the land of apartheid was anathema to people from one end of the planet to the other. The Reverend Jesse Jackson, who had recently become a national African American leader, said the Bophuthatswana location would only condone the actions of a racist regime.

In an attempt at damage control, promoter Bob Arum met with representatives of both the Organization of African Unity and the NAACP to seek a compromise. Arum then announced that he was shifting the site from Bophuthatswana to Mauritius, an island nation in the Indian Ocean that was the home of the extinct dodo bird. However, once news got out that Southern Sun Hotels would still have a piece of the action, pressure from civil rights and anti-apartheid activists forced Arum to withdraw from Mauritius as well.

With his overseas prospects as dead as the dodo, Arum ended up looking stateside for a venue. He settled on the 85,000-seat Superdome in New Orleans. His co-promoters would be Louisiana Sports, Inc., and the live gate was estimated at $5 million.

Working on the theory that nothing exceeds like excess, Arum added three other title fights to the card, billing it as the "Carnival of Champions." It would be the first time in history that four championship bouts would occur in the same arena. New Orleans, famous for its party atmosphere, now became caught up in fight mania.

As fight day approached, Ali dispelled doubts concerning his condition by working his way to fighting trim at 221 pounds. Spinks, at 201, also appeared to be in excellent shape. The few extra pounds sat well on his frame.

Veteran cornerman George Benton, who had helped Sam Solomon train Leon in February, returned to the Spinks camp a few weeks before the rematch. Benton offered some canny insights concerning the upcoming "Battle of New Orleans."

He believed Spinks would have to control the fight, belying the old adage that the challenger had to carry the momentum in order to win. The difference was Ali's immense popularity. For that reason, Benton felt that even though Spinks was champion, he'd have to "fight like he's the challenger."

As far as Benton was concerned, Spinks possessed all the physical and psychological tools he needed to repeat his victory over Ali. Any mental barriers such as awe of Ali's status should have been broken down once and for all in February. In their first fight, the question as to whether Leon could sustain his aggression for 15 rounds was a major issue; now it was not.

Regarding physical conditioning, Benton gave that edge to Spinks as well. Although he was well aware that Ali had whipped himself into excellent shape, George pointed out that it was "36-year-old shape," which was no match for the condition of which a 25-year-old like Spinks was capable of achieving.

Benton's bottom line was that Leon had the upper hand despite the odds in Ali's favor. He also said he wouldn't be surprised if Spinks won by knockout.

For his part, Spinks tried to avoid the appearance of overconfidence. He expected a stronger performance from Ali in the rematch. He knew that Ali would be in top form and desperately wanted to win the title for a third time.

Ali did indeed want it "bad," despite his earlier motivation problems. It was hardly a secret that this was probably his final fight. He constantly referred to it as "the last dance."

Many doubted the authenticity of his hints at retirement, and who could blame them? They'd heard the same words too many times before. In the minds of most fans, Ali would fight on if he regained the title. Spinks thought Ali would continue even if his challenge was turned back. And Ali added fuel to the fire by declaring that "when" he won, he would "stay around six months or so. Give the people a chance to see me as champion."

In striking contrast to the first fight, Ali's mouth was running in high gear. He spoke of his superiority over Spinks, predicting that he would win easily. He made fun of Leon's dental distinctions, as well as his brushes with the law. "If he stays out of jail, I'll whip his tail," Ali taunted.

Leon stayed out of jail, and the fighters finally stepped into the ring for their much-anticipated rematch. Spinks would be paid $3.7 million, while Ali had to be satisfied with a mere $3,250,000.

Viewed in strictly objective terms, the fight wasn't worth that much. It was Ali's show from the opening bell. Of course, the fighter in the ring wasn't vintage Ali. But he was still good enough to dominate the action throughout the contest. All he had to do was utilize the advantages in size and experience he had squandered in February.

As well, Spinks fought in a disoriented, unfocused manner. To his credit, he never stopped trying. But he simply could not cope with a well-conditioned Ali, even one in "36-year-old" shape.

Leon's corner proved more hindrance than help this time. There were too many people telling him too many things at once. At the end of every round, Spinks was met by a babble of voices that drowned out what he really needed to hear: the advice of trainers Benton and Solomon.

In fact, Benton became so disgusted he left after the fifth round. With all the disarray in Leon's corner, the commissioner jumped into the ring at one point and threatened to fine them. There were so many people crowding around in Spinks's corner that Benton simply walked away.

Chaos in the corner was nothing new to Spinks. During the Ledoux fight, everyone was shouting at him. His younger brother, Michael, ran around the ring apron yelling encouragement while others in his entourage screamed instructions from the corner and ringside. As a bemused Ledoux put it, "The only one not advising Leon was Ann Landers."

Things didn't get any better in the Superdome. As Spinks was getting ready in his dressing room, it was discovered that someone had forgotten to bring an very important piece of equipment: a protective cup. After a mad scramble, Mike Rossman, who had won the light heavyweight title from Victor Galindez earlier in the evening, saved the day by lending Leon his own family jewels protector.

That fiasco was a portent of things to come. Round after round went by with Spinks swinging and missing while Ali hit and held. The only stanza Leon won on all three scorecards was the fifth, and that was only because Referee Lucien Joubert took the round away from Ali for holding Spinks behind the head.

Spinks had a few fleeting moments of success. For the most part, though, the fight was little more than a 15-round boxing lesson administered by the master.

At the end, the crowd cheered anyway, not because they had seen a great fight, but because they had witnessed history in the making. The decision was a mere formality, with Ali winning by a landslide. In the end, Spinks appeared more relieved than disappointed.

When he went to congratulate Ali on his victory, Muhammad's cornermen rudely shoved him out of camera range.

The aftermath of Ali's third coronation provided more infighting than the bout in the ring, with the Louisiana promoters accusing each other of skimming revenues. Eventually, Jake Di Maggio and Philip Ciaccio of Louisiana Sports, Inc. filed suit against co-promoters Sherman Copelin, Don Hubbard, and Butch Lewis. The latter three were black, and when Ali caught wind of the lawsuit, he accused Ciaccio and Di Maggio of racism. The two promoters immediately sued Ali for defamation of character. However, they promised to drop the suit provided Ali issued a public apology for referring to them as "two white dagoes."[15]

At first, Ali refused. "Me, Muhammad Ali, go down there and apologize? Never! Apologize for what? For telling the truth?"[16] Later, he admitted that he'd been fed misleading information on the events leading up to Di Maggio and Ciaccio's initial legal action against the black promoters. Ali then apologized for the accusation of racism and for the "dago" slur. "I should not have called them a name," Ali said. "Particularly a name which offends a whole nationality of people."[17]

In the meantime, Copelin and Hubbard filed their own suits against Ciaccio and Di Maggio. It was hardly an auspicious beginning for Ali's third reign as champion.

The post-fight controversies didn't end there, however. Bob Arum, openly disgusted with Spinks's showing, slammed the ex-champion in the press, stating that Leon was "not sober one night" when he was in New Orleans before the fight.[18]

Arum also expressed doubt that Spinks would ever fight again. Leon's attorneys announced that the promoter's remarks were slanderous and unfounded, and threatened to slap the promoter with a defamation suit. They also declared Spinks's promotional contract with Arum, which still had five fights to go, "null and void."

Spinks then began negotiations with Don King, and the two reached a verbal agreement. When Arum caught wind of the arrangement, he threatened to sue Spinks and King the moment they signed any contract. Arum and Spinks finally resolved their differences. Leon's stock had fallen considerably, but he was still a marketable commodity and would remain a pawn in the King–Arum promotional wars for several years to come.

As for Ali, the once and future champion reiterated his intention of enjoying the title before making any further decisions regarding his boxing career. No one pressured one way or another. The two Spinks fights had clearly indicated that the Ali era had run its course. Still, sentiment dictated that Ali be allowed to end it in whatever way he chose.

The thought of boxing without Ali was almost unimaginable. However, if he had to go, most fans wanted him to go out on top. Only the diehard "Clay"-haters would relish Ali's hanging on until he was seriously injured.

As 1978 ended, there were two champions, Ali and Larry Holmes. For 1979, two questions loomed. First, would Ali finally retire for good? Second, would Holmes be Ali's true successor?

Twelve

1979 and Beyond

Farewell to Ali

Compared to the tumult and turnover of 1978, 1979 was something of an anticlimax, with no bona fide superfights and little memorable action. The decade that had begun like a sizzling five-punch combination to the jaw appeared to be ending like a 15th-round clinch between a pair of bone-tired pugs.

Still, the final year of the '70s laid the foundation for a new era in the division. The names and faces that had dominated heavyweight headlines for most of the decade — Frazier, Foreman, Norton, Shavers, Quarry, Lyle — were gone or fading, and the ranks of the top ten were opening to a new crop of hopefuls. Leon Spinks was still a hot name in the division, and the other young lions beginning to roar included white hope Gerry Cooney and former amateur standouts John Tate and Michael Dokes. Whether or not these newcomers could match the feats of the contenders they replaced remained to be seen.

Yet as 1979 began, the oldest, most familiar face in boxing still shone brightly at the helm of the sport's flagship division. Muhammad Ali was still heavyweight champion of the world, in the eyes of the World Boxing Association, as well as those who believed the WBC had been wrong in stripping Spinks of title recognition for fighting Ali instead of Ken Norton in his first defense.

Having regained at least part of his title from Spinks, Ali kept the sporting world guessing concerning his next move. He had several options at hand, and plenty of time to make his final decision.

Would he retire as champion? Would he attempt to unify the title in a final superfight against World Boxing Council king Larry Holmes? Or would he attempt one or more easy defenses to round out his third title reign, even though at age 37 no defense would be easy? Spinks had taught him that lesson, if nothing else.

As speculation about his future continued, Ali embarked on a worldwide exhibition tour, a valedictory in which he would be seen in the ring for perhaps the last time. Unfortunately, he often appeared in woefully flabby condition. In India, he was actually jeered by spectators who were disappointed by his sloppy condition.

It was as though Ali was content to act as champion in name only, simply marking time until the WBA's title defense deadline expired. This wasn't the way most fans expected Ali's third reign to finish.

Finally, on June 26, 1979, Muhammad ended the suspense and officially resigned from his position as WBA champion. It was the fourth time in his career that Ali and the WBA crown had parted company, and the first occasion on which that event occurred voluntarily. His record-setting third acquisition of the title appeared a fitting finale to a career that had lasted nearly 20 years. Indeed, many of Ali's fans had literally grown up with him. Now he was gone.

When a dominant champion like Ali retires, boxing historians dust off their record books and begin to argue over the fighter's place in the history of the sport. Before Ali, four heavyweights stood out as truly great champions in terms of ability, accomplishments, and significance. Those four were Jack Johnson, Jack Dempsey, Joe Louis, and Rocky Marciano. In debates over who the greatest champion of all time might be, those four names were mentioned time and again. How, then, did Ali's achievements measure up to those of his predecessors?

His record speaks for itself. His three reigns added up to eight years, comparing favorably to Louis's record 12, Johnson's eight, Dempsey's seven, and Marciano's four. In addition, Ali's 19 title defenses were second only to Louis's 25, and far overshadowed the 8 registered by Johnson and the six and five by Marciano and Dempsey.

In knockout percentage, Ali's .627 lagged well behind Marciano's .878 and Louis's .742, but his inside-the-distance output was on a par with Dempsey's .620. Johnson, at .374, had one of the lowest kayo ratios in championship history.

Ali's total of 59 bouts at the time of his 1979 retirement placed him above only Marciano's 49. Johnson had 107 recorded bouts, Dempsey 79 and Louis 66.

Numbers, however, don't tell the full story of a champion's significance. Primo Carnera, for example, scored more knockouts than any other heavyweight champion. But no one would argue that the Italian giant should be mentioned in the same breath with Louis and Dempsey, or even Floyd Patterson.

Other, less tangible factors define greatness. Johnson's defensive artistry was so superlative that he literally toyed with most of his opponents. Dempsey's sheer ferocity in the ring kept the fans of his era on the edge of their seats. Louis's combination of punching power and boxing skill could destroy anyone foolish enough to step into the ring with him. And Marciano's grit and determination carried him to the only undefeated record among the heavyweight champions.

Again, Ali measures up well. During his first reign, he dazzled his opponents with unparalleled speed of hand and foot. When those attributes diminished during his second championship tenure, he relied on courage, guile, and durability to carry him to victory. In effect, he dominated two full generations of heavyweights in two entirely different ways.

When it comes to significance outside the ring, each legendary champion carved out a unique reputation. Johnson was an iconoclast who rebelled against the racial restrictions of his time. Dempsey symbolized the devil-may-care spirit of the Roaring Twenties. Louis was the first black hero to be embraced by a majority of the white population. And Marciano reflected the can-do dynamism of post–World War II America.

But Ali may have outdone all the other champions by personifying the most tumultuous time period of the 20th century: the 1960s and early '70s.

As Arthur Daley wrote in his October 25, 1970, column in the *New York Times* concerning "the Greatest's" significance: "Virtually no one feels neutral about Cassius. As a matter of fact, few ever did, even in the old days when his vainglorious boasting irritated a lot of people who wanted to see him get his block knocked off. Now they feel the same for other reasons. For others he became an anti-war or pro-black symbol, or both, unjustly persecuted by Whitey's establishment."

By any imaginable criteria, then, Ali definitely deserved to take his place next to the great champions who preceded him. His shoes would be difficult, if not impossible, to fill. But that didn't stop other fighters from making the attempt.

With the WBA title vacated, only one heavyweight champion remained in the post-Ali era: Larry Holmes. Of course, Holmes still held only the WBC version of the title, and the WBA wasn't about to hand him its recognition on a silver platter. Yet Holmes believed that Ali, not the WBA, stood between him and universal acclaim. Unfortunately, Larry was unable to accept the reality that he could never match or even come close to Ali's level of popularity, no matter what he accomplished in and out of the ring.

Holmes had plenty of company in the misery of trying to succeed a popular champion. Gene Tunney and Ezzard Charles, both excellent fighters in their own right, were always overshadowed by their immediate predecessors, Jack Dempsey and Joe Louis.

But Holmes's problem was more than historical. Quite simply, Larry lacked Ali's natural charm and charisma, attributes that were unique to the "Louisville Lip." Other fighters had come to their own personal terms with that truism. Before his ill-fated defense against Ali in 1974, George Foreman acknowledged that even were he to conquer his adversary, he could never match Muhammad's level of celebrity.

"I can beat him and knock him out in the first or second round, but that doesn't mean that people are going to follow me with the same enthusiasm as they did him," Foreman said. "It's just something God gave him to have."[1]

Foreman may have resigned himself to the inevitable, but Holmes always felt shortchanged. Still, Larry admired and respected his friend and former employer and wished him well in his retirement.

A truly larger-than-life figure, Ali was and is many things to many people. For boxing fans, he was the man who rescued the "sweet science" from the brink of a plummet into a sea of mediocrity and raised it to a new plateau of worldwide popularity.

Ali once boasted that he was bigger than the Kentucky Derby, World Series and Indy 500. Not exactly the most humble of self-assessments, but accurate nonetheless. People who had never heard of the New York Yankees or the Dallas Cowboys readily recognized the name and face of Muhammad Ali.

Ring magazine editor Bert Randolph Sugar wrote in the November 1979 issue what Ali's departure would mean to the sport: "Ali so dominated the boxing scene and the boxing fan's fancy that all a magazine had to do for a quick sale was put his picture on the cover. Forget that more than occasionally no story went with the cover. Just Ali was enough."

Even Ali's sharpest critics couldn't deny his positive influence on the sport. Joe Louis, who never supported Ali's antiwar stance, said in 1974 that Ali had done more for boxing than any man in history. That was high praise indeed, coming from a man who was probably the most beloved heavyweight champion in history. It also indicated the tremendous distance Ali had traveled since his early days as champion.

Back then, in 1964 and 1965, Ali was hardly considered boxing's savior. The stench surrounding his two fights with Sonny Liston actually threatened to kill the sport. And when he converted to the Nation of Islam and refused to be drafted into the U.S. Army, Ali became a virtual pariah in his homeland.

During the 1970s, however, attitudes toward Ali underwent a gradual but profound change. His opposition to the Vietnam War was forgiven, if not forgotten. The injustice represented by his forced exile from boxing came to be widely recognized. As well, as the Nation of Islam toned down its anti-white rhetoric, Ali's religion became less controversial.

Like Louis, Ali eventually transcended his profession. He made many headlines on issues beyond boxing, and he became a symbol of hope and strength for millions of people who had never seen him fight. Ali's concern for the plight of blacks in the United States and around the world and his countless acts of personal and financial generosity became the building blocks of legend.

Examples of his beneficence abound. He was instrumental in the mid-1970s campaign to free ex-middleweight Rubin "Hurricane" Carter from imprisonment on a trumped-up murder charge, and he talked a young black man out of committing suicide. His money always "floated like a butterfly" out of his hands and into the pockets of anyone with a story to tell.

Ali wasn't just part of an era; he literally embodied it. In the February 1, 1974, issue of the *New York Times*, Tom Wicks wrote an article that compared the cultural influences of Ali and singer Bob Dylan.

According to Wicks, "Ali, whatever they say, is as sharp a symbol as Dylan of a time in American life when young men and women rebelled passionately against the world they saw, and made what Eugene McCarthy called 'deep, even dangerous commitments' to a new age of openness and generosity in which they thought, 'peace will guide the planets and love will steer the stars.'"

The imagination that Ali sparked enabled many people to shed their shackles and fly along with him, even for a brief moment. Ali stood for so many things outside the ring, and was such an exciting figure inside the squared circle, that his fights, especially the big ones, took on a far grander significance than that of a mere sporting event. Ali-Frazier I is only one example.

As Howard Cosell once said, Ali's name was destined to appear in history books as well as sports pages. When Ali said he was the most famous person on Earth, he was only telling the truth. Thus any other fighter, regardless of his fistic accomplishments, would invariably pale in comparison to "The Greatest."

But Larry Holmes could never accept that truth, even though the public's relatively indifferent reaction to him wasn't anything personal. Anyone who followed Ali's reign would have received a similar reception. As Dave Anderson prophesied before the Holmes–Norton fight in 1978: "In the next heavyweight era, all the fighters and all the fights will be measured against what Ali has accomplished."

Anderson's forecast proved painfully accurate. Still, Ali's fans greeted his retirement with an almost universal sigh of relief. Everyone wanted to see him go out on top and unhurt; no one wanted to endure the sad spectacle of an Ali reduced to the status of ring victim like so many other great champions before him.

Ali had retired so many times in the past that each announcement was greeted with ever-increasing skepticism. This time, though, he appeared to mean what he said when he vowed never to fight again. His true fans fervently hoped he would keep his word.

In the meantime, Ali's confirmation of the end of his ring career solidified Bob Arum's plans to set up a tournament to crown a new champion. No one could fill the void left by Ali's departure, but Arum added spice to the succession process by arranging a four-man elimination tournament that would pit two black Americans, Leon Spinks and John Tate, against a pair of whites from South Africa: Kallie Knoetze and Gerrie Coetzee. It was the Soul Brothers vs. the Boer Brothers.

Controversy over quality appeared to be the name of Arum's new game. He was willing to do almost anything to divert attention from Holmes, who was controlled by arch-rival Don King.

New Generation

In 1979 a top heavyweight made headlines on a political level. However, it was Kallie Knoetze, not Muhammad Ali, who stirred up tension and passion that year.

Knoetze had burst onto the boxing scene with an upset third-round KO of Duane Bobick in 1978. At 6'2" and 220 pounds, the Afrikaner was a brutish slugger with a powerful right hand, a South African version of Luis Firpo. He showed a great deal of promise, and the win over Bobick propelled him into the ratings even though the only other "name" opponent on Knoetze's 17–2 record was Richard Dunn.

However, Knoetze carried some serious political baggage. In the mid- to late 1970s, the blacks of South Africa stepped up their resistance to the apartheid system, and the authorities of that system in turn stepped up their repression. As a member of the South African police force in 1977, Knoetze chased down and shot a black youth at point-blank range. The victim's alleged offense was making a black power salute and throwing a stone.

In the aftermath, the youth's leg had to be amputated and Knoetze was pressured into leaving the force. As well, his right to fight outside South Africa became a major moral and political issue in 1978 and '79.

The debate hit its peak in January of 1979 when Knoetze traveled to Miami Beach to fight a lower-echelon white hope named Bill Sharkey. On a competitive level, the bout was far from noteworthy. Sharkey was a decent fighter, but he lacked the size and skills to cope with Knoetze's punching power. The American folded in the fourth round.

However, the fact that the fight was staged on U.S. soil prompted a political tug-of-war. On one side of the rope were anti-apartheid activists opposed to the idea of a South African fighting in the states. The Reverend Jesse Jackson led a demonstration outside the arena on fight night. He believed that to allow someone like Knoetze to practice his trade in America was tantamount to condoning apartheid.

Those who supported Knoetze's right to fight weren't necessarily in favor of the apartheid system. Their main line of argument was that sports and politics should never mix. Their bottom line was that as long as a man is willing and physically able to step into the ring, he should be permitted to do so regardless of his creed or philosophy.

In an ironic way, the furor resembled the Sonny Liston debate of the early 1960s. Liston, of course, was a convicted felon, while Knoetze was basically a rogue cop. However, the underlying issue—who determines the moral fitness of a fighter to challenge for the championship?—was similar.

Boxing Illustrated editor Reg Noble summed up the Knoetze controversy by calling it a "political football." However, it was also a publicity coup for Bob Arum. As Knoetze's promoter, Arum came under critical fire from a variety of sources. And he loved every minute of it. The more media attention his blacks vs. Afrikaners tournament received, the less Ali's absence would be noted. For a while, Arum's ingenious if unscrupulous ploy actually worked.

The first bout in the WBA elimination series pitted Knoetze against John Tate on June 2 in Mmabatho, the capital of the pseudo-independent South African homeland of Bophuthatswana.

Tate, an Arkansas native who now resided in Knoxville, Tennessee, was a member of the celebrated 1976 U.S. Olympic team that included Leon and Michael Spinks, Sugar Ray Leonard, and Howard Davis Jr. But Big John failed to register success on the level enjoyed by his teammates. In the semifinals of the heavyweight competition, Tate suffered a first-round knockout at the hands of Cuban superman Teofilo Stevenson.

But John didn't depart Montreal empty-handed. Reaching the semifinals guaranteed him a bronze medal. However, bronze doesn't glitter as brightly as gold, and Tate's accomplishment was overlooked when he returned to the U.S.

As well, his quick exit at Stevenson's hands caused skeptical observers to doubt his potential as a pro. But the skeptics ignored Tate's 74–8 record over some of the best amateur talent in the world. Besides, losing to Stevenson was no disgrace. The Cuban, who probably had the most destructive right hand in boxing, amateur or pro, defeated every American opponent he fought and would go on to win an unprecedented third gold medal in the 1980 Olympics.

Tate turned pro on May 7, 1977, with a fifth-round stoppage of Jerry Thompkins on the undercard of a Leon Spinks fight. Although John didn't receive the type of media exposure accorded to Spinks early in his career, he did possess some important attributes his fellow prospect lacked.

One of those attributes was size. At 6'4" and 230 solid pounds, Tate was bigger than most fighters in the heavyweight top ten, never mind Leon Spinks. However, attitude provided an even bigger contrast between the two. Whereas Spinks's training habits were at best lackadaisical, Tate plunged enthusiastically into the demanding routine of conditioning. He desperately wanted to go places in the boxing world and well understood the sacrifices he would have to make to get there.

Over the next two years, Tate trudged patiently up the ladder, measuring his progress one opponent at a time. On May 13, 1978, he stopped rugged trial horse Raul Gorosito in two rounds. Gorosito held a disqualification win over Knoetze, although the South African later avenged that loss via 10-round decision.

After the win over Gorosito, Tate's record stood at 12–0 with 10 knockouts. Nevertheless, some critics believed the towering Olympian would meet his doom at the hands of his next opponent, Bernardo Mercado. When the two big men met at Madison Square Garden on June 22, Mercado, a native of Colombia, had already gained a reputation as one of the division's premier punchers. His 20–0 record placed him in the top ten, and he was being mentioned as a possible challenger for Larry Holmes. Mercado's supporters viewed Tate as nothing more than just another knockout victim.

But it was Mercado who fell in two short rounds to Tate's bludgeoning fists. And boxing fans suddenly began to pay more attention to the man nicknamed "The Fighting Machine."

Tate racked up four more victories in 1978 and moved into 1979 with a high-profile fight against another former Olympian, Duane Bobick. In the wake of his upset loss to Knoetze, Bobick had compiled eight consecutive knockout wins over a motley crew of ham-and-eggers. Now, against Tate, Duane faced yet another crossroads in his career.

The outcome of the Tate–Bobick matchup would answer some outstanding questions about both fighters. Bobick's diehard adherents dismissed the Norton and Knoetze losses as flukes that belied Duane's true potential. However, a loss to the inexperienced Tate would end Bobick's career.

For Tate's part, Bobick retained sufficient credibility to constitute a true test of his progress. If he lost, he could always go back to the drawing board. And if he won it would lift him higher in the ratings.

The fact that Tate did indeed win was not so shocking as the manner in which he achieved the victory. At the opening bell, he came out of his corner like a grizzly bear and mauled Bobick into submission in less than a round. In the aftermath, Tate's fistic stock soared.

As for Bobick, he had once again failed in the spotlight. Duane's manager at the time, Dave Wolf, concluded: "He simply froze. Appears the real problem is that he can't handle extreme pressure situations."[2]

Bobick fought one more time, losing on cuts to George Chaplin before hanging up his gloves for good.

The victory over Bobick earned Tate his slot opposite Knoetze in Arum's tournament. Opinion on the outcome was mixed. Tate appeared to be the better ring technician, but Knoetze's right hand gave him a puncher's chance. As well, many remembered the sight of Tate collapsing under the impact of Teofilo Stevenson's right during the Olympics.

On fight day in Mmabatho, Knoetze lived up to his boorish reputation before the opening bell by snatching an American flag from Tate's hand and hurling it to the canvas. Earlier, during the weigh-in, Knoetze had shoved the American off the scales. If the South African hoped those actions would intimidate Big John, the tactic backfired.

Knoetze took the first round through sheer aggression. In the second, however, the taller, more skillful American took control, working behind a stiff left jab. From that point onward, Tate gained momentum and confidence. By the eighth round, a battered, bleeding Knoetze was reeling defenselessly around the ring.

Finally, at the 2:52 mark of the round, referee Isidore Rodriguez halted the massacre. Tate would advance to the final against the winner of the Leon Spinks–Gerrie Coetzee matchup scheduled for June 24.

As for Knoetze, the drubbing Tate administered exposed him as limited slugger who was easy pickings for anyone with decent boxing skills. His career took a tailspin after the Tate fight, and he retired in 1981 after suffering several more knockout defeats. Though his fistic significance turned out to be minimal, the controversy surrounding Knoetze made him the most talked-about fighter of 1979.

The other South African heavyweight in the tournament, Gerrie Coetzee, tended to be overshadowed by the notoriety of his countryman. However, it was Coetzee, not Knoetze, who held the South African heavyweight title. And in the fighters' lone encounter back in 1976, Gerrie won a narrow 10-round decision over the ex-policeman.

As a fighter and as a man, Coetzee was Knoetze's antithesis. While the latter's notorious past spoke for itself, Coetzee was viewed as a mild-mannered gentleman. If Knoetze was comparable to Sonny Liston, Gerrie Coetzee was South Africa's equivalent to Floyd Patterson.

In the ring, Gerrie was a boxer, not a slugger. At 6'3" and 220 pounds, he fit the mold of the modern, "big" heavyweight. His primary weakness was a fragile right hand. After an operation that fused some of the bones in the hand together, Coetzee became known as the man with the "Bionic Right," a weapon with a mystique similar to that of Ingemar Johansson's "Hammer of Thor."

Unlike Knoetze, whose racial views were several notches below tolerant, Coetzee viewed himself as a potential source of harmony between blacks and whites in South Africa. His idol was Muhammad Ali, and when Coetzee married in 1980, he chose Randy Stephens, a black American who had lost to Gerrie in the ring, as his best man.

As he approached the Spinks fight, which would be held in Monte Carlo, the 23-year-old Coetzee boasted a perfect 21–0 record with 11 knockouts. Other than Knoetze, his "name" victims were one-time prospect Johnny Boudreaux and Ibar Arrington. Because all his fights had taken place in South Africa, Gerrie was something of a mystery man to most boxing fans outside his homeland.

His opponent, Leon Spinks, was far from a mystery. The Coetzee encounter would be Leon's first ring encounter since he lost his WBA title to Muhammad Ali in New Orleans. That loss robbed "Neon Leon" of a great deal of glitter. Yet he was still the favorite going into the elimination series.

Although his tenure as heavyweight champion was at that time the shortest in history, Spinks was still only 25 years old. Despite his meager pro record of 7-1-1, he had spent thirty rounds in the ring with Muhammad Ali, and that experience was like getting an instant diploma in the finer points of boxing.

Still, there were many questions to be answered about Leon Spinks. Had he learned to refine his crude boxing skills? Had the letdown of losing his title diminished his desire? Could he handle a young, hungry, well-conditioned contender like Coetzee?

Questions aside, most observers agreed that a trained, focused Spinks could remain a force in the division for a long time to come. After their second fight Ali stated: "He's a great fighter. Spinks will go down as one of the greatest of all time."[3]

In the Monte Carlo ring, Spinks started with his customary madman's rush, forcing the larger Coetzee into the ropes. Then the South African landed a solid right to Spinks's head. Leon laughed the blow off. A moment later, he was on the canvas. No longer laughing, the shaken Spinks tried to hold on, but Coetzee floored him two more times for a stunning first-round stoppage.

Coetzee's credentials were now firmly established. In less than a round, he had done what Ali couldn't do in 30. For Spinks, the future promised a long, hard climb back to respectability, let alone another shot at the title.

The stage was now set for an October 20 WBA final that would feature two young, undefeated contenders in Coetzee and John Tate. Some critics decried the contest on the basis of Coetzee's nationality, regardless of his merits as an individual. Others deplored the site Bob Arum chose for the contest: Loftus Versfeld Stadium in Pretoria, the capital of South Africa. The bout would be promoted by Arum in conjunction with Southern Sun Hotels.

As expected, the fight came under extreme fire from anti-apartheid activists throughout the world. Arum's strategy in countering that fire was to straddle both sides of the fence. To white South Africans, Arum was the man who vindicated their athletes' right to compete in the face of an international sports boycott. However, before agreeing to the deal with Southern Sun, he laid down stipulations regarding racial policy, demanding and receiving integrated seating at Loftus Versfeld on the night of the fight.

Then Arum took matters a step further and pushed for the desegregation of all sports facilities in South Africa. In Canada's *MacLean's* magazine, sportswriter Joe Flaherty commented that Arum had "donned the mantle of a contemporary Lincoln ... you begin to get the feeling he wouldn't be happy until he gets shot in a theatre."

Arum's conscience may have been soothed by his gestures, but his opening of the stadium doors to black spectators was viewed by most as small consolation for the positive exposure the fight would bestow on a nation whose political core was based on systemic racism. Besides, the majority of the black population was too impoverished to afford the price of a ticket. The 80,000-plus crowd at the Loftus Versfeld would include only a few black faces.

As an African American, Tate came under almost as much fire as Arum for his participation in the fight. Several American civil rights leaders expressed deep disappointment in Tate's decision to perform in the land of apartheid.

South African blacks were, for the most part, split in their opinion of Tate. Some adopted him as a symbol of hope in the battle against the white oppressor. Others saw him as nothing more than a mercenary who compromised principles for money. Tate's manager, Ace Miller, said money was indeed the primary motivation for fighting Coetzee. Dr. Nthatho

Motlana, a civic leader in the black township of Soweto, dismissed Tate as an "honorary white."

Don King naturally seized the opportunity to lash out at Arum and Tate. "It's a sad commentary on a man [Arum] who's willing to make his money off a country whose policy is the oppression of blacks," King proclaimed. "Now he's taking an illiterate like John Tate who doesn't know one thing from another and sending him into the lion's den. Some people will do anything for money."[4]

"Some people" included Don King, who eventually promoted in South Africa as well.

Staging a heavyweight title fight in South Africa in 1979 was a captivating experience for the entire nation, both black and white. As Brian Ross-Adams wrote in the *Rand Daily Mail* on the day of the match: "To imagine that Ali's successor could be a boy from the plots, from the forgotten backyards of the world, South Africa, is to move into the realm of miracles."[5]

Strategically speaking, Tate–Coetzee was a difficult fight to call. Based on their most recent performances, the contest promised to be a real slam-banger pitting Coetzee, the conqueror of Spinks, against the Tennessee giant who had disposed of Bobick and Knoetze. Both men were big and possessed above-average punching power.

On the other hand, Tate and Coetzee were actually boxing strategists rather than straight-ahead sluggers. Consequently, there was a 50–50 chance their bout would end up creating more yawns than thrills.

Unfortunately for the spectators, the former proved true. The capacity pro–Coetzee crowd would have seen more action at a chess match. Although the hometown boy did well in the early rounds, he did virtually nothing after the sixth stanza. Tate, who was incredibly fit for a 240-pounder, controlled the rest of the action. But he never came close to putting Coetzee away, and the bout lasted the full 15 rounds.

The judges seemed as apathetic as the fighters, scoring a total of 19 even rounds among them. In the end, Tate came away with the decision and the WBA crown.

In retrospect, the inglorious end to the WBA tournament was an appropriate launching for a crown that would be blasted from brow to brow over the majority of the 1980s. As time passed, the significance of the WBA champions diminished in comparison to the reign of Larry Holmes.

King Larry

As he began his WBC title reign, Holmes was determined to make his mark on the boxing world by defending his crown often and impressively. After a five-month layoff to recover from his grueling war against Ken Norton, Larry made his first defense in Las Vegas on November 10, 1978. His opponent was Alfredo Evangelista.

Evangelista hadn't done much since his title fight with Ali back in 1977. Still, the fact that he had gone the distance lent at least a modicum of respectability to his name. Against Holmes, for the first six rounds it looked as though Alfredo would once again last the full 15 rounds. Holmes's left jab landed again and again, but Evangelista continued to march forward while accomplishing little.

In the seventh round Holmes lashed out with a short, quick right to Evangelista's jaw. Alfredo fell flat on his face and stayed in that position until referee Richard Greene counted him out.

For the first time since Ali stopped Richard Dunn in 1976, a heavyweight title bout had been decided by a knockout. Holmes's reign appeared to be off to an auspicious beginning.

"That was my first title defense," Holmes stated. "There will be more, much more! I'll be around a long time."[6]

Larry's next challenger was Puerto Rican Ossie "Jaws" Ocasio. Ocasio had earned his title shot by virtue of back-to-back decision wins over Jimmy Young. At that time, Young was still a highly rated contender, so Ossie's pair of victories over the crafty Philadelphian were a noteworthy credential. However, Ocasio's 14–0 record included only 9 knockouts, and at 5'11" and 207 pounds, he was small for a heavyweight.

On March 23, 1979, Holmes and Ocasio faced each other in a Las Vegas ring. Once again, Holmes dominated the fight with his left jab. Ocasio fought defensively, using some of the tactics he had learned during 20 rounds of chasing Young. However, Ossie's offensive output was so minimal that after six rounds, the crowd was becoming restless.

As in the Evangelista bout, the seventh round proved lucky for Holmes. He caught Ocasio with a battering-ram straight left that dropped the Puerto Rican. From that point on, it was all over for Ossie as Holmes proceeded to deck him three more times before referee Carlos Padilla called a halt at 2:38 of the round.

The thoroughness of his defeat prompted Ocasio to drop down to the newly-formed cruiserweight class. Three years later, he won the WBA title in that division.

Although the WBC champion had performed well, the main event was almost overshadowed by an undercard bout matching Ken Norton against Earnie Shavers. Norton-Shavers was an official eliminator to determine Holmes's next challenger.

Norton, the last of the Old Guard of the 1970s, was still considered one of the best heavyweights in the world. He wanted nothing more than a rematch with Holmes, but Larry wasn't in a hurry to tangle with Norton any time soon. Thus, Ken found himself in a familiar position, and time was not on his side.

He maintained his WBC #1 ranking by nearly decapitating Randy Stephens with a thunderous left hook in the third round of a bout that was on the undercard of Holmes-Evangelista. The box-off against Shavers wasn't Ken's idea, but he was willing to take the chance because a victory would guarantee him a rematch with Holmes.

Unfortunately for Norton, his weakness was big punchers, and nobody punched harder than Earnie Shavers. It took the bald bomber less than a round to smash Norton to the canvas twice, securing yet another spectacular victory and his own second crack at Holmes.

Norton had intended to drag Shavers into the later rounds and capitalize on Earnie's questionable stamina. "That's what I hoped to do. He just came out and did to me what I planned to do to him."[7]

Norton's career was now at its lowest ebb since his disastrous defeat by George Foreman in 1974. Back then, Norton was young enough to rebound. In 1979, however, he was a tired 36-year-old who was nearing the end of the line.

Ken's decline was proven beyond the shadow of a doubt on August 19, 1979, when he fought Scott Ledoux. After controlling most of the bout with his superior skills, Norton absorbed a bad beating in the tenth and final round. Ledoux's rally left the former WBC champ reeling helplessly at the bell.

The officials called the fight a draw, but it was a moral victory for Ledoux. The Norton fight breathed new life into LeDoux's career. Although he lost a decision to future champ Mike Weaver in his next fight, he rebounded to hand hot prospect Marty Monroe his first defeat on March 3, 1980. That victory launched Scott into a long-hoped-for crack at the title against Larry Holmes on July 7, 1980. Holmes easily stopped LeDoux due to an eye injury in seven frames.

The Fighting Frenchman never reached those heights again, although he did win seven of the remaining eleven contests of his career. He retired after being stopped by Frank Bruno in three rounds on May 3, 1983. LeDoux's final record stood at 33–13–4 with 22 KOs. Sadly, Scott passed away from ALS (Lou Gehrig's Disease) on August 11, 2011, at the age of 62.

A combination of the near defeat by Ledoux and the death of manager and friend Bob Biron finally prompted Norton to pack it in. The two men had once vowed that they would stay in boxing only as a team, and if one should leave for any reason, the other would follow.

"That's why, when Bob hung them up for good in September, I had to announce my retirement," Norton wrote in an article published in the January 1980 issue of *The Ring*.

On October 29, Norton held a press conference at Gallagher's in New York to officially announce his retirement. Ever the gentleman, Norton took the opportunity to thank certain members of the press for their support over the years. He also acknowledged that the disappointing 1976 loss to Ali had sapped his love for the sport. Ken claimed that he was at his peak the night of his rubber match with Ali.

Although Norton will always be remembered as the heavyweight champion who never won a title fight, he was also one of the best fighters in a great era.

With Norton gone, Shavers became the final standard-bearer for the great heavyweights of the earlier part of the decade. Given the ease with which Holmes had beaten him in 1978, it appeared that their rematch would end the same way. But Holmes decided to pick up some pocket change in a tune-up bout before honoring his promise to fight the Shavers–Norton winner. Larry's designated victim was a muscular ex–Marine named Mike Weaver.

The 27-year-old Weaver, who had been fighting since 1972, carried a spotty 19–8 record into his unlikely title challenge. Two of those losses had come at the hands of the Bobick brothers. However, Mike did hold wins over the likes of Pedro Lovell, Bernardo Mercado, and Stan Ward. In fact, going into the Holmes fight, Weaver had reeled off five straight knockout wins and had annexed the largely meaningless United States heavyweight title.

In his early days, Weaver, a Texas native now fighting out of Diamond Bar, California, had taken a job as a sparring partner for Ken Norton. Norton was so impressed with Weaver's physique that he nicknamed him "Hercules." At 6'1", Weaver packed 202 well-distributed pounds on his frame. Mike hated the "Hercules" nickname, but it stuck with him throughout his career.

On the eve of his June 22 date with Destiny, Weaver was actually more reminiscent of Sylvester Stallone's *Rocky* character than Hercules. The fight was held at Madison Square Garden, but Weaver was deemed such a prohibitive underdog that no TV network would carry it. Holmes considered it little more than a pre–Shavers workout.

Once the bout got underway, though, Larry quickly realized that Weaver's mediocre record was misleading. Although Holmes was scoring well with his jab, Weaver kept up the pressure and landed jolting blows of his own. In the fourth round, a right by Weaver sent Holmes to the canvas, but referee Harold Valan ruled it a slip. Weaver kept up his relentless attack, and the crowd of 14,136 began to sense an upset in the making. The tenth round saw Holmes rocked by another Weaver right hand.

Then, in the eleventh, Larry stormed back with a vicious right uppercut that dropped Weaver. Mike got up at 8 and was saved by the bell. After an all-out assault by Holmes at the beginning of the 12th, Referee Valan called a halt at the 44-second mark.

Holmes had saved his title, but the difficulties Weaver posed sent the WBC champion's stock down a few notches. In a commentary on the fight in the September 1979 issue of *The Ring*, Nat Loubet wrote: "It is doubtful if Holmes will want anymore of Weaver who on several occasions during their meeting came within a smidgen of winning the WBC crown."

Loubet was right, to a point. It took 21 years until the two tangled again. By then both men were in the neighborhood of 50, and the result, another KO for Holmes, lacked any significance. However, Mike's sterling performance in their 1979 fight led to a 1980 shot at John Tate's WBA title. Hopelessly behind on points, Weaver knocked Tate senseless with a left hook in the waning seconds of the 15th round. Many efforts were made to match Weaver and Holmes in a title-unification bout, but the promotion never came off.

As for Holmes, he had learned his lesson: never underestimate your opponent, and that included the upcoming Shavers. Yes, Earnie Shavers was 35 years old; and yes, Holmes had won nearly every round in their 1978 encounter. But Shavers was a harder puncher than Weaver, and Holmes knew he would have to be in excellent condition to repeat his victory.

He also knew Shavers would be highly motivated. This was probably Earnie's last opportunity to win a title, and the Ohio hitman was capable of putting away anyone he hit. Shavers was the underdog, but his one-round blowout of Norton, who had given Holmes hell over 15 close rounds, caused some sentimental fans to believe Earnie stood a legitimate puncher's chance against Holmes.

Shavers's long-time trainer, Frank Luca, agreed. He pointed out that Earnie was dealing with stressful managerial issues before their first bout. Coupled with the fact that Shavers only had four weeks of training, his troubles resulted in a sub-par Earnie.

Luca went on to draw the inevitable comparison between the fighters' performances against Norton. He assumed since his fighter dismantled Norton in less than a round, and Holmes just barely won a decision, that it posed some relevance in regards to their rematch.

Shortly before the fight, which was hosted by Caesars Palace in Las Vegas, Holmes tried a little psychological warfare on his old friend. In an interview with Howard Cosell, Larry accused Shavers of having "some dog in him." The insult may or may not have been meant seriously, but it was clear Shavers didn't appreciate any accusation of cowardice. If Holmes wanted a grudge fight, so be it.

On September 28, the past and future of the 1970s heavyweights met in the person of Shavers and Holmes. And over the first six rounds, the future looked secure as Holmes speared Shavers repeatedly with jabs and combinations. Earnie smiled every time Holmes landed a hard blow. But Shavers could not land anything significant of his own, and he was falling hopelessly behind on points.

Also, Holmes had opened cuts over both of Shavers's eyes. In the seventh stanza, Holmes tried to take Earnie out, and got nailed with a crushing overhand right to the jaw. Down went Holmes!

Larry was in considerably more trouble than he'd been during the Weaver fight, and he had to call on all the courage and resilience in his body to lift himself off the canvas. Shavers tried desperately to put Holmes away, but he couldn't land another hard blow.

The rest of the fight was anticlimactic. Holmes hit Shavers with everything but the kitchen sink, but couldn't put him away. In the meantime, Earnie's eyes bled and swelled, and his punches hit nothing but air. Holmes did go down again in the ninth, but Referee Davey Pearl ruled it a slip.

Finally, in the eleventh, Shavers was backed against the ropes while Holmes hit him at will. Two minutes into the round, Pearl stopped the fight. As Steven C. Losch wrote in the January 1980 issue of *Boxing Digest*, "All that remained of Earnie Shavers in the 11th round was his enormous heart, and a heart can't throw punches."

Larry acknowledged that heart in a post-fight interview, telling Shavers that he hadn't meant the "dog" gibe. Then he reached across Howard Cosell and shook Shavers's hand, saying: "You're a man, Earnie." It was a classy ending to the last major heavyweight fight of the decade.

Shavers fought on into 1995 (age 50), but he never won another important bout. His overall log was 74–14–1 (68 KOs).

By the end of 1979, Holmes had successfully defended his title for the fourth time in a year, all by knockout. He had exhibited both superb boxing skills and an ability to come back from adversity. Yet he considered himself boxing's version of Rodney Dangerfield, getting none of the respect he felt he deserved.

Part of Holmes's problem was the Ali factor. Another was a phenomenal increase in recognition of champions in the lighter weight divisions. When Ali was champion, great fighters like Jose Napoles, Carlos Monzon, Emile Griffith, Bob Foster, and Ruben Olivares received only a sliver of the spotlight, especially in the lucrative American market.

Once Ali retired, the smaller men came into their own. Superstars like Sugar Ray Leonard, Marvelous Marvin Hagler, Thomas Hearns, Alexis Arguello, Roberto Duran, Aaron Pryor, and Ray "Boom Boom" Mancini commanded purses and publicity at a level comparable to that of the heavyweight champion. The spotlight usually commanded by the heavyweight king became crowded during Holmes's reign.

Holmes's mission became the unification of the title and the removal of the shadow of Ali from his career. And Ali, who was growing restless in retirement, was beginning to talk comeback.

Throughout 1980, rumors of Ali's imminent return to the ring dominated the sports pages. However, early reports indicated that "The Greatest" intended to challenge Tate, not Holmes. Then, after Tate's unexpected demise at the hands of Mike Weaver, an Ali–Weaver showdown became a hot item. There were also hints that Ali had signed to fight a tune-up against Scott Ledoux before taking on Weaver or Holmes.

Ledoux ended up with a title shot against Holmes, who easily dispatched him in 7 rounds. Prior to that, Holmes had stopped Lorenzo Zanon in six rounds and big Leroy Jones in eight. Finally, Ali made his intentions clear.

"I want Holmes!" he shouted for the world to hear.

And what Ali wanted, Ali got.

Holmes was no fool. He knew that for all the millions an Ali fight would pour into his bank account, he was in a no-win situation. In reality, it was a fight he didn't want. But it was also a fight he couldn't avoid.

The bout was scheduled for October 2, 1980. Ali, who had been out of action more than a year, was approaching his 39th birthday; Holmes was a month away from 31. Ali was training hard and he returned to his old loudmouthed ways during the pre-fight build up, labeling Holmes "Peanut Head," among other things.

Holmes tried to take Ali's insults in stride. Although on one level he resented Muhammad's popularity, the ex-champ had also been Larry's idol and mentor. He said the Ali fight would finally "get the monkey off my back." Deep down, though, he must have known that would never happen.

Beating an old, washed-up Ali would only hinder Holmes's already precarious relations with the boxing public. The same fate faced by Ezzard Charles when he defeated Joe Louis and Gene Tunney when he retired Jack Dempsey now beckoned Holmes. Larry would, at least, be well-paid for destroying a legend.

And that's exactly what happened on fight night at Caesars Palace. Ali, who had weighed in at a light but weak 217 pounds due to a drug he had taken to reduce his poundage, could do nothing against his former sparring partner. His guile wasn't enough; Holmes knew all Ali's moves and had worked out ways to counter them.

As round after painful round went by, Holmes administered a thorough and systematic thrashing to Ali. Only Muhammad's iron chin, or perhaps a combination of that and Holmes's compassion, kept Ali on his feet for ten rounds. At the start of the eleventh, a beaten and embarrassed Ali remained on his stool at the insistence of Angelo Dundee.

Holmes was awarded a TKO victory. But the win was, at best, bittersweet. Throughout the rest of the first half of the 1980s, he remained champion, although he never achieved his dream of universal recognition. Larry Holmes proudly carried the torch of 1970s excellence. Unfortunately, there were no Fraziers, Foremans, Quarrys, or Lyles in Holmes's supporting cast, and by the time another great fighter, Mike Tyson, came along, Larry was too old to offer him serious competition.

They Always Come Back

Ali wasn't the only top-notch fighter of the 1970s who had difficulty remaining in retirement. For those men, boxing wasn't merely a profession; it became an obsession. For better or worse, it was in their blood, and they could not accept the fact that the era of excellence they created had come to an end.

The roar of the crowd and the allure of being called "Champ" is as intoxicating to a boxer as drugs and alcohol are to the rest of us. For those who have been fortunate enough to drink from the cup of glory only to have that cup taken away, the quest for one more taste is usually futile. For fighters, the dream dies slowly, one punch at a time.

Due to the nature and demands of professional sports, athletes are forced to retire at a relatively young age. Only in sports could a 35-year-old man be referred to as "ancient." Most athletes, including boxers, retire sometime in their early to mid-thirties, reluctantly passing the torch to the next generation.

Fighters tend to be critical of each other, and they are prone to finding fault in those who take their places in the ratings. The ex-boxer, still relatively youthful, begins to fancy his chances against the new breed. Remembering past renown and forgetting the drudgery of training, many fighters return hopefully to the gyms of which they had previously grown weary.

"The gym owns them," Dave Anderson once wrote in an article about comebacking fighters. He tells of how, after years of training, most boxers grow to despise the monk-like monotony of training. "When they stop boxing," Anderson continued, "they discover that just as they could not live with the gym, now they cannot live without it."

The '70s heavyweights were not exceptions to that rule.

Boxing is an individual sport, and consequently most have to learn hard truths for themselves. The pugilistic retirement pasture has a fence that is temptingly low, and the former champions and contenders who felt they were still spry enough to clear the barrier did so.

Ignoring the telltale signs of physical deterioration, the heroes of the '70s found themselves magnetically attracted to the ring by a force that obscured reason and allowed emotion to rule. And, for the most part, these foolhardy comebacks were encouraged by fans who longed for one last glimpse of the decade's glory even though the press condemned them.

As well, the drastic escalation of purses during the early '80s could only magnify the temptation to come back. Whether the rebounding fighter could ever again put forth an honest effort in the ring was often of only secondary importance. The lure of a quick, substantial dollar became sufficient incentive for many to take the plunge.

Ken Norton was the first to follow Ali out of retirement. Fifteen months after his struggle against Scott Ledoux, Norton was back in action. On November 7, 1980, he won a tough 10-round decision over Randall "Tex" Cobb. Then he began negotiations for a big-money crossroads meeting with the latest White Hope, Gerry Cooney. The bout was scheduled for May 11, 1981.

But why come back at all? Norton explained that he didn't like the way his career had ended. He also said he had regained the motivation that had abandoned him after the third Ali fight. However, motivation was no longer enough for a man who was rapidly approaching his thirty-eighth birthday.

On the surface, though, Norton was a remarkably well-preserved specimen. It was difficult to detect any flaws in his spectacular physique as fight approached. Nevertheless, Ken's bulging muscles belied the fact that his reflexes had dulled and his legs had lost their bounce. Even Norton's trainer, Bill Slayton, saw the difference. He didn't like the looks of Ken's legs in training, but reasoned that they were still good enough to beat Cooney.

Norton's confidence going into the Cooney fight was understandable. Ken had always been hell on white fighters, destroying the likes of Duane Bobick, Jerry Quarry, and Boone Kirkman. In Cooney, however, Norton was facing a 6'6", 225-pound power hitter, and that kind of fighter, black, white, or polka-dot, had always been the ex–WBC champion's nemesis.

It took Cooney only 54 seconds to leave Norton sitting battered and bleary-eyed on the bottom strand of the ropes. Before Referee Tony Perez pulled Cooney away, it appeared Norton's life may have been endangered.

The one-sided thrashing convinced Ken that his days in boxing were over. His two-fight comeback was a fistic failure, but financially speaking it would be difficult to view it as anything other than a roaring success. The $150,000 he made against Cobb and his $850,000 purse for the Cooney fight added up to a cool million.

Norton had already earned more than $16 million prior to his comeback, ranking him second only to Ali in terms of monetary success in the 1970s. Through careful management and smart investment of his money, Norton is financially secure today, even though a 1986 car crash left him with injuries from which he is still recovering.

But Ken's monetary status is an exception to the rule. Most ex-champions and contenders find that their post-boxing activities are rarely as lucrative as punching for pay. Some hang on to their careers as long as they can, chasing the fast buck long after the rest of their dreams have died. As younger men, most fighters don't have the time, opportunity, or inclination to develop skills that will serve them outside the ring. Consequently, when they reach the point at which they should get out of the game, they fight on for smaller and smaller purses because in many cases the only alternative is unemployment.

A prime example of a '70s fighter who kept going long after his desire had faded was Jimmy Young. After his heartbreaking loss to Norton in 1977, Young allowed his remarkable skills to corrode. His apathetic approach to his profession was evident in the condition in which he entered his bouts. Layers of flab now jiggled on his once-lean frame as he lost to fighters he should have beaten with ease. He fought throughout most of the 1980s, losing as many fights as he won. For him, boxing was no longer a chance to grasp the brass ring of immortality; it was just a job.

In contrast, no one ever worked harder or displayed more desire throughout his career than Smokin' Joe Frazier, who had wisely hung up his gloves after his second loss to George Foreman. Despite his absence from competition, Frazier stayed in shape by working out in his now-famous Philadelphia gym.

In some respects, it is sensible for a former athlete to maintain a regular workout schedule to remain fit; on the other, it can be a flirtation with temptation. When an ex-fighter begins to feel, or imagine, that old bounce in his step and snap in his punches, he begins to believe he has miraculously recaptured his lost youth. Early in 1978, Frazier began to take serious steps toward a comeback. Proposed fights against Earnie Shavers, Kallie Knoetze, and Scott Ledoux were in the works when fate intervened and laid Joe low with a case of hepatitis. For a while, Joe was literally in a life-or-death situation, and after he recovered his comeback was shelved.

Three years later, the comeback itch returned, fueled once again by Frazier's daily trips to the gym. Unlike other ex-fighters who sometimes hang around gyms like Banquo's ghost, Frazier was training a promising stable of prospects that included his son, Marvis. The temptation to see what he could do in the ring himself became overpowering.

Joe discussed the idea of coming back with his family, who grudgingly agreed after observing him in a few sparring sessions. But the media and fans weren't as easy to convince. Frazier hadn't fought since June of 1976 and hadn't won a fight since his March 1975 stoppage of Jimmy Ellis. Joe understood and appreciated the concern of his family and friends but assured them that at only 37, he was still capable in the ring.

Frazier's comeback opponent was a humongous ex-convict named Floyd "Jumbo" Cummings. Jumbo had melded a pumped-up physique through weight training during his prison years. Despite his near superhuman strength, though, Cummings was slow and ponderous. He would have been easy prey for the Frazier who nearly made Ali quit during the "Thrilla in Manila."

But this was December 3, 1981, not October 1, 1975, and a lardy, rusty Frazier was lucky to escape with a draw against Cummings. Not only did he lack his old fire and fury, Joe was also fighting without Eddie Futch in his corner. Always loyal to Frazier's best interests, Futch was opposed to the comeback, so Frazier didn't ask his old trainer to work his corner that night.

For Frazier, it took the dismal showing against Cummings to convince him that his "smokin'" days were over. He was luckier than most, however. Even though he no longer participated in boxing, he could continue vicariously through his son Marvis and the other fighters he trained.

Joe Frazier remained close to boxing and his gym for the remainder of his life. Guiding his son Marvis to a fateful November 1983 thrashing at the hands of Larry Holmes, Frazier's popularity among fans grew stronger over the years as his true greatness was truly recognized.

Frazier passed away of liver cancer on November 7, 2011, leaving behind one of the greatest legacies in sports history.

Eight days after the Frazier–Cummings fight, Joe's old rival, Muhammad Ali, was himself back in action. And Ali's fans could only shake their heads in sorrow. After the terrible thrashing he had suffered at the hands of Larry Holmes fourteen months earlier, what could possibly have induced him to try again a month short of his fortieth birthday? The answer is quite simple: he missed the challenge.

As well, Ali had an explanation for his abysmal performance against Holmes. He said he had taken thyroid pills to aid him in his struggle to lose weight. At the beginning of his training for Holmes, Ali had weighed a blubbery 253 pounds, 36 more than his weight on fight night. Unfortunately, his sleek exterior masked a debilitated interior. The drastic weight reduction left him so dehydrated that he couldn't even break a sweat. In his weakened condition, he couldn't do a thing against Holmes.

Even so, it is extremely doubtful that the Ali of 1980 could have handled Holmes even in the best condition of which he was capable at age 38. But the thyroid pills did provide a convenient rationalization.

With the Holmes debacle explained away, Ali began to train for his December 11 bout against Trevor Berbick. The location would be Nassau, capital of the Bahamas. Berbick, a Jamaican-born bulk of muscle, was then fighting out of Halifax, Nova Scotia. His claims to fame were a knockout of former WBA champion John Tate and a respectable, albeit losing, 15-round effort against Holmes.

Ali intended to use Berbick as a stepping stone to another shot at the title. Like his arch-rival Frazier, Muhammad's primary objective was glory rather than money. The idea of claiming the heavyweight championship of the world for a fourth time intrigued him.

Neither Ali nor Frazier, whose names were once again linked in the headlines, could attract the interest of a single television network for their 1981 comeback efforts. In Frazier's case, CBS boxing advisor Mort Sharnik said the network turned down the Cummings fight because they didn't want to encourage Joe to continue his quest.

Ferdie Pacheco, speaking on behalf of the peacock network, stated: "We don't want a requiem for a heavyweight played on NBC."

Serious concern was expressed for the safety of the two legends. Frazier grew somewhat annoyed with all the pre-fight alarm. Ali, on the other hand, found the worrywarts amusing.

However, there were some real indications that concerns about Ali's health were justified. Over the past few years, many observers had begun to notice a sluggishness creeping into his speech and movement. Some argued that he had simply matured and was no longer the hyperactive kid he had been years ago. But others were worried that the considerable physical damage he had absorbed since his 1970 return to the ring was finally catching up with him. With that anxiety in mind, one of the stipulations for the sanctioning of the Ali–Berbick bout was public disclosure of a series of neurological exams Ali had undergone in December of 1980. In the report, Dr. Dennis W. Cope of the UCLA Medical Center's Division of Endocrinology stated that there was nothing in his tests that should prevent Ali from fighting.

Thus, Ali went ahead with what was billed as the "Drama in the Bahamas." Having learned a lesson from the Holmes fight, he conceded the extra poundage a middle-aged man carries and went into the bout at a heavy but comfortable 236. He fought hard and did his best, and even three years earlier he would have boxed rings around Berbick. But

Berbick walked through Ali's punches and scored enough of his own to capture a unanimous 10-round verdict.

Afterwards, in a slurred voice, Ali admitted that "Father Time" had indeed caught up with him. He never fought again.

In 1984, he was diagnosed as suffering from Parkinson's Syndrome, which has slowed both his speech and movement, but hasn't affected his quick wits.

Leon Spinks was only 27 years old in 1980, but he had fallen so far so fast that the rest of his career qualified as a perpetual comeback. For the most part, boxing fans still enjoyed his Pier 6 brand of fighting, and they cheered him as he brawled his way back into contention with knockouts over Alfredo Evangelista and Bernardo Mercado.

Those wins lifted Spinks to the #1 contender's slot, and caused many observers to wonder if he had finally begun to achieve the potential he had shown the night he beat Ali. On the strength of his ex-champion status, Leon received a shot at Larry Holmes's WBC title on June 12, 1981, in Detroit.

Because of his pressuring style, Spinks was given an excellent chance against the champion. But Holmes was too big and two skillful, and he demolished Leon in three rounds.

At that point, Spinks decided it was time to shed about ten pounds and campaign in the new cruiserweight class. But the lighter class posed problems as well, and on March 6, 1983, Leon was stopped in six rounds by Carlos De Leon, who was between reigns as WBC champion.

Spinks fought on and made his final grab at a title on March 23, 1986, when he challenged WBA junior heavyweight king Dwight Muhammad Qawi. Looking weak at 190 pounds, Spinks was battered into defeat in six frames.

From that point, Spinks plummeted into oblivion, becoming an easy mark for up-and-coming fighters. His life became a sad rags-to-riches-to-rags story. He had once stood at the pinnacle of boxing success; now he was fighting, and losing, for pittances on small-town undercards.

Did Spinks's harrowing seven-month reign as champion subconsciously kill any motivation he may have had to reach those heights again? Only Leon knows for sure. In May of 1988, Leon announced his retirement after a first-round KO loss to Canadian Tony Morrison.

Like most, the retirement didn't stick. Leon hung on until December 4, 1995.

In his last bout Spinks was decisioned in eight rounds by another '70s holdout, Fred "Young Sanford" Houpe. At that stage, at 42 years of age and seeing his record plummet to 26–17–3, Leon hung up his gloves for good.

No matter what happened in this latter stage of his career, Leon Spinks can say with pride that he was once the undisputed heavyweight champion of the world. No one can ever take that distinction away from him.

Of course, Spinks wasn't the only '70s heavyweight still on the scene in the nineties. As we have already seen, the Foreman comeback, which started off as a lark and culminated in unimagined success, is the extreme exception to the rule. "Big George's" personal and financial glory only fueled others to chase the same dream. Foreman has been joined on the 40-something comeback trail by none other than Larry Holmes. In 1981, Holmes had insisted that the urge that had driven Ali and Frazier to return to the ring would never affect him. In the meantime, Larry held onto his WBC title until 1983, defending it a total of 17 times.

His most lucrative and satisfying defense came against Gerry Cooney, who fell in 13 rounds on June 11, 1982. Then the WBC threatened to strip him of his title for not signing for a defense against Greg Page.

Holmes then relinquished the WBC's belt and was proclaimed champion by the newly formed International Boxing Federation. Larry was still considered the "real" champion by most, but now he had to share recognition with two other titleholders.

Fighting on under the IBF banner, Holmes compiled three more defenses, bringing his record to 48–0, one shy of Rocky Marciano's perfect 49–0 slate. But on the night of September 25, 1985, Michael Spinks made history by scoring an upset 15-round decision over Holmes. Spinks thus became the first reigning light heavyweight champion to win the heavyweight title.

On April 19, 1986, Holmes attempted to regain the IBF title from Spinks, but again lost by decision. At that point, Larry retired, leaving a trail of bitterness behind him.

In the following years, a new force appeared on the heavyweight scene, a youthful power-puncher named Mike Tyson.

By 1987, Tyson had unified the WBC, WBA, and IBF titles, a feat Holmes had never accomplished. Despite his earlier disclaimers, a 38-year-old Holmes could not resist the call of fame and money. He came back against Tyson on January 22, 1988, and was destroyed in four rounds.

Once again, Holmes retired. Then, in the wake of Tyson's unexpected downfall at the hands of Buster Douglas and Holyfield's subsequent defeat of Douglas, Larry launched another comeback in 1991, beating five nonentities before winning a surprise 12-round decision over a rated contender named Ray Mercer. The win earned him a crack at Holyfield on June 19, 1992. Ironically, it was the first time in his career that Holmes challenged for the "undisputed" heavyweight title. Despite a game effort, Holmes lost a unanimous verdict.

On the strength of his showing against Holyfield, Holmes pressed on, reeling off seven straight victories which earned him a shot at then WBC champ Oliver McCall on April 8, 1995. He lost a razor-thin decision. Holmes fought on for seven more years, and retired after beating Eric "Butterbean" Esch on July 27, 2002, at the age of 52. Larry's final record stands at a very respectable 69–6 (44 KOs) against the best the division had to offer over a thirty-year span. He was inducted into the Hall of Fame in 2008.

More than thirty years later, appreciation for the great fights and fighters of the 1970s has increased. Boxing fans now look back and reminisce not only over the accomplishments of Ali, but also the many exciting moments provided by Frazier, Norton, Foreman, and Holmes. The more recent successes of the latter two provide a connection to those days of blood and glory.

In retrospect, the decade of the 1970s measures more than favorably compared to the other great eras of the past. The credit goes entirely to the fighters, from the great champions to contenders like Quarry, Ellis, Shavers, Lyle, Bugner, Young, Middleton, Bonavena, and a host of lesser lights. Their names alone conjure fond memories of an unparalleled period of ring excellence. They have come to mean as much to boxing as boxing has meant to them. Because of these fighters, boxing is in our blood, too.

Chapter Notes

Chapter One

1. John L. Sullivan, "Negro Champion Led All The Way — Jeffries Slow and Clumsy, *New York Times*, July 5, 1910, p. 9.
2. W.H. Rocap, "Victory Little to Boast of," *New York Times*, June 28, 1914.
3. John L. Sullivan, "I'll Win ... Jeffries; Can't Lose ... Johnson," *New York Times*, July 4, 1910, p. 14.
4. Robert Ripley, *1925 Everlast Record Book*.
5. *Ibid*.
6. *1976 Ring Record Book*.
7. Robert Ripley, *1929 Everlast Record Book*.
8. Murray Levin, *New York Daily Mirror*, 1928.
9. *Ibid*.
10. Lisle Shoemaker, *San Diego Sun*, 1938.
11. W.D. McMillan, *Morning Sun*, 1938.
12. *1976 Ring Record Book*.
13. Joseph C. Nichols, "Layne is 5–9 Choice to Beat Marciano," *New York Times*, July 12, 1951, p. 29.

Chapter Two

1. Arthur Daley, "Sports of the Times: The Big Bear," *New York Times*, February 24, 1964, p. 30.
2. Howard M. Tucker, "Right Hand Punch Finishes German." *New York Times*, December 5, 1961, p. 55.
3. Arthur Daley, "Sports of the Times: A Boy on a Man's Errand," *New York Times*, February 23, 1964, p. V:3.
4. Leonard Koppett, "Liston Is Sharp Outside of Ring," *New York Times*, February 21, 1964, p. 22.
5. *Ibid*.
6. Leonard Koppett, "Clay Ends Drills, but Not His Talk," *New York Times*, February 22, 1964, p. 25.
7. *Ibid*.
8. Leonard Koppett, "TV Fight Facing Integration Snag." *New York Times*, February 24, 1964, p. 30.
9. Arthur Daley. "Sports of the Times: Day of Decision," *New York Times*, April 28, 1967.
10. Robert Lipsyte, "U.S. Court Rejects Appeal by Clay," *New York Times*, April 28, 1967.
11. Associated Press, "Clay Asks Court to Stay Induction," *New York Times*, April 26, 1967, p. 60.
12. *Ibid*.
13. Robert Lipsyte, "Clay Puts His Affairs in Order as Day of Decision Approaches," *New York Times*, April 27, 1967, p. 59.
14. *Ibid*.
15. Robert Lipsyte, "Clay Refuses Army Oath; Stripped of Boxing Crown," *New York Times*, April 29, 1967, p. 1.
16. *Ibid*.
17. "No Mission Impossible for the Greatest," Ali–Frazier III Album, *Boxing Illustrated 1975*, p. 8.

Chapter Three

1. Dave Anderson, "Rough Grindstone Ahead for Ellis' Damaged Nose," *New York Times*, February 14, 1970, p. 16.
2. Mark Kram, "Showbiz Is Out, Boxing Is In," *Sports Illustrated*, February 16, 1970, 32:14–15.
3. Arthur Daley, "Sports of the Times: Something to Sell," *New York Times*, February 15, 1970.
4. Anderson, "Rough Grindstone."
5. Arthur Daley, "Frazier Spars 4 Rounds for a Total of 20," *New York Times*, February 11, 1970, p. 58.
6. Daley, "Sports of the Times: Something to Sell."
7. Dave Anderson, "Style Gives Ellis Good Chance Against Heavily Favored Frazier Tomorrow," *New York Times*, February 15, 1970.
8. Anderson, "Rough Grindstone."
9. *Ibid*.
10. Dave Anderson, "Clay Picks Old Mate, Picks Ellis in Eight." *New York Times*, February 10, 1970, p. 34.
11. *Ibid*.
12. *Ibid*.
13. Robert Lipsyte, "Sports of the Times: One More Time," *New York Times*, February 16, 1970.
14. Dave Anderson, "Clay Picks Old Mate," *New York Times*, February 10, 1970, p. 34.
15. Daley, "Frazier Spars."
16. Dave Anderson, "Frazier Flattens Ellis and Wins Undisputed Heavyweight Title," *New York Times*, February 17, 1970, p. 46.
17. *Ibid*.
18. *Ibid*.
19. Arthur Daley, "Sports of the Times: Alone at the Top," *New York Times*, February 18, 1970, p. 54.
20. *Ibid*.
21. Steve Cady, "Ellis Says He Let Frazier Run Bout," *New York Times*, February 17, 1970, p. 46.
22. *Ibid*.
23. Dave Anderson, "Ali Rated 17-to-5 Choice Over Quarry Tomorrow," *New York Times*, October 25, 1970, p. V:3.
24. *Ibid*.
25. Tex Maule, "Once and Future King? Scramble for Ali's Title," *Sports Illustrated*, November 6, 1967, 27:18–21.
26. *Ibid*.
27. *Ibid*.
28. Dave Anderson, "Ali's Speed After Layoff Is Big Question in Quarry Bout Tonight," *New York Times*, October 26, 1970, p. 51.
29. Dave Anderson, "Ali Finds Crown Fits and Wears It," *New York Times*, September 11, 1970, p. 52.
30. Dave Anderson, "Politicians Spar Over the Ali–Quarry Bout," *New York Times*, October 23, 1970, p. 51.
31. *Ibid*.
32. Robert Lipsyte, "Sports of The Times: The Return," *New York Times*, October 26, 1970, p. 51.

33. Anderson, "Ali Rated 17-to-5," *New York Times*, October 25, 1970, p. V:3.
34. *Ibid*.
35. Dave Anderson, "Ali Scores Third-Round Knockout Over Quarry in Successful Return to Ring," *New York Times*, October 27, 1970, p. 56.
36. *Ibid*.
37. *Ibid*.
38. *Ibid*.
39. Robert Lipsyte, "Ali Says Frazier Will Be Easier," *New York Times*, October 27, 1970, p. 56.
40. *Ibid*.
41. *Ibid*.
42. Pat Putnam, "One Round of Boxing Was More Than Enough," *Sports Illustrated*, November 30, 1970, 33:20–21.
43. *Ibid*.
44. *Ibid*.
45. *Ibid*.
46. *Ibid*.
47. *Ibid*.
48. *Ibid*.
49. Lester Bromberg, "Isn't It Time Ringo Showed Up for More Of Those Yankee $?" *Ring Magazine*, March 1974, p. 50.
50. Steve Cady, "Ali Starts Drive to Make Mountain Out of Bonavena," *New York Times*, November 6, 1970, p. 30.
51. *Ibid*.
52. Dave Anderson, "Prediction: Rhyme Calls for Bonavena to Fall in Nine," *New York Times*, December 1, 1970, p. 63.
53. *Ibid*.
54. Robert Lipsyte, "Sports of the Times: Are You Crazy?" *New York Times*, December 5, 1970, p. 43.
55. *Ibid*.
56. Mark Kram, "Muddle, Then a Zinger," *Sports Illustrated*, December 14, 1970, 33:20–1.
57. *Ibid*.
58. Lipsyte, "Sports of the Times: Are You Crazy?"
59. *Ibid*.
60. Daley, "Sports of the Times: The Toreador."
61. *Ibid*.
62. Dave Anderson, "Ali Calls Bonavena 'Perfect Test' of Whether He Still Has Champion's Touch," *New York Times*, December 6, 1970.
63. *Ibid*.
64. Dave Anderson, "Ali Orders His Block of Tickets so the Chips Fall Everywhere," *New York Times*, December 4, 1970, p. 64.
65. *Ibid*.
66. Dave Anderson, "Argentine Incurs First Knockout," *New York Times*, December 8, 1970, p. 64.
67. Gerald Eskenazi, "Bonavena Predicts Ali Will Defeat Frazier for Title," *New York Times*, December 8, 1970, p. 64.
68. Arthur Daley, "Sports of the Times: Not Too Impressive," *New York Times*, December 9, 1970.
69. Anderson, "Argentine Incurs."
70. *Ibid*.
71. Jerry Kirshenbaum, "Boxing," *Sports Illustrated*, January 25, 1971.

Chapter Four

1. United Press International, "Way is Cleared for Title Match," *New York Times*, January 12, 1971, p. 40.
2. Jerry Kirshenbaum, "Boxing," *Sports Illustrated*, January 25, 1971.
3. *Ibid*.
4. *Ibid*.
5. *Ibid*.
6. Dave Anderson, "Durham Demanding Referee Who Can Control Ali," *New York Times*, March 1, 1971.
7. Dave Anderson, "Frazier and Ali: Morality Drama Unfolds," *New York Times*, March 7, 1971, p. V:3.
8. Anderson, "Frazier and Ali"; *New York Times*, March 6, 1971, p. 15.
9. Anderson, "Frazier and Ali"; *New York Times*, March 6, 1971, p. 15.
10. Dave Anderson, "Pilot Wants Frazier to Retire," *New York Times*, March 6, 1971.
11. Arthur Daley, "Sports of the Times: The Fight," *New York Times*, March 7, 1971 p. V:3.
12. *Ibid*.
13. Anderson, "Durham Demanding Referee."
14. Dave Anderson, "Frazier Puts Hook Into Victory Party," *New York Times*, March 5, 1971, p. 41.
15. Anderson, "Frazier and Ali: Morality Drama Unfolds."
16. Joe Nichols, "Ali Accepts Underdog Role," *New York Times*, March 5, 1971, p. 41.
17. *Ibid*.
18. Dave Anderson, "Frazier Gleams in Dawn's Early Light," *New York Times*, February 28, 1971, p. VI:6.
19. Dave Anderson, "Bomb Call at Inn," *New York Times*, March 8, 1971, p. 45.
20. Dave Anderson, "Frazier Outpoints Ali and Keeps Title," *New York Times*, March 9, 1971, p. 29.
21. *Ibid*.
22. *Ibid*.
23. Arthur Daley, "Epic Worth the Price," *New York Times*, March 9, 1971, p. 29.
24. *Ibid*.
25. *Ibid*.
26. *Ibid*.
27. Deane McGowen, "Frazier Says Blows to Body Won," *New York Times*, March 9, 1971, p. 29.
28. *Ibid*.
29. *Ibid*.
30. *Ibid*.
31. Neil Amdur, "Ali Is Silent on Way to Hospital," *New York Times*, March 9, 1971, p. 29.
32. *Ibid*.
33. Dave Anderson, "Manager Foresees No Fights for Frazier Before Next Year," *New York Times*, March 10, 1971, p. 49.
34. Dave Anderson, "Frazier Outpoints Ali and Keeps Title," *New York Times*, March 9, 1971, p. 29.
35. Dave Anderson, "Tired Champion Relaxes While Undergoing Tests," *New York Times*, March 18, 1971, p. 49.
36. "Violent Coronation in Kinshasa," *Time Magazine*, September 23, 1974.
37. Randy Gordon, "The George Foreman Story," *Superfight Magazine*, 1974, p. 37.
38. *Ibid*.
39. Bob Ruiz, "George Chuvalo: Canadian Heavyweight with True Grit," *Boxing Guide*, October 1974, p. 58.
40. M. Kane, "Salute the Grand Old Flag-Raiser George Foreman," *Sports Illustrated*, August 17, 1970, 33:56–57.
41. *Ibid*.
42. Marshall Reed, "Foreman Lowers the Boone," *Boxing Illustrated*, February 1971, p. 61.
43. Arthur Daley, "Sports of the Times: A Boring Fight," *New York Times*, July 27, 1971, p. 25.

44. *Ibid.*
45. *Ibid.*
46. Dave Anderson, "Victor at 220_ in Command of Houston Bout," *New York Times*, July 27, 1971, p. 25.
47. *Ibid.*
48. Howard Cosell, *Wide World of Sports*, ABC TV, November 29, 1971.
49. Tex Maule, "Got to Look Good for Allah," *Sports Illustrated*, November 29, 1971, 35:28–29.
50. *Ibid.*
51. *Ibid.*

Chapter Five

1. Dave Anderson, "Manager Foresees No Fights for Frazier Before Next Year," *New York Times*, March 10, 1971, p. 49.
2. R. Fimrite, "Back to School Time for Terry Daniels," *Sports Illustrated*, January 24, 1972, 36:22–23.
3. Red Smith, "Fight Is Stopped with Challenger Draped Over Ring Ropes," *New York Times*, January 16, 1972.
4. Fimrite, "Back to School Time for Terry Daniels."
5. *Ibid.*
6. *Ibid.*
7. Mark Kram, "Bluffs Butcher Gets Tenderized," *Sports Illustrated*, June 5, 1972, 36:26–27.
8. Dave Anderson, "Frazier Stops Stander in Fifth Round to Keep Title," *New York Times*, May 26, 1972.
9. Mark Kram, "Bluffs Butcher Gets Tenderized," *Sports Illustrated*, June 5, 1972, 36:26–27.
10. Leslie Nakashima, "Not Only Foster Got Stung." *Sports Illustrated*, April 10, 1972, 36:80.
11. *Ibid.*
12. Dick Beddoes, "By Dick Beddoes," *Globe and Mail*, May 1, 1972, p. 51.
13. Robert F. Jones, "Blast Was One Big Bust," *Sports Illustrated*, May 15, 1972, 36:38–40.
14. Dick Beddoes, "Ali Wins but Still Unable to Deck Chuvalo," *Globe and Mail*, May 2, 1972, p. 32.
15. *Ibid.*
16. Bob Ruiz, "George Chuvalo: Canadian Heavyweight with True Grit," *Boxing Guide*, October 1974, p. 56.
17. *Ibid.*
18. Tex Maule, "Boxing," *Sports Illustrated*, July 10, 1972.
19. *Ibid.*
20. Wikipedia.
21. Robert Lipsyte, "A Star Is Reborn," *New York Times*, September 12, 1972, p. 20.
22. Red Smith, "Patterson Gains Decision Over Bonavena at Garden," *New York Times*, February 12, 1972.
23. *Ibid.*
24. *Ibid.*
25. Edwin Shrake, "Boxing," *Sports Illustrated*, December 4, 1972.
26. *Ibid.*
27. *Ibid.*
28. *Ibid.*
29. *Ibid.*

Chapter Six

1. Dan Daniel, "Boxing," *Ring Magazine*, November 1972.
2. George Plimpton, "You Better Believe It," *Sports Illustrated*, February 3, 1973, 38:20–4.
3. Dan Shockett, "Frazier Dropped Six Times! Foreman Wins Title," *Superfight Magazine*, 1974, p. 27.
4. *Ring Record Book 1976.*
5. Edwin Shrake, "Meet the New Champ!" *Sports Illustrated*, January 29, 1973, 38:12–13.
6. Shockett, "Frazier Dropped Six Times!"
7. Arthur Daley, "An Abrupt End to the Frazier Reign," *New York Times*, January 23, 1973.
8. Red Smith, "Foreman Stops Frazier in 2nd, Wins Title," *New York Times*, January 23, 1973.
9. Neil Allen, "Ali Antics Just Another Las Vegas Turn, Says Bugner," *London Times*, February 13, 1973, p. 14.
10. Neil Allen, "Heavier Going This Time for Ali the Orator," *London Times*, February 15, 1973, p. 12.
11. Dan Levin, "Bury His Heart at Wounded Jaw," *Sports Illustrated*, April 9, 1973, 38:28–29.
12. *Ibid.*
13. "The Man Who Whupped Muhammad Ali," *Ebony Magazine*, June 1973, 28:152–4.
14. Levin, "Bury His Heart at Wounded Jaw."
15. William Wallace, "Norton 5–1 Underdog, Breaks Ali's Jaw, Wins Split Decision," *New York Times*, April 1, 1973, p. V:1.
16. Randy Gordon, "The Muhammad Ali Story," *Superfight Magazine*, 1974, p. 66.
17. Tex Maule, "The Mouth That Nearly Roared," *Sports Illustrated*, April 23, 1973, 38:28–30.
18. Pat Putnam, "One Little Move a Giant Step," *Sports Illustrated*, June 18, 1973, 38:22–4.
19. *Ibid.*
20. Pat Putnam, "Bugle Call Champion," *Sports Illustrated*, June 12, 1978, 48:34–35.
21. Edwin Shrake, "It Was the Mouth by a Whisker," *Sports Illustrated*, September 17, 1973, 39:42–3.
22. Steve Randel, "If I Hadn't Trained Like I Did Norton Would've Whipped Me," *World Boxing*, January 1974, p. 36.
23. Mark Kram, "Jawful Test on the Mountain," *Sports Illustrated*, September 3, 1973, 39:24–6.
24. Shrake, "It Was the Mouth by a Whisker."
25. *Ibid.*
26. Randel, "If I Hadn't Trained Like I Did."
27. *Ibid.*
28. Neil Allen, "Bugner Loses to Frazier in Relentless Struggle," *London Times*, July 3, 1973, p. 11.
29. Muhammad Ali, "Frazier's All Punched Out," *Boxing Illustrated*, January 1974, p. 13.
30. Frank Hastings, "Ali Whips Lubbers for 12, Reserving Right for Joe," *Ring Magazine*, January 1974, p. 8.
31. Dan Levin, "Boxing," *Sports Illustrated*, October 9, 1972, 37:88.
32. *Ibid.*
33. *Ibid.*
34. *Ibid.*
35. *Ibid.*
36. Robert Lipsyte, "Sports of the Times: The Fighters," *New York Times*, February 21, 1964, p. 22.
37. *Sports Illustrated*, February 19, 1973.
38. Jack Welsh, "Quarry Risks High Stakes in Garden," *Boxing Illustrated*, January 1974, p. 31.
39. Teddy Brenner, "Boxing," *Schenectady Gazette*, December 14, 1973.
40. Dan Shockett, "Quarry Kayoes Shavers," *International Boxing*, April 1974, p. 36.
41. Deane McGowen, "Sweet Victory Soured by Wrist Injury," *New York Times*, December 15, 1973, p. 39.
42. Kram, "Jawful Test."
43. *Ibid.*

44. Robert J. Thornton, "At Ringside," *World Boxing*, March 1974, p. 6.
45. Kram, "Jawful Test."
46. *Ibid.*
47. *Ibid.*
48. "Revenge for Pearl Harbor," *World Boxing*, January 1974, p. 53.
49. *Ibid.*

Chapter Seven

1. "Picking Foreman's Foe," *Time Magazine*, January 28, 1974, 103:59.
2. Dan Shockett, "Ali Insists: This Time It'll Be Different," *World Boxing*, March 1974, p. 35.
3. Gerald Eskenazi, "Ali Favored Over Frazier in Battle of Ex-Champs," *New York Times*, January 27, 1974, p. V:1.
4. Dave Anderson, "Old-Timers Night," *New York Times*, January 27, 1974, p. V:5.
5. "Picking Foreman's Foe," *Time Magazine*.
6. Muhammad Ali, "Frazier's All Punched Out," *Boxing Illustrated*, January 1974, p. 13.
7. Dave Anderson, "Playful Ali Is 212, Frazier 209, Quiet," *New York Times*, January 28, 1974, p. 21.
8. Red Smith, "Demeaning What," *New York Times*, January 28, 1974, p. 21.
9. Pete Axthelm, "End of the Road: Ali and Frazier," *Newsweek*, February 11, 1974, 88:65.
10. Dave Anderson, "I'm Not Ignorant, Stand Up Man," *New York Times*, January 24, 1974, p. 29.
11. *Ibid.*
12. *Ibid.*
13. Anderson, "I'm Not Ignorant."
14. *Ibid.*
15. Steve Cady, "Ali Taunts Frazier Into Shoving Match," *New York Times*, January 24, 1974.
16. *Ibid.*
17. *Ibid.*
18. Gerald Eskenazi, "Ali, Frazier Are Fined for 'Demeaning' Boxing," *New York Times*, January 26, 1974, p. 23.
19. Anderson, "Playful Ali is 212."
20. *Ibid.*
21. *Ibid.*
22. Eskenazi, "Ali Favored Over Frazier."
23. Anderson, "Playful Ali is 212."
24. Gerald Eskenazi, "Ali's Hand Treatments Stir a Mystery in Camp," *New York Times*, January 20, 1974, p. V:1.
25. *Ibid.*
26. Anderson, "I'm Not Ignorant."
27. Dave Anderson, "Ali Beats Frazier on Decision Here," *New York Times*, January 29, 1974, p. 1.
28. *Ibid.*
29. *Ibid.*
30. *Ibid.*
31. Stephen Randel, "California Grapevine," *International Boxing*, April 1974, p. 12.
32. *Ibid.*
33. *Ibid.*
34. *Ibid.*
35. *Ibid.*
36. Jerry Quarry, "I'll Fight Ali — Winner-Take-All," *World Boxing*, July 1974, p. 32.
37. Steve Ende, "Joe Frazier's Dramatic Comeback," *International Boxing*, October 1974, p. 54.
38. *Ibid.*
39. "Violent Coronation in Zaire," *Time Magazine*, September 23, 1974.
40. *Ibid.*
41. Red Smith, "Don King, Mini-Conglomerate," *New York Times*, August 10, 1974, p. V:3.
42. Dave Anderson, "Boxing," *New York Times*, September 28, 1974, p. V:1.
43. *Ibid.*
44. *Ibid.*
45. *Ibid.*
46. Dan Shockett, "I'll Knock Ali Out Early," *World Boxing*, November 1974, p. 35.
47. Jack Welsh, "Countdown to Super Showdown Begins," *Boxing Illustrated*, October 1974, p. 19.
48. *Ibid.*
49. G. Bonventure, "A Machine Named George," *Newsweek*, April 8, 1974, 83:45.
50. Tommy Kaye, "Foreman vs. Ali — The Big One Finally On Its Way," *Boxing Guide*, October 1974, p. 8.
51. "Violent Coronation in Zaire," *Time Magazine*, September 23, 1974.
52. Welsh, "Countdown to Super Showdown."
53. Randel, "California Grapevine."
54. Joe Louis, "Muhammad Will Learn Like Frazier How Big, Strong Foreman Is," *Boxing Illustrated*, October 1974, p. 21.
55. Joe Louis, "Foreman by Kayo in Seven," *Superfight '74*, p. 51.
56. Muhammad Ali, "Why I'll Beat George Foreman," *International Boxing*, October 1974, p. 35.
57. P. Axthelm, "Muhammad on the Mountaintop," *Newsweek*, November 11, 1974, 85:70–1.
58. *Ibid.*
59. *Ibid.*
60. *Ibid.*

Chapter Eight

1. Stephen Brunt, "Wepner Still Fond of Fast Life, Fast Ladies," *Globe and Mail*, August 1, 1987, p. A8.
2. Mark Kram, "They Have Kept Him in Stitches," *Sports Illustrated*, March 24, 1975, 42:22.
3. *Ibid.*
4. Dave Anderson, "Boxing," *New York Times*, February 15, 1975, p. 45.
5. Peter Bonventure, "Fool's Gold," *Newsweek*, April 7, 1975, 85:59.
6. Robert Lipsyte, "A Fight for the Fans of Marcus Welby," *New York Times*, March 23, 1975, p. V:2.
7. Joe Nichols, "Ali Will Donate Purse to Minority Poor," *New York Times*, February 11, 1975, p. 49.
8. "Boxing," *Sports Illustrated*, October 9, 1975.
9. "In Stitches," *Time Magazine*, April 7, 1975, 105:63.
10. Dave Anderson, "Winner's Fall in 9th Ranked Knockdown," *New York Times*, March 25, 1975.
11. Dave Anderson, "Nobody Laughs at Chuck Wepner Now," *New York Times*, March 26, 1975, p. 53.
12. "Ron Lyle Must Begin Again," *World Boxing*, July 1975, p. 33.
13. Tex Maule, "When Right Makes Might," *Sports Illustrated*, May 26, 1975, 42:74.
14. Neil Allen, "Ali's Non-Stop Sparring Has Trainer and Two Partners Gasping," *London Times*, June 28, 1975, p. 23.
15. Ron Olver, "Press and Fans Criticize Bugner for Kuala Lumpur Fight," *Ring Magazine*, October 1975, p. 68.

16. Neil Allen, "Manila is to Host Next Big Deal," *London Times*, July 2, 1975, p. 11.
17. Randy Gordon, "Frazier You're Next!" *World Boxing*, November 1975, p. 45.
18. *Ibid.*
19. *Ibid.*
20. Dave Anderson, "Old-Timers Night." *New York Times*, January 27, 1974.
21. Eddie Futch, "Joe Handled Him Before and He'll Do It Again," Ali–Frazier III Album, *Boxing Illustrated 1975*, p. 31.
22. *Ibid.*
23. Dave Anderson, "Battered Frazier's Pilot Ends Brutal Manila Bout," *New York Times*, October 1, 1975, p. 31.
24. *Ibid.*
25. *Ibid.*
26. Red Smith, "Joe Was Still Coming In," *New York Times*, October 1, 1975, p. 31.

Chapter Nine

1. "Ron Lyle: Defeat Without Dishonor," *International Boxing*, June 1976, p. 39.
2. "Round of the Year," *Boxing Illustrated*, March 1977, p. 37.
3. Randy Gordon, "The Superbrawl in Las Vegas," *International Boxing*, June 1976, p. 59.
4. *Ibid.*
5. *Ibid.*
6. Reg Noble, "End of an Era," *Boxing Illustrated*, July 1976, p. 10.
7. Dave Anderson, "Ali at 226 for Bout Tonight," *New York Times*, February 20, 1976, p. 41.
8. Dave Anderson, "Champion Has Little Trouble in Victory," *New York Times*, February 21, 1976, p. 17.
9. Dave Anderson, "Coopman Not in Ali's Plan," *New York Times*, February 18, 1976, p. 29.
10. Dave Anderson, "God Ain't Gonna Let Me Burn Up," *New York Times*, February 19, 1976, p. 47.
11. *Ibid.*
12. Reg Noble, "End of an Era," *Boxing Illustrated*, July 1976, p. 10.
13. Red Smith, "And the Belgi are the Bravest," *New York Times*, February 21, 1976, p. 20.
14. Mark Kram, "One-Nighter in San Juan," *Sports Illustrated*, March 1, 1976, 44:14–17.
15. *Ibid.*
16. "Young Stuns Lyle," *Philadelphia Evening Bulletin*, February 12, 1975, p. 46.
17. "Young-Shavers," *Philadelphia Evening Bulletin*, February 20, 1973.
18. Pat Putnam, "Boxing," *Sports Illustrated*, October 31, 1977.
19. Dave Anderson, "'Remember San Diego' and Ali Does," *New York Times*, April 29, 1976, p. 47.
20. Pat Putnam, "Boxing," *Sports Illustrated*, October 31, 1977.
21. "Ron Lyle Must Begin Again," *World Boxing*, July 1975, p. 33.
22. Dave Anderson, "Champion Has Little Trouble in Victory," *New York Times*, February 21, 1976, p. 17.
23. *Ibid.*
24. Dave Anderson, "'Remember San Diego.'"
25. *Ibid.*
26. *Ibid.*
27. *Ibid.*
28. Greg Nolan, "The Fight Ali Can't Avoid," *Boxing Illustrated*, August 1977, p. 7.
29. Dave Anderson, "Ali Struggles But Keeps Title on Unanimous Decision Over Young," May 1, 1976, p. 17.
30. *Ibid.*
31. Greg Nolan, "The Fight Ali Can't Avoid," *Boxing Illustrated*, August 1977, p. 7
32. Associated Press, "Ali Says He Felt His Age," *New York Times*, May 2, 1976, p. V:1.
33. Dave Anderson, "The Most Subjective Sport," *New York Times*, May 2, 1976, p. V:5.
34. Neil Allen, "The Sun Rises and Sets On Hemingway Hero," *London Times*, May 27, 1976, p. 8.
35. Reuters, "Dunn Planning Aggressive Tactics for Ali," *London Times*, May 4, 1976, p. 11.
36. Reuters, "Dunn Wins His Demand for Better Facilities," *London Times*, May 13, 1976, p. 13.
37. Reuters, "Dunn for Action, Not Words," *London Times*, May 12, 1976, p. 9.
38. Reuters, "Dunn Planning Aggressive Tactics for Ali," *London Times*, May 4, 1976, p. 11.
39. Reuters, "Stiff Workout by Dunn in Impoverished Hall," *London Times*, May 22, 1976, p. 24.
40. Reuters, "There Comes a Time When Even Ali Cannot Hold the Stage," *London Times*, May 24, 1976.
41. Neil Allen, "Dunn Has Short Neck Advantage," *London Times*, May 24, 1976.
42. Neil Allen, "The Sun Rises and Sets On Hemingway Hero," *London Times*, May 27, 1976, p. 8.
43. "Bugner Boosts British Boxing," *Boxing Illustrated*, May 1977, p. 42.
44. Reuters, "Bugner Returns to Prove Point Against Dunn," *London Times*, July 5, 1976.
45. "Bugner Boosts British Boxing," *Boxing Illustrated*, May 1977, p. 42.
46. Ron Olver, "A New Bugner Regains European and Commonwealth Crowns," *Ring Magazine*, January 1977, p. 42.
47. Associated Press, "Ali Says He Felt His Age," *New York Times*, May 2, 1976, p. V:1.
48. Robert H. Boyle, "Smokin' Joe Burns Out," *Sports Illustrated*, June 28, 1976, 44:68.
49. *Ibid.*
50. Red Smith, "This Was for Auld Lang Syne," *New York Times*, September 29, 1976.
51. *Ibid.*
52. Dave Anderson, "Champion Awarded 8 of 15 Rounds — No Knockdowns," *New York Times*, September 29, 1976.
53. *Ibid.*
54. Gerald Eskenazi, "Norton: First Shock, Then Tears," *New York Times*, September 29, 1976.
55. Michael Katz, "Ali Finds Non-Believers in His Dressing Room," *New York Times*, September 29, 1976.
56. Peter Axthelm, "Mirror, Mirror on the Wall," *Newsweek*, October 11, 1976, 88:82–3.
57. Mark Kram, "Not the Greatest Way to Go," *Sports Illustrated*, October 11, 1976, 45:36–38.
58. Nat Loubet, "Editorial," *Ring Magazine*, January 1977, p. 5.

Chapter Ten

1. Greg Nolan, "White Hope or No Hope," *Boxing Illustrated*, July 1976, p. 16.
2. Douglas S. Looney, "He's Not Pretty, He's Just Persistent," *Sports Illustrated*, May 9, 1977, 46:40–2.
3. Michael Katz, "Bobick Faces Sternest Test in Bout with Norton Tonight," *New York Times*, May 11, 1977, p. 19.

4. Dan Shockett, "I'd Rather Take a Beating Than Have a 9 to 5 Job," *World Boxing*, March 1974, p. 40.
5. Dan Levin, "Couple of Hit and Miss Propositions," *Sports Illustrated*, July 31, 1972, 37:20–22.
6. Nolan, "White Hope or No Hope."
7. "What Happens to the Heavyweight Division Now," *International Boxing*, December 1974, p. 31.
8. Gary Morgenstein, "Duane Bobick: What Went Wrong," *Big Book of Boxing*, July 1979, p. 24.
9. *Ibid.*
10. Nolan, "White Hope or No Hope."
11. Douglas S. Looney, "He's Not Pretty, He's Just Persistent," *Sports Illustrated*, May 9, 1977, 46:40–2.
12. Jack Obermayer, "Duane Bobick: Great White Hope or Dope," *World Champion*, July 1977, p. 12.
13. Michael Katz, "Ali Suggests Norton Beat Young First," *New York Times*, May 13, 1977, p. A21.
14. Michael Katz, "Ali Toys With Evangelista and Scores a Unanimous Decision," *New York Times*, May 17, 1977, p. 39.
15. *Ibid.*
16. Michael Katz, "Ali, Foe Look Soft For Title Bout," *New York Times*, May 16, 1977, p. 40.
17. *Ibid.*
18. *Ibid.*
19. Michael Katz, "Ali Toys With Evangelista."
20. *Ibid.*
21. *Ibid.*
22. Deane McGowen, "Shavers, in Lieu of Any Verbal Jab, Gives Ali a Gift and Gets Some Gab," *New York Times*, September 24, 1977, p. 11.
23. *Ibid.*
24. Associated Press, "Ellis Floors Ali Twice," *New York Times*, September 22, 1977, p. B7.
25. Steve Cady, "Ali Pondering Retirement, But Maybe Not Right Now," *New York Times*, October 1, 1977, p. 13.
26. *Ibid.*
27. Nat Loubet, "Editorial," *Ring Magazine*, July 1977, p. 5.
28. Nat Loubet, "Norton Short Circuits Bobick," August 1977, p. 11.
29. Pat Putnam, "Win Some, Lose Some, Split the Rest," *Sports Illustrated*, November 14, 1977, 47:36–38.
30. Reg Noble, "The Fight Ali Can't Lose," *Boxing Illustrated*, April 1978, p. 7.
31. Pat Putnam, "Win Some, Lose Some."
32. Shirley Norman, "Norton–Young Stirs Controversy," *Ring Magazine*, February 1978, p. 8.

Chapter Eleven

1. Al Bernstein, "Ali's Charitable Exhibition Encouragement for Norton," *Boxing Illustrated*, May 1978, p. 45.
2. John Ort, "It's Spinks vs. Ali!" *Ring Magazine*, February 1978.
3. Shirley Norman, "End of an Era ... Spinks is Heavyweight Champ!" *Ring Magazine*, April 1978, p. 31.
4. James Tuite, "Split Decision Gives Championship to Challenger, 24," *New York Times*, February 16, 1978, p. 1.
5. Pat Putnam, "Don't Hate 'Em, Just Hit 'Em," *Sports Illustrated*, November 6, 1978, 49:46–51.
6. *Ibid.*
7. *Ibid.*
8. "Larry Holmes — Fighter of the Year," *World Boxing*, March 1979, p. 34.
9. Putnam, "Don't Hate 'Em."
10. "Larry Holmes — Fighter of the Year," *World Boxing*.
11. *Ibid.*
12. Howard Cosell, "Norton vs. Holmes," ABC TV, June 9, 1978.
13. "Is There Anyone Who Cannot Beat Leon Spinks," *World Boxing*, July 1978, p. 34.
14. Reg Noble, "Why Ali Won't Call It Quits," *Boxing Illustrated*, December 1978, p. 2.
15. Robert J. Thornton, "At Ringside," *International Boxing*, February 1979, p. 6.
16. *Ibid.*
17. *Ibid.*
18. *Ibid.*

Chapter Twelve

1. "Violent Coronation in Kinshasa," *Time Magazine*, September 23, 1974, 104:100–2.
2. Gary Morgenstein, "Duane Bobick: What Went Wrong," *Big Book of Boxing*, July 1979.
3. Reg Noble, "Why Ali Won't Call it Quits," *Boxing Illustrated*, December 1978, p. 14.
4. Allen F. Long, "John Tate: The Great Black Hope," *Boxing Illustrated*, October 1979, p. 33.
5. Brian Ross-Adams, "Boxing," *Rand Daily Mail*, October 20, 1979.
6. "Fighter of the Year." *World Boxing*, March 1979, p. 36.
7. "Shavers Kayoes Norton in First Round," *World Boxing*, July 1979, p. 32.

Bibliography

Ali, Muhammad. "Frazier's All Punched Out." *Boxing Illustrated*, January 1974, p. 13.

_____. "Why I'll Beat George Foreman." *International Boxing*, October 1974, p. 35.

Allen, Neil. "Ali's Antics Just Another Las Vegas Turn Says Bugner." *London Times*, February 13, 1973, p. 14.

_____. "Ali's Non-Stop Sparring Has Trainer and Two Partners Gasping." *London Times*, June 28, 1975, p. 23.

_____. "Bugner Loses to Frazier in Relentless Struggle." *London Times*, July 3, 1973, p. 11.

_____. "Dunn Has Short Neck Advantage." *London Times*, May 24, 1976.

_____. "Heavier Going This Time for Ali the Orator." *London Times*, February 15, 1973, p. 12.

_____. "Manila to Host Next Big Deal." *London Times*, July 2, 1975, p. 11.

_____. "The Sun Rises and Sets on Hemingway Hero." *London Times*, May 27, 1976, p. 8

Amdur, Neil. "Ali Is Silent on Way to Hospital." *New York Times*, March 9, 1971, p. 29.

Anderson, Dave. "Ali at 226 for Bout Tonight." *New York Times*, February 20, 1976, p. 41.

_____. "Ali Beats Frazier on Decision Here." *New York Times*, January 29, 1974, p. 1.

_____. "Ali Calls Bonavena 'Perfect Test' of Whether He Still Has Champion's Touch." *New York Times*, December 6, 1970.

_____. "Ali Finds Crown Fits and Wears It." *New York Times*, September 11, 1970, p. 52.

_____. "Ali Orders His Block of Tickets So the Chips Fall Everywhere." *New York Times*, December 4, 1970, p. 64.

_____. "Ali Rated 17-to-5 Choice Over Quarry Tomorrow." *New York Times*, October 25, 1970, p. V3.

_____. "Ali Scores Third Round Knockout Over Quarry in Successful Return to Ring." *New York Times*, October 27, 1970, p. 56.

_____. "Ali's Speed After Layoff Is Big Question in Quarry Bout Tonight." *New York Times*, October 26, 1970, p. 51.

_____. "Ali Struggles But Keeps Title on Unanimous Decision Over Young." *New York Times*, May 1, 1976, p. 17.

_____. "Argentine Incurs First Knockout." *New York Times*, December 8, 1970, p. 64.

_____. "Battered Frazier's Pilot Ends Brutal Manila Bout." *New York Times*, October 1, 1975, p. 31.

_____. "Bomb Call at Inn." *New York Times*, March 8, 1971, p. 45.

_____. "Champion Awarded 8 of 15 Rounds — No Knockdowns." *New York Times*, September 29, 1976.

_____. "Champion Has Little Trouble in Victory." *New York Times*, February 21, 1976, p. 17.

_____. "Clay Picks Old Mate, Picks Ellis In Eight." *New York Times*, February 10, 1970.

_____. "Coopman Not in Ali's Plan." *New York Times*, February 18, 1976, p. 29.

_____. "Durham Demanding Referee Who Can Control Ali." *New York Times*, March 1, 1971.

_____. "Frazier and Ali: Morality Drama Unfolds." *New York Times*, March 7, 1971, p. V:3.

_____. "Frazier Flattens Ellis and Wins Undisputed Heavyweight Title." *New York Times*, February 17, 1970, p. 46.

_____. "Frazier Gleams in Dawn's Early Light." *New York Times*, February 28, 1971, p. VI:6.

_____. "Frazier Outpoints Ali and Keeps Title." *New York Times*, Mach 9, 1971, p. 29.

_____. "Frazier Puts Hook into Victory Party." *New York Times*, March 5, 1971, p. 41

_____. "Frazier Stops Stander in Fifth Round to Keep Title." *New York Times*, May 26, 1972.

_____. "God Ain't Gonna Let Me Burn Up." *New York Times*, February 19, 1976, p. 47.

_____. "I'm Not Ignorant, Stand Up Man." *New York Times*, January 24, 1974, p. 29.

_____. "Manager Foresees No Fights For Frazier Before Next Year." *New York Times*, March 10, 1971, p. 49.

_____. "The Most Subjective Sport." *New York Times*, May 2, 1976, V:5.

_____. "Nobody Laughs at Chuck Wepner Now." *New York Times*, March 26, 1975, p. 53.

_____. "Old-Timer's Night." *New York Times*, January 27, 1974, p. V:5.

_____. "Pilot Wants Frazier to Retire." *New York Times*, March 6, 1971, p. 15

_____. "Playful Ali Is 212, Frazier 209, Quiet." *New York Times*, January 28, 1974, p. 21.

_____. "Politicians Spar Over the Ali–Quarry Bout." *New York Times*, October 23, 1970, p. 51.

_____. "Prediction in Rhyme Calls for Bonavena to Fall in Nine." *New York Times*, December 1, 1970, p. 63.

_____. "Rough Grindstone Ahead for Ellis' Damaged Nose." *New York Times*, February 14, 1970, p. 16.

_____. "Style Gives Ellis Good Chance Against Heavily Favored Frazier Tomorrow." *New York Times*, February 15, 1970.

_____. "Tired Champion Relaxes While Undergoing Tests." *New York Times*, March 18, 1971, p. 49.

_____. "Victor, at 220 1/2 in Command of Houston Bout." *New York Times*, July 27, 1971, p. 25.

_____. "'Remember San Diego' and Ali Does." *New York Times*, April 29, 1976, p. 47.

_____. "Winner's Fall in 9th Ranked Knockdown." *New York Times*, March 25, 1975.

Associated Press. "Ali Says He Felt His Age." *New York Times*, May 2, 1976, p. V:1.

_____. "Clay Asks Court To Stay Induction." *New York Times*, April 26, 1967, p. 60.

_____. "Ellis Floors Ali." *New York Times*, September 22, 1977, p. B7.

Axthelm, Peter. "The End of the Road." *Newsweek*, February 11, 1974, p. 55.

_____. "Mirror, Mirror on the Wall." *Newsweek*, October 11, 1976, 88:82–83.

_____. "Muhammad on the Mountaintop." *Newsweek*, November 11, 1974, p. 70.

Beddoes, Dick. "Ali Wins but Still Unable to Deck Chuvalo." *Globe and Mail*, May 2, 1972, p. 32.

_____. "By Dick Beddoes." *Globe and Mail*, May 1, 1972, p. 52.

Bernstein, Al. "Ali's Charitable Exhibition Encouragement for Ken Norton." *Boxing Illustrated*, May 1978, p. 45.

Bonventure, P. "Fool's Gold." *Newsweek*, April 7, 1975, 85:59.

_____. "A Machine Named George." *Newsweek*, April 8, 1974, 83:45.

Boyle, Robert H. "Smokin' Joe Burns Out." *Sports Illustrated*, June 28, 1976, 44:68.

Brenner, Teddy. "Boxing." *Schenectady Gazette*, December 14, 1973.

Bromberg, Lester. "Isn't It Time Ringo Showed Up for More of Those Yankee $?" *Ring Magazine*, March 1974, p. 50.

Brunt, Stephen. "Wepner Still Fond of Fast Life, Fast Ladies." *Globe and Mail*, August 1, 1987, p. A8.

"Bugner Boosts British Boxing." *Boxing Illustrated*, March 1977, p. 42.

Cady, Steve. "Ali Pondering Retirement, nut Maybe Not Right Now." *New York Times*, October 1, 1977, p. 13.

_____. "Ali Starts Drive to Make Mountain Out of Bonavena." *New York Times*, November 6, 1970, p. 30.

_____. "Ali Taunts Frazier into Shoving Match." *New York Times*, January 24, 1974, p. 24.

_____. "Ellis Says He Let Frazier Run Bout." *New York Times*, February 17, 1970, p. 46.

Cosell, Howard. "Norton vs. Holmes." ABC-TV, June 9, 1978.

_____. *Wide World of Sports*, ABC-TV, November 17, 1971.

Daley, Arthur. "An Abrupt End to the Frazier Reign." *New York Times*, January 23, 1973, p. 29.

_____. "Day of Decision." *New York Times*, April 28, 1967.

_____. "Epic Worth the Price." *New York Times*, March 9, 1971, p. 29.

_____. "Frazier Spars 4 Rounds for Total of 20." *New York Times*, February 11, 1970, p. 58.

_____. "Sports of the Times: Alone at the Top." *New York Times*, February 18, 1970, p. 54.

_____. "Sports of the Times: The Big Bear." *New York Times*, February 24, 1964, p. 30.

_____. "Sports of the Times: A Boring Fight." *New York Times*, July 27, 1971, p. 25.

_____. "Sports of the Times: A Boy on a Man's Errand." *New York Times*, February 23, 1964, p. V:3.

_____. "Sports of the Times: The Fight." *New York Times*, March 7, 1971, p. V:3.

_____. "Sports of the Times: Not Too Impressive." *New York Times*, December 9, 1970.

_____. "Sports of the Times: Something to Sell." *New York Times*, February 15, 1970.

_____. "Sports of the Times: The Toreador." *New York Times*, December 6, 1970.

Daniel, Dan. "Boxing." *Ring*, November 1972.

Ende, Steve. "Joe Frazier's Dramatic Comeback." *International Boxing*, October 1974, p. 54.

Eskenazi, Gerald. "Ali Favored Over Frazier in Battle of Ex-Champs." *New York Times*, January 27, 1974, p. V:1.

_____. "Ali, Frazier Are Fined For 'Demeaning' Boxing." *New York Times*, January 26, 1974, p. 23.

_____. "Ali's Hand Treatments Stir a Mystery in Camp." *New York Times*, January 20, 1974 p. V:1.

_____. "Bonavena Predicts Ali Will Defeat Frazier for Title." *New York Times*, December 8, 1970, p. 64.

_____. "Norton: First Shock Then Tears." *New York Times*, September 29, 1976.

"Fight of the Year." *World Boxing*. March 1979, p. 32.

"Fighter of the Year." *World Boxing*. March 1979, p. 36.

Fimrite, R. "Back to School Time for Terry Daniels." *Sports Illustrated*, January 24, 1972, 36:22–3.

Futch, Eddie. "Joe Handled Him Before and He'll Do It Again." Ali–Frazier III Album, *Boxing Illustrated 1975*, p. 31.

Gordon, Randy. "Frazier You're Next." *World Boxing*. November 1975, p. 45.

_____. "The George Foreman Story." *Superfight Magazine 1974*, p. 37.

_____. "The Muhammad Ali Story." *Superfight Magazine 1974*, p. 66.

_____. "The Superbrawl in Las Vegas." *International Boxing*, June 1976, p. 59.

Hastings, Frank. "Ali Whips Lubbers for 12, Reserving Right For Joe." *Ring Magazine*, January 1974, p. 8.

"In Stitches." *Time Magazine*, April 7, 1975, 105:63.

"Is There Anyone Who Cannot Beat Leon Spinks." *World Boxing*. July 1978, p. 34.

Jones, Robert F. "Blast Was One Big Bust." *Sports Illustrated*, May 15, 1972, 36:38–40.

Kane, M. "Salute the Grand Old Flag-Raiser George Foreman." *Sports Illustrated*, August 17, 1971, 33:56–57.

Katz, Michael. "Ali Finds Non-Believers in His Dressing Room." *New York Times*, September 29, 1976.

_____. "Ali Suggests Norton Beat Young First." *New York Times*, May 13, 1977, p. A17.

_____. "Ali Toys With Evangelista and Scores a Unanimous Decision." *New York Times*, May 17, 1977, p. 39.

_____. "Ali, Foe Look Soft for Title Bout." *New York Times*, May 16, 1977, p. 37.

_____. "Bobick Faces Sternest Test In Bout With Norton Tonight." *New York Times*, May 11, 1977, p. 19.

Kaye, Tommy. "Foreman vs. Ali—The Big One Finally on Its Way." *Boxing Guide*, October 1974, p. 8.

Kirshenbaum, Jerry. "Boxing." *Sports Illustrated*, January 25, 1971.

Koppett, Leonard. "Clay Ends Drills, but Not His Talk." *New York Times*, February 22, 1964, p. 25.

_____. "Liston Is Sharp Outside of Ring." *New York Times*, February 21, 1964, p. 22.

_____. "TV Fight Facing Integration Snag." *New York Times*, February 24, 1964, p. 30.

Kram, Mark. "Bluffs Butcher Gets Tenderized." *Sports Illustrated*, June 5, 1972, 36:26–7.

_____. "Jawful Test on the Mountain." *Sports Illustrated*, 39:24–26.

_____. "Muddle Then a Zinger." *Sports Illustrated*, December 14, 1970, 33:26–27.

_____. "Not the Greatest Way to Go." *Sports Illustrated*, October 11, 1976, 45:36–38.

_____. "One-Nighter in San Juan." *Sports Illustrated*, March 1, 1976, 44:14–17.

_____. "Show Biz Is Out, Boxing Is In." *Sports Illustrated*, February 16, 1970, 32:14–15.

_____. "They Kept Him In Stitches." *Sports Illustrated*, March 24, 1975, 42:22–24.

"Larry Holmes—Fighter of the Year." *World Boxing*, March 1979, p. 34.

Levin, Dan. "Boxing." *Sports Illustrated*, October 9, 1972.

_____. "Bury His Heart at Wounded Jaw." *Sports Illustrated*, April 9, 1973, 38:28–29.

Levin, Murray. *New York Daily Mirror*, 1928.

Lipsyte, Robert. "Ali Says Frazier Will Be Easier." *New York Times*, October 27, 1970, p. 56.

_____. "Clay Puts His Affairs in Order." *New York Times*, April 27, 1967, p. 59.

_____. "Clay Refuses Army Oath; Stripped of Boxing Crown." *New York Times*, April 29, 1967, p. 1.

_____. "A Fight for the Fans of Marcus Welby." *New York Times*, March 23, 1975, p. V:2.

_____. "Sports of the Times: Are You Crazy." *New York Times*, December 5, 1970.

_____. "Sports of the Times: The Fighters." *New York Times*, February 21, 1964, p. 22.

_____. "Sports of the Times: One More Time." *New York Times*, February 14, 1970.

_____. "Sports of the Times: The Return." *New York Times*, October 26, 1970, p. 51.

_____. "A Star Is Born." *New York Times*, September 12, 1970, p. 20.

_____. "U.S. Court Rejects Appeal by Clay." *New York Times*, April 28, 1967.

Long, Allen F. "John Tate: The Great Black Hope." *Boxing Illustrated*, October 1979, p. 33.

Looney, Douglas S. "He's Not Pretty, He's Just Persistent." *Sports Illustrated*, May 9, 1977, 46:40–2.

Loubet, Nat. "Editorial." *Ring Magazine*, January 1977, p. 5.

_____. "Editorial." *Ring Magazine*, July 1977, p. 5.

_____. "Norton Short Circuits Bobick." *Ring Magazine*, August 1977, p. 11.

Louis, Joe. "Foreman By Kayo in Seven." *Superfight '74*, p. 51.

_____. "Muhammad Will Learn Like Frazier How Big, Strong Foreman Is." *Boxing Illustrated*, October 1974, p. 21.

"The Man Who Whipped Muhammad Ali." *Ebony Magazine*, 28:152–4.

Maule, Tex. "Boxing." *Sports Illustrated*, July 10, 1972.

_____. "Got to Look Good for Allah." *Sports Illustrated*, November 29, 1971, 35:28–9.

_____. "The Mouth That Nearly Roared." *Sports Illustrated*, April 9, 1973, 38:28–29.

_____. "Once and Future King? Scramble for Ali's

Title." *Sports Illustrated*, November 6, 1967, 27:18–21.
_____. "When Right Made Might." *Sports Illustrated*, May 26, 1975, 42:22–24.
McGowen, Deane. "Frazier Says Blows to Body Won." *New York Times*, March 9, 1971, p. 29.
_____. "Shavers, in Lieu of Any Verbal Jab, Gives Ali a Gift and Gets Some Gab." *New York Times*, September 24, 1977, p. 11.
_____. "Sweet Victory Soured by Wrist Injury." *New York Times*, December 15, 1973, p. 39.
McMillan, W.D. *Morning Sun*, 1938.
Morgenstein, Gary. "Duane Bobick: What Went Wrong." *Big Book of Boxing*, July 1979, pp. 24, 60.
Nakashima, Leslie. "Not Only Foster Got Stung." *Sports Illustrated*, April 10, 1972, 36:80.
Nichols, Joe. "Ali Accepts Underdog Role." *New York Times*, March 5, 1971, p. 41.
_____. "Ali Will Donate Purse to Minority Poor." *New York Times*, February 11, 1975, p. 49.
Nichols, Joseph C. "Layne Is 5–9 Choice to Beat Marciano." *New York Times*, July 12, 1951, p. 29.
1976 Ring Record Book.
"No Mission Impossible for the Greatest." Ali–Frazier III Album, *Boxing Illustrated 1975*, p. 8.
Noble, Reg. "End of an Era." *Boxing Illustrated*, July 1976, p. 10.
_____. "The Fight Ali Can't Lose." *Boxing Illustrated*, April 1978, p. 7.
_____. "Why Ali Won't Call It Quits." *Boxing Illustrated*, December 1978, pp. 2, 14.
Nolan, Greg. "The Fight Ali Can't Avoid." *Boxing Illustrated*, August 1977, p. 7.
_____. "White Hope or No Hope." *Boxing Illustrated*, July 1976, p. 16.
Norman, Shirley. "End of an Era ... Spinks Is Heavyweight Champ." April 1978, p. 31.
_____. "Norton–Young Stirs Controversy." *Ring Magazine*, February 1978, p. 8.
Obermayer, Jack. "Duane Bobick—Great White Hope or Dope." *World Champion Magazine*, July 1977, p. 12.
Olver, Ron. "A New Bugner Regains European and Commonwealth Crowns." *Ring Magazine*, January 1977, p. 42.
_____. "Press and Fans Criticize Bugner for Kuala Lumpur Fight." *Ring Magazine*, October 1975, p. 68.
Ort, John. "It's Spinks vs. Ali!" *Ring Magazine*, February 1978.
Plimpton, George. "You Better Believe It." *Sports Illustrated*, February 3, 1973, 38:20–24.
Putnam, Pat. "Boxing." *Sports Illustrated*, October 31, 1977.
_____. "Bugle Call Champion." *Sports Illustrated*, June 12, 1978, 48:34–35.
_____. "Don't Hate 'Em, Just Hit 'Em." *Sports Illustrated*, November 6, 1978, 49:46–51.
_____. "One Little Move, a Giant Step." *Sports Illustrated*, June 18, 1973, 38:22–4.
_____. "One Round of Boxing was more than Enough." *Sports Illustrated*, November 30, 1970, 33:20–21.
_____. "Win Some, Lose Some, Split the Rest." *Sports Illustrated*, November 14, 1977, 47:36–38.
Quarry, Jerry. "I'll Fight Ali—Winner-Take-All." *World Boxing*, July 1974, p. 32.
Randel, Stephen. "California Grapevine." *International Boxing*, April 1974, p. 12.
_____. "California Grapevine." *International Boxing*, August 1974, p. 12.
_____. "California Grapevine." *World Boxing*, November 1974, p. 50.
Randel, Steve. "If I Hadn't Trained Like I Did Norton Would've Whipped Me." *World Boxing Magazine*, January 1974, p. 36.
Reed, Marshall. "Foreman Lowers the Boone." *Boxing Illustrated*, February 1971, p. 61.
Reuters, "Bugner Returns to Prove Point Against Dunn." *London Times*, July 5, 1976.
_____. "Dunn For Action, Not Words." *London Times*, May 12, 1976, p. 9.
_____. "Dunn Planning Aggressive Tactics for Ali." *London Times*, May 4, 1976, p. 11.
_____. "Dunn Wins His Demand For Better Facilities." *London Times*, May 13, 1976, p. 13.
_____. "Stiff Workout By Dunn in Impoverished Hall." *London Times*, May 22, 1976, p. 24.
_____. "There Comes a Time When Even Ali Cannot Hold the Stage." *London Times*, May 24, 1976.
"Revenge For Pearl Harbor." *World Boxing*, Magazine, January 1974, p. 53.
Ring Record Book 1976.
Ripley, Robert. *1925 Everlast Record Book*.
_____. *1929 Everlast Record Book*.
Rocap, W.H. "Victory Little to Boast of." *New York Times*, June 28, 1914.
"Ron Lyle: Defeat Without Dishonor." *International Boxing*, June 1976, p. 39.
"Ron Lyle Must Begin Again." *World Boxing*, July 1975, p. 33.
Ross-Adams, Brian. "Boxing." *Rand Daily Mail*, October 20, 1979.
"Round of the Year." *Boxing Illustrated*, March 1977, p. 37.
Ruiz, Bob. "George Chuvalo: Canadian Heavyweight with True Grit." *Boxing Guide*, October 1974, pp. 56, 58.
"Shavers Kayoes Norton in First Round." *World Boxing*, July 1979, p. 32.
"Shavers–Young." *Philadelphia Evening Bulletin*, February 20, 1973.
Shockett, Dan. "Frazier Dropped Six Times! Foreman Wins Title." *Superfight Magazine 1974*, p. 27.

_____. "I'd Rather Take a Beating Than Have a 9 to 5 Job." *World Boxing Magazine*, March 1974, p. 40.
_____. "I'll Knock Ali Out Early." *World Boxing*, November 1974, p. 35.
_____. "Muhammad Ali Insists: This Time It'll Be Different." *World Boxing*, March 1974, p. 35.
_____. "Quarry Kayoes Shavers." *International Boxing*, April 1974, p. 36.
Shoemaker, Lisle. *San Diego Sun*, 1938.
Shrake, Edwin. "Boxing." *Sports Illustrated*, December 4, 1972.
_____. "It Was the Mouth by a Whisker." *Sports Illustrated*, September 17, 1973, 38:42–43.
_____. "Meet the New Champ!" *Sports Illustrated*, January 29, 1973, 38:12–13.
Smith, Red. "And the Belgi are the Bravest." *New York Times*, February 21, 1976, p. 20.
_____. "Demeaning What." *New York Times*, January 28, 1974, p. 21.
_____. "Don King—Mini Conglomerate." *New York Times*, August 10, 1974, p. V:3.
_____. "Fight Is Stopped with Challenger Draped Over Ring Ropes." *New York Times*, January 16, 1972.
_____. "Foreman Stops Frazier in Two Rounds, Wins Title." *New York Times*, January 23, 1973, p. 1.
_____. "Joe Was Still Coming In." *New York Times*, October 1, 1975, p. 31.
_____. "Patterson Gains Decision Over Bonavena at Garden." *New York Times*, February 12, 1972.
_____. "This Was for Auld Lang Syne." *New York Times*, September 29, 1976.
Sullivan, John L. "I'll Win ... Jeffries; Can't Lose ... Johnson." *New York Times*, July 4, 1910, p. 14.
_____. "Negro Champion Led All the Way—Jeffries Slow and Clumsy." *New York Times*, July 5, 1910, p. 9.
Thornton, Robert J. "At Ringside." *International Boxing*, February 1979, p. 6.
Tucker, Howard M. "Right Hand Punch Finishes German." *New York Times*, December 5, 1961, p. 55.
Tuite, James. "Split Decision Gives Championship to Challenger, 24." *New York Times*, February 16, 1978, p. 1.
United Press International. "Way Is Cleared for Title Match." *New York Times*, January 12, 1971, p. 40.
"Violent Coronation in Kinshasa." *Time Magazine*, September 23, 1974, 104:100–2.
Wallace, William. "Norton, 5–1 Underdog, Breaks Ali's Jaw, Wins Split Decision." *New York Times*, April 1, 1973, V:1.
Welsh, Jack. "Quarry Risks High Stakes In Garden." *Boxing Illustrated*, January 1974, p. 31.
"What Happens to the Heavyweight Division Now." *International Boxing*, December 1974, p. 34.
"Young Stuns Lyle." *Philadelphia Evening Bulletin*, February 12, 1976, p. 46.

Index

Aaron, Hank 174
AAU heavyweight title 95, 132, 177
ABC Sports 88, 144–146, 164 185, 238, 254, 271
Africa 162, 165, 166, 170, 174, 234
African American 282
Afrikaner 279
Agosto, Pedro 106, 229, 251, 252, 263
Aidala, Artie 72
Aird, Billy 210
Alabama 11
Albuquerque, New Mexico 53
Aldeyou, Raymond 247
Alexander, Joe 156, 157, 219
Ali, Muhammad (Cassius Marcellus Clay, Jr.) 4, 6, 14, 18, 22, 128, 130, 131, 133, 136, 138–141, 153–155, 158–161, 228–229, 231, 233, 234, 236, 244–251, 263, 266, 269; Bonavena 56–61; Bugner 116–121, 188–191; comeback (Quarry 1) 46–52; Coopman, Young and Dunn 203–218; early life and career 26–29; Ellis 83–86; Evangelista 237–239; Foreman and Zaire 162–175; Frazier 64–75, 142–151, 192–202; importance of Dundee 68–69; Liston 1 29–31; Lyle 183–187; Nation of Islam *see* Muslims; Norton 123–127, 219–227; Patterson 104–107; retirement 281–284; roadshow 96–109; Shavers 240–243; Spinks 254–262, 270–278; stripped of title 34–41; Supreme Court overturns conviction 85; Vietnam War and military service 34–37; Wepner 176–182
Ali, Rahman 145
Allah 190
Allen, Neil 118, 120, 130, 190, 191, 211, 214
Allied troops 13
Alongi, Tony 48, 79
ALS (Lou Gehrig's Disease) 285
Alzheimer's Disease 107
Anderson, Dave 124, 127, 143, 144, 146, 151, 167, 178, 179, 181, 204, 269, 278, 288
Anderson, Ray 66, 92
Andre the Giant 216
Araneta Coliseum 193

Argentina 28, 43, 57, 60, 61, 77, 102, 103, 111, 184, 185, 220, 221, 263
Arguello, Alexis 287
Arkansas 279
Army and Navy Relief 13
Arrington, Dale "Ibar" 265, 281
Arum, Bob 45, 116, 142, 146, 159, 161, 205, 212, 250, 254, 259–261, 270, 272, 274, 278, 279, 281–283
Asia 98
Associated Press 75, 106, 197, 209
Atlanta, Georgia 46, 50, 101
Atlantic City 177
Atlas, Charles 219
August, Berndt 211
Australia 36, 187, 215
Axthelm, Peter 144, 155, 226

Baer, Buddy 13, 241
Baer, Max 11, 13, 209, 234
Bailey, Lou 81, 102, 135, 184, 220
Baker, Bob 17
Baker, Carl 188
Baldwin, Dr. F. Bruce 36
Ball, Lynn 230
Ballard, Harold 45
Ballard, Jody 199, 244, 245, 263
Baltimore, Maryland 221
Banks, Al 82
Banks, Sonny 28, 181
Baresi, Mrs. 180
Barnes, Millard "Mitt" 250
Barnum, P.T. 159, 161
Barone, Nick 14
Barone, Pep 25
Baruzzi, Mario 237
Basque 89, 139
Bassey, Hogan "Kid" 211
Battle of the Long Count 9
Bayonne, New Jersey 35, 176, 180
Beattie, Jim 86
Beaufort, South Carolina 36
Beaumont, Texas 110
Bedford, England 116
Beirut, Lebanon 74
Belfast, N. Ireland 104
Belgian Congo *see* Zaire
Belgium 166, 172, 203, 204, 239
Bentham, Teddy 47, 51, 52
Bentley, Junior 252
Benton, George 39, 272, 273
Berbick, Trevor 18, 291, 292
Bernstein, Al 265

Beshore, Freddie 14
Besmanoff, Willie 28, 53, 78
Beverly Hills, California 64
Bicentennial 198
Biddles, George 211–213, 215
Biggs, Tyrell 18
Biron, Bob 122, 125, 154, 226, 245, 254, 259–261, 285
Black, Julian 161
Black Muslims *see* Muslims
Blackburn, Jack (Chappie) 125
Blin, Jurgen 88, 89, 112, 118, 128, 129, 135, 184
Bobick, Duane 221, 227, 229, 233–237, 239, 243, 244, 248, 251, 252, 262, 264, 278, 280, 281, 283, 289
Bobick, Rodney 251, 262, 263, 265, 266
Bodell, Jack 102, 118
Bonavena, Oscar 35, 37, 38, 40, 41, 44, 53, 233, 293; contract sold to Conforte 220; early career and financial savvy 56–62, 66, 69, 71, 79, 82–84, 89, 96, 103, 105, 106, 109, 111, 113, 184, 191, 216; tragic death 221
Boone, Clarence 110, 139
Bophuthatswana 271, 272, 279
Borden, Leslie 80
Boston, Charlie 82
Boston, Massachusetts 9, 32
Boswell, Mike 95, 118, 119, 133, 229
Boudreaux, Johnny "Black Knight" 241, 252, 281
Bowe, Riddick 20–22
Bowlus, Minnesota 233, 263
Boxing Digest 286
Boxing Illustrated 24, 28, 29, 39, 92, 265, 279
Boxing Writer's Association 89
Boxing Yearbook 1974 169
Braddock, Jim 11, 12 15, 209, 233, 241
Brassell, Rufus 46, 77, 102
Bratton, Johnny 73
Braverman, Al 139, 140, 176, 177, 180, 181
Brazell, Grady 122
Brazil 82, 133
Brennan, Bill 7
Brenner, Teddy 56, 60, 140, 162, 178
Brewster Center (Detroit) 125

307

Brezhnev, Leonid 271
Briggs, Shannon 21
Briscoe, Bennie 36, 205
British Boxing Board of Control 118, 215
British Columbia 99
British heavyweight champion 102, 118, 128, 191, 211, 215
Bronx, New York 224
Brooklyn, New York 229
Brooks, Eddie 199
Brooks, Reco 95, 136
Brown, Drew "Bundini" 51, 52, 69, 72–74, 112, 115, 174
Brown, Elmo 139
Brown, Paul 117
Brown, Vic 105
Brown Distilleries Corporation 27
Brownsville, New York 18
Bruce, Mike 36, 37, 81
Bruno, Frank 19
Buck, Harold 259, 269
Budapest, Hungary 190
Buenos Aires, Argentina 56, 58, 221
Bugner, Joe 22, 82, 88–90, 99, 102, 109, 133, 138, 140, 141, 177, 180, 203, 212–215, 219, 221, 233, 293; Ali 118–123, 188–192; early life and career 116–118; Frazier 128–130
"Bum of the Month" 11, 13, 14, 215
Burman, Clarence "Red" 13
Burns, Tommy 235
Burns, Tommy (Noah Brusso) 4, 53
Burton, Willie 82
Butkus, Dick 78
Butterbean (Eric Esch) 293

Caesar's Palace, Las Vegas 119, 246, 267, 269, 286, 288
Caldwell, Leroy 82, 133, 220
California 40, 47, 91, 97, 102, 109, 133, 155, 182, 221, 243
California State Heavyweight Championship 240
Camden, New Jersey 68
Campanis, Al 161
Campbell, Dr. Edward 82, 133, 147, 148
Campbell, Rocky 210
Canada 19, 21, 37, 64, 79, 82, 85, 89, 101, 176, 235, 251, 292
Canadian heavyweight title 78, 99, 101
Cane, Dante 80
Capone, Al 116
Caracas, Venezuela 151–154, 160, 162, 175, 206
Carlos, John 165
Carnera, Primo 11, 53, 276
"Carnival of Champions" 272
Carpentier, Georges 7, 8, 53
Carson, Bill 251
Carter, Rubin "Hurricane" 39, 277
Cassina, Loren 221
Castellano, Tony 106, 150

Cavanaugh, Jerome P. 45
Cayton, Bill 18, 19
CBS TV 254, 260, 291
Chamberlain, Neville 212
Chamberlain, Wilt 83
Chaplin, George 281
Charles, Ezzard 14–16, 22, 53, 118, 277, 288
Charlie's Angels 254
Chartwell Artists, Ltd. 64
Chase, Charlie 89, 99
Checchini, Harry 220
Chepulis, Ionas 76
Chicago, Illinois 9, 26, 32, 64, 84, 116
Chicago Tribune 26
Chile 13
Christianity 66, 165
Chuvalo, George 33, 37, 38, 49, 56–59, 78–83, 87, 88, 96, 99–101, 105, 109–112, 123, 127, 176, 233
Ciaccio, Philip 274
Clancy, Gil 59, 133, 137, 141, 152, 155, 199, 201, 202, 230
Clark, Lamar 27
Clark, Henry 97, 98, 169, 221, 240, 241
Clay, Cassius, Jr. *see* Ali, Muhammad
Clay, Cassius, Sr. 27
Clayton, Zack 49, 172–174
Cleroux, Robert 78, 101
Cleveland, Ohio 91, 92, 137, 159, 160, 162, 178, 180, 262
Cleveland Coliseum 176
Cliffside, New Jersey 134
Cloverlay, Inc. 37, 39, 62
Cobb, Randall "Tex" 289
Cobo Hall, Detroit
Cockell, Don 16, 189
Coetzee, Gerrie 278, 281–283
Colombia 280
color line 10
Colorado 183
Colorado State Athletic Commission 200
Colorado State Penitentiary 131
Comiskey Park, Chicago 26
Commonwealth heavyweight title 102, 118, 128, 211, 215
Condon, John 158, 164
Conn, Billy 13, 14, 22, 53, 206
Conn, Mark 60
Conrad, Harold 104
Cooke, Jack Kent 63–65, 83, 91, 142
Cooney, Gerry 17, 230, 275, 289
Cooper, "Smokin'" Bert 20
Cooper, Henry 28, 29, 68, 118, 127, 170, 176, 181, 189, 191, 233
Coopman, Jean Pierre 203–207, 212, 215, 239, 254
Cope, Dr. Dennis W. 291
Copelin, Sherman 274
Corbett, James J. 4, 23
Cordoza, Paul 70
Corletti, Eduardo 102, 103, 117
Cosby, Bill 67

Cosell, Howard 87, 88, 114, 144–146, 252, 268, 278, 286, 287
Council Bluffs, Iowa 95
Covington, Hayden 34
Croke Park, Dublin 104
Cuba 234, 235, 237, 249, 279, 280
Culpepper, Henry 240
Cummings, Floyd " Jumbo " 290, 291
Cuthbert, Georgia 261

Dakin, Roland 120
Daley, Arthur 29, 31, 52, 74, 276
Dallas Cowboys 277
Daly, Bill 139, 141
Daly, John 162
D'Amato, Cus 18, 19, 25, 26, 38, 86
Dangerfield, Rodney 270
Daniel, Dan 111
Daniels, Bill 132, 235
Daniels, Terry 91–96, 105, 110–112, 139, 140, 178, 198, 199, 203, 212, 251
Daredevil Jack 7
Darwin, Charles 3
Daskiewicz, Joe 255
Davey, Chuck 45, 54
Davila, Roberto 77, 83, 177
Davis, Howard 249, 279
Dawson, James P. 14
Dean, Dr. Michael 123
Declaration of Independence 198
Deer Lake, Pennsylvania 126, 147, 262
deJaeger, Karl 203
DeJohn, Mike 23, 79
DeLeon, Carlos 292
Dempsey, Jack 4, 6–10, 14, 18, 22, 23, 41, 48, 53, 69, 118, 166, 171, 180, 197, 202, 216, 222, 275, 277, 288
Dennis, John "Dino" 218, 252
Denver, Colorado 89, 131, 133, 184, 200, 220
Denver Boxing Club 185
Denver Rocks 132
Detroit, Michigan 11, 45, 46
DeVanney, Jimmy 211
Diamond Bar, California 285
DiFuria, Pat 97
DiMaggio, Jake 273
Dokes, Michael 20, 275
Dooley, Edwin B. 34, 60, 146
Dorazio, Gus 13
Douglas, James "Buster" 12, 19, 293
Doyle, Tony 47, 48, 62, 83, 102, 133, 135, 221, 240
Drover, Bill 82, 133
Drum 222
Dublin, Ireland 103, 104, 106
Duff, Mickey 128
Dugent, Duke 36
Duncan, Pat 188, 189, 263
Dundee, Angelo 28, 29, 39, 42–46, 51, 52, 59, 68, 69, 73, 84, 85, 109, 112, 115, 123, 127, 147,

Index

170, 172–174, 186, 188, 189, 192, 194, 196, 204, 207, 208, 210, 223, 225, 238, 239, 242, 257, 263, 288
Dundee, Chris 140
Dundee, Jimmy 74
Dunn, Janet 211
Dunn, Richard 203, 205, 206, 208, 210–215, 238, 254, 255, 279, 284
Dupree, Rodell 262
Duran, Roberto 287
Durelle, Yvon 78
Durham, Yancey (Yank) 36, 37, 45–47, 52, 55, 59, 67–70, 74, 91, 93, 94, 96, 112–114, 128, 130, 144
Dutch 118, 130, 131
Dutra, Harold 122
Dutrieux, Herman 93
Dylan, Bob 278

Earls, Willis 92
Eastling, Aaron 77, 122
Easton, Pennsylvania 261, 266
Ebony magazine 123
Edson, Jay 86, 140
Ekwelum, Ngozika 210
Ellington, Duke 70
Elliott, Alexander 215
Ellis, Jimmy 35, 90, 99, 104, 109, 111, 112, 136, 137, 141, 148, 177, 185, 194, 221, 242, 263, 290, 293; Ali 39, 83–87; Dundee 39, 84; Frazier and retirement 187–189; unification fight with Frazier 42–45; WBA champion 40, 41
El Paso, Texas 82
Ende, Steven 159
Eppy, Joe 61
Erlichman, Marty 138
Erskine, Joe 78
Eskin, Lew 104
ESPN Sports 265
Ettiene, Clifford 21
Europe 88, 89, 203, 211, 237
European Boxing Union 203, 205
European heavyweight title 89, 102, 118–120, 128, 203, 205, 211, 214, 215
Evangelista, Alfredo 205, 237–241, 244, 254, 283, 292
Evans, M. Clifford 34
Everlast Record Book 6, 9

Fariello, Joe 38, 87
Farleigh Dickinson University 134
Farley, James A., Jr. 226
Farr, Tommy 12, 117, 189
Farrar, Reginald 177
Faversham, William, Jr. 27, 37
Felstein, Bob "Pretty Boy" 101
Ferguson, Jesse 20
Ferrara, Chickie 186
Fighter's Heaven 147
Fimrite, Ron 93
Firpo, Luis 6–8, 10, 40, 202, 279
Fitzpatrick, John 206

Fitzsimmons, Bob 4, 53
Flaherty, Joe 282
Fleischer, Nat 5, 38, 42, 65
Florida 69
Flynn, "Fireman" Jim 33
Foley, Zora 17, 23, 28, 33, 40, 53, 57, 58, 78, 79, 94
Fonda, Jane 64
Ford, Pres. Gerald 175
Foreman, George 5, 15, 120, 121, 124–133, 157–161, 180, 182–185, 187, 190, 192, 196, 197, 205, 215, 223, 224, 227, 228, 240–249, 251, 252, 256, 257, 263, 264, 269–271, 275, 277, 284, 288, 290, 292, 293; Ali and Zaire 162–178; contractual disputes 137, 138; early life and career 75–84, 89, 99, 106; first retirement and comeback 232–235; Frazier 109–116, 216–218; Lyle 198–202; Norton 151–156; regains title 20–22, 62, 232; Roman 137–143; Young 229–232
Forte, Levi 77, 105, 189
Foster, Bob 46, 52–56, 66, 69, 103, 107–112, 119, 134, 169, 188, 287
Foster, Mac 49, 50, 90, 97–100, 112, 123, 130, 133, 135, 140, 156, 168, 184, 188
Foxx, Redd 264
France 205, 247
Frankfurt, W. Germany 184
Frazier, Florence 36, 151
Frazier, Joe 22, 133, 137–141, 163–166, 171, 173, 175, 178, 180–183, 187–189, 203–205, 208, 208, 213, 215, 222, 224, 233–237, 241, 249, 251, 255, 256, 266, 269, 270, 275, 278, 288, 291, 293; Ali 64–75, 142–152, 192–200; Bugner 128–131; Daniels 91–94; death 290; early life and career 36–41; Ellis 42–45; Foreman 110–116, 216–220; Foster 53–56; importance of Durham 67, 68; 1981 comeback 290; Quarry 155–159; Stander 94–96
Frazier, Marvis 290
Freeman, Peter 251
Fresno, California 97
Fried, Franklin 64
Fried, Jack 206
Fullmer, Gene 78
Futch, Eddie 121, 123–127, 144–146, 149, 150, 158, 194–197, 217, 218, 233, 235–237, 245, 290

Gainford, George 161
Galento, "Two Ton" Tony 12, 12, 94, 241
Galindez, Victor 273
Gallagher's 285
Garcia, Jose Luis 39, 122, 123, 135, 153, 184, 188, 206, 219, 220
Garland, Judy 65
Garrett, Sam 160

Gault, Pappy 234
Gelb, Frank 207
General Motors strike 55
Geoff, Dr. Julian 43
Georgetti, Jose 57
Georgia 46, 50, 234
Germany 10, 12, 21, 23, 40, 88, 89, 211, 212, 234
Giachetti, Richie 262
Gibbons, Tommy 7, 8
Gibbs, Harry 129, 177
Gillian, Ludene !38, 140, 141
Gilmore, Jimmy 97
Glick, Abe 39
God 277
Godfrey, George 10
Godoy, Arturo 13
Goldberg, Marvin 57
Golden Gloves 36, 47, 177, 205, 206, 234
Goldman, Charley 15, 57, 86
Golota, Andrew 20
Gone with the Wind 63
Gonzalez, Manuel A. 146
Goodman, Bobby 173
Goodman, Mack 105
Goodwin, Murphy 95, 110, 139
Gordon, Jack 61, 150
Gore, Bill 54, 55
Gorgeous George 27
Gorosito, Raul 263, 280
Gosha, Richie (Dick) 136
Goss, Woody 36
Gotch, Frank 215
Gould, Will 9
Grant's Pass, Oregon 75
Great Britain 10, 12, 16, 19, 21, 30, 48, 68, 69, 82, 102, 116–120, 128–130, 162, 176, 188–192, 203, 205
The Greatest 50, 153, 163
Greb, Harry 7, 8
Green, Charlie "Devil" 104, 105, 203
Greene, Abe J. 177
Greene, Richard 283
Griffith, Emile 146, 287
Guiffre, Dr. James 74, 75
Gullick, Ted 110

Hagler, Marvelous Marvin 287
Halifax, Nova Scotia 291
Hallenstadion (Zurich) 88
Hamid, George 39, 177
Hamilton, Gene 47
Hannay, Judge Allen B. 34
Hansen, Knute 10
Harris, Charlie "Emperor" 105, 136
Harris, Stamford 80, 82
Hart, Marvin 4
Hayden, Mike 263
Hayes, Mike 220
Hearns, Thomas 287
Heeney, Tom 9
Hemsdale Leisure Corporation 162
Hepburn, Obie 211
Hernandez, Fred 187
High Sierra Theatre 108
Hill, George 46

Hinke, Terry 178
Hitler, Adolf 12
Hodges, Clay 205
Holland 203
Hollywood, California 7, 182, 222, 236, 237
Holmes, Larry 6, 11, 14, 56, 160, 244, 248, 274, 276–278, 280, 290–293; Ali's sparring partner 262; early life and career 261–266; Norton 267–270; reign compared to Louis' 17, 18, 20, 22; title reign and domination 283–288
Holyfield, Evander 19–22, 232, 293
Honolulu 185, 207, 262
Houpe, Fred *see* Sanford, Young
House of Sports, Inc. 46
Houston, Texas 33, 34, 39, 64, 76, 85, 119, 138, 161, 170, 244
Houston Astrodome 39, 62, 63, 83, 85, 86, 91, 113
Howard, Ron 220
Hubbard, Don 274
Huber, Hans 36
Hudgins, Johnny 46
Hungary 116
Hunsaker, Tunney 27
Hurley, Jack 81

I Only Talk Winning 84
Illinois 38
In the Corner 124, 144
Indianapolis, Indiana 19
Indris, Dato Harun 188
Indy 500 277
Inglewood Forum 64
Inoki, Antonio 215, 216
International Boxing Federation (IBF) 7, 18, 21, 293
International Boxing Hall of Fame 21, 293
International Boxing League 132
Iron Curtain 190
Isaac, Kevin 202, 229, 262
Iselin, Jimmy 88
Islamic *see* Muslims
Italy 11, 183, 234, 237, 239, 244, 246, 247, 253
Iwama, Frank 139

Jackson, Rev. Jesse 272, 279
Jackson, Morris 128
Jackson, Peter 4
Jacksonville, Illinois 122
Jacobs, Jim 18, 19
Jacobs, Mike 161
Jaggi, Hansrudi 88, 89
Jakarta, Indonesia 130
Jamaica 18, 110–117, 138, 151, 188, 217, 291
James, Charlie 219, 220, 241
Japan 13, 60, 97, 98, 151
Japanese Boxing Association 97
Jeannette, Joe 5, 22
Jeffries, James J. 4–6, 12, 23, 33, 215
Jensen, Marv 27

Jesus Christ 191
Job Corps 75
Johansson, Ingomar 17, 23, 32, 233, 238, 281
John, Elton 162
Johnson, Alonzo 28, 198, 199
Johnson, Bunny 210, 211
Johnson, George "Scrapiron" 77, 81, 117, 128, 133
Johnson, Greg 244
Johnson, Harold 16
Johnson, Jack 4–6, 10–12, 22, 32–34, 41, 47, 53, 99, 171, 215, 216, 233, 275
Johnson, "Battling" Jim 5
Johnson, Leroy R. 46
Johnson, Maynard 50
Johnson, Sarge 255
Joiner, Billy 221
Jones, Doug 28, 29, 33, 38, 53, 69, 79, 81, 99
Jones, Florida Al 219
Jones, Leroy 244, 287
Jones, Memphis Al 185, 187, 207
Joubert, Lucien 273
Judge, Jerry 198, 199

Kangaroo, Captain 147
Kaplan, Mike 102
Katz, George 25
Kearns, Jack "Doc" 81, 180
Keel, Earl 86
Kelleher, Neil W. 60
Kelly, Tom 209
Kennedy, Pres. John F. 26
Kentucky 26
Kentucky Derby 277
Ketchel, Stanley 5
King, Coretta Scott 67
King, Don 19, 178, 198, 202, 205, 227, 232, 238, 243, 244, 250, 252, 259–264, 266, 267, 274, 278, 283; criminal past 159; manager of Shavers, Merritt & Holmes 136, 137; promotional beginnings (Zaire) 160–162, 166, 169
King, Howard 23, 78
Kingston, Jamaica 110–113
Kinshasa, Zaire 161, 162, 166, 167
Kirkman, Boone 81, 110, 170, 185, 187, 188, 198, 199, 251, 289
Kleiman, Dr. A. Harry 80, 242
Klitschko, Vitali 4, 22
Klitschko, Wladimir 4, 22
Knoetze, Kallie 278–283, 290
Knoxville, Tennessee 279
Kou, Yoshio 97
Kram, Mark 42, 47
Krueger, Terry 220, 263
Ku Klux Klan 234
Kuala Lumpur, Malaysia 188–191, 213

Landover, Maryland 187, 205, 220, 237, 263
Langford, Sam 5, 6, 22, 67
LaStarza, Roland 16
Latka, George 127

Lavorante, Alejandro 28
Layne, Rex 16
Leavenworth 45
Lederman, Harold 225
LeDoux, Scott 218, 221, 230, 251–257, 263, 273, 284, 285, 287, 289, 290
Leonard, Sugar Ray 249, 279, 287
Lesnevich, Gus 14
Levene, Harry 214, 215
Levin, Jack 243, 247
Lewin, Murray 10
Lewis, Al "Blue" 103–106, 112, 119, 184
Lewis, Butch 250, 257, 274
Lewis, John Henry 12, 53
Lewis, Lennox 20–22
Lewis, Ted "Kid" 8
Lewiston, Maine 32, 55
Lincoln, Abraham 282
Lincoln, Amos 86
Lingala language 172
Lipsyte, Robert 37, 179
Liston, Charles "Sonny" 17, 55, 66, 68, 73, 80, 97, 113, 115, 126, 127, 131, 133, 138, 165, 167, 168, 171, 172, 174, 177, 180, 227, 230, 233, 242, 256, 259, 268, 270, 277, 279, 281; Ali and WBA suspension 32–36; early beginnings 23–26; mentor to Foreman 76, 77; mysterious death 35; negative image and Patterson 23–26; upset loss to Clay (Ali) 27–31
Liston, Geraldine 35
Lloyd, Robert 207
LoBianco, Johnny 50, 82, 105, 106, 183
London, Brian 33, 48, 117, 176
London, England 28, 64, 102, 128, 162, 190, 206
London Observer 191
London Times 118, 120, 130, 211
Lonsdale belt 215
Lord, Doug 92, 93
Los Angeles, California 47, 82, 91, 110
Los Angeles Dodgers 161
Los Angeles Forum 91
Los Angeles Kings 64
Los Angeles Lakers 64, 83
Losch, Steven C. 286
Loubet, Nat 42, 227, 238, 245, 286
Loughran, Tommy 10, 11, 53
Louis, Joe 4, 6, 11–14, 17, 18, 22–26, 37, 41, 52, 53, 66, 84, 94, 113, 117, 118, 125, 157, 158, 161, 164, 171
Louisiana Sports, Inc. 272, 274
Louisiana State Athletic Commission 92
Louisville, Kentucky 27, 39, 44, 84
Louisville Group 27, 28, 31, 36
Lovell, Alberto 58, 219
Lovell, Pedro 220, 285
Lubbers, Rudi 118, 128–131, 147, 203, 237

Luca, Frank 243, 286
Lundeen, Dr. William 124
Lurie, Art 259
Lutrell, Cowboy 216
Lux, Frank 247
Lyle, Ron 22, 89, 90, 109, 110, 123, 137, 138, 141, 156, 175, 178, 189, 190, 197205, 207, 208, 215–217, 219, 220, 227–229, 233, 235, 240, 244, 245, 247, 248, 264, 275, 288; Ali 184–188; death 293; decline, retirement and comeback 230; early beginnings 131–133; Foreman 200–202; Quarry 133–135; Shavers 198–200; Young 230

Maas, Peter 254
Mac, Johnny 95
Machado, Danny 89
Machen, Eddie 17, 32, 37, 38, , 47, 48, 78
MacLean's magazine 282
Maddox, Lester 46, 50
Madison Square Garden 26, 28, 35, 38, 42–44, 50, 56, 57, 60, 62–65, 70, 77, 80, 81, 104–106, 113, 133
Madrid, Spain 237
Mafuz, Dr. Edward 239
Maine 38
Malaysia 188, 189, 191, 193
Malitz, Mark 37
Maloney, Jim 10
Mancini, Ray "Boom Boom" 287
Mandingo 222
Mandunga, Bula 170
Manila, Philippines 193, 195, 219, 224, 263, 266, 269
Mann, Nathan 12
Mann Act 5, 6, 33, 34
Maple Leaf Gardens 45, 198
Marantz, Steve 165
Marciano, Rocky 14–18, 22, 24, 41, 48, 53, 57, 78, 86, 132, 166, 172, 189, 233, 275, 293
Marcos, Pres. Ferdinand 193
Marcos, Imelda 193
Marion Correctional Institute (Ohio) 159
Markson, Harry 56, 62, 81
Marques of Queensbury 4, 60, 100, 140, 152, 169, 216
Marshall, Texas 75
Martin, Joe 27
Martin, Leotis 35, 36, 39, 40, 44, 57
Maryland State Athletic Commission 252
Mashburn, Bob 219
Massachusetts 15, 38
Mathis, Buster 36, 38, 80, 86–89, 101, 111, 112, 119, 133, 180, 244
Mattux, Clifford 132
Maule, Tex 41
Mauriello, Tami 14
Mauritius 272
Maxim, Joey 14, 16, 53
McAliden, Danny 128, 133, 210, 211, 221

McBride, Kevin 21
McCall, Oliver 21, 293
McCarthy, Eugene 278
McCoy, Al 13
McGann, Sparrow 10, 11
McGill, Sam 98
McIllvaney, Hugh 191
McIntyre, Jerry 251
McLeay, Earl 101
McMillan, W.D. 12
McMurray, Bill 169, 170
McMurtry, "Irish" Pat 78
McNeeley, Tom 57, 105
Meilleur, Jimmy 60
Melbourne, Australia 187
Meno, Jose 58
Mercado, Bernardo 280, 285, 292
Mercante, Arthur 70–72 80, 81, 106, 113–115, 137, 224, 225
Mercer, Ray 293
Merchant Marines 74
Merritt, Jeff "Candy Slim" 39, 136, 159, 160
Mexico 39, 80, 132
Mexico City 76, 249
Miami, Florida 69, 77, 79, 105, 140, 174, 279
Michigan Boxing Commission 54
Michigan State University 45
Middleton, Larry 90, 102, 109, 118, 133, 135, 184, 187, 221, 222, 235, 236, 240, 251, 293
Midwest heavyweight title 94
Mildenberger, Karl 33, 35, 40, 57, 66, 204, 211, 233
Miller, Ace 282, 283
Mims, Terry 253
Minneapolis 251, 252
Minneapolis, Minnesota 236, 251–253, 263
Miske, Billy 7
Miss Black America Pageant 19
Missouri 247
Miteff, Alex 28, 78
Mmabatho 279, 281
Mobutu Sese Seko 161, 162, 166, 169, 170, 188
Monroe, Marty 284
Monte Carlo 282
Montevideo, Uruguay 237
Montgomery, Alabama 25
Montreal, Quebec 78, 99, 247, 250, 251, 255, 279
Monzon, Carlos 287
Moore, Archie 16, 17, 28, 53, 78, 113, 121, 136, 174, 198
Moore, Sonny 53, 62, 93
Moorer, Michael 15, 20, 21, 233
Moran, Frank 5, 6
Morehouse College 46
Morrison, Tony 292
Mosa, Ralph 120
Moses 192
Motlana, Dr. Nthatho 282, 283
Muhammad, Hon. Elijah 31, 124
Muhammad, Herbert 31, 64, 126, 161, 186, 204, 208, 244, 246
Muhammad, Matthew Saad 205
Munich, Germany 210, 212, 234

Munich Hilton Hotel 212
Municipal Stadium (Philadelphia) 15
Muslims 30–32, 65, 66, 106, 126, 130, 144, 165, 190, 227, 277
Mussell, Sam 46
Musto, Tony 13

NAACP 25, 272
Nagler, Barney 53
Napoles, Jose 287
Nappi, Pat 255
Nassau, Bahamas 291
Nation of Islam *see* Muslims
National Boxing Association 8, 14, 24
National Football League 5, 78, 91, 95
National Hockey League 64
National Sports, Ltd. 113
National Stadium (Jamaica) 113
Nazis 12, 25
NBC TV 242, 254, 291
Nebraska 94, 95
Negro Baseball League 255
Neiman, Leroy 72
Neumann, Randy 19, 134, 178, 205, 223, 233, 235, 265
Nevada 160
New Jersey 77, 133
New Jersey Athletic Commission 177
New Jersey State Heavyweight title 134
New Orleans, Louisiana 25, 91, 270, 272, 274, 281
New York City 35, 36, 48, 56, 57, 63, 69, 70, 133, 146, 154, 156, 157, 163, 165, 185, 285
New York Daily Mirror 10
New York State 26, 35, 38, 60; taxes 162
New York State Athletic Commission 8, 14, 43, 57, 60, 69, 73, 80, 82, 107, 142, 146, 147, 226, 242
New York Times 5, 6, 14, 16, 25, 28, 29, 37, 52, 66, 78, 127, 130, 167, 178, 209, 223, 243, 254, 276, 278
New York Yankees 277
New Zealand 9
Newsweek magazine 125, 144, 155, 226
Newton, Wendell 135, 184
Nichols, Joseph C. 16
Nigeria 211
Nilon, Jack 35
Noble, Reg 265, 279
Norris, Jim 161
Norris, Rochell 221
North American Heavyweight Championship 82, 132, 148
Northwest Missouri State University 122
Norton, Ken 17, 22, 109, 112
Norway 189
Nova, Lou 13

Oakland, California 264
O'Brien, Philadelphia Jack 53

Ocasio, Osvaldo "Jaws" 247, 284
O'Connell, Jack 83
O'Connor, Ulich 213
O'Grady, Pat 226
O'Halloran, Jack 77, 92, 95, 117, 133, 139, 140, 240
Ohio 159, 160, 244, 286
Ohio University 160
Olivares, Ruben 287
Olympics 20, 27, 31, 36, 38, 39, 62, 76, 77, 80, 116, 165, 198, 228, 234, 235, 246, 249–251, 253–255, 262
Oma, Lee 14
Omaha, Nebraska 94, 96, 128
Omaha Civic Auditorium 96
Onasis, Aristotle 64
Order of Canada 101
Organization of African Unity 272

Pacheco, Dr. Ferdie 73, 124, 126, 180, 216, 227, 239, 240, 254, 291
Pacific Coliseum 100
Padilla, Carlos 195, 196, 284
Paez, Miguel 58, 111
Page, Greg 292
Paladino, Dr. Roberto 62
Palermo, Frank "Blinky" 24, 25, 247
Pan American Games 107, 122, 177, 234, 235, 249
Papp, Lazlo 116
Paret, Benny "Kid" 146
Paris 216
Parker, James J. 78
Parkinson's Syndrome 292
Pastor, Bob 13
Pastrano, Willie 23
Patterson, Floyd 17, 18, 29, 32, 33, 35, 40, 53, 57, 59, 62, 66, 76, 79, 81, 83, 90, 92, 109, 112, 115, 119, 127, 163, 177, 220, 234, 238, 256, 281; Ali 104–107; Ellis 41, 42; Quarry fights 48; showdown with Liston 23–26
Patterson, Thomas 105
Patterson, Tracy 107
Paycheck, Johnny 13
Pearl Harbor 13, 60, 160
Peers Management 86, 88
Peltz, J. Russell 125
Penn Central Railroad 68
Pennsylvania 8, 38, 160
Pentecostal 131
Pep, Willie 66
Peralta, Gregorio 43, 57, 58, 77, 82, 110, 135, 168, 184
Perenchio, Jerry 63–65, 162, 199, 216, 217
Perez, Tony 51, 133, 148–150, 180, 181, 194, 289
Persol, Johnny 40
Peru 77, 83, 177
Pett, Harry 46
Pezim, Murray 99, 100
Philadelphia 8, 15, 36, 43, 45, 68, 69, 130, 133, 147, 185, 197, 205–207, 230, 231, 255, 284, 290

Philadelphia Arena 229
Philadelphia Bulletin 206
Philippine Islands 193
Pini, Piero 203
Pires, Luis 58, 82, 133, 167, 168
Pleasanton, California 75
Poland 20
Police Athletic League(PAL) 36, 68, 205, 262
Polite, Charlie 77, 105, 117, 128, 139, 198, 199, 219
Polo Grounds 13
Porat, Otto von 10
Powell, Charlie 28
Prater, Tom 252, 264, 265
Prescott, Johnny 117
Presley, Elvis 120
Pretoria, S.A. Pearl, Davey 286
prostrate cancer 107
Pruitt-Igoe housing project 249, 250
Pryor, Aaron 287
Puerto Rican heavyweight champion 139, 251
Puerto Rico 106, 139, 141, 207, 231, 247, 251, 284
pugilistica dementia 183, 247
Putnam, Pat 55, 205, 265

Qawi, Dwight Muhammad 292
Quarry, Jack 47, 83, 84, 101
Quarry, James 47, 183
Quarry, Jerry 22, 35, 40, 41, 44, 46, 55, 58–60, 62, 83, 87, 89, 97, 99, 104, 109, 112, 123, 126, 152, 160, 175, 184–185, 187, 188, 194, 197, 199, 219, 221, 233, 240, 267, 275, 288, 289, 293; Ali 50–53, 101–103; Chuvalo disaster 80, 81; early life and career 47–50; Frazier 155–159; Lyle and Shavers (rise of the Phoenix) 133–141; Norton 182, 183; pugilistic dementia and death 183
Quarry, Mike 103, 134, 183
Quezon City, Philippines 193

Rademacher, Pete 256
Ramos, Manuel 39, 41, 58, 80, 92, 95, 128, 132, 133
Rand Daily Mail 283
Randolph, Leo 249
Recht, Bill 72, 106
Red Cross 179
Redding, California 48
Regis, Ulric 117
Reno, Charlie 80, 125
Reno, Nevada 5, 221
Renton, Washington 187
Ricci, Gino 80
Rickard, Tex 8, 161
Righetti, Alfio 246, 247, 253–256
Riley, Don 235
Ring magazine 5, 18, 28, 29, 38, 42, 44, 49, 61, 65, 92, 95, 105, 111, 133, 136, 165, 203, 207, 211, 227, 238
Rio de Janeiro, Brazil 243

Ripley, Robert 6, 7
Rischer, Roger 78, 97
Risko, Johnny 10
Rivkin Art 122, 125, 154
Roberto Clemente Coliseum 204, 231
Robinson, Horace "Big City" 264
Robinson, Sugar Ray 24, 73, 85, 99, 161, 206
Rockwell, Norman 26
Rocky 181, 211, 238, 239, 285
Rodriguez, Isidore 281
Rodriguez, Lucien 205, 237
Rogan, lou 229
Roman, Joe "King" 138–141, 151, 152, 178, 207, 231, 264
Rome, Italy 27
Rondeau, Jimmy 152–154, 247
Rondon, Vincente 133, 263
Rooney, Kevin 19
Roper, Bob 7
Roper, Jack 12
Ros, Bepi 130, 237
Ross-Adams, Brian 283
Rossman, Mike 273
Roth, Charlie 202
Royal Air Force Institute of Aviation 189
Rudd, Irving 235
Ruddock, Donovan "Razor" 19, 21
Rudi, Bjorn 189
Ruiz, John 21
Rumble in the Jungle 162–175, 231
Russell, Roger 77, 105, 221
Russia 216, 271
Ruth, Babe 174

Saddler, Sandy 77, 78, 113, 198
Sadler, Dick 77, 78, 110, 111, 115, 125, 137, 138, 140, 141, 151, 152, 154, 167, 169–171, 174, 198
St. Ives, England 116
St. Louis, Missouri 249, 255, 256
St. Luke's Hospital (Philadelphia) 74
St. Paul, Minnesota 219
St. Paul Pioneer Press 235
St. Valentine's Day Massacre 116
Salt Lake City, Utah 47, 111
San Antonio, Texas 220
San Diego, California 121, 123, 2008, 222
San Diego Sun 12
Sanford, Young (Fred Houpe) 235, 244, 264, 265, 292
San Francisco, California 199
San Juan, Puerto Rico 204, 239, 245, 246, 259, 260, 266, 269
Sarajevo 81
Satterfield, Bob 16, 240
Savannah Morning News 12
Savarese, Lou 19
Scandinavia 10
Schmeling, Max 10–14, 25, 66, 164, 241
Schmidt, Waldemar 231
Schneider, Jimmy "the Greek" 69
Schultz, Axel 21
Schwartz, Hank 154, 160

Index

Scott, Bruce 251, 255
Scott, Phil 10
Scott, Vic 82
Seattle, Washington 45, 77, 81, 187
Sesquicentenial Stadium 8
Shannon, Mickey 262
Sharkey, Bill 279
Sharkey, Jack 9–11
Sharnik, Mort 291
Shavers, Earnie 3, 22, 95, 138–139, 141, 156, 159, 160, 187, 244–245, 248, 253, 255, 256, 265, 266, 275, 290, 293; Ali 240–243; early beginnings 136–137; Holmes 261–262, 285–287; Lyle 199–200; Norton 284; Young 206, 207, 221, 230
Sherwood, Kenneth N. 146
Shoemaker, Leslie 12
Simon, Abe 13
Skog, Harold 203
Slayton, Bill 222, 267, 289
Smith, Andy 116, 117, 119, 129, 215
Smith, Howard "KO" 221, 240, 241
Smith, James "Bonecrusher" 18
Smith, "Lightning" Bob 251
Smith, Red 143, 146, 147, 151, 161, 226
Smith, Tommie 165
Smith, Tommy 62
Soldier's Field 9
Solomon, Sam 255, 256, 272, 273
Soria, Sixto 249, 250
Sorrels, Terry 111, 220
Soto, Pedro 252
South Africa 271, 272, 278–283
South America 82, 154, 220, 237
South American Heavyweight Title 57, 82
Southern Methodist University 91
Southern Sun Hotels Corporation 272, 282
Soviet Union 36, 76, 271
Soweto 283
Spain 10, 205, 237, 239
Spencer, Thad 35, 39, 40, 49, 95, 97, 117, 170, 219
Spinks, Kay 257
Spinks, Leon, Sr. 250
Spinks, Michael 17, 18, 56, 249, 250, 273, 279, 293
Sports Illustrated 41, 42, 47, 54, 93, 133, 139, 205, 262
Sports, Inc. 37
Stallings, Bob 99, 133, 135, 184, 221
Stallone, Sylvester 181, 182, 211, 238, 285
Stander, Darlene 95, 211
Stander, Ron 94–96, 109, 111, 112, 178, 220, 240, 251, 263
Staples, A.J. 132
Stateline, Nevada 107
Stevens, Les 206
Stevenson, Teofilo 234, 235, 279–281
Stewart, Alex 19
Stockholm, Sweden 41

Street, Bob 95
Streisand, Barbra 138
Stribling, Young 10
Sugar, Bert Randolph 277
Sulaiman, Jose 204, 239, 245, 246, 259, 260, 266, 269
Sullivan, John L. 4, 5
Sun City, S.A. 272
Superdome 272
Swessel, Joe 269

Talbot, Lou 120, 259, 269
Talese, Gay 26
Tate, John 275, 278–283, 286, 287, 291
Taylor, Elizabeth 64
Taylor, Ernie 86
Tennessee 283
Terrell, Ernie 32, 33, 35, 39, 53, 59, 62, 79, 100, 127, 177, 180, 219
Texas 62, 92, 110, 138, 285
Texas Boxing Commission 62
Thomas, Don 75
Thomas, Harry 12
Thomas, John 127
Thomas, Pinklon 18
Thompkins, Jerry 280
Thompson, Ben 243, 244
Thrilla in Manila 192–198, 202, 214, 216, 219, 243, 257, 262, 290
Tiger, Billy 80
Tiger, Dick 54
Tillman, Henry 19
Todd, Michael 159
Tokyo, Japan 19, 36, 97, 98, 100, 138, 140, 215, 216
Toledo, Ohio 8
Top Rank, Inc. 142, 159, 212, 235, 260
Toronto, Ontario 45, 46, 78, 198, 199
Toronto Maple Leafs 45
Tubbs, Tony 18
Tucker, Tony 18
Tuite, James 155
Tunero, Kid 237
Tunney, Gene 6, 8–10, 12, 14, 22, 93, 118, 197, 277, 288
Turkey 227
Turley, Bob 140
Turnbow, Mel 62, 82, 86, 133
Twenty Mai Stadium (Kinshasa) 162, 171–173
Tyson, Mike 4, 12, 17–22, 288, 293

UCLA Medical Centre 291
Uganda 36
Uncle Tom 67, 74, 107, 144, 164, 165, 193
Ungerman, Irving 78, 80, 99, 100
Uniondale, New York 216
United States Army 13, 34, 277
United States Boxing Championships controversy 238, 252, 264
United States Heavyweight Championship 177, 178, 285

United States Marine Corps 97, 122, 250, 285
United States Navy 234
United States Supreme Court 34, 42, 63, 85
Urtain, Jose 89, 118, 139, 205, 210, 237
Uruguay 205, 237
Uzcudun, Paolino 10, 11

Val Barker Award 249
Valan, Harold 177, 218, 285, 286
Valdez, Nino 16, 17, 23
Valentino, Pat 14
Vancouver, British Columbia 99, 100
Vancouver Athletic Commission 100
Velasquez, Ramon 140, 178
Venezuela 122, 152, 154, 161, 219
Ventura, Tony 139
Video Techniques, Inc. 160
Viet Cong 33, 34
Vietnam War 4, 34, 74, 97, 98, 122, 164, 192, 212, 277
Vingo, Carmine 16
Viscusi, Lou 53
Visini, Angelo 237

Waco, Texas 25
Walcott, Jersey Joe 14–16, 22, 32
Waldheim, Don 77
Wales 12, 78
Wallace, Coley 16
Wallace, Roy "Cookie" 220, 251, 263
War Bonds 13
Ward, Forest 122, 177
Ward, Stan 230, 244, 285
Warner, Don 70
Warren, Ohio 136, 240
Washington, Desiree 19
Washington State Boxing Commission 46
Watergate 4
Waters, Bob 29, 74
Wayne, John 163
Weaver, Mike 240, 263, 285–287
Weill, Al 16, 17
Wells Fargo 100
Wembley Stadium 214
Wepner, Chuck 35, 77, 117, 133, 139, 140, 170, 176–184, 188, 189, 204, 213, 216, 218, 233, 235, 236, 238, 263
Werleman, Ireno 203
West Germany 36, 88, 184, 210
West Virginia 229
Westphal, Albert 23
White, Walter 263
White Heavyweight Championship 33, 35
white hopes 5, 40, 47, 81, 94, 156, 170, 179, 233, 234, 251, 275, 279
White House 174, 175
Whitehurst, Bert 53
Whynter, Billy 211

Wicks, Tom 278
Wide World of Sports 66, 145, 146
Wiler, Gary "Hobo" 77
Wiley, Harry 85
Willard, Jess 6–8
Williams, Carl "The Truth" 19
Williams, Cleveland 23, 33, 69, 88, 240
Williams, Danny 21
Williams, Roy 133, 205, 221, 240, 255, 256, 263, 264
Wills, Harry 6, 8–11, 22
Wilson, Ollie 82
Wipperman, Dick 57, 86
Witherspoon, Tim 18
The Wizard of Oz 65
Wolfe, Dave 280
Woodward, Dr. Paul 123
Woody, James J. 58, 77, 87, 135, 219
World Boxing Association (WBA) 7, 18, 21, 24, 249, 253, 259, 261, 263, 266, 270, 275, 284, 291–293; Ali vacates title 276; Ellis crowned 42, 43, 49, 57, 77, 79, 83, 92, 103, 105, 111, 133, 135, 139, 152, 177, 185, 187; 1967 tournament 34–41; reaffirms Spinks as champion 260; sanctions Ali–Coopman 204; strips Ali of title first time 32, 33; strips Ali of title second time 34–36; supports Ali 245; Tate wins title 283; tourney to replace Ali 277–282
World Boxing Commission (WBC) 7, 17–20, 21, 49, 111, 139, 140, 178, 189, 227, 237, 239, 246, 254, 256, 259, 266, 267, 269, 275–277, 283–285, 289, 292, 293; strips Spinks of title 260–261; threatens to strip Ali 245; withholds sanction of Ali–Coopman 204
World Boxing Hall of Fame 183
World Boxing Magazine 109, 159, 240
World Boxing Organization (WBO) 20
World Martial Arts Championship 216
World Series 277
World War II 13, 68, 74, 276
Wright, Bruce 62

Yankee Stadium 12, 216, 224, 250
Yemelyanov, Vadim 36
Yokosaka, Japan 98
Young, Dick 127, 209, 214
Young, Jimmy 3, 22, 134, 185, 186, 197, 199, 202, 212, 213, 219, 220, 223, 227, 237, 238, 240, 243–245, 254, 258, 260, 263, 264, 284, 290, 293; Ali 207–210; early career 205–207; Foreman 229–233; Norton 246–247; pugilistic dementia and death 247; ring decline 247
Youngstown, Ohio 229

Zaire 153, 161–167, 170–172, 175, 178, 193, 198, 229, 257
Zanon, Lorenzo 183, 237–239, 244, 245, 287
Zouski, Steve 232
Zurich, Switzerland 88
Zyglewicz, Dave 41, 170